CONTENTS

CHAPTER 1: INTRODUCTION   **1**

1.1   INTRODUCTION TO PROGRAMMING   2
Machine Language   2
Assembly Languages   2
Low- and High-Level Languages   3
Procedure and Object Orientations   4
Application and System Software   4
Programming Languages   5

1.2   PROBLEM SOLUTION AND SOFTWARE DEVELOPMENT   9
Phase I. Development and Design   10
Phase II. Documentation   15
Phase III. Maintenance   16
Backup   16

1.3   ALGORITHMS   17

1.4   COMMON PROGRAMMING ERRORS   23

1.5   CHAPTER SUMMARY   23

1.6   CHAPTER APPENDIX: COMPUTER HARDWARE AND STORAGE CONCEPTS   24
Computer Storage   26
Two's Complement Numbers   27
Words and Addresses   28

PART ONE: PROCEDURE-ORIENTED PROGRAMMING IN C++

CHAPTER 2: PROBLEM SOLVING USING C++   **33**

2.1   INTRODUCTION TO C++   34
The main() Function   37
The cout Object   38

2.2   PROGRAMMING STYLE   45
Comments   46

2.3   DATA VALUES AND ARITHMETIC OPERATIONS   49
Integer Values   49
Floating-Point Numbers   50
Character Values   52
Escape Sequences   54
Arithmetic Operations   54
Integer Division   57

	A Unary Operator (Negation)	58
	Operator Precedence and Associativity	59
2.4	VARIABLES AND DECLARATION STATEMENTS	63
	Declaration Statements	65
	Multiple Declarations	68
	Memory Allocation	70
	Displaying a Variable's Address	72
2.5	INTEGER QUALIFIERS	77
	Data Type Conversions	79
	Determining Storage Size	80
2.6	APPLYING THE SOFTWARE DEVELOPMENT PROCEDURE	81
2.7	APPLICATIONS	87
	Application 1: Radar Speed Traps	87
	Application 2: Telephone Switching Networks	89
2.8	COMMON PROGRAMMING ERRORS	96
2.9	CHAPTER SUMMARY	98
CHAPTER 3: COMPLETING THE BASICS		**101**
3.1	ASSIGNMENT OPERATIONS	102
	Assignment Variations	107
	Accumulating	108
	Counting	110
3.2	FORMATTING NUMBERS FOR PROGRAM OUTPUT	117
3.3	USING MATHEMATICAL LIBRARY FUNCTIONS	131
	Casts	135
3.4	PROGRAM INPUT USING THE cin OBJECT	140
3.5	THE const QUALIFIER	152
	Placement of Statements	153
3.6	APPLICATIONS	158
	Application 1: Acid Rain	158
	Application 2: Approximating the Exponential Function	161
3.7	COMMON PROGRAMMING ERRORS	168
3.8	CHAPTER SUMMARY	169
3.9	CHAPTER APPENDIX: A CLOSER LOOK AT ERRORS	171
	Compile-Time and Run-Time Errors	171
	Syntax and Logic Errors	171

CHAPTER 4: SELECTION STRUCTURES   177

4.1	SELECTION CRITERIA	178
	Logical Operators	180
	A Numerical Accuracy Problem	182
4.2	THE `if-else` STATEMENT	184
	Compound Statements	187
	Block Scope	189
	One-Way Selection	190
	Problems Associated with the `if-else` Statement	192
4.3	NESTED `if` STATEMENTS	197
	The `if-else` Chain	199
4.4	THE `switch` STATEMENT	207
4.5	APPLICATIONS	213
	Application 1: Data Validation	213
	Application 2: Solving Quadratic Equations	215
4.6	COMMON PROGRAMMING ERRORS	221
4.7	CHAPTER SUMMARY	222
4.8	CHAPTER APPENDIX: A CLOSER LOOK AT PROGRAM TESTING	225

CHAPTER 5: REPETITION STRUCTURES   227

5.1	INTRODUCTION	228
	Pretest and Posttest Loops	229
	Fixed-Count versus Variable-Condition Loops	230
5.2	`while` LOOPS	231
5.3	INTERACTIVE `while` LOOPS	240
	Sentinels	248
	`break` and `continue` Statements	249
	The Null Statement	251
5.4	`for` LOOPS	253
5.5	LOOP PROGRAMMING TECHNIQUES	266
	Technique 1: Interactive Input within a Loop	266
	Technique 2: Selection within a Loop	267
	Technique 3: Evaluating Functions of One Variable	269
	Technique 4: Interactive Loop Control	271
5.6	NESTED LOOPS	274
5.7	`do while` LOOPS	279
	Validity Checks	281

5.8   COMMON PROGRAMMING ERRORS   283

5.9   CHAPTER SUMMARY   284

CHAPTER 6: MODULARITY USING FUNCTIONS   289

6.1   FUNCTION AND PARAMETER DECLARATIONS   290
       Function Prototypes   292
       Calling a Function   292
       Defining a Function   294
       Placement of Statements   298
       Function Stubs   299
       Functions with Empty Parameter Lists   301
       Default Arguments   301
       Function Templates   302
       Reusing Function Names (Overloading)   306

6.2   RETURNING A SINGLE VALUE   310
       In-Line Functions   316

6.3   RETURNING MULTIPLE VALUES   321
       Passing and Using Reference Parameters   321

6.4   APPLICATIONS   331
       Application 1: Rectangular to Polar Coordinate Conversion   332
       Application 2: Simulation   339

6.5   VARIABLE SCOPE   350
       Scope Resolution Operator   353
       Misuse of Globals   355

6.6   VARIABLE STORAGE CLASS   359
       Local Variable Storage Classes   359
       Global Variable Storage Classes   363

6.7   COMMON PROGRAMMING ERRORS   368

6.8   CHAPTER SUMMARY   368

PART TWO: OBJECT-ORIENTED PROGRAMMING

CHAPTER 7: I/O FILE STREAMS AND DATA FILES   375

7.1   I/O FILE STREAM OBJECTS AND METHODS   376
       Files   376
       File Stream Objects and Modes   377
       File Stream Methods   378
       Embedded and Interactive File Names   384
       Closing a File   387

7.2	READING AND WRITING FILES	388
	Standard Device Files	396
	Other Devices	396
7.3	RANDOM FILE ACCESS	399
7.4	FILE STREAMS AS FUNCTION ARGUMENTS	403
7.5	COMMON PROGRAMMING ERRORS	407
7.6	CHAPTER SUMMARY	407
7.7	CHAPTER APPENDIX: THE iostream CLASS LIBRARY	409
	File Stream Transfer Mechanism	409
	Components of the iostream Class Library	410
	In-Memory Formatting	411

CHAPTER 8: INTRODUCTION TO CLASSES — **415**

8.1	ABSTRACT DATA TYPES IN C++ (classes)	416
	Abstract Data Types	418
	Class Construction	420
	Terminology	429
8.2	CONSTRUCTORS	432
	Calling Constructors	435
	Overloaded and inline Constructors	435
	Destructors	439
8.3	APPLICATIONS	442
	Application 1: Constructing an Elevator Object	442
	Application 2: A Single Object Gas Pump Simulation	446
8.4	COMMON PROGRAMMING ERRORS	454
8.5	CHAPTER SUMMARY	454

CHAPTER 9: CLASS FUNCTIONS AND CONVERSIONS — **457**

9.1	ASSIGNMENT	458
	Copy Constructors	462
	Base/Member Initialization	465
9.2	ADDITIONAL CLASS FEATURES	467
	Class scope	467
	Static Class Members	468
	Friend Functions	473
9.3	OPERATOR FUNCTIONS	478
	Operator Functions as Friends	484

9.4   DATA TYPE CONVERSIONS   487
       Built-In to Built-In Conversion   487
       Built-In to Class Conversion   488
       Class to Built-In Conversion   490
       Class to Class Conversion   492

9.5   APPLICATION—A MULTI-OBJECT GAS PUMP SIMULATION   496

9.6   CLASS INHERITANCE   504
       Access Specifications   506
       An Example   507

9.7   POLYMORPHISM   512

9.8   COMMON PROGRAMMING ERRORS   517

9.9   CHAPTER SUMMARY   518

PART THREE: DATA STRUCTURES

CHAPTER 10: ARRAYS   523

10.1   ONE-DIMENSIONAL ARRAYS   524
       Input and Output of Array Values   529

10.2   ARRAY INITIALIZATION   535

10.3   DECLARING AND PROCESSING TWO-DIMENSIONAL ARRAYS   538
       Larger Dimensional Arrays   542

10.4   APPLICATIONS   545
       Application 1: Statistical Analysis   545
       Application 2: Curve Plotting   548

10.5   ARRAYS AS ARGUMENTS   558

10.6   COMMON PROGRAMMING ERRORS   566

10.7   CHAPTER SUMMARY   566

10.8   CHAPTER APPENDIX: SEARCHING AND SORTING   567
       Search Algorithms   568
       Big O Notation   575
       Sort Algorithms   575

CHAPTER 11: POINTERS   583

11.1   ADDRESSES AND POINTERS   584
       Storing Addresses   585
       Using Addresses   586
       Declaring Pointers   587
       References and Pointers   589

11.2	ARRAY NAMES AS POINTERS	596
	Dynamic Array Allocation	602
11.3	POINTER ARITHMETIC	606
	Pointer Initialization	609
11.4	PASSING ADDRESSES	610
	Passing Arrays	616
	Advanced Pointer Notation	619
11.5	COMMON PROGRAMMING ERRORS	624
11.6	CHAPTER SUMMARY	626

CHAPTER 12: RECORDS AS DATA STRUCTURES — **627**

12.1	SINGLE RECORDS	628
12.2	ARRAYS OF STRUCTURES	634
12.3	STRUCTURES AS FUNCTION ARGUMENTS	639
	Passing a Pointer	642
	Returning Structures	645
12.4	LINKED LISTS	649
12.5	DYNAMIC DATA STRUCTURE ALLOCATION	657
12.6	UNIONS	664
12.7	COMMON PROGRAMMING ERRORS	667
12.8	CHAPTER SUMMARY	668

PART FOUR: ADDITIONAL TOPICS

CHAPTER 13: NUMERICAL METHODS — **671**

13.1	INTRODUCTION TO ROOT FINDING	672
13.2	THE BISECTION METHOD	675
13.3	REFINEMENTS TO THE BISECTION METHOD	681
	Regula Falsi Method	682
	Modified Regula Falsi Method	684
	Summary of the Algorithms Based on Bisection	689
13.4	THE SECANT METHOD	691
13.5	INTRODUCTION TO NUMERICAL INTEGRATION	694
13.6	THE TRAPEZOIDAL RULE	695
	Computational Form of the Trapezoidal Rule Equation	697
	Example of a Trapezoidal Rule Calculation	699

13.7   SIMPSON'S RULE   700
       Example of Simpson's Rule as an Approximation to an Integral   702

13.8   COMMON PROGRAMMING ERRORS   704

13.9   CHAPTER SUMMARY   704

CHAPTER 14: BIT OPERATIONS   707

14.1   THE AND OPERATOR   708

14.2   THE INCLUSIVE OR OPERATOR   711

14.3   THE EXCLUSIVE OR OPERATOR   713

14.4   THE COMPLEMENT OPERATOR   715

14.5   DIFFERENT-SIZE DATA ITEMS   716

14.6   THE SHIFT OPERATORS   717

14.7   CHAPTER SUMMARY   722

APPENDIX A: OPERATOR PRECEDENCE TABLE   723

APPENDIX B: ASCII CHARACTER CODES   725

APPENDIX C: PROGRAM ENTRY, COMPILATION, AND EXECUTION   727

APPENDIX D: FLOATING POINT NUMBER STORAGE   733

APPENDIX E: COMMAND LINE ARGUMENTS   737

APPENDIX F: NAMESPACES   743

APPENDIX G: THE STANDARD TEMPLATE LIBRARY   747

APPENDIX H: SOLUTIONS TO SELECTED
             ODD-NUMBERED EXERCISES   753

INDEX   859

PREFACE

The C++ programming language has become the preeminent applications language of the 1990s in almost every area except the engineering sciences. Ironically, both C+ and its predecessor, C, were developed at ATT Bell Laboratories (now part of Lucent Technology), considered by many to be one of the premier engineering and scientific facilities in the world. Slowly, however, C++ has gained a hold even here and is rapidly becoming acknowledged within the engineering and scientific community as the programming language of choice. This has happened for a variety of reasons and, interestingly, mirrors the acceptance of C and C++ as the standard programming language used within Bell Laboratories.

The C programming language was designed in conjunction with the development of the UNIX operating system and was identified as an advanced operating systems language. Engineers at Bell Laboratories, however, noticed that C had characteristics that also made it extremely useful for engineering and scientific purposes. In addition to C's standard capabilities that were common to FORTRAN, C provided many additional machine-level capabilities that made real-time processing possible, without resorting to assembly-level programming. With the addition of object-oriented capabilities, C evolved into the C++ programming language in the early 1980s. These additional object-oriented capabilities made programming graphical interfaces, such as color monitors, much easier than was previously possible, and provided a significant advance to the simple character input and display associated with both C and FORTRAN.

For most people, employing the full potential of a hybrid language such as C++, which contains both procedural and object-oriented features, requires a gradual refinement of programming skills from a procedural to an object orientation. This is the approach taken by this text. It was written with the intention of adjusting to a complete object-oriented approach as rapidly as possible within the confines of a pedagogically sound and achievable progression.

In practical terms, this text has been written to support a one or two semester C++ programming course. It intentionally has been written to be sufficiently flexible so that professors can still mold the text to their individual preference of topic presentation. This is achieved in the following way.

Excluding Chapter One, which presents computer literacy material for those who require this background, Part I presents the basic procedural syntax, flow control, and modularity topics that are needed for an effective understanding of C++'s object features. When the topics of arrays (Chapter 10), files (Chapter 7), and classes (Chapter 8) are added to this material, a comprehensive one-semester course will have been completed. The presentation order of these last three topics is entirely up to the discretion of the professor, as each of these chapters has been specifically written to be dependent only on the material contained in Part I. Additionally, depending on time and inclination, the numerical techniques presented in Chapter 13 may also be presented at any point after Part I has been completed. Figure 1 illustrates this one-semester topic dependency.

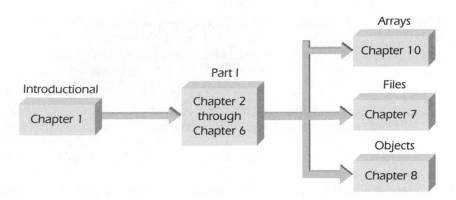

Figure 1. Topic Dependency for a One-Semester Course

A specific feature of this text is that Part II, on object-oriented programming, and Part III on data structures, are interchangeable. Thus, if you want to present object-oriented programming early, you would follow a Part I – Part II – Part III progression. On the other hand, if you want to continue with additional procedural programming reinforcement and present object-oriented programming toward the end of the course, you would use the sequence Part I – Part III – Part II. In either case, the material on files presented in Chapter 7, the material on arrays presented in Chapter 10, the material on classes presented in Chapter 8, and the material on numerical techniques presented in Chapter 13 can be introduced at any time after Part I.

Figure 2, the topic dependency chart, illustrates the flexibility of introducing topics within the overall context of procedural programming, object-oriented programming, and data structures.

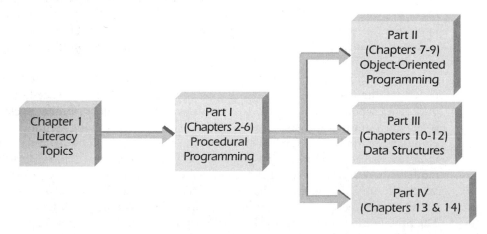

Figure 2. Topic Dependency Chart

In using this text, students should be familiar with fundamental algebra, but no other pre-requisites are assumed. Chapter 1 presents the computer literacy material for students who need this background. Large numbers of examples are drawn from various engineering and scientific disciplines. The instructor may choose applications that match students' experience or for a particular course emphasis.

Distinctive Features of This Book

Writing Style

The one thing that I have found most important in my own teaching is that regardless of what is written about, it must be written so that students can read it. Once the professor sets the stage, the selected textbook must encourage, nurture, and assist the student in acquiring and "owning" the material presented in class. My primary concern, and one of the distinctive features of this book, is that it has been written for the student. Thus, I feel the writing style used to convey the concepts presented is an important and distinctive aspect of the text.

Modularity

To produce readable and maintainable code, modularity is essential. C++, by its nature, is a modular language. Thus, the connection between C++ functions and modules is made early in the text, in Section 2.1, and sustained throughout the book. The idea of parameter passing into modules also is made early in Section 3.3, using C++'s function library, introducing students to functions and argument passing as natural techniques of programming. Chapter 7 introduces object-oriented programming techniques, thus both continuing and strengthening this modular emphasis.

Software Engineering

Rather than simply introduce students to programming in C++, this text provides students with the fundamentals of software engineering from both procedural and object-oriented viewpoints. Section 1.2 introduces the software development cycle, presenting one of the main themes of the text, emphasizing problem solving techniques: the importance of understanding a problem, selecting and refining the solution, and understanding the relationship between analysis, design, coding, and testing. Immediately following this, Section 1.3 introduces algorithms.

Applications

Starting with Chapter 2, each chapter contains an Applications section with an average of two completed applications per chapter. Each application demonstrates effective problem solving within the context of a complete program solution. This is done for both procedural and object-oriented designs.

Program Testing

Every single C++ program in this text has been successfully compiled and run under Version 6.0 of Microsoft's Visual C++ Development System. A source diskette of all programs is included with the text. This will permit students to both experiment and extend the existing programs and more easily modify them as required by a number of end-of-section exercises.

Pedagogical Features

To facilitate the goal of making C++ accessible as a first level course, the following pedagogical features have been incorporated into the text:

End of Section Exercises

Almost every section in the book contains numerous and diverse skill builder and programming exercises. Additionally, solutions to selected odd-numbered exercises are provided in Appendix H.

Pseudocode Descriptions

Pseudocode is stressed throughout the text. Flowchart symbols are presented, but are used only in visually presenting flow-of-control constructs.

Common Programming Errors and Chapter Review

Each chapter ends with a section on common programming errors and a review of the main topics covered in the chapter.

Enrichment Sections

Given the many different emphases that can be applied in teaching C++, a number of enrichment sections have been included as chapter appendices. These allow you to provide different emphases with different students or different C++ classes.

Point of Information Boxes

A set of shaded boxes that provides additional brief clarification of commonly used and/or difficult concepts, such as abstraction, lvalues, and rvalues, values versus identities, flags, and stream formatting.

Programming Notes

A set of shaded boxes that highlights alternative and advanced programming techniques.

Career Choices

A set of shaded boxes that describes various engineering career choices, such as electrical, chemical, mechanical, aeronautical, and so forth.

Appendices and Supplements

An expanded set of appendices is provided. These include appendices on operator precedence, ASCII codes, program entry and compilation, and floating point number storage. Additionally, solutions to selected odd-numbered exercises are included in the text, and a 3½" IBM-PC compatible diskette contains all of the source code for programs presented in the text.

A Note to FORTRAN Programmers

The emerging acceptance of C++ from both the C and FORTRAN user community is now clearly discernable. Because there is sometimes a slight initial confusion with three fundamental C++ features, I have briefly summarized these features.

The first concept that is unique to both C and C++ is that they do not have a built-in LOGICAL (that is, true or false) data type (although such a type is being implemented in the current ANSI draft standard for C++). Because this data type is not a built-in data type within the C language and has not traditionally been a part of C++, a tested expression conventionally does not evaluate to a LOGICAL value. Thus, the syntax

```
if(LOGICAL expression)
    execute this statement;
```

is also not built into C and rarely found in C++. Rather, both C and C++ use the more encompassing syntax

```
if(expression)
    execute this statement;
```

where "expression" is any expression that evaluates to a numeric value. If the result of the tested expression is a non-zero value it is treated as if it were true, and only a zero value is treated as false. Conversely, the result of a relational expression that is true evaluates to a numeric value of 1, while a relational expression that is false evaluates to a 0.

The second feature that is unique to both C and C++ is their construction and use of pointers. In C++, a pointer is a variable that is used to store a memory address. Although pointer variables are primarily used with the indirection operator, *, to explicitly dereference the pointer and obtain the desired "pointed to" target, C++'s pointers are much richer than those found in FORTRAN 90. This is because the contents of a pointer variable can be displayed or manipulated much like any other variable and arithmetic on pointers is supported.

Finally, C++ does not impose rigid rules on the placement of statements. In this regard, the only really relevant rule in C++ is that an identifier must be declared before it is used. Although a sensible placement of statements is always a good programming practice, C++ does not impose a placement order to the extent that FORTRAN does.

ACKNOWLEDGMENTS

This book began as an idea. It became a reality only due to the encouragement, skills, and efforts supplied by many people. I would like to acknowledge their contribution.

First, I would like to thank Suzanne Jeans, my editor at Brooks/Cole Publishing Company. With the incorporation of PWS within the larger Brooks/Cole publishing community, Suzanne provided a continuity and constancy that I sincerely appreciate and that ensured the publication of this text on schedule.

Additionally, I would like to express my gratitude to the following individual reviewers: Farzan Aminian, Trinity University, San Antonio; Jeffrey Blessing, Milwaukee School of Engineering; Don Hearn, University of Illinois at Urbana-Champaign; Jo Perry, North Carolina State University; Warren N. White, Kansas State University; and Linda F. Wilson, Dartmouth College.

Each of these reviewers supplied extremely detailed and constructive reviews of both the original manuscript and a number of revisions. Their suggestions, attention to detail, and comments were extraordinarily helpful to me as the manuscript evolved and matured through the editorial process.

Once the review process was completed, the task of turning the final manuscript into a textbook depended on many people other than me. For this, I especially want to thank the production coordinator, Kelsey McGee, the copy editor, Kathy Cobb, and the compositor, Karla Russell of GEX Publishing Services. The dedication of these people was incredible and very important to me. Almost from the moment the book moved to the production stage this team seemed to take personal ownership of the text and I am very grateful to them. I also very much appreciate the suggestions and work of marketing manager Nathan Wilbur.

Special acknowledgment goes to two of my colleagues, Emil Neu of Stevens Institute of Technology and G.J. Borse of Lehigh University, who provided material for this text. Specifically, their contributions include almost all of Chapter 13, and the information contained within the Career Choice boxes, which Dr. Borse graciously permitted me to use from his FORTRAN 77 text (copyright held by PWS Publishing).

I also acknowledge with gratitude the direct encouragement and support of Fairleigh Dickinson University, especially the positive academic climate provided by the university and the constant encouragement and support of my dean, Paul Lerman, and my chairperson, Joel Harmon, without which this text could not have been written. I would also like to thank Karen Langbert for providing specific incites and mathematical verification on a number of engineering applications.

Finally, I deeply appreciate the patience, understanding, and love provided by my friend, wife, and partner, Rochelle.

Gary Bronson
1999

CHAPTER 1

Introduction

TOPICS

1.1 INTRODUCTION TO PROGRAMMING

1.2 PROBLEM SOLUTION AND SOFTWARE DEVELOPMENT

1.3 ALGORITHMS

1.4 COMMON PROGRAMMING ERRORS

1.5 CHAPTER SUMMARY

1.6 CHAPTER APPENDIX: COMPUTER HARDWARE AND STORAGE CONCEPTS

1.1 ▷ INTRODUCTION TO PROGRAMMING

A computer is a machine and like other machines, such as an automobile or lawn mower, it must be turned on and then driven, or controlled, to do the task it was meant to do. In an automobile, for example, control is provided by the driver, who sits inside of and directs the car. In a computer, the driver is a set of instructions, called a program. More formally, a **computer program** is a self-contained set of instructions used to operate a computer to produce a specific result. Another term for a program or set of programs is **software**, and we will use both terms interchangeably throughout the text.[1]

The process of writing a program, or software, is called **programming**, while the set of instructions that can be used to construct a program is called a **programming language**. Available programming languages come in a variety of forms and types.

Machine Language

At its most fundamental level the only programs that can actually be used to operate a computer are **machine language programs**. Such programs, which are also referred to as **executable programs**, or **executables** for short, consist of a sequence of instructions composed of binary numbers such as:[2]

    11000000 000000000001 000000000010

    11110000 000000000010 000000000011

Such machine language instructions consist of two parts: an instruction part and an address part. The instruction part, which is referred to as the **opcode** (short for operation code), is usually the leftmost set of bits in the instruction and tells the computer the operation to be performed, such as add, subtract, multiply, etc., while the rightmost bits specify the memory addresses of the data to be used. For example, assuming that the eight leftmost bits of the first instruction listed above is the operation code to add, and the next two groups of twelve bits are the addresses of the two operands to be added, this instruction would be a command to "add the data in memory location 1 to the data in memory location 2."[3] Similarly, assuming that the opcode 11110000 means multiply, the next instruction is a command to "multiply the data in memory location 2 by the data in location 3."

Assembly Languages

Although each class of computer—such as IBM PCs, Apple Macintoshes, and DEC VAX computers—has its own particular machine language, it is very tedious and time consuming to write such machine language programs. One of the first advances in programming was the substitution of word-like symbols, such as ADD, SUB, MUL, for the binary opcodes and

---

[1]More inclusively, the term software is also used to denote both the programs and the data that the programs will operate on.

[2]Review the appendix at the end of this chapter if you are unfamiliar with binary numbers.

[3]To obtain the address values as decimal numbers, convert the binary values to decimal using the method presented in the chapter appendix.

both decimal numbers and labels for memory addresses. For example, using these symbols and decimal values for memory addresses, the previous two machine language instructions can be written as

ADD 1, 2

MUL 2, 3

Programming languages that use this type of symbolic notation are referred to as **assembly languages**. Since computers can only execute machine language programs, the set of instructions contained within an assembly language program must be translated into a machine language program before it can be executed on a computer. Translator programs that perform this function for assembly language programs are known as **assemblers** (see Figure 1.1).

An assembly Language Program → Translation Program (assembler) → Machine Language Program

Figure 1.1 *Assembly programs must be translated.*

Low- and High-Level Languages

Both machine level and assembly languages are classified as **low-level languages**. This is because both of these language types use instructions that are directly tied to one type of computer. As such, an assembly language program is limited in that it can only be used with the specific computer type for which the program is written. Such programs do, however, permit using special features of a particular computer and generally execute at the fastest level possible.

In contrast to low-level languages are high-level languages. A **high-level language** uses instructions that resemble written languages, such as English, and can be run on a variety of computer types. FORTRAN, BASIC, Pascal, and C++ are all examples of high-level languages.[4] Using C++, an instruction to add two numbers together and multiply by a third number can be written as:

```
result = (first + second) * third;
```

Programs written in a computer language (high or low level) are referred to interchangeably as both **source programs** and **source code**. Once a program is written in a high level language it must also, like a low-level assembly program, be translated into the machine language of the computer on which it will be run. This translation can be accomplished in two ways.

When each statement in a high-level source program is translated individually and executed immediately upon translation, the programming language used is called an **interpreted language**, and the program doing the translation is called an **interpreter**.

---

[4]C++ is sometimes classified as a middle-level language to convey the fact that although C++ is written as a high-level language, it can also take advantage of machine features that historically could only be accessed with assembly or machine languages.

When all of the statements in a high-level source program are translated as a complete unit before any one statement is executed, the programming language used is called a **compiled language**. In this case, the program doing the translation is called a **compiler**. Both compiled and interpreted versions of a language can exist, although typically one predominates. For example, although compiled versions of BASIC do exist, BASIC is predominantly an interpreted language. Similarly, although interpreted versions of C++ exist, C++ is predominantly a compiled language.

Procedure and Object Orientations

In addition to classifying programming languages as high or low level, they are also classified by orientation as either procedure- or object-oriented. In a **procedure-oriented language** the available instructions are used to create self-contained units, referred to as **procedures**. The purpose of a procedure is to accept data as input and transform the data in some manner to produce a specific result as an output. For the last 25 years most high-level programming languages have been procedure-oriented.

Within the past few years a second orientation, referred to as object oriented has taken center stage. One of the motivations for **object-oriented languages** was the development of graphical screens and support for graphical user interfaces (GUIs) capable of displaying multiple windows. In such an environment each window on the screen can conveniently be considered an object, with associated characteristics, such as color, position, and size. Using an object approach a program must first define the characteristics of the objects it will be manipulating and then be constructed of units that pass information to each object to produce the desired results. C++, which is formally classified as an object-oriented language, contains features found in both procedural- and object-oriented languages.

Application and System Software

Two logical categories of computer programs are application software and system software. **Application software** consists of those programs written to perform particular tasks required by the users. Most of the programs in this book are examples of application software.

System software is the collection of programs that must be readily available to any computer system in order for it to operate at all. In the early computer environments of the 1950s and 1960s, the user had to initially load the system software by hand to prepare the computer to do anything at all. This was done by using rows of switches on a front panel. Those initial, hand-entered commands were said to **boot** the computer, an expression derived from "pulling oneself up by the bootstraps." Today the so-called **bootstrap loader** is a permanent, automatically executed component of the computer's system software.

Additionally, before the 1960s, it was not uncommon for the user to also have to load a separate set of programs necessary for reading from and writing to the input and output devices that were being used. Similarly, it was the user's responsibility to find the code that would translate an application program to the computer's internal machine language so that it could be executed. Typically, most of these **utilities** are now kept on either a hard disk or floppy diskette and are booted into the computer either automatically when the system is powered up or on command by the user.

Various terms are used by different manufacturers for the collection of system utilities called the **operating system**. Often, the system software name ends with *OS* or *DOS* (for Disk Operating System). Additional tasks handled by modern operating systems include memory, input and output, and secondary storage management. Many systems handle very large programs, as well as multiple users concurrently, by dividing programs into segments or pages that are moved between the disk and memory as needed. Such operating systems create a **virtual memory,** which appears to be as large as necessary to handle any job, and a **multi-user** environment is produced that gives each user the impression that the computer and peripherals are his or hers alone. Additionally, many operating systems, including most windowed environments, permit each user to run multiple programs. Such operating systems are referred to as **multitasking** systems.

Most system operations are *transparent* to the user; that is, they take place internally without user intervention. However, some operating system commands are provided intentionally for you to interact directly with the system. The most common of these commands are those that allow the handling of data files on disk. Some of these are listed in Table 1.1 by the names with which they are implemented in both MS-DOS and UNIX operating systems.

Table 1.1 Common Operating System Commands

Task	DOS command	UNIX command
Display the directory of all files available	DIR	ls
Delete a specified file or group of files	ERASE or DELETE filename(s)	rm filename(s)
List the contents of a program to the monitor	TYPE filename	cat filename
Print the contents of a program to the printer	PRINT filename	lp or lpr filename
Copy a file	COPY source destination	cp source destination
Rename a file	RENAME oldname newname	mv oldname newname
Force a permanent halt to a running program	CTRL Break or CTRL Z or CTRL C	Del key, CTRL Break, or \
Force a temporary suspension of the current operation	CTRL S or Pause	CTRL S
Resume the current operation (recover from a CTRL S)	CTRL S	CTRL S

Programming Languages

On a fundamental level, all computer programs do the same thing (Figure 1.2); they direct a computer to accept data (input), to manipulate the data (process), and to produce reports (output). This implies that all computer programming languages that support a procedure orientation must provide essentially the same capabilities for performing these operations.

These capabilities are provided either as specific instruction types or "pre-packaged" groups of instructions that can be called to do specific tasks. In C++, the "pre-packaged" groups of instructions are contained in **object libraries** (in C they were called function libraries). Table 1.2 lists the fundamental set of instructions provided by FORTRAN, COBOL, Pascal, C, and C++ for performing input, processing, and output tasks.

Figure 1.2 All programs perform the same operations.

If all programming languages provide essentially the same features, why are there so many of them? The answer is that there are vast differences in the types of input data, calculations needed, and output reports required by various applications. For example, scientific and engineering applications require high-precision numerical outputs, accurate to many decimal places. In addition, these applications typically use many algebraic or trigonometric formulae to produce their results. For example, calculating the bacterial concentration level in a polluted pond, as illustrated in Figure 1.3, requires evaluating an exponential equation to a high degree of numerical accuracy. The FORTRAN programming language, with its algebra-like instructions, was initially developed for such applications. FORTRAN, whose name is an acronym derived from FORmula TRANslation, was introduced in 1957. It was the first commercially available high-level language and is the oldest high-level language still in use.

Table 1.2 Fundamental Programming Language Instruction Summary

Operation	FORTRAN	BASIC	COBOL	Pascal	C	C++
Input (Get the data)	READ	INPUT READ/DATA	READ ACCEPT	READ READLN	scanf() gets() getchar()	cin cin.get cin.getline
Processing (Use the data)	= IF/ELSE DO	LET IF/ELSE FOR WHILE UNTIL	COMPUTE IF/ELSE PERFORM	:= IF/ELSE FOR WHILE REPEAT	= if/else for while do	= if/else for while do
	+	+	ADD	+	+, =+, ++	+, =+, ++
	−	−	SUBTRACT	−	−, =−, −−	−, =−, −−
	*	*	MULTIPLY	*	*, =*	*, =*
	/	/	DIVIDE	/	/, =/	/, =/
	**	^		**	pow()	pow()
Output (Display the data)	WRITE PRINT	PRINT PRINT/ USING	WRITE DISPLAY	WRITE WRITELN	printf() puts() putchar()	cout

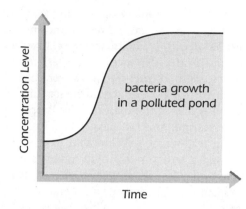

Figure 1.3 FORTRAN was developed for scientific and engineering applications.

Business applications usually deal in whole numbers, representing inventory quantities, for example, or dollar and cents data accurate to only two decimal places. These applications require simpler mathematical calculations than scientific applications. The outputs required from business programs frequently consist of reports containing extensive columns of neatly formatted dollar and cents numbers and totals. For these applications the COBOL programming language, with its picture output formats, is an ideal language (see Figure 1.4). COBOL, which was commercially introduced in the 1960s, stands for COmmon Business Oriented Language.

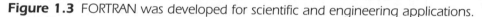

Part No.	Description	Quantity	Price
12225	#4 Nails, Common	25 boxes	1.09
12226	#6 Nails, Common	30 boxes	1.09
12227	#8 Nails, Common	65 boxes	1.29
12228	#10 Nails, Common	57 boxes	1.35
12229	#12 Nails, Common	42 boxes	
12230	#16 Nails, Common		

Figure 1.4 COBOL was developed for business applications.

Teaching programming to students has its own set of requirements. Here a relatively straightforward, easy-to-understand language is needed that does not require detailed knowledge of a specific application. Both the BASIC and Pascal programming languages were developed for this purpose. BASIC stands for Beginners All-purpose Symbolic Instruction Code and was developed in the 1960s at Dartmouth College. BASIC is ideal for creating small, easily developed, interactive programs.

Pascal was developed in the 1971 to provide students with a firmer foundation in modular and structured programming than was provided by early versions of BASIC.[5]

---

[5]Current versions of both BASIC and FORTRAN do provide the same structures found in Pascal.

Modular programs consist of many small subprograms, each of which performs a clearly defined and specific task that can be tested and modified without disturbing other sections of the program. Pascal is not an acronym, like the words FORTRAN, COBOL, and BASIC, but is named after the seventeenth-century mathematician, Blaise Pascal. The Pascal language is so rigidly structured, however, that there are no escapes from the structured modules when such escapes would be useful. This is unacceptable for many real-world projects and is one of the reasons why Pascal did not become widely accepted in the scientific, engineering, and business fields. The design philosophy, called **structured programming**, that lead to the development of Pascal is, however, very relevant to C++ programmers. Using a structured programming approach results in readable, reliable, and maintainable programs. We introduce the elements of this program-design philosophy in the next section and continue to expand on it and use it throughout the text.

C++ began as an extension to C, which is a procedure-oriented language developed in the 1970s at AT&T Bell Laboratories by Ken Thompson, Dennis Ritchie, and Brian Kernighan. In the early 1980s, Bjarne Stroustrup (also at AT&T) used his simulation-language background to develop C++. A central feature of simulation languages is that they model real-life situations as objects. This object orientation, which was ideal for graphical screen objects such as rectangles and circles, was combined with existing C features to form the C++ language. Thus, C++ retained the extensive set of capabilities provided by C and is itself a true general-purpose programming language. As such, it can be used for everything from simple, interactive programs to highly sophisticated and complex engineering and scientific programs, within the context of a truly structured language.

Exercises 1.1

1. Define the following terms:
   a. computer program
   b. programming
   c. programming language
   d. high-level language
   e. low-level language
   f. machine language
   g. assembly language
   h. procedure-oriented language
   i. object-oriented language
   j. source program
   k. compiler
   l. interpreter

2. Describe the purpose and primary uses of application and system software.

3. a. Describe the difference between high- and low-level languages.
   b. Describe the difference between procedure- and object-oriented languages.

4. Describe the similarities and differences between assemblers, interpreters, and compilers.

5. a. Given the following operation codes,

```
11000000 means add the 1st operand to the 2nd operand
10100000 means subtract the 1st operand from the 2nd operand
11110000 means multiply the 2nd operand by the 1st operand
11010000 means divide the 2nd operation by the 1st operand
```

translate the following instructions into English:

opcode	Address of 1st operand	Address of 2nd operand
11000000	000000000001	0000000000010
11110000	000000000010	0000000000011
10100000	000000000100	0000000000011
11010000	000000000101	0000000000011

b. Assuming the following locations contain the given data, determine the result produced by the instructions listed in Exercise 5.a. For this exercise assume each instruction is executed independently of any instruction.

Address	Initial value (in decimal) stored at this address
00000000001	5
00000000010	3
00000000011	6
00000000100	14
00000000101	4

6. Rewrite the machine-level instructions listed in Exercise 5.a using assembly language notation. Use the symbolic names ADD, SUB, MUL, and DIV for addition, subtraction, multiplication, and division operations, respectively. In writing the instructions use decimal values for the addresses.

1.2 PROBLEM SOLUTION AND SOFTWARE DEVELOPMENT

No matter what field of work you choose or what your lifestyle may be, you will have to solve problems. Many of these, such as adding up the change in your pocket, can be solved quickly and easily. Others, such as riding a bicycle, require some practice but soon become automatic. Still others require considerable planning and forethought if the solution is to be appropriate and efficient. For example, constructing a cellular telephone network or creating an inventory management system for a department store are problems for which trial-and-error solutions could prove expensive and disastrous.

Creating a program is no different, because a program is a solution developed to solve a particular problem. As such, writing a program is almost the last step in a process of first determining what the problem is and the method that will be used to solve the problem. Each field of study has its own name for the systematic method used to solve problems by designing suitable solutions. In science and engineering the approach is referred to as the **scientific method,** while in quantitative analysis the approach is referred to as the **systems approach.**

The method used by professional software developers for understanding the problem that is being solved and for creating an effective and appropriate software solution is called the **software development procedure.** This procedure, as illustrated in Figure 1.5 consists of three overlapping phases:

- Development and Design
- Documentation
- Maintenance

As a discipline, **software engineering** is concerned with creating readable, efficient, reliable, and maintainable programs and systems, and it uses the software development procedure to achieve this goal.

Figure 1.5 The three phases of program development.

Phase I. Development and Design

Phase I begins with either a statement of a problem or a specific request for a program, which is referred to as a **program requirement.** Once a problem has been stated or a specific request for a program solution has been made, the development and design phase begins. This phase consists of the four well-defined steps as illustrated in Figure 1.6 and summarized next.

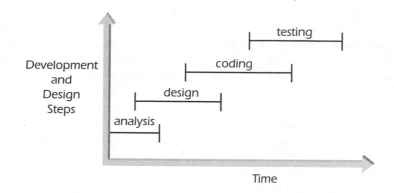

Figure 1.6 *The development and design steps.*

Step 1 Analyze the Problem

This step is required to ensure that the problem is clearly defined and understood. The determination that the problem is clearly defined is made only after the person doing the analysis understands what outputs are required and what inputs will be needed. To accomplish this the analyst must have an understanding of how the inputs can be used to produce the desired output. For example, assume that you receive the following assignment:

> *Write a program that gives the information we need about circles.*
> *Complete by tomorrow.*
>
> *— Management*

A simple analysis of this program requirement reveals that it is not a well-defined problem at all because we do not know exactly what output information is required. As such, it would be a major mistake to begin immediately writing a program to solve it. To clarify and define the problem statement your first step should be to contact "Management" to define exactly what the program is to produce (its outputs). Suppose you do this and you learn that what is really desired is a program to calculate and display the circumference of a circle when given the radius. Since a formula exists for converting the input to the output, you may proceed to the next step. If we are not sure of how to obtain the required output or exactly what inputs are needed, a more in-depth analysis is called for. This typically means obtaining more background information about the problem or application. It also frequently entails doing one or more hand calculations to ensure that we understand what inputs are needed and how they must be combined to achieve the desired output.

Countless hours have been spent writing computer programs that either have never been used or have caused considerable animosity between programmer and user because the programmer did not produce what the user needed or expected. Successful programmers understand and avoid this by ensuring that the problem's requirements are understood. This is the first step in creating a program and the most important because in it the specifications for the final program solution are determined. If the requirements are not fully and completely understood before programming begins, the results are almost always disastrous.

For example, imagine designing and building a house without fully understanding the architect's specifications. After the house is completed, the architect tells you that a bathroom is required on the first floor, where you have built a wall between the kitchen and the dining room. In addition, that particular wall is one of the main support walls for the house and contains numerous pipes and electrical cables. In this case, adding one bathroom requires a rather major modification to the basic structure of the house.

Experienced programmers understand the importance of analyzing and understanding a program's requirements before coding, especially if they too have constructed programs that later had to be entirely dismantled and redone. The key to success here, which ultimately determines the success of the final program, is to determine the main purpose of the system as seen by the person making the request. For large systems, the analysis is usually conducted by a systems analyst. For smaller systems or individual programs, the analysis is typically performed directly by the programmer.

Regardless of how the analysis is done, or by whom, at its conclusion there should be a clear understanding of

- What the system or program must do

- What outputs must be produced

- What inputs are required to create the desired outputs

Step 2   Develop a Solution

In this step we select the exact set of steps, called an algorithm, that we will use to solve the problem. The solution is typically obtained by a series of refinements, starting with the initial algorithm found in the analysis step, until an acceptable and complete algorithm is obtained. This algorithm must be checked, if this was not already done in the analysis step, to ensure that it correctly produces the desired outputs. The check is typically done by doing one or more hand calculations not already done.

For small programs the selected algorithm may be extremely simple and consist of only one or more calculations that must be performed. More typically, the initial solution must be refined and organized into smaller subsystems, with specifications for how the subsystems will interface with each other. To achieve this goal, the description of the algorithm starts from the highest level (topmost) requirement and proceeds downward to the parts that must be constructed to achieve this requirement. To make this more meaningful, consider a computer program that is required to track the number of parts in inventory. The required output for this program is a description of all parts carried in inventory and the number of units of each item in stock; the given inputs are the initial inventory quantity of each part, the number of items sold, the number of items returned, and the number of items purchased.

For these specifications, a designer could initially organize the requirements for the program into the three sections illustrated in Figure 1.7. This is called a **top-level structure diagram** because it represents the first overall structure of the program selected by the designer.

Figure 1.7 *First-level structure diagram.*

Once an initial structure is developed, it is refined until the tasks indicated in the boxes are completely defined. For example, both the data entry and report modules shown in Figure 1.7 would be further refined. The data-entry module certainly must include provisions for entering the data. Since it is the system designer's responsibility to plan for contingencies and human error, provisions must also be made for changing incorrect data after an entry has been made and for deleting a previously entered value altogether. Similar subdivisions for the report module can also be made. Figure 1.8 illustrates a second level structure diagram for an inventory tracking system that includes these further refinements.

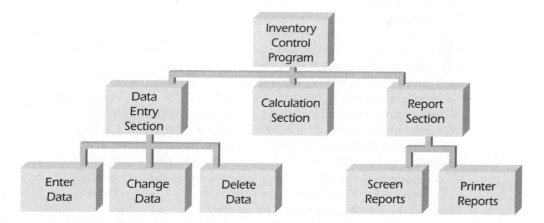

Figure 1.8 *Second-level refinement structure diagram.*

The process of refining a solution continues until the smallest requirement is included within the solution. Notice that the design produces a treelike structure where the levels branch out as we move from the top of the structure to the bottom. When the design is complete each task designated in a box is typically coded with separate sets of instructions that are executed as they are called on by tasks higher up in the structure.

Step 3   Code the Solution

This step, which is also referred to as writing the program and implementing the solution, consists of translating the chosen design solution into a computer program. If the analysis and solution steps have been correctly performed, the coding step becomes rather mechanical in nature. In a well-designed program, the statements making up the program will, however, conform to certain well-defined patterns or structures that have been defined in the solution step. These structures control how the program executes and consist of the following types:

1. Sequence

2. Selection

3. Iteration

4. Invocation

Sequence defines the order in which instructions are executed by the program. The specification of which instruction comes first, which comes second, and so on, is essential if the program is to achieve a well-defined purpose.

Selection provides the capability to make a choice between different operations, depending on the result of some condition. For example, the value of a number can be checked before a division is performed. If the number is not zero, it can be used as the denominator of a division operation, otherwise the division will not be performed and the user will be issued a warning message.

Iteration, which is also referred to as *looping* and *repetition*, provides the ability for the same operation to be repeated based on the value of a condition. For example, grades might be repeatedly entered and added until a negative grade is entered. In this case the entry of a negative grade is the condition that signifies the end of the repetitive input and addition of grades. At that point a calculation of an average for all the grades entered could be performed.

Invocation involves invoking, or summoning, a set of statements as it is needed. For example, the computation of a person's net pay involves the tasks of obtaining pay rates and hours worked, calculating the net pay, and providing a report or check for the required amount. Each of these individual tasks would typically be coded as separate units that are called into execution, or invoked, as they are needed.

Step 4   Test and Correct the Program

The purpose of testing is to verify that a program works correctly and actually fulfills its requirements. In theory, testing would reveal all existing program errors (in computer terminology, a program error is called a **bug**[6]). In practice, this would require checking all possible combinations of statement execution. Because of the time and effort required, this is usually an impossible goal except for extremely simple programs. (We illustrate why this is generally an impossible goal in Section 4.8)

---

[6]The derivation of this term is rather interesting. When a program stopped running on the Mark I, at Harvard University in September 1945, Grace Hopper traced the malfunction to a dead insect that had gotten into the electrical circuits. She recorded the incident in her logbook at 15:45 hours as "Relay #70. . . . (moth) in relay. First actual case of bug being found."

Because exhaustive testing is not feasible for most programs, different philosophies and methods of testing have evolved. At its most basic level, however, testing requires a conscious effort to ensure that a program works correctly and produces meaningful results. This means that careful thought must be given to what the test is meant to achieve and the data that will be used in the test. If testing reveals an error (bug), the process of debugging, which includes locating, correcting, and verifying the correction, can be initiated. It is important to realize that although testing may reveal the presence of an error, it does not necessarily indicate the absence of one. Thus, the fact that a test revealed one bug does not indicate that another one is not lurking somewhere else in the program.

To catch and correct errors in a program it is important to develop a set of test data by which to determine whether the program gives correct answers. In fact, an accepted step in formal software development many times is to plan the test procedures and create meaningful test data before writing the code. This tends to help the person be more objective about what the program must do because it essentially circumvents any subconscious temptation after coding to choose test data that will not work. The procedures for testing a program should examine every possible situation under which the program will be used. The program should be tested with data in a reasonable range as well as at the limits and in areas where the program should tell the user that the data are invalid. Developing good test procedures and data for sophisticated problems can be more difficult than writing the program code itself.

Table 1.3 lists the relative amount of effort that is typically expended on each of these four development and design steps in large commercial programming projects. As this listing demonstrated, coding is not the major effort in this phase. Many new programmers have trouble because they spend the majority of their time writing the program, without spending sufficient time understanding the problem or designing an appropriate solution. In this regard, it is worthwhile to remember the programming proverb, "It is impossible to write a successful program for a problem or application that is not fully understood." A somewhat equivalent and equally valuable proverb is "The sooner you start coding a program the longer it usually takes to complete."

Table 1.3 Effort Expended in Phase I.

Step	Effort
Analyze the problem	10%
Develop a solution	20%
Code the solution	20%
Test the program	50%

Phase II. Documentation

So much work becomes useless or lost and so many tasks must be repeated because of inadequate documentation that it could be argued that documenting your work is the most important step in problem solving. Actually, many of the critical documents are created during the analysis, design, coding, and testing steps. Completing the documentation requires collecting these documents, adding additional material, and presenting it in a form that is most useful to you and your organization.

Although not everybody classifies them in the same way, there are essentially five documents for every problem solution:

1. Program description
2. Algorithm development and changes
3. Well-commented program listing
4. Sample test runs
5. Users' manual

"Putting yourself in the shoes" of a member of a large organization's team that might use your work—anyone from the secretary to the programmer/analysts and management—should help you to make the content of the important documentation clear. The documentation phase formally begins in the development and design phase and continues into the maintenance phase.

Phase III Maintenance

This phase is concerned with ongoing correction of problems, revisions to meet changing needs, and adding new features. Maintenance is often the major effort, the primary source of revenue, and the longest lasting of the engineering phases. While development may take days or months, maintenance may continue for years or decades. The better the documentation is, the more efficiently this phase can be performed, and the happier the customer and user will be.

Backup

Although not part of the formal design process, it is critical to make and keep backup copies of the program at each step of the programming and debugging process. It is easy to delete or change the current working version of a program beyond recognition. Backup copies allow the recovery of the last stage of work with a minimum of effort. The final working version of a useful program should be backed up at least twice. In this regard, another useful programming proverb is "Backup is unimportant if you don't mind starting all over again."

Many organizations keep at least one backup on site, where it can be easily retrieved, and another backup copy either in a fireproof safe or at a remote location.

Exercises 1.2

1. **a.** List and describe the four steps required in the design and development stage of a program.
   b. In addition to the design and development stage, what are the other two stages required in producing a program and why are they required?

2. A note from your supervisor, Mr. J. Bosworth says

    Solve our lighting problems.
    — J. Bosworth

    a. What should be your first task?
    b. How would you accomplish this task?
    c. How long would you expect this to take, assuming everyone cooperates?

3. Program development is only one phase in the overall software development procedure. Assuming that documentation and maintenance require 60% of the total software effort in designing a system, and using Table 1.3, determine the amount of effort required for initial program coding as a percentage of total software effort.

4. Many people requesting a program or system for the first time consider coding to be the most important aspect of program development. They feel that they know what they need and think that the programmer can begin coding with minimal time spent in analysis. As a programmer, what pitfalls can you envision in working with such people?

5. Many first-time computer users try to contract with programmers for a fixed fee (total amount to be paid is fixed in advance). What is the advantage to the user in having this arrangement? What is the advantage to the programmer in having this arrangement? What are some disadvantages to both user and programmer in this arrangement?

6. Many programmers prefer to work on an hourly rate basis. Why do you think this is so? Under what conditions would it be advantageous for a programmer to give a client a fixed price for the programming effort?

7. Experienced users generally want a clearly written statement of programming work to be done, including a complete description of what the program will do, delivery dates, payment schedules, and testing requirements. What is the advantage to the user in requiring this? What is the advantage to a programmer in working under this arrangement? What disadvantages does this arrangement have for both user and programmer?

1.3 ALGORITHMS

Before a program is written, the programmer must clearly understand what data are to be used, the desired result, and the procedure to be used to produce this result. The procedure, or solution, selected is referred to as an algorithm. More precisely, an **algorithm** is defined as a step-by-step sequence of instructions that must terminate and describes how the data is to be processed to produce the desired outputs. In essence, an algorithm answers the question "What method will you use to solve this problem?"

Only after we clearly understand the data that we will be using and select an algorithm (the specific steps required to produce the desired result) can we code the program.

Seen in this light, programming is the translation of a selected algorithm into a language that the computer can use.

To illustrate an algorithm, we shall consider a simple problem. Assume that a program must calculate the sum of all whole numbers from 1 through 100. Figure 1.9 illustrates three methods we could use to find the required sum. Each method constitutes an algorithm.

Method 1 - Columns: Arrange the numbers from 1 to 100 in a column and add them

$$
\begin{array}{r}
1 \\
2 \\
3 \\
4 \\
\cdot \\
\cdot \\
\cdot \\
98 \\
99 \\
+100 \\
\hline
5050
\end{array}
$$

Method 2 - Groups: Arrange the numbers in groups that sum to 101 and multiply the number of groups by 101

$$
\left.\begin{array}{l}
1+100=101 \\
2+99=101 \\
3+98=101 \\
4+97=101 \\
\quad\cdot\qquad\cdot \\
\quad\cdot\qquad\cdot \\
\quad\cdot\qquad\cdot \\
49+52=101
\end{array}\right\} \text{50 groups}
$$

(50x101=5050)

Method 3 - Formula: Use the formula

$$\text{sum} = \frac{n(a+b)}{2}$$

where

n= number of terms to added (100)
a= first number to be added (1)
b= last number to be added (100)

$$\text{sum} = \frac{100(1+100)}{2} = 5050$$

Figure 1.9 Summing the numbers 1 through 100.

Clearly, most people would not bother to list the possible alternatives in a detailed step-by-step manner, as we have done here, and then select one of the algorithms to solve the problem. But then most people do not think algorithmically; they tend to think intuitively.

Symbol	Name	Description
	Terminal	Indicates the beginning or end of a program
	Input/Output	Indicates an input or output operation
	Process	Indicates computation or data manipulation
	Flow Lines	Used to connect the other flowchart symbols and indicate the logic flow
	Decision	Indicates a program branch point
	Loop	Indicates the initial, limit, and increment values of a loop
	Predefined Process	Indicates a predefined process, as in calling a function
	Connector	Indicates an entry to, or exit from, another part of the flowchart or a connection point
	Report	Indicates a written output report

Figure 1.10 Flowchart symbols.

For example, if you had to change a flat tire on your car, you would not think of all the steps required—you would simply change the tire or call someone else to do the job. This is an example of intuitive thinking.

Unfortunately, computers do not respond to intuitive commands. A general statement such as "add the numbers from 1 to 100" means nothing to a computer because the computer can only respond to algorithmic commands written in an acceptable language such as C++. To program a computer successfully, you must clearly understand this difference between algorithmic and intuitive commands. A computer is an "algorithm-responding" machine; it is not an "intuitive-responding" machine. You cannot tell a computer to change a tire or to add the numbers from 1 through 100. Instead, you must give the computer a detailed step-by-step set of instructions that, collectively, forms an algorithm. For example, the following set of instructions forms a detailed method, or algorithm, for determining the sum of the numbers from 1 through 100:

> *Set n equal to 100*
> *Set a = 1*
> *Set b equal to 100*
> *Calculate sum* $= \dfrac{n(a + b)}{2}$
>
> *Print the sum*

Notice that these instructions are not a computer program. Unlike a program, which must be written in a language the computer can respond to, an algorithm can be written or described in various ways. When English-like phrases are used to describe the algorithm (the processing steps), as in this example, the description is called **pseudocode**. When mathematical equations are used, the description is called a **formula**. When diagrams that employ the symbols shown in Figure 1.10 are used, the description is referred to as a **flowchart**. Figure 1.11 illustrates the use of these symbols in depicting an algorithm for determining the average of three numbers.

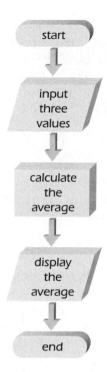

Figure 1.11 Flowchart for calculating the average of three numbers.

Because flowcharts are cumbersome to revise and can easily support unstructured programming practices, they have fallen out of favor by professional programmers, while the use of pseudocode to express the logic of algorithms has gained increasing acceptance. In describing an algorithm using pseudocode, short English phrases are used. For example, acceptable pseudocode for describing the steps needed to compute the average of three numbers is

> *Input the three numbers into the computer's memory*
> *Calculate the average by adding the numbers and dividing the sum by three*
> *Display the average*

Only after an algorithm has been selected and the programmer understands the steps required can the algorithm be written using computer-language statements. The writing of an algorithm using computer-language statements is called coding the algorithm, which is the third step in our program development procedure (see Figure 1.12). Most of Part I of this text is devoted to showing you how to develop and code algorithms into C++.

Figure 1.12 Coding an algorithm.

Exercises 1.3

1. Determine a step-by-step procedure (list the steps) to do the following tasks. (*Note: There is no one single correct answer for each of these tasks. The exercise is designed is to give you practice in converting intuitive-type commands into equivalent algorithms and making the shift between the thought processes involved in the two types of thinking.*)

    a. Fix a flat tire

    b. Make a telephone call

    c. Login to a computer

    d. Roast a turkey

2. Are the procedures you developed for Exercise 1 algorithms? Discuss why or why not.

3. Determine and write an algorithm (list the steps) to interchange the contents of two cups of liquid. Assume that a third cup is available to hold the contents of either cup temporarily. Each cup should be rinsed before any new liquid is poured into it.

4. Write a detailed set of instructions, in English, to calculate the resistance of the following resistors connected in series: n resistors, each having a resistance of 56 ohms, m resistors, each having a resistance of 33 ohms, and p resistors, each having a resistance of 15 ohms. Note that the total resistance of resistors connected in series is the sum of all individual resistances.

5. Write a set of detailed, step-by-step instructions, in English, to find the smallest number in a group of three integer numbers.

6. a. Write a set of detailed, step-by-step instructions, in English, to calculate the fewest number of dollar bills needed to pay a bill of amount TOTAL. For example, if TOTAL were $97 the bills would consist of one $50 bill, two $20 bills, one $5 bill and two $1 bills. (For this exercise assume that only $100, $50, $20, $10, $5, and $1 bills are available.)

    b. Repeat Exercise 6a, but assume the bill is to be paid only in $1 bills.

7. a. Write an algorithm to locate the first occurrence of the name JEANS in a list of names arranged in random order.

    b. Discuss how you could improve your algorithm for Exercise 7a if the list of names were arranged in alphabetical order.

8. Write an algorithm to determine the total occurrences of the letter e in any sentence.

9. Determine and write an algorithm to sort four numbers into ascending (from lowest to highest) order.

1.4 > COMMON PROGRAMMING ERRORS

The most common errors associated with the material presented in this chapter are as follows.

1. A major programming error made by most beginning programmers is the rush to write and run a program before fully understanding what is required, including the algorithms that will be used to produce the desired result. A symptom of this haste to get a program entered into the computer is the lack of any documentation or even a program outline or a written program itself. Many problems can be caught just by checking a copy of the program or even a description of the algorithm written in pseudocode.

2. A second major error is not backing up a program. Almost all new programmers make this mistake until they lose a program that has taken considerable time to code.

3. The third error made by many new programmers is the lack of understanding that computers respond only to explicitly defined algorithms. Telling a computer to add a group of numbers is quite different than telling a friend to add the numbers. The computer must be given the precise instructions for doing the addition in a programming language.

1.5 > CHAPTER SUMMARY

1. The programs used to operate a computer are referred to as *software*.

2. Programming languages come in a variety of forms and types. *Machine language* programs, also known as *executable programs*, contain the binary codes that can be executed by a computer. *Assembly languages* permit the use of symbolic names for mathematical operations and memory addresses. Programs written in assembly languages must be converted to machine language, using translator programs called *assemblers*, before the programs can be executed. Assembly and machine languages are referred to as *low-level languages*.

   Compiler and *interpreter languages* are referred to as *high-level languages*. This means that they are written using instructions that resemble a written language, such as English, and can be run on a variety of computer types. Compiler languages require a *compiler* to translate the program into a binary language form, whereas interpreter languages require an *interpreter* to do the translation.

3. As a discipline, *software engineering* is concerned with creating readable, efficient, reliable, and maintainable programs and systems.

4. The software development procedure consists of three phases:

- Program development and design

- Documentation

- Maintenance

5. The program development and design phase consists of four well-defined steps:

- Analyze the problem

- Develop a solution

- Code the solution

- Test and correct the solution

6. An *algorithm* is a step-by-step procedure that must terminate and describes how a computation or task is to be performed.

7. A *computer program* is a self-contained unit of instructions used to operate a computer to produce a specific result. More formally, a computer program is a description of an algorithm written in a language that can be processed by a computer.

8. The four fundamental control structures used in coding an algorithm are

- Sequence

- Selection

- Iteration

- Invocation

1.6 CHAPTER APPENDIX: COMPUTER HARDWARE AND STORAGE CONCEPTS

All computers, from large super computers costing millions of dollars to smaller desktop personal computers, must perform a minimum set of functions and provide the capability to

1. Accept input

2. Display output

3. Store information in a logically consistent format (traditionally binary)

4. Perform arithmetic and logic operations on either the input or stored data

5. Monitor, control, and direct the overall operation and sequencing of the system

Figure 1.13 illustrates the computer hardware components that support these capabilities. Specifically, this hardware consists of arithmetic and logic, control, memory, and input/output units.

The **arithmetic and logic Unit (ALU)** performs all the arithmetic and logic functions, such as addition, subtraction, provided by the computer.

The **control unit** directs and monitors the overall operation of the computer. It keeps track of where in memory the next instruction resides, issues the signals needed to both read data from and write data to other units in the system, and controls execution of all instructions.

The **memory unit** stores information in a logically consistent format. Typically, both instructions and data are stored in memory, usually in separate and distinct areas.

The **input and output (I/O) unit** provides the interface to which peripheral devices such as keyboards, monitors, printers, and card readers are attached.

In the first commercially available computers of the 1950s, all hardware units were built using relays and vacuum tubes. The resulting computers were extremely large pieces of equipment, capable of making thousands of calculations per second, and costing millions of dollars.

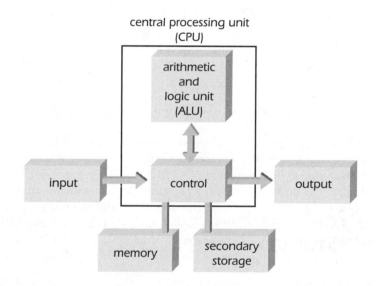

Figure 1.13 Basic hardware units of a computer.

With the introduction of transistors in the 1960s, both the size and cost of computer hardware were reduced. The transistor was approximately one-twentieth the size of its vacuum tube counterpart. The transistors small size allowed manufacturers to combine the arithmetic and logic unit with the control unit into a single new unit. This combined unit is called the **central processing unit (CPU)**. The combination of the ALU and control units into one CPU made sense because a majority of control signals generated by a program are directed to the ALU in response to arithmetic and logic instructions within the program. Combining the ALU with the control unit simplified the interface between these two units and provided improved processing speed.

The mid-1960s saw the introduction of integrated circuits (ICs), which resulted in still another significant reduction in the space required to produce a CPU. Initially, integrated circuits were manufactured with up to 100 transistors on a single 1 cm² chip of silicon. Such devices are referred to as small-scale integrated (SSI) circuits. Current versions of these chips contain hundreds of thousands to over a million transistors and are referred to as very large scale integrated (VLSI) chips.

VLSI chip technology has provided the means of transforming the giant computers of the 1950s into today's desktop and notebook personal computers. Each individual unit required to form a computer (CPU, memory, and I/O) is now manufactured on an individual VLSI chip, respectively, and the single-chip CPU is referred to as a **microprocessor**. Figure 1.14 illustrates how these chips are connected internally within current personal computers, such as the IBM-PCs.

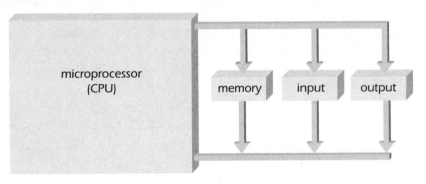

Figure 1.14 VLSI chip connections for a desktop computer.

Concurrent with the remarkable reduction in computer hardware size has been an equally dramatic decrease in cost and increase in processing speeds. Equivalent computer hardware that cost over a million dollars in 1950 can now be purchased for less than five hundred dollars. If the same reductions occurred in the automobile industry, for example, a Rolls Royce could now be purchased for ten dollars! The processing speeds of current computers have also increased by a factor of a thousand over their 1950s predecessors, with the computational speeds of current machines being measured in both millions of instructions per second (MIPS) and billions of instructions per second (BIPS).

Computer Storage

The physical components used in manufacturing a computer require that the numbers and letters inside its memory unit are not stored using the same symbols that people use. The number 126, for example, is not stored using the symbols 1, 2, and 6. Nor is the letter that we recognize as *A* stored using this symbol. In this section we will see why this is so and how computers store numbers. In Chapter 2 we will see how letters are stored.

The smallest and most basic data item in a computer is called a **bit**. Physically, a bit is really a switch that can be either open or closed. The convention we will follow is that the open and closed positions of each switch are represented as a 0 and a 1, respectively.[7]

A single bit that can represent the values 0 and 1, by itself, has limited usefulness. All computers, therefore, group a set number of bits together, both for storage and transmission. The grouping of eight bits to form a larger unit is an almost universal computer standard. Such groups are referred to as **bytes**. A single byte consisting of eight bits, where each bit is either a 0 or 1, can represent any one of 256 distinct patterns. These consist of the pattern 00000000 (all eight switches open) to the pattern 11111111 (all eight switches closed), and all possible combinations of 0s and 1s in between. Each of these patterns can be used to represent either a letter of the alphabet, other single characters, such as a dollar sign, comma, etc., a single digit, or numbers containing more than one digit. The collection of patterns consisting of 0s and 1s used to represent letters, single digits, and other single characters are called **character codes** (two such codes, called the ASCII and EBCDIC codes, are presented in Section 2.1). The patterns used to store numbers are called **number codes**, one of which is presented below.

Two's Complement Numbers

The most common number code for storing integer values inside a computer is called the **two's complement** representation. Using this code, the integer equivalent of any bit pattern, such as 10001101, is easy to determine and can be found for either positive or negative integers with no change in the conversion method. For convenience we will assume byte-sized bit patterns consisting of a set of eight bits each, although the procedure carries directly over to larger size bit patterns.

The easiest way to determine the integer represented by each bit pattern is to first construct a simple device called a value box. Figure 1.15 illustrates such a box for a single byte. Mathematically, each value in the box illustrated in Figure 1.15 represents an increasing power of two. Since two's complement numbers must be capable of representing both positive and negative integers, the leftmost position, in addition to having the largest absolute magnitude, also has a negative sign.

```
-128| 64 | 32 | 16 |  8 |  4 |  2 |  1
----|----|----|----|----|----|----|---
    |    |    |    |    |    |    |
```

Figure 1.15 *An eight-bit value box.*

Conversion of any binary number, for example 10001101, simply requires inserting the bit pattern into the value box and adding the values having ones under them. Thus, as illustrated in Figure 1-16, the bit pattern 10001101 represents the integer number –115.

---

[7]This convention, unfortunately, is rather arbitrary, and you will frequently encounter the reverse correspondence where the open and closed positions are represented as 1 and 0, respectively.

```
-128 | 64 | 32 | 16 |  8 |  4 |  2 |  1
----|----|----|----|----|----|----|---
   1 |  0 |  0 |  0 |  1 |  1 |  0 |  1
-128 +  0 +  0 +  0 +  8 +  4 +  0 +  1 = -115
```

Figure 1.16 *Converting 10001101 to a base 10 number.*

The value box can also be used in reverse, to convert a base 10 integer number into its equivalent binary bit pattern. Some conversions, in fact, can be made by inspection. For example, the base 10 number −125 is obtained by adding 3 to −128. Thus, the binary representation of −125 is 10000011, which equals −128 + 2 + 1. Similarly, the two's complement representation of the number 40 is 00101000, which is 32 plus 8.

Although the value box conversion method is deceptively simple, the method is directly related to the underlying mathematical basis of two's complement binary numbers. The original name of the two's complement code was the weighted-sign code, which correlates directly to the value box. As the name **weighted sign** implies, each bit position has a weight, or value, of two raised to a power and a sign. The signs of all bits except the leftmost bit are positive and the sign of the leftmost bit is negative.

In reviewing the value box, it is evident that any two's complement binary number with a leading 1 represents a negative number, and any bit pattern with a leading 0 represents a positive number. Using the value box it is easy to determine the most positive and negative values capable of being stored. The most negative value that can be stored in a single byte is the decimal number −128, which has the bit pattern 10000000. Any other nonzero bit will simply add a positive amount to the number. Additionally, it is clear that a positive number must have a 0 as its leftmost bit. From this you can see that the largest positive 8-bit two's complement number is 01111111 or 127.

Words and Addresses

One or more bytes may themselves be grouped into larger units, called **words,** which facilitate faster and more extensive data access. For example, retrieving a word consisting of four bytes from a computer's memory results in more information than that obtained by retrieving a word consisting of a single byte. Such a retrieval is also considerably faster than four individual byte retrievals. This increase in speed and capacity, however, is achieved by an increase in the computer's cost and complexity.

Early personal computers, such as the Apple IIe and Commodore machines, internally stored and transmitted words consisting of single bytes. The first IBM-PCs used word sizes consisting of two bytes, while more current Pentium based PCs store and process words consisting of four bytes each.

The number of bytes in a word determines the maximum and minimum values that can be represented by the word. Table 1.4 lists these values for 1, 2, and 4 byte words (each of the values listed can be derived using 8-, 16-, and 32-bit value boxes, respectively).

Table 1.4 Integer Values and Word Size.

Word Size	Maximum Integer Value	Minimum Integer Value
1 Byte	127	−128
2 Bytes	32,767	−32,768
4 Bytes	2,147,483,647	−2,147,483,648

In addition to representing integer values, computers must also store and transmit numbers containing decimal points, which are mathematically referred to as real numbers. The codes used for real numbers, which are more complex than those used for integers, are presented in Appendix D.

Aeronautical/Aerospace Engineering

Among the youngest of the engineering disciplines, aeronautical/aerospace engineering is concerned with all aspects of the design, production, testing, and utilizing of vehicles or devices that fly in air (aeronautical) or in space (aerospace), from hang gliders to space shuttles. Since the science and engineering principles involved are so broad based, aeroengineers usually specialize in a subarea that may overlap with other engineering fields such as mechanical, metallurgical/materials, chemical, civil, or electrical engineering. Such subareas include the following.

1. Aerodynamics. The study of the flight characteristics of various structures or configurations. Typical considerations are the drag and lift associated with airplane design or the onset of turbulent flow. A knowledge of fluid dynamics is essential. The modeling and testing of all forms of aircraft is part of this discipline.

2. Structural design. The design, production, and testing of aircraft and spacecraft to withstand the wide range of in-flight demands on these vehicles, such as underwater vessels, are in the province of the structural engineer.

3. Propulsion systems. The design of internal combustion, jet, and liquid- and solid-fuel rocket engines and their coordination in the overall design of the vehicle. Rocket engines, especially, require innovative engineering to accommodate the extreme temperatures of storing, mixing, and burning fuels such as liquid oxygen.

4. Instrumentation and guidance. The aerospace industry has been a leader in developing and utilizing solid-state electronics in the form of microprocessors to monitor and adjust the operations of hundreds of air- and spacecraft functions. This field uses the expertise of both electrical engineers and aeroengineers.

5. Navigation. The computation of orbits within and outside the atmosphere, and the determination of the orientation of a vehicle with respect to points on the earth or in space.

Part One
Procedure-Oriented Programming in C++

CHAPTERS

2 Problem Solving Using C++

3 Completing the Basics

4 Selection Structures

5 Repetition Structures

6 Modularity Using Functions

Although C++ is an object-oriented language, it was developed as an extension to C, which is a procedural-oriented language. As such, C++ is a hybrid language having both procedural and object features. Because of this hybrid nature it is not only possible to write a complete C++ program using only procedural code, it is impossible to write an object-oriented program in C++ that does not include procedural elements. Thus, a proper start to learning C++ requires familiarity with its procedural aspects.

CHAPTER 2

Problem Solving Using C++

TOPICS

2.1 INTRODUCTION TO C++
THE main() FUNCTION
THE cout OBJECT

2.2 PROGRAMMING STYLE
COMMENTS

2.3 DATA VALUES AND ARITHMETIC OPERATIONS
INTEGER VALUES   ARITHMETIC OPERATIONS
FLOATING-POINT NUMBERS   INTEGER DIVISION
CHARACTER VALUES   A UNARY OPERATOR (NEGATION)
ESCAPE SEQUENCES   OPERATOR PRECEDENCE AND ASSOCIATIVITY

2.4 VARIABLES AND DECLARATION STATEMENTS
DECLARATION STATEMENTS   MEMORY ALLOCATION
MULTIPLE DECLARATIONS   DISPLAYING A VARIABLE'S ADDRESS

2.5 INTEGER QUALIFIERS
DATA TYPE CONVERSIONS
DETERMINING STORAGE SIZE

2.6 APPLYING THE SOFTWARE DEVELOPMENT PROCEDURE
STEP 1: ANALYZE THE PROBLEM   STEP 3: CODE THE SOLUTION
STEP 2: DEVELOP A SOLUTION   STEP 4: TEST AND CORRECT THE PROGRAM

2.7 APPLICATIONS
APPLICATION 1: RADAR SPEED TRAPS
APPLICATION 2: TELEPHONE SWITCHING NETWORKS

2.8 COMMON PROGRAMMING ERRORS

2.9 CHAPTER SUMMARY
LOOKING AT CAREER CHOICES: ELECTRICAL ENGINEERING

2.1 ▷ INTRODUCTION TO C++

A well-designed program is constructed using a design philosophy similar to that used in constructing a well-designed building: It doesn't just happen; it depends on careful planning and execution if the final design is to accomplish its intended purpose. Just as an integral part of the design of a building is its structure, the same is true for a program.

Programs whose structure consists of interrelated segments, arranged in a logical and easily understandable order to form an integrated and complete unit, are referred to as **modular programs** (Figure 2.1). Modular programs are noticeably easier to develop, correct, and modify than programs constructed in some other manner. In programming terminology, the smaller segments used to construct a modular program are referred to as **modules**.

Each module is designed and developed to perform a specific task and is really a small subprogram all by itself. A complete C++ program is constructed by combining as many modules as necessary to produce the desired result. The advantage of modular construction is that the overall design of the program can be developed before any single module is written. Once the requirements for each module are finalized, the modules can be programmed and integrated within the overall program as they are completed.

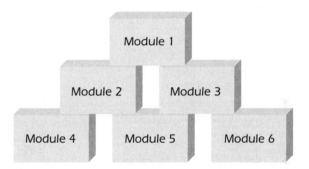

Figure 2.1 A well-designed program is built using modules.

In C++ modules can be either classes or functions. It helps to think of a **function** as a small machine that transforms the data it receives into a finished product. For example, Figure 2.2 illustrates a function that accepts two numbers as inputs and multiplies the two numbers to produce one output. As shown, the interface to the function is its inputs and results. The process of converting the inputs to results is both encapsulated and hidden within the function. In this regard the function can be thought of as a single unit providing a special purpose operation. A similar analogy is appropriate for a **class**.

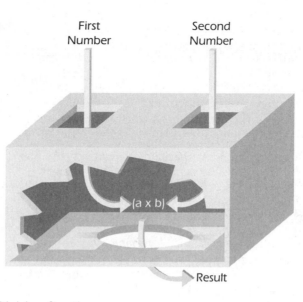

Figure 2.2 *A multiplying function.*

A **class** is a more complicated unit than a function because it contains both data and functions appropriate for manipulating the data. Thus, unlike a function, which is used to encapsulate a set of operations, a class encapsulates both data and one or more sets of operations. As such, each class contains all of the elements required for the input, output, and processing of its objects and can be thought of as a small dedicated computer. Initially, we will be predominantly concerned with the more basic function module.

One important requirement for designing a good function or class is to give it a name that conveys to the reader some idea of what the function or class does. The names permissible for functions and classes are also used to name other elements of the C++ language and are collectively referred to as **identifiers**. Identifiers can be made up of any combination of letters, digits, or underscores (_) selected according to the following rules.

1. The first character of the name must be a letter or underscore (_).

2. Only letters, digits, or underscores may follow the initial letter. Blank spaces are not allowed; either use the underscore to separate words in a name consisting of multiple words or capitalize the first letter of one or more words.

3. A function name cannot be one of the keywords listed in Table 2.1. (A **keyword** is a word that is set aside by the language for a special purpose and can only be used in a specified manner.[1])

4. The maximum number of characters in a function name is 31.[2]

---

[1]Keywords in C are also reserved words, which means they must be used only for their specified purpose. Attempting to use them for any other purpose will generate an error message.

[2] This tends to be compiler specific. For Microsoft Visual C++, the length of an identifier is 247 characters.

Examples of valid C++ identifiers are

```
DegToRad     intersect     addNums     slope
bessel1      mult_two      FindMax     density
```

Examples of invalid identifiers are

1AB3 (Begins with a number, which violates rule 1.)

E*6   (Contains a special character, which violates rule 2.)

while (This is a keyword, which violates rule 3.)

In addition to conforming to C++'s identifier rules, a C++ function name must always be followed by parentheses (the reason for this is explained shortly). Also, a good function name should be a mnemonic. A **mnemonic** (pronounced nii-monic) is a word or name designed as a memory aid. For example, the function name DegToRad() (note that we have included the required parentheses after the identifier, which clearly marks this as a function name) is a mnemonic if it is the name of a function that converts degrees to radians. Here, the name itself helps to identify what the function does.

Examples of valid function names that are not mnemonics are

```
easy()     c3po()     r2d2()     TheForce()     mike()
```

Function names that are not mnemonic should not be used because they convey no information about what the function does.

Additionally, function names can be typed in mixed upper and lowercase letters. This is becoming increasingly common in C++, although it is not absolutely necessary. All uppercase identifiers are usually reserved for symbolic constants, a topic covered in Section 3.5.

Additionally, C++ is a **case-sensitive** language. This means that the compiler distinguishes between uppercase and lowercase letters. Thus, in C++, the names TOTAL, total, and TotaL represent three distinct names.

Table 2.1 Keywords

auto	default	goto	public	this
break	do	if	register	template
case	double	inline	return	typedef
catch	else	int	short	union
char	enum	long	signed	unsigned
class	extern	new	sizeof	virtual
const	float	overload	static	void
continue	for	private	struct	volatile
delete	friend	protected	switch	while

The `main()` Function

A distinct advantage of using functions and classes in C++ is that the overall structure of the program in general, and individual modules in particular, can be planned in advance, including provision for testing and verifying each module's operation. Each function and class can then be written to meet its intended objective.

To provide for the orderly placement and execution of modules, each C++ program must have one and only one function named `main()`. The `main()` function is referred to as a **driver function**, because it drives, or tells the other modules the sequence in which they are to execute (Figure 2.3).[3]

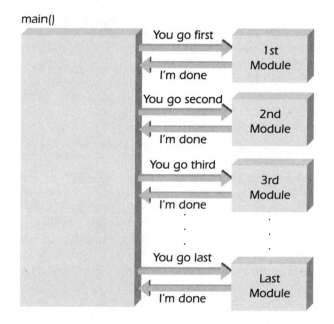

Figure 2.3 The `main()` function directs all other functions.

Figure 2.4 illustrates a structure for the `main()` function. The first line of the function, in this case `int main()` is referred to as a **function header line**. A function header line, which is always the first line of a function, contains three pieces of information:[4]

1. What type of data, if any, is returned from the function.

2. The name of the function.

3. What type of data, if any, is sent into the function.

The keyword before the function name defines the type of value the function returns when it has completed operating. When placed before the function's name the keyword

---

[3]Modules executed from `main()` may, in turn, execute other modules. Each module, however, always returns to the module that initiated its execution. This is true even for `main()`, which returns control to the operating system in effect when `main()` was initiated.

[4]A class method must also begin with a header line that adheres to these same rules.

`int` (see Table 2.1) designates that the function will return an integer value. Similarly, when the parentheses following the function name are empty, it signifies that no data will be transmitted into the function when it is run. (Data transmitted into a function at run time are referred to as **arguments** of the function.) The braces, { and }, determine the beginning and end of the function body and enclose the statements making up the function. The statements inside the braces determine what the function does. Each statement inside the function must end with a semicolon (;).

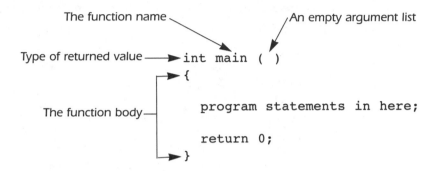

Figure 2.4 The structure of a `main()` function.

You will be naming and writing many of your own C++ functions. In fact, the rest of this book is primarily about the statements required to construct useful functions and how to combine functions and data into useful classes and programs. Each program, however, must have one and only one `main()` function. Until we learn how to pass data into a function and return data from a function (the topics of Chapter 6), the header line illustrated in Figure 2.4 will serve us for all the programs we need to write. For simple programs consider that the first two lines until they are explained more fully,

```
int main()
{
```

simply designate that "the program begins here," while the last two lines

```
    return 0;
}
```

designate the end of the program. Fortunately, many useful functions and classes have already been written for us. We will now see how to use an object created from one of these classes to create our first working C++ program.

The `cout` **Object**

One of the most versatile and commonly used objects provided in C++ is named `cout` (pronounced "see out"). This object, whose name was derived from Console OUTput, is an output object that sends data given to it to the standard output display device.[5] For

---

[5] The `cout` object is formally created from the `ostream` class, which is described in detail in Chapter 7.

most systems this display device is a video screen. The `cout` object displays on the monitor whatever is passed to it. For example, if the data `Hello there world!` is passed to `cout`, this data is printed (or displayed) on your terminal screen. The data `Hello there world!` is passed to the `cout` object by simply putting the insertion ("put to") symbol, `<<`, before the message and after the object's name, as shown in Figure 2.5.

```
cout << "Hello there world!";
```

Figure 2.5 *Passing a message to* `cout`.

Now let's put all this together into a working C++ program that can be run on your computer. Consider Program 2.1.

Program 2.1

```
#include <iostream.h>

int main()
{
    cout << "Hello there world!";

    return 0;
}
```

The first line of the program

```
#include <iostream.h>
```

is a preprocessor command. Preprocessor commands begin with a pound sign, (#) and perform some action before the compiler translates the source program into machine code. Specifically, the `#include` preprocessor command causes the contents of the named file, in this case `iostream.h` to be inserted where the `#include` command appears.[6] The file `iostream.h` is referred to as a **header file** because it is placed at the top, or head, of a C++ program using the `#include` command. In particular, the `iostream.h` file provide descriptions of two classes, `istream` and `ostream`. These two classes contain the actual data definitions and operations used for data input and output.[7] This header file must be included in all programs that use `cout`. As also indicated in Program 2.1, preprocessor commands do not end with a semicolon.

---

[6] Two other alternatives that use the `iostream` designation without the `.h` suffix are explained in Appendix F.

[7] Formally, `cout` is an object of the class ostream.

Point of Information

What Is Syntax?

A programming language's **syntax** is the set of rules for formulating grammatically correct language statements. In practice this means that a C++ statement with correct syntax has the proper form specified for the compiler. As such, the compiler will accept the statement and not generate an error message.

It should be noted that an individual statement or program can be syntactically correct and still be logically incorrect. Such a statement or program would be correctly structured but produce an incorrect result. This is similar to an English statement that is grammatically correct but makes no sense. For example, although the sentence "The tree is a ragged cat" is grammatically correct, it makes no sense.

The preprocessor command is followed by the start of the program's `main()` function. The `main()` function begins with the header line developed in the previous section and the body of the function, enclosed in braces, consists of only one statement. Remember that all statements end with a semicolon (;). The statement in `main()` passes one message to the `cout` object. The message is the string `Hello there world!`.

Since `cout` is an object of a prewritten class, we do not have to write it; it is available for use just by activating it correctly. Like all C++ objects, `cout` can only perform certain well-defined actions. For `cout`, the action is to assemble data for output display. When a string of characters is passed to `cout`, the object sees to it that the string is correctly displayed on your monitor, as shown in Figure 2.6.

```
Hello there world!
```

Figure 2.6 The output from Program 2.1.

Strings in C++ are any combination of letters, numbers, and special characters enclosed in double quotes ("string in here"). The double quotes are used to delimit (mark) the beginning and ending of the string and are not considered part of the string. Thus, the string of characters making up the message sent to `cout` must be enclosed in double quotes, as we have done in Program 2.1.

Let us write another program to illustrate `cout`'s versatility. Read Program 2.2 to determine what it does.

Program 2.2

```
#include <iostream.h>

int main()
{
  cout << "Computers, computers everywhere";
  cout << "\n   as far as I can C";

  return 0;
}
```

When Program 2.2 is run, the following is displayed:

```
Computers, computers everywhere
      as far as I can C
```

You might be wondering why the \n did not appear in the output. The two characters \
and n, when used together, are called a newline escape sequence. They tell cout to send
instructions to the display device to move to a new line. In C++, the backslash (\) character provides an "escape" from the normal interpretation of the character following it
by altering the meaning of the next character. If the backslash was omitted from the second cout call in Program 2.2, the n would be printed as the letter n and the program
would print out:

```
Computers, computers everywheren   as far as I can C
```

Newline escape sequences can be placed anywhere within the message passed to cout. See
if you can determine the display produced by Program 2.3.

Program 2.3

```
#include <iostream.h>

int main()
{
  cout << "Computers everywhere\n as far as\n\nI can see";

  return 0;
}
```

The output for Program 2.3 is:

```
Computers everywhere
 as far as

I can see
```

Exercises 2.1

1. State whether the following are valid function names. If they are valid, state whether they are mnemonic names. (Recall that a mnemonic function name conveys some idea about the function's purpose). If they are invalid names, state why.

power	density	m1234$	newamp	1234	abcd
total	tangent	absval	computed	b34a	34ab
volts$	a2-b3	while	minVal	sine	$sine
cosine	speed	netdistance	sum	return	stack

2. Assume that the following functions have been written:

   ```
   getLentgh(),  getWidth(),  calcArea(),  displayArea()
   ```

   a. From the functions' names, what do you think each function might do?
   b. In what order do you think a `main()` function might execute these functions (based on their names)?

3. Assume that the following functions have been written:

   ```
   speed(),  distance(),  acceleration()
   ```

   From the functions' names, what do you think each function might do?

4. Determine names for functions that do the following:
   a. Find the average of a set of numbers.
   b. Find the area of a rectangle.
   c. Find the minimum value in a set of numbers.
   d. Find the density of a steel door.
   e. Sort a set of numbers from lowest to highest.

5. Just as the keyword `int` is used to signify that a function will return an integer, the keywords `void`, `char`, `float`, and `double` are used to signify that a function will return no value, a character, a floating-point number, and a double-precision number. Using this information, write header lines for a `main()` function that will receive no arguments but will return
   a. no value
   b. a character
   c. a floating-point number
   d. a double-precision number

6. **a.** Using `cout`, write a C++ program that displays your name on one line, your street address on a second line, and your city, state, and zip code on the third line.

   b. Run the program you have written for Exercise 6a on a computer. (*NOTE:* You must understand the procedures for entering and running a C++ program on the particular computer installation you are using.)

7. **a.** Write a C++ program to display the following:

```
The cosecant of an angle
    is equal to one over
        the sine of the angle.
```

   b. Compile and run the program you have written for Exercise 7a on a computer.

8. **a.** How many `cout` statements would you use to display the following:

Degrees	Radians
0	0.0000
90	1.5708
180	3.1416
270	4.7124
360	6.2832

   b. What is the minimum number of `cout` statements that could be used to print the table in Exercise 8a?

   c. Write a complete C++ program to produce the output illustrated in Exercise 8a.

   d. Run the program you have written for Exercise 8c on a computer.

9. In response to a newline escape sequence, cout positions the next displayed character at the beginning of a new line. This positioning of the next character actually represents two distinct operations. What are they?

10. **a.** Assuming a case insensitive compiler, determine which of these program unit names are equivalent:

AVERAG	averag	MODE	BESSEL	Mode
Total	besseL	TeMp	Densty	TEMP
denSTY	MEAN	total	mean	moDE

   b. Redo Exercise 10a assuming a case sensitive compiler.

Project Structuring Exercises

Most projects, both programming and nonprogramming, can usually be structured into smaller subtasks or units of activity. These smaller subtasks can often be delegated to different people so that when all the tasks are finished and integrated, the project or program is completed. For Exercises 11 through 16, determine a set of subtasks that, taken together, complete the project. Be aware that there are many possible solutions for each exercise. The only requirement is that the set of subtasks selected, when taken together, complete the required task.

NOTE: *The purpose of these exercises is to have you consider the different ways that complex tasks can be structured. Although there is no one correct solution to these exercises, there are incorrect solutions and solutions that are better than others. An incorrect solution is one that does not fully specify the task. One solution is better than another if it more clearly or easily identifies what must be done.*

11. You are given the task of wiring and installing lights in the attic of your house. Determine a set of subtasks that, taken together, will accomplish this. (*Hint:* The first subtask would be to determine the placement of the light fixtures.)

12. You are given the job of preparing a complete meal for five people next weekend. Determine a set of subtasks, that taken together, accomplish this. (*Hint:* One subtask, not necessarily the first one, would be to buy the food.)

13. You are a sophomore in college and are planning to go to graduate school for a Master's degree in electrical engineering after you graduate. List a set of major objectives that you must fulfill to meet this goal. (*Hint:* One subtask is "Determine the correct courses to take.")

14. You are given the job of planting a vegetable garden. Determine a set of subtasks that accomplish this. (*Hint:* One such subtask would be to plan the layout of the garden.)

15. You are responsible for planning and arranging the family camping trip this summer. List a set of subtasks that, taken together, accomplish this objective successfully. (*Hint:* One subtask would be to select the camp site.)

16. **a.** A national medical testing laboratory desires a new computer system to analyze its test results. The system must be capable of processing each day's results. Additionally, the laboratory wants the capability to retrieve and output a printed report of all results that meet certain criteria, for example, all results obtained for a particular doctor or all results obtained for hospitals in a particular state. Determine three or four major program units into which this system could be separated. (*Hint:* One possible program unit is "Prepare Daily Results" to create each day's reports.)

    b. Suppose someone enters incorrect data for a particular test result, which is discovered after the data has been entered and stored by the system. What program unit is needed to take care of correcting this problem? Discuss why such a program unit might or might not be required by most systems.

    c. Assume a program unit exists that allows a user to alter or change data that has been incorrectly entered and stored. Discuss the need for including an "audit trail" that would allow for a later reconstruction of the changes made, when they were made, and who made them.

2.2 PROGRAMMING STYLE

C++ programs start execution at the beginning of the `main()` function. Since a program can have only one starting point, every C++ language program must contain one and only one `main()` function. As we have seen, all of the statements that make up the `main()` function are then included within the braces `{}` following the function name. Although the `main()` function must be present in every C++ program, C++ does not require that the word main, the parentheses `()`, or the braces `{}` be placed in any particular form. The form used in the last section

```
int main()
{
  program statements in here;

  return 0;
}
```

was chosen strictly for clarity and ease in reading the program.[8] For example, the following general form of a `main()` function would also work:

```
int main
 (
 ) { first statement;second statement;
        third statement;fourth
statement;
return 0;}
```

Notice that more than one statement can be put on a line, or one statement can be written across lines. Except for strings, double quotes, identifiers, and keywords, C++ ignores all white space (white space refers to any combination of one or more blank spaces, tabs, or new lines). For example, changing the white space in Program 2.1 and making sure not to split the string Hello there world! across two lines results in the following valid program:

```
#include <iostream.h>

int main
(
){
cout <<
"Hello there world!";
 return 0;
}
```

---

[8]If one of the program statements uses cout, the #include <iostream.h> preprocessor command is required.

Although this version of main() does work, it is an example of extremely poor programming style. It is difficult to read and understand. For readability, the main() function should always be written in standard form as:

```
int main()
 {
    program statements in here;

    return 0;
 }
```

In this standard form the function name starts in column 1 and is placed with the required parentheses on a line by itself. The opening brace of the function body follows on the next line and is placed under the first letter of the line containing the function name. Similarly, the closing function brace is placed by itself in column 1 as the last line of the function. This structure serves to highlight the function as a single unit.

Within the function itself, all program statements are indented at least two spaces. Indentation is another sign of good programming practice, especially if the same indentation is used for similar groups of statements. Review Program 1.2 to see that the same indentation was used for both cout object calls.

As you progress in your understanding and mastery of C++, you will develop your own indentation standards. Just keep in mind that the final form of your programs should be consistent and should always serve as an aid to the reading and understanding of your programs.

Comments

Comments are explanatory remarks made within a program. When used carefully, comments can be very helpful in clarifying what the complete program is about, what a specific group of statements is meant to accomplish, or what one line is intended to do. C++ supports two types of comments: line and block. Both types of comments can be placed anywhere within a program and have no effect on program execution. The computer ignores all comments—they are there strictly for the convenience of anyone reading the program.

A line comment begins with two slashes (//) and continues to the end of the line. For example, the following lines are all line comments:

```
// this is a comment
// this program prints out a message
// this program calculates a square root
```

The symbols //, with no white space between them, designate the start of the line comment. The end of the line on which the comment is written designates the end of the comment.

A line comment can be written either on a line by itself or at the end of the same line containing a program statement. Program 2.4 illustrates the use of line comments within a program.

Program 2.4

```
// this program displays a message
#include <iostream.h>

int main()
{
    cout << "Hello there world!"; // this produces the display

    return 0;
}
```

The first comment appears on a line by itself at the top of the program and describes what the program does. This is generally a good location to include a short comment describing the program's purpose. If more comments are required, they can be placed, one per line. Thus, when a comment is too long to be contained on one line, it can be separated into two or more line comments, with each separate comment preceded by the double slash symbol set //. The comment

```
// this comment is invalid because it
    extends over two lines
```

will result in a C++ error message on your computer. This comment is correct when written as

```
// this comment is used to illustrate a
// comment that extends across two lines
```

Comments that span across two or more lines are, however, more conveniently written as C-type block comments rather than as multiple line comments. Such comments begin with the symbols /* and end with the symbols */. For example,

```
/* This is a block comment that
    spans
    across three lines */
```

In C++, a program's structure is intended to make the program readable and understandable, making the use of extensive comments unnecessary. This is reinforced if function, class, and variable names, described in the next chapter, are carefully selected to convey their meaning to anyone reading the program. However, if the purpose of a function, class, or statement is still not clear from its structure, name, or context, include comments where clarification is needed. Obscure code with no comments is a sure sign of bad programming when the program must be maintained or read by others. Similarly, excessive comments are also a sign of bad programming, because they imply that insufficient thought was given to having the code itself be self-explanatory. Typically, any program that you write should begin with a set of initial program comments that include a short program description, your name, and the date that the program was last modified. For space considerations, and because all programs in this text were written by the author, initial comments will only be used for short program descriptions when they are not provided as part of the accompanying descriptive text.

Exercises 2.2

1. **a.** Will the following program work?

```
#include <iostream.h>
int main() {cout << "Hello there world!"; return 0;}
```

   b. Why is the program given in Exercise 1a not a good program?

2. Rewrite the following programs to conform to good programming practice.

   a.
```
#include <iostream.h>
   int main(
   ){
   cout           <<
   "The time has come"
   ; return 0;}
```

   b.
```
#include <iostream.h>
   int main
   (    ){cout << "Newark is a city\n";cout <<
   "In New Jersey\n"; cout <<
   "It is also a city\n"
   ; cout << "In Delaware\n"
   ; return 0;}
```

   c.
```
#include <iostream.h>
   int main() {cout << Reading a program\n";cout <<
   "is much easier\n"
   ; cout << "if a standard form for main is used\n")
   ; cout
   <<"and each statement is written\n";cout
   <<            "on a line by itself\n")
   ; return 0;}
```

   d.
```
#include <iostream.h>
   int main
   (    ){ cout << "Every C++ program"
   ; cout
   <<"\nmust have one and only one"
   ;
   cout << "main function"
   ;
```

```
cout <<
"\n the escape sequence of characters")
; cout <<
  "\nfor a newline can be placed anywhere"
; cout
<<"\n within the message passed to cout"
; return 0;}
```

3. a. When used in a message, the backslash character alters the meaning of the character immediately following it. If we wanted to print the backslash character, we would have to tell `cout` to escape from the way it normally interprets the backslash. What character do you think is used to alter the way a single backslash character is interpreted?

  b. Using your answer to Exercise 3a, write the escape sequence for printing a backslash.

4. a. A **token** of a computer language is any sequence of characters that, as a unit, with no intervening characters or white space, has a unique meaning. Using this definition of a token, determine whether escape sequences, function names, and the keywords listed in Table 1.2 are tokens of the C++ language.

  b. Discuss whether adding white space to a message alters the message. Discuss whether messages can be considered tokens of C++.

  c. Using the definition of a token given in Exercise 4a, determine whether the following statemen is true: "Except for tokens of the language, C++ ignores all white space."

2.3 ▷ DATA VALUES AND ARITHMETIC OPERATIONS

C++ programs can process different types of data in different ways. For example, calculating the bacteria growth in a polluted pond requires mathematical operations on numerical data, while sorting a list of names requires comparison operations using alphabetical data. In this section we introduce C++'s elementary data types and the operations that can be performed on them. Additionally, we show how to use the `cout` object function to display the results of these operations.

The three basic data values used in C++ are integers, floating-point numbers, and character values. Each of these data values is described in the following subsections.

Integer Values

An **integer value** is zero, or any positive or negative number without a decimal point. Examples of valid integer values are

```
0    5    -10    +25    1000    253    -26351    +36
```

As these examples illustrate, integers may be signed (have a leading + or – sign) or unsigned (no leading + or – sign). No commas, decimal points, or special symbols, such as the dollar sign, are allowed. Examples of invalid integer values are

$255.62   2,523   3.   6,243,892   1,492.89   +6.0

Different computer types have their own internal limit on the largest (most positive) and smallest (most negative) integer values that can be used in a program. These limits depend on the amount of storage each computer sets aside for an integer; as such, they are said to be implementation dependent. The more commonly used storage allocations are listed in Table 2.2. (Review Section 1.6 if you are unfamiliar with the concept of a byte.) By referring to your computer's reference manual or using the `sizeof` operator introduced in Section 2.5 you can determine the actual number of bytes allocated by your computer for each integer value. To store integer values greater than those supported by the memory allocation shown in Table 2.2 requires using integer qualifiers. These qualifiers are described in Section 2.5.

Table 2.2 Integer Values and Word Size[9]

Word Size	Maximum Integer Value	Minimum Integer Value
1 Byte	127	–128
2 Bytes	32,767	–32,768
4 Bytes	2,147,483,647	–2,147,483,648

Floating-Point Numbers

A **floating-point number**, which is also called a **real number**, is any signed or unsigned number having a decimal point. Examples of floating-point numbers are:

+10.625   5.   –6.2   3251.92   0.0   0.33   –6.67   +2.

Notice that the numbers 5., 0.0, and +2. are classified as floating-point numbers, while the same numbers written without a decimal point (5, 0, +2) would be integer values. As with integer values, special symbols, such as the dollar sign and the comma, are not permitted in floating-point numbers. Examples of invalid floating-point numbers are

5,326.25   24   123   6,459 $10.29

C++ supports three different categories of floating-point numbers: float, double, and long double. The difference between these numbers is the amount of storage that a computer uses for each type. Most computers use twice the amount of storage for doubles than for floats, which allows a double to have approximately twice the precision of a float (for this reason floats are sometimes referred to as **single precision** numbers and doubles as

---

[9] It is interesting to note that in all cases the magnitude of the most negative integer allowed is always one more than the magnitude of the most positive integer. This is due to the method most commonly used to represent integers, called two's complement representation. For an explanation of two's complement representation see the appendix at the end of Chapter 1.

double precision numbers). Similarly, long double numbers typically use twice the storage used for doubles, with a consequent increase in precision. The actual storage allocation for each data type, however, depends on the particular compiler. In compilers that allocate the same amount of storage for double, and single precision numbers, these two data types become identical. The same is true for long doubles, and the `sizeof` operator introduced in Section 2.5 will allow you to determine the amount of storage reserved by your compiler for each of these data types. A float number is indicated to the compiler by appending either an F or f after the number and a double is created by appending either an L or l to the number. In the absence of these suffixes, a floating-point number is considered as a double. For example:

> `9.234`   indicates a double
>
> `9.234f`   indicates a float
>
> `9.234L`   indicates a long double

The only difference in these numbers is the amount of storage the computer may use to store them. For numbers having more than six significant digits to the right of the decimal point, this storage becomes important. Appendix D describes the binary storage format typically used for real values and its impact on number precision. The exact difference, if any, in allocated storage is compiler dependent. The only requirement made by C++ is that a long double must provide at least the same precision as a double and that a double must provide at least the same precision as a float.

Exponential Notation

Floating-point numbers can be written in exponential notation, which is similar to scientific notation and is commonly used to express both very large and very small numbers in a compact form. The following examples illustrate how numbers with decimals can be expressed in exponential and scientific notation.

Decimal Notation	Exponential Notation	Scientific Notation
1625.	1.625e3	1.625×10^3
63421.	6.3421e4	6.3421×10^4
.00731	7.31e–3	$7.31 \times 10{-}3$
.000625	6.25e–4	$6.25 \times 10{-}4$

In exponential notation the letter e stands for exponent. The number following the e represents a power of 10 and indicates the number of places the decimal point should be moved to obtain the standard decimal value. The decimal point is moved to the right if the number after the e is positive, or moved to the left if the number after the e is negative. For example, the e3 in the number 1.625e3 means move the decimal place three places to the right, so that the number becomes 1625. The e–3 in the number 7.31e–3 means move the decimal point three places to the left, so that 7.31e–3 becomes 0.00731.

Character Values

The third basic type of data recognized by C++ are characters. Characters include the letters of the alphabet (both uppercase and lowercase), the ten digits 0 through 9, and special symbols such as + $. , – !. A single **character value** is any one letter, digit, or special symbol enclosed by single quotes. Examples of valid character values are

```
'A'   '$'   'b'   '7'   'y'   '!'   'M'   'q'
```

Character values are typically stored in a computer using either the ASCII or EBCDIC codes. **ASCII**, pronounced AS-KEY, is an acronym for American Standard Code for Information Interchange. **EBCDIC**, pronounced either as EBB-SAH-DICK or EBB-SEE-DICK, is an acronym for Extended Binary Coded Decimal Interchange Code. Each of these codes assigns individual characters to a specific pattern of 0s and 1s. Table 2.3 lists the correspondence between bit patterns and the uppercase letters of the alphabet used by the ASCII and EBCDIC codes.

Point of Information

Boolean Data

Boolean data is restricted to one of two values, either **true** or **false**. Traditionally, both C and C++ did not support built-in boolean data.

As specified by the draft ANSI/IOS Standard C++ will now incorporate a boolean data type and permit using the two boolean values, **true** and **false**. In C++ compilers currently implementing a boolean data type, the actual values represented by the two boolean values, **true** and **false**, have been the integer values 1 and 0, respectively.

In actual practice, boolean data is most useful when examining a specific condition, and as a result of the condition being **true** or **false**, taking a prescribed course of action. As the examination of conditions is considered in Chapter 4, we will encounter boolean data once again in that chapter.

Table 2.3 The ASCII and EBCDIC Uppercase Letter Codes

Letter	ASCII Code	EBCDIC Code	Letter	ASCII Code	EBCDIC Code
A	01000001	11000001	N	01001110	11010101
B	01000010	11000010	O	01001111	11010110
C	01000011	11000011	P	01010000	11010111
D	01000100	11000100	Q	01010001	11011000
E	01000101	11000101	R	01010010	11011001
F	01000110	11000110	S	01010011	11100010
G	01000111	11000111	T	01010100	11100011
H	01001000	11001000	U	01010101	11100100
I	01001001	11001001	V	01010110	11100101
J	01001010	11010001	W	01010111	11100110
K	01001011	11010010	X	01011000	11100111
L	01001100	11010011	Y	01011001	11101000
M	01001101	11010100	Z	01011010	11101001

Using Table 2.3, we can determine how the characters 'B', 'A', 'R', 'T', 'E', and 'R', for example, are stored inside a computer that uses the ASCII character code. Using the ASCII code, this sequence of characters requires six bytes of storage (one byte for each letter) and would be stored as illustrated in Figure 2.7.

Figure 2.7 The letters BARTER stored inside a computer in ASCII character code.

Escape Sequences

When a backslash (\) is used directly in front of a select group of characters, the backslash tells the computer to escape from the way these characters would normally be interpreted. For this reason, the combination of a backslash and these specific characters are called **escape sequences**. We have already encountered an example of this in the newline escape sequence, \n. Table 2.4 lists C++'s most commonly used escape sequences.

Table 2.4 Escape Sequences

Escape Sequence	Meaning
\b	move back one space
\f	move to next page
\n	move to next line
\r	carriage return
\t	move to next tab setting
\\	backslash character
\'	single quote
\nnn	treat nnn as an octal number

Although each escape sequence listed in Table 2.4 is made up of two distinct characters, the combination of the two characters with no intervening white space causes the computer to store one character code. Table 2.5 lists the ASCII code byte patterns for the escape sequences listed in Table 2.4.

Table 2.5 The ASCII Escape Sequence Codes

C++ Escape Sequence	Meaning	Computer Code
\b	backspace	00001000
\f	form feed	00001100
\n	newline	00001010
\r	carriage return	00001101
\\	backslash	01011100
\'	single quote	00100111
\"	double quote	00100010

Arithmetic Operations

Integers and real numbers can be added, subtracted, multiplied, and divided. Although it is usually better not to mix integers and real numbers when performing arithmetic operations, predictable results are obtained when different data types are used in the same arithmetic expression. Somewhat surprising is the fact that character data can also be added and subtracted with both character and integer data to produce useful results.

The operators used for arithmetic operations are called **arithmetic operators** and are listed next:

Operation	Operator
Addition	+
Subtraction	−
Multiplication	*
Division	/
Modulus Division	%

A *simple arithmetic expression* consists of an arithmetic operator connecting two operands in the form

```
operand operator operand
```

Examples of arithmetic expressions are

```
3 + 7
18 – 3
12.62 + 9.8
.08 * 12.2
12.6 / 2.
```

The spaces around the arithmetic operators in these examples are inserted strictly for clarity and can be omitted without affecting the value of the expression.

The value of any arithmetic expression can be displayed on the standard output device using cout. To do this we must pass the desired value to this object. For example, the statement

```
cout << (6 + 15);
```

yields the display 21. Strictly speaking, the parentheses surrounding the expression 6 + 15 are not required to indicate that it is the value of the expression, which is 21, that is being placed on the output stream.[10]

In addition to displaying a numerical value, a string identifying the output can also be displayed by passing the string to cout as we did in Section 2.1. For example, the statement

```
cout << "The sum of 6 and 15 is " <<  (6 + 15);
```

causes two pieces of data to be sent to cout, a string and a value. Individually, each set of data is sent to the cout preceded by its own insertion operator symbol (<<). Here, the first data sent to the stream is the string "The sum of 6 and 15 is ", and the second item sent to the stream is the value of the expression 6 + 15. The display produced by this statement is

```
The sum of 6 and 15 is 21
```

Notice that the space between is and the number 21 is caused by the space placed within

---

[10] This is because the + operator has a higher precedence than the << operator, as explained later in this section.

the string passed to `cout`. As far as `cout` is concerned, its input is simply a set of characters that are then sent on to be displayed in the order they are received. Characters from the input are queued, one behind the other, and sent to an output stream for display. Placing a space in the input causes this space to be part of the output stream that is ultimately displayed. For example, the statement

```
cout << "The sum of 12.2 and 15.754 is " <<  (12.2 + 15.754);
```

yields the display

```
The sum of 12.2 and 15.754 is 27.954
```

We should mention that insertion of data into the output stream can be made over multiple lines and is only terminated by a semicolon. Thus, the prior display is also produced by the statement

```
cout << "The sum of 12.2 and 15.754 is "
        <<  (12.2 + 15.754);
```

The requirements in using multiple lines are that a string contained within double quotes cannot be split across lines and that the terminating semicolon appear only on the last line. Within a line multiple insertion symbols can be used.

As the last display indicates, floating-point numbers are displayed with sufficient decimal places to the right of the decimal place to accommodate the fractional part of the number. This is true if the number has six or fewer decimal digits. If the number has more than six decimal digits, the fractional part is rounded to six decimal digits, and if the number has no decimal digits, neither a decimal point nor any decimal digits are displayed.[11]

Character data can also be displayed using `cout`. For example, the statement

```
cout << "The first letter of the alphabet is an " << 'a';
```

causes the display

```
The first letter of the alphabet is an a
```

Program 2.5 illustrates using `cout` to display the results of an expression within the statements of a complete program.

---

[11]It should be noted that none of this output is defined as part of the C++ language. Rather it is defined by a set of classes and routines provided with each C++ compiler.

Program 2.5

```
#include <iostream.h>

int main()
{
  cout << "15.0 plus 2.0 equals "        << (15.0 + 2.0) << '\n'
       << "15.0 minus 2.0 equals "       << (15.0 - 2.0) << '\n'
       << "15.0 times 2.0 equals "       << (15.0 * 2.0) << '\n'
       << "15.0 divided by 2.0 equals " << (15.0 / 2.0) << '\n';

  return 0;
}
```

The output of Program 2.5 is

```
15.0 plus 2.0 equals 17
15.0 minus 2.0 equals 13
15.0 times 2.00 equals 30
15.0 divided by 2.0 equals 7.5
```

Expression Types

An **expression** that contains only integer operands is called an **integer expression,** and the result of the expression is an integer value. Similarly, an expression containing only floating-point operands (single and double-precision) is called a **floating-point** expression, and the result of such an expression is a floating-point value. An expression containing both integer and floating-point operands is called a **mixed-mode** expression. Although it is usually better not to mix integer and floating-point operands in an arithmetic operations, the data type of each operation is determined by the following rules:

1. If both operands are integers, the result of the operation is an integer.

2. If one operand is a floating-point value, the result of the operation is a double-precision value.

Note that the result of an arithmetic expression is never a single-precision (float) number. This is because the computer temporarily converts all floats to double-precision numbers when arithmetic is being done.

Integer Division

The division of two integers can produce rather strange results for the unwary. For example, dividing the integer 15 by the integer 2 yields an integer result. Since integers cannot contain a fractional part, the expected result, 7.5, is not obtained. In C++, the fractional part of the result obtained when dividing two integers is dropped (truncated). Thus, the value of 15/2 is 7, the value of 9/4 is 2, and the value of 19/5 is 3.

Often, however, we would like to retain the remainder of an integer division. To do this C++ provides an arithmetic operator that captures the remainder when two integers are divided. This operator, called the modulus operator, has the symbol %. The modulus operator can be used only with integers. For example,

```
 9 % 4 is 1
17 % 3 is 2
14 % 2 is 0
```

A Unary Operator (Negation)

Besides the binary operators for addition, subtraction, multiplication, and division, C++ also provides unary operators. One of these unary operators uses the same symbol that is used for binary subtraction (–). The minus sign used in front of a single numerical operand negates (reverses the sign of) the number.

Table 2.6 summarizes the six arithmetic operations we have described so far and lists the data type of the result produced by each operator based on the data type of the operands involved.

Table 2.6 Summary of Arithmetic Operators

Operation	Operator	Type	Operand	Result
Addition	+	Binary	Both integers One operand not an integer	Integer Double precision
Subtraction	–	Binary	Both integers One operand not an integer	Integer Double precision
Multiplication	*	Binary	Both integers One operand not an integer	Integer Double precision
Division	/	Binary	Both integers One operand not an integer	Integer Double precision
Modulus	%	Binary	Both integers One integer	Integer Integer
Negation	–	Unary	One floating-point or double-precision operand	Double precision

Operator Precedence and Associativity

Besides such simple expressions as 5 + 12 and .08 * 26.2, we frequently need to create more complex arithmetic expressions. C++, like most other programming languages, requires that certain rules be followed when writing expressions containing more than one arithmetic operator. These rules are

1. Two binary arithmetic operator symbols must never be placed side by side. For example, 5 * %6 is invalid because the two operators * and % are placed next to each other.

2. Parentheses should be used to form groupings, and all expressions enclosed within parentheses are evaluated first. For example, in the expression (6 + 4) / (2 + 3), the 6 + 4 and 2 + 3 are evaluated first to yield 10 / 5. The 10 / 5 is then evaluated to yield 2.

3. Sets of parentheses may also be enclosed by other parentheses. For example, the expression (2 * (3 + 7)) / 5 is valid. When parentheses are used within parentheses, the expressions in the innermost parentheses are always evaluated first. The evaluation continues from innermost to outermost parentheses until the expressions of all parentheses have been evaluated. The number of right-facing parentheses, (, must always equal the number of left-facing parentheses,), so that there are no unpaired sets.

4. Parentheses cannot be used to indicate multiplication. The multiplication operator, *, must be used. For example, the expression (3 + 4) (5 + 1) is invalid. The correct expression is (3 + 4) * (5 + 1).

Parentheses should be used to specify logical groupings of operands and to indicate clearly to both the computer and programmers the intended order of arithmetic operations. In the absence of parentheses, expressions containing multiple operators are evaluated by the priority, or precedence, of the operators. Table 2.7 lists both the precedence and associativity of the operators considered in this section.

Table 2.7 Operator Precedence and Associativity

Precedence	Associativity
unary –	right to left
* / %	left to right
+ –	left to right

The precedence of an operator establishes its priority relative to all other operators. Operators at the top of Table 2.7 have a higher priority than operators at the bottom of the table. In expressions with multiple operators, the operator with the higher precedence is used before an operator with a lower precedence. For example, in the expression 6 + 4 / 2 + 3, the division is done before the addition, yielding an intermediate result of 6 + 2 + 3. The additions are then performed to yield a final result of 11.

Expressions containing operators with the same precedence are evaluated according to their associativity. This means that evaluation is either from left to right or from right to left as each operator is encountered. For example, in the expression 8 + 5 * 7 % 2 * 4, the multiplication and modulus operator are of higher precedence than the addition operator and are evaluated first. Both of these operators, however, are of equal precedence. Therefore, these operators are evaluated according to their left-to-right associativity, yielding

```
8 +  5 * 7 % 2 * 4  =
   8 + 35 % 2 * 4  =
        8 + 1 * 4  =
         8 + 4  =   12
```

Exercises 2.3

1. Determine data types appropriate for the following data:
  a. the average of four speeds
  b. the number of transistors in a circuit
  c. the length of the Golden Gate Bridge
  d. the part numbers in a machine
  e. the distance from Brooklyn, NY to Newark, NJ
  f. the names or circuit components

2. Convert the following numbers into standard decimal form:

  6.34e5   1.95162e2   8.395e1   2.95e-3   4.623e-4

3. Write the following decimal numbers using exponential notation:

  126.   656.23   3426.95   4893.2   .321   .0123   .006789

4. Listed below are correct algebraic expressions and incorrect C++ expressions corresponding to them. Find the errors and write corrected C++ expressions.

Algebra	*C++ Expression*
a. (2)(3) + (4)(5)	(2)(3) + (4)(5)
b. $\dfrac{6 + 18}{2}$	6 + 18 / 2
c. $\dfrac{4.5}{12.2 - 3.1}$	4.5 / 12.2 - 3.1
d. 4.6(3.0 + 14.9)	4.6(3.0 + 14.9)
e. (12.1 + 18.9)(15.3 - 3.8)	(12.1 + 18.9)(15.3 - 3.8)

5. Determine the value of the following integer expressions:
  a. 3 + 4 * 6
  b. 3 * 4 / 6 + 6
  c. 2 * 3 / 12 * 8 / 4
  d. 10 * (1 + 7 * 3)
  e. 20 - 2 / 6 + 3
  f. 20 - 2 / (6 + 3)
  g. (20 - 2) / 6 + 3
  h. (20 - 2) / (6 + 3)
  i. 50 % 20
  j. (10 + 3) % 4

6. Determine the value of the following floating-point expressions:

a. 3.0 + 4.0 * 6.0
b. 3.0 * 4.0 / 6.0 + 6.0
c. 2.0 * 3.0 / 12.0 * 8.0 / 4.0
d. 10.0 * (1.0 + 7.0 * 3.0)
e. 20.0 - 2.0 / 6.0 + 3.0
f. 20.0 - 2.0 / (6.0 + 3.0)
g. (20.0 - 2.0) / 6.0 + 3.0
h. (20.0 - 2.0) / (6.0 + 3.0)

7. Assume that distance has the integer value 1, v has the integer value 50, n has the integer value 10, and t has the integer value 5, evaluate the following expressions:

a. n / t + 3
b. v / t + n - 10 * distance
c. v - 3 * n + 4 * distance
d. distance / 5
e. 18 / t
f. -t * n
g. -v / 20
h. (v + n) / (t + distance)
i. v + n / t + distance

8. Using the system reference manuals for your computer, determine the character code used by your computer.

9. Determine the output of the following program:

```
#include <iostream.h>
int main()  // a program illustrating integer truncation
{
    cout << "answer1 is the integer " << 9/4 << '/n';
    cout << "answer2 is the integer " << 17/3 << '/n';

    return 0;
}
```

10. Determine the output of the following program:

```
#include <iostream.h>

int main()  // a program illustrating the % operator
{
  cout << "The remainder of 9 divided by 4 is " << 9 % 4 << '/n';
  cout << "The remainder of 17 divided by 3 is " << 17 % 3 << '/n';

 return 0;
}
```

11. Write a C++ program that displays the results of the expressions `3.0 * 5.0`, `7.1 * 8.3 - 2.2` and `3.2 / (6.1 * 5)`. Calculate the value of these expressions manually to verify that the displayed values are correct.

12. Write a C++ program that displays the results of the expressions `15 / 4`, `15 % 4`, and `5 * 3 - (6 * 4)`. Calculate the value of these expressions manually to verify that the displayed values are correct.

13. **a.** Show how the name PULLEY would be stored inside a computer that uses the ASCII code. That is, draw a figure similar to Figure 2.7 for the letters PULLEY.
    b. Show how the name PULLEY would be stored inside a computer that uses the EBCDIC code.

14. **a.** Repeat Exercise 13a using the letters of your own last name.
    b. Repeat Exercise 13b using the letters of your own last name.

15. Enter, compile, and run Program 2.5 on your computer system.

16. Since computers use different representations for storing integer, floating-point, double-precision, and character values, discuss how a program might alert the computer to the data types of the various values it will be using.

17. Although we have concentrated on operations involving integer, and floating-point numbers, C++ allows characters and integers to be added or subtracted. This can be done because C++ always converts a character to an equivalent integer value whenever a character is used in an arithmetic expression. Thus, characters and integers can be freely mixed in such expressions. For example, if your computer uses the ASCII code, the expression `'a' + 1` equals `'b'`, and `'z' - 1` equals `'y'`. Similarly, `'A' + 1` is `'B'`, and `'Z' - 1` is `'Y'`. With this as background, determine the character results of the following expressions (assume that all characters are stored using the ASCII code).
    a. `'m' - 5`
    b. `'m' + 5`
    c. `'G' + 6`
    d. `'G' - 6`
    e. `'b' - 'a'`
    f. `'g' - 'a' + 1`
    g. `'G' - 'A' + 1`

NOTE: *For the following exercise the reader should have an understanding of basic computer storage concepts. Specifically, if you are unfamiliar with the concept of a byte, refer to Section 1.6 before doing the next exercise.*

18. Although the total number of bytes varies from computer to computer, memory sizes of 65,536 to more than several million bytes are not uncommon. In computer language, the letter K is used to represent the number 1024, which is 2 raised to the 10th power and M is used to represent the number 1,048,576, which is 2 raised to the 20th power. Thus, a memory size of 640K is really 640 times 1024,

or 655,360 bytes, and a memory size of 4M is really 4 times 1,048,576, which is 4,194,304 bytes. Using this information, calculate the actual number of bytes in

a. a memory containing 512 K bytes
b. a memory containing 2 M bytes
c. a memory containing 8 M bytes
d. a memory containing 16 M bytes
e. a memory consisting of 4 M words, where each word consists of 2 bytes
f. a memory consisting of 4 M words, where each word consists of 4 bytes
g. a floppy diskette that can store 1.44 M bytes

2.4 VARIABLES AND DECLARATION STATEMENTS

All integer, floating-point, and other values used in a computer program are stored and retrieved from the computer's memory unit. Conceptually, individual memory locations in the memory unit are arranged like the rooms in a large hotel. Like hotel rooms, each memory location has a unique address ("room number"). Before high-level languages such as C++ existed, memory locations were referenced by their addresses. For example, to store the integer values 45 and 12 in the memory locations 1652 and 2548 (See Figure 2.8), respectively, required instructions equivalent to

Put a 45 in location 1652
Put a 12 in location 2548

To add the two numbers just stored and save the result in another memory location, for example at location 3000, we need a statement comparable to

Add the contents of location 1652
to the contents of location 2548
and store the result into location 3000

Figure 2.8 Enough storage for two integers.

Clearly this method of storage and retrieval is a cumbersome process. In high-level languages like C++, symbolic names are used in place of actual memory addresses. These symbolic names are called **variables**. A variable is simply a name given by the programmer that is used to refer to computer storage locations. The term variable is used because the value stored in the variable can change, or vary. For each name that the programmer uses, the computer keeps track of the actual memory address corresponding to that name. In our hotel room analogy, this is equivalent to putting a name on the door of a room and referring to the room by this name, such as the BLUE room, rather than using the actual room number.

In C++ the selection of variable names is left to the programmer as long as the following rules are observed:

1. The variable name must begin with a letter or underscore (_), and may contain only letters, underscores, or digits. It cannot contain any blanks, commas, or special symbols, such as ( ) & , $ # . ! \ ?

2. A variable name cannot be a keyword (see Table 2.1).

3. The variable name cannot consist of more than 31 characters.

These rules are similar to those used for selecting function names. As with function names, variable names should be mnemonics that give some indication of the variable's use. For example, a good name for a variable used to store a value that is the total of some other values would be `sum` or `total`. Variable names that give no indication of the value stored, such as `r2d2`, `linda`, `bill`, and `getum` should not be selected. As with function names, variable names can be typed in uppercase and lowercase letters.

Now assume that the first memory location illustrated in Figure 2.9, which has address 1652, is given the name `num1`. Also assume that memory location 2548 is given the variable name `num2`, and memory location 3000 is given the variable name `total`, as illustrated in Figure 2.9.

Figure 2.9 Naming storage locations.

Using these variable names, the operation of storing 45 in location 1652, storing 12 in location 2548, and adding the contents of these two locations is accomplished by the C++ statements

```
num1 = 45;
num2 = 12;
total = num1 + num2;
```

Each of these three statements is called an **assignment statement** because it tells the computer to assign (store) a value into a variable. Assignment statements always have an equal (=) sign and one variable name immediately to the left of this sign. The value on the right of the equal sign is determined first and this value is assigned to the variable on the left of the equal sign. The blank spaces in the assignment statements are inserted for readability. We will have much more to say about assignment statements in the next chapter, but for now we can use them to store values in variables.

A variable name is useful because it frees the programmer from concern over where data is physically stored inside the computer. We simply use the variable name and let the compiler worry about where in memory the data is actually stored. Before storing a value into a variable, however, C++ requires that we clearly declare the type of data that is to be stored in it. We must tell the compiler, in advance, the names of the variables that will be used for characters, the names that will be used for integers, and the names that will be used to store the other C++ data types.

Declaration Statements

Naming a variable and specifying the data type that can be stored in it are accomplished using **declaration statements**. A declaration statement has the general form

data-type variable name;

where *data-type* designates a valid C++ data type and *variable name* is a user-selected variable name. For example, variables used to hold integer values are declared using the keyword `int` to specify the data type and have the form:

`int` *variable-name;*

Thus, the declaration statement

```
int sum;
```

declares sum as the name of a variable capable of storing an integer value.

In addition to the reserved word `int` used to specify an integer, the reserved word **long**, which is considered a data type qualifier, is used to specify a long integer.[12] For example, the statement

```
long int datenum;
```

---

[12] Additionally, the reserved words `unsigned int` are used to specify an integer that can only store nonnegative numbers and the reserved words `short int` are used to specify a short integer.

Point of Information

Atomic Data
The variables we have declared have all been used to store atomic data values. An atomic data value is a value that is considered a complete entity by itself and is not decomposable into a smaller data type supported by the language. For example, although an integer can be decomposed into individual digits, C++ does not have a numerical digit type. Rather, each integer is regarded as a complete value by itself and, as such, is considered atomic data. Similarly, since the integer data type only supports atomic data values, it is said to be an atomic data type. As you might expect, floats, chars, and bools are atomic data types also.

declares datenum as a variable that will be used to store a long integer. When using the long qualifier the keyword int can omitted. Thus, the previous declaration can be written as

        long datenum;

Variables used to hold single-precision floating-point values are declared using the keyword **float**, whereas variables that will be used to hold double-precision values are declared using the keyword **double**. For example, the statement

        float firstnum;

declares firstnum as a variable that will be used to store a floating-point number. Similarly, the statement

        double secnum;

declares that the variable secnum will be used to store a double-precision number.
    Although declaration statements may be placed anywhere within a function, declarations are typically grouped together and placed immediately after the function's opening brace. In all cases, however, a variable must be declared before it can be used, and like all C++ statements, declaration statements must end with a semicolon. If the declaration statements are placed after the opening function brace, a simple main() function containing declaration statements would have the general form

```
#include <iostream.h>

int main()
{
  declaration statements;

  other statements;

  return 0;
}
```

Program 2.6 illustrates this form in declaring and using four floating-point variables, with the cout object used to display the contents of one of the variables.

Program 2.6

```
#include <iostream.h>

int main()
{
  float grade1;  // declare grade1 as a float variable
  float grade2;  // declare grade2 as a float variable
  float total;   // declare total as a float variable
  float average; // declare average as a float variable

  grade1 = 85.5;
  grade2 = 97.0;
  total = grade1 + grade2;
  average = total/2.0;  // divide the total by 2.0
  cout << "The average grade is " << average << endl;

  return 0;
}
```

The placement of the declaration statements in Program 2.6 is straightforward, although we will shortly see that the four individual declarations can be combined into a single declaration. When Program 2.6 is run, the following output is displayed:

```
The average grade is 91.25
```

Notice that when a variable name is sent to `cout`, the value stored in the variable is placed on the output stream and displayed. Also notice the use of the term `endl` as the last item to be inserted into the output stream. The keyword `endl` is an example of a C++ **manipulator**, which is an item used to manipulate how the output stream of characters is displayed. In particular the `endl` manipulator first causes a newline character (\n) to be added to the output stream and then forces an immediate flushing of the output stream. When used with the `cout` object this has the effect of ensuring an immediate display of the stream on the terminal. (Section 3.2 contains a list of the more commonly used manipulators.)

Just as integer and real (floating-point, double-precision, and long-double) variables must be declared before they can be used, a variable used to store a single character must also be declared. Character variables are declared using the reserved word `char`. For example, the declaration

```
char ch;
```

declares `ch` to be a character variable. Program 2.7 illustrates this declaration and the use of `cout` to display the value stored in a character variable.

Program 2.7

```cpp
#include <iostream.h>

int main()
{
  char ch;       // this declares a character variable

  ch = 'a';      // store the letter a into ch
  cout << "The character stored in ch is " << ch << endl;
  ch = 'm';      // now store the letter m into ch
  cout << "The character now stored in ch is "<< ch << endl;

  return 0;
}
```

When Program 2.7 is run, the output produced is:

```
The character stored in ch is a
The character now stored in ch is m
```

Notice in Program 2.7 that the first letter stored in the variable ch is a and the second letter stored is m. Since a variable can only be used to store one value at a time, the assignment of m to the variable automatically causes a to be overwritten.

Multiple Declarations

Variables having the same data type can always be grouped together and declared using a single declaration statement. The common form of such a declaration is

data-type variable list;

For example, the four separate declarations used in Program 2.6,

```cpp
        float grade1;
        float grade2;
        float total;
        float average;
```

can be replaced by the single declaration statement

```cpp
        float grade1, grade2, total, average;
```

Similarly, the two character declarations,

```cpp
        char ch;
        char key;
```

can be replaced with the single declaration statement

```
char ch, key;
```

Note that declaring multiple variables in a single declaration requires that the data type of the variables be given only once, that all the variables names be separated by commas, and that only one semicolon be used to terminate the declaration. The space after each comma is inserted for readability and is not required.

Declaration statements can also be used to store an initial value into declared variables. For example, the declaration statement

```
int num1 = 15;
```

both declares the variable `num1` as an integer variable and sets the value of 15 into the variable. When a declaration statement is used to store a value into a variable, the variable is said to be **initialized**. Thus, in this example it is correct to say that the variable `num1` has been initialized to 15. Similarly, the declaration statements

```
float grade1 = 87.0;
float grade2 = 93.5;
float total;
```

declare three floating-point variables and initializes two of them. When initializations are used, good programming practice dictates that each initialized variable be declared on a line by itself. Constants, expressions using only constants (such as 87.0 + 12 − 2), and expressions using constants and previously initialized variables can all be used as initializers within a function. For example, Program 2.6 with declaration initialization becomes Program 2.6a.

Program 2.6a

```cpp
#include <iostream.h>

int main()
{
  float grade1 = 85.5;
  float grade2 = 97.0;
  float total, average;

  total = grade1 + grade2;
  average = total/2.0;  // divide the total by 2.0
  cout << "The average grade is " << average << endl;

  return 0;
}
```

Notice the blank line after the last declaration statement. Inserting a blank line after the variable declarations placed at the top of a function body is a good programming practice. It improves both a program's appearance and its readability.

An interesting feature of C++ is that variable declarations may be freely intermixed and even contained with other statements; the only requirement is that a variable must be declared prior to its use. For example, the variable `total` in Program 2.6a could have been declared when it is first used using the statement `float total = grade1 + grade2`. In very restricted situations (such as debugging as described in Section 3.9 or in a for loop, described in Section 5.4), declaring a variable at its point of use can be helpful. In general, it is preferable not to disperse declarations but rather to group them, in as concise and clear manner as possible, at the top of each function.

Memory Allocation

The declaration statements we have introduced have performed both software and hardware tasks. From a software perspective, declaration statements always provide a list of all variables and their data types. In this software role, variable declarations also help to control an otherwise common and troublesome error caused by the misspelling of a variable's name within a program. For example, assume that a variable named `distance` is declared and initialized using the statement

```
int distance = 26;
```

Now assume that this variable is inadvertently misspelled in the statement

```
mpg = distnce / gallons;
```

In languages that do not require variable declarations, the program would treat `distnce` as a new variable and either assign an initial value of zero to the variable or use whatever value happened to be in the variable's storage area. In either case a value would be calculated and assigned to `mpg`, and finding the error or even knowing that an error occurred could be extremely troublesome. Such errors are impossible in C++ because the compiler will flag `distnce` as an undeclared variable. The compiler cannot, of course, detect when one declared variable is typed in place of another declared variable.

In addition to their software role, declaration statements can also perform a distinct hardware task. Since each data type has its own storage requirements, the computer can allocate sufficient storage for a variable only after knowing the variable's data type. Because variable declarations provide this information, they can be used to force the compiler to reserve sufficient physical memory storage for each variable. Declaration statements used for this hardware purpose are also called **definition statements** because they define or tell the compiler how much memory is needed for data storage.

All the declaration statements we have encountered so far have also been definition statements. Later, we will see cases of declaration statements that do not cause any new storage to be allocated and are used simply to declare or alert the program to the data types of variables that are created elsewhere in the program.

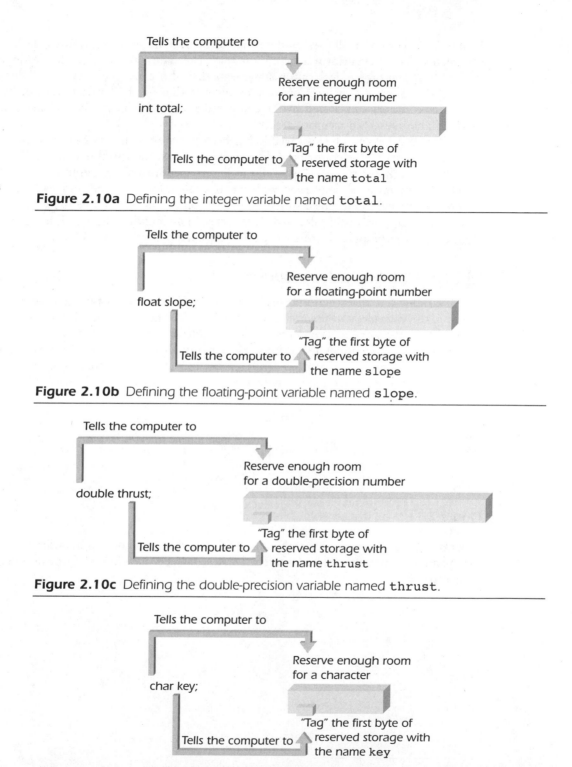

Figure 2.10a Defining the integer variable named `total`.

Figure 2.10b Defining the floating-point variable named `slope`.

Figure 2.10c Defining the double-precision variable named `thrust`.

Figure 2.10d Defining the character variable named `key`.

Figure 2.10 (parts a-d) illustrates the series of operations set in motion by declaration statements that also perform a definition role. The figure shows that definition statements (or, if you prefer, declaration statements that also cause memory to be allocated) "tag" the first byte of each set of reserved bytes with a name. This name is, of course, the variable's name and is used by the computer to correctly locate the starting point of each variable's reserved memory area.

Within a program, after a variable has been declared, it is typically used by a programmer to refer to the contents of the variable (that is, the variable's value). Where in memory this value is stored is generally of little concern to the programmer. The compiler, however, must be concerned with where each value is stored and with correctly locating each variable. In this task the computer uses the variable name to locate the first byte of storage previously allocated to the variable. Knowing the variable's data type then allows the compiler to store or retrieve the correct number of bytes.

Displaying a Variable's Address[13]

Every variable has three major items associated with it: its data type, the actual value stored in the variable, and the address of the variable. The value stored in the variable is referred to as the variable's contents, while the address of the first memory location used for the variable constitutes its address. How many locations are actually used for the variable, as we have just seen, depends on the variable's data type. The relationship between these three items (type, contents, location) is illustrated in Figure 2.11.

Figure 2.11 A typical variable.

Programmers are usually concerned only with the value assigned to a variable (its contents) and give little attention to where the value is stored (its address). For example, consider Program 2.8.

---

[13] This topic may be omitted on first reading without loss of subject continuity

> **Program 2.8**
>
> ```cpp
> #include <iostream.h>
>
> int main()
> {
>   int num;
>
>   num = 22;
>   cout << "The value stored in num is " << num << endl;
>
>   return 0;
> }
> ```

The output displayed when Program 2.8 is run is

```
The value stored in num is 22
```

Program 2.8 merely prints the value 22, which is the contents of the variable num. We can go further, however, and ask "where is the number 22 actually stored?" Although the answer is "in num," this is only half of the answer. The variable name num is simply a convenient symbol for real, physical locations in memory, as illustrated in Figure 2.12.

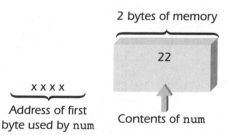

Figure 2.12 *Somewhere in memory.*

To determine the address of num, we can use C++'s address operator, &, which means "the address of." Except when used in an expression, the address operator placed in front of a variable's name refers to the address of the variable.[14] For example, &num means *the address of* num, &total means *the address of* total, and &price means *the address of* price. Program 2.9 uses the address operator to display the address of the variable num.

---

[14]When used in declaring reference variables and arguments, which is presented in Chapter 7, the ampersand refers to the data type *preceding* it. Thus, the declaration float &num is read as "num is the address of a float", or more commonly as "num is a reference to a float".

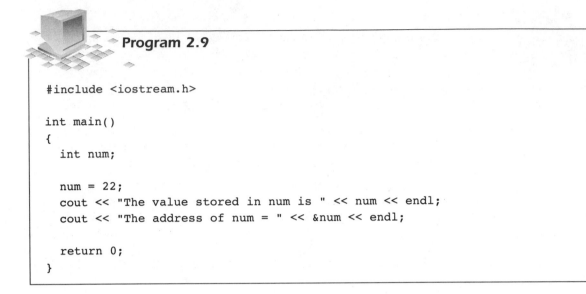

Program 2.9

```
#include <iostream.h>

int main()
{
  int num;

  num = 22;
  cout << "The value stored in num is " << num << endl;
  cout << "The address of num = " << &num << endl;

  return 0;
}
```

The output of Program 2.9 is

```
The value stored in num is 22
The address of num = 0x8f5afff4
```

Figure 2.13 illustrates the additional address information provided by the output of Program 2.9.

Figure 2.13 A more complete picture of the variable **num**.

Clearly, the address output by Program 2.9 depends on the computer used to run the program. Every time Program 2.9 is executed, however, it displays the address of the first memory location used to store the variable num. As illustrated by the output of Program 2.9, the display of addresses is in hexadecimal notation. This display has no effect on how addresses are used internal to the program; it merely provides us with a means of displaying addresses that is helpful in understanding them. As we shall see in Chapters 6 and 11, using addresses as opposed to only displaying them is an extremely important and powerful programming tool.

Exercises 2.4

1. State whether the following variable names are valid or not. If they are invalid, state the reason why.

   ```
   prod_a      c1234       abcd        _c3         12345
   newamp      watts       $total      new$al      a1b2c3d4
   9ab6        sum.of      average     volts1      finvolt
   ```

2. State whether the following variable names are valid or not. If they are invalid, state the reason why. Also indicate which of the valid variable names should not be used because they convey no information about the variable.

   ```
   current     a243        r2d2        first_num   cc_al
   harry       sue         c3p0        total       sum
   maximum     okay        a           awesome     goforit
   3sum        for         tot.al      c$five      netpower
   ```

3. **a.** Write a declaration statement to declare that the variable `count` will be used to store an integer.
   b. Write a declaration statement to declare that the variable `volt` will be used to store a floating-point number.
   c. Write a declaration statement to declare that the variable `power` will be used to store a double-precision number.
   d. Write a declaration statement to declare that the variable `keychar` will be used to store a character.

4. Write declaration statements for the following variables.
   a. `num1`, `num2`, and `num3` used to store integer numbers
   b. `amps1`, `amps2`, `amps3`, and `amps4` used to store floating-point numbers
   c. `volts1`, `volts2`, and `volts3` used to store double-precision numbers
   d. `code-a`, `code-b`, `code-c`, `code-d`, and `code-e` used to store character types

5. Write declaration statements for the following variables.
   a. `firstnum` and `secnum` used to store integers
   b. `speed`, `acceleration`, and `distance` used to store floating-point numbers
   c. `thrust` used to store a double-precision number

6. Rewrite each of these declaration statements as three individual declarations.
   a. `int month, day = 30, year;`
   b. `double hours, volt, power = 15.62;`
   c. `float price, amount, taxes;`
   d. `char in_key, ch, choice = 'f';`

7. a. Determine what each statement causes to happen in the following program.

```
#include <iostream.h>

int main()
{
  int num1, num2, total;
  num1 = 25;
  num2 = 30;
  total = num1 + num2;
  cout << "The total of" << num1 << " and "
       << num2 << " is " << total << endl;

  return 0;
}
```

b. What is the output that will be printed when the program listed in Exercise 7a is run?

8. Every variable has three items associated with it. What are these three items?

NOTE FOR EXERCISES 9 THROUGH 11: *Assume that a character requires one byte of storage, an integer two bytes, a floating-point number four bytes, a double-precision number eight bytes, and that variables are assigned storage in the order they are declared (review Section 1.6 if you are unfamiliar with the concept of a byte).*

Addresses

Figure 2.14 Memory bytes for exercises 9, 10, and 11.

9. a. Using Figure 2.14 and assuming that the variable name `rate` is assigned to the byte having memory address 159, determine the addresses corresponding to each variable declared in the following statements. Also fill in the appropriate bytes with the initialization data included in the declaration statements (use letters for the characters, not the computer codes that would actually be stored).

```
float rate;
char ch1 = 'w', ch2 = 'o', ch3 = 'w', ch4 = '!';
double taxes;
int num, count = 0;
```

b. Repeat Exercise 9a, but substitute the actual byte patterns that a computer using the ASCII code would use to store the characters in the variables ch1, ch2, ch3, and ch4. (*Hint:* Use Table 2.2.)

10. a. Using Figure 2.14 and assuming that the variable named cn1 is assigned to the byte at memory address 159, determine the addresses corresponding to each variable declared in the following statements. Also fill in the appropriate bytes with the initialization data included in the declaration statements (use letters for the characters and not the computer codes that would actually be stored).

```
char cn1 = 'a', cn2 = ' ', cn3 = 'b', cn4 = 'u', cn5 = 'n';
char cn6 = 'c', cn7 = 'h', key = '\\', sch = '\'', inc = 'o';
char inc1 = 'f';
```

b. Repeat Exercise 10a, but substitute the actual byte patterns that a computer using the ASCII code would use to store the characters in each of the declared variables. (*Hint:* Use Table 2.2.)

11. Using Figure 2.14 and assuming that the variable name miles is assigned to the byte at memory address 159, determine the addresses corresponding to each variable declared in the following statements.

```
float miles;
int count, num;
double dist, temp;
```

2.5 ▷ INTEGER QUALIFIERS

Integer numbers are generally used in programs as counters to keep track of the number of times that something has occurred. For most applications, the counts needed are less than 32,767, which is the maximum signed integer value that can be stored in two bytes. Since most computers allocate at least two bytes for integers, there is usually no problem.

Cases do arise, however, where larger integer numbers are needed. In financial applications, for example, dates such as 7/12/89 are typically converted to the number of days from the turn of the century. This conversion makes it possible to store and sort dates using a single number for each date. Unfortunately, for dates after 1987, the number of days from the turn of the century is larger than the maximum value of 32,767 allowed when only two bytes are allocated for each integer variable.

To accommodate real application requirements such as this, C++ provides long-integer, short-integer, and unsigned-integer data types. These three additional integer data types are obtained by adding the qualifiers `long`, `short`, or `unsigned`, respectively, to the normal integer declaration statements. For example, the declaration statement

```
long int days;
```

declares the variable days to be a long-integer. The word `int` in a long-integer declaration statement is optional, so the previous declaration statement can also be written as `long days;`. The amount of storage allocated for a long integer depends on the compiler being used. Although you would expect that a long integer variable would be allocated more space than a standard integer, this may not be the case. About all that can be said is that long integers will provide no less space than regular integers. The actual amount of storage allocated by your computer should be checked using the `sizeof` operator described at the end of this section.

Once a variable is declared as a long integer, integer values may be assigned as usual for standard integers, or an optional letter L (either uppercase or lowercase, with no space between the number and letter) may be appended to the integer. For example, the declaration statement

```
long days = 38276L;
```

declares days to be of type long-integer and assigns the long-integer constant 38276 to the variable days.

In addition to the long qualifier, C++ also provides for a short qualifier. Although you would expect a short integer to conserve computer storage by reserving fewer bytes than used for an integer, this is not always the case. Some compilers allocate the same amount of storage for both integers and short integers. Again, the amount of memory space allocated for a short integer data type depends on your compiler and can be checked using the `sizeof` operator (described at the end of this section). As with long integers, short integers may be declared using the terms `short` or `short int` in a declaration statement. Once a variable is declared as a short integer, values are assigned as normally done with integers.

The final integer data type is the unsigned integer. This data type is obtained by prefixing the reserved word `int` with the qualifier unsigned. For example, the declaration statement

```
unsigned int days;
```

declares the variable days to be of type unsigned. Unsigned integers are generally only used for positive integers and effectively doubles the positive value that can be stored without increasing the number of bytes allocated to an integer. This is accomplished by effectively treating all unsigned integers as positive numbers, as illustrated in Figure 2.15.

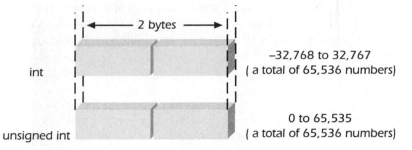

Figure 2.15 *Unsigned integers storage using two bytes.*

Figure 2.16 illustrates all of C++'s fundamental data types and their relationship to each other.

Figure 2.16 *C++'s fundamental data types.*

Data Type Conversions

The general rules for converting integer and floating-point operands in mixed-mode arithmetic expressions were presented in the Section 2.4. A more complete set of conversion rules for arithmetic operators, which includes character, short, and long integer operands, is provided in Table 2.8, where the rules are applied in order, starting with Rule 1.

Table 2.8 Conversion rules for arithmetic operators

1. If both operands are either character or integer operands then:
   a. when both operands are character, short, or integer data types the result of the expression is an integer value.
   b. when one of operands is a long integer the result is a long integer, unless one of the operands is an unsigned integer. In this latter case the other operand is converted to an unsigned integer value and the resulting value of the expression is an unsigned value.

2. If any one operand is a floating-point value then:
   a. when one or both operands are floats the result of the operation is a float value.
   b. when one or both operands are doubles the result of the operation is a double value.
   c. when one or both operands are long doubles the result is a long double value.

Note that these rules apply to each individual arithmetic operation in their correct order of evaluation. For example, in the expression 14.78F - 4 * 3L, the multiplication, which has a higher precedence than the subtraction, is performed first. For this multiplication of two integer operands, the integer 4 is converted to a long integer value, and the result of the expression is 12L (Rule 1b). The result of the next operation, 14.78F - 12L, is the single-precision (float) value 2.78 (Rule 2a).

Determining Storage Size[15]

C++ provides an operator for determining the amount of storage your compiler allocates for each data type. This operator, called the sizeof() operator, returns the number of bytes of the variable or data type included in the parentheses. Unlike a function, which itself is made of C++ statements, the sizeof() operator is an integral part of the C++ language itself. Examples using the sizeof operator are

        sizeof(num1)   sizeof(int)   sizeof(float)

If the item in parentheses is a variable, as in the example sizeof(num1), sizeof() returns the number of bytes of storage that the computer reserved for the variable. If the item following the word sizeof is a data type, such as int or char, sizeof will return the number of bytes of storage that the computer uses for the given data type. Using either approach, we can use sizeof to determine the amount of storage used by different data types. Consider Program 2.10.

Program 2.10

```
#include <iostream.h>

int main()
{
  char ch;
  int num1;
  cout << "Bytes of storage used by a character: "
       << sizeof(ch) << endl;
  cout << "Bytes of storage used by an integer: "
       << sizeof(num1) << endl;

  return 0;
}
```

Program 2.10 declares that the variable ch is used to store a character and that the variable num1 is used to store an integer. From our discussion in the last section, we know that each of these declaration statements is also a definition statement. As such, the first declaration statement instructs the compiler to reserve enough storage for a character,

---

[15]This section assumes a basic understanding of computer storage concepts and terms. If you are unfamiliar with these concepts, please review Section 1.6.

and the second declaration statement instructs the compiler to reserve enough storage for an integer. The `sizeof()` operator is then used to tell us how much room the computer really set aside for these two variables. When Program 2.10 is run on an IBM personal computer the following output is obtained:

```
Bytes of storage used by a character: 1
Bytes of storage used by an integer: 2
```

Exercises 2.5

1. **a.** Run Program 2.10 to determine how many bytes your computer uses to store character and integer data types.

   b. Expand Program 2.10 to determine how many bytes your computer uses for short integers, long integers, and unsigned integers.

2. After running the program written for Exercise 1b, use Table 2.2 to determine the maximum and minimum numbers that can be stored in integer, short integer, and long integer variables for your computer.

3. Program 2.10 did not actually store any values into the variables `ch` and `num1`. Why was this not necessary?

4. **a.** Expand Program 2.10 to determine how many bytes your computer uses to store floating-point and double-precision numbers.

   b. Although there is no long float data class, double-precision numbers are sometimes considered as the equivalent long form for floating-point numbers. Why is this so? Does the output of the program written for Exercise 4a support this statement?

2.6 ▶ APPLYING THE SOFTWARE DEVELOPMENT PROCEDURE

Recall from Section 1.2 that writing a C++ program is essentially the third step in the programming process. The first two steps in the process are determining what is required and selecting the algorithm to be coded into C++. In this section we show how the steps presented in Section 1.2 are applied in practice when converting programming problems into working C++ programs. To review, once a program requirement or problem is stated, the software development procedure consists of the following steps.

◆ Step 1: Analyze the Problem

The analysis of a problem can consist of up to two parts. The first part is a **basic analysis** that must be performed on all problems and consists of extracting the complete input and output information supplied by the problems. That is, you must

1. Determine and understand the desired output items that the program must produce

2. Determine the input items

Together these two items are referred to as the problem's input/output, or I/O, for short. Only after a problem's I/O has been determined is it possible to select an algorithm for transforming the inputs into the desired outputs. At this point it is sometimes necessary and/or useful to perform a hand calculation to verify that the output can indeed be obtained from the inputs. Clearly, if a formula is given that relates the inputs to the output, this step can be omitted at this stage. If the required inputs are available and the desired output(s) can be produced, the problem is said to be clearly defined and can be solved.

For a variety of reasons it may not be possible to complete a basic analysis. If this is the case, an extended analysis may be necessary. An **extended analysis** simply means that you must obtain additional information about the problem so that you thoroughly understand what is being asked for and how to achieve the result. In this text any additional information required for an understanding of the problem will be supplied along with the problem statement.

◆ Step 2:   Develop a Solution

This step is frequently referred to as the design step, and we will use the terms **design** and **development** interchangeably. In this step you must settle on an algorithm for transforming the input items into the desired outputs and refine it as necessary so that it adequately defines all of the features that you want your program to have. If you haven't performed a hand calculation using the algorithm in the analysis step, you should do so here, using specific input values.

In designing a solution, the specific approach we will take is often referred to as the **top-down approach**. This approach consists of starting with the most general solution and refining it in a manner such that the final program solution consists of clearly defined tasks that can be accomplished by individual program functions.

◆ Step 3:   Code the Solution

At this point you actually write the C++ program that corresponds to the solution developed in Step 2.

◆ Step 4:   Test and Correct the Program

This is done by means of selected test data and is used make corrections to the program when errors are found. One set of test data that should always be used is the data used in your previous hand calculation.

To see how each of these steps can be implemented in practice, we now apply it to the following simple programming problem.

The electrical resistance, r, of a metal wire, in ohms, is given by the formula $r = (ml)/a$ where m is the resistivity of the metal; l is the length of the wire, in feet; and a is the cross-sectional area of the wire, in circular mils. Using this information, write a C++ program to calculate the resistance of a wire that is 125 feet long, has a cross-sectional area of 500 circular mils, and is copper. The resistivity of copper, m, is 10.4.

Step 1   Analyze the Problem

The first step in developing a program for this problem statement is to perform a basic analysis. We begin by determining the required outputs. Frequently, the statement of the problem will use such words as *calculate, print, determine, find,* or *compare*, which can be used to determine the desired outputs.

For our sample problem statement, the key phrase is "to calculate the resistance of a wire." This clearly identifies an output item. Since there are no other such phrases in the problem, only one output item is required.

After we have clearly identified the desired output, the basic analysis step continues with the identification of all input items. It is essential at this stage to distinguish between input items and input values. An **input item** is the name of an input quantity, whereas an **input value** is a specific number or quantity that the input item can be. For example, in our sample problem statement, the input items are the resistivity, m, the length or the wire, l, and the cross-sectional area of the wire, a. Although these input item have specific numerical values, these input item values are generally not of importance at this stage.

The reason that input values are not needed at this point is that the selection of an algorithm is typically independent of specific input values. The algorithm depends on knowing what the output and input items are and if there are any special limits. Let us see why this is so.

From the problem statement it is clear that the algorithm for transforming the input items to the desired output is given by the formula $r = (ml)/a$. Notice that this formula can be used regardless of the specific values assigned to m, l, or a. Although we cannot produce an actual numerical value for the output item (resistance) unless we have actual numerical values for the input item, the correct relationship between inputs and outputs is expressed by the formula. Recall that this is precisely what an algorithm provides: a description of how the inputs are to be transformed into outputs that works for all inputs.

Step 2   Develop a Solution

The basic algorithm for transforming the inputs into the desired output is provided by the given formula. We must now refine it by listing, in detail, how the inputs, outputs, and algorithm are to be combined to produce a solution. This listing indicates the steps that will be taken by the program to solve the problem. As such it constitutes an outline of the final form that will be followed by the program code. Using pseudocode, the complete algorithm for solving this problems is

> *Assign values to m, l, and a*
> *Calculate the resistance using the formula r = (ml)/a*
> *Display the result*

Notice that the structure of this algorithm conforms to the sequential control structure presented in Section 1.2.

Having selected and refined the algorithm, the next step in the design (if it was not already done in the analysis step) is to check the algorithm by hand using specific data. Performing a manual calculation, either by hand or using a calculator, helps to ensure that you really do understand the problem. An added advantage of doing a manual calculation is that the results can be used later to verify program operation in the testing phase.

Then, when the final program is used with other data, you will have established a degree of confidence that a correct result is being calculated.

Doing a manual calculation requires that we have specific input values that can be assigned and used by the algorithm to produce the desired output. For this problem three input values are given: a resistivity of 10.4, a cross-sectional area of 500 circular mils, and a length of 125 feet. Substituting these values into the formula, we obtain a resistance = (10.4)(125)/500 = 2.60 ohms for the copper wire.

Step 3   Code the Solution

Since we have carefully developed a program solution, all that remains is to code the solution algorithm in C++. This means declaring appropriate input and output variables, initializing the input variables appropriately, computing the resistance, and printing the calculated resistance value. Program 2.11 performs these steps.

Program 2.11

```
#include <iostream.h>
int main()
{
  float resistivity, area, length, resistance;

  resistivity = 10.4;
  area = 500;
  length = 125;
  resistance = (resistivity * length) / area;

  cout << "The resistance of the wire (in ohms) is "
       << resistance << endl;

  return 0;
}
```

When program 2.11 is executed, the following output is produced:

```
The resistance of the wire (in ohms) is 2.6
```

Now that we have a working program that produces a result, the final step in the development process, testing the program, can begin.

Step 4   Test and Debug the Program

The purpose of testing is to verify that a program works correctly and actually fulfills its requirements. Once testing has been completed the program can be used to calculate outputs for differing input data without the need for retesting. This is, of course, one of the real values in writing a program; the same program can be used over and over with new input data.

The simplest test method is to verify the program's operation for carefully selected sets of input data. One set of input data that should always be used is the data that was selected for the hand calculation made previously in Step 2 of the development procedure. In this case the program is relatively simple and performs only one calculation. Because the output produced by the test run agrees with our hand calculation we have a good degree of confidence that it can be used to correctly calculate the resistance for any input values.

Exercises 2.6

NOTE: *In each of these exercises a programming problem is given. Read the problem statement first and then answer the questions pertaining to the problem.* **Do not** write a program to solve the problems, but simply answer the questions following the program specification.

1. Assume that a C++ program is to be written to calculate the total resistance of a series circuit. In such a circuit the total resistance is the sum of all individual resistance values. Assume that the circuit consists of a number of 56 ohm, 33 ohm, and 15 ohm resistors.
   a. For this programming problem how many outputs are required?
   b. How many inputs does this problem have?
   c. Determine an algorithm for converting the input items into output items. Assume that the number of 56 ohm resistors is m, the number of 33 ohm resistors is n, the number of 15 ohm resistors is p.
   d. Test the algorithm written for part c using the following sample data: $m = 17$, $n = 24$, and $p = 12$.

2. Assume that a program is to be written to calculate the value of *distance*, in miles, given the relationship:

   distance = rate * elapsed time

   a. For this programming problem how many outputs are required?
   b. How many inputs does this problem have?
   c. Determine an algorithm for converting the input items into output items.
   d. Test the algorithm written for part c using the following sample data: *rate* is 55 miles per hour and *elapsed time* is 2.5 hours.
   e. How must the algorithm you determined in part c be modified if the elapsed time were given in minutes instead of hours.

3. Assume that a program is to be written to determine the value of *Ergies*, given the relationships:

   $Ergies = Fergies * \sqrt{Lergies}$
   $Lergies = 2 * \pi * e^{\mu}$

   a. For this programming problem how many outputs are required?
   b. How many inputs does this problem have?

   c. Determine an algorithm for converting the input items into output items.

   d. Test the algorithm written for part c using the following sample data:
    Fergies = 14.65, π = 3.1416, μ = 1.672, and *e* = 2.7818.

4. Assume that a program is to be written to display the following specifications:

Voltage Amplification: 35

Power output: 2.5 watts

Bandwidth: 15KHz

   a. For this program problem how many lines of output are required?

   b. How many inputs does this problem have?

   c. Determine an algorithm for converting the input items into output items.

5. Write a C++ program to determine how far a car has traveled after 10 seconds assuming the car is initially traveling at 60 miles per hour and the driver applies the brakes to uniformly decelerate at a rate of 12 miles/sec². Use the fact that *distance* = $s - (1/2)dt^2$, where *s* is the initial speed of the car, *d* is the deceleration, and *t* is the elapsed time.

   a. For this programming problem how many outputs are required?

   b. How many inputs does this problem have?

   c. Determine an algorithm for converting the input items into output items.

   d. Test the algorithm written for part c using the data given in the problem.

6. Consider the following programming problem: In 1627, Manhattan Island was sold to the Dutch settlers for approximately $24. If the proceeds of that sale had been deposited in a Dutch bank paying 5% interest, compounded annually, what would the principal balance be at the end of 2002? A display is required as follows: Balance as of December 31, 2002 is: xxxxxx, where xxxxxx is the amount calculated by your program.

   a. For this programming problem how many outputs are required?

   b. How many inputs does this problem have?

   c. Determine an algorithm for converting the input items into output items.

   d. Test the algorithm written for part c using the data given in the problem statement.

7. Write a program that calculates and displays the output voltages of two electrical circuits and the sum of the two voltages. The output voltage for the first circuit is given by the equation (150) *V* / *0.38f* and the output voltage for the second circuit is given by the equation

$$\frac{230V}{\sqrt{56^2 + (0.98f)^2}}$$

where *V* is the input voltage to the circuit and *f* is the frequency in Hertz.

   a. For this programming problem how many outputs are required?

   b. How many inputs does this problem have?

   c. Determine an algorithm for converting the input items into output items.

d. Test the algorithm written for part c using the following sample data: The first circuit is operated with an input voltage of 1.2 volts at a frequency of 144 Hertz and the second circuit is operated with an input voltage of 2.3 volts at 100 Hertz.

8. Consider the following programming problem: The formula for the standard normal deviate, z, used in statistical applications is

$$z = \frac{X - \mu}{\sigma}$$

where μ refers to a mean value and σ to a standard deviation. Using this formula, write a program that calculates and displays the value of the standard normal deviate when $X = 85.3$, $\mu = 80$, and $\sigma = 4$.

a. For this programming problem how many outputs are required?
b. How many inputs does this problem have?
c. Determine an algorithm for converting the input items into output items.
d. Test the algorithm written for part c using the data given in the problem.

9. The equation of the normal (bell-shaped) curve used in statistical applications is

$$y = \frac{1}{\sigma \sqrt{2\pi}} e^{-(1/2)[(x - \mu)/\sigma]^2}$$

Using this equation, assume that a C++ program is to be written that calculates the value of y.

a. For this programming problem how many outputs are required?
b. How many inputs does this problem have?
c. Determine an algorithm for converting the input items into output items.
d. Test the algorithm written for part c assuming $\mu = 90$, $\sigma = 4$, $x = 80$, and $\pi = 3.1416$.

2.7 APPLICATIONS

In this section the software development procedure presented in the previous section is applied to two specific programming problems. Although each problem is different, the development procedure works for both situations. This procedure can be applied to any programming problem to produce a completed program and forms the foundation for all programs developed in this text.

Application 1: Radar Speed Traps

A common highway-patrol speed detection radar emits a beam of microwaves at a frequency f_0. The beam is reflected off an approaching car, and the reflected beam is picked up and analyzed by the radar unit. The frequency of the reflected beam is shifted slightly from f_0 to f_1 due to the motion of the car. The relationship between the speed of the car, v, in miles per hour, and the two microwave frequencies is

$$v = (6.685 \times 10^8)(f_1 - f_0) / (f_1 + f_0)$$

where the emitted waves have a frequency of $f_0 = 2 \times 10^{10}$ sec^{-1}. Using the given formula, write a C++ program to calculate and display the speed corresponding to a received frequency of 2.000004×10^{10} sec^{-1}.

We now apply the software development procedure to this problem.

Step 1   Analyze the Problem

For this problem a single output is required by the program: the speed of the car. The input items required to solve for the speed are the emitted frequency, f_0 and the received frequency, f_1.

Step 2   Develop a Solution

The algorithm given for transforming the three input items into the desired output item is given by the formula $v = 6.685 \times 10^8(f_1 - f_0)/ (f_1 + f_0)$. Thus, the complete algorithm for our program solution is

> *Assign values to f_1 and f_0*
> *Calculate the speed using the formula $v = 6.685 \times 10^8(f_1 - f_0)/ (f_1 + f_0)$.*
> *Display the result.*

A hand calculation, using the data that $f_0 = 2 \times 10^{10}$ sec^{-1} and $f_1 = 2.000004 \times 10^{10}$ sec^{-1} yields a speed of 66.85 miles per hour.

Step 3   Code the Solution

Program 2.12 provides the necessary code.

Program 2.12

```cpp
#include <iostream.h>

int main()
{
  double speed, f0, f1;

  f0 = 2e-10;
  f1 = 2.0000004e-10;

  speed = 6.685e8 * (f1 - f0) / (f1 + f0);
  cout << "The speed is " << speed << " miles/hour " <<endl;

  return 0;
}
```

Program 2.12 begins with an `#include` preprocessor command followed by a `main()` function. This function starts with the keyword `main` and ends with the closing brace, `}`. Additionally, Program 2.12 contains one declaration statement, three assignment statements, and one output statement. The assignment statements `f0 = 2e-10` and `f1 = 2.0000004e-10` are used to initialize the `f0` and `f1` variables, respectively. The assignment statement

```
speed = 6.685e8 * (f1 - f0) / (f1 + f0);
```

calculates a value for the variable named `speed`. When Program 2.12 is compiled and executed the following output is produced.

```
The speed is 66.85 miles/hour
```

Step 4   Test and Correct the Program

The last step in the development procedure is to test the output. Because the single calculation and displayed value agrees with the previous hand calculation, we have verified the correct program operation. This permits us to use the program for different values of received frequencies. Note that if the parentheses were not correctly placed in the assignment statement that calculated a value for speed, the displayed value would not agree with our previous hand calculation. This would have alerted us to the fact there was an error in the program.

Application 2: Telephone Switching Networks

A directly connected telephone network is one in which all telephones in the network are directly connected and do not require a central switching station to establish calls between two telephones. For example, financial institutions on Wall Street use such a network to maintain direct and continuously open phone lines between firms.

The number of direct lines needed to maintain a directly connected network for n telephones is given by the formula

$$lines = n(n - 1)/2$$

For example, directly connecting four telephones requires 6 individual lines (see Figure 2.17). Adding a fifth telephone to the network illustrated in Figure 2.17 would require an additional 4 lines for a total of 10 lines.

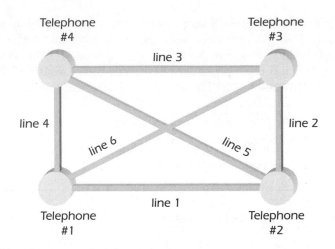

Figure 2.17 Directly connecting four telephones.

Using the given formula, write a C++ program that determines the number of direct lines required for 100 telephones, and the additional lines required if 10 new telephones were added to the network.

Step 1   Analyze the Problem

For this program two outputs are required: the number of direct lines for 100 telephones and the additional number of lines needed when 10 new telephones are added to the existing network. The input item required for this problem is the number of telephones, which is denoted as *n* in the formula.

Step 2   Develop a Solution

The first output is easily obtained using the formula

> $lines = n(n - 1)/2$

Although there is no formula given for additional lines, we can use the given formula to determine the total number of lines needed for 110 subscribers. Subtracting the number of lines for 100 subscribers from the number of lines needed for 110 subscribers will then yield the number of additional lines required. Thus, the complete algorithm for our program, in pseudocode, is

Calculate the number of direct lines for 100 subscribers
Calculate the number of direct lines for 110 subscribers
Calculate the additional lines needed, which is the difference between the second and first calculation
Display the number of lines for 100 subscribers
Display the additional lines needed

Checking this algorithm by hand, using the data given, yields the answer:

$lines = 100(100 - 1)/2 = 100(99)/2 = 4950$

for 100 telephones and

lines = 5995

for 110 telephones. Thus, an additional 1045 lines would be needed to directly connect the ten additional telephones into the existing network.

Step 3   Code the Solution

Program 2.13 provides the necessary code.

Program 2.13

```cpp
#include <iostream.h>

int main()
{
  int numin1, numin2, lines1, lines2;

  numin1 = 100;
  numin2 = 110;
  lines1 = numin1 * (numin1 - 1)/2;
  lines2 = numin2 * (numin2 - 1)/2;
  cout << "The number of initial lines is " << lines1 << ". "<<endl;
  cout << "There are " << lines2 - lines1
       << " additional lines needed."<<endl;

  return 0;
}
```

As before, the C++ program includes the `iostream.h` header file and consists of one `main()` function. The body of this function begins with the opening brace, {, and ends with the closing brace, }. Since the number of lines between subscribers must be an integer (a fractional line is not possible) the variables `lines1` and `lines2` are specified as integer variables. The first two assignment statements initialize the variables `numin1` and `numin2`. The next assignment statement calculates the number of lines needed for 100 subscribers and the last assignment statement calculates the number of lines for 110 subscribers. The first `cout` statement is used to display a message and the result of the first calculation. The next `cout` statement is used to display the difference between the two calculations. The following output is produced when Program 2.13 is compiled and executed.

```
The number of initial lines is 4950.
There are 1045 additional lines needed.
```

Step 4   Test and Correct the Program

As the two calculations and displayed values agree with the previous hand calculation, we have verified correct operation of the program.

Exercises 2.7

1. **a.** Modify Program 2.12 to calculate the speed of a car whose return radar frequency is $2.00000035 \times 10^{10}$ sec^{-1}.
   b. Compile and execute the program written for Exercise 1a on a computer.

2. **a.** Modify Program 2.12 to determine the frequency that will be returned by a car traveling at 55 miles per hour. Your program should produce the following display:

`The returned frequency corresponding to 55 miles per hour is_____`

   where the underline is replaced by the actual value calculated by your program.
   b. Compile and execute the program written for Exercise 2a on a computer. Make sure to do a hand calculation so that you can verify the results produced by your program.
   c. After you have verified the results of the program written in Exercise 2a, modify the program to calculate the returned frequency of a car traveling at 75 miles per hour.

3. **a.** Modify Program 2.13 to calculate and display the total number of lines needed to connect 1000 individual phones directly to each other.
   b. Compile and execute the program written for Exercise 3a on a computer.

4. **a.** Modify Program 2.13 so that a new variable `numfin`, the additional number of subscribers to be connected to the existing network, is initialized to 10. Make any other changes in the program so that the program produces the same display as Program 2.13.
   b. Compile and execute the program written for Exercise 4a on a computer. Check that the display produced by your program matches the display shown in the text.

5. **a.** Design, write, compile, and execute a C++ program to convert temperature in degrees Fahrenheit to degrees Celsius. The equation for this conversion is

   Celsius = 5.0/9.0 (Fahrenheit - 32.0).

   Have your program convert and display the Celsius temperature corresponding to 98.6 degrees Fahrenheit. Your program should produce the following display:

`For a fahrenheit temperature of _____ degrees,`
`    the equivalent celsius temperature is_____ degrees.`

   where appropriate values are inserted by your program in place of the underlines.

b. Check the values computed by your program by hand. After you have verified that your program is working correctly, modify it to convert 86.5 degrees Fahrenheit into its equivalent Celsius value.

6. a. Write, compile, and execute a C++ program to calculate the resistance of a series circuit consisting of twelve 56-ohm, twenty 39-ohm, thirty-two 27-ohm, and twenty-seven 15-ohm resistors. Use the fact that the resistance of a series circuit is the sum of the resistances of all individual resistances. Your program should produce the following display:

`The total resistance, in ohms, is xxxx`

where xxx is replaced by the actual resistance value calculated by your program.

b. Check the values computed by your program by hand. After you have verified that your program is working correctly, modify it to calculate the resistance of a series circuit consisting of no 56-ohm resistors, seventeen 39-ohm resistors, nineteen 27-ohm resistors, and forty-two 15-ohm resistors.

7. a. Design, write, compile, and execute a C++ program to calculate the elapsed time it took to make a 183.67 mile trip. The equation for computing elapsed time is

elapsed time = total distance / average speed

Assume that the average speed during the trip was 58 miles per hour.

b. Check the values computed by your program by hand. After you have verified that your program is working correctly, modify it to determine the elapsed time it takes to make a 372-mile trip at an average speed of 67 miles/hour.

8. a. Design, write, compile, and execute a C++ program to calculate the sum of the numbers from 1 to 100. The formula for calculating this sum is

$$sum = (n/2) \ (\ 2*a + (n - 1)d \ )$$

where n = number of terms to be added, a = the first number, and d = the difference between each number.

b. Check the values computed by your program by hand. After you have verified that your program is working correctly, modify it to determine the sum of the integers from 100 to 1000.

NOTE: *Exercises 9, 10, and 11 require raising a number to a power. This can be accomplished using C++'s power function* pow(). *For example, the statement* pow(2.0,5.0); *raises the number 2.0 to the 5th power, and the statement* pow(num1,num2); *raises the variable* num1 *to the* num2 *power. To use the power function either place an* #include math.h *preprocessor command on a line by itself after the* #include iostream.h *command or include the declaration statement* double pow(); *with the variable declaration statements used in your program. The power function is explained in more detail in Section 3.3.*

9. a. Newton's law of cooling states that when an object with an initial temperature T is placed in a surrounding substance of temperature A, it will reach a temperature *TFIN* in t minutes according to the formula

$$TFIN = (T - A) \ e^{-kt} + A$$

In this formula e is the irrational number 2.71828 rounded to five decimal places, commonly known as Euler's number, and k is a thermal coefficient, which depends on the material being cooled. Using this formula write, compile, and execute a C++ program that determines the temperature reached by an object after 20 minutes when it is placed in a glass of water whose temperature is 60 degrees. Assume that the object initially has a temperature of 150 degrees and has a thermal constant of 0.0367.

b. Check the value computed by your program by hand. After you have verified that your program is working correctly, modify it to determine the temperature reached after 10 minutes when it is placed in a glass of water whose temperature is 50 degrees.

10. a. The voltage gain of an amplifier is given by the formula

$$voltage\ gain = [23\ /\ (\ 23^2 + (0.5f)^2\ )^{1/2}\ ]^n$$

where f is the frequency, in Hertz, and n is the number of stages in the amplifier. Using this formula write, compile, and execute a C++ program that determines the value of the voltage gain for a 4-stage amplifier operating at a frequency of 120 Hertz. Your program should produce the following display:

```
At a frequency of xxxxx hertz, the voltage gain is yyyyy
```

where xxxxx is replaced by the frequency and yyyyy by the voltage gain.

b. Check the value computed by your program by hand. After you have verified that your program is working correctly, modify it to determine the voltage gain of a 12.stage amplifier operating at a frequency of 9500 Hertz.

11. a. The electrical current, i, in amps, that flows through the circuit illustrated in Figure 2.18 is given by the equation

$$i = \frac{E(1-e)}{R}^{-(R/L)t}$$

where E is the voltage of the battery in volts, R is the value of the resistor in ohms, L is the value of the inductor in henrys, t is the time in seconds after the switch is closed, and e is euler's number, which is 2.718 accurate to 3 decimal places. Using this formula, write, compile, and run a C++ program to determine the current flowing in the circuit illustrated in Figure 2.18 when t is 0.12 seconds.

Figure 2.18 A series RL circuit.

b. Check the value computed by your program by hand. After you have verified that your program is working correctly, modify it to determine the current in 0.12 seconds if E is 25 volts, R is 33 ohms, and L is 15 henrys.

12. a. The electrical current, i, in amps, that flows through the circuit illustrated in Figure 2.19 is given by the following equation:

$$i = \frac{(E)e^{-t/RC}}{R}$$

where E is the voltage of the battery in volts, R is the value of the resistor in ohms, C is the value of the capacitor in farads, t is the time in seconds after the switch is closed, and e is euler's number, which is 2.718 accurate to 3 decimal places. Using this formula, write, compile, and run a C++ program to determine the voltage across the capacitor illustrated in Figure 2.19 when t is 0.31 seconds.

Figure 2.19 A series RC circuit.

b. Check the value computed by your program by hand. After you have verified that your program is working correctly, modify it to determine the current in 0.85 seconds if E is 25 volts, R is 220 ohms, and C is 0.00039 farads.

13. a. The electrical voltage, V, in volts, across the capacitor, C, illustrated in Figure 2.20 is given by the equation

$$V = \frac{E\left[1 - e^{-t/RC}\right]}{R}$$

where E is the voltage of the battery in volts, R is the value of the resistor in ohms, C is the value of the capacitor in farads, t is the time in seconds after the switch is closed, and e is euler's number, which is 2.718 accurate to 3 decimal places. Using this formula, write, compile, and run a C++ program to determine the voltage across the capacitor illustrated in Figure 2.20 when t is 0.42 seconds.

Figure 2.20 A series RC circuit.

b. Check the value computed by your program by hand. After you have verified that your program is working correctly, modify it to determine the current in 0.85 seconds if E is 25 volts, R is 220 ohms, and C is 0.00039 farads.

14. a. The set of linear equations

$$a_{11}X_1 + a_{12}X_2 = c_1$$

$$a_{21}X_1 + a_{22}X_2 = c_2$$

can be solved using Cramer's rule:

$$X_1 = \frac{c_1 a_{22} - c_2 a_{12}}{a_{11} a_{22} - a_{12} a_{21}}$$

$$X_2 = \frac{c_2 a_{11} - c_1 a_{21}}{a_{11} a_{22} - a_{12} a_{21}}$$

Using these equations, write, compile, and execute a C++ program to solve for the X_1 and X_2 values that satisfy the following equations

$$3X_1 + 4X_2 = 40$$

$$5X_1 + 2X_2 = 34$$

b. Check the values computed by your program by hand. After you have verified that your program is working correctly, modify it to solve the following set of equations:

$$3X_1 + 12.5X_2 = 22.5$$

$$4.2X_1 - 6.3X_2 = 30$$

2.8 COMMON PROGRAMMING ERRORS

Part of learning any programming language is making the elementary mistakes commonly encountered as you begin to use the language. These mistakes tend to be quite frustrating, since each language has its own set of common programming errors waiting for the unwary. The more common errors made when initially programming in C++ include the following.

1. Omitting the parentheses after `main`.

2. Omitting or incorrectly typing the opening brace { that signifies the start of a function body.

3. Omitting or incorrectly typing the closing brace } that signifies the end of a function.

4. Misspelling the name of an object or function, for example, typing `cot` instead of `cout`.

5. Forgetting to close a string sent to `cout` with a double quote symbol.

6. Forgetting to separate individual data streams passed to `cout` with an insertion ("put-to") symbol, `<<`.

7. Omitting the semicolon at the end of each C++ statement.

8. Adding a semicolon at the end of the `#include` preprocessor command.

9. Forgetting the `\n` to indicate a new line.

10. Incorrectly typing the letter O for the number zero (0), or vice versa. Incorrectly typing the letter l, for the number 1, or vice versa.

11. Forgetting to declare all the variables used in a program. This error is detected by the compiler and an error message is generated for all undeclared variables.

12. Storing an inappropriate data type in a declared variable. This error is detected by the compiler and the assigned value is converted to the data type of the variable it is assigned to.

13. Using a variable in an expression before a value has been assigned to the variable. Here, whatever value happens to be in the variable will be used when the expression is evaluated, and the result will be meaningless.

14. Dividing integer values incorrectly. This error is usually disguised within a larger expression and can be a very troublesome error to detect. For example, the expression

    3.425 + 2/3 + 7.9

yields the same result as the expression

    3.425 + 7.9

because the integer division of 2/3 is 0.

15. Mixing data types in the same expression without clearly understanding the effect produced. Since C++ allows expressions with "mixed" data types, it is important to understand the order of evaluation and the data type of all intermediate calculations. As a general rule it is better never to mix data types in an expression unless a specific effect is desired.

    The third, fifth, seventh, eighth, and ninth errors in this list are initially the most common, while even experienced programmers occasionally make the tenth error. It is worthwhile for you to write a program and specifically introduce each of these errors, one at a time, to see what error messages are produced by your compiler.

Then when these error messages appear due to inadvertent errors, you will have had experience in understanding the messages and correcting the errors.

On a more fundamental level, a major programming error made by all beginning programmers is the rush to code and run a program before the programmer fully understands what is required and the algorithms and procedures that will be used to produce the desired result. A symptom of this haste to get a program entered into the computer is the lack of either an outline of the proposed program or a written program itself. Many problems can be caught just by checking a copy of the program, either handwritten or listed from the computer, before it is ever compiled.

 2.9 ## CHAPTER SUMMARY

1. A C++ program consists of one or more modules called functions. One of these functions must be called `main()`. The `main()` function identifies the starting point of a C++ program.

2. The simplest C++ program consists of the single function `main()`.

3. Following the function name, the body of a function has the following general form:

```
{
    All C++ statements in here;
}
```

4. All C++ statements must be terminated by a semicolon.

5. Three types of data were introduced in this chapter: integer, floating-point, and character data. Each of these types of data is typically stored in a computer using different amounts of memory. C++ recognizes each of these data types, in addition to other types yet to be presented.

6. The `cout` object can be used to display all of C++'s data types.

7. When the `cout` object is used within a program, the preprocessor command `#include <iostream.h>` must be placed at the top of the program. Preprocessor commands do not end with a semicolon.

8. Every variable in a C++ program must be declared as to the type of value it can store. Declarations within a function may be placed anywhere within a function, although a variable can only be used after it is declared. Variables may also be initialized when they are declared. Additionally, variables of the same type may be declared using a single declaration statement. Variable declaration statements have the general form:

data-type variable-name(s);

9. A simple C++ program containing declaration statements has the typical form

```
#include <iostream.h>

int main()
{
   declaration statements;

   other statements;

   return 0;
}
```

Although declaration statements may be placed anywhere within the function's body, a variable may only be used after it is declared.

10. Declaration statements always play a software role of informing the compiler of a function's valid variable names. When a variable declaration also causes the computer to set aside memory locations for the variable, the declaration statement is also called a definition statement. (All the declarations we have used in this chapter have also been definition statements.)

11. The `sizeof()` operator can be used to determine the amount of storage reserved for variables.

Electrical Engineering

Electrical engineering deals with the application of the principles of electricity and electromagnetism to the manufacture of all forms of machines and devices that either use electricity or produce electrical energy. The field is the largest of all engineering fields. In its beginning in the mid 1800s it was concerned solely with generating electrical energy. It has evolved into a field with broad boundaries, encompassing communication, computers, robotics, and solid-state devices such as transistors.

1. Power. This area involves generation of electrical energy in large fossil-fuel, nuclear, solar, or hydroelectric plants or the efficient utilization of electrical energy by means of motors or illumination devices. Also important are the transmission and distribution of electrical energy through overhead lines, microwaves, light pipes, and superconducting lines.

2. Solid-State Electronics. Through modern physics and materials science, exotic semiconducting materials are being developed and used to construct microcircuitry for monitoring and controlling the operations of all kinds of devices, from video games to assembly-line robots. The improved reliability, rapidly shrinking size, and reduced power requirements of modern miniaturized electrical components have created limitless opportunities for applications.

3. Communications. Communications involves the design and construction of equipment used in the transmission of information via electricity or electromagnetic waves (radio, light, microwaves, etc.) The use of the laser for communication is a topic of modern concern, whereas antenna characteristics and radar are somewhat older.

4. Computers and Robotics. While electronics deals with the principles associated with the functions of components, computer engineers are concerned with designing the complex circuitry that interweaves the components into a computer. Microprocessors, or small computers, are designed to constantly monitor and control the operations of a particular piece of equipment such as a lathe or an autopilot.

CHAPTER 3

Completing the Basics

TOPICS

3.1 ASSIGNMENT OPERATIONS
ASSIGNMENT VARIATIONS
ACCUMULATING
COUNTING

3.2 FORMATTING NUMBERS FOR PROGRAM OUTPUT

3.3 USING MATHEMATICAL LIBRARY FUNCTIONS
CASTS

3.4 PROGRAM INPUT USING THE cin OBJECT

3.5 THE const QUALIFIER
PLACEMENT OF STATEMENTS

3.6 APPLICATIONS
APPLICATION 1: ACID RAIN
APPLICATION 2: APPROXIMATING THE EXPONENTIAL FUNCTION

3.7 COMMON PROGRAMMING ERRORS

3.8 CHAPTER SUMMARY

3.9 CHAPTER APPENDIX: A CLOSER LOOK AT ERRORS
COMPILE-TIME AND RUN-TIME ERRORS
SYNTAX AND LOGIC ERRORS
LOOKING AT CAREER CHOICES: MECHANICAL ENGINEERING

In the last chapter we explored how results are displayed using C++'s cout object and how numerical data is stored and processed using variables and assignment statements. In this chapter we complete our introduction to C++ by presenting additional processing and input capabilities.

3.1 > ASSIGNMENT OPERATIONS

We have already encountered simple assignment statements in Chapter 2. Assignment statements are the most basic C++ statements for both assigning values to variables and performing computations. This statement has the syntax:

variable = expression;

The simplest expression in C++ is a single constant. In each of the following assignment statements, the operand to the right of the equal sign is a constant:

```
length = 25;
width = 17.5;
```

In each of these assignment statements the value of the constant to the right of the equal sign is assigned to the variable on the left of the equal sign. It is important to note that the equal sign in C++ does not have the same meaning as an equal sign in algebra. The equal sign in an assignment statement tells the computer first to determine the value of the operand to the right of the equal sign and then to store (or assign) that value in the locations associated with the variable to the left of the equal sign. In this regard, the C++ statement `length = 25;` is read "length is assigned the value 25." The blank spaces in the assignment statement are inserted for readability only.

Recall that a variable can be initialized when it is declared. If an initialization is not done within the declaration statement, the variable should be assigned a value with an assignment statement or input operation before it is used in any computation. Subsequent assignment statements can, of course, be used to change the value assigned to a variable. For example, assume the following statements are executed one after another and that `slope` was not initialized when it was declared:

```
slope = 3.7;
slope = 6.28;
```

The first assignment statement assigns the value of 3.7 to the variable named `slope`.[1] The next assignment statement causes the computer to assign a value of 6.28 to `slope`. The 3.7 that was in `slope` is overwritten with the new value of 6.28 because a variable can store only one value at a time. It is sometimes useful to think of the variable to the left of the equal sign as a temporary parking spot in a huge parking lot. Just as an individual parking spot can be used only by one car at a time, each variable can store only one value at a time. The "parking" of a new value in a variable automatically causes the program to remove any value previously parked there.

---

[1] Since this is the first time a value is explicitly assigned to this variable it is frequently referred to as an initialization. This stems from historical usage that said a variable was initialized the first time a value was assigned to it. Under this usage it is correct to say that "total is initialized to 3.7." From an implementation viewpoint, however, this later statement is incorrect. This is because the assignment operation is handled differently by the C++ compiler than an initialization performed when a variable is created by a declaration statement. This difference is only important when using C++'s class features and is explained in detail in Section 9.1.

In addition to being a constant, the operand to the right of the equal sign in an assignment statement can be a variable or any other valid C++ expression. An **expression** is any combination of constants, variables, and function calls that can be evaluated to yield a result. Thus, the expression in an assignment statement can be used to perform calculations using the arithmetic operators introduced in Section 2.3. Examples of assignment statements using expressions containing these operators are

```
sum = 3 + 7;
diff = 15 - 6;
product = .05 * 14.6;
tally = count + 1;
newtotal = 18.3 + total;
taxes = .06 * amount;
totalWeight = factor * weight;
average = sum / items;
slope = (y2 - y1) / (x2 - x1);
```

As always in an assignment statement, the computer first calculates the value of the expression to the right of the equal sign and then stores this value in the variable to the left of the equal sign. For example, in the assignment statement `totalWeight = factor * weight;` the arithmetic expression `factor * weight` is first evaluated to yield a result. This result, which is a number, is then stored in the variable `totalWeight`.

In writing assignment expressions, you must be aware of two important considerations. Since the expression to the right of the equal sign is evaluated first, all variables used in the expression must previously have been given valid values if the result is to make sense. For example, the assignment statement `totalWeight = factor * weight;` causes a valid number to be stored in `totalWeight` only if the programmer first takes care to assign valid numbers to `factor` and `weight`. Thus the sequence of statements

```
factor = 1.06;
weight = 155.0;
totalWeight = factor * weight;
```

tells us the values being used to obtain the result that will be stored in `totalWeight`. Figure 3.1 illustrates the values stored in the variables `factor`, `weight`, and `totalWeight`.

Figure 3.1 *Values stored in the variables.*

The second consideration to keep in mind is that since the value of an expression is stored in the variable to the left of the equal sign, only one variable can be listed in this position. For example, the assignment statement

```
amount + 1892 = 1000 + 10 * 5;
```

is invalid. The right-side expression evaluates to the integer 1050, which can only be stored in a variable. Since amount + 1892 is not a valid variable name, the computer does not know where to store the calculated value. Program 3.1 illustrates the use of assignment statements to calculate the volume of a cylinder. As illustrated in Figure 3.2, the volume of a cylinder is determined by the formula, $Volume = \pi r^2 h$, where r is the radius of the cylinder, h is the height, and π is the constant 3.1416 (accurate to four decimal places).

Figure 3.2 Determining the volume of a cylinder.

Program 3.1

```
//   this program calculates the volume of a cylinder,
//      given its radius and height
#include <iostream.h>

int main()
{
  float radius, height, volume;

  radius = 2.5;
  height = 16.0;
  volume = 3.1416 * radius * radius * height;
  cout << "The volume of the cylinder is " << volume << endl;

  return 0;
}
```

When Program 3.1 is compiled and executed, the output is

    The volume of the cylinder is 314.16

Consider the flow of control that the computer uses in executing Program 3.1. Program execution begins with the first statement within the body of the main() function and continues sequentially, statement by statement, until the closing brace of main is encountered.

This flow of control is true for all programs. The computer works on one statement at a time, executing that statement with no knowledge of what the next statement will be. This explains why all operands used in an expression must have values assigned to them before the expression is evaluated. When the computer executes the statement

```
volume = 3.1416 * radius * radius * height;
```

in Program 3.1, it uses whatever value is stored in the variables `radius` and `height` at the time the assignment statement is executed.[2] If no values have been specifically assigned to these variables before they are used in the assignment statement, the computer uses whatever values happen to occupy these variables when they are referenced (on some systems all variables are automatically initialized to zero). The computer does not "look ahead" to see if you assign values to these variables later in the program.

It is important to realize that in C++, the equal sign, =, used in assignment statements is itself an operator, which differs from the way most other high-level languages process this symbol. In C++ (as in C), the = symbol is called the **assignment operator**, and an expression using this operator, such as `interest = principal * rate`, is an assignment expression. Since the assignment operator has a lower precedence than any other arithmetic operator, the value of any expression to the right of the equal sign will be evaluated first, prior to assignment.

Like all expressions, assignment expressions themselves have a value. The value of the complete assignment expression is the value assigned to the variable on the left of the assignment operator. For example, the expression `a = 5` both assigns a value of 5 to the variable `a` and results in the expression itself having a value of 5. The value of the expression can always be verified using a statement such as

```
cout << "The value of the expression is " << (a = 5);
```

Here, the value of the expression itself is displayed and not the contents of the variable `a`. Although both the contents of the variable and the expression have the same value, it is worthwhile realizing that we are dealing with two distinct entities.

From a programming perspective, it is the actual assignment of a value to a variable that is significant in an assignment expression; the final value of the assignment expression itself is of little consequence. However, the fact that assignment expressions have a value has implications that must be considered when C++'s relational operators are presented.

Any expression that is terminated by a semicolon becomes a C++ statement. The most common example of this is the assignment statement, which is simply an assignment expression terminated with a semicolon. For example, terminating the assignment expression `a = 33` with a semicolon results in the assignment statement `a = 33;` , which can be used in a program on a line by itself.

Since the equal sign is an operator in C++, multiple assignments are possible in the same expression or its equivalent statement. For example, in the expression `a = b = c = 25` all the assignment operators have the same precedence. Since the

---

[2] Since C++ does not have an exponentiation operator, the square of the radius is obtained by the term radius * radius. In Section 3.3 we introduce C++'s power function pow(), which allows us to raise a number to a power.

assignment operator has a right-to-left associativity, the final evaluation proceeds in the sequence

```
c = 25
b = c
a = b
```

In this case, this has the effect of assigning the number 25 to each of the variables individually and can be represented as

```
a = (b = (c = 25))
```

Appending a semicolon to the original expression results in the multiple assignment statement

```
a = b = c = 25;
```

This latter statement assigns the value 25 to the three individual variables equivalent to the following order:

```
c = 25;
b = 25;
a = 25;
```

Note that data type conversions can take place across assignment operators; that is, the value of the expression on the right side of the assignment operator is converted to the data type of the variable to the left of the assignment operator. Thus, assigning an integer value to a real variable causes the integer to be converted to a real value. Similarly, assigning a real value to an integer variable forces conversion of the real value to an integer, which always results in the loss of the fractional part of the number due to truncation. For example, if `temp` is an integer variable, the assignment `temp = 25.89` causes the integer value 25 to be stored in the integer variable `temp`.[3]

A more complete example of data type conversions, which includes both mixed-mode and assignment conversion, is the evaluation of the expression

```
a = b * d
```

where `a` and `b` are integer variables and `d` is a floating-point variable. When the mixed-mode expression `b * d` is evaluated[4], the value of `d` used in the expression is converted to a double-precision number for purposes of computation (it is important to note that the value stored in `d` remains a floating-point number). Since one of the operands is a double-precision variable, the value of the integer variable `b` is converted to a double-precision number for the computation (again, the value stored in `b` remains an integer) and the resulting value of the expression `b * d` is a double-precision number. Finally, data type conversion across the assignment operator comes into play. Since the left side of the assignment operator is an integer variable, the double-precision value of the expression `(b * d)` is truncated to an integer value and stored in the variable `a`.

---

[3] The correct integer portion, clearly, is retained only when it is within the range of integers allowed by the compiler.

[4] Review the rules in Section 2.3 for the evaluation of mixed-mode expressions, if necessary.

Point of Information

lvalues and rvalues

The terms `lvalue` and `rvalue` are frequently used terms in programming technology. Both of these terms are language independent and mean the following: An **lvalue** can have a value assigned to it while an **rvalue** cannot.

In both C and C++ this means that an `lvalue` can appear on both the left and right sides of an assignment operator while an `rvalue` can only appear on the right side of an assignment operator. For example, each variable we have encountered can be either an `lvalue` or `rvalue`, while a number can only be an `rvalue`. Not all variables, however, can be `lvalues` and `rvalues`. For example, an array type, which is introduced in Chapter 10, cannot be an `lvalue` or an `rvalue`, while individual array elements can be both.

Assignment Variations

Although only one variable is allowed immediately to the left of the equal sign in an assignment expression, the variable on the left of the equal sign can also be used on the right of the equal sign. For example, the assignment expression `sum = sum + 10` is valid. Clearly, as an algebraic equation sum could never be equal to itself plus 10. But in C++, the expression `sum = sum + 10` is not an equation—it is an expression that is evaluated in two major steps. The first step is to calculate the value of `sum + 10`. The second step is to store the computed value in `sum`. See if you can determine the output of Program 3.2.

Program 3.2

```cpp
#include <iostream.h>

int main()
{
  int sum;

  sum = 25;
  cout << "The number stored in sum is " << sum << endl;
  sum = sum + 10;
  cout << "The number now stored in sum is " << sum << endl;

  return 0;
}
```

The assignment statement sum = 25; tells the computer to store the number 25 in sum, as shown in Figure 3.3.

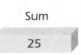

Sum

25

Figure 3.3 The integer 25 is stored in sum.

The first cout statement causes the value stored in sum to be displayed by the message **The number stored in sum is 25.** The second assignment statement in Program 3.2, sum = sum + 10; causes the program to retrieve the 25 stored in sum and add 10 to this number, yielding the number 35. The number 35 is then stored in the variable on the left side of the equal sign, which is the variable sum. The 25 that was in sum is simply over-written with the new value of 35, as shown in Figure 3.4.

Sum

Old value is overwritten

25

New value (35) is stored

Figure 3.4 sum = sum + 10; causes a new value to be stored in sum.

Assignment expressions like sum = sum + 25, which use the same variable on both sides of the assignment operator, can be written using the following shortcut **assignment operators:**

      +=   -=   *=   /=   %=

For example, the expression sum = sum + 10 can be written as sum += 10. Similarly, the expression price *= rate is equivalent to the expression price = price * rate.

In using these new assignment operators it is important to note that the variable to the left of the assignment operator is applied to the complete expression on the right. For example, the expression price *= rate + 1 is equivalent to the expression price = price * (rate + 1), not price = price * rate + 1.

Accumulating

Assignment expressions like sum += 10 or its equivalent, sum = sum + 10, are very common in programming. These expressions are required in accumulating subtotals when data is entered one number at a time. For example, if we want to add the numbers 96, 70, 85, and 60 in calculator fashion, the following statements could be used:

Statement	Value in sum
sum = 0;	0
sum = sum + 96;	96
sum = sum + 70;	166
sum = sum + 85;	251
sum = sum + 60;	311

The first statement initializes sum to 0. This removes any number ("garbage value") stored in sum that would invalidate the final total. As each number is added, the value stored in sum is increased accordingly. After completion of the last statement, sum contains the total of all the added numbers. Program 3.3 illustrates the effect of these statements by displaying sum's contents after each addition is made.

Program 3.3

```
#include <iostream.h>

int main()
{
  int sum;

  sum = 0;
  cout << "The value of sum is initially set to " << sum << endl;
  sum = sum + 96;
  cout << "  sum is now " << sum << endl;
  sum = sum + 70;
  cout << "  sum is now " << sum << endl;
  sum = sum + 85;
  cout << "  sum is now " << sum  << endl;
  sum = sum + 60;
  cout << "  The final sum is " << sum << endl;

  return 0;
}
```

The output displayed by Program 3.3 is:

```
The value of sum is initially set to 0
    sum is now 96
    sum is now 166
    sum is now 251
    The final sum is 311
```

Although Program 3.3 is not a practical program (it is easier to add the numbers by hand), it does illustrate the subtotaling effect of repeated use of statements having the form

variable = variable + new_value;

We will find many uses for this type of statement when we become more familiar with the repetition statements introduced in Chapter 5.

Counting

An assignment statement that is very similar to the accumulating statement is the counting statement. Counting statements have the form

variable = variable + fixed_number;

Examples of counting statements are

```
i = i + 1;
n = n + 1;
count = count + 1;
j = j + 2;
m = m + 2;
kk = kk + 3;
```

In each of these examples the same variable is used on both sides of the equal sign. After the statement is executed the value of the respective variable is increased by a fixed amount. In the first three examples the variables i, n, and count have all been increased by one. In the next two examples the respective variables have been increased by two, and in the final example the variable kk has been increased by three.

For the special case in which a variable is either increased or decreased by one, C++ provides two unary operators. Using the increment operator,[5] ++, the expression variable = variable + 1 can be replaced by either the expression variable++ or ++variable. Examples of the increment operator are

Expression	Alternative
i = i + 1	i++ or ++i
n = n + 1	n++ or ++n
count = count + 1	count++ or ++count

---

[5]As an historical note, the ++ in C++ was inspired from the increment operator symbol. It was used to indicate that C++ was the next increment to the C language.

Program 3.4 illustrates the use of the increment operator.

Program 3.4

```cpp
#include <iostream.h>

int main()
{
  int count;

  count = 0;
  cout << "The initial value of count is " << count << endl;
  count++;
  cout << "   count is now " << count << endl;
  count++;
  cout << "   count is now " << count << endl;
  count++;
  cout << "   count is now " << count << endl;
  count++;
  cout << "   count is now " << count << endl;

  return 0;
}
```

The output displayed by Program 3.4 is:

```
The initial value of count is 0
      count is now 1
      count is now 2
      count is now 3
      count is now 4
```

When the ++ operator appears before a variable it is called a **prefix increment operator**; when it appears after a variable it is called a **postfix increment operator**. The distinction between a prefix and postfix increment operator is important when the variable being incremented is used in an assignment expression. For example, the expression k = ++n does two things in one expression. Initially the value of n is incremented by one and then the new value of n is assigned to the variable k. Thus, the statement k = ++n; is equivalent to the two statements

```
n = n + 1;    // increment n first
k = n;        // assign n's value to k
```

The assignment expression k = n++, which uses a postfix increment operator, reverses this procedure. A postfix increment operates after the assignment is completed. Thus, the statement k = n++; first assigns the current value of n to k and then increments the value of n by one. This is equivalent to the two statements

```
k = n;        // assign n's value to k
n = n + 1;    // and then increment n
```

In addition to the increment operator, C++ also provides a decrement operator, --. As you might expect, the expressions variable-- and --variable are both equivalent to the expression variable = variable - 1.

Examples of the decrement operator are:

Expression	Alternative
i = i - 1	i-- or --i
n = n - 1	n-- or --n
count = count - 1	count-- or --count

When the -- operator appears before a variable it is called a **prefix decrement operator**. When the decrement appears after a variable it is called a **postfix decrement operator**. For example, both of the expressions n-- and --n reduce the value of n by one. These expressions are equivalent to the longer expression n = n - 1. As with the increment operators, however, the prefix and postfix decrement operators produce different results when used in assignment expressions. For example, the expression k = --n first decrements the value of n by one before assigning the value of n to k, while the expression k = n-- first assigns the current value of n to k and then reduces the value of n by one.

Exercises 3.1

1. Write an assignment statement to calculate the circumference of a circle having a radius of 3.3 inches. The equation for determining the circumference, c, of a circle is $c = 2\pi r$, where r is the radius and π equals 3.1416.

2. Write an assignment statement to calculate the area of a circle. The equation for determining the area, a, of a circle is $a = \pi r^2$, where r is the radius and $\pi = 3.1416$.

3. Write an assignment statement to convert temperature in degrees Fahrenheit to degrees Celsius. The equation for this conversion is Celsius = 5/9 (Fahrenheit – 32).

4. Write an assignment statement to calculate the round-trip distance, d, in feet, of a trip that is s miles long, one way.

5. Write an assignment statement to calculate the elapsed time, in minutes, that it takes to make a trip. The equation for computing elapsed time is elapsed *time = total distance / average speed*. Assume that the distance is in miles and the average speed is in miles/hour.

6. Write an assignment statement to calculate the nth term in an arithmetic sequence. The formula for calculating the value, v, of the nth term is $v = a + (n - 1)d$, where a = the first number in the sequence and d = the difference between any two numbers in the sequence.

7. Write an assignment statement to calculate the linear expansion in a steel beam as a function of temperature increase. The formula for linear expansion, l, is $l = l_o[1+\propto(T_f-T_o)]$, where l_o is the length of the beam at temperature T_o, $\propto$ is the coefficient of linear expansion, and T_f is the final temperature of the beam.

8. Coulomb's law states that the force F, acting between two electrically charged spheres is given by the formula $F = kq_1q_2/r^2$, where q_1 is the charge on the first sphere, q_2 is the charge on the second sphere, r is the distance between the centers of the two spheres, and k is a proportionality constant. Write an assignment statement to calculate the force, F.

9. Write an assignment statement to determine the maximum bending moment, M, of a beam. The formula for maximum bending moment is, $M = XW(L - X)/L$, where X is the distance from the end of the beam that a weight, W, is placed, and L is the length of the beam.

10. Determine the output of the following program:

```cpp
#include <iostream.h>

int main() // a program illustrating integer truncation
{
    int num1, num2;

    num1 = 9/2;
    num2 = 17/4;
    cout << "the first integer displayed is " << num1 << endl;
    cout << "the second integer displayed is " << num2 << endl;

    return 0;
}
```

11. Determine and correct the errors in the following programs.

    a.
```cpp
#include <iostream.h>

    int main()
    {
      width = 15
      area = length * width;
      cout << "The area is " << area

    }
```

b. `#include <iostream.h>`

```
int main()
{
  int length, width, area;
  area = length * width;
  length = 20;
  width = 15;
  cout << "The area is " << area;

  return 0;
```

c. `#include <iostream.h>`

```
int main()
{
  int length = 20; width = 15, area;
  length * width = area;
  cout << "The area is " , area;

  return 0;
}
```

12. By mistake a student reordered the statements in Program 3.3 as follows:

```
#include <iostream.h>

int main()
{
  int sum;
  sum = 0;
  sum = sum + 96;
  sum = sum + 70;
  sum = sum + 85;
  sum = sum + 60;
  cout << "The value of sum is initially set to " << sum << endl;
  cout << "  sum is now " << sum << endl;
  cout << "  sum is now " << sum << endl;
  cout << "  sum is now " << sum << endl;
  cout << "  The final sum is " << sum << endl;

  return 0;
}
```

Determine the output that this program produces.

13. Using Program 3.1, determine the volume of cylinders having the following radii and heights.

Radius (in.)	Height (in.)
1.62	6.23
2.86	7.52
4.26	8.95
8.52	10.86
12.29	15.35

14. The area of an ellipse (see Figure 3.5) is given by the formula Area = πab.

Using this formula, write a C++ program to calculate the area of an ellipse having a minor axis of 2.5 inches and a major axis of 6.4 inches.

Figure 3.5 The minor axis *a* and the major axis *b* of an ellipse.

15. Modify Program 3.1 to calculate the weight, in pounds, of the steel cylinder whose volume was found by the program. The formula for determining the weight is weight = 0.28 $(\pi)(r^2)(h)$, where *r* is the radius (in inches) and *h* is the height (in inches) of the cylinder.

16. The circumference of an ellipse (see Figure 3.5) is given by the formula:

$$\text{Circumference} = \pi\sqrt{2^2\left(a+b\right)^2}$$

Using this formula, write a C++ program to calculate the area of an ellipse having a minor radius of 2.5 inches and a major radius of 6.4 inches. (*Hint:* The square root can be taken by raising the quantity 2[$a^2 + b^2$] to the 0.5 power).

17. a. The combined resistance of three resistors connected in parallel, as shown in Figure 3.6, is given by the equation

$$\text{Combined resistance} = \frac{1}{\dfrac{1}{R_1} + \dfrac{1}{R_2} + \dfrac{1}{R_3}}$$

Write a C++ program to calculate and display the combined resistance when the three resistors $R_1 = 1000$, $R_2 = 1000$, and $R_3 = 1000$ are connected in parallel. Your program should produce the display "The combined resistance, in ohms, is xxxxx", where the xs are replaced by the value of the combined resistance computed by your program.

Figure 3.6 Three resistors connected in parallel.

   b. How do you know that the value calculated by your program is correct?

   c. Once you have verified the output produced by your program, modify it to determine the combined resistance when the resistors R_1 = 1500, R_2 = 1200, and R_3 = 2000 are connected in parallel.

18. a. Write a C++ program to calculate and display the value of the slope of the line connecting the two points whose coordinates are (3,7) and (8,12). Use the fact that the slope between two points having coordinates (x_1,y_1) and (x_2,y_2) is slope = $(y_2 - y_1) / (x_2 - x_1)$. Your program should produce the display The slope is xxxx, where the xs are replaced by the value calculated by your program.

   b. How do you know that the result produced by your program is correct?

   c. Once you have verified the output produced by your program, modify it to determine the slope of the line connecting the points (2,10) and (12,6).

19. a. Write a C++ program to calculate and display the coordinates of the midpoint of the line connecting the two points given in Exercise 27a. Use the fact that the coordinates of the midpoint between two points having coordinates (x_1,y_1) and (x_2,y_2) are $[(x_1 + x_2)]/2, [(y_1 + y_2)]/2)$. Your program should produce the following display:

```
The x midpoint coordinate is xxx
The y midpoint coordinate is xxx
```

   where the xs are replaced with the values calculated by your program.

   b. How do you know that the midpoint values calculated by your program are correct?

   c. Once you have verified the output produced by your program, modify it to determine the midpoint coordinates of the line connecting the points (2,10) and (12,6).

20. a. For the electrical circuit shown in Figure 3.7, the branch currents, i_1, i_2, and, i_3 can be determined using the formulas

$$i_1 = \frac{E_2 R_3 + E_1(R_1 + R_3)}{(R_1 + R_3)(R_2 + R_3) - (R_3)^2}$$

$$i_2 = \frac{E_1 R_3 + E_2(R_1 + R_3)}{(R_1 + R_3)(R_2 + R_3) - (R_3)^2}$$

$$i_3 = i_1 - i_2$$

Using these formulas write a C++ program to compute the branch currents when $R_1 = 10$ ohms, $R_2 = 4$ ohms, $R_3 = 6$ ohms, $E_1 = 12$ volts, and $E_2 = 9$ volts. The display produced by your program should be

```
Branch current 1 is xxxx
Branch current 2 is xxxx
Branch Current 3 is xxxx
```

where the xs are replaced by the values determined in your program.

b. How do you know that the loop currents calculated by your program are correct?

c. Once you have verified the output produced by your program, modify it to determine the branch currents for the following values: $R_1 = 1500$, $R_2 = 1200$, $R_3 = 2000$, $E_1 = 15$, and $E_2 = 12$.

Figure 3.7 An electical circuit.

3.2 FORMATTING NUMBERS FOR PROGRAM OUTPUT

Besides displaying correct results, it is extremely important for a program to present its results attractively. Most programs are judged, in fact, on the perceived ease of data entry and the style and presentation of their output. For example, displaying a monetary result as 1.897000 is not in keeping with accepted report conventions. The display should be either $1.90 or $1.89, depending on whether rounding or truncation is used.

The format of numbers displayed by cout can be controlled by field width manipulators included in each output stream. Table 3.1 lists the most commonly used manipulators available for this purpose.[6]

---

[6]As was noted in Chapter 2, the endl manipulator inserts a newline and then flushes the stream.

Table 3.1 Commonly Used Stream Manipulators

Manipulator	Action
setw(n)	Set the field width to n
setprecision(n)	Set the floating-point precision to n places
setiosflags(flags)	Set the format flags (see Table 2-9 for flag settings)
dec	Set output for decimal display
hex	Set output for hexadecimal display
oct	Set output for octal display

For example, the statement

```
cout << "The sum of 6 and 5 is" << setw(3) <<  21;
```

causes the printout

```
The sum of 6 and 15 is 21
```

The setw(3) field-width manipulator included in the stream of data passed to cout is used to set the displayed field-width. The 3 in this manipulator sets the default field-width for the next number in the stream to be three spaces wide. This field-width setting causes the 21 to be printed in a field of three spaces, which includes one blank and the number 21. As illustrated, integers are right-justified within the specified field.

Field-width manipulators are useful in printing columns of numbers so that the numbers in each column align correctly. For example, Program 3.5 illustrates how a column of integers would align in the absence of field-width manipulators.

Program 3.5

```cpp
#include <iostream.h>

int main()
{
  cout << 6 << endl
       << 18 << endl
       << 124 << endl
       << "---\n"
       << (6+18+124) << endl;

  return 0;
}
```

The output of Program 3.5 is

```
  6
 18
124
---
148
```

Since no field-width manipulators are given, the cout object allocates enough space for each number as it is received. To force the numbers to align on the units digit requires a field width wide enough for the largest displayed number. For Program 3.5, a width of three suffices. The use of this field width is illustrated in Program 3.6.

Program 3.6

```cpp
#include <iostream.h>
#include <iomanip.h>

int main()
{
  cout << setw(3) << 6 << endl
       << setw(3) << 18 << endl
       << setw(3) << 124 << endl
       << "---\n"
       << (6+18+124) << endl;

  return 0;
}
```

The output of Program 3.6 is

```
  6
 18
124
---
148
```

Notice that the field-width manipulator must be included for each occurrence of a number inserted onto the data stream sent to cout, and that the manipulator only applies to the next insertion of data immediately following it. Also notice that if manipulators are to be included within an output display, the iomanip.h header file must be included as part of the program. This is accomplished by the preprocessor command #include <iomanip.h>.[7]

---

[7]Since the iomanip.h header file will include the iostream.h header file if it has not already been included, the #include statement for iostream.h can be omitted.

Formatted floating-point numbers require the use of three field-width manipulators. The first manipulator sets the total width of the display, including the decimal point; the second manipulator sets the output type (exponent or conventional decimal display) and the third manipulator determines how many digits can be printed to the right of the decimal point. For example, the statement

```
cout << "|" << setw(10) <<  setiosflags(ios::fixed)<< setprecision(3) << 25.67 << "|";
```

causes the printout

```
|    25.670|
```

the bar symbol, |, in the example is used to delimit (mark) the beginning and end of the display field. The `setw` manipulator tells `cout` to display the number in a total field of 10, while the `setprecision` manipulator tells `cout` to display a three digits to the right of the decimal point. The `setiosflags` manipulator using the `ios::fixed` flag ensures that the output is displayed in conventional decimal format; that is, as a fixed-point rather then an exponential number.

For all numbers (integers, floating-point, and double-precision), `cout` ignores the `setw` manipulator specification if the total specified field width is too small, and allocates enough space for the integer part of the number to be printed. The fractional part of both floating-point and double-precision numbers is displayed up to the precision set with the `setprecision` manipulator (in the absence of a `setprecision` manipulator, the default precision is set to 6 decimal places). If the fractional part of the number to be displayed contains more digits than called for in the `setprecision` manipulator, the number is rounded to the indicated number of decimal places; if the fractional part contains fewer digits than specified, the number is displayed with the fewer digits. Table 3.2 illustrates the effect of various format manipulator combinations. Again, for clarity, the bar symbol, |, is used to clearly delineate the beginning and end of the output fields.

Table 3.2 Effect of Format Manipulators[8]

Manipulators	Number	Display	Comments
`setw(2)`	3	| 3|	Number fits in field
`setw(2)`	43	|43|	Number fits in field
`setw(2)`	143	|143|	Field width ignored
`setw(2)`	2.3	|2.3|	Field width ignored

`setw(5)`
`setiosflags(ios::fixed)`
`setprecision(2)`
	2.366	| 2.37|	Field width of 5 with 2 decimal digits

`setw(5)`
`setiosflags(ios::fixed)`
`setprecision(2)`
	42.3	|42.30|	Number fits in field

---

[8]If either the manipulator flags ios::fixed or ios::scientific are not in effect, the setprecision value indicates the total number of significant digits displayed rather than the number of digits after the decimal point.

Table 3.2 Effect of Format Manipulators (continued)

Manipulators	Number	Display	Comments

`setw(5)`
`setiosflags(ios::fixed)`
`setprecision(2)`
	142.364	|142.36|	Field width ignored but precision specification is used

`setw(5)`
`setiosflags(ios::fixed)`
`setprecision(2)`
	142.366	|142.37|	Field width ignored but precision specification is used

`setw(5)`
`setiosflags(ios::fixed)`
`setprecision(2)`
	142	| 142|	Field width used, precision irrelevant

In addition to the `setw` and `setprecision` manipulators, a field-justification manipulator is also available. As we have seen, numbers sent to `cout` are normally displayed right justified in the display field, while strings are displayed left justified. To alter the default justification for a stream of data, the `setiosflags` manipulator can be used. For example, the statement

```
cout << "|" << setw(10) << setiosflags(ios::left) << 142 << "|";
```

causes the following left-justified display

```
|142       |
```

As we have previously seen, since data passed to `cout` may be continued across multiple lines, the previous display would also be produced by the statement

```
cout << "|" << setw(10)
            << setiosflags(ios::left)
            << 142 << "|";
```

As always, the field-width manipulator is only in effect for the next single set of data passed to `cout`. Right justification for strings in a stream is obtained by the manipulator `setiosflags(ios::right)`. The symbols `ios` in both the function name and the `ios::right` argument comes from the first letters of the words input output stream.

In addition to the left and right flags that can be used with the `setiosflags()` manipulator, other flags may also be used to affect the output. The most commonly used flags for this manipulator are listed in Table 3.3.

What Is a Flag?

In current programming usage the term **flag** refers to an item, such as a variable or argument, that sets a condition usually considered as either active or nonactive. Although the exact origin of this term in programming is not known it probably originates from the use of real flags to signal a condition, such as the Stop, Go, Caution, and Winner flags commonly used at car races.

In a similar manner each flag argument to the `setiosflags()` manipulator function activates a specific condition. For example, the `ios::dec` flag sets the display format to decimal, while the flag `ios::oct` activates the octal display format. Since these conditions are mutually exclusive, which means that only one condition can be active at a time, activating one such flag automatically deactivates the other flags.

Flags that are not mutually exclusive, such as `ios::dec`, `ios::showpoint`, and `ios::fixed` can all be set on at the same time. This can be done using three individual `setiosflag()` calls or combining all arguments into one call as follows:

```
cout << setiosflags(ios::dec || ios::showpoint || ios::fixed);
```

Table 3.3 Format Flags for Use with setiosflags()

Flag	Meaning
`ios::showpoint`	always display a deciaml point. In the adsence of the ios::fixed flag, a numerical value with a decimal point is displayed with a default of 6 significant digits. If the integer part of the number requires more than 6 digits the display will be in exponential notation, unless the ios::fixed flag is in effect. For example, the value 12345567. is displayed as 1.23457e0 unless the ios::fixed flag is in effect. This flag has no effect on integer values
`ios::showpos`	display a leading + sign when the number is positive
`ios::fixed`	display the number in conventional fixed-point decimal notation (that is, with an integer and fractional part separated by decimal point), and not in exponential notation
`ios::scientific`	use exponential notation on output
`ios::dec`	display as a decimal number (this is the default)
`ios::oct`	display as an octal number
`ios::hex`	display as a hexadecimal number
`ios::left`	left justify output
`ios::right`	right justify output

Notice that all of the flags in Table 3.3 are used as arguments to the `setiosflags()` manipulator function. Another name for a manipulator function that uses arguments is

Point of Information

Formatting cout Stream Data

The data in a cout output stream can be formatted in precise ways. One of the most common format requirements is to display numbers in a monetary format by always displaying two digits after the decimal point, such as 123.45. This can be done with the following statement:

```
cout << setiosflags(ios::fixed)
     << setiosflags(ios::showpoint)
     << setprecision(2);
```

The first manipulator flag, ios::fixed, forces all numbers placed on the cout stream to be placed in conventional decimal point notation. The next flag, ios::showpoint, tells the stream to always display a decimal point. Thus, a value such as 1.0 will appear as 1.0, and not as a 1 with no displayed decimal value. Finally, the setprecision manipulator tells the stream to always display 2 decimal values after the decimal point. Thus, the number 1.0 for example, will appear as 1.00.

Instead of using manipulators, you can also used the cout stream functions setf() and precision(). For example, the previous formatting can also be accomplished using the code:

```
cout.setf(ios::fixed);
cout.setf(ios::showpoint);
cout.precision(2);
```

Note the syntax here: the name of the object, cout, is separated from the function with a period. As we shall see in Chapter 8 this is the standard way of specifying a function and connecting it to a specific object.

Which style you select is a matter of preference. In both cases the formats need only be specified once and remain in effect for every number subsequently inserted into the cout stream.

a **parameterized manipulator.** As an example of using **parameterized manipulator** functions, consider the statement

```
cout << setiosflags(ios::fixed) << setiosflags(ios::showpoint) << setprecision(4);
```

This forces all subsequent floating-point numbers sent to the output stream to be displayed with a decimal point and four decimal digits. If the number has fewer than four decimal digits it will be padded with trailing zeros.

In addition to outputting integers in decimal notation, the ios::oct and ios:hex flags permit conversions to octal and hexadecimal, respectively. Program 3.7 illustrates the use of these flags. Since decimal is the default display, an ios::dec flag is not required in the first output stream.

Program 3.7

```
// a program to illustrate output conversions
#include <iostream.h>
#include <iomanip.h>

int main()
{
  cout << "The decimal (base 10) value of 15 is " << 15 << endl
       << "The octal (base 8) value of 15 is "
       << setiosflags(ios::oct) << 15 << endl
       << "The hexadecimal (base 16) value of 15 is "
       << setiosflags(ios::hex) << 15 << endl;

  return 0;
}
```

The output produced by Program 3.7 is

```
The decimal (base 10) value of 15 is 15
The octal (base 8) value of 15 is 17
The hexadecimal (base 16) value of 15 is f
```

In place of the conversion flags ios::dec, ios::oct, and ios::hex, three simpler manipulators, dec, oct, and hex are provided in <iostream.h>. These simpler manipulators, unlike their longer counterparts, leave the conversion base set for all subsequent output streams. Using these simpler manipulators, Program 3.7 can be rewritten as

```
#include <iostream.h>

int main()  // a program to illustrate output conversions
{
  cout << "The decimal (base 10) value of 15 is " << 15 << endl
       << "The octal (base 8) value of 15 is " << oct << 15 << endl
       << "The hexadecimal (base 16) value of 15 is " << hex << 15 << endl;

  return 0;
}
```

The display of integer values in one of the three possible number systems (decimal, octal, and hexadecimal) does not affect how the number is actually stored inside a computer. All numbers are stored using the computer's own internal codes. The manipulators sent to cout simply tell the object how to convert the internal code for output display purposes.

Besides displaying integers in octal or hexadecimal form, integer constants can also be written in a program in these forms. To designate an octal integer constant, the number must have a leading zero. The number 023, for example, is an octal number in C++. Hexadecimal numbers are denoted using a leading 0x. The use of octal and hexadecimal integer constants is illustrated in Program 3.8.

Program 3.8

```
#include <iostream.h>

int main()
{
  cout << "The decimal value of 025 is " << 025 << endl
       << "The decimal value of 0x37 is "<< 0x37 << endl;

  return 0;
}
```

When Program 3.8 is run, the following output is obtained:

```
The decimal value of 025 is 21
The decimal value of 0x37 is 55
```

The relationship between the input, storage, and display of integers is illustrated in Figure 3.8.

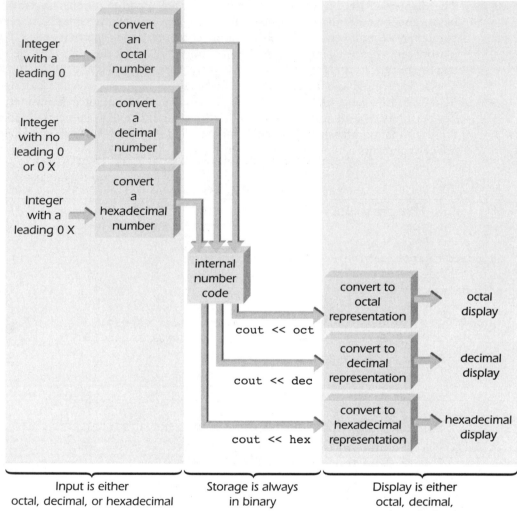

Figure 3.8 Input, storage, and display of integers.

Exercises 3.2

1. Determine the output of the following program:

```
#include <iostream.h>
int main()  // a program illustrating integer truncation
{
  cout << "answer1 is the integer " <<  9/4
       << "\nanswer2 is the integer " <<  17/3 << endl;

  return 0;
}
```

2. Determine the output of the following program:

```
#include <iostream.h>
int main()  // a program illustrating the % operator
{
  cout << "The remainder of 9 divided by 4 is " <<  9 % 4
       << "\nThe remainder of 17 divided by 3 is " <<  17 % 3 << endl;

  return 0;
}
```

3. Write a C++ program that displays the results of the expressions 3.0 * 5.0, 7.1 * 8.3 − 2.2, and 3.2 / (6.1 * 5). Calculate the value of these expressions manually to verify that the displayed values are correct.

4. Write a C++ program that displays the results of the expressions 15 / 4, 15 % 4, and 5 * 3 − (6 * 4). Calculate the value of these expressions manually to verify that the display produced by your program is correct.

5. Determine the errors in each of the following statements:

    a. cout << "\n << " 15)
    b. cout << "setw(4)" << 33;
    c. cout << "setprecision(5)" << 526.768;
    d. "Hello World!" >> cout;
    e. cout << 47 << setw(6);
    f. cout << set(10) << 526.768 << setprecision(2);

6. Determine and write out the display produced by the following statements:

    a. cout << "|" << 5 <<"|";
    b. cout << "|" << setw(4) << 5 << "|";
    c. cout << "|" << setw(4) << 56829 << "|";
    d. cout << "|" << setw(5) << setiosflags(ios::fixed)
           << setprecision(2) << 5.26 << "|";
    e. cout << "|" << setw(5) << setiosflags(ios::fixed)
           << setprecision(2) << 5.267 << "|";
    f. cout << "|" << setw(5) << setiosflags(ios::fixed)
           << setprecision(2) << 53.264 << "|";
    g. cout << "|" << setw(5) << setiosflags(ios::fixed)
           << setprecision(2) << 534.264 << "|";
    h. cout << "|" << setw(5) << setiosflags(ios::fixed)
           << setprecision(2) << 534. << "|";

7. Write out the display produced by the following statements.

    a. cout << "The number is " << setw(6) << setiosflags(ios::fixed)
           << setprecision(2) << 26.27 << endl;
      cout << "The number is " << setw(6) << setiosflags(ios::fixed)
           << setprecision(2) << 682.3 << endl;
      cout << "The number is " << setw(6) << setiosflags(ios::fixed)
           << setprecision(2) << 1.968 << endl;

b.
```
cout << setw(6) << setiosflags(ios::fixed)
        << setprecision(2) << 26.27 << endl;
cout << setw(6) << setiosflags(ios::fixed)
        << setprecision(2) << 682.3 << endl;
cout << setw(6) << setiosflags(ios::fixed)
        << setprecision(2) << 1.968 << endl;
cout << "------\n";
cout << setw(6) << setiosflags(ios::fixed)
        << setprecision(2)
        << 27.27 + 682.3 + 1.968 << endl;
```
c.
```
cout << setw(5) << setiosflags(ios::fixed)
        << setprecision(2) << 26.27 << endl;
cout << setw(5) << setiosflags(ios::fixed)
        << setprecision(2) << 682.3 << endl;
cout << setw(5) << setiosflags(ios::fixed)
        << setprecision(2) << 1.968 << endl;
cout << "-----\n";
cout << setw(5) << setiosflags(ios::fixed)
        << setprecision(2)
        << 27.27 + 682.3 + 1.968 << endl;
```
d.
```
cout << setw(5) << setiosflags(ios::fixed)
        << setprecision(2) << 36.164 << endl;
cout << setw(5) << setiosflags(ios::fixed)
        << setprecision(2) << 10.003 << endl;
cout << "-----" << endl;
```

8. The following table lists the correspondence between the decimal numbers 1 through 15 and their octal and hexadecimal representation.

Decimal:	1	2	3	4	5	6	7	8	9	10	11	12	13	14	15
Octal:	1	2	3	4	5	6	7	10	11	12	13	14	15	16	17
Hexadecimal:	1	2	3	4	5	6	7	8	9	a	b	c	d	e	f

Using the above table, determine the output of the following program.

```
#include <iostream.h>
#include <iomanip.h>

int main()
{
  cout << "\nThe value of 14 in octal is " << oct << 14 <<
       << "\nThe value of 14 in hexadecimal is " << hex << 14
       << "\nThe value of 0xA in decimal is " << dec << 0xA
       << "\nThe value of 0xA in octal is " << oct << 0xA
       << endl;

  return 0;
}
```

9. The combined resistance of three resistors connected in parallel, as shown in Figure 3.9 is given by the equation

$$\text{Combined resistance} = \frac{1}{\dfrac{1}{R_1} + \dfrac{1}{R_2} + \dfrac{1}{R_3}}$$

Using this formula, write a C++ program to calculate and display the combined resistance when the three resistors R_1 = 1000, R_2 = 1000, and R_3 = 1000 are connected in parallel. The output should produce the display

`The combined resistance is xxxx.xx ohms,`

where xxxx.xx denotes that the calculated value should be placed in a field width of 7 columns, with two positions to the right of the decimal point.

Figure 3.9 Three resistors connected in parallel.

10. Write a C++ program to calculate and display the value of the slope of the line connecting the two points whose coordinates are (3,7) and (8,12). Use the fact that the slope between two points having coordinates (x1,y1) and (x2,y2) is slope = (y2 − y1) / (x2 − x1). The display produced by your program should be: The value of the slope is xxx.xx, where xxx.xx denotes that the calculated value should be placed in a field wide enough for three places to the left of the decimal point, and two places to the right of it.

11. Write a C++ program to calculate and display the coordinates of the midpoint of the line connecting the two points whose coordinates are (3,7) and (8,12). Use the fact that the coordinates of the midpoint between two points having coordinates (x1,y1) and (x2,y2) are ((X1 + X2)/2, (Y1 + Y2)/2). The display produced by your program should be:

`The x coordinate of the midpoint is xxx.xx`
`The y coordinate of the midpoint is xxx.xx`

where xxx.xx denotes that the calculated value should be placed in a field wide enough for three places to the left of the decimal point, and two places to the right of it.

12. Write a C++ program to calculate and display the maximum bending moment, *M*, of a beam, which is supported on both ends (see Figure 3.10). The formula for maximum bending moment is, $M = XW (L − X) / L$, where *X* is the distance from the end of the beam that a weight, W, is placed, and L is the length of the beam. The display produced by your program should be

```
The maximum bending moment is xxxx.xxxx
```

where xxxx.xxxx denotes that the calculated value should be placed in a field wide enough for four places to the right and left of the decimal point.

Figure 3.10 Calculating the maximum bending moment.

13. For the electrical circuit shown in Figure 3.11, the branch currents, i_1, i_2, and, i_3 can be determined using the formulas

$$i_1 = \frac{E_2 R_3 + E_1(R_1 + R_3)}{(R_1 + R_3)(R_2 + R_3) - (R_3)^2}$$

$$i_2 = \frac{E_1 R_3 + E_2(R_1 + R_3)}{(R_1 + R_3)(R_2 + R_3) - (R_3)^2}$$

$$i_3 = i_1 - i_2$$

Using these formulas write a C++ program to compute the branch currents when $R_1 = 10$ ohms, $R_2 = 4$ ohms, $R_3 = 6$ ohms, $E_1 = 12$ volts, and $E_2 = 9$ volts. The display produced by your program should be

```
Branch current 1 is xx.xxxxx
Branch current 2 is xx.xxxxx
Branch current 3 is xx.xxxxx
```

where xx.xxxx denotes that the calculated value should be placed in a field wide enough for two places to the left of the decimal point and four places to the right of it.

Figure 3.11 Calculating loop currents in an electrical circuit.

3.3 ▷ USING MATHEMATICAL LIBRARY FUNCTIONS

As we have seen, assignment statements can be used to perform arithmetic computations. For example, the assignment statement

```
volts = resistance * current;
```

multiplies the value in `current` times the value in `resistance` and assigns the resulting value to `volts`. Although addition, subtraction, multiplication, and division are easily accomplished using C++'s arithmetic operators, no such operators exist for raising a number to a power, finding the square root of a number, or determining trigonometric values. To facilitate such calculations, C++ provides standard preprogrammed functions that can be included in a program.

Before using one of C++'s mathematical functions, you need to know

- The name of the desired mathematical function

- What the mathematical function does

- The type of data required by the mathematical function

- The data type of the result returned by the mathematical function

- How to include the library

To illustrate the use of C++'s mathematical functions, consider the mathematical function named `sqrt`, which calculates the square root of a number. The square root of a number is computed using the expression

```
sqrt(number)
```

where the function's name, in this case `sqrt`, is followed by parentheses containing the number for which the square root is desired. The purpose of the parentheses following the function name is to provide a funnel through which data can be passed to the function (see Figure 3.12). The items that are passed to the function through the parentheses are called arguments of the function and constitute its input data. For example, the following expressions are used to compute the square root of the arguments 4, 17.0, 25, 1043.29, and 6.4516, respectively:

```
sqrt(4)
sqrt(17.0)
sqrt(25)
sqrt(1043.29)
sqrt(6.4516)
```

Figure 3.12 *Passing data to the* `sqrt()` *function.*

Notice that the argument to the `sqrt` function can be either an integer or real value. This is an example of C++'s function overloading capabilities. Function overloading permits the same function name to be defined for different argument data types. In this case there are really five square root functions named `sqrt()`—one defined for integer, long integer, float, double, and long double arguments. The correct `sqrt` function is called depending on the type of value given it. The `sqrt()` function determines the square root of its argument and returns the result as a double. The values returned by the previous expressions are

Expression	Value Returned
`sqrt(4)`	2.0
`sqrt(17.0)`	4.123106
`sqrt(25)`	5.0
`sqrt(1043.29)`	32.3
`sqrt(6.4516)`	2.54

In addition to the `sqrt` function, Table 3.4 lists the more commonly used mathematical functions provided in C++. To access these functions in a program requires that the mathematical header file named `math.h`, which contains appropriate declarations for the mathematical function, be included with the function. This is done by placing the following preprocessor statement at the top of any program using a mathematical function:

```
#include <math.h>  ◄————————no semicolon
```

Although some of the mathematical functions listed require more than one argument, all functions, by definition, can directly return at most one value. Additionally, all of the functions listed are overloaded: this means the same function name can be used with integer and real arguments. Table 3.5 illustrates the value returned by selected functions using example arguments.

Table 3.4 Common C++ functions

Function Name	Description	Returned Value
abs(a)	absolute value	same data type as argument
pow(a1,a2)	a1 raised to the a2 power	data type of argument a1
sqrt(a)	square root of a	same data type as argument
sin(a)	sine of a (a in radians)	double
cos(a)	cosine of a (d in radians)	double
tan(a)	tangent of a (d in radians)	double
log(a)	natural logarithm of a	double
log10(a)	common log (base 10) of a	double
exp(a)	e raised to the a power	double

Table 3.5 Selected function examples

Example	Returned Value
abs(-7.362)	7.362000
abs(-3)	3
pow(2.0,5.0)	32.00000
pow(10,3)	1000
log(18.697)	2.928363
log10(18.697)	1.271772
exp(-3.2)	0.040762

In each case that a mathematical function is used it is called into action by giving the name of the function and passing any data to it within the parentheses following the function's name (see Figure 3.13).

function-name (data passed to the function);

This identifies   This passes data to
the called   the function
function

Figure 3.13 Using and passing data to a function.

The arguments that are passed to a function need not be single constants. Expressions can also be arguments provided that the expression can be computed to yield a value of the required data type. For example, the following arguments are valid for the given functions:

```
sqrt(4.0 + 5.3 * 4.0)          abs(2.3 * 4.6)
sqrt(16.0 * 2.0 - 6.7)         sin(theta - phi)
sqrt(x * y - z/3.2)            cos(2.0 * omega)
```

The expressions in parentheses are first evaluated to yield a specific value. Thus, values would have to be assigned to the variables theta, phi, x, y, z, and omega before their use in the above expressions. After the value of the argument is calculated, it is passed to the function.

Functions may also be included as part of larger expressions. For example,

```
    4 * sqrt(4.5 * 10.0 - 9.0) - 2.0
  = 4 * sqrt(36.0) - 2.0
  = 4 * 6.0 - 2.0
  = 24.0 - 2.0
  = 22.0
```

The step-by-step evaluation of an expression such as

```
3.0 * sqrt(5 * 33 - 13.71) / 5
```

is

Step	Result
1. Perform multiplication in argument	`3.0 * sqrt(165 - 13.71) / 5`
2. Complete argument calculation	`3.0 * sqrt(151.29) / 5`
3. Return a function value	`3.0 * 12.3 / 5`
4. Perform the multiplication	`36.9 / 5`
5. Perform the division	`7.38`

Program 3.9 illustrates the use of the **sqrt** function to determine the time it takes a ball to hit the ground after it has been dropped from an 800-foot tower. The mathematical formula used to calculate the time, in seconds, that it takes to fall a given distance, in feet, is

```
time = sqrt(2 * distance / g)
```

where g is the gravitational constant equal to 32.2 ft/sec².

The output produced by Program 3.9 is

```
It will take 7.049074 seconds to fall 800 feet.
```

As used in Program 3.9, the value returned by the **sqrt** function is assigned to the variable **time**. In addition to assigning a function's returned value to a variable, the returned value may be included within a larger expression, or even used as an argument to another function. For example, the expression

```
sqrt( sin( abs(theta) ) )
```

is valid. Since parentheses are present, the computation proceeds from the inner to the outer pairs of parentheses. Thus, the absolute value of **theta** is computed first and used as an argument to the **sin** function. The value returned by the **sin** function is then used as an argument to the **sqrt** function.

Program 3.9

```cpp
#include <iostream.h>  // this line may be placed second instead of first
#include <math.h>      // this line may be placed first instead of second

int main()
{
  int height;
  double time;

  height = 800;
  time = sqrt(2 * height / 32.2);
  cout << "It will take " << time << " seconds to fall "
       << height << " feet.\n";

  return 0;
}
```

Note that the arguements of all trigonometric functions (sin, cos, etc.) must be in radians. Thus, to obtain the sine of an angle that is given in degrees the angle must first be converted to radian measure. This is easily accomplished by multiplying the angle by the term (3.1416/180.) For example, to obtain the sine of 30 degrees, the expression sin (30 * 3.1416/180.) may be used.

Casts

We have already seen the conversion of an operand's data type within mixed-mode arithmetic expressions (Section 2.3) and across assignment operators (Section 3.1). In addition to these implicit data type conversions that are automatically made within mixed-mode arithmetic and assignment expressions, C++ also provides for explicit user-specified type conversions. The operator used to force the conversion of a value to another type is the cast operator. This is a unary operator having the form *data-type (expression)*, where *data-type* is the desired data type of the expression following the cast. For example, the expression

```cpp
int (a * b)
```

ensures that the value of the expression a * b is converted to an integer value.[9]

---

[9]The C type cast syntax, in this case, (int) (a * b), where the parentheses are placed around the keyword int, also works in C++.

Exercises 3.3

1. Write function calls to determine:
   a. The square root of 6.37.
   b. The square root of x − y.
   c. The sine of 30 degrees.
   d. The sine of 60 degrees.
   f. The absolute value of $a^2 − b^2$.
   h. The value of e raised to the 3rd power.

2. For $a = 10.6$, $b = 13.9$, $c = −3.42$, determine the following values:
   a. `int (a)`
   b. `int (b)`
   c. `int (c)`
   d. `int (a + b)`
   e. `int (a) + b + c`
   f. `int (a + b) + c`
   g. `int (a + b + c)`
   h. `float (int (a)) + b`
   i. `float (int (a + b))`
   j. `abs(a) + abs(b)`
   k. `sqrt(abs(a - b))`

3. Write C++ statements for the following:
   a. $b = \sin x − \cos x$
   b. $b = \sin^2 x − \cos^2 x$
   c. $area = (c * b * \sin a)/2$
   d. $c = \sqrt{a^2 + b^2}$
   e. $p = \sqrt{|m − n|}$
   f. $sum = \dfrac{a(r^n − 1)}{r − 1}$

4. Write, compile, and execute a C++ program that calculates and returns the 4th root of the number 81.0, which is 3. When you have verified that your program works correctly, use it to determine the fourth root of 1,728.896400. Your program should make use of the **sqrt** function.

5. Write, compile, and execute a C++ program that calculates the distance between two points whose coordinates are (7, 12) and (3, 9). Use the fact that the distance between two points having coordinates (x_1, y_1) and (x_2, y_2) is *distance* = sqrt($[x_1 − x_2]^2 + [y_1 − y_2]^2$). When you have verified that your program works correctly, by calculating the distance between the two points manually, use your program to determine the distance between the points (−12, −15) and (22, 5).

6. If a 20-foot ladder is placed on the side of a building at a 85-degree angle, as illustrated on Figure 3.14, the height at which the ladder touches the building can be calculated as *height* = 20 * sin 85°. Calculate this height by hand and then write, compile, and execute a C++ program that determines and displays the value of the height. When you have verified that your program works correctly, use it to determine the height of a 25-foot ladder placed at an angle of 85 degrees.

Figure 3.14 *Calculating the height of a ladder against a building.*

7. The maximum height reached by a ball thrown with an initial velocity v, in meters/sec, at an angle of θ is given by the formula *height* = $(.5 * v^2 * \sin^2 \theta) / 9.8$. Using this formula, write, compile, and execute a C++ program that determines and displays the maximum height reached when the ball is thrown at 5 miles/hour at an angle of 60 degrees. (*Hint*: make sure to convert the initial velocity into the correct units. There are 1609 meters in a mile.) Calculate the maximum height manually and verify the result produced by your program. After you have verified that your program works correctly, use it to determine the height reached by a ball thrown at 7 miles/hour at an angle of 45 degrees.

8. For small values of x, the value of $\sin(x)$ can be approximated by the power series:

$$x - \frac{x^3}{6} + \frac{x^5}{120} - \cdots$$

As with the sin function, the value of x must be in radians. Using this power series, write, compile, and execute a C++ program that approximates the sine of 180/3.1416 degrees, which equals one radian. Additionally, have your program use the sin function to calculate the sine and display both calculated values and the absolute difference of the two results. Verify the approximation produced by your program by hand. After you have verified your program is working correctly, use it to approximate the value of the sine of 62.2 degrees.

9. The polar coordinates of a point consist of the distance, r, from a specified origin and an angle, θ, with respect to the x axis. The x and y coordinates of the point are related to its polar coordinates by the formulas

   ```
   x = r cos θ
   y = r sin θ
   ```

   Using these formulas, write a C++ program that calculates the x and y coordinates of the point whose polar coordinates are $r = 10$ and $\theta = 30$ degrees. Verify the results produced by your program by calculating the results manually. After you have verified your program is working correctly, use it to convert the polar coordinates $r = 12.5$ and $\theta = 67.8°$ into rectangular coordinates.

10. A model of worldwide population growth, in billions of people, since 1990 is given by the equation:

    $$\textit{Population} = 5.5 \ (1 + e^{0.02(\textit{Year} - 1990)})$$

    Using this formula, write, compile, and execute a C++ program to estimate the worldwide population in the year 2000. Verify the result displayed by your program by calculating the answer manually. After you have verified your program is working correctly, use it to estimate the world's population in the year 2012.

11. A model to estimate the number of grams of a certain radioactive isotope left after N years is given by the formula

    $$\textit{Remaining material} = (\textit{Original material}) \ e^{-0.00012N}$$

    Using this formula, write, compile, and execute a C++ program to determine the amount of radioactive material remaining after 1000 years, assuming an initial amount of 100 grams. Verify the display produced by your program using a hand calculation. After you have verified your program is working correctly, use it to determine the amount of radioactive material remaining after 275 years, assuming an initial amount of 250 grams.

12. The number of years that it takes for a certain isotope of uranium to decay to one-half of an original amount is given by the formula

    $$\textit{Half-life} = \ln(2)/k$$

    where k equals 0.00012. Using this formula, write, compile, and execute a C++ program that calculates and displays the half-life of this uranium isotope. Verify the result produced by your program using a hand calculation. After you have verified your program is working correctly, use it to determine the half-life of a uranium isotope having a $k = 0.00026$.

13. The amplification of electronic circuits is measured in units of decibels, which is calculated as

    $$10 \ \text{LOG} \ (P_o/P_i)$$

where P_o is the power of the output signal and P_i is the power of the input signal. Using this formula, write, compile, and execute a C++ program that calculates and displays the decibel amplification in which the output power is 50 times the input power. Verify the result displayed by your program using a hand calculation. After you have verified your program is working correctly, use it to determine the amplification of a circuit whose output power is 4.639 watts and input power is 1 watt.

14. The loudness of a sound is measured in units of decibels, which is calculated as

```
10 LOG (SL/RL)
```

where *SL* is intensity of the sound being measured and *RL* is a reference sound intensity level. Using this formula write a C++ program that calculates and displays the decibel loudness of a busy street having a sound intensity of 10,000,000 *RL*. Verify the result produced by your program using a hand calculation. After you have verified your program is working correctly, use it to determine the sound level, in decibels, of the following sounds:
   a. A whisper of sound intensity 200 *RL*
   b. A rock band playing at a sound intensity of 1,000,000,000,000 *RL*
   c. An airplane taking off at a sound intensity of 100,000,000,000,000 *RL*

15. When a particular rubber ball is dropped from a given height (in meters) its impact speed (in meters/second) when it hits the ground is given by the formula *speed* = sqrt(2 * g * *height*). The ball then rebounds to 2/3 the height from which it last fell. Using this information write, test, and run a C++ program that calculates and displays the impact speed of the first three bounces and the rebound height of each bounce. Test your program using an initial height of 2.0 meters. Run the program twice and compare the results for dropping the ball on Earth ($g = 9.81$ meters/sec^2) and on the moon ($g = 1.67$ meters/sec^2).

16. a. A balance has the following size weights: 100 lb., 50 lb., 10 lb., 5 lb., and 1 lb. The number of 100 lb. and 50 lb. weights required to weigh an object whose weight is WEIGHT pounds can be calculated using the following C++ statements:

```
// Determine the number of 100 lb. Weights
    w100 = int(WEIGHT/100)
// Determine the number of 50 lb. Weights
    w50 = int((WEIGHT - w100 * 100)/50)
```

Using these statements as a starting point, write a C++ program that calculates the number of each type of weight necessary to weigh a 789 lb. object.
   b. Without compiling or executing your program check the effect, by hand, of each statement in the program and determine what is stored in each variable as each statement is encountered.
   c. When you have verified that your algorithm works correctly, compile and execute your program. Verify that the results produced by your program are correct. After you have verified your program is working correctly, use it to determine the weights required to weigh a 626 lb. object.

3.4 ▷ PROGRAM INPUT USING THE `cin` OBJECT

Data for programs that are only going to be executed once may be included directly in the program. For example, if we wanted to multiply the numbers 30.0 and 0.05, we could use Program 3.10.

Program 3.10

```cpp
#include <iostream.h>

int main()
{
  float num1, num2, product;

  num1 = 30.0;
  num2 = 0.05;
  product = num1 * num2;
  cout << "30.0 times 0.05 is " << product << endl;

  return 0;
}
```

The output displayed by Program 3.10 is

        30.0 times 0.05 is 1.5

Program 3.10 can be shortened, as illustrated in Program 3.11. Both programs, however, suffer from the same basic problem in that they must be rewritten in order to multiply different numbers. Both programs lack the facility for entering different numbers on which to operate.

Program 3.11

```cpp
#include <iostream.h>

int main()
{
  cout << "30.0 times 0.05 is " << 30.0 * 0.05 << endl;

  return 0;
}
```

Except for the practice provided to the programmer of writing, entering, and running the program, programs that do the same calculation only once, on the same set of numbers, are clearly not very useful. After all, it is simpler to use a calculator to multiply two numbers than to enter and run either Program 3.10 or 3.11.

This section presents the cin object, which is used to enter data into a program while it is executing. Just as the cout object displays a copy of the value stored inside a variable, the cin object allows the user to enter a value at the terminal (see Figure 3.15). The value is then stored directly in a variable.

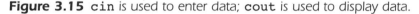

Figure 3.15 cin is used to enter data; cout is used to display data.

When a statement such as cin >> num1; is encountered, the computer stops program execution and accepts data from the keyboard. When a data item is typed, the cin object stores the item into the variable listed after the extraction ("get from") operator, >>. The program then continues execution with the next statement after the call to cin. To see this, consider Program 3.12.

Program 3.12

```cpp
#include <iostream.h>

int main()
{
  float num1, num2, product;

  cout << "Please type in a number: ";
  cin  >> num1;
  cout << "Please type in another number: ";
  cin  >> num2;
  product = num1 * num2;
  cout << num1 << " times " << num2 << " is " << product << endl;

  return 0;
}
```

The first cout statement in Program 3.12 prints a string that tells the person at the terminal what should be typed. When an output string is used in this manner it is called a **prompt**. In this case the prompt tells the user to type a number. The computer then executes the next statement, which uses a cin object. The cin object puts the computer into a temporary pause (or wait) state for as long as it takes the user to type a value. Then the user signals the cin object that the data entry is finished by pressing the return key after the value has been typed. The entered value is stored in the variable to the right of the extraction symbol, and the computer is taken out of its paused state. Program execution then proceeds with the next statement, which in Program 3.12 is another statement using cout. This statement causes the next message to be displayed. The following statement then uses cin to again put the computer into a temporary wait state while the user types a second value. This second number is stored in the variable num2.

The following sample run was made using Program 3.12.

```
Please type in a number: 30
Please type in another number: 0.05
30 times 0.05 is 1.5
```

In Program 3.12, each time cin is invoked it is used to store one value into a variable. The cin object, however, can be used to enter and store as many values as there are extraction symbols, >>, and variables to hold the entered data. For example, the statement

```
cin >> num1 >> num2;
```

results in two values being read from the terminal and assigned to the variables num1 and num2. If the data entered at the terminal was

0.052 245.79

the variables num1 and num2 would contain the values 0.052 and 245.79, respectively. Notice that when actually entering numbers such as 0.052 and 245.79, there must be at least one space between the numbers. The space between the entered numbers clearly indicates where one number ends and the next begins. Inserting more than one space between numbers has no effect on cin.

The same spacing also is applicable to entering character data; that is, the extraction operator, >>, will skip blank spaces and store the next nonblank character in a character variable. For example, in response to the statements

```
char ch1, ch2, ch3;  // declare three character variables
cin >> ch1 >> ch2 >> ch3;  // accept three characters
```

The input

a   b   c

causes the letter a to be stored in the variable ch1, the letter b to be stored in the variable ch2, and the variable c to be stored in the variable ch3. Since a character variable can only be used to store one character, the input

abc

can also be used.

Any number of statements using the `cin` object may be made in a program, and any number of values may be input using a single `cin` statement. Program 3.13 illustrates using the cin object to input three numbers from the keyboard. The program then calculates and displays the average of the numbers entered.

Program 3.13

```
#include <iostream.h>

int main()
{
  int num1, num2, num3;
  float average;

  cout << "Enter three integer numbers: ";
  cin >> num1 >> num2 >> num3;
  average =  (num1 + num2 + num3) / 3.0;
  cout << "The average of the numbers is " << average << endl;

  return 0;
}
```

The following sample run was made using Program 3.13:

```
Enter three integer numbers: 22 56 73
The average of the numbers is 50.333333
```

Note that the data typed at the keyboard for this sample run consists of the input

```
22 56 73
```

In response to this stream of input, Program 3.13 stores the value 22 in the variable num1, the value 56 in the variable num2, and the value 73 in the variable num3 (see Figure 3.16). Since the average of three integer numbers can be a floating-point number, the variable average, which is used to store the average, is declared as a floating-point variable. Note also that the parentheses are needed in the assignment statement `average = (num1 + num2 + num3) / 3.0;`. Without these parentheses, the only value that would be divided by three would be the integer in num3 (because division has a higher precedence than addition).

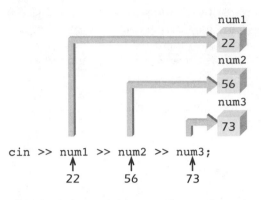

num1

22

num2

56

num3

73

cin >> num1 >> num2 >> num3;

22   56   73

Figure 3.16 Inputting data into the variables num1, num2, and num3.

The cin extraction operation, like the cout insertion operation, is "clever" enough to make a few data-type conversions. For example, if an integer is entered in place of a floating-point or double-precision number, the integer will be converted to the correct data type.[10] Similarly, if a floating-point or double-precision number is entered when an integer is expected, only the integer part of the number will be used. For example, assume the following numbers are typed in response to the statement cin >> num1 >> num2 >> num3;, where num1 and num3 have been declared as floating-point variables and num2 is an integer variable

56 22.879 33.923

The 56 will be converted to 56.0 and stored in the variable num1. The extraction operation continues extracting data from the input stream sent to it, expecting an integer value. As far as cin is concerned, the decimal point after the 22 in the number 22.879 indicates the end of an integer and the start of a decimal number. Thus, the number 22 is assigned to num2. Continuing to process its input stream, cin takes the .879 as the next floating-point number and assigns it to in num3. As far as cin is concerned, 33.923 is extra input and is ignored. If, though, you do not initially type enough data, the cin object will continue to make the computer pause until sufficient data has been entered.

Exercises 3.4

1. For the following declaration statements, write a statement using the cin object that will cause the computer to pause while the appropriate data is typed by the user.
   a. int firstnum;
   b. float grade;
   c. double secnum;
   d. char keyval;

---

[10]Strictly speaking, what comes in from the keyboard is not any data type, such as an int or float, but is simply a sequence of characters. The extraction operation handles the conversion from the character sequence to a defined data type.

e. `int month years;`
`float average;`

f. `char ch;`
`int num1,num2;`
`double grade1,grade2;`

g. `float interest, principal, capital;`
`double price, yield;`

h. `char ch,letter1,letter2;`
`int num1,num2,num3;`

i. `float temp1,temp2,temp3;`
`double volts1,volts2;`

2. a. Write a C++ program that first displays the following prompt:

`Enter the temperature in degrees Celsius:`

Have your program accept a value entered from the keyboard and convert the temperature entered to degrees Fahrenheit, using the formula *Fahrenheit* = (9.0 / 5.0) * *Celsius* + 32.0. Your program should then display the temperature in degrees Celsius, using an appropriate output message.

b. Compile and execute the program written for Exercise 2a. Verify your program by calculating, by hand, and then using your program, the Fahrenheit equivalent of the following test data:

Test data set 1: 0 degrees Celsius
Test data set 2: 50 degrees Celsius
Test data set 3: 100 degrees Celsius

When you are sure your program is working correctly, use it to complete the following table:

Celsius	Fahrenheit
45	
50	
55	
60	
65	
70	

3. Write, compile, and execute a C++ program that displays the following prompt:

`Enter the radius of a circle:`

After accepting a value for the radius, your program should calculate and display the area of the circle. (*Hint: area = 3.1416 * radius²*.) For testing purposes, verify your program using a test input radius of 3 inches. After manually determining that the result produced by your program is correct, use your program to complete the following table:

Radius (in.)	Area (sq. in.)
1.0	
1.5	
2.0	
2.5	
3.0	
3.5	

4. **a.** Write, compile, and execute a C++ program that displays the following prompts:

```
Enter the miles driven:
Enter the gallons of gas used:
```

After each prompt is displayed, your program should use a cin statement to accept data from the keyboard for the displayed prompt. After the gallons of gas used number has been entered, your program should calculate and display miles per gallon obtained. This value should be included in an appropriate message and calculated using the equation *miles per gallon = miles / gallons* used. Verify your program using the following test data:

Test data set 1: Miles = 276, Gas = 10 gallons
Test data set 2: Miles = 200, Gas = 15.5 gallons

When you have completed your verification, use your program to complete the following table:

Miles driven	Gallons used	MPG
250	16.00	
275	18.00	
312	19.54	
296	17.39	

b. For the program written for Exercise 4a, determine how many verification runs are required to ensure the program is working correctly and give a reason supporting your answer.

5. a. Write, compile, and execute a C++ program that displays the following prompts:

```
Enter a number:
Enter a second number:
Enter a third number:
Enter a fourth number:
```

After each prompt is displayed, your program should use a cin statement to accept a number from the keyboard for the displayed prompt. After the fourth number has been entered, your program should calculate and display the average of the numbers. The average should be included in an appropriate message. Check the average displayed by your program using the following test data:

Test data set 1: 100, 100, 100, 100
Test data set 2: 100, 0, 100, 0

When you have completed your verification, use your program to complete the following table:

Numbers	Average
92, 98, 79, 85	
86, 84, 75, 86	
63, 85, 74, 82	

b. Repeat Exercise 5a, making sure that you use the same variable name, `number`, for each number input. Also use the variable `sum` for the sum of the numbers. (*Hint:* To do this, you may use the statement `sum = sum + number` after each number is accepted. Review the material on accumulating presented in Section 2.3.)

6. a. Write, compile, and execute a C++ program that computes and displays the value of the second-order polynomial $ax^2 + bx + c$ for any user input values of the coefficients a, b, c, and the variable x. Have your program first display a message informing the user as to what the program will do, and then display suitable prompts to alert the user to enter the desired data. (*Hint:* Use a prompt such as `Enter the coefficient of the x-squared term:`)

b. Check the result produced by the your program written for Exercise 6a using the following test data:

Test data set 1: $a = 0$, $b = 0$, $c = 22$, $x = 56$
Test data set 2: $a = 0$, $b = 22$, $c = 0$, $x = 2$
Test data set 3: $a = 22$, $b = 0$, $c = 0$, $x = 2$
Test data set 4: $a = 2$, $b = 4$, $c = 5$, $x = 2$
Test data set 5: $a = 5$, $b = -3$, $c = 2$, $x = 1$

When you have completed your verification, use your program to complete the following table:

a	b	c	x	polynomial value
2.0	17.0	−12.0	1.3	
3.2	2.0	15.0	2.5	
3.2	2.0	15.0	−2.5	
−2.0	10.0	0.0	2.0	
−2.0	10.0	0.0	4.0	
−2.0	10.0	0.0	5.0	
−2.0	10.0	0.0	6.0	
5.0	22.0	18.0	8.3	
4.2	−16	−20	−5.2	

7. The number of bacteria, B, in a certain culture that is subject to refrigeration can be approximated by the equation $B = 300000 \, e^{-0.032t}$, where e is the irrational number 2.71828 (rounded to five decimal places), known as Euler's number, and t is the time, in hours, that the culture has been refrigerated. Using this equation, write, compile, and execute a single C++ program that prompts the user for a value of time, calculates the number of bacteria in the culture, and displays the result. For testing purposes, check your program using a test input of 10 hours. When you have verified the operation of your program, use it to determine the number of bacteria in the culture after 12, 18, 24, 36, 48, and 72 hours.

8. Write, compile, and execute a program that calculates and displays the square-root value of a user-entered real number. Verify your program by calculating the square roots of the following data: 25, 16, 0, and 2. When you completed your verification, use your program to determine the square root of 32.25, 42, 48, 55, 63, and 79.

9. Write, compile, and execute a program that calculates and displays the 4th root of a user-entered number. Recall from elementary algebra that the 4th root of a number can be found by raising the number to the ¼ power. (*Hint*: do not use integer division—can you see why?) Verify your program by calculating the fourth root of the following data: 81, 16, 1, and 0. When you have completed your verification, use your program to determine the fourth root of 42, 121, 256, 587, 1240, and 16,256.

10. For the series circuit shown in Figure 3.17, the voltage drop, V_2, across resistor, R_2, and the power, P_2, delivered to this resistor are given by the equations $V_2 = I R_2$ and $P_2 = I V_2$, where $I = E / (R_1 + R_2)$. Using these equations, write, compile, and execute a C++ program that prompts the user for values of E, R_1, and R_2, calculates the voltage drop and power delivered to R_2, and displays the results. Check your program using the test data: $E = 10$ volts, $R_1 = 100$ ohms, and $R_2 = 200$ ohms. When you have completed your verification, use your program to complete the following table:

E (volts)	R_1 (ohms)	R_2 (ohms)	Voltage drop (volts)	Power delivered (watts)
10	100	100		
10	100	200		
10	200	200		
20	100	100		
20	100	200		
20	200	200		

Figure 3.17 Calculating the voltage drop.

11. Write, compile, and execute a C++ program that computes the combined resistance of three parallel resistors. The values of each resistor should be accepted using a Cin statement (use the formula for combined resistance given in Exercise 9 of Section 3.2). Verify the operation of your program by using the following test data:

    Test data set 1: $R_1 = 1000$, $R_2 = 1000$, and $R_3 = 1000$.
    Test data set 2: $R_1 = 1000$, $R_2 = 1500$, and $R_3 = 500$.

    When you have completed your verification, use your program to complete the following table:

R1 (volts)	R2 (ohms)	R3 (ohms)	Combined Resistance (ohms)
3000	3000	3000	
6000	6000	6000	
2000	3000	1000	
2000	4000	5000	
4000	2000	1000	
10000	100	100	

12. Using `input` statements, write, compile, and execute a C++ program that accepts the x and y coordinates of two points. Have your program determine and display the midpoints of the two points (use the formula given in Exercise 11 of Section 3.2). Verify your program using the following test data:

Test data set 1: Point 1 = (0, 0) and Point 2 = (16, 0)
Test data set 2: Point 1 = (0, 0) and Point 2 = (0, 16)
Test data set 3: Point 1 = (0, 0) and Point 2 = (–16, 0)
Test data set 4: Point 1 = (0, 0) and Point 2 = (0, –16)
Test data set 5: Point 1 = (–5, –5) and Point 2 = (5, 5)

When you have completed your verification, use your program to complete the following table.

Point 1	Point 2	Midpoint
(4, 6)	(16, 18)	
(22, 3)	(8, 12)	
(–10, 8)	(14, 4)	
(–12, 2)	(14, 3.1)	
(3.1, –6)	(20, 16)	
(3.1, –6)	(–16, –18)	

13. Write, compile, and execute a C++ program that calculates and displays the value of the current flowing through an RC circuit. The circuit consists of a battery that is connected in series to a switch, resistor, and a capacitor. When the switch is closed the current, i, that flows through the circuit is given by the equation:

$$i = (E/R)\ e^{-t/\tau}$$

where E is the voltage of the battery (in volts), R is the resistance (in ohms), τ is termed the time constant, and t is the time (in seconds) since the switch was closed.

The program should prompt the user to enter appropriate values and use input statements to accept the data. In constructing the prompts, use statements such as `Enter the voltage of the battery`. Verify the operation of your program by calculating, by hand, the current for the following test data:

Test data set 1: Voltage = 20 volts, R = 10 ohms, τ = 0.044, t = 0.023 seconds.
Test data set 2: Voltage = 35, R = 10 ohms, τ = 0.16, t = 0.067 seconds.

When you have completed your verification, use your program to determine the value of the current for the following cases:

a. Voltage = 35, R = 10 ohms, τ = 0.16, t = 0.11 seconds.
b. Voltage = 35, R = 10 ohms, τ = 0.16, t = 0.44 seconds.
c. Voltage = 35, R = 10 ohms, τ = 0.16, t = 0.83 seconds.

d. Voltage = 15, R = 10 ohms, τ = 0.55, t = 0.11 seconds.
e. Voltage = 15, R = 10 ohms, τ = 0.55, t = 0.44 seconds.
f. Voltage = 15, R = 10 ohms, τ = 0.55, t = 0.067 seconds.
g. Voltage = 6, R = 1000 ohms, τ = 2.6, t = 12.4 seconds.

14. Program 3.12 prompts the user to input two numbers, where the first value entered is stored in `num1` and the second value is stored in `num2`. Using this program as a starting point, write a program that swaps the values stored in the two variables.

15. Repeat Exercise 5a, making sure that you use the same variable name, `number`, for each number input. Also use the variable `sum` for the sum of the numbers. (*Hint*: To do this, you must use the statement `sum = sum + number;` after each number is accepted. Review the material on accumulating presented in Section 3.1.)

16. Write a C++ program that prompts the user to type in a number. Have your program accept the number as an integer and immediately display the integer using a `cout` object call. Run your program three times. The first time you run the program enter a valid integer number, the second time enter a floating-point number, and the third time enter a character. Using the output display, see what number your program actually accepted from the data you entered.

17. Repeat Exercise 16 but have your program declare the variable used to store the number as a floating-point variable. Run the program four times. The first time enter an integer, the second time enter a decimal number with less than six decimal places, the third time enter a number having more than six decimal places, and the fourth time enter a character. Using the output display, keep track of what number your program actually accepted from the data you typed in. What happened, if anything, and why?

18. Repeat Exercise 16 but have your program declare the variable used to store the number as a double-precision variable. Run the program four times. The first time enter an integer, the second time enter a decimal number with less than six decimal places, the third time enter a number having more than six decimal places, and the fourth time enter a character. Using the output display, keep track of what number your program actually accepted from the data you typed in. What happened, if anything, and why?

19. **a.** Why do you think that successful applications programs contain extensive data-input validity checks? (*Hint*: Review Exercises 16, 17, and 18.)
    b. What do you think is the difference between a data-type check and a data reasonableness check?
    c. Assume that a program requests that a month, day, and year be entered by the user. What are some checks that could be made on the data entered?

3.5 THE const QUALIFIER

Certain constants used within a program have a more general meaning that is recognized outside the context of the program. Examples of these types of constants include the number 3.1416, which is π accurate to four decimal places; 32.2 ft/sec^2, which is the gravitational constant; and the number 2.71828, which is Euler's number accurate to five decimal places.

The meaning of certain other constants appearing in a program are defined strictly within the context of the application being programmed. For example, in determining the weight of various sized objects, the density of the material being used takes on a special significance. By themselves the density numbers are quite ordinary, but in the context of a particular application they have a special meaning. Numbers such as these are sometimes referred to by programmers as **magic numbers**. Frequently, the same magic number appears repeatedly within the same program. This recurrence of the same constant throughout a program is a potential source of error should the constant have to be changed. For example, if interest rates or sales-tax rates change, as rates are prone to do, the programmer would have the cumbersome task of changing the value everywhere it appears in the program. Multiple changes, however, are subject to error—if just one rate value is overlooked and not changed, the result obtained when the program is run will be incorrect and the source of the error difficult to locate.

To avoid the problem of having a magic number spread throughout a program in many places and to permit clear identification of more universal constants, such as π, C++ allows the programmer to give these constants their own symbolic name. Then, instead of using the number throughout the program, the symbolic name is used instead. If the number ever has to be changed, the change need only be made once at the point where the symbolic name is equated to the actual number value. Equating numbers to symbolic names is accomplished using the const declaration qualifier. The const qualifier specifies that the declared identifier can only be read after it is initialized; it cannot be changed. Three examples using this qualifier are

```
const float PI = 3.1416;
const double DENSITY = 0.238;
const int MAXNUM = 100;
```

The first declaration statement creates a floating-point constant named PI and initializes it with the value 3.1416, while the second declaration statement creates the double-precision constant named DENSITY and initializes it to 0.238. Finally, the third declaration creates an integer constant named MAXNUM and initializes it with the value 100.

Once a const identifer is created and initialized, the value stored in it cannot be changed. Thus, for all practical purposes the name of the constant and its value are linked together for the duration of the program that declares them.

Although we have typed the `const` identifiers in uppercase letters, lowercase letters could have been used. It is common in C++, however, to use uppercase letters for `const` identifiers to easily identify them as such. Then, whenever a programmer sees uppercase letters in a program, he or she will know the value of the constant cannot be changed within the program.

Once declared, a `const` identifier can be used in any C++ statement in place of the number it represents. For example, the assignment statements

```
circum = 2 * PI * radius;
weight = DENSITY * volume;
```

are both valid. These statements must, of course, appear after the declarations for all their variables. Since a `const` declaration effectively equates a constant value to an identifier, and the identifier can be used as a direct replacement for its initializing constant, such identifier are commonly referred to as **symbolic constants** or **named constants**. We shall use these terms interchangeably.

Placement of Statements

At this stage we have introduced a variety of statement types. The general rule in C++ for statement placement is simply that a variable or named constant must be declared before it can be used. Although this rule permits both preprocessor directives and declaration statements to be placed throughout a program, doing so results in a very poor program structure. As a matter of good programming form, the following statement ordering should be used:

```
Preprocessor directives

int main()
{
  Named constants
  main function declarations

  other executable statements

  return value
}
```

As new statement types are introduced we will expand this placement structure to accommodate them. Notice that comment statements can be freely intermixed anywhere within this basic structure.

Program 3.14 illustrates the use of a symbolic constant to calculate the weight of a steel cylinder. The density of the steel is 0.284 lb/in^3.

Program 3.14

```cpp
// This program determines the weight of a steel cylinder
//   by multiplying the volume of the cylinder times its density
// The volume of the cylinder is given by the formula PI * pow(radius,2) * height.
#include <iostream.h>
#include <iomanip.h>
#include <math.h>

int main()
{
  const double PI = 3.1416;
  const double DENSITY = 0.284;
  double radius, height, weight;

  cout << "Enter the radius of the cylinder (in inches): ";
  cin  >> radius;
  cout << "Enter the height of the cylinder (in inches): ";
  cin  >> height;
  weight = DENSITY * PI * pow(radius,2) * height;
  cout << setiosflags(ios:: fixed)
        << setiosflags(ios::showpoint)
        << setprecision(4)
        << "The cylinder weighs " << weight << " pounds" << endl;

  return 0;
}
```

Notice in Program 3.14 that two named constants have been defined: PI and DENSITY. The following run was made to determine the weight of a cylinder with a radius of three inches and a height of 12 inches.

```
Enter the radius of the cylinder (in inches): 3
Enter the height of the cylinder (in inches): 12
The cylinder weighs 96.3592 pounds
```

The advantage of using the named constant PI in Program 3.14 is that it clearly identifies the value of 3.1416 in terms recognizable to most people. The advantage of using the named constant DENSITY is that it permits a programmer to change the value of the density for another material without having to search through the program to see where the density is used. If, of course, many different materials are to be considered, the density should be changed from a named constant to a variable. A natural question arises, then, as to the difference between named constants and variables.

The value of a variable can be altered anywhere within a program. By its nature a named constant is a constant value that must not be altered after it is defined. Naming a constant rather than assigning the value to a variable ensures that the value in the constant can not be subsequently altered. Whenever a named constant appears in an instruction it has the same effect as the constant it represents. Thus, DENSITY in Program 3.14 is simply another way of representing the number 0.284. Since DENSITY and the number 0.284 are equivalent, the value of DENSITY may not be subsequently changed within the program. Once DENSITY has been defined as a constant, an assignment statement such as

```
DENSITY = 0.156;
```

is meaningless and will result in an error message, because DENSITY is not a variable. Since DENSITY is only a stand-in for the value 0.284, this statement is equivalent to writing the invalid expression 0.284 = 0.156. In addition to using a const statement to name constants, as in Program 3.14, this statement can also be used to equate the value of a constant expression to a symbolic name. A constant expression is an expression consisting of operators and constants only. For example, the statement

```
const double DEG_TO_RAD = 3.1416/180.0;
```

equates the value of the constant expression 3.1416/180.0 to the symbolic name DEG_TO_RAD. The symbolic name, as always, can be used in any statement following its definition. For example, since the expression 3.1416/180.0 is required for converting degrees to radians, the symbolic name selected for this conversion factor can be conveniently used whenever such a conversion is required. Thus, in the assignment statement

```
height = distance * sin(angle * DEG_TO_RAD);
```

the symbolic constant DEG_TO_RAD is used to convert the value in angle to radian measure.

A previously defined named constant can also be used in a subsequent const statement. For example, the following sequence of statements are valid:

```
const double PI = 3.1416;
const double  DEG_TO_RAD = PI / 180.0;
```

Since the constant 3.1416 has been equated to the symbolic name PI, it can be used legitimately in any subsequent definition, even within another const statement. Program 3.15 uses the named constant DEG_TO_RAD to convert a user entered angle, in degrees, into its equivalent radian measure for use by the sin function.

Program 3.15

```
#include <iostream.h>
#include <iomanip.h>
#include <math.h>

int main()
{
  const double PI = 3.1416;
  const double DEG_TO_RAD = PI/180.0;
  double angle;

  cout << "Enter the angle (in degrees): ";
  cin >> angle;
  cout << setiosflags(ios:: fixed)
       << setiosflags(ios::showpoint)
       << setprecision(4)
       << "The sine of the angle is " << sin(angle * DEG_TO_RAD) << endl;

  return 0;
}
```

The following sample run was made using Program 3.15.

```
Enter the angle (in degrees): 30
The sine of the angle is 0.5000
```

Although we have used the const qualifier to construct symbolic constants, we will encounter this data type once again in Chapter 6, where we will show that they are useful as function arguments in ensuring that the argument is not modified within the function.

Exercises 3.5

1. Modify Program 3.9 to use the named constant GRAY in place of the value 32.2 used in the program. Compile and execute your program to verify it produces the same result as shown in the text.

2. Rewrite the following program to use the named constant FACTOR in place of the expression (5.0/9.0) contained within the program.

```cpp
#include <iostream.h>

int main()
{
  float fahren, celsius;
  cout << "Enter a temperature in degrees Fahrenheit: ";
  cin  >> fahren;
  celsius = (5.0/9.0) * (fahren - 32.0);
  cout << "The equivalent Celsius temperature is "
       << celsius << endl;

  return 0;
}
```

3. Rewrite the following program to use the named constant PRIME-RATE in place of the value 0.08 contained within the program.

```cpp
#include <iostream.h>

int main()
{
  float prime, amount, interest;
  prime = 0.08;        // prime interest rate
  cout << <Enter the amount: ";
  cin  >> amount;
  interest = prime * amount;
  cout << "The interest earned is"
       << interest << " dollars" << endl;

  return 0;
}
```

4. Rewrite the following program so that the variable volts is changed to a named constant.

```cpp
#include <iostream.h>

int main()
{
  float current, resistance, volts;

  volts = 12;
  cout << " Enter the resistance: ";
  cin >> resistance;
  current = volts / resistance;
  cout << "The current is " << current << endl;

  return 0;
}
```

3.6 > APPLICATIONS

In this section we present two applications to further illustrate both the use of `cin` statements to accept user input data and the use of library functions for performing calculations.

Application 1: Acid Rain

The use of coal as the major source of steam power began with the Industrial Revolution. Currently coal is one of the principal sources of electrical power generation in many industrialized countries.

Since the middle of the 19th century it has been known that the oxygen used in the burning process combines with the carbon and sulfur in the coal to produce both carbon dioxide and sulfur dioxide. When these gases are released into the atmosphere the sulfur dioxide combines with the water and oxygen in the air to form sulfuric acid, which itself is transformed into separate hydronium ions and sulfates (see Figure 3.18). It is the hydronium ions in the atmosphere that fall to earth, as components of rain, that change the acidity levels of lakes and forests.

The acid level of rain and lakes is measured on a pH scale using the formula

$$pH = -\log_{10} (\text{Concentration of hydronium ions})$$

where the concentration of hydronium ions is measured in units of moles/liter. A pH value of 7 indicates a neutral value (neither acid nor alkaline), whereas levels below 7 indicate the presence of an acid, and levels above 7 indicate the presence of an alkaline substance. For example, sulfuric acid has a pH value of approximately 1, lye has a pH value of approximately 13, and water typically has a pH value of 7. Marine life usually cannot survive in water with a pH level below 4.

Using the formula for pH, we will write a C++ program that calculates the pH level of a substance based on a user input value for the concentration of hydronium ions. Using the development procedure described in Section 2.6 we have the following steps.

Step 1   Analyze the Problem

Although the statement of the problem provides technical information on the composition of acid rain, from a programming viewpoint this is a rather simple problem. Here there is only one required output (a pH level) and one input (the concentration of hydronium ions).

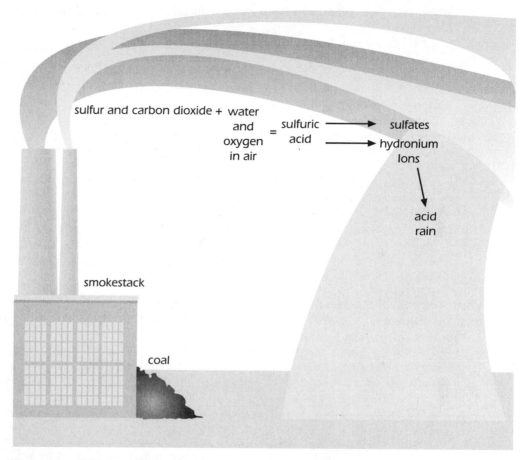

Figure 3.18 The formation of acid rain.

Step 2   Develop a Solution

The algorithm required to transform the input to the required output is a rather straight forward use of the pH formula that is provided. The pseudocode representation of the complete algorithm for entering the input data, processing the data to produce the desired output, and displaying the output is:

> *Display a prompt to enter an ion concentration level.*
> *Read a value for the concentration level.*
> *Calculate a pH level using the given formula.*
> *Display the calculated value.*

To ensure that we understand the formula used in the algorithm, we will do a hand calculation. The result of this calculation can then be used to verify the result produced by the program. Assuming a hydronium concentration of 0.0001 (any value would do), the pH level is calculated as $-\log_{10} 10^{-4}$. Either by knowing that the logarithm of 10 raised to a power is the power itself, or by using a log table, the value of this expressions is $-(-4) = 4$.

Step 3   Code the Solution

Program 3.16 describes the selected algorithm in C++. The choice of variable names is arbitrary.

Program 3.16

```
#include <iostream.h>
#include <math.h>

int main()
{
  float hydron, pHlevel;

  cout << "Enter the hydronium ion concentration: ";
  cin  >> hydron;
  pHlevel = -log10(hydron);
  cout << "The pH level is " << pHlevel << endl;

  return 0;
}
```

Program 3.16 begins with two `#include` preprocessor statements, followed by the function `main()`. Within `main()`, a declaration statement declares two floating-point variables, `hydron` and `pHlevel`. The program then displays a prompt requesting input data from the user. After the prompt is displayed, a `cin` statement is used to store the entered data in the variable `hydron`. Finally, a value for `pHlevel` is calculated, using the logarithmic library function, and displayed. As always, the program is terminated with a closing brace.

Step 4   Test and Correct the Program

A test run using Program 3.16 produced the following:

```
Enter the hydronium ion concentration level: 0.0001
The pH level is 4
```

Because the program performs a single calculation, and the result of this test run agrees with our previous hand calculation, the program has been completely tested. It can now be used to calculate the pH level of other hydronium concentrations with confidence that the results being produced are accurate.

Application 2: Approximating the Exponential Function

The exponential function e^x, where e is known as Euler's number (and has the value 2.718281828459045...) appears many times in descriptions of natural phenomena. For example, radioactive decay, population growth, and the normal (bell-shaped) curve used in statistical applications all can be described using this function.

The value of e^x can be approximated using the series[11]

$$1 + \frac{x}{1} + \frac{x^2}{2} + \frac{x^3}{6} + \frac{x^4}{24} + \frac{x^5}{120} + \frac{x^6}{720} \cdots$$

Using this polynomial as a base, write a program that approximates e raised to a user input value of x using the first 4 terms of this series. For each approximation display the value calculated by C++'s exponential function, `exp()`, the approximate value, and the absolute difference between the two. Make sure to verify your program using a hand calculation. Once the verification is complete, use the program to approximate e^4. Using the development procedure described in Section 2.6 we perform the following steps.

Step 1   Analyze the Problem

The statement of the problem specifies that four approximations are to be made, using one, two, three, and four terms of the approximating polynomial, respectively. For each approximation three output values are required: the value of e^x produced by the exponential function, the approximated value, and the absolute difference between the two values. Figure 3.19 illustrates, in symbolic form, the structure of the required output display.

e^x	Approximation	Difference
library function value	1st approximate value	1st difference
library function value	2nd approximate value	2nd difference
library function value	3rd approximate value	3rd difference
library function value	4th approximate value	4th difference

Figure 3.19 *Required output display.*

The output indicated on Figure 3.19 can be used to get a "feel" for what the program must look like. Realizing that each line in the display can only be produced by executing a `cout` statement, it should be clear that four such statements must be executed. Additionally, since each output line contains three computed values, each `cout` statement will have three items in its expression list.

The only input to the program consists of the value of x. This will, of course, require a single prompt and a `cin` statement to input the necessary value.

---

[11]The formula from which this is derived is

$$e^x = \frac{x^0}{0!} + \frac{x^1}{1!} + \frac{x^2}{2!} + \frac{x^3}{3!} + \cdots + \frac{x^n}{n!}$$

Step 2   Develop a Solution

Before any output items can be calculated, it will be necessary to have the program prompt the user for a value of x and then have the program accept the entered value. The actual output display consists of two title lines followed by four lines of calculated data. The title lines can be produced using two cout statements. Now let's see how the actual data being displayed is produced.

The first item on the first data-output line illustrated on Figure 3.19 can be obtained using the exp() library function. The second item on this line, the approximation to e^x, can be obtained by using the first term in the polynomial that was given in the program specification. Finally, the third item on the line can be calculated using the fabs() library function on the difference between the first two items. When all of these items are calculated a single cout statement can be used to display the three results on the same line.

The second output line illustrated in Figure 3.19 displays the same type of items as the first line, except that the approximation to e^x requires the use of two terms of the approximating polynomial. Notice also that the first item on the second line, the value obtained by the exp() function, is the same as the first item on the first line. This means that this item does not have to be recalculated and the value calculated for the first line can simply be displayed a second time. Once the data for the second line has been calculated a single cout statement can be used to display the required values.

Finally, only the second and third items on the last two output lines shown in Figure 3.19 need to be recalculated, since the first item on these lines is the same as previously calculated for the first line.

Thus, for this problem, the complete algorithm described in pseudocode is

> *Display a prompt for the input value of x*
> *Read the input value*
> *Display the heading lines*
> *Calculate the exponential value of x using the exp() function*
> *Calculate the first approximation*
> *Calculate the first difference*
> *Print the first output line*
> *Calculate the second approximation*
> *Calculate the second difference*
> *Print the second output line*
> *Calculate the third approximation*
> *Calculate the third difference*
> *Print the third output line*
> *Calculate the fourth approximation*
> *Calculate the fourth difference*
> *Print the fourth output line*

To ensure that we understand the processing used in the algorithm we will do a hand calculation. The result of this calculation can then be used to verify the result produced by the program that we write. For test purposes we will use a value of 2 for x, which produces the following approximations.

Using the first term of the polynomial the approximation is

$$e^2 = 1$$

Using the first two terms of the polynomial the approximation is

$$e^2 = 1 + \frac{2}{1} = 3$$

Using the first three terms of the polynomial the approximation is

$$e^2 = 3 + \frac{2^2}{2} = 5$$

Using the first four terms of the polynomial the approximation is

$$e^2 = 5 + \frac{2^3}{6} = 6.3333$$

Notice that in using four terms of the polynomial it was not necessary to recalculate the value of the first three terms; instead, we used the previously calculated value.

Step 3   Code the Solution

Program 3.17 represents a description of the selected algorithm in C++.

Program 3.17

```cpp
// this program approximates the function e raised to the x power
// using one, two, three, an four terms of an approximating polynomial
#include <iostream.h>
#include <iomanip.h>
#include <math.h>

int main()
{
  float x, func_val, approx, difference;

  cout << "\nEnter a value of x: ";
  cin  >> x;

    // print two title lines
  cout << " e to the x        Approximation       Difference\n";
  cout << "-------------       -------------       -------------\n";

  func_val = exp(x);      // use the library function

    // calculate the first approximation
```

(Continued)

(Continued)

```
    approx = 1;
    difference = fabs(func_val - approx);
    cout << setw(10) << setiosflags(ios::showpoint) << func_val
         << setw(18) << approx
         << setw(18) << difference << endl;

      // calculate the second approximation
    approx = approx + x;
    difference = fabs(func_val - approx);
    cout << setw(10) << setiosflags(ios::showpoint) << func_val
         << setw(18) << approx
         << setw(18) << difference << endl;

      // calculate the third approximation
    approx = approx + pow(x,2)/2.0;
    difference = fabs(func_val - approx);
    cout << setw(10) << setiosflags(ios::showpoint) << func_val
         << setw(18) << approx
         << setw(18) << difference << endl;

      // calculate the fourth approximation
    approx = approx + pow(x,3)/6.0;
    difference = fabs(func_val - approx);
    cout << setw(10) << setiosflags(ios::showpoint) << func_val
         << setw(18) << approx
         << setw(18) << difference << endl;

    return 0;
}
```

In reviewing Program 3.17 notice that the input value of *x* is obtained first. The two title lines are then printed prior to any calculations being made. The value of the e^x is then computed using the `exp()` library function and assigned to the variable `func_val`. This assignment permits this value to be used in the four difference calculations and displayed four times without the need for recalculation.

Since the approximation to the e^x is "built up" using more and more terms of the approximating polynomial, only the new term for each approximation is calculated and added to the previous approximation. Finally, to permit the same variables to be used over, the values in them are immediately printed before the next approximation is made. The following is a sample run produced by Program 3.17.

```
Enter a value of x: 2
   e to the x          Approximation          Difference
 -------------        -------------          -------------
    7.389056            1.000000              6.389056
    7.389056            3.000000              4.389056
    7.389056            5.000000              2.389056
    7.389056            6.333333              1.055723
```

Step 4   Test and Correct the Program

The first two columns of output data produced by the sample run agree with our hand calculation. A hand check of the last column verifies that it also correctly contains the difference in values between the first two columns.

Because the program only performs nine calculations, and the result of the test run agrees with our hand calculations, it appears that the program has been completely tested. However, it is important to understand that this is because of our choice of test data. Selecting a value of 2 for x forced us to verify that the program was, in fact, calculating 2 raised to the required powers. A choice of 0 or 1 for our hand calculation would not have given us the verification that we need. Do you see why this is so?

Using these latter two values would not adequately test whether the program used the pow( ) function correctly, or even if it used it at all! That is, an incorrect program that did not use the pow( ) function could have been constructed to produce correct values for x = 0 and x = 1, but for no other values of x. Since the test data we used does adequately verify the program, however, we can use it with confidence in the results produced. Clearly, however, the output demonstrates that to achieve any level of accuracy with the program, more terms than four would be required.

Exercises 3.6

1. Enter, compile, and run Program 3.16 on your computer system.

2. a. Enter, compile, and run Program 3.17 on your computer system.
   b. Determine how many terms of the approximating polynomial should be used to achieve an error of less than 0.0001 between the approximation and the value of e^2 as determined by the exp( ) function.

3. By mistake a student wrote Program 3.17 as follows:

```
// this program approximates the function e raised to the x power
// using one, two, three, an four terms of an approximating polynomial
#include <iostream.h>
#include <iomanip.h>
#include <math.h>

int main()
{
  float x, func_val, approx, difference;
```

```
    // print two title lines
cout << " e to the x          Approximation       Difference\n";
cout << "-------------         -------------       -------------\n";

cout << "\nEnter a value of x: ";
cin >> x;
func_val = exp(x);        // use the library function

    // calculate the first approximation
approx = 1;
difference = fabs(func_val - approx);
cout << setw(10) << setiosflags(ios::showpoint) << func_val
     << setw(18) << approx
     << setw(18) << difference << endl;

    // calculate the second approximation
approx = approx + x;
difference = fabs(func_val - approx);
cout << setw(10) << setiosflags(ios::showpoint) << func_val
     << setw(18) << approx
     << setw(18) << difference << endl;

    // calculate the third approximation
approx = approx + pow(x,2)/2.0;
difference = fabs(func_val - approx);
cout << setw(10) << setiosflags(ios::showpoint) << func_val
     << setw(18) << approx
     << setw(18) << difference << endl;

    // calculate the fourth approximation
approx = approx + pow(x,3)/6.0;
difference = fabs(func_val - approx);
cout << setw(10) << setiosflags(ios::showpoint) << func_val
     << setw(18) << approx
     << setw(18) << difference << endl;

    return 0;
}
```

Determine the output that will be produced by this program.

4. The value of π can be approximated by the series

$$4\left(1-\frac{1}{3}+\frac{1}{5}-\frac{1}{7}+\cdots\right)$$

Using this formula, write a program that calculates and displays the value of π using 2, 3, and 4 terms of the series.

5. **a.** The formula for the standard normal deviate, z, used in statistical applications is

$$z = \frac{x - \mu}{\sigma}$$

where μ refers to a mean value and σ to a standard deviation. Using this formula, write a program that calculates and displays the value of the standard normal deviate when $x = 85.3$, $\mu = 80$, and $\sigma = 4$.

b. Rewrite the program written in Exercise 5a to accept the values of x, μ, and σ as user inputs while the program is executing.

6. **a.** The equation of the normal (bell-shaped) curve used in statistical applications is

$$y = \frac{1}{\sigma\sqrt{2\pi}} e^{-\left(\frac{1}{2}\right)\left[(x-\mu)/\sigma\right]^2}$$

Using this equation, and assuming $\mu = 90$ and $\sigma = 4$, write a program that determines and displays the value of y when $x = 80$.

b. Rewrite the program written in Exercise 6a to accept the values of x, μ, and σ as user inputs while the program is executing.

7. **a.** Write, compile, and execute a C++ program that calculates and displays the voltage gain of a three stage amplifier at a frequency of 1000 Hertz. The voltage gains of the stages are:

Stage 1 gain: $23/[2.3^2 + (0.044f)^2]^{1/2}$
Stage 2 gain: $12/[6.7^2 + (0.34f)^2]^{1/2}$
Stage 3 gain: $17/[1.9^2 + (0.45f)^2]^{1/2}$

where f is the frequency in Hertz. The voltage gain of the amplifier is the product of the gains of the individual stages.

b. Redo Exercise 7a assuming that the frequency will be entered when the program is run.

8. The volume of oil stored in a underground 200-foot deep cylindrical tank is determined by measuring the distance from the top of the tank to the surface of the oil. Knowing this distance and the radius of the tank, the volume of oil in the tank can be determined using the formula *volume = π radius^2 (200 – distance)*. Using this information, write, compile, and execute a C++ program that accepts the radius and distance measurements, calculates the volume of oil in the tank, and displays the two input values and the calculated volume. Verify the results of your program by doing a hand calculation using the following test data: radius equals 10 feet and distance equals 12 feet.

9. The perimeter, approximate surface area, and approximate volume of an in-ground pool are given by the following formulas:

perimeter = 2(length + width)
*volume = length * width * average depth*
*underground surface area = 2(length + width)average depth + length * width*

Using these formulas as a basis, write a C++ program that accepts the length, width, and average depth measurements, and then calculates the perimeter, volume, and underground surface area of the pool. In writing your program make the following two calculations immediately after the input data has been entered: *length * width* and *length + width*. The results of these two calculations should then be used, as appropriate, in the assignment statements for determining the perimeter, volume, and underground surface area without recalculating them for each equation. Verify the results of your program by doing a hand calculation using the following test data: length equals 25 feet, width equals 15 feet, and average depth equals 5.5 feet. When you have verified that your program is working, use it to complete the following table.

Length	Width	Depth	Perimeter	Volume	Underground Surface Area
25	10	5.0			
25	10	5.5			
25	10	6.0			
25	10	6.5			
30	12	5.0			
30	12	5.5			
30	12	6.0			
30	12	6.5			

3.7 ▷ COMMON PROGRAMMING ERRORS

In using the material presented in this chapter, be aware of the following possible errors

1. Forgetting to assign or initialize values for all variables before the variables are used in an expression. Such values can be assigned by assignment statements, initialized within a declaration statement, or assigned interactively by entering values using the `cin` object.

2. Using a mathematical library function without including the preprocessor statement `#include <math.h>` (and on a UNIX based system forgetting to include the `-lm` argument on the `cc` command line).

3. Using a library function without providing the correct number or arguments having the proper data type.

4. Applying either the increment or decrement operator to an expression. For example, the expression

```
(count + n)++
```

is incorrect. The increment and decrement operators can only be applied to individual variables.

5. Forgetting to separate all variables passed to `cin` with an extraction symbol, `>>`.

6. Being unwilling to test a program in depth. After all, since you wrote the program you assume it is correct or you would have changed it before it was compiled. It is extremely difficult to back away and honestly test your own software. As a programmer you must constantly remind yourself that just because you think your program is correct does not make it so. Finding errors in your own program is a sobering experience, but one that will help you become a master programmer.

7. A more exotic and less common error occurs when the increment and decrement operators are used with variables that appear more than once in the same expression. This error occurs because C++ does not specify the order in which operands are accessed within an expression. For example, the value assigned to result in the statement

```
result = i + i++;
```

is compiler dependent. If your compiler accesses the first operand, `i`, first, the above statement is equivalent to

```
result = 2 * i;
i++;
```

However, if your compiler accesses the second operand, `i++`, first, the value of the first operand will be altered before it is used the second time and the value $2i + 1$ is assigned to result. As a general rule, therefore, do not use either the increment or decrement operator in an expression when the variable it operates on appears more than once in the expression.

 ## 3.8 CHAPTER SUMMARY

1. An expression is a sequence of one or more operands separated by operators. An operand is a constant, a variable, or another expression. A value is associated with an expression.

2. Expressions are evaluated according to the precedence and associativity of the operators used in the expression.

3. The assignment symbol, `=`, is an operator. Expressions using this operator assign a value to a variable; additionally, the expression itself takes on a value. Since assignment is an operation in C++, multiple uses of the assignment operator are possible in the same expression.

4. The increment operator, ++, adds one to a variable, while the decrement operator, --, subtracts one from a variable. Both of these operators can be used as prefixes or postfixes. In prefix operation the variable is incremented (or decremented) before its value is used. In postfix operation the variable is incremented (or decremented) after its value is used.

5. C++ provides library functions for calculating square root, logarithmic, and other mathematical computations. Each program using one of these mathematical functions must either include the statement #include <math.h> or have a function declaration for the mathematical function before it is called.

6. Every mathematical library function operates on its arguments to calculate a single value. To use a library function effectively, you must know what the function does, the name of the function, the number and data types of the arguments expected by the function, and the data type of the returned value.

7. Data passed to a function are called arguments of the function. Arguments are passed to a library function by including each argument, separated by commas, within the parentheses following the function's name. Each function has its own requirements for the number and data types of the arguments that must be provided.

8. Functions may be included within larger expressions.

9. The `cin` object is used for data input. This object accepts a stream of data from the keyboard and assigns the data to variables. The general form of a statement using `cin` is:

```
cin >> var1 >> var2 . . . >> varn;
```

The extraction symbol, >>, must be used to separate the variable names.

10. When a `cin` statement is encountered the computer temporarily suspends further statement execution until sufficient data has been entered for the number of variables contained in the `cin` statememt.

11. It is good programming practice to display a message, prior to a `cin` statement, that alerts the user as to the type and number of data items to be entered. Such a message is called a **prompt**.

12. Values can be equated to a single constant, using the `const` keyword. This creates a named constant that is read-only after it is initialized within the declaration statement. This declaration has the syntax

```
const data-type constant-name = initial value;
```

and permits the constant to be used instead of the initial value anywhere in the program after the declaration.

3.9 CHAPTER APPENDIX: A CLOSER LOOK AT ERRORS

The ideal in programming is to efficiently produce readable, error-free programs that work correctly and can be modified or changed with a minimum of testing required for reverification. In this regard it is useful to know the different types of errors that can occur, when they are detected, and how to correct them.

Compile-Time and Run-Time Errors

A program error can be detected at a variety of times:

1. Before a program is compiled,

2. While the program is being compiled,

3. While the program is being run,

4. After the program has been executed and the output is being examined, and

5. Not at all.

Errors detected by the compiler are formally referred to as **compile-time errors** and errors that occur while the program is being run are formally referred to as **run-time errors**.

Methods are available for detecting errors before a program is compiled and after it has been executed. The method for detecting errors after a program has been executed is called **program verification and testing**. The method for detecting errors before a program is compiled is called **desk checking**. Desk checking refers to the procedure of checking a program, by hand, at a desk or table for syntax and logic errors, which are described next. Debugging programs are also available for detecting errors while a program is being executed.

Syntax and Logic Errors

Computer literature distinguishes between two primary types of errors, called syntax and logic errors, respectively. A **syntax error** is an error in the structure or spelling of a statement. For example the statements

```
cout << "There are four syntax errors here\n
cot " Can you find tem";
```

contain four syntax errors. These errors are:

1. A closing quote is missing in line 1.

2. A terminating semicolon (;) is missing in line 1.

3. The keyword `cout` is misspelled in line 2.

4. The insertion symbol is missing in line 2.

All of these errors will be detected by the compiler when the program is compiled. This is true of all syntax errors—since they violate the basic rules of C++, if they are not discovered by desk checking, the compiler will detect them and display an error message indicating that a syntax error exists.[12] In some cases the error message is extremely clear and the error is obvious; in other cases it takes a little detective work to understand the error message displayed by the compiler. Since all syntax errors are detected at compile time, the terms compile-time errors and syntax errors are frequently used interchangeably. Strictly speaking, however, compile-time refers to when the error was detected and syntax refers to the type of error detected. Note that the misspelling of the word `tem` in the second `cout` statement is not a syntax error. Although this spelling error will result in an undesirable output line being displayed, it is not a violation of C++'s syntactical rules. It is a simple case of a typographical error, commonly referred to as a "typo".

Logic errors are characterized by erroneous, unexpected, or unintentional errors that are a direct result of some flaw in the program's logic. These errors, which are never caught by the compiler, may either be detected by desk-checking, by program testing, by accident when a user obtains an obviously erroneous output, while the program is executing, or not at all. If the error is detected while the program is executing a run-time error occurs that results in an error message being generated and/or abnormal and premature program termination.

Since logic errors may not be detected by the computer, they are always more difficult to detect than syntax errors. If not detected by desk checking, a logic error will reveal itself in two main ways. In one instance the program executes to completion but produces incorrect results. Logic errors of this type include

> *No output:* This is either caused by an omission of a `cout` statement or a sequence of statements that inadvertently bypasses a `cout` statement.
>
> *Unappealing or misaligned output:* This is caused by an error in a `cout` statement.
>
> *Incorrect numerical results:* This is caused by either incorrect values assigned to the variables used in an expression, the use of an incorrect arithmetic expression, an omission of a statement, roundoff error, or the use of an improper sequence of statements.

See if you can detect the logic error in Program 3.18.

---

[12]They may not, however, all be detected at the same time. Frequently, one syntax error "masks" another error and the second error is only detected after the first error is corrected.

Program 3.18

```cpp
#include <iostream.h>
#include <iomanip.h>
#include <math.h>

int main()     // a compound interest program
{
  float capital, amount, rate, nyrs;

  cout << "This program calculates the amount of money\n"
       << "in a bank account for an initial deposit\n"
       << "invested for n years at an interest rate r.\n\n"
       << "Enter the initial amount in the account: ";
  cin  >> amount;
  cout << "Enter the number of years: ";
  cin  >> nyrs;
  capital = amount * pow((1 + rate/100.0), nyrs);

    // set output formats
  cout << setiosflags(ios::fixed)
       << setiosflags(ios::showpoint)
       << setprecision(2);

  cout << "\nThe final amount of money is "
       << setw(8) << '$' << capital << endl;

  return 0;
}
```

Following is a sample run of Program 3.18.

```
This program calculates the amount of money
in a bank account for an initial deposit
invested for n years at an interest rate r.

Enter the initial amount in the account: 1000.
Enter the number of years: 5

The final amount of money is $ 1000.00
```

As indicated in the output, the final amount of money is identical to the initial amount input. Did you spot the error in Program 3.18 that produced this apparently erroneous output?

Unlike a misspelled output message, the error in Program 3.18 causes a mistake in a computation. Here the error is that the program does not initialize the variable `rate` before this variable is used in the calculation of `capital`. When the assignment statement that calculates `capital` is executed the program uses whatever value is stored in `rate`. On those systems that initialize all variables to zero, the value zero will be used for `rate`. However, on those systems that do not initialize all variables to zero, the program will use whatever "garbage" value happens to occupy the storage locations corresponding to the variable `rate`. (The manuals supplied with your compiler will indicate which of these two actions your compiler takes.) In either case an error is produced.

Although the logic error in this example program did not cause premature program termination, faulty or incomplete program logic can cause run-time errors. Examples of this type of logic error are attempts to divide by zero or to take the square root of a negative number.

Any program testing that is done should be well thought out to maximize the possibility of locating errors. An important programming realization is that although a single test can reveal the presence of an error, it does not verify the absence of one. The fact that one error is revealed by a particular verification run does not indicate that another error is not lurking somewhere else in the program; the fact that one test revealed no errors does not indicate that there are no errors.

Although there are no hard and fast rules for isolating the cause of an error, some useful techniques can be applied. The first of these is a preventive technique. Frequently many errors are simply introduced by the programmer in the rush to code and run a program before fully understanding what is required and how the result is to be achieved. A symptom of this haste to get a program entered into the computer is the lack of an outline of the proposed program (pseudocode or flowcharts) or a hand-written program itself. Many errors can be eliminated simply by checking a copy of the program before it is ever entered or compiled by desk checking the program.

A second useful technique is to mimic the computer and execute each statement, by hand, as the computer would. This means writing down each variable as it is encountered in the program and listing the value that should be stored in the variable as each input and assignment statement is encountered. Doing this also sharpens your programming skills, because it requires that you fully understand what each statement in your program causes to happen. Such a check is called **program tracing**.

A third and very powerful debugging technique is to use one or more diagnostic `cout` statements to display the values of selected variables. For example, consider again Program 3.18. Since this program produced an incorrect value for `capital`, it is worthwhile to place a `cout` statement immediately before the assignment statement for `capital` to display the value of all variables used in the computation. If the displayed values are correct, then the problem is in the assignment statement; if the values are incorrect, we must determine where the incorrect values were actually obtained.

In this same manner, another use of `cout` statements in debugging is to immediately display the values of all input data. This technique is referred to as **echo printing** and is useful in establishing that the computer is correctly receiving and interpreting the input data.

One of the most powerful debugging techniques is to use a debugger program, which traces program execution as the program is executing. The discussion of such programs is beyond the scope of this text.

Finally, no discussion of program verification is complete without mentioning the primary ingredient needed for successful isolation and correction of errors. This is the attitude and spirit you bring to the task. Since you wrote the program, your natural assumption is that it is correct or you would have changed it before it was compiled. It is extremely difficult to back away and honestly test and find errors in your own software. As a programmer you must constantly remind yourself that just because you *think* your program is correct does not make it so. Finding errors in your own programs is a sobering experience, but one that will help you become a master programmer. It can also be exciting and fun if approached as a detection problem with you as the master detective.

Looking at Career Choices

Mechanical Engineering

Generally speaking, mechanical engineers are concerned with machines or systems that produce or apply energy. The range of technological activities that are considered part of mechanical engineering is probably broader than in any other engineering field. The field can be roughly subdivided into four categories:

1. Power. Design of power-generating machines and systems such as boiler-turbine engines for generating electricity, solar power, heating systems, and heat exchanges.

2. Design. Innovative design of machine parts or components from the most intricate and small to the gigantic. For example, mechanical engineers work alongside electrical engineers to design automatic control systems such as robots.

3. Automotive. Design and testing of transportation vehicles and the machines used to manufacture them.

4. Heating, ventilation, air conditioning, and refrigeration. Design of systems to control our environment both indoors and out and to control pollution.

Mechanical engineers usually have a thorough background in subjects like thermodynamics, heat transfer, statics and dynamics, and fluid mechanics.

CHAPTER 4

Selection Structures

TOPICS

4.1 SELECTION CRITERIA
LOGICAL OPERATORS
A NUMERICAL ACCURACY PROBLEM

4.2 THE `if-else` STATEMENT
COMPOUND STATEMENTS
BLOCK SCOPE
ONE-WAY SELECTION
PROBLEMS ASSOCIATED WITH THE `if-else` STATEMENT

4.3 NESTED `if` STATEMENTS
THE `if-else` CHAIN

4.4 THE `switch` STATEMENT

4.5 APPLICATIONS
APPLICATION 1: DATA VALIDATION
APPLICATION 2: SOLVING QUADRATIC EQUATIONS

4.6 COMMON PROGRAMMING ERRORS

4.7 CHAPTER SUMMARY

4.8 CHAPTER APPENDIX: A CLOSER LOOK AT PROGRAM TESTING
LOOKING AT CAREER CHOICES: CIVIL ENGINEERING

*Many advances have occurred in the theoretical foundations of programming since the inception of high-level languages in the late 1950s. One of the most important of these advances was the recognition in the late 1960s that any algorithm, no matter how complex, could be constructed using combinations of four standardized **flow of control** structures: sequential, selection, repetition, and invocation.*

*The term **flow of control** refers to the order in which a program's statements are executed. Unless directed otherwise, the normal flow of control for all programs is **sequential**. This means that statements are executed in sequence, one after another, in the order in which they are placed within the program.*

Selection, repetition and invocation structures permit the sequential flow of control to be altered in precisely defined ways. As you might have guessed, the selection structure is used to select which statements are to be performed next and the repetition structure is used to repeat a set of statements. In this chapter we present C++'s selection statements. Repetition and invocation techniques are presented in Chapters 5 and 6.

4.1 > SELECTION CRITERIA

In the solution of many problems, different actions must be taken depending upon the value of the data. Examples of simple situations include calculating an area *only if* the measurements are positive, performing a division *only if* the divisor is not zero, printing different messages *depending upon* the value of a grade received, and so on.

The `if-else` statement in C++ is used to implement such a decision structure in its simplest form – that of choosing between two alternatives. The most commonly used pseudocode syntax of this statement is

```
if (condition)
    statement executed if condition is "true";
else
    statement executed if condition is "false";
```

When an executing program encounters the `if` statement, the condition is evaluated to determine its numerical value, which is then interpreted as either true or false. If the condition evaluates to any positive or negative nonzero numerical value, the condition is considered as a "true" condition and the statement following the `if` is executed. If the condition evaluates to a zero numerical value, the condition is considered as a "false" condition and the statement following the `else` is executed. The `else` part of the statement is optional and may be omitted.

The condition used in an `if` statement can be any valid C++ expression (including, as we will see, even an assignment expression). The most commonly used expressions, however, are called **relational expressions**. A **simple relational expression** consists of a relational operator that compares two operands as shown in Figure 4.1.

Figure 4.1 Anatomy of a simple relational expression.

While each operand in a relational expression can be either a variable or constant, the relational operators must be one of those listed in Table 4.1. These relational operators may be used with integer, float, double, or character operands, but must be typed exactly as given in Table 4.1. Thus, while the following examples are all valid:

```
age > 40        length <= 50        temp > 98.6

     3 < 4       flag == done        id_num == 682

day != 5        2.0 > 3.3           hours > 40
```

the following are invalid:

```
length =< 50    // operator out of order

2.0 >> 3.3      // invalid operator

flag = = done   // spaces are not allowed
```

Table 4.1

Relational operator	Meaning	Example
<	less than	age < 30
>	greater than	height > 6.2
<=	less than or equal to	taxable <= 20000
>=	greater than or equal to	temp >= 98.6
==	equal to	grade == 100
!=	not equal to	number != 250

Relational expressions are sometimes called **conditions** and we will use both terms to refer to these expressions. Like all C++ expressions, relational expressions are evaluated to yield a numerical result.[1] In the case of a relational expression, the value of the expression can only be the integer value of 1 or 0, which is interpreted as true and false, respectively. *A relational expression that we would interpret as true evaluates to an integer value of 1, and a false relational expression results in an integer value of 0.* For example, because the relationship 3 < 4 is always true, this expression has a value of 1, and because the relationship 2.0 > 3.3 is always false, the value of the expression itself is 0. This can be verified using the statements

```
cout << "The value of 3 < 4 is " << (3 < 4) << endl;
cout << "The value of 2.0 > 3.0 is " << (2.0 > 3.3) << endl;
```

which results in the display

```
The value of 3 < 4 is 1
The value of 2.0 > 3.0 is 0
```

---

[1]In this regard C++ differs from other high-level computer languages that yield a Boolean (true, false) result.

The value of a relational expression such as `hours > 40` depends on the value stored in the variable `hours`.

In a C++ program, a relational expression's value is not as important as the interpretation C++ places on the value when the expression is used as part of a selection statement. In these statements, which are presented in the next section, we will see that a zero value is used by C++ to represent a false condition and any nonzero value is used to represent a true condition. The selection of which statement to execute next is then based on the value obtained.

In addition to numerical operands, character data can also be compared using relational operators. For example, in the ASCII code the letter 'A' is stored using a code having a lower numerical value than the letter 'B', the code for a 'B' is lower in value than the code for a 'C', and so on. For character sets coded in this manner, the following conditions are evaluated as listed below.

Expression	Value	Interpretation
`'A' > 'C'`	0	False
`'D' <= 'Z'`	1	True
`'E' == 'F'`	0	False
`'G' >= 'M'`	0	False
`'B' != 'C'`	1	True

Comparing letters is essential in alphabetizing names or using characters to select a particular choice in decision-making situations.

Logical Operators

In addition to using simple relational expressions as conditions, more complex conditions can be created using the logical operators AND, OR, and NOT. These operators are represented by the symbols `&&`, `||`, and `!`, respectively.

When the AND operator, `&&`, is used with two simple expressions, the condition is true only if both individual expressions are true by themselves. Thus, the logical condition

```
(voltage > 48) && (milliamp < 10)
```

is true only if `voltage` is greater than 48 and `milliamp` is less than 10. Since relational operators have a higher precedence that logical operators, the parentheses in this logical expression could have been omitted.

The logical OR operator, `||`, is also applied between two expressions. When using the OR operator, the condition is satisfied if either one or both of the two expressions is true. Thus, the condition

```
(voltage > 48) || (milliamp < 10)
```

is true if either `voltage` is greater than 48, `milliamp` is less than 10, or if both conditions are true. Again, the parentheses surrounding the relational expressions are included to make the expression easier to read. Because of the higher precedence of relational operators with respect to logical operators the same evaluation would be made even if the parentheses were omitted.

For the declarations

```
int i, j;
float a, b, complete;
```

the following represent valid conditions:

```
a > b
(i == j) || (a < b) || complete
(a/b > 5) && (i <= 20)
```

Before these conditions can be evaluated, the values of a, b, i, j, and complete must be known. Assuming a = 12.0, b = 2.0, i = 15, j = 30, and complete = 0.0 the previous expressions yield the following results:

Expression	Value	Interpretation
a > b	1	True
(i == j) || (a < b) || complete	0	False
(a/b > 5) && (i <= 20)	1	True

The NOT operator is used to change an expression to its opposite state; that is, if the expression has any nonzero value (true), !expression produces a zero value (false). If an expression is false to begin with (has a zero value), !expression is true and evaluates to 1. For example, assuming the number 26 is stored in the variable age, the expression age > 40 has a value of zero (it is false), while the expression !(age > 40) has a value of 1. Since the NOT operator is used with only one expression, it is a unary operator.

The relational and logical operators have a hierarchy of execution similar to the arithmetic operators. Table 4.2 lists the precedence of these operators in relation to the other operators we have used.

Table 4.2

Operator	Associativity
! unary − ++ --	right to left
* / %	left to right
+ −	left to right
< <= > >=	left to right
== !=	left to right
&&	left to right
||	left to right
= += −= *= /=	right to left

The following example illustrates the use of an operator's precedence and associativity to evaluate relational expressions, assuming the following declarations:

```
char key = 'm';
int i = 5, j = 7, k = 12;
double x = 22.5;
```

Expression	Equivalent Expression	Value	Interpretation
i + 2 == k - 1	(i + 2) == (k - 1)	0	False
3 * i - j < 22	(3 * i) - j < 22	1	True
i + 2 * j > k	(i + (2 * j)) > k	1	True
k + 3 <= -j + 3 * i	(k + 3) <= ((-j) + (3*i))	0	False
'a' + 1 == 'b'	('a' + 1) == 'b'	1	True
key - 1 > 'p'	(key - 1) > 'p'	0	False
key + 1 == 'n'	(key + 1) == 'n'	1	True
25 >= x + 1.0	25 >= (x + 1.0)	1	True

As with all expressions, parentheses can be used to alter the assigned operator priority and improve the readability of relational expressions. By evaluating the expressions within parentheses first, the following compound condition is evaluated as

```
(6 * 3 == 36 / 2) || (13 < 3 * 3 + 4) && !(6 - 2 < 5)
    (18 == 18) ||     (13 < 9 + 4)    && !(4 < 5)
            1 ||        (13 < 13)      && !1
            1 ||            0          &&  0
            1 ||            0
                      1
```

A Numerical Accuracy Problem

A problem that can occur with C++'s relational expressions is a subtle numerical accuracy problem relating to floating point and double precision numbers. Due to the way computers store these numbers, tests for equality of floating point and double precision values and variables using the relational operator == should be avoided.

The reason for this is that many decimal numbers, such as 0.1, for example, cannot be represented exactly in binary using a finite number of bits. Thus, testing for exact equality for such numbers can fail. When equality of noninteger values is desired it is better to require that the absolute value of the difference between operands be less than some extremely small value. Thus, for floating-point and double-precision operands the general expression

operand_1 == operand_2

should be replaced by the condition

fabs(operand_1 – operand_2) < 0.000001

where the value 0.000001 can be altered to any other acceptably small value. Thus, if the difference between the two operands is less than 0.000001 (or any other user selected amount), the two operands are considered essentially equal. For example if x and y are floating point variables, a condition such as

```
x/y == 0.35
```

should be programmed as

```
fabs(x/y - 0.35) < epsilon
```

where `epsilon` can be a constant set to any acceptably small value, such as 0.000001.[2] This latter condition ensures that slight inaccuracies in representing noninteger numbers in binary do not affect evaluation of the tested condition. Since all computers have an exact binary representation of zero, comparisons for exact equality to zero don't encounter this numerical accuracy problem.

Exercises 4.1

1. Determine the value of the following expressions. Assume a = 5, b = 2, c = 4, d = 6, and e = 3.

   a. `a > b`
   b. `a != b`
   c. `d % b == c % b`
   d. `a * c != d * b`
   e. `d * b == c * e`
   f. `!(a * b)`
   g. `!(a % b * c)`
   h. `!(c % b * a)`
   i. `b % c * a`

2. Using parentheses, rewrite the following expressions to correctly indicate their order of evaluation. Then evaluate each expression assuming a = 5, b = 2, and c = 4.

   a. `a % b * c && c % b * a`
   b. `a % b * c || c % b * a`
   c. `b % c * a && a % c * b`
   d. `b % c * a || a % c * b`

3. Write relational expressions to express the following conditions (use variable names of your own choosing):

   a. The distance is equal to 30 feet.
   b. The ambient temperature is 86.4.
   c. A speed is 55 MPH.
   d. The current month is 12 (December).
   e. The letter input is K.

---

[2]Using the `fabs()` function requires inclusion of the `math.h` header file. This is done by placing the preprocessor statement `#include<math.h>` either immediately before or after the `#include<iostream.h>` preprocessor statement. UNIX based systems also require specific inclusion of the math library at compile time with a `-lm` command line argument.

f. A length is greater than two feet and less than three feet.

g. The current day is the 15th day of the 1st month.

h. The automobile's speed is 35 MPH and its acceleration is greater than 4 MPH per second.

i. An automobile's speed is greater than 50 MPH and it has been moving for at least 5 hours.

j. The code is less than 500 characters and takes more than 2 microseconds to transmit.

4. Determine the value of the following expressions, assuming a = 5, b = 2, c = 4, and d = 5.

a. `a == 5`

b. `b * d == c * c`

c. `d % b * c > 5 || c % b * d < 7`

4.2 THE `if-else` STATEMENT

The `if-else` structure directs the computer to perform a series of one or more instructions based on the result of a comparison. For example, suppose we are to calculate the area of a circle given the radius as an input value. If the input is a negative number we are to print a message that the radius cannot be a negative value, otherwise we are to calculate and print the circle's area. The `if-else` structure can be used in this situation to select the correct operation based on whether the radius is negative or not. The general syntax of the `if-else` statement is

    `if` *(expression) statement1;*

    `else` *statement2;*

The expression is evaluated first. If the value of the expression is nonzero, *statement1* is executed. If the value is zero the statement after the keyword else is executed. Thus, one of the two statements (either *statement1* or *statement2*, but not both) is always executed depending on the value of the expression. Notice that the tested expression must be put in parentheses and a semicolon is placed after each statement

For clarity, the `if-else` statement generally is written on four lines using the form

    `if` *(expression)* ◄——————— no semicolon here

       statement1;

    `else` ◄——————— no semicolon here

       statement2;

The form of the if-else statement that is selected typically depends on the length of statements 1 and 2. However, when using the second form, do not put a semicolon after the parentheses or the keyword else. The semicolons go only after the ends of the statements.

The flowchart for the if-else statement is shown in Figure 4.2.

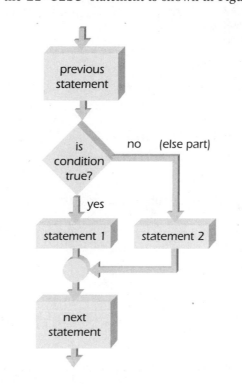

Figure 4.2 The if-else flowchart.

As a specific example of an if-else structure, we will construct a C++ program for determining the area of a circle by first examining the value of the radius. The condition to be tested is whether the radius is less than zero. An appropriate if-else statement for this situation is:

```
if (radius < 0.0)
  cout << "A negative radius is invalid" << endl;
else
  cout << "The area of this circle is " << 3.1416 * pow(radius,2) << endl;
```

Here we have used the relational operator << to represent the relation "less than." If the value of radius is less than 0, the condition is true (has a value of 1) and the statement cout >> "A negative radius is invalid"; is executed. If the condition is not true, the value of the expression is zero, and the statement after the keyword else is executed. Program 4.1 illustrates the use of this statement in a complete program.

Program 4.1

```cpp
#include <iostream.h>
#include <math.h>

int main()
{
  float radius;

  cout << "Please type in the radius: ";
  cin  >> radius;

  if (radius < 0.0)
    cout << "A negative radius is invalid" << endl;
  else
    cout << "The area of this circle is " << 3.1416 * pow(radius,2) << endl;

  return 0;
}
```

A blank line was inserted before and after the `if-else` statement to highlight it in the complete program. We will continue to do this throughout the text to emphasize the statement being presented.

To illustrate selection in action, Program 4.1 was run twice with different input data. The results were

```
Please type in the radius: -2.5
A negative radius is invalid
```

and:

```
Please type in the radius: 2.5
The area of this circle is 19.635
```

In reviewing this output observe that the radius in the first run of the program was less than 0 and the `if` part of the `if-else` structure correctly executed the `cout` statement telling the user that a negative radius is invalid. In the second run, the radius is not negative and the `else` part of the `if-else` structure was used to yield a correct area computation of

$$3.1416 * (2.5)^2 = 19.635$$

Although any expression can be tested by an `if-else` statement, relational expressions are predominately used. However, statements such as

```
if (num)
  cout << "Bingo!";
else
  cout << "You lose!";
```

are valid. Since num, by itself, is a valid expression, the message Bingo! is displayed if num
has any nonzero value and the message You lose! is displayed if num has a value of zero.

Compound Statements

Although only a single statement is permitted in both the if and else parts of the if-else
statement, this statement can be a single compound statement. A **compound statement** is
a sequence of single statements contained between braces, as shown in Figure 4.3.

```
{
    statement1;
    statement2;
    statement3;
        .
        .
        .
    last statement;
}
```

Figure 4.3 A compound statement consists of individual statements enclosed
within braces.

The use of braces to enclose a set of individual statements creates a single block of statements, which may be used anywhere in a C++ program in place of a single statement.
The next example illustrates the use of a compound statement within the general form of
an if-else statement.

```
if (expression)
{
    statement1;    // as many statements as necessary
    statement2;    // can be put within the braces
    statement3;    // each statement must end with a ;

}
else
{
    statement4;
    statement5;
        .
        .
    statementn;
}
```

Program 4.2 illustrates the use of a compound statement in an actual program.

Program 4.2

```cpp
#include <iostream.h>
#include <iomanip.h>

// a temperature conversion program
int main()
{
  char temp_type;
  float temp, fahren, celsius;

  cout << "Enter the temperature to be converted: ";
  cin  >> temp;
  cout << "Enter an f if the temperature is in Fahrenheit";
  cout << "\n or a c if the temperature is in Celsius: ";
  cin  >> temp_type;

    // set output formats
  cout << setiosflags(ios::fixed)
       << setiosflags(ios::showpoint)
       << setprecision(2);

  if (temp_type == 'f')
  {
    celsius = (5.0 / 9.0) * (temp - 32.0);
    cout << "\nThe equivalent Celsius temperature is "
         << celsius << endl;
  }
  else
  {
    fahren =  (9.0 / 5.0) * temp + 32.0;
    cout << "\nThe equivalent Fahrenheit temperature is "
         << fahren << endl;
  }

  return 0;
}
```

Program 4.2 checks whether the value in `temp_type` is f. If the value is f, the compound statement corresponding to the `if` part of the `if-else` statement is executed. Any other letter results in execution of the compound statement corresponding to the `else` part. A sample run of Program 4.2 follows.

```
Enter the temperature to be converted: 212
Enter an f if the temperature is in Fahrenheit
 or a c if the temperature is in Celsius: f

The equivalent Celsius temperature is 100.00
```

Block Scope

All statements contained within a compound statement constitute a single block of code and any variable declared within such a block only has meaning between its declaration and the closing braces defining the block. For example, consider the following section of code, which consists of two blocks of code:

```
{   // start of outer block
  int a = 25;
  int b = 17;

  cout << "The value of a is " << a
      <<" and b is " << b << endl;

  {    // start of inner block
    float a = 46.25;
    int c = 10;

    cout << "a is now " << a
        << " b is now " << b
        << " and c is " << c << endl;
  }   // end of inner block

  cout << "a is now " << a
      << " and b is " << b << endl;

}   // end of outer block
```

The output that is produced by this section of code is:

```
The value of a is 25 and b is 17
a is now 46.25 b is now 17 and c is 10
a is now 25 and b is 17
```

This output is produced as follows: The first block of code defines two variables named a and b, which may be used anywhere within this block after their declaration, including any block contained inside of it. Within the inner block, two new variables have been declared, named a and c. At this stage then, we have created four different variables, two of which have the same name. Any referenced variable first results in an attempt to access a variable correctly declared within the block containing the reference. If no variable is defined within the block, an attempt is made to access a variable in the next immediate outside block until a valid access results.

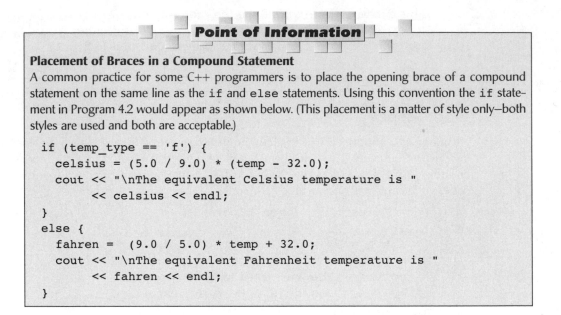

Point of Information

Placement of Braces in a Compound Statement

A common practice for some C++ programmers is to place the opening brace of a compound statement on the same line as the `if` and `else` statements. Using this convention the `if` statement in Program 4.2 would appear as shown below. (This placement is a matter of style only—both styles are used and both are acceptable.)

```
if (temp_type == 'f') {
   celsius = (5.0 / 9.0) * (temp - 32.0);
   cout << "\nThe equivalent Celsius temperature is "
        << celsius << endl;
}
else {
   fahren =  (9.0 / 5.0) * temp + 32.0;
   cout << "\nThe equivalent Fahrenheit temperature is "
        << fahren << endl;
}
```

Thus, the values of the variables a and c referenced within the inner block use the values of the variables a and c declared in that block. Since no variable named b was declared inside the inner block, the value of b displayed from within the inner block is obtained from the outer block. Finally, the last `cout` object, which is outside of the inner block, displays the value of the variable a declared in the outer block. If an attempt was made to display the value of c anywhere in the outer block, the compiler would issue an error message stating that c is an undefined symbol.

The area within a program where a variable can be used is formally referred to as the **scope of the variable**, and we will have much more to say on this subject in Chapter 6.[3]

One-Way Selection

A useful modification of the `if-else` statement involves omitting the `else` part of the statement altogether. In this case, the `if` statement takes the shortened and frequently useful form

> `if` *(expression)*
> *statement;*

---

[3]Blocks consisting of definition statements only can be given explicit names. Such named blocks are referred to as *namespaces* and are described in Appendix F.

The statement following `if (expression)` is only executed if the expression has a nonzero value (a true condition). As before, the statement may be a compound statement. The flowchart for this statement is illustrated on Figure 4.4.

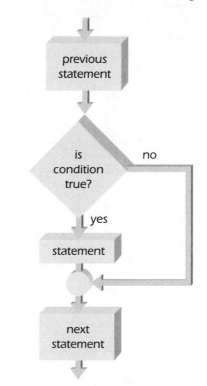

Figure 4.4 Flowchart for the one-way `if` statement.

This modified form of the `if` statement is called a one-way if statement. Program 4.3 uses this statement to selectively display a message for cars that have been driven more than 3000.0 miles.

Program 4.3

```cpp
#include <iostream.h>

int main()
{
  const float LIMIT = 3000.0;
  int id_num;
  float miles;

  cout << "Please type in car number and mileage: ";
  cin  >> id_num >> miles;

  if(miles > LIMIT)
    cout << "  Car " << id_num << " is over the limit.\n";

  cout << "End of program output.\n";

  return 0;
}
```

As an illustration of its one-way selection criteria in action, Program 4.3 was run twice, each time with different input data. Only the input data for the first run causes the message `Car 256 is over the limit` to be displayed.

```
Please type in car number and mileage: 256 3562.8
  Car 256 is over the limit.
End of program output.
```

and

```
Please type in car number and mileage: 23 2562.3
End of program output.
```

Problems Associated with the `if-else` Statement

Two of the most common problems encountered in initially using C++'s `if-else` statement are:

1. Misunderstanding the full implications of what an expression is, and
2. Using the assignment operator, =, in place of the relational operator ==.

Recall that an expression is any combination of operands and operators that yields a result. This definition is extremely broad and more encompassing than is initially apparent. For example, all of the following are valid C++ expressions:

```
age + 5
age = 30
age == 40
```

Assuming that the variables are suitably declared, each of the above expressions yields a result. Program 4.4 uses the cout object to display the value of these expressions when age = 18.

Program 4.4

```
#include <iostream.h>

int main()
{
  int age = 18;

  cout << "The value of the first expression is " << (age + 5) << endl;
  cout << "The value of the second expression is " << (age = 30) << endl;
  cout << "The value of the third expression is " << (age == 40) << endl;

  return 0;
}
```

The display produced by Program 4.4 is:

```
The value of the first expression is 23
The value of the second expression is 30
The value of the third expression is 0
```

As the output of Program 4.4 illustrates, each expression, by itself, has a value associated with it. The value of the first expression is the sum of the variable age plus 5, which is 23. The value of the second expression is 30, which is also assigned to the variable age. The value of the third expression is zero, since age is not equal to 40, and a false condition is represented in C++ with a value of zero. If the value in age had been 40, the relational expression a == 40 would be true and would have a value of 1.

Point of Information

The Boolean Data Type

Traditionally, both C and C++ did not have a built-in boolean data type with its two boolean values, **true** and **false**. Since this data type was not originally a part of the language, a tested expression could not evaluate to a boolean value. Thus, the syntax

> *if(boolean expression is true)*
> *execute this statement;*

was also not built-in to either C or C++. Rather, both C and C++ use the more encompassing syntax:

> *if(expression)*
> *execute this statement;*

where *expression* is any expression that evalutes to a numeric value. If the value of the tested expression is a non-zero value it is considered as true, and only a zero value is considered as false.

As specified by the ANSI/ISO C++ draft standard, C++ will have a new boolean data type containing the two values, **true** and **false**. Boolean variables will be declared using the keyword **bool**. As currently implemented, the actual values represented by the two boolean values, **true** and **false**, are the integer values 1 and 0, respectively. For example, consider the following program, which declares two boolean variables.

```
#include <iostream.h>
int main()
{
  bool t1, t2;

  t1 = true;
  t2 = false;

  cout <<"The value of t1 is " << t1
       << "\n and the value of t2 is " << t2 << endl;

  return 0;
}
```

The output produced by this program is:

```
The value of t1 is 1
and the value of t2 is 0
```

As seen by the output, the boolean values **true** and **false**, are represented by the integer values 1 and 0, respectively. The boolean values true and false have the following relationships.

```
!true=false
!false=true
```

Additionally, applying either a postfix or prefix ++ operator to a variable of type bool will set the boolean value to **true**. the postfix and prefix -- operators cannot be applied to boolean variables.

Boolean values can also be compared, as illustrated in the following code:

```
if (t1 == t2)
  cout << "The values are equal" << endl;
else
  cout << "The values are not equal" << endl;
```

Lastly, assigning any non-zero value to a boolean variable results in the varieable being set to **true**; that is, a value of 1, and assigning a zero value to a boolean results in the variable being set to **false**; that is, a value of 0.

Now assume that the relational expression age == 40 was intended to be used in the if statement

```
if (age == 40)
  cout << "Happy Birthday!";
```

but was mistyped as age = 40, resulting in

```
if (age = 40)
  cout << "Happy Birthday!";
```

Since the mistake results in a valid C++ expression, and any C++ expression can be tested by an if statement, the resulting if statement is valid and will cause the message Happy Birthday! to be printed regardless of what value was previously assigned to age. Can you see why?

The condition tested by the if statement does not compare the value in age to the number 40, but assigns the number 40 to age. That is, the expression age = 40 is not a relational expression at all, but an assignment expression. At the completion of the assignment the expression itself has a value of 40. Since C++ treats any nonzero value as true, the cout statement is executed. Another way of looking at this is to realize that the if statement is equivalent to the following two statements:

```
age = 40;      // assign 40 to age
if (age)       // test the value of age
  cout << "Happy Birthday!";
```

Since a C++ compiler has no means of knowing that the expression being tested is not the desired one, you must be especially careful when writing conditions.

Exercises 4.2

1. Write appropriate if statements for each of the following conditions:
   a. If an angle is equal to 90 degrees print the message "The angle is a right angle," else print the message that "The angle is not a right angle."
   b. If the temperature is above 100 degrees display the message "above the boiling point of water" else display the message "below the boiling point of water."
   c. If the number is positive add the number to possum, else add the number to negsum.
   d. If the slope is less than 0.5 set the variable flag to zero, else set flag to one.
   e. If the difference between volts1 and volts2 is less than 0.001, set the variable approx to zero, else calculate approx as the quantity (volts1 – volts2) / 2.0.
   f. If the frequency is above 60, display the message "The frequency is too high."
   g. If the difference between temp1 and temp2 exceeds 2.3 degrees, calculate error as (temp1 – temp2) * factor.
   h. If x is greater than y and z is less than 20, read in a value for p.
   i. If distance is greater than 20 and it is less than 35, read in a value for time.

2. Write if statements corresponding to the conditions illustrated by each of the following flow charts.

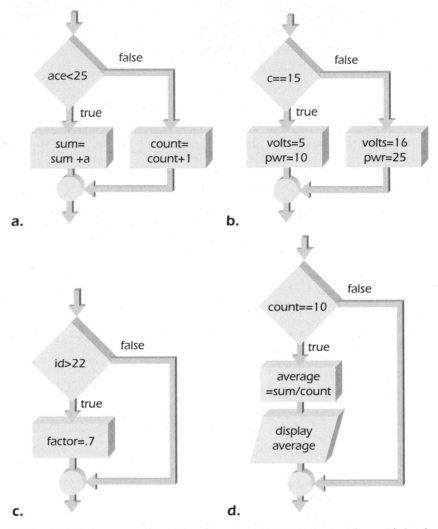

a.

b.

c.

d.

3. Write a C++ program that asks the user to input two numbers. If the first number entered is greater than the second number the program should print the message "The first number is greater," else it should print the message "The first number is smaller." Test your program by entering the numbers 5 and 8 and then using the numbers 11 and 2. What do you think your program will display if the two numbers entered are equal? Test this case.

4. a. A certain waveform is 0 volts for time less than 2 seconds and 3 volts for time equal to or greater than 2 seconds (such waveforms are referred to as step functions). Write a C++ program that accepts time into the variable named `time` and display the appropriate voltage depending on the input value.

   b. How many runs should you make for the program written in Exercise 4a to verify that it is operating correctly? What data should you input in each of the program runs?

5. a. An insulation test for a wire requires that the insulation withstand at least 600 volts. Write a C++ program that accepts a test voltage and prints either the message "PASSED VOLTAGE TEST" or the message "FAILED VOLTAGE TEST," as appropriate.

6. a. Write a C++ program to compute the value of pressure in pounds per square inch (psi) of a waveform described as follows:

For time, t, equal to or less than 35 seconds the pressure is $0.46t$ psi and for time equal to or greater than 35 seconds the pressure is $0.19t + 9.45$ psi.

The program should request the time as input and should display the pressure as output.

   b. How many runs should you make for the program written in Exercise 6a to verify that it is operating correctly? What data should you input in each of the program runs?

7. a. Write a C++ program that displays either the message "PROCEED WITH TAKEOFF" or "ABORT TAKEOFF" depending on the input. If the character g is entered in the variable **code**, the first message should be displayed; otherwise the second message should be displayed.

   b. How many runs should you make for the program written in Exercise 7a to verify that it is operating correctly? What data should you input in each of the program runs?

8. a. A small factory generates its own power with a 20 Kilowatt generator and a 50 Kilowatt generator. The plant manager indicates which generator is required by typing a character code. Write a C++ program that accepts this code as input. If code s is typed a message directing the plant foreman to use the smaller generator should be displayed; otherwise a message directing the use of the larger generator should be output.

4.3 NESTED `if` STATEMENTS

As we have seen, an **if-else** statement can contain simple or compound statements. Any valid C++ statement can be used, including another **if-else** statement. Thus, one or more **if-else** statements can be included within either part of an **if-else** statement. The inclusion of one or more **if** statements within an existing **if** statement is called a *nested* **if** statement. For example, substituting the one-way **if** statement

```
if (distance > 500)
   cout << "snap";
```

for **statement1** in the following **if** statement

```
if (hours < 9)
  statement1;
else
  cout << "pop";
```

results in the nested `if` statement

```
if (hours < 9)
{
  if (distance > 500)
    cout << "snap";
}
else
  cout << "pop";
```

The braces around the inner one-way `if` are essential because in their absence C++ associates an `else` with the closest unpaired `if`. Thus, without the braces, the above statement is equivalent to

```
if (hours < 9)
  if (distance > 500)
    cout << "snap";
  else
    cout << "pop";
```

Here the `else` is paired with the inner `if`, which destroys the meaning of the original `if-else` statement. Notice also that the indentation is irrelevant as far as the compiler is concerned. Whether the indentation exists or not, *the statement is compiled by associating the last* `else` *with the closest unpaired* `if, unless braces are used to alter the default pairing.*

The process of nesting `if` statements can be extended indefinitely, so that the `cout << "snap";` statement could itself be replaced by either a complete `if-else` statement or another one-way `if` statement.

Figure 4.5 illustrates the general form of a nested `if-else` statement when an `if-else` statement is nested (a) within the `if` part of an `if-else` statement and (b) within the `else` part of an `if-else` statement.

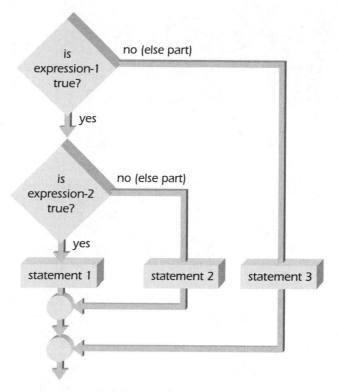

Figure 4.5a if-else *statement nested in an* if.

The if-else Chain

In general, the nesting illustrated in Figure 4.5a tends to be confusing and is best avoided in practice. However, an extremely useful construction occurs for the nesting illustrated in Figure 4.5b, which has the form

```
if (expression_1)
   statement1;
else
   if (expression_2)
      statement2;
   else
      statement3;
```

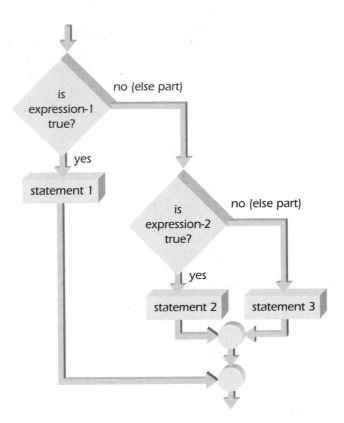

Figure 4.5b if-else *statement nested in an* else.

As with all C++ programs, since white space is ignored, the indentation shown is not required. More typically, the preceding construction is written using the following arrangement:

```
if (expression_1)
   statement1;
else if (expression_2)
   statement2;
else
   statement3;
```

This form of a nested if statement is extremely useful in practice, and is formally referred to as an if-else chain. Each condition is evaluated in order, and if any condition is true the corresponding statement is executed and the remainder of the chain is terminated. The statement associated with the final else is only executed if none of the previous conditions is satisfied. This serves as a default or catch-all case that is useful for detecting an impossible or error condition.

The chain can be continued indefinitely by repeatedly making the last statement another `if-else` statement. Thus, the general form of an `if-else` chain is:

```
if (expression_1)
    statement1;
else if (expression_2)
    statement2;
else if (expression_3)
    statement3;
           .
           .
           .
else if (expression_n)
    statement_n;
else
    last_statement;
```

Each condition is evaluated in the order it appears in the statement. For the first condition that is true, the corresponding statement is executed, and the remainder of the statements in the chain are not executed. Thus, if `expression_1` is true, only `statement1` is executed; otherwise `expression_2` is tested. If `expression_2` is then true, only `statement2` is executed; otherwise `expression_3` is tested, and so on. The final else in the chain is optional, and `last_statement` is only executed if none of the previous expressions was true.

To illustrate using and `if-else` chain, Program 4.5 displays an item's specification status corresponding to a letter input. The following letter codes are used:

Specification Status	Input Code
Space Exploration	S
Military Grade	M
Commercial Grade	C
Toy Grade	T

Program 4.5

```cpp
#include <iostream.h>

int main()
{
  char code;

  cout << "Enter a specification code: ";
  cin  >> code;

  if (code == 'S')
      cout << "The item is space exploration grade.";
  else if (code == 'M')
    cout << "The item is military grade.";
  else if (code == 'C')
    cout << "The item is commercial grade.";
  else if (code == 'T')
      cout << "The item it toy grade.";
  else
      cout << "An invalid code was entered.";
  cout << endl;

  return 0;
}
```

As a further example of an `if-else` chain, we determine the output of a digital converter unit using the following input/output relationship:

Input Weight	Output Reading
greater than or equal to 90 lbs	1111
less than 90 lbs but greater than 80 lbs	1110
less than 80 lbs but greater than or equal to 70 lbs	1101
less than 70 lbs but greater than or equal to 60 lbs	1100
less than 60 lbs	1011

The following statements can be used to determine the correct output reading, where the variable `inlbs` is used to store the input reading:

```cpp
if (inlbs >= 90)
    digout = 1111;
```

```
        else if (inlbs >= 80)
            digout = 1110;
        else if (inlbs >= 70)
            digout = 1101;
        else if (inlbs >= 60)
            digout = 1100;
        else
            digout = 1011;
```

Notice that this example makes use of the fact that the chain is stopped once a true condition is found. This is accomplished by checking for the highest input weight first. If the input value is less than 90, the `if-else` chain continues checking for the next highest weight, and so on, until the correct weight category is obtained.

Program 4.6 uses an `if-else` chain to calculate and display the correct output reading corresponding to the weight input in the `cin` statement.

Program 4.6

```
#include <iostream.h>

int main()
{
  int digout;
  float inlbs;

  cout << "Enter the input weight: ";
  cin  >> inlbs;

  if (inlbs >= 90)
      digout = 1111;
  else if (inlbs >= 80)
      digout = 1110;
  else if (inlbs >= 70)
    digout = 1101;
  else if (inlbs >= 60)
    digout = 1100;
  else
    digout = 1011;

  cout << "The digital output is " << digout << endl;

  return 0;
}
```

A sample run using Program 4.6 is illustrated below.

```
Enter the input weight: 72.5
The digital output is 1101
```

As with all C++ statements, each individual statement within an `if-else` chain can be replaced by a compound statement bounded by the braces { and }.

Exercises 4.3

1. Modify Program 4.5 to accept both lower and uppercase letters as marriage codes. For example, if a user enters either an m or an M, the program should display the message "The item is military grade."

2. Write nested if statements corresponding to the conditions illustrated in each of the following flowcharts.

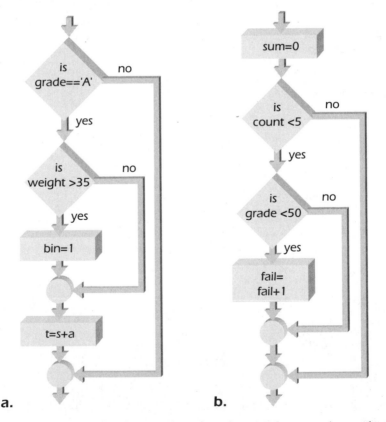

a.   **b.**

3. An angle is considered acute if it is less than 90 degrees, obtuse if it is greater than 90 degrees, and a right angle if it is equal to 90 degrees. Using this information write a C++ program that accepts an angle, in degrees, and displays the type of angle corresponding to the degrees entered.

4. The grade level of undergraduate college students is typically determined according to the following schedule:

Number of Credits Completed	Grade Level
less than 32	Freshman
32 to 63	Sophomore
64 to 95	Junior
96 or more	Senior

Using this information, write a C++ program that accepts the number of credits a student has completed, determines the student's grade level, and displays the grade level.

5. A student's letter grade is calculated according to the following schedule:

Numerical grade	Letter grade
greater than or equal to 90	A
less than 90 but greater than or equal to 80	B
less than 80 but greater than or equal to 70	C
less than 70 but greater than or equal to 60	D
less than 60	F

Using this information, write a C++ program that accepts a student's numerical grade, converts the numerical grade to an equivalent letter grade, and displays the letter grade.

6. The tolerance of critical components in a system is determined by the application according to the following schedule:

Specification Status	Tolerance
Space Exploration	Less than 0.1%
Military Grade	Greater than or equal to 0.1% and less than 1%
Commercial Grade	Greater than or equal to 1% and less than 10%
Toy Grade	Greater than or equal to 10%

Using this information, write a C++ program that accepts the tolerance reading of a component and determines the specification that should be assigned to the component.

7. Write a C++ program that accepts a number followed by one space and then a letter. If the letter following the number is f, the program is to treat the number entered as a temperature in degrees Fahrenheit, convert the number to the equivalent degrees Celsius, and print a suitable display message. If the letter following the number is c, the program is to treat the number entered as a temperature in Celsius, convert the number to the equivalent degrees Fahrenheit, and print a suitable display message. If the letter is neither an f or c, the program is to print a message that the data entered is incorrect and terminate. Use an `if-else` chain in your program and make use of the conversion formulas:

$Celsius = (5.0 / 9.0) * (Fahrenheit - 32.0)$
$Fahrenheit = (9.0 / 5.0) * Celsius + 32.0$

8. Using the relationships from Program 4.6, the following program calculates the digital output:

```cpp
int main()
{
   int digout;
   float inlbs;

   cout << "Enter the input weight: ";
   cin  >> inlbs;

   if (inlbs >= 90) digout = 1111;
   if (inlbs >= 80) && (inlbs <= 90) digout = 1110;
   if (inlbs >= 70) && (inlbs <= 80) digout = 1101;
   if (inlbs >= 60) && (inlbs <= 70) digout = 1100;
   if (inlbs < 1000) digout = 1011;

   cout << "The digital output is " << digout << endl;

   return 0;
}
```

   a. Will this program produce the same output as Program 4.6?
   b. Which program is better and why?

9. The following program was written to produce the same result as Program 4.6:

```cpp
int main()
{
   int digout;
   float inlbs;

   cout << "Enter the input weight: ";
   cin  >> inlbs;

   if (inlbs < 60)
```

```
      digout = 1011;
   else if (inlbs >= 60)
      digout = 1100;
   else if (inlbs >= 70)
     digout = 1101;
   else if (inlbs >= 80)
     digout = 1110;
   else if (inlbs >= 90)
     digout = 1111;

   cout << "The digital output is " << digout << endl;

   return 0;
}
```

a. Will this program run?
b. What does this program do?
c. For what values of input pounds does this program calculate the correct digital output?

4.4 THE switch STATEMENT

The if-else chain is used in programming applications where one set of instructions must be selected from many possible alternatives. The switch statement provides an alternative to the if-else chain for cases that compare the value of an integer expression to a specific value. The general form of a switch statement is

```
switch (expression)
{    // start of compound statement
  case value_1: ◄─────────────── terminated with a colon
     statement1;
     statement2;
         .
         .
     break;
  case value_2: ◄─────────────── terminated with a colon
     statementm;
     statementn;
         .
         .
     break;
         .
         .
```

```
      case value_n: ◄─────────────── terminated with a colon
         statementw;
         statementx;
              .
              .
         break;
      default:        ◄─────────────── terminated with a colon
         statementaa;
         statementbb;
              .
   }     // end of switch and compound statement
```

The `switch` statement uses four new keywords: `switch`, `case`, `break`, and `default`. Let's see what each of these words does.

The keyword `switch` identifies the start of the `switch` statement. The expression in parentheses following this word is evaluated and the result of the expression compared to various alternative values contained within the compound statement. The expression in the `switch` statement must evaluate to an integer result or a compilation error results.

Internal to the `switch` statement, the keyword `case` is used to identify or label individual values that are compared to the value of the `switch` expression. The `switch` expression's value is compared to each of these `case` values in the order in which these values are listed until a match is found. When a match occurs, execution begins with the statement immediately following the match. Thus, as illustrated in Figure 4.6, the value of the expression determines where in the `switch` statement execution actually begins.

Any number of `case` labels may be contained within a `switch` statement, in any order. If the value of the expression does not match any of the `case` values, however, no statement is executed unless the keyword `default` is encountered. The word `default` is optional and operates the same as the last `else` in an `if-else` chain. If the value of the expression does not match any of the case values, program execution begins with the statement following the word `default`.

Once an entry point has been located by the `switch` statement, all further `case` evaluations are ignored and execution continues through the end of the compound statement unless a `break` statement is encountered. This is the reason for the `break` statement, which identifies the end of a particular `case` and causes an immediate exit from the `switch` statement. Thus, just as the word `case` identifies possible starting points in the compound statement, the `break` statement determines terminating points. If the `break` statements are omitted, all cases following the matching `case` value, including the `default` case, are executed.

Figure 4.6 The expression determines an entry point.

When writing a switch statement, you can use multiple case values to refer to the same set of statements; the default label is optional. For example, consider the following:

```
switch (number)
{
  case 1:
    cout << "Have a Good Morning\n";
    break;
  case 2:
    cout << "Have a Happy Day\n";
    break;
  case 3:
  case 4:
```

```
      case 5:
        cout << "Have a Nice Evening\n";
   }
```

If the value stored in the variable number is 1, the message `Have a Good Morning` is displayed. Similarly, if the value of number is 2, the second message is displayed. Finally, if the value of number is 3 or 4 or 5, the last message is displayed. Since the statement to be executed for these last three cases is the same, the cases for these values can be "stacked together" as shown in the example. Also, since there is no `default`, no message is printed if the value of number is not one of the listed `case` values. Although it is good programming practice to list `case` values in increasing order, this is not required by the `switch` statement. A `switch` statement may have any number of `case` values, in any order; only the values being tested for need be listed.

Program 4.7 uses a switch statement to select the arithmetic operation (addition, multiplication, or division) to be performed on two numbers depending on the value of the variable `opselect`.

Program 4.7 was run twice. The resulting display clearly identifies the case selected. The results are

```
      Please type in two numbers: 12 3
      Enter a select code:
              1 for addition
              2 for multiplication
              3 for division : 2
      The product of the numbers entered is 36
```

and:

```
      Please type in two numbers: 12 3
      Enter a select code:
              1 for addition
              2 for multiplication
              3 for division : 3
      The first number divided by the second is 4
```

In reviewing Program 4.7 notice the `break` statement in the last `case`. Although this `break` is not necessary, it is a good practice to terminate the last `case` in a `switch` statement with a `break`. This prevents a possible program error later if an additional `case` is subsequently added to the `switch` statement. With the addition of a new `case`, the `break` between `cases` becomes necessary; having the `break` in place ensures you will not forget to include it at the time of the modification.

Program 4.7

```cpp
#include <iostream.h>

int main()
{
  int opselect;
  double fnum, snum;

  cout << "Please type in two numbers: ";
  cin  >> fnum >> snum;
  cout << "Enter a select code: ";
  cout << "\n         1 for addition";
  cout << "\n         2 for multiplication";
  cout << "\n         3 for division : ";
  cin  >> opselect;

  switch (opselect)
  {
    case 1:
      cout << "The sum of the numbers entered is " << fnum+snum;
      break;
    case 2:
      cout << "The product of the numbers entered is " << fnum*snum;
      break;
    case 3:
      cout << "The first number divided by the second is " << fnum/snum;
      break;
  }      // end of switch

  cout << endl;

  return 0;
}
```

Because character data types are always converted to integers in an expression, a switch statement can also be used to "switch" based on the value of a character expression. For example, assuming that choice is a character variable, the following switch statement is valid:

```cpp
switch(choice)
{
  case 'a':
  case 'e':
  case 'i':
  case 'o':
  case 'u':
```

```
      cout << "The character in choice is a vowel\n";
      break;
   default:
      cout << "The character in choice is not a vowel\n";
      break;    // this break is optional
}    // end of switch statement
```

Exercises 4.4

1. Rewrite the following `if-else` chain using a `switch` statement:

```
if (let_grad == 'A')
  cout << "The numerical grade is between 90 and 100\n";
else if (let_grad == 'B')
  cout << "The numerical grade is between 80 and 89.9\n";
else if (let_grad == 'C')
  cout << "The numerical grade is between 70 and 79.9\n";
else if (let_grad == 'D';
  cout << "How are you going to explain this one\n";
else
{
  cout << "Of course I had nothing to do with my grade.\n";
  cout << "It must have been the professor's fault.\n";
}
```

2. Rewrite the following `if-else` chain using a `switch` statement:

```
if (factor == 1)
  pressure = 25.0
else if (factor == 2)
  pressure = 36.0
else if (factor == 3)
 pressure = 45.0
else if (factor == 4) || (factor == 5) || (factor == 6)
  pressure = 49.0
```

3. Each disk drive in a shipment of these devices is stamped with a code from 1 through 4, which indicates a drive of manufacturers as follows:

Code	Disk Drive Manufacturer
1	3M Corporation
2	Maxell Corporation
3	Sony Corporation
4	Verbatim Corporation

Write a C++ program that accepts the code number as an input and based on the value entered displays the correct disk drive manufacturer.

4. Rewrite Program 4.5 using a `switch` statement.

5. Determine why the `if-else` chain in Program 4.6 cannot be replaced with a `switch` statement.

6. Rewrite Program 4.7 using a character variable for the select code. (*Hint*: Review Section 3.4 if your program does not operate as you think it should.)

4.5 APPLICATIONS

Two major uses of C++'s if statements are to select appropriate processing paths and to prevent undesirable data from being processed at all. In this section examples of both uses are provided.

Application 1: Data Validation

An important use of C++'s if statements is to validate data by checking for clearly invalid cases. For example, a date such as 5/33/86 contains an obviously invalid day. Similarly, the division of any number by zero within a program, such as 14/0, should not be allowed. Both of these examples illustrate the need for a technique called **defensive programming**, in which the program includes code to check for improper data before an attempt is made to process it further. The defensive programming technique of checking user input data for erroneous or unreasonable data is referred to as **input data validation**.

Consider the case where we are to write a C++ program to calculate the square root and the reciprocal of a user entered number. Before calculating the square root, validate that the number is not negative, and before calculating the reciprocal, check that the number is not zero.

Step 1 Analyze the Problem

The statement of the problem requires that we accept a single number as an input, validate the entered number, and based on the validation produce two possible outputs: If the number is nonnegative we are to determine its square root and if the input number is not zero we are to determine its reciprocal.

Step 2 Develop a Solution

Since the square root of a negative number does not exist as a real number, and the reciprocal of zero cannot be taken, our program must contain input data validation statements to screen the user input data and avoid these two cases. The pseudocode describing the processing required is:

Display a program purpose message
Accept a user input number

>   *If the number is negative*
>   *print a message that the square root cannot be taken*
>   *Else*
>   *calculate and display the square root*
>   *Endif*
>   *If the number is zero then*
>   *print a message that the reciprocal cannot be taken*
>   *Else*
>   *calculate and display the reciprocal*
>   *Endif*

Step 3   Code the Solution

The C++ code corresponding to our pseudocode solution is listed in Program 4.8.

Program 4.8

```cpp
#include <iostream.h>
#include <math.h>

int main()
{
   double usenum;

   cout << "This program calculates the square root and\n"
        << "reciprocal (1/number) of a number\n"
        << "\nPlease enter a number: ";
   cin  >> usenum;
   if (usenum < 0.0)
     cout << "The square root of a negative number does not exist.\n";
   else
     cout << "The square root of " << usenum
          << " is " << sqrt(usenum) << endl;
   if (usenum == 0.0)
     cout << "The reciprocal of zero does not exist.\n";
   else
     cout << "The reciprocal of " << usenum
          << " is " <<  (1.0/usenum) << endl;

   return 0;
}
```

Program 4.8 is a rather straightforward program containing two separate (nonnested) `if` statements. The first `if` statement checks for a negative input number; if the number is negative a message indicating that the square root of a negative number cannot be taken is displayed, else the square root is taken. The second `if` statement checks whether the entered number is zero; if it is a message indicating that the reciprocal of zero cannot be taken is displayed, else the reciprocal is taken.

Step 4   Test and Correct the Program

Test values should include a positive number, and values for the limiting cases, such as a negative and zero input value. Test runs follow for two of these cases:

```
This program calculates the square root and
reciprocal (1/number) of a number

Please enter a number: 5

The square root of 5 is 2.236068
The reciprocal of 5 is 0.2
```

and

```
This program calculates the square root and
reciprocal (1/number) of a number

Please enter a number: -6

The square root of a negative number does not exist
The reciprocal of -6 is -0.166667
```

Application 2: Solving Quadratic Equations

A **quadratic equation** is an equation that has the form $ax^2 + bx + c = 0$ or that can be algebraically manipulated into this form. In this equation x is the unknown variable, and a, b, and c are known constants. Although the constants b and c can be any numbers, including zero, the value of the constant a cannot be zero (if a is zero, the equation would become a **linear equation** in x). Examples of quadratic equations are

$$5x^2 + 6x + 2 = 0$$
$$x^2 - 7x + 20 = 0$$
$$34x^2 + 16 = 0$$

In the first equation $a = 5$, $b = 6$, and $c = 2$; in the second equation $a = 1$, $b = -7$, and $c = 20$; and in the third equation $a = 34$, $b = 0$, and $c = 16$.

The real roots of a quadratic equation can be calculated using the quadratic formula as:

$$\text{root } 1 = \frac{-b + \sqrt{b^2 - 4ac}}{2a}$$

and

$$\text{root } 2 = \frac{-b - \sqrt{b^2 - 4ac}}{2a}$$

Using these equations we will write a C++ program to solve for the roots of a quadratic equation.

Step 1   Analyze the Problem

The problem requires that we accept three inputs—the coefficients a, b, and c of a quadratic equation and compute the roots of the equation using the given formulas.

Step 2   Develop a Solution

A first attempt at a solution would be to use the user-entered values of a, b, and c to calculate directly a value for each of the roots. Thus, our first solution would be

> *Display a program purpose message*
> *Accept user-input values for a, b, and c*
> *Calculate the two roots*
> *Display the values of the calculated roots*

However, this solution must be refined further to account for a number of possible input conditions. For example, if a user entered a value of 0 for both a and b, the equation is neither quadratic nor linear and has no solution (this is referred to as a degenerate case). Another possibility is that the user supplies a nonzero value for b but makes a zero. In this case the equation becomes a linear one with a single solution of $-c / b$. A third possibility is that the value of the term $b^2 - 4ac$, which is called the **discriminant,** is negative. Since the square root of a negative number cannot be taken, this case will have no real roots. Finally, when the discriminant is zero, both roots are the same (this is referred to as the repeated roots case).

Taking into account all four of these limiting cases, a refined solution for correctly determining the roots of a quadratic equation is expressed by the following pseudocode:

> *Display a program purpose message*
> *Accept user-input values for a, b, and c*
> *If a = 0 and b = 0 then*
> > *display a message saying that the equation has no solution*
> *Else if a = zero then*
> > *calculate the single root equal to −c/b*
> > *display the single root*
> *Else*
> > *calculate the discriminant*

> *If the discriminant > 0 then*
> > *solve for both roots using the given formulas*
> > *display the two roots*
> *Else if the discriminant < 0 then*
> > *display a message that there are no real roots*
> *Else*
> > *calculate the repeated root equal to $-b/(2a)$*
> > *display the repeated root*
> *Endif*
Endif

Notice in the pseudocode that we have used nested `if-else` statements. The outer `if-else` statement is used to validate the entered coefficients and determine that we have a valid quadratic equation. The inner `if-else` statement is then used to determine if the equation has two real roots (discriminant > 0), two imaginary roots (discriminant < 0), or repeated roots (discriminant = 0).

Step 3   Code the Solution

The equivalent C++ code corresponding to our pseudocode solution is listed in Program 4.9.

Step 4   Test and Correct the Program

Test values should include values for a, b, and c that result in two real roots, plus limiting values for a and b that result in either a linear equation ($a = 0$, $b \neq 0$), a degenerate equation ($a = 0$, $b = 0$), and a negative and zero discriminant. Two such test runs of Program 4.9 follow:

```
This program calculates the roots of a
   quadratic equation of the form
            2
         ax + bx + c = 0
Please enter values for a, b, and c: 1 2 -35

The two real roots are 5 and -7
```

and

```
This program calculates the roots of a
   quadratic equation of the form
            2
         ax + bx + c = 0

Please enter values for a, b, and c: 0 0 16

The equation is degenerate and has no roots.
```

Program 4.9

```cpp
#include <iostream.h>
#include <math.h>

// this program solves for the roots of a quadratic equation
int main()
{
  double a, b, c, disc, root1, root2;

  cout << "This program calculates the roots of a\n";
  cout << "   quadratic equation of the form\n";
  cout << "                2\n";
  cout << "            ax + bx + c = 0\n\n";
  cout << "Please enter values for a, b, and c: ";
  cin >>  a >>  b >> c;
  if ( a == 0.0 && b == 0.0)
    cout << "The equation is degenerate and has no roots.\n";
  else if (a == 0.0)
    cout << "The equation has the single root x = "
       << -c/b << endl;
  else
  {
    disc = pow(b,2.0) - 4 * a * c;     // calculate discriminant
    if (disc > 0.0)
    {
      disc = sqrt(disc);
      root1 = (-b + disc) / (2 * a);
      root2 = (-b - disc) / (2 * a);
      cout << "The two real roots are "
   << root1 << " and " << root2 << endl;
    }
    else if (disc < 0.0)
      cout << "Both roots are imaginary.\n";
    else
      cout << "Both roots are equal to " << -b / (2 * a) << endl;
  }

  return 0;
}
```

The first run solves the quadratic equation $x^2 + 2x - 35 = 0$, which has the real roots $x = 5$ and $x = -7$. The input data for the second run results in the equation $0x^2 + 0x + 16 = 0$. Because this degenerates into the mathematical impossibility of $16 = 0$, the program correctly identifies this as a degenerate equation. We leave it as an exercise to create test data for the other limiting cases checked for by the program.

Exercises 4.5

1. a. Write a program that accepts two real numbers from a user and a select code. If the entered select code is 1, have the program add the two previously entered numbers and display the result; if the select code is 2, the numbers should be multiplied, and if the select code is 3, the first number should be divided by the second number.

    b. Determine what the program written in Exercise 1a does when the entered numbers are 3 and 0, and the select code is 3.

    c. Modify the program written in Exercise 1a so that division by 0 is not allowed and an appropriate message is displayed when such a division is attempted.

2. a. Write a program to display the following two prompts:

```
Enter a month (use a 1 for Jan, etc.):
Enter a day of the month:
```

    Have your program accept and store a number in the variable `month` in response to the first prompt, and accept and store a number in the variable `day` in response to the second prompt. If the month entered is not between 1 and 12 inclusive, print a message informing the user that an invalid month has been entered. If the day entered is not between 1 and 31, print a message informing the user that an invalid day has been entered.

    b. What will your program do if the user types a number with a decimal point for the month? How can you ensure that your `if` statements check for an integer number?

    c. In a non-leap year February has 28 days, the months January, March, May, July, August, October, and December have 31 days, and all other months have 30 days. Using this information, modify the program written in Exercise 2a to display a message when an invalid day is entered for a user entered month. For this program ignore leap years.

3. a. The quadrant in which a line drawn from the origin resides is determined by the angle that the line makes with the positive x axis as follows:

Angle from the positive x axis	Quadrant
Between 0 and 90 degrees	I
Between 90 and 180 degrees	II
Between 180 and 270 degrees	III
Between 270 and 360 degrees	IV

Using this information, write a C++ program that accepts the angle of the line as user input and determines and displays the quadrant appropriate to the input data. (*NOTE:* If the angle is exactly 0, 90, 180, or 270 degrees the corresponding line does not reside in any quadrant but lies on an axis.)

   b. Modify the program written for Exercise 3a so that a message is displayed that identifies an angle of zero degrees as the positive *x* axis, an angle of 90 degrees as the positive *y* axis, an angle of 180 degrees as the negative *x* axis, and an angle of 270 degrees as the negative *y* axis.

4. a. All years that are evenly divisible by 400 or are evenly divisible by four and not evenly divisible by 100 are leap years. For example, since 1600 is evenly divisible by 400, the year 1600 was a leap year. Similarly, since 1988 is evenly divisible by four but not by 100, the year 1988 was also a leap year. Using this information, write a C++ program that accepts the year as user input, determines if the year is a leap year, and displays an appropriate message that tells the user if the entered year is or is not a leap year.

   b. Using the code written in Exercise 4a redo Exercise 2c such that leap years are taken into account.

5. Based on an automobile's model year and weight the state of New Jersey determines the car's weight class and registration fee using the following schedule:

Model Year	Weight	Weight Class	Registration Fee
1970 or earlier	Less than 2700 lbs	1	$16.50
	2700 to 3800 lbs	2	25.50
	More than 3800 lbs	3	46.50
1971 to 1979	Less than 2700 lbs	4	27.00
	2700 to 3800 lbs	5	30.50
	More than 3800 lbs	6	52.50
1980 or later	Less than 3500 lbs	7	19.50
	3500 or more lbs	8	52.50

Using this information write a C++ program that accepts the year and weight of an automobile and determines and displays the weight class and registration fee for the car.

6. Modify Program 4.9 so that the imaginary roots are calculated and displayed when the discriminant is negative. For this case the two roots of the equation are:

$$x_1 = \frac{-b}{2a} + \frac{\mathrm{sqrt}[-(b^2 - 4ac)]}{2a} i$$

and

$$x_2 = \frac{-b}{2a} - \frac{\text{sqrt}[-(b^2 - 4ac)]}{2a}\,i$$

where i is the imaginary number symbol for the square root of –1. (*Hint:* calculate the real and imaginary parts of each root separately.)

7. In the game of Blackjack the cards 2 through 10 are counted at their face values, regardless of suit, all face cards (jack, queen, and king) are counted as 10, and an ace is counted as either a 1 or an 11, depending on the total count of all the cards in a player's hand. The ace is counted as 11 only if the resulting total value of all cards in a player's hand does not exceed 21, else it is counted as a 1. Using this information write a C++ program that accepts three card values as inputs (a 1 corresponding to an ace, a 2 corresponding to a two, and so on), calculates the total value of the hand appropriately, and displays the value of the three cards with a printed message.

4.6 ▷ COMMON PROGRAMMING ERRORS

Three programming errors are common to C++'s selection statements.

1. Using the assignment operator, =, in place of the relational operator, ==. This can cause an enormous amount of frustration because any expression can be tested by an `if-else` statement. For example, the statement

```
if (opselect = 2)
    cout << "Happy Birthday";
else
    cout << "Good Day";
```

always results in the message `Happy Birthday` being printed, regardless of the initial value in the variable `opselect`. The reason for this is that the assignment expression `opselect = 2` has a value of 2, which is considered a true value in C++. The correct expression to determine the value in `opselect` is `opselect == 2`.

2. Letting the `if-else` statement appear to select an incorrect choice. In this typical debugging problem, the programmer mistakenly concentrates on the tested condition as the source of the problem. For example, assume that the following `if-else` statement is part of your program:

```
if (key == 'F')
{
    contemp = (5.0/9.0) * (intemp - 32.0;
    cout << "Conversion to Celsius was done";
}
```

```
else
{
  contemp = (9.0/5.0) * intemp + 32.0;
  cout << "Conversion to Fahrenheit was done";
}
```

This statement will always display `Conversion to Celsius` was done when the variable `key` contains an `F`. Therefore, if this message is displayed when you believe `key` does not contain `F`, investigation of `key`'s value is called for. As a general rule, whenever a selection statement does not act as you think it should, test your assumptions about the values assigned to the tested variables by displaying their values. If an unanticipated value is displayed, you have at least isolated the source of the problem to the variables themselves, rather than the structure of the `if-else` statement. From there you will have to determine where and how the incorrect value was obtained.

3. Using nested `if` statements without including braces to indicate the desired structure. Without braces the compiler defaults to pairing `else`s with the closest unpaired `if`s, which sometimes destroys the original intent of the selection statement. To avoid this problem and to create code that is readily adaptable to change, it is useful to write all `if-else` statements as compound statements in the form

```
if (expression)
{
  one or more statements in here
}
else
{
  one or more statements in here
}
```

By using this form, no matter how many statements are added later, the original integrity and intent of the `if` statement is maintained.

4.7 CHAPTER SUMMARY

1. Relational expressions, which are also called **conditions**, are used to compare operands. If a relational expression is true, the value of the expression is the

integer 1. If the relational expression is false, it has an integer value of 0. Relational expressions are created using the following relational operators.

Relational Operator	Meaning	Example
<	Less than	`age < 30`
>	Greater than	`height > 6.2`
<=	Less than or equal to	`taxable <= 20000`
>=	Greater than or equal to	`temp >= 98.6`
==	Equal to	`grade == 100`
!=	Not equal to	`number != 250`

2. More complex conditions can be constructed from relational expressions using C++'s logical operators, `&&` (AND), `||` (OR), and `!` (NOT).

3. An `if-else` statement is used to select between two alternative statements based on the value of an expression. Although relational expressions are usually used for the tested expression, any valid expression can be used. In testing an expression, `if-else` statements interpret a nonzero value as true and a zero value as false. The general form of an `if-else` statement is:

```
if (expression)
   statement1;
else
   statement2;
```

This is a two-way selection statement. If the expression has a nonzero value it is considered as true and `statement1` is executed; otherwise `statement2` is executed.

4. An `if-else` statement can contain other `if-else` statements. In the absence of braces, each `else` is associated with the closest preceding unpaired `if`.

5. The `if-else` chain is a multiway selection statement having the general form

```
if (expression_1)
   statement_1;
else if (expression_2)
   statement_2;
else if (expression_3)
   statement_3;
         .
         .
         .
else if (expression_m)
   statement_m;
else
   statement_n;
```

Each expression is evaluated in the order in which it appears in the chain. Once an expression is true (has a nonzero value), only the statement between that expression and the next `else if` or `else` is executed, and no further expressions are tested. The final `else` is optional, and the statement corresponding to the final `else` is only executed if none of the previous expressions is true.

6. A compound statement consists of any number of individual statements enclosed within the brace pair, { and }. Compound statements are treated as a single unit and can be used anywhere a single statement is used.

7. The switch statement is a multiway selection statement. The general form of a switch statement is

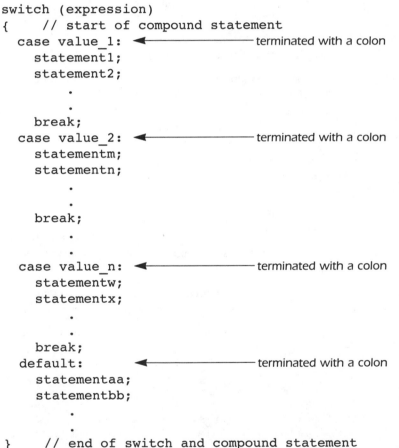

```
switch (expression)
{     // start of compound statement
  case value_1:  ◀————————————— terminated with a colon
     statement1;
     statement2;

        .
        .

     break;
  case value_2:  ◀————————————— terminated with a colon
     statementm;
     statementn;

        .
        .

     break;

        .
        .

  case value_n:  ◀————————————— terminated with a colon
     statementw;
     statementx;

        .
        .

     break;
  default:       ◀————————————— terminated with a colon
     statementaa;
     statementbb;

        .
        .

}     // end of switch and compound statement
```

For this statement the value of an integer expression is compared to a number of integer or character constants or constant expressions. Program execution is transferred to the first matching case and continues through the end of the `switch` statement unless an optional `break` statement is encountered. The cases in a `switch` statement can appear in any order and an optional `default` case can be included. The `default` case is executed if none of the other cases is matched.

4.8 CHAPTER APPENDIX: A CLOSER LOOK AT PROGRAM TESTING

In theory, a comprehensive set of test runs would reveal all possible program errors and ensure that a program will work correctly for any and all combinations of input and computed data. In practice this requires checking all possible combinations of statement execution. Due to the time and effort required, this is an impossible goal except for extremely simple programs. Let us see why this is so. Consider Program 4.10.

Program 4.10

```
#include <iostream.h>

int main()
{
  int num;

  cout << "Enter a number: ";
  cin  >> num;
  if (num == 5)
    cout << "Bingo!\n";
  else
    cout << "Bongo!\n";

  return 0;
}
```

Program 4.10 has two paths that can be traversed as the program progresses from its opening brace to its closing brace. The first path, which is executed when the input number is 5, is in the sequence

```
cout << "Enter a number";
cin  >> num;
cout << "Bingo!\n";
```

The second path, which is executed whenever any number except 5 is input, includes the sequence of instructions

```
cout << "Enter a number";
cin  >> num;
cout << "Bongo!\n";
```

To test each possible path through Program 4.10 requires two runs of the program, with a judicious selection of test input data to ensure that both paths of the if statement are exercised. The addition of one more if statement in the program increases the number of possible execution paths by a factor of two and requires four (2^2) runs of the program for complete testing. Similarly, two additional if statements increase the number of paths by a factor of four and requires eight (2^3) runs for complete testing and three additional if statements would produce a program that required sixteen (2^4) test runs.

Now consider a modestly sized application program consisting of only ten modules, each module containing five if statements. Assuming the modules are always called in the same sequence, there are 32 possible paths through each module (2 raised to the fifth power) and more than 1,000,000,000,000,000 (2 raised to the fiftieth power) possible paths through the complete program (all modules executed in sequence). The time needed to create individual test data to exercise each path and the actual computer run time required to check each path make the complete testing of such a program impossible to achieve.

The inability to fully test all combinations of statement execution sequences has led to the programming saying that "there is no error-free program." It has also led to the realization that any testing that is done should be well thought out to maximize the possibility of locating errors. At a minimum, test data should include appropriate values for input values, illegal input values that the program should reject, and limiting values that are checked by selection statements within the program.

Looking at Career Choices

Civil Engineering

The field of civil engineering is concerned primarily with large-scale structures and systems used by a community. A civil engineer designs, constructs, and operates bridges, dams, tunnels, buildings, airports, roads and other large-scale public works. Civil engineers are also responsible for the effects these large-scale systems have on society and the environment. Thus, civil engineers are involved in water resources, flood control, waste disposal, and overall urban planning. The field can be subdivided into three categories.

1. Structures. Design, construction, and operation of large-scale edifices such as dams, buildings, and roads. The properties of materials, geology, soil mechanics, and statics and dynamics are important elements of the background training. For example, how tall a building can be constructed before it will buckle under its own weight is a question involving all of these subjects.

2. Urban planning. Planning, design, and construction of transportation systems (road, railroads, river development, airports) and general land use. Surveying and mapmaking are necessary skills.

3. Sanitation. Waste treatment, water supply, and sewage systems. Fluid mechanics, hydrology, pollution control, irrigation, and economics are important considerations.

CHAPTER 5

Repetition Structures

TOPICS

5.1 INTRODUCTION
PRETEST AND POSTTEST LOOPS
FIXED-COUNT VERSUS VARIABLE-CONDITION LOOPS

5.2 while LOOPS

5.3 INTERACTIVE while LOOPS
SENTINELS
break AND continue STATEMENTS
THE NULL STATEMENT

5.4 for LOOPS

5.5 LOOP PROGRAMMING TECHNIQUES
TECHNIQUE 1: INTERACTIVE INPUT WITHIN A LOOP
TECHNIQUE 2: SELECTION WITHIN A LOOP
TECHNIQUE 3: EVALUATING FUNCTIONS OF ONE VARIABLE
TECHNIQUE 4: INTERACTIVE LOOP CONTROL

5.6 NESTED LOOPS

5.7 do while LOOPS
VALIDITY CHECKS

5.8 COMMON PROGRAMMING ERRORS

5.9 CHAPTER SUMMARY
LOOKING AT CAREER CHOICES: INDUSTRIAL ENGINEERING

The programs examined so far have illustrated the programming concepts involved in input, output, assignment, and selection capabilities. By this time you should have gained enough experience to be comfortable with these concepts and the mechanics of implementing them using C++. Many problems, however, require a repetition capability in which the same calculation or sequence of instructions is repeated, over and over, using different sets of data. Examples of such repetition include continual checking of user data entries until an acceptable entry, such as a valid password, is entered;

counting and accumulating running totals; and constant acceptance of input data and recalculation of output values that only stops upon entry of a sentinel value.

*This chapter explores the different methods that programmers use in constructing repeating sections of code and how they can be implemented in C++. More commonly, a section of code that is repeated is referred to as a **loop**, because after the last statement in the code is executed the program branches, or loops, back to the first statement and starts another repetition through the code. Each repetition is also referred to as an **iteration** or **pass through the loop.***

5.1 INTRODUCTION

The real power of a program is realized when the same type of operation must be made over and over. For example, consider Program 3.17 in Section 3.6, where the same set of instructions is repeated three times. Retyping this same set of instructions is tedious, time consuming, and subject to error. It certainly would be convenient if we could type such repeating instructions only once and then have a method of informing the program to repeat execution of the instructions three times. Such a method is available using repetitive sections of code.

Constructing a repetitive section of code requires that four elements be present. The first necessary element is a repetition statement. This **repetition statement** both defines the boundaries containing the repeating section of code and controls whether the code will be executed or not. In general there are three different forms of repetition structures, all of which are provided in C:

1. `while` structure

2. `for` structure

3. `do while` structure

Each of these structures requires a condition that must be evaluated, which is the second required element for constructing repeating sections of code. Valid conditions are identical to those used in selection statements. If the condition is true, the code is executed; otherwise, it is not.

The third required element is a statement that initially sets the condition. This statement must always be placed before the condition is first evaluated to ensure correct loop execution the first time the condition is evaluated.

Finally, there must be a statement within the repeating section of code that allows the condition to become false. This is necessary to ensure that, at some point, the repetitions stop.

Pretest and Posttest Loops

The condition being tested can be evaluated at either the beginning or the end of the repeating section of code. Figure 5.1 illustrates the case where the test occurs at the beginning of the loop. This type of loop is referred to as a **pretest loop** because the condition is tested before any statements within the loop are executed. If the condition is true, the executable statements within the loop are executed. If the initial value of the condition is false, the executable statements within the loop are never executed at all and control transfers to the first statement after the loop. To avoid infinite repetitions, the condition must be updated within the loop. Pretest loops are also referred to as **entrance-controlled loops**. Both the `while` and `for` loop structures are examples of such loops.

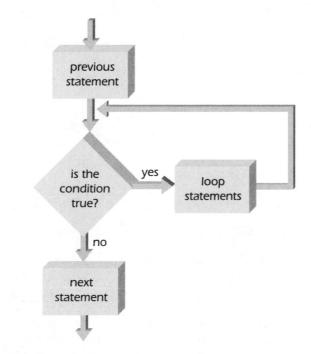

Figure 5.1 A pretest loop.

A loop that evaluates a condition at end of the repeating section of code, as illustrated in Figure 5.2, is referred to as **posttest** or **exit-controlled loop**. Such loops always execute the loop statements at least once before the condition is tested. Since the executable statements within the loop are continually executed until the condition becomes false, there always must be a statement within the loop that updates the condition and permits it to become false. The `do while` construct is an example of a posttest loop.

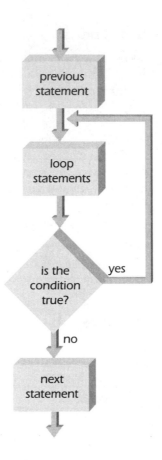

Figure 5.2 A posttest loop.

Fixed-Count versus Variable-Condition Loops

In addition to where the condition is tested (pretest or posttest), repeating sections of code are also classified as to the type of condition being tested. In a **fixed count loop**, the condition is used to keep track of how many repetitions have occurred. For example, we might want to produce a table of 10 numbers, including their squares and cubes, or a fixed design such as

```
*************************
*************************
*************************
*************************
```

In each of these cases, a fixed number of calculations is performed or a fixed number of lines are printed, at which point the repeating section of code is exited. All of C++'s repetition statements can be used to produce fixed count loops.

In many situations the exact number of repetitions is not known in advance or the items are too numerous to count beforehand. For example, when entering a large amount of experimental data we might not want to take the time to count the number of actual data items that are to be entered. In cases like this a variable condition loop is used. In a **variable condition loop** the tested condition does not depend on a count being reached, but rather on a variable that can change interactively with each pass through the loop. When a specified value is encountered, regardless of how many iterations have occurred, repetitions stop. All of C++'s repetition statements can be used to create variable condition loops.[1] In this chapter we will encounter examples of both fixed count and variable condition loops.

5.2 while **Loops**

In C++, a **while loop** is constructed using a while statement. The syntax of this statement is

>   *while (expression)*
>   *statement;*

The expression contained within parentheses is the condition tested to determine if the statement following the parentheses is executed. The expression is evaluated in exactly the same manner as that contained in an if-else statement; the difference is in how the expression is used. As we have seen, when the expression is true (has a nonzero value) in an if-else statement, the statement following the expression is executed once. In a while statement the statement following the expression is executed repeatedly as long as the expression evaluates to a nonzero value. Considering just the expression and the statement following the parentheses, the process used by the computer in evaluating a while statement is

1. Test the expression
2. If the expression has a nonzero (true) value
   a. execute the statement following the parentheses
   b. go back to step 1
else
   exit the while *statement and execute the next executable statement following the* while *statement*

Notice that step 2b forces program control to be transferred back to step 1. This transfer of control back to the start of a while statement in order to reevaluate the expression is what forms the program loop. The while statement literally loops back on itself to recheck the expression until it evaluates to zero (becomes false). This naturally means that somewhere in the loop provision must be made that permits the value of the tested expression to be altered. As we will see, this is indeed the case.

---

[1]In this C++ differs from most other languages such as BASIC, FORTRAN, and Pascal. In each of these languages the for structure (which is implemented using a DO statement in FORTRAN) can only be used to produce fixed count loops. C++'s for statement, as we will see shortly, is virtually interchangeable with its while statement.

This looping process produced by a `while` statement is illustrated in Figure 5.3. A diamond shape is used to show the two entry and two exit points required in the decision part of the `while` statement.

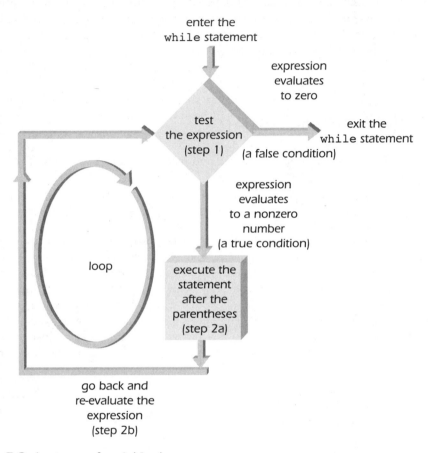

Figure 5.3 Anatomy of a `while` loop.

To make this a little more tangible, consider the relational expression `count <= 10` and the statement `cout << count;`. Using these, we can write the following valid `while` statement:

```
while (count <= 10)
    cout << count;
```

Although the above statement is valid, the alert reader will realize that we have created a situation in which the `cout` object either is called forever (or until we stop the program) or is not called at all. Let us see why this happens.

If count has a value less than or equal to 10 when the expression is first evaluated, a call to cout is made. The while statement then automatically loops back on itself and retests the expression. Since we have not changed the value stored in count, the expression is still true and another call to cout is made. This process continues forever, or until the program containing this statement is prematurely stopped by the user. However, if count starts with a value greater than 10, the expression is false to begin with and the cout object call is never made.

How do we set an initial value in count to control what the while statement does the first time the expression is evaluated? The answer, of course, is to assign values to each variable in the tested expression before the while statement is encountered. For example, the following sequence of instructions is valid:

```
count = 1;
while (count <= 10)
   cout << count;
```

Using this sequence of instructions, we have ensured that count starts with a value of 1. We could assign any value to count in the assignment statement—the important thing is to assign some value. In practice, the assigned value depends on the application.

We must still change the value of count so that we can finally exit the while statement. To do this requires an expression such as count = count + 1 to increment the value of count each time the while statement is executed. The fact that a while statement provides for the repetition of a single statement does not prevent us from including an additional statement to change the value of count. All we have to do is replace the single statement with a compound statement. For example,

```
count = 1;          // initialize count
while (count <= 10)
{
   cout << count;
   count++;          // increment count
}
```

Note that, for clarity, we have placed each statement in the compound statement on a different line. This is consistent with the convention adopted for compound statements in the last chapter. Let us now analyze the above sequence of instructions.

The first assignment statement sets count equal to 1. The while statement is then entered and the expression is evaluated for the first time. Since the value of count is less than or equal to 10, the expression is true and the compound statement is executed. The first statement in the compound statement is a call to the cout object to display the value of count. The next statement adds 1 to the value currently stored in count, making this value equal to 2. The while statement now loops back to retest the expression. Since count is still less than or equal to 10, the compound statement is again executed. This process continues until the value of count reaches 11. Program 5.1 illustrates these statements in an actual program.

Program 5.1

```
#include <iostream.h>

int main()
{
  int count;

  count = 1;                 // initialize count
  while (count <= 10)
  {
    cout << count << "   ";
    count++;                 // increment count
  }

  return 0;
}
```

The output for Program 5.1 is:

       1   2   3   4   5   6   7   8   9   10

There is nothing special about the name count used in Program 5.1. Any valid integer variable could have been used.

Before we consider other examples of the while statement two comments concerning Program 5.1 are in order. First, the statement count++ can be replaced with any statement that changes the value of count. A statement such as count = count + 2, for example, would cause every second integer to be displayed. Second, it is the programmer's responsibility to ensure that count is changed in a way that ultimately leads to a normal exit from the while. For example, if we replace the expression count++ with the expression count--, the value of count will never exceed 10 and an infinite loop will be created. An **infinite loop** is a loop that never ends; the program just keeps displaying numbers until you realize that the program is not working as you expected.

Now that you have some familiarity with the while statement, see if you can read and determine the output of Program 5.2.

Program 5.2

```
#include <iostream.h>

int main()
{
  int i;

  i = 10;
  while (i >= 1)
  {
    cout << i << "   ";
    i--;                    // subtract 1 from i
  }

  return 0;
}
```

The assignment statement in Program 5.2 initially sets the int variable i to 10. The while statement then checks to see if the value of i is greater than or equal to 1. While the expression is true, the value of i is displayed by the cout object and the value of i is decremented by 1. When i finally reaches zero, the expression is false and the program exits the while statement. Thus, the following display is obtained when Program 5.2 is run:

```
10   9   8   7   6   5   4   3   2   1
```

To illustrate the power of the while statement, consider the task of printing a table of numbers from 1 to 10 with their squares and cubes. This can be done with a simple while statement as illustrated by Program 5.3.

When Program 5.3 is run, the following display is produced:

NUMBER	SQUARE	CUBE
------	------	----
1	1	1
2	4	8
3	9	27
4	16	64
5	25	125
6	36	216
7	49	343
8	64	512
9	81	729
10	100	1000

Program 5.3

```cpp
#include <iostream.h>
#include <iomanip.h>

int main()
{
  int num;

  cout << "NUMBER     SQUARE      CUBE\n"
       << "------     ------      ----\n";

  num = 1;
  while (num < 11)
  {
    cout << setw(3) << num << "          "
         << setw(3) << num * num      << "       "
         << setw(4) << num * num * num << endl;
    num++;           // increment num
  }
  return 0;
}
```

Note that the expression used in Program 5.3 is num < 11. For the integer variable num, this expression is exactly equivalent to the expression num <= 10. The choice of which to use is entirely up to you.

If we want to use Program 5.3 to produce a table of 1000 numbers, all we do is change the expression in the while statement from i < 11 to i < 1001. Changing the 11 to 1001 produces a table of 1000 lines—not bad for a simple five-line while statement.

All the program examples illustrating the while statement are examples of fixed-count loops because the tested condition is a counter that checks for a fixed number of repetitions. A variation on the fixed-count loop can be made where the counter is not incremented by one each time through the loop, but by some other value. For example, consider the task of producing a Celsius to Fahrenheit temperature conversion table. Assume that Fahrenheit temperatures corresponding to Celsius temperatures ranging from 5 to 50 degrees are to be displayed in increments of five degrees. The desired display can be obtained with the series of statements

```
celsius = 5;      // starting Celsius value
while (celsius <= 50)
{
  fahren = (9.0/5.0) * celsius + 32.0;
  cout << celsius
       << fahren;
  celsius = celsius + 5;
}
```

As before, the while statement consists of everything from the word while through the closing brace of the compound statement. Prior to entering the while loop we have made sure to assign a value to the counter being evaluated, and there is a statement to alter the value of the counter within the loop (in increments of 5 Celsius) to ensure an exit from the while loop. Program 5.4 illustrates the use of this code in a complete program.

Program 5.4

```
#include <iostream.h>
#include <iomanip.h>

// a program to convert Celsius to Fahrenheit
int main()
{
  const int MAX_CELSIUS = 50;
  const int START_VAL = 5;
  const int STEP_SIZE = 5;
  int celsius;
  float fahren;

  cout << "DEGREES    DEGREES\n"
       << "CELSIUS   FAHRENHEIT\n"
       << "-------    ----------\n";

  celsius = START_VAL;

    // set output formats for floating point numbers only
  cout << setiosflags(ios::showpoint)
       << setprecision(2);
```

(Continued)

(Continued)

```
    while (celsius <= MAX_CELSIUS)
    {
      fahren = (9.0/5.0) * celsius + 32.0;
      cout << setw(4)   << celsius
           << setw(13) << fahren << endl;
      celsius = celsius + STEP_SIZE;
    }

    return 0;
}
```

The display obtained when Program 5.4 is executed is

| DEGREES | DEGREES |
CELSIUS	FAHRENHEIT
5	41.00
10	50.00
15	59.00
20	68.00
25	77.00
30	86.00
35	95.00
40	104.00
45	113.00
50	122.00

Exercises 5.2

1. Rewrite Program 5.1 to print the numbers 2 to 10 in increments of two. The output of your program should be

   2   4   6   8   10

2. Rewrite Program 5.3 to produce a table that starts at a Celsius value of −10 and ends with a Celsius value of 60, in increments of ten degrees.

3. **a.** For the following program determine the total number of items displayed. Also determine the first and last numbers printed.

```
# include <iostream.h>

int main()
{
   int num = 0;
   while (num <= 20)
   {
      num++;
      cout << num << " ";
   }

   return 0;
}
```

   b. Enter and run the program from Exercise 3a on a computer to verify your answers to the exercise.

   c. How would the output be affected if the two statements within the compound statement were reversed (that is, if the cout call were made before the ++n statement)?

4. Write a C++ program that converts gallons to liters. The program should display gallons from 10 to 20 in one-gallon increments and the corresponding liter equivalents. Use the relationship that 1 gallon contains 3.785 liters.

5. Write a C++ program that converts feet to meters. The program should display feet from 3 to 30 in three-foot increments and the corresponding meter equivalents. Use the relationship that there are 3.28 feet to a meter.

6. A machine purchased for $28,000 is depreciated at a rate of $4000 a year for seven years. Write and run a C++ program that computes and displays a depreciation table for seven years. The table should have the form

Year	Depreciation	End-of-YearValue	Accumulated Depreciation
1	4000	24000	4000
2	4000	20000	8000
3	4000	16000	12000
4	4000	12000	16000
5	4000	8000	20000
6	4000	4000	24000
7	4000	0	28000

7. An automobile travels at an average speed of 55 miles per hour for four hours. Write a C++ program that displays the distance driven, in miles, that the car has traveled after, 1, 2, etc., hours until the end of the trip.

8. a. An approximate conversion formula for converting Fahrenheit to Celsius temperatures is

   Celsius = (Fahrenheit – 30) / 2

   Using this formula, and starting with a Fahrenheit temperature of zero degrees, write a C++ program that determines when the approximate equivalent Celsius temperature differs from the exact equivalent value by more than four degrees. (*Hint*: Use a `while` loop that terminates when the difference between approximate and exact Celsius equivalents exceeds four degrees.)

   b. Using the approximate Celsius conversion formula given in Exercise 8a, write a C++ program that produces a table of Fahrenheit temperatures, exact Celsius equivalent temperatures, approximate Celsius equivalent temperatures, and the difference between the correct and approximate equivalent Celsius values. The table should begin at zero degrees Fahrenheit, use two-degree Fahrenheit increments, and terminate when the difference between exact and approximate values differs by more than four degrees.

9. The value of Euler's number, *e*, can be approximated using the formula

   e = 1 + 1/1! + ½! + 1/3! + 1/4! + 1/5! + · · ·

   Using this formula, write a C++ program that approximates the value of *e* using a `while` loop that terminates when the difference between two successive approximations differs by less than 10 e–9.

10. The value of sin *x* can be approximated using the formula

$$\sin\ x = x\ -\frac{x^3}{3!}+\frac{x^5}{5!}-\frac{x^7}{7!}+\frac{x^9}{9!}\cdots$$

   Using this formula, determine how many terms are needed to approximate the value returned by the intrinsic `sin()` function with an error less than 1 e–6, when *x* = 30 degrees. (*Hints*: Use a `while` loop that terminates when the difference between the value returned by the intrinsic `sin()` function and the approximation is less than 1 e–6. Also note that *x* must first be converted to radian measure and that the alternating sign in the approximating series can be determined as $(-1)*(n+1)$ where *n* is the number of terms used in the approximation.)

5.3 ▷ INTERACTIVE `while` LOOPS

Combining interactive data entry with the repetition capabilities of the `while` statement produces very adaptable and powerful programs. To understand the concept involved, consider Program 5.5, where a `while` statement is used to accept and then display four user-entered numbers, one at a time. Although it uses a very simple idea, the program highlights the flow of control concepts needed to produce more useful programs.

Program 5.5

```cpp
#include <iostream.h>
#include <iomanip.h>

int main()
{
  const int MAXNUMS = 4;
  int count;
  float num;

  cout << "\nThis program will ask you to enter "
       << MAXNUMS << " numbers.\n";
  count = 1;
  while (count <= MAXNUMS)
  {
    cout << "\nEnter a number: ";
    cin  >> num;
    cout << "The number entered is " << num;
    count++;
  }
  cout << endl;

  return 0;
}
```

The following is a sample run of Program 5.5.

```
This program will ask you to enter 4 numbers.

Enter a number: 26.2
The number entered is 26.2
Enter a number: 5
The number entered is 5
Enter a number: 103.456
The number entered is 103.456
Enter a number: 1267.89
The number entered is 1267.89
```

Let us review the program so we clearly understand how the output was produced. The first message displayed is caused by execution of the first `cout` object call. This call is outside and before the `while` statement, so it is executed once before any statement in the `while` loop.

Once the `while` loop is entered, the statements within the compound statement are executed while the tested condition is true. The first time through the compound statement, the message `Enter a number:` is displayed. The program then calls `cin`, which forces the computer to wait for a number to be entered at the keyboard. Once a number is typed and the Return or Enter key is pressed, the `cout` object displays the number. The variable `count` is then incremented by one. This process continues until four passes through the loop have been made and the value of `count` is 5. Each pass causes the message `Enter a number:` to be displayed, causes one call to `cin` to be made, and causes the message `The number entered is` to be displayed. Figure 5.4 illustrates this flow of control.

Rather than simply displaying the entered numbers, Program 5.5 can be modified to use the entered data. For example, let us add the numbers entered and display the total. To do this, we must be very careful about how we add the numbers, since the same variable, num, is used for each number entered. Because of this the entry of a new number in Program 5.5 automatically causes the previous number stored in num to be lost. Thus, each number entered must be added to the total before another number is entered. The required sequence is

> *Enter a number*
> *Add the number to the total*

How do we add a single number to a total? A statement such as `total = total + num` does the job perfectly. This is the accumulating statement introduced in Section 3.1. After each number is entered, the accumulating statement adds the number into the total, as illustrated in Figure 5.5. The complete flow of control required for adding the numbers is illustrated in Figure 5.6.

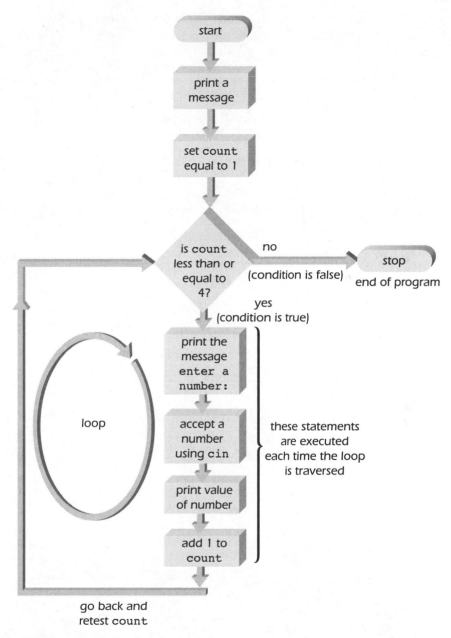

Figure 5.4 Flow of control diagram for Program 5.5.

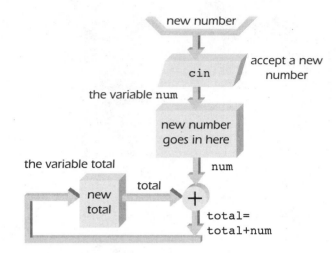

Figure 5.5 Accepting and adding a number to a total.

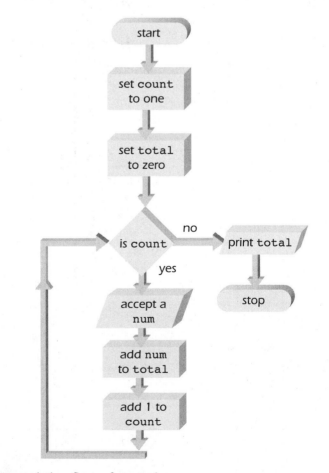

Figure 5.6 Accumulation flow of control.

In reviewing Figure 5.6, observe that we have made a provision for initially setting the total to zero before the while loop is entered. If we were to clear the total inside the while loop, it would be set to zero each time the loop was executed and any value previously stored would be erased.

Program 5.6 incorporates the necessary modifications to Program 5.5 to total the numbers entered. As indicated in the flow diagram shown in Figure 5.6, the statement total = total + num; is placed immediately after the cin statement. Putting the accumulating statement at this point in the program ensures that the entered number is immediately "captured" into the total.

Program 5.6

```cpp
#include <iostream.h>
#include <iostream.h>
#include <iomanip.h>

int main()
{
  const int MAXNUMS = 4;
  int count;
  float num, total;

  cout << "\nThis program will ask you to enter "
       << MAXNUMS << " numbers.\n";
  count = 1;
  total = 0;

  while (count <= MAXNUMS)
  {
    cout << "\nEnter a number: ";
    cin  >> num;
    total = total + num;
    cout << "The total is now " << total;
    count++;
  }

  cout << "\nThe final total is " << total << endl;

  return 0;
}
```

Let us review Program 5.6. The variable `total` was created to store the total of the numbers entered. Prior to entering the `while` statement the value of `total` is set to zero. This ensures that any previous value present in the storage location(s) assigned to the variable `total` is erased. Within the `while` loop the statement `total = total + num;` is used to add the value of the entered number into `total`. As each value is entered, it is added into the existing total to create a new total. Thus, `total` becomes a running subtotal of all the values entered. Only when all numbers are entered does `total` contain the final sum of all the numbers. After the `while` loop is finished, the last `cout` statement is used to display this sum.

Using the same data we entered in the sample run for Program 5.5, the following sample run of Program 5.6 was made:

```
This program will ask you to enter 4 numbers.

Enter a number: 26.2
The total is now 26.2
Enter a number: 5
The total is now 31.2
Enter a number: 103.456
The total is now 134.656
Enter a number: 1267.89
The total is now 1402.546

The final total is 1402.546
```

Having used an accumulating assignment statement to add the numbers entered, we can now go further and calculate the average of the numbers. Where do we calculate the average—within the `while` loop or outside of it?

In the case at hand, calculating an average requires that both a final sum and the number of items in that sum be available. The average is then computed by dividing the final sum by the number of items. At this point, we must ask, "At what point in the program is the correct sum available, and at what point is the number of items available?" In reviewing Program 5.6 we see that the correct sum needed for calculating the average is available after the `while` loop is finished. In fact, the whole purpose of the `while` loop is to ensure that the numbers are entered and added correctly to produce a correct sum. After the loop is finished, we also have a count of the number of items used in the sum. However, due to the way the `while` loop was constructed, the number in `count` (5) when the loop is finished is 1 more than the number of items (4) used to obtain the total. Knowing this, we simply subtract one from `count` before using it to determine the average. With this as background, see if you can read and understand Program 5.7.

Program 5.7

```cpp
#include <iostream.h>
#include <iomanip.h>

int main()
{
  const int MAXNUMS = 4;
  int count;
  float num, total, average;

  cout << "\nThis program will ask you to enter "
       << MAXNUMS << " numbers.\n";
  count = 1;
  total = 0;

  while (count <= MAXNUMS)
  {
    cout << "Enter a number: ";
    cin  >> num;
    total = total + num;
    count++;
  }

  count--;
  average = total / count;
  cout << "The average of the numbers is " << average << endl;

  return 0;
}
```

Program 5.7 is almost identical to Program 5.6, except for the calculation of the average. We have also removed the constant display of the total within and after the while loop. The loop in Program 5.7 is used to enter and add four numbers. Immediately after the loop is exited, the average is computed and displayed.

A sample run of Program 5.7 follows:

```
This program will ask you to enter 4 numbers.

Enter a number: 26.2
Enter a number: 5
Enter a number: 103.456
Enter a number: 1267.89

The average of the numbers is 350.6365
```

Sentinels

All of the loops we have created thus far have been examples of fixed count loops, where a counter has been used to control the number of loop iterations. By means of a `while` statement variable condition loops may also be constructed. For example, when entering grades we may not want to count the number of grades that will be entered, but would prefer to enter the grades continuously and, at the end, type in a special data value to signal the end of data input.

In computer programming, data values used to signal either the start or end of a data series are called **sentinels**. The sentinel values must, of course, be selected so as not to conflict with legitimate data values. For example, if we were constructing a program to process a student's grades, and assuming that no extra credit is given that could produce a grade higher than 100, we could use any grade higher than 100 as a sentinel value. Program 5.8 illustrates this concept. In Program 5.8 data is continuously requested and accepted until a number larger than 100 is entered. Entry of a number higher than 100 alerts the program to exit the `while` loop and display the sum of the numbers entered.

We show a sample run using Program 5.8 below. As long as grades less than or equal to 100 are entered, the program continues to request and accept additional data. When a number less than or equal to 100 is entered, the program adds this number to the total. When a number greater than 100 is entered, the loop is exited and the sum of the grades that were entered is displayed.

```
To stop entering grades, type in any number
 greater than 100.

Enter a grade: 95
Enter a grade: 100
Enter a grade: 82
Enter a grade: 101

The total of the grades is 277
```

Program 5.8

```
#include <iostream.h>

int main()
{
  const int HIGHGRADE = 100;
  float grade, total;

  grade = 0;
  total = 0;
  cout << "\nTo stop entering grades, type in any number";
  cout << "\n greater than 100.\n\n";

  while (grade <= HIGHGRADE)
  {
    total = total + grade;
    cout << "Enter a grade: ";
    cin  >> grade;
  }

  cout << "\nThe total of the grades is " << total << endl;
  return 0;
}
```

break **and** continue **Statements**

Two useful statements in connection with repetition statements are the **break** and **continue** statements. We have encountered the break statement in relation to the switch statement. The syntax of this statement is

break;

A break statement, as its name implies, forces an immediate break, or exit, from switch, while, and the for and do-while statements presented in the next sections.

For example, execution of the following while loop is immediately terminated if a number greater than 76 is entered.

```
while(count <= 10)
{
  cout << "Enter a number: ";
  cin  >> num;
  if (num > 76)
  {
    cout << "You lose!\n";
    break;        // break out of the loop
  }
  else
    cout << "Keep on trucking!\n";
 count++
}
// break jumps to here
```

The break statement violates pure structured programming principles because it provides a second, nonstandard exit from a loop. Nevertheless, the break statement is extremely useful and valuable for breaking out of loops when an unusual condition is detected. The break statement is also used to exit from a switch statement, but this is because the desired case has been detected and processed.

The continue statement is similar to the break statement but applies only to loops created with while, do-while, and for statements. The general format of a continue statement is

continue;

When continue is encountered in a loop, the next iteration of the loop is immediately begun. For while loops this means that execution is automatically transferred to the top of the loop and reevaluation of the tested expression is initiated. Although the continue statement has no direct effect on a switch statement, it can be included within a switch statement that itself is contained in a loop. Here the effect of continue is the same: the next loop iteration is begun.

As a general rule the continue statement is less useful than the break statement, but it is convenient for skipping over data that should not be processed while remaining in a loop. For example, invalid grades are simply ignored in the following section of code and only valid grades are added to the total:[2]

---

[2]The continue is not essential, however, and the selection could have been written as

```
If (grade >= 0 && grade <= 100)
{
  total = total + grade;
  count++;
}
```

```
while (count < 30)
{
  cout << "Enter a grade: ";
  cin  >> grade;
  if(grade < 0 || grade > 100)
    continue;
  total = total + grade;
  count++;
}
```

The Null Statement

All statements must be terminated by a semicolon. A semicolon with nothing preceding it is also a valid statement, called the Null statement. Thus, the statement

```
;
```

is a null statement. This is a do-nothing statement that is used where a statement is syntactically required, but no action is called for. Null statements typically are used with either `while` or `for` statements. An example of a `for` statement using a null statement is found in Program 5.10c in the next section.

Exercises 5.3

1. Rewrite Program 5.6 to compute the total of eight numbers.

2. Rewrite Program 5.6 to display the prompt:

   `Please type in the total number of data values to be added:`

   In response to this prompt, the program should accept a user-entered number and then use this number to control the number of times the `while` loop is executed. Thus, if the user enters 5 in response to the prompt, the program should request the input of five numbers and display the total after five numbers have been entered.

3. a. Write a C++ program to convert Celsius degrees to Fahrenheit. The program should request the starting Celsius value, the number of conversions to be made, and the increment between Celsius values. The display should have appropriate headings and list the Celsius value and the corresponding Fahrenheit value. Use the relationship

   $Fahrenheit = (9.0 / 5.0) * Celsius + 32.0$

   b. Run the program written in Exercise 3a on a computer. Verify that your program starts at the correct starting Celsius value and contains the exact number of conversions specified in your input data.

4. a. Modify the program written in Exercise 3 to request the starting Celsius value, the ending Celsius value, and the increment. Thus, instead of the condition checking for a fixed count, the condition will check for the ending Celsius value.

b. Run the program written in Exercise 4a on a computer. Verify that your output starts at the correct beginning value and ends at the correct ending value.

5. Rewrite Program 5.7 to compute the average of ten numbers.

6. Rewrite Program 5.7 to display the following prompt:

`Please type in the total number of data values to be averaged:`

In response to this prompt, the program should accept a user-entered number and then use this number to control the number of times the `while` loop is executed. Thus, if the user enters 6 in response to the prompt, the program should request the input of six numbers and display the average of the next six numbers entered.

7. By mistake, a programmer put the statement `average = total / count;` within the `while` loop immediately after the statement `total = total + num;` in Program 5.7. Thus, the while loop becomes

```
while (count <= MAXNUMS)
{
  cout << "Enter a number: ";
  cin  >> num;
  total = total + num;
  average = total / count;
  count++;
}
```

Will the program yield the correct result with this `while` loop?
From a programming perspective, which `while` loop is better to use and why?

8. An arithmetic series is defined by

$$a + (a + d) + (a + 2d) + (a + 3d) + \cdots + [(a + (n - 1)d)]$$

where a is the first term, d is the "common difference," and n is the number of terms to be added. Using this information write a C++ program that uses a `while` loop to both display each term and determine the sum of the arithmetic series having $a = 1$, $d = 3$, and $n = 100$. Make sure that your program displays the value it has calculated.

9. A geometric series is defined by

$$a + ar + ar^2 + ar^3 + \cdots + ar^{n-1}$$

where a is the first term, r is the "common ratio," and n is the number of terms in the series. Using this information write a C++ program that uses a `while` loop to both display each term and determine the sum of a geometric series having $a = 1$, $r = .5$, and $n = 10$. Make sure that your program displays the value it has calculated.

10. In addition to the arithmetic average of a set of numbers, both a geometric and harmonic mean can be calculated. The geometric mean of a set of n numbers x_1, $x_2, \ldots x_n$ is defined as

$$\sqrt[n]{x_1 \cdot x_2 \cdot \cdots \cdot x_n}$$

and the harmonic mean as

$$\frac{n}{\dfrac{1}{x_1} + \dfrac{1}{x_2} + \cdots + \dfrac{1}{x_n}}$$

Using these formulas, write a C++ program that continues to accept numbers until the number 999 is entered and then calculates and displays both the geometric and harmonic means of the entered numbers. (*Hint*: It will be necessary for your program to correctly count the number of values entered.)

11. **a.** The following data were collected on a recent automobile trip.

Mileage	Gallons
22495	Full tank
22841	12.2
23185	11.3
23400	10.5
23772	11.0
24055	12.2
24434	14.7
24804	14.3
25276	15.2

Write a C++ program that accepts a mileage and gallons value and calculates the miles-per-gallon (mpg) achieved for that segment of the trip. The miles-per-gallon is obtained as the difference in mileage between fill-ups divided by the number of gallons of gasoline used in the fill-up.

b. Modify the program written for Exercise 11a to additionally compute and display the cumulative mpg achieved after each fill-up. The cumulative mpg is calculated as the difference between each fill-up mileage and the mileage at the start of the trip divided by the sum of the gallons used to that point in the trip.

5.4 for LOOPS

In C++, a **for loop** is constructed using a `for` statement. This statement performs the same functions as the `while` statement, but uses a different form. In many situations, especially those that use a fixed count condition, the `for` statement format is easier to use than its `while` statement equivalent.

The syntax of the for statement is

for (initializing list; expression; altering list)
    statement;

Although the for statement looks a little complicated, it is really quite simple if we consider each of its parts separately.

Within the parentheses of the for statement are three items, separated by semicolons. Each of these items is optional and can be described individually, but the semicolons must be present.

In its most common form, the *initializing* list consists of a single statement used to set the starting (initial value) of a counter, the *expression* contains the maximum or minimum value the counter can have and determines when the loop is finished, and the *altering* list provides the increment value that is added to or subtracted from the counter each time the loop is executed. Examples of simple for statements having this form are

```
for (count = 1; count < 10; count = count + 1)
    cout << count;
```

and

```
for (i = 5; i <= 15; i = i + 2)
    cout << i;
```

In the first for statement, the counter variable is named count, the initial value assigned to count is 1, the loop continues as long as the value in count is less than 10, and the value of count is incremented by one each time through the loop. In the next for statement, the counter variable is named i, the initial value assigned to i is 5, the loop continues as long as i's value is less than or equal to 15, and the value of i is incremented by 2 each time through the loop. In both cases a cout statement is used to display the value of the counter. Another example of a for loop is given in Program 5.9.

When Program 5.9 is executed, the following display is produced:

```
NUMBER     SQUARE ROOT
------     -----------
  1          1.000000
  2          1.414214
  3          1.732051
  4          2.000000
  5          2.236068
```

The first two lines displayed by the program are produced by the two cout statements placed before the for statement. The remaining output is produced by the for loop. This loop begins with the for statement and is executed as follows.

The initial value assigned to the counter variable count is 1. Since the value in count does not exceed the final value of 5, the execution of the cout statement within the loop produces the display

```
  1          1.000000
```

Control is then transferred back to the for statement, which then increments the value in count to 2, and the loop is repeated, producing the display

```
  2          1.414214
```

Program 5.9

```cpp
#include <iostream.h>
#include <iomanip.h>
#include <math.h>

int main()
{
  const int MAXCOUNT = 5;
  int count;

  cout << "NUMBER     SQUARE ROOT\n";
  cout << "------     -----------\n";

  cout << setiosflags(ios::showpoint);
  for (count = 1; count <= MAXCOUNT; count++)
    cout << setw(4) << count
         << setw(15) << sqrt(count) << endl;

  return 0;
}
```

This process continues until the value in `count` exceeds the final value of 5, producing the complete output table. For comparison purposes, a `while` loop equivalent to the `for` loop contained in Program 5.9 is:

```cpp
cout << setiosflags(ios::showpoint);
count = 1
while (count <= MAXCOUNT)
{
    cout << setw(4) << count
         << setw(15) << sqrt(count) << endl;
    count++;
}
```

As seen in this example, the difference between the `for` and `while` loops is the placement of the initialization, condition test, and incrementing items. The grouping of these items in the `for` statement is very convenient when fixed-count loops must be constructed. See if you can determine the output produced by Program 5.10.

Program 5.10

```
#include <iostream.h>

int main()
{
  int count;

  for (count = 2; count <= 20; count = count + 2)
    cout << count << "  ";

  return 0;
}
```

Did you figure it out? The loop starts with a `count` initialized to 2, stops when `count` exceeds 20, and increments `count` in steps of 2. The output of Program 5.10 is

    2   4   6   8   10   12   14   16   18   20

The `for` statement does not require that any of the items in parentheses be present or that they be used for initializing or altering the values in the expression statements. However, the two semicolons must be present within the `for`'s parentheses. For example, the construction `for ( ; count <= 20 ;)` is valid.

If the initializing list is missing, the initialization step is omitted when the `for` statement is executed. This, of course, means that the programmer must provide the required initializations before the `for` statement is encountered. Similarly, if the altering list is missing, any expressions needed to alter the evaluation of the tested expression must be included directly within the statement part of the loop. The `for` statement only ensures that all expressions in the initializing list are executed once, before evaluation of the tested expression, and that all expressions in the altering list are executed at the end of the loop before the tested expression is rechecked. Thus, Program 5.10 can be rewritten in any of the three ways shown in Programs 5.10a, 5.10b, and 5.10c.

Program 5.10a

```
#include <iostream.h>

int main()
{
  int count;

  count = 2;    // initializer outside for statement
  for ( ; count <= 20; count = count + 2)
    cout << count << "   ";

  return 0;
}
```

Program 5.10b

```
#include <iostream.h>

int main()
{
  int count;

  count = 2;    // initializer outside for loop
  for( ; count <= 20; )
  {
    cout << count << "   ";
    count = count + 2;     // alteration statement
  }

  return 0;
}
```

Program 5.10c

```
#include <iostream.h>

int main()    // all expressions within the for's parentheses
{
  int count;

  for (count = 2; count <= 20; cout << count << "   ", count = count + 2);

  return 0;
}
```

In Program 5.10a, `count` is initialized outside the `for` statement and the first list inside the parentheses is left blank. In Program 5.10b, both the initializing list and the altering list are removed from within the parentheses. Program 5.10b also uses a compound statement within the `for` loop, with the expression-altering statement included in the compound statement. Finally, Program 5.10c has included all items within the parentheses, so there is no need for any useful statement following the parentheses. Here the null statement satisfies the syntactical requirement of one statement to follow the `for`'s parentheses.

Observe also in Program 5.10c that the altering list (last set of items in parentheses) consists of two items, and that a comma has been used to separate these items. The use of commas to separate items in both the initializing and altering lists is required if either of these two lists contains more than one item. Last, note the fact that Programs 5.10a, 5.10b, and 5.10c are all inferior to Program 5.10 and although you may encounter them in your programming career, you should not use them. Adding items other than loop control variables and their updating conditions within the `for` statement tends to confuse its readability and can introduce unwanted effects. Keeping the loop control structure "clean," as is done in Program 5.10 is important and a good programming practice.

Although the initializing and altering lists can be omitted from a `for` statement, omitting the tested expression results in an infinite loop. For example, such a loop is created by the statement

```
for (count = 2;  ; count = count + 1)
  cout << count;
```

As with the `while` statement, both `break` and `continue` statements can be used within a `for` loop. The `break` forces an immediate exit from the `for` loop, as it does in the `while` loop. The `continue`, however, forces control to be passed to the altering list in a `for` statement, after which the tested expression is reevaluated. This differs from the action of a `continue` in a `while` statement, where control is passed directly to the reevaluation of the tested expression.

Point of Information

Where to Place the Opening Braces

There are two styles of writing `for` loops that are used by professional C++ programmers. These styles only come into play when the `for` loop contains a compound statement. The style illustrated and used in the text takes the form

> *for (expression)*
> *{*
> *compound statement in here*
> *}*

An equally acceptable style that is used by many programmers places the initial brace of the compound statement on the first line. Using this style a `for` loop appears as

> *for (expression) {*
> *compound statement in here*
> *}*

The advantage of the first style is that the braces line up under one another, making it easier to locate brace pairs. The advantage of the second style is that it makes the code more compact and saves a line, permitting more code to be viewed in the same display area. Both styles are used but are almost never intermixed. Select whichever style appeals to you and be consistent in its use. As always, the indentation you use within the compound statement (two or four spaces, or a tab) should also be consistent throughout all of your programs. The combination of styles that you select becomes a "signature" for your programming work.

Figure 5.7 illustrates the internal workings of a `for` loop. As shown, when the `for` loop is completed control is transferred to the first executable statement following the loop. To avoid the necessity of always illustrating these steps, a simplified set of flowchart symbols is available for describing `for` loops. Using the fact that a `for` statement can be represented by the flowchart symbol

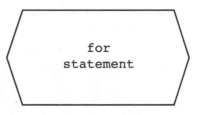

complete `for` loops can alternatively be illustrated as shown on Figure 5.8.

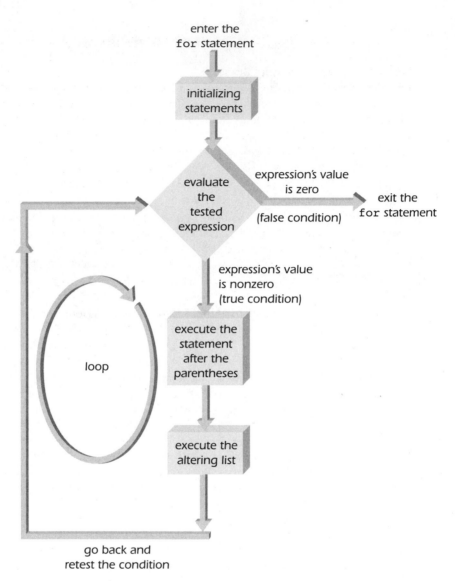

Figure 5.7 `for` loop flowchart.

Point of Information

Do You Use a for or while Loop?
A commonly asked question by beginning programmers is which loop structure should they use—a for or while loop. This is a good question because both of these loop structures are pretest loops that, in C++, can be used to construct both fixed-count and variable condition loops.

In almost all other computer languages, including Visual Basic and Pascal, the answer is relatively straight forward, because the for statement can only be used to construct fixed-count loops. Thus, in these languages for statements are used to construct fixed-count loops and while statements are generally used only when constructing variable-condition loops.

In C++, this easy distinction does not hold, since each statement can be used to create each type of loop. The answer in C++, then, is really a matter of style. Since a for and while loop are interchangeable in C++, either loop is appropriate. Some professional programmers always use a for statement for every pretest loop they create and almost never use a while statement—others always use a while statement and rarely use a for statement. Still a third group tends to retain the convention used in other languages—a for loop is generally used to create fixed-count loops and a while loop is used to create variable-condition loops. In C++ it is all a matter of style and you will encounter all three styles in your programming career.

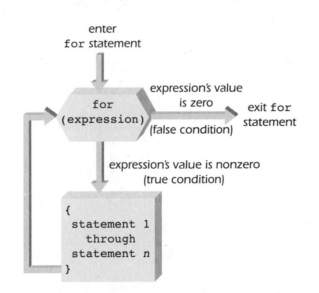

Figure 5.8 Simplified for loop flowchart.

To understand the enormous power of for loops, consider the task of printing a table of numbers from 1 to 10, including their squares and cubes, using this statement. Such a table was previously produced using a while loop in Program 5.3. You may wish to review Program 5.3 and compare it to Program 5.11 to get a further sense of the equivalence between for and while loops.

Program 5.11

```cpp
#include <iostream.h>
#include <iomanip.h>

int main()
{
  const int MAXNUMS = 10;
  int num;

  cout << "NUMBER    SQUARE    CUBE\n"
       << "------    ------    ----" << endl;

  for (num = 1; num <= MAXNUMS; num++)
    cout << setw(3) << num << "        "
         << setw(3) << num * num << "       "
         << setw(4) << num * num * num << endl;

  return 0;
}
```

When Program 5.11 is run, the display produced is

NUMBER	SQUARE	CUBE
1	1	1
2	4	8
3	9	27
4	16	64
5	25	125
6	36	216
7	49	343
8	64	512
9	81	729
10	100	1000

Simply changing the number 10 in the for statement of Program 5.11 to a 1000 creates a loop that is executed 1000 times and produces a table of numbers from 1 to 1000. As with the while statement this small change produces an immense increase in the processing and output provided by the program. Notice also that the expression num++ was used in the altering list in place of the usual num = num + 1.

Exercises 5.4

1. Write individual for statements for the following cases.
    a. Use a counter named i that has an initial value of 1, a final value of 20, and an increment of 1.
    b. Use a counter named icount that has an initial value of 1, a final value of 20, and an increment of 2.
    c. Use a counter named j that has an initial value of 1, a final value of 100, and in increment of 5.
    d. Use a counter named icount that has an initial value of 20, a final value of 1, and an increment of –1.
    e. Use a counter named icount that has an initial value of 20, a final value of 1, and an increment of –2.
    f. Use a counter named count that has an initial value of 1.0, a final value of 16.2, and an increment of 0.2.
    g. Use a counter named xcnt that has an initial value of 20.0, a final value of 10.0, and an increment of –0.

2. Determine the number of times that each for loop is executed for the for statements written for Exercise 1.

3. Determine the value in total after each of the following loops is executed.
    a.
```
total = 0;
for (i = 1; i <= 10; i = i + 1)
   total = total + 1;
```
    b.
```
total = 1;
for (count = 1; count <= 10; count = count + 1)
   total = total * 2;
```
    c.
```
total = 0
for (i = 10; i <= 15; i = i + 1)
   total = total + i;
```
    d.
```
total = 50
for (i = 1; i <=10; i = i + 1)
   total = total - i;
```
    e.
```
total = 1
for (icnt = 1; icnt <= 8; ++icnt)
   total = total * icnt;
```
    f.
```
total = 1.0
for (j = 1; j <= 5; ++j)
   total = total / 2.0;
```

4. Determine the output of the following program.

```
#include <iostream.h>

int main()
{
  int i;

  for (i = 20; i >= 0; i = i - 4)
    cout << i << " ";

  return 0;
}
```

5. Modify Program 5.11 to produce a table of the numbers zero through 20 in increments of 2, with their squares and cubes.

6. Modify Program 5.11 to produce a table of numbers from 10 to 1, instead of 1 to 10 as it currently does.

7. Write and run a C++ program that displays a table of 20 temperature conversions from Fahrenheit to Celsius. The table should start with a Fahrenheit value of 20 degrees and be incremented in values of 4 degrees. Recall that

$$Celsius = (5.0/9.0) * (Fahrenheit - 32)$$

8. Modify the program written for Exercise 7 to initially request the number of conversions to be made.

9. The expansion of a steel bridge as it is heated to a final Celsius temperature, T_F, from an initial Celsius temperature, T_0, can be approximated using the formula

$$Increase\ in\ length = a * L * (T_F - T_0)$$

where a is the coefficient of expansion (which for steel is 11.7 e–6) and L is the length of the bridge at temperature T_0. Using this formula, write a C++ program that displays a table of expansion lengths for a steel bridge that is 7365 meters long at 0 degrees Celsius, as the temperature increases to 40 degrees in 5 degree increments.

10. The probability that an individual telephone call will last less than t minutes can be approximated by the exponential probability function

$$Probability\ that\ a\ call\ lasts\ less\ than\ t\ minutes = 1 - e^{-t/a}$$

where a is the average call length and e is Euler's number (2.71828). For example, assuming that the average call length is 2 minutes, the probability that a call will last less than 1 minute is calculated as $1 - e^{-1/2} = 0.3297$.

Using this probability equation, write a C++ program that calculates and displays a list of probabilities of a call lasting less than 1 to less than 10 minutes, in one minute increments.

11. **a.** The arrival rate of customers in a busy New York bank can be estimated using the Poisson probability function

$$P(x) = \frac{\lambda^x e^{-\lambda}}{x!}$$

where x = the number of customer arrivals per minute; λ = the average number of arrivals per minute; and e = Euler's number (2.71828). For example, if the average number of customers entering the bank is three customers per minute, then λ is equal to three. Thus, the probability of one customer arriving in any one minute is

$$P(x = 1) = \frac{3^1 e^{-3}}{1!} = 0.149561$$

and the probability of two customers arriving in any one minute is

$$P(x = 2) = \frac{3^2 e^{-3}}{2!} = 0.224454$$

Using the Poisson probability function, write a C++ program that calculates and displays the probability of 1 to 10 customer arrivals in any one minute when the average arrival rate is 3 customers per minute.

b. The formula given in Exercise 11a is also applicable for estimating the arrival rate of planes at a busy airport (here, an arriving "customer" is an incoming airplane). Using this same formula modify the program written in Exercise 11a to accept the average arrival rate as an input data item. Then run the modified program to determine the probability of 0 to ten planes attempting to land in any one minute period at an airport during peak arrival times. Assume that the average arrival rate for peak arrival times is two planes per minute.

12. A golf ball is dropped from an airplane. The distance, d, the ball falls in t seconds is given by the equation $d = (½)gt^2$, where g is the acceleration due to gravity and is equal to 32 ft/sec². Using this information, write and run a C++ program that displays the distance fallen in each one second interval for ten seconds and the total distance the golf ball falls at the end of each interval. The output should complete the following table:

TIME	DISTANCE IN CURRENT INTERVAL	TOTAL DISTANCE
0	0.0	0.0
1	16.0	16.0
.	.	.
.	.	.
.	.	.
10	.	.

13. Assume the airplane in Exercise 12 is flying at a height of 50,000 feet. Modify the program written for Exercise 12 to determine how long it will take the ball to reach the ground. In order to increase the accuracy of your result without an undue number of calculations, decrease the time interval from 1 second to 0.1 second as the ball nears the ground.

14. The Fibonacci sequence is 0, 1, 1, 2, 3, 5, 8, 13, ... where the first two terms are 0 and 1, and each term thereafter is the sum of the two preceding terms; that is $Fib[n] = Fib[n - 1] + Fib[n - 2]$. Using this information, write a C++ program that calculates the nth number in a Fibonacci sequence, where n is interactively entered into the program by the user. For example, if $n = 6$, the program should display the value 5.

5.5 LOOP PROGRAMMING TECHNIQUES

In this section we present four common programming techniques associated with pretest (for and while) loops. All of these techniques are common knowledge to experienced programmers.

Technique 1: Interactive Input within a Loop

In Section 5.2 we presented the effect of including a cin statement within a while loop. Interactively entering data within a loop is a general technique that is equally applicable to for loops. For example, in Program 5.12 a cin statement is used to allow a user to interactively input a set of numbers. As each number is input, it is added to a total. When the for loop is exited, the average is calculated and displayed.

The for statement in Program 5.12 creates a loop that is executed four times. The user is prompted to enter a number each time through the loop. After each number is entered, it is immediately added to the total. Notice that total is initialized to zero as part of the initializing list of the for statement is executed. The loop in Program 5.12 is executed as long as the value in count is less than or equal to four and is terminated when count becomes five (the increment to five, in fact, is what causes the loop to end). The output produced by Program 5.12 is essentially the same as Program 5.7.

Program 5.12

```cpp
#include <iostream.h>

// This program calculates the average of MAXCOUNT
// user-entered numbers
int main()
{

  const int MAXCOUNT = 4;
  int count;
  float num, total, average;

  total = 0.0;

  for (count = 0; count < MAXCOUNT; count++)
  {
    cout << "Enter a number: ";
    cin  >> num;
    total = total + num;
  }

  average = total / MAXCOUNT;
  cout << "The average of the data entered is "
       << average << endl;
  return 0;
}
```

Technique 2: Selection within a Loop

Another common programming technique is to use either a `for` or `while` loop to cycle through a set of numbers and select those numbers that meet one or more criteria. For example, assume that we want to find both the positive and negative sum of a set of numbers. The criteria here is whether the number is positive or negative, and the logic for implementing this program is given by the pseudocode

> *While the loop condition is true*
>   *Enter a number*
>   *If the number is greater than zero*
>   *add the number to the positive sum*
>   *Else*
>   *add the number to the negative sum*
>   *Endif*
> *Endwhile*

Program 5.13 describes this algorithm in C++ for a fixed count loop where five numbers are to be entered.

Program 5.13

```cpp
#include <iostream.h>

// this program computes the positive and negative sums of a set
// of MAXNUMS user entered numbers
int main()
{
  const int MAXNUMS = 5;
  int i;
  float usenum, postot, negtot;

  postot = 0; // this initialization can be done in the declaration
  negtot = 0; // this initialization can be done in the declaration

  for (i = 1; i <= MAXNUMS; i++)
  {
    cout << "Enter a number (positive or negative) : ";
    cin  >> usenum;
    if (usenum > 0)
      postot = postot + usenum;
    else
      negtot = negtot + usenum;
  }
  cout << "The positive total is " << postot << endl;
  cout << "The negative total is " << negtot << endl;

  return 0;
}
```

The following is a sample run using Program 5.13.

```
Enter a number (positive or negative) : 10
Enter a number (positive or negative) : -10
Enter a number (positive or negative) : 5
Enter a number (positive or negative) : -7
Enter a number (positive or negative) : 11
The positive total is 26.000000
The negative total is -17.000000
```

Technique 3: Evaluating Functions of One Variable

Loops can be conveniently constructed to determine and display the values of a single variable mathematical function for a set of values over any specified interval. For example, assume that we want to know the values of the function

$$y = 10x^2 + 3x - 2$$

for x between 2 and 6. Assuming that x has been declared as an integer variable, the following `for` loop can be used to calculate the required values.

```
for (x = 2; x <= 6; x++)
{
    y = 10 * pow(x,2) + 3 * x - 2;
    cout << setw(4) << x
         << setw(11) << y << endl;
}
```

For this loop we have used the variable x as both the counter variable and the unknown (independent variable) in the function. For each value of x from two to five a new value of y is calculated and displayed. This `for` loop is contained within Program 5.14, which also displays appropriate headings for the values printed.

Program 5.14

```cpp
#include <iostream.h>
#include <iomanip.h>
#include <math.h>

int main()
{
  int x, y;

  cout << "x value   y value\n"
       << "-------   --------" << endl;
  for (x = 2; x <= 6; ++x)
  {
    y = 10 * pow(x,2) + 3 * x - 2;
    cout << setw(4) << x
         << setw(11) << y << endl;
  }

  return 0;
}
```

The following is displayed when Program 5.14 is executed:

```
x value     y value
-------     --------
   2           44
   3           97
   4          170
   5          263
   6          376
```

Two items are of importance here. The first is that any equation with one unknown can be evaluated using a single for or an equivalent while loop. The method requires substituting the desired equation into the loop in place of the equation used in Program 5.14, and adjusting the counter values to match the desired solution range.

The second item of note is that we are not constrained to using integer values for the counter variable. For example, by specifying a noninteger increment, solutions for fractional values can be obtained. This is shown in Program 5.15, where the equation $y = 10x^2 + 3x - 2$ is evaluated in the range $x = 2$ to $x = 6$ in increments of 0.5.

Program 5.15

```cpp
#include <iostream.h>
#include <iomanip.h>
#include <math.h>

int main()
{
  float x, y;

  cout << "x value       y value\n";
       << "--------     ----------" << endl;
  cout << setiosflags(ios::fixed)
       << setiosflags(ios::showpoint)
       << setprecision(6);
  for (x = 2.0; x <= 6.0; x = x + 0.5)
  {
    y = 10.0 * pow(x,2.0) + 3.0 * x - 2.0;
    cout << setw(7) <<   x
         << setw(14) << y << endl;
  }

  return 0;
}
```

Notice that x and y have been declared as floating point variables in Program 5.15 to allow these variables to take on fractional values. The following is the output produced by this program.

```
x value          y value
--------         ----------
2.000000         44.000000
2.500000         68.000000
3.000000         97.000000
3.500000        131.000000
4.000000        170.000000
4.500000        214.000000
5.000000        263.000000
5.500000        317.000000
6.000000        376.000000
```

Technique 4: Interactive Loop Control

Values used to control a loop may be set using variables rather than constant values. For example, the four statements

```
i = 5;
j = 10;
k = 1;
for (count = i; count <= j; count = count + k)
```

produce the same effect as the single statement

```
for (count = 5; count <= 10; count = count + 1)
```

Similarly, the statements

```
i = 5;
j = 10;
k = 1;
count = i;
while (count <= j)
  count = count + k;
```

produce the same effect as the following `while` loop

```
count = 5;
while (count <= 10)
  count = count + 1;
```

The advantage of using variables in the initialization, condition, and altering expressions is that it allows us to assign values for these expressions external to either the `for` or while statement. This is especially useful when a cin statement is used to set the actual values. To make this a little more tangible, consider Program 5.16.

Program 5.16

```cpp
#include <iostream.h>
#include <iomanip.h>

// this program displays a table of numbers, their squares and cubes
// starting from the number 1. The final number in the table is
// input by the user

int main()
{
  int num, final;

  cout << "Enter the final number for the table: ";
  cin  >> final;

  cout << "NUMBER SQUARE CUBE\n";
  cout << "------ ------ ----\n";

  for (num = 1; num <= final; num++)
    cout << setw(3) << num
         << setw(8) << num*num
         << setw(7) << num*num*num << endl;

  return 0;
}
```

In Program 5.16, we have used a variable to control the condition (middle) expression. Here a cin statement has been placed before the loop to allow the user to decide what the final value should be. Notice that this arrangement permits the user to set the size of the table at run time, rather than having the programmer set the table size at compile time. This also makes the program more general, since it now can be used to create a variety of tables without the need for reprogramming and recompiling.

Exercises 5.5

1. **cin within a loop:** Write and run a C++ program that accepts six Fahrenheit temperatures, one at a time, and converts each value entered to its Celsius equivalent before the next value is requested. Use a `for` loop in your program. The conversion required is *Celsius = (5.0/9.0) · (Fahrenheit – 32)*.

2. **cin within a loop:** Write and run a C++ program that accepts 10 individual values of gallons, one at a time, and converts each value entered to its liter equivalent before the next value is requested. Use a `for` loop in your program. Use the fact that there are 3.785 liters in one gallon.

3. **Interactive loop control:** Modify the program written for Exercise 2 to initially request the number of data items that will be entered and converted.

4. **Interactive loop control:** Modify Program 5.13 so that the number of entries to be input is specified by the user when the program is executed.

5. **Selection:** Modify Program 5.13 so that it displays the average of the positive and negative numbers. (*Hint:* Be careful not to count the number zero as a negative number.) Test your program by entering the numbers 17, –10, 19, 0, –4. The positive average displayed by your program should be 18 and the negative average, –7.

6. **a. Selection:** Write a C++ program that selects and displays the maximum value of five numbers that are to be entered when the program is executed. (*Hint:* Use a `for` loop with both a `cin` and `if` statement internal to the loop.)
   b. Modify the program written for Exercise 6a so that it displays both the maximum value and the position in the input set of numbers where the maximum occurs.

7. **Selection:** Write a C++ program that selects and displays the first 20 integer numbers that are evenly divisible by 3.

8. **Selection:** A child's parents promised to give the child $10 on her 12th birthday and double the gift on every subsequent birthday until the gift exceeded $1000. Write a C++ program to determine how old the child will be when the last amount is given, and the total amount received.

9. **Mathematical functions:** Modify Program 5.15 to produce a table of y values for the following:
   a. $y = 3x^5 - 2x^3 + x$
      for x between 5 and 10 in increments of 0.2

   b. $y = 1 + x + \dfrac{x^2}{2} + \dfrac{x^3}{6} + \dfrac{x^4}{24}$
      for x between 1 and 3 in increments of 0.1
   c. $y = 2e^{0.8t}$ for t between 4 and 10 in increments of 0.2

10. **Mathematical Functions:** A model of worldwide population, in billions of people, is given by the equation

    $$Population = 4.88(1 + e^{0.02t})$$

    where t is the time in years ($t = 0$ represents January 1985 and $t = 1$ represents January 1986). Using this formula, write a C++ program that displays a yearly population table for the years January 1994 though January 2005.

11. **Mathematical Functions:** The x and y coordinates, as a function of time, t, of a projectile fired with an initial velocity v at an angle of θ with respect to the ground is given by:

    $$x = v\, t\, \cos(\theta)$$
    $$y = v\, t\, \sin(\theta)$$

    Using these formulas, write a C++ program that displays a table of x and y values for a projectile fired with an initial velocity of 500 ft/sec at an angle of 22.8 degrees. (*Hint:* Remember to convert to radian measure.) The table should contain values corresponding to the time interval 0 to 10 seconds in increments of $\frac{1}{2}$ seconds.

5.6 ▷ NESTED LOOPS

In many situations it is convenient to use a loop contained within another loop. Such loops are called **nested loops**. A simple example of a nested loop is

```
for(i = 1; i <= 5; i++)          // start of outer loop
{
   cout << "\ni is now " << i << endl;

   for(j = 1; j <= 4; j++)       // start of inner loop
      cout << "  j = " << j;      // end of inner loop
}                                 // end of outer loop
```

The first loop, controlled by the value of i, is called the *outer loop*. The second loop, controlled by the value of j, is called the *inner loop*. Notice that all statements in the inner loop are contained within the boundaries of the outer loop and that we have used a different variable to control each loop. For each single trip through the outer loop, the inner loop runs through its entire sequence. Thus, each time the i counter increases by 1, the inner for loop executes completely. This situation is illustrated in Figure 5.9.

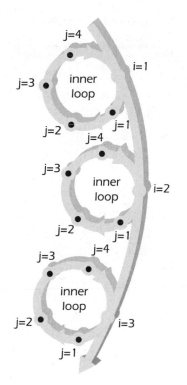

Figure 5.9 For each `i`, `j` loops.

Program 5.17 includes the preceding code in a working program.

The output of a sample run of Program 5.17 is

```
i is now 1
   j = 1   j = 2   j = 3   j = 4
i is now 2
   j = 1   j = 2   j = 3   j = 4
i is now 3
   j = 1   j = 2   j = 3   j = 4
i is now 4
   j = 1   j = 2   j = 3   j = 4
i is now 5
   j = 1   j = 2   j = 3   j = 4
```

Program 5.17

```cpp
#include <iostream.h>

int main()
{
  const int MAXI = 5;
  const int MAXJ = 4;
  int i, j;

  for(i = 1; i <= MAXI; i++)     // start of outer loop <----+
  {                              //                          |
    cout << "\ni is now " << i << endl;  //                  |
                                 //                          |
    for(j = 1; j <= MAXJ; j++)   // start of inner loop      |
      cout << "  j = " << j;     // end of inner loop        |
  }                              // end of outer loop  <-----+

  cout << endl;

  return 0;
}
```

To illustrate the usefulness of a nested loop, we will use one to compute the average grade for each student in a class of 20 students. Each student has taken four exams during the course of the semester. The final grade is calculated as the average of these examination grades. The pseudocode describing how this computation can be done is

> *For 20 times*
> > *Set the student grade total to zero*
> > *For 4 times*
> > > *input a grade*
> > > *add the grade to the total*
> > *Endfor // end of inner for loop*
> > *Calculate student's average grade*
> > *Print the student's average grade*
> *Endfor // end of outer for loop*

As described by the pseudocode, an outer loop consisting of 20 passes will be used to compute the average grade for each student. The inner loop will consist of 4 passes. One examination grade is entered in each inner loop pass. As each grade is entered it is added to the total for the student, and at the end of the loop the average is calculated and displayed.

Since both outer and inner loops are fixed count loops of 20 and 4, respectively, we will use `for` statements to create these loops. Program 5.18 provides the C++ code corresponding to the pseudocode.

Program 5.18

```cpp
#include <iostream.h>

int main()
{

  const int NUMGRADES = 4;
  const int NUMSTUDENTS = 20;
  int i, j;
  float grade, total, average;

  for (i = 1; i <= NUMSTUDENTS; i++) // start of outer loop
  {
    total = 0;                        // clear the total for this student
    for (j = 1; j <= NUMGRADES; j++) // start of inner loop
    {
      cout << "Enter an examination grade for this student: ";
      cin  >> grade;
      total = total + grade;          // add the grade into the total
    }                                 // end of the inner for loop
    average = total / NUMGRADES;      // calculate the average
    cout << "\nThe average for student " << i
         << " is " << average << "\n\n";
  }                                   // end of the outer for loop

  return 0;
}
```

In reviewing Program 5.18, pay particular attention to the initialization of `total` within the outer loop, before the inner loop is entered. `total` is initialized 20 times, once for each student. Also notice that the average is calculated and displayed immediately after the inner loop is finished. Since the statements that compute and print the average are also contained within the outer loop, 20 averages are calculated and displayed. The entry and addition of each grade within the inner loop use techniques we have seen before, which should now be familiar to you.

Exercises 5.6

1. Four experiments are performed, each experiment consisting of six test results. The results for each experiment are given below. Write a program using a nested loop to compute and display the average of the test results for each experiment.

   1st experiment results: 23.2 31 16.9 27 25.4 28.6
   2nd experiment results: 34.8 45.2 27.9 36.8 33.4 39.4
   3rd experiment results: 19.4 16.8 10.2 20.8 18.9 13.4
   4th experiment results: 36.9 39 49.2 45.1 42.7 50.6

2. **a.** Modify the program written for Exercise 1 so that the number of test results for each experiment is entered by the user. Write your program so that a different number of test results can be entered for each experiment.
   b. Rewrite the program written for Exercise 2a to eliminate the inner loop. To do this, you will have to input six results for each experiment rather than one at a time.

3. **a.** An electrical manufacturer tests five generators by measuring their output voltages at three different times. Write a C++ program that uses a nested loop to enter each generator's test results and then computes and displays the average voltage for each generator. Assume the following generator test results:

   1st generator: 122.5 122.7   123.0
   2nd generator: 120.2 127.0   125.1
   3rd generator: 121.7 124.9   126.0
   4th generator: 122.9 123.8   126.7
   5th generator: 121.5 124.7   122.6

   b. Modify the program written for Exercise 3a to calculate and display the average voltage for all the generators. (*Hint:* Use a second variable to store the total of all the generator's voltages.)

4. Rewrite the program written for Exercise 3a to eliminate the inner loop. To do this, you will have to input three voltages for each generator rather than one at a time. Each voltage must be stored in its own variable name before the average is calculated.

5. Write a program that calculates and displays values for y when

   $$y = xz/(x - z)$$

   Your program should calculate y for values of x ranging between 1 and 5 and values of z ranging between 2 and 6. The x variable should control the outer loop and be incremented in steps of 1 and z should be incremented in steps of 1. Your program should also display the message Function Undefined when the x and z values are equal.

6. Assembly languages for some microprocessors do not have a multiply operation. While there are sophisticated algorithms for performing multiplication in such cases, a simple method multiplies by repeated addition. In this case the efficiency

of the algorithm can be increased by using nested loops. For example, to multiply a number by twelve, first add the number three times and then add the result four times. This requires only seven additions as opposed to twelve. Using this information write a C++ program that multiplies 33, 47, and 83 by 1001 using a nest of three loops and then displays the result. (*Hint:* $1001 = 7 \cdot 11 \cdot 13$)

5.7 do while **Loops**

Both the `while` and `for` statements evaluate an expression at the start of the repetition loop; as such they are always used to create pretest loops. Posttest loops, which are also referred to as exit-controlled loops can also be constructed in C++. The basic structure of such a loop, which is referred to as a do while loop is illustrated in Figure 5.10. Notice that a do while loop continues iterations through the loop while the condition is true and exits the loop when the condition is false.

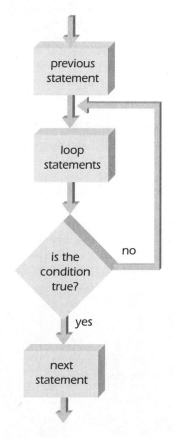

Figure 5.10 do while *loop structure.*

In C++, a posttest do while loop is created using a do statement. As its name implies, this statement allows us to do some statements before an expression is evaluated at the end of the loop. The general form of C++'s do statement is

> *do*
> *statement;*
> *while (expression);* ◄─────────── don't forget the final **;**

As with all C++ programs, the single statement in the do may be replaced with a compound statement. A flow-control diagram illustrating the operation of the do statement is shown in Figure 5.11.

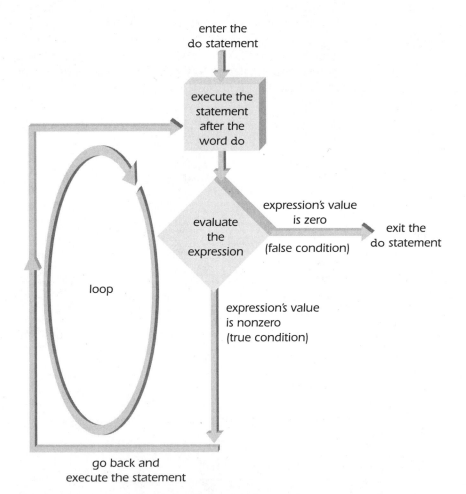

Figure 5.11 The do statement's flow of control.

As illustrated, all statements within the do statement are executed at least once before the expression is evaluated. Then, if the expression has a nonzero value, the statements are executed again. This process continues until the expression evaluates to zero (becomes false). For example, consider the following do statement:

```
do
{
  cout << "\nEnter a price: ";
  cin  >> price;
  if (abs(price - SENTINEL) < 0.0001)
    break;
  salestax = RATE * price;
  cout << setiosflags(ios::showpoint)
       << setprecision(2)
       << "The sales tax is $ " << salestax;
}
while (price != SENTINEL);
```

Observe that the prompt and cin statement are included within the loop because the tested expression is evaluated at the end of the loop.

As with all repetition statements, the do statement can always replace or be replaced by an equivalent while or for statement. The choice of which statement to use depends on the application and the style preferred by the programmer. In general, the while and for statements are preferred because they clearly let anyone reading the program know what is being tested "right up front" at the top of the program loop.

Validity Checks

The do statement is particularly useful in filtering user-entered input and providing data validation checks. For example, assume that an operator is required to enter a valid customer identification number between the numbers 1000 and 1999. A number outside this range is to be rejected and a new request for a valid number made. The following section of code provides the necessary data filter to verify the entry of a valid identification number:

```
do
{
  cout << "\nEnter an identification number: ";
  cin  >> id_num;
}
while (id_num < 1000 || id_num > 1999);
```

Here, a request for an identification number is repeated until a valid number is entered. This section of code is "bare bones" in that it neither alerts the operator to the cause of the new request for data nor allows premature exit from the loop if a valid identification number cannot be found. An alternative removing the first drawback is

```
do
{
  cout << "\nEnter an identification number: ";
  cin  >> id_num;
  if (id_num < 1000 || id_num > 1999)
  {
    cout << "An invalid number was just entered\n";
    cout << "Please check the ID number and re-enter\n";
  }
  else
    break;     // break if a valid id num was entered
} while(1);   // this expression is always true
```

Here we have used a `break` statement to exit from the loop. Since the expression being evaluated by the `do` statement is always 1 (true), an infinite loop has been created that is only exited when the `break` statement is encountered.

Exercises 5.7

1. a. Using a do statement, write a program to accept a grade. The program should request a grade continuously as long as an invalid grade is entered. An invalid grade is any grade less than 0 or greater than 100. After a valid grade has been entered, your program should display the value of the grade entered.

   b. Modify the program written for Exercise 1a so that the user is alerted when an invalid grade has been entered.

   c. Modify the program written for Exercise 1b so that it allows the user to exit the program by entering the number 999.

   d. Modify the program written for Exercise 1b so that it automatically terminates after five invalid grades are entered.

2. a. Write a program that continuously requests a grade to be entered. If the grade is less than 0 or greater than 100, your program should print an appropriate message informing the user that an invalid grade has been entered, else the grade should be added to a total. When a grade of 999 is entered the program should exit the repetition loop and compute and display the average of the valid grades entered.

   b. Run the program written in Exercise 2a on a computer and verify the program using appropriate test data.

3. a. Write a program to reverse the digits of a positive integer number. For example, if the number 8735 is entered, the number displayed should be 5378. (*Hint:* Use a do statement and continuously strip off and display the units digit of the number. If the variable num initially contains the number entered, the units digit is obtained as (num % 10). After a units digit is displayed, dividing the number by 10 sets up the number for the next iteration. Thus, (8735 % 10) is 5 and

(8735 / 10) is 873. The do statement should continue as long as the remaining number is not zero.

b. Run the program written in Exercise 3a on a computer and verify the program using appropriate test data.

4. Repeat any of the exercises in Section 5.3 using a do statement rather than a for statement.

5. Given a number n, and an approximation for its square root, a closer approximation to actual square root can be obtained using the formula:

$$new\ approximation = \frac{(n\ /\ previous\ approximation) + previous\ approximation}{2}$$

Using this information, write a C++ program that prompts the user for a number and an initial guess at its square root. Using this input data your program should calculate an approximation to the square root that is accurate to 0.00001 (*Hint:* Stop the loop when the difference between two approximation is less than 0.00001.)

6. Here is a challenging problem for those who know a little calculus. The Newton–Raphson method can be used to find the roots of any equation $y(x) = 0$. In this method the $(i + 1)$st approximation, x_{i+1}, to a root of $y(x) = 0$ is given in terms of the ith approximation, x_i, by the formula

$x_{i+1} = x_i - y(x_i)\ /\ y'(x_i)$

For example, if $y(x) = 3x^2 + 2x - 2$, then $y'(x) = 6x + 2$, and the roots are found by making a reasonable guess for a first approximation x_1 and iterating using the equation

$x_{i+1} = x_i - (3x_i^2 + 2x_i - 2)\ /\ (6x_i + 2)$

a. Using the Newton–Raphson method, find the two roots of the equation $3x^2 + 2x - 2 = 0$. (*Hint:* There is one positive root and one negative root.)

b. Extend the program written for Exercise 6a so that it will find the roots of any function $y(x) = 0$, when the function for $y(x)$ and the derivative of $y(x)$ are placed in the code.

5.8 COMMON PROGRAMMING ERRORS

Six errors are commonly made by beginning C++ programmers when using repetition statements. The most troublesome of these for new programmers is the "off by one" error, where the loop executes either one too many or one too few times than was intended. For example, the loop created by the statement for(i = 1; i < 11; i++) executes ten times, not eleven, even though the number 11 is used in the statement. Thus, an equivalent loop can be constructed using the statement for(i = 1; i <= 10; i ++). However, if the loop is started with an initial value of i = 0, using the statement for(i = 0; i < 11; i++), the loop will be traversed 11 times, as will a loop constructed with the statement for(i = 0; i <= 10; i++). Thus, in constructing loops, you must pay particular attention to both initial and final conditions used to control the loop to ensure that number of loop traversals is not off by one too many or one too few executions.

The next two errors pertain to the tested expression, and have already been encountered with the `if` and `switch` statements. The first is the inadvertent use of the assignment operator, =, for the equality operator, ==, in the tested expression. An example of this error is typing the assignment expression a = 5 instead of the desired relational expression a==5. Since the tested expression can be any valid C++ expression, including arithmetic and assignment expressions, this error is not detected by the compiler.

As with the `if` statement, repetition statements should not use the equality operator, ==, when testing floating-point or double-precision operands. For example, the expression `fnum == 0.01` should be replaced by a test requiring that the absolute value of `fnum - 0.01` be less than an acceptable amount. The reason for this is that all numbers are stored in binary form. Using a finite number of bits, decimal numbers such as 0.01 have no exact binary equivalent, so that tests requiring equality with such numbers can fail.

The next two errors are particular to the `for` statement. The most common is to place a semicolon at the end of the `for`'s parentheses, which frequently produces a `do-nothing` loop. For example, consider the statements

```
for(count = 0; count < 10; count++);
    total = total + num;
```

Here the semicolon at the end of the first line of code is a null statement. This has the effect of creating a loop that is executed 10 times with nothing done except the incrementing and testing of `count`. This error tends to occur because C++ programmers are used to ending most lines with a semicolon.

The next error occurs when commas are used to separate the items in a `for` statement instead of the required semicolons. An example of this is the statement

```
for (count = 1, count < 10, count++)
```

Commas must be used to separate items within the initializing and altering lists, but semicolons must be used to separate these lists from the tested expression.

The last error occurs when the final semicolon is omitted from the `do` statement. This error is usually made by programmers who have learned to omit the semicolon after the parentheses of a `while` statement and carry over this habit when the reserved word `while` is encountered at the end of a `do` statement.

5.9 ▷ CHAPTER SUMMARY

1. A section of repeating code is referred to as a *loop*.

The loop is controlled by a repetition statement that tests a condition to determine whether the code will be executed. Each pass through the loop is referred to as a *repetition* or *iteration*. The tested condition must always be explicitly set prior to its first evaluation by the repetition statement. Within the loop there must always be a statement that permits altering of the condition so that the loop, once entered, can be exited.

2. There are three basic type of loops:

a. `while`

b. `for`

c. `do while`

The `while` and `for` loops are *pretest* or *entrance controlled loops*. In this type of loop the tested condition is evaluated at the beginning of the loop, which requires that the tested condition be explicitly set prior to loop entry. If the condition is true, loop repetitions begin; otherwise the loop is not entered. Iterations continue as long as the condition remains true. In C++, `while` and `for` loops are constructed using `while` and `for` statements, respectively.

The `do while` loop is a *posttest* or *exit controlled loop*, where the tested condition is evaluated at the end of the loop. This type of loop is always executed at least once. As long as the tested condition remains true, `do while` loops continue to execute.

3. Loops are also classified as to the type of tested condition. In a *fixed count loop*, the condition is used to keep track of how many repetitions have occurred. In a *variable condition loop* the tested condition is based on a variable that can change interactively with each pass through the loop.

4. In C++, a `while` loop is constructed using a `while` statement. The most commonly used form of this statement is

while (expression)
{
   statements;
}

The expression contained within parentheses is the condition tested to determine if the statement following the parentheses, which is generally a compound statement, is executed. The expression is evaluated in exactly the same manner as that contained in an `if-else` statement; the difference is how the expression is used. In a `while` statement the statement following the expression is executed repeatedly as long as the expression retains a nonzero value, rather than just once, as in an `if-else` statement. An example of a `while` loop is

```
count = 1;                    // initialize count
while (count <= 10)
{
  cout << count << "  ";
  count++;                    // increment count
}
```

The first assignment statement sets `count` equal to 1. The `while` statement is then entered and the expression is evaluated for the first time. Since the value of `count` is less than or equal to 10, the expression is true and the compound statement is executed. The first statement in the compound statement uses the `cout` object to display the value of `count`. The next statement adds 1 to the value currently stored in `count`, making this value equal to 2. The `while` statement now loops back to retest the expression. Since `count` is still less than or equal to 10, the compound statement is again executed. This process continues until the value of `count` reaches 11.

The `while` statement always checks its expression at the top of the loop. This requires that any variables in the tested expression must have values assigned before the `while` is encountered. Within the `while` loop there must be a statement that alters the tested expression's value.

5. In C++, a `for` loop is constructed using a `for` statement. This statement performs the same functions as the `while` statement, but uses a different form. In many situations, especially those that use a fixed-count condition, the `for` statement format is easier to use than its `while` statement equivalent. The most commonly used form of the `for` statement is

```
for (initializing list; expression; altering list)
{
   statements;
}
```

Within the parentheses of the `for` statement are three items, separated by semi-colons. Each of these items is optional but the semicolons must be present.

The initializing list is used to set any initial values before the loop is entered; generally it is used to initialize a counter. Statements within the initializing list are only executed once. The expression in the `for` statement is the condition being tested: It is tested at the start of the loop and prior to each iteration. The altering list contains loop statements that are not contained within the compound statement: generally it is used to increment or decrement a counter each time the loop is executed. Multiple statements within a list are separated by commas. An example of a `for` loop is

```
for (total = 0, count = 1; count < 10; count++)
{
   cout << "Enter a grade: ";
   total = total + grade;
}
```

In this `for` statement, the initializing list is used to initialize both `total` and `count`. The expression determines that the loop will execute as long as the value in count is less than 10, and the value of `count` is incremented by one each time through the loop.

6. The `for` statement is extremely useful in creating fixed-count loops. This is because the initializing statements, the tested expression, and statements affecting the tested expression can all be included in parentheses at the top of a `for` loop for easy inspection and modification.

7. The `do` statement is used to create posttest loops because it checks its expression at the end of the loop. This ensures that the body of a do loop is executed at least once. Within a do loop there must be at least one statement that alters the tested expression's value.

Industrial Engineering

Each of the traditional engineering disciplines (civil, mechanical, electrical, chemical, and metallurgical/mining) relies on a particular area of natural science for its foundation. Industrial engineering, however, incorporates the knowledge of the social sciences into designing improvements in human-machine systems. Industrial engineers are responsible for designing, installing, and evaluating machines and systems and also for monitoring their interface with people to improve overall productivity. This job may involve understanding human behavioral characteristics and their effects on the design of machines or the workplace. Industrial engineers draw heavily on knowledge in economics, business management, and finance, as well as in the natural sciences. The areas of specialization of the industrial engineer may be divided into four categories:

1. Operations research. This area involves the application of analytical techniques and mathematical models to phenomena such as inventory control, simulation, decision theory, and queuing theory to optimize the total systems necessary for the production of goods.

2. Management or administrative engineering. The increasingly complex interplay of management and production skills in modern industrial operations has resulted in a need for technically trained managers. These managers evaluate and plan corporate ventures and interact with labor, engineering departments, and subcontractors. A management engineer may also participate in the financial operations of a company, drawing on knowledge in economics, business management, and law.

3. Manufacturing and production engineering. Before a product is produced, the complete manufacturing process must be designed and set up to optimize the economics involved and the final quality of the item. This task requires a broad knowledge of process design, plant layouts, tool design, robotics, and human-machine interactions.

4. Information systems. This area involves the use of computers to gather and analyze data for decision making and planning and to improve human–machine activity.

The following list includes the most common responsibilities of industrial engineers who responded to a recent survey by the American Institute of Industrial Engineers:

Facilities planning and design	Cost control
Methods engineering	Inventory control
Work systems design	Energy conservation
Production engineering	Computerized process control
Management information and control systems	Product packaging, handling, and testing
Organization analysis and design	Tool and equipment selection
Work measurement	Production control
Wage administration	Product improvement study
Quality control	Preventive maintenance
Project management	Safety programs
	Training programs

CHAPTER 6

Modularity Using Functions

TOPICS

6.1 FUNCTION AND PARAMETER DECLARATIONS
FUNCTION PROTOTYPES
CALLING A FUNCTION
DEFINING A FUNCTION
PLACEMENT OF STATEMENTS
FUNCTION STUBS

FUNCTIONS WITH EMPTY PARAMETER LISTS
DEFAULT ARGUMENTS
FUNCTION TEMPLATES
REUSING FUNCTION NAMES (OVERLOADING)

6.2 RETURNING A SINGLE VALUE
IN-LINE FUNCTIONS

6.3 RETURNING MULTIPLE VALUES
PASSING AND USING REFERENCE PARAMETERS

6.4 APPLICATIONS
APPLICATION 1: RECTANGULAR TO POLAR COORDINATE CONVERSION
APPLICATION 2: SIMULATION

6.5 VARIABLE SCOPE
SCOPE RESOLUTION OPERATOR
MISUSE OF GLOBALS

6.6 VARIABLE STORAGE CLASS
LOCAL VARIABLE STORAGE CLASSES   GLOBAL VARIABLE STORAGE CLASSES

6.7 COMMON PROGRAMMING ERRORS

6.8 CHAPTER SUMMARY
LOOKING AT CAREER CHOICES: CHEMICAL ENGINEERING

Professional programs are designed, coded, and tested very much like hardware: as a set of modules that are integrated to perform a completed whole. A good analogy of this is an automobile where one major module is the engine, another is the transmission, a third the braking system, a fourth the body, and so on. Each of these modules are linked together and ultimately placed under the control of the driver, which can be compared to a supervisor or main program module. The whole now operates as a complete unit, able to do useful work, such as driving to the store. During the assembly process, each module is individually constructed, tested, and found to be free of defects (bugs) before it is installed in the final product.

Now think of what you might do if you wanted to improve your car's performance. You might alter the existing engine or remove it altogether and bolt in a new engine. Similarly, you might change the transmission or tires or shock absorbers, making each modification individually as your time and budget allowed. In each case the majority of the other modules can stay the same, but the car now operates differently.

In this analogy, each of the major components of a car can be compared to a function. For example, the driver calls on the engine when the gas pedal is pressed. The engine accepts inputs of fuel, air, and electricity to turn the driver's request into a useful product—power—and then sends this output to the transmission for further processing. The transmission receives the output of the engine and converts it to a form that can be used by the drive axle. An additional input to the transmission is the driver's selection of gears (drive, reverse, neutral, etc.).

In each case, the engine, transmission, and other modules only "know" the universe bounded by their inputs and outputs. The driver need know nothing of the internal operation of the engine, transmission, air-conditioning, and other modules that are being controlled. All that is required is an understanding of what each unit does and how to use it. The driver simply "calls" on a module, such as the engine, brakes, air conditioning, and steering when that module's output is required. Communication between modules is restricted to passing needed inputs to each module as it is called upon to perform its task, and each module operates internally in a relatively independent manner. This same modular approach is used by engineers to create and maintain reliable C++ programs using functions.

As we have seen, each C++ program must contain a `main()` *function. In addition to this required function, C++ programs may also contain any number of additional functions. In this chapter we learn how to write these functions, pass data to them, process the passed data, and return a result.*

6.1 ▷ FUNCTION AND PARAMETER DECLARATIONS

In creating C++ functions we must be concerned with both the function itself and how it interacts with other functions, such as `main()`. This includes correctly passing data into a function when it is called and in returning values from a function. In this section we describe the first part of the interface, passing data to a function and having the function correctly receive, store, and process the transmitted data.

As we have already seen with mathematical functions, a function is called, or used, by giving the function's name and passing any data to it, as arguments, in the parentheses following the function name (see Figure 6.1).

function-name (*data passed to function*);

This identifies the This passes data
called function   to the function

Figure 6.1 Calling and passing data to a function.

The called function must be able to accept the data passed to it by the function doing the calling. Only after the called function successfully receives the data can the data be manipulated to produce a useful result.

To clarify the process of sending and receiving data, consider Program 6.1, which calls a function named FindMax(). The program, as shown, is not yet complete. Once the function FindMax() is written and included in Program 6.1, the completed program, consisting of the functions main() and FindMax(), can be compiled and executed.

Program 6.1

```
#include <iostream.h>

void FindMax(int, int);   // the function declaration (prototype)

int main()
{
  int firstnum, secnum;

  cout << "\nEnter a number: ";
  cin  >> firstnum;
  cout << "Great! Please enter a second number: ";
  cin  >> secnum;

  FindMax(firstnum, secnum); // the function is called here

  return 0;
}
```

Let us examine the declaration and calling of the function FindMax() from main(). We will then write FindMax() to accept the data passed to it and determine the largest or maximum value of the two passed values.

The function FindMax() is referred to as the **called function**, since it is called or summoned into action by its reference in main(). The function that does the calling, in this case main(), is referred to as the **calling function**. The terms called and calling come from standard telephone usage, where one party calls the other on a telephone. The party initiating the call is referred to as the calling party, and the party receiving the call is referred to as the called party. The same terms describe function calls. The called function, in this case FindMax(), is declared as a function that expects to receive two integer numbers and to return no value (a void) to main(). This declaration is formally referred to as a function prototype. The function is then called by the last statement in the program.

Function Prototypes

Before a function can be called, it must be declared to the function that will do the calling. The declaration statement for a function is referred to as a **function prototype**. The function prototype tells the calling function the type of value that will be formally returned, if any, and the data type and order of the values that the calling function should transmit to the called function. For example, the function prototype previously used in Program 6.1

```
void FindMax(int, int);
```

declares that the function `FindMax()` expects two integer values to be sent to it, and that this particular function formally returns no value (void). Function prototypes may be placed with the variable declaration statements of the calling function, above the calling function name, as in Program 6.1, or in a separate header file that will be included using an `#include` preprocessor statement. Thus, the function prototype for `FindMax()` could have been placed either before or after the statement `#include <iostream.h>`, prior to `main()`, or within `main()`. (The reasons for the choice of placement are presented in Section 6.3). The general form of function prototype statements is:

return-data-type function-name(list of argument data types);

where the data type refers to the type of the value that will be formally returned by the function. Examples of function prototypes are

```
int fmax(int, int);
float swap(int, char, char, double);
void display(double, double);
```

The function prototype for `fmax()` declares that this function expects to receive two integer arguments and will formally return an integer value. The function prototype for `swap()` declares that this function requires four arguments consisting of an integer, two characters, and a double precision argument, in this order, and will formally return a floating-point number. Finally, the function prototype for `display()` declares that this function requires two double precision arguments and does not return any value. Such a function might be used to display the results of a computation directly, without returning any value to the called function.

The use of function prototypes permits error checking of data types by the compiler. If the function prototype does not agree with data types defined when the function is written, an error message (typically `Undefined symbol`) will occur. The prototype also serves another task; it ensures conversion of all arguments passed to the function to the declared argument data type when the function is called.

Calling a Function

Calling a function is a rather easy operation. The only requirements are that the name of the function be used and that any data passed to the function be enclosed within the parentheses following the function name using the same order and type as declared in the function prototype. The items enclosed within the parentheses are called **arguments** of the called function (see Figure 6.2).

$$\underbrace{FindMax}\ \underbrace{(firstnum,\ secnum)};$$

| This identifies the `FindMax()` function | This causes two values to be passed to `FindMax()` |

Figure 6.2 Calling and passing two values to `FindMax()`.

If a variable is one of the arguments in a function call, the called function receives a copy of the value stored in the variable. For example, the statement `FindMax(firstnum, secnum);` calls the function `FindMax()` and causes the values currently residing in the variables `firstnum` and `secnum` to be passed to `FindMax()`. The variable names in parentheses are arguments that provide values to the called function. After the values are passed, control is transferred to the called function.

As illustrated in Figure 6.3, the function `FindMax()` *does not receive the variables named* `firstnum` *and* `secnum` *and has no knowledge of these variable names.*[1] The function simply receives the values in these variables and must itself determine where to store these values before it does anything else. Although this procedure for passing data to a function may seem surprising, it is really a safety procedure for ensuring that a called function does not inadvertently change data stored in a variable. The function gets a copy of the data to use. It may change its copy and, of course, change any variables declared inside itself. However, unless specific steps are taken to do so, a function is not allowed to change the contents of variables declared in other functions.

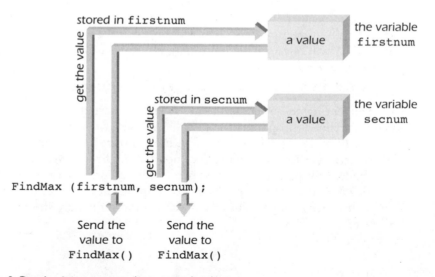

Figure 6.3 `FindMax()` receives actual values.

Now we will begin writing the function `FindMax()` to process the values passed to it.

---

[1]This is significantly different from computer languages such as FORTRAN, where functions and subroutines receive access to these variables and can pass data back through them. In Section 6.3 we will see how, using reference variables, that C++ also permits direct access to the calling function's variables.

Defining a Function

A function is defined when it is written. Each function is defined once (that is, written once) in a program and can then be used by any other function in the program that suitably declares it.

Like the `main()` function, every C++ function consists of two parts, a **function header** and a **function body**, as illustrated in Figure 6.4. The purpose of the function header is to identify the data type of the value returned by the function, provide the function with a name, and specify the number, order, and type of arguments expected by the function. The purpose of the function body is to operate on the passed data and directly return, at most, one value back to the calling function. (We will see, in Section 6.5, how a function can be made to return multiple values.)

Figure 6.4 General format of a function.

The function header is always the first line of a function and contains the function's returned value type, its name, and the names and data types of its arguments. Since `FindMax()` will not formally return any value and is to receive two integer arguments, the following header line can be used:

```
void FindMax(int x, int y) ◄──── no semicolon
```

The argument names in the header are formally referred to as **formal parameters** of the function.[2] Thus, the parameter `x` will be used to store the first value passed to `FindMax()` and the parameter `y` will be used to store the second value passed at the time of the function call. The function does not know where the values come from when the call is made from `main()`. The first part of the call procedure executed by the computer involves going to the variables `firstnum` and `secnum` and retrieving the stored values. These values are then passed to `FindMax()` and ultimately stored in the parameters `x` and `y` (see Figure 6.5).

---

[2]The portion of the function header that contains the function name and parameters is formally referred to as a *function declarator*.

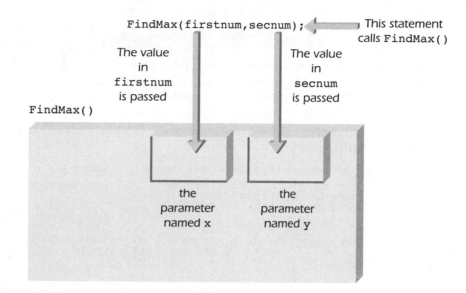

Figure 6.5 Storing values into parameters.

The function name and all parameter names in the header, in this case `FindMax`, `x`, and `y`, are chosen by the programmer. Any names selected according to the rules used to choose variable names can be used. All parameters listed in the function header line must be separated by commas and must have their individual data types declared separately.

Now that we have written the function header for the `FindMax()` function, we can construct its body. Let us assume that the `FindMax()` function selects and displays the larger of the two numbers passed to it.

As illustrated in Figure 6.6, a function body begins with an opening brace, `{`, contains any necessary declarations and other C++ statements, and ends with a closing brace, `}`. This should be familiar to you because it is the same structure used in all the `main()` functions we have written. This should not be a surprise because `main()` is itself a function and must adhere to the rules required for constructing all legitimate functions.

```
{
    named constant declarations,
    variable declarations, and
    other C++ statements
}
```

Figure 6.6 Structure of a function body.

Point of Information

Function Definitions and Function Prototypes

A **function definition** defines a function. Thus, when you write a function, you are really writing a function definition. Each definition begins with a header line that includes a parameter list, if any, enclosed in parentheses and ends with the closing brace that terminates the function's body. The parentheses are required whether or not the function uses any parameters. A commonly used syntax for a function definition is:

```
return-data-type function-name(parameter list)
{
  constant declarations
  variable declarations

  other C++ statements

  return value
}
```

A **function prototype** declares a function. The syntax for a function prototype, which provides the return data type of the function, the function's name, and the function's argument list is:

```
return-data-type function-name(list of parameter data types);
```

As such, the prototype along with pre- and postcondition comments (see Point of Information box on page 297) should provide a user with all the programming information needed to successfully call the function.

Generally, all functions prototypes are placed at the top of the program, and all definitions are placed after the `main()` function. However, this placement can be changed. The only requirement in C++ is that a function cannot be called before it has been either declared or defined.

In the body of the function `FindMax()`, we will declare one variable to store the maximum of the two numbers passed to it. We will then use an `if—else` statement to find the maximum of the two numbers. Finally, a `cout` object stream will be used to display the maximum. The complete function definition for the `FindMax()` function is:

```
void FindMax(int x, int y)
{                       // start of function body
  int maxnum;           // variable declaration

  if (x >= y)           // find the maximum number
    maxnum = x;
  else
    maxnum = y;

  cout << "\nThe maximum of the two numbers is "
       << maxnum << endl;

}  // end of function body and end of function
```

Point of Information

Preconditions and Postconditions

Preconditions are any set of conditions required by a function to be true if it is to operate correctly. For example, if a function uses the named constant MAXCHARS, which must have a positive value, a precondition is that MAXCHARS be declared with a positive value before the function is called.

Similarly, a postcondition is a condition that will be true after the function is executed, assuming that the preconditions are met.

Pre- and postconditions are typically documented as user comments. For example, consider the following declaration and comments:

```
int leapyr(int)
// Preconditions: the integers must represent a year in a four
//              : digit form, such as 1999
// Postcondition: a 1 is be returned if the year is a leap year;
//              : otherwise a 0 will be returned
```

Pre- and postcondition comments should be included with both function prototypes and function definitions whenever clarification is needed.

Notice that the parameter declarations are made within the header line and the variable declaration is made immediately after the opening brace of the function's body. This is in keeping with the concept that parameter values are passed to a function from outside the function, and that variables are declared and assigned values from within the function body.

Program 6.2 includes the FindMax() function within the program code previously listed in Program 6.1.

Program 6.2 can be used to select and print the maximum of any two integer numbers entered by the user. A sample run using Program 6.2 follows:

```
Enter a number: 25
Great! Please enter a second number: 5

The maximum of the two numbers is 25
```

The placement of the FindMax() function after the main() function in Program 6.2 is a matter of choice. We will always list main() first because it is the driver function that should give anyone reading the program an idea of what the complete program is about before encountering the details of each function. In no case, however, can the definition of FindMax() be placed inside main(). This is true for all C++ functions, which must be defined by themselves outside any other function. Each C++ function is a separate and independent entity with its own parameters and variables; nesting of functions is never permitted.

Program 6.2

```cpp
#include <iostream.h>

void FindMax(int, int);   // the function prototype

int main()
{
  int firstnum, secnum;

  cout << "\nEnter a number: ";
  cin  >> firstnum;
  cout << "Great! Please enter a second number: ";
  cin  >> secnum;

  FindMax(firstnum, secnum); // the function is called here

  return 0;
}

// following is the function FindMax()

void FindMax(int x, int y)
{                     // start of function body
  int maxnum;         // variable declaration

  if (x >= y)         // find the maximum number
    maxnum = x;
  else
    maxnum = y;

  cout << "\nThe maximum of the two numbers is "
       << maxnum << endl;

  return;
} // end of function body and end of function
```

Placement of Statements

C++ does not impose a rigid statement-ordering structure on the programmer. The general rule for placing statements in a C++ program is simply that all preprocessor directives, named constants, variables, and functions must be either declared or defined before they can be used. As we have noted previously, although this rule permits both preprocessor directives and declaration statements to be placed throughout a program, doing so results in a very poor program structure.

As a matter of good programming form, the following statement ordering should form the basic structure around which all of your C++ programs are constructed.

```
preprocessor directives

function prototypes

int main()
{
  named constants
  variable declarations

  other executable statements

  return value
}

function definitions
```

As always, comment statements can be freely intermixed anywhere within this basic structure.

Function Stubs

An alternative to completing each function required in a complete program is to write the main() function first, and add the functions later, as they are developed. The problem that arises with this approach, however, is the same problem that occurred with Program 6.1; that is, the program cannot be run until all of the functions are included. For convenience we have reproduced the code for Program 6.1 below.

```
#include <iostream.h>

void FindMax(int, int);  // the function declaration (prototype)

int main()
{
  int firstnum, secnum;

  cout << "\nEnter a number: ";
  cin  >> firstnum;
  cout << "Great! Please enter a second number: ";
  cin  >> secnum;

  FindMax(firstnum, secnum); // the function is called here

  return 0;
}
```

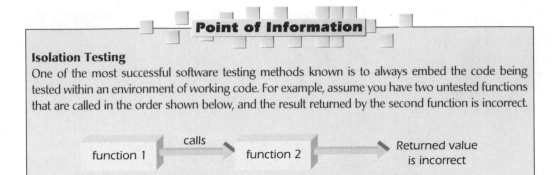

Isolation Testing

One of the most successful software testing methods known is to always embed the code being tested within an environment of working code. For example, assume you have two untested functions that are called in the order shown below, and the result returned by the second function is incorrect.

From the information shown on this figure, one or possibly both of the functions could be operating incorrectly. The first order of business is to isolate the problem to a specific function.

One of the most powerful methods of performing this code isolation is to decouple the functions. This is done by either testing each function individually or by testing one function first and only when you know it is operating correctly reconnecting it to the second function. Then, if an error occurs you have isolated the error to either the transfer of data between functions or the internal operation of the second function.

This specific procedure is an example of the *basic rule of testing*, which states that each function should only be tested in a program in which all other functions are known to be correct. This means that one function must first be tested by itself, using stubs if necessary for any called functions, and a second tested function should be tested either by itself or with a previously tested function, and so on. This ensures that each new function is isolated within a test bed of correct functions, with the final program effectively built up of tested function code.

This program would be complete if there were a function definition for `FindMax`. But we really don't need a *correct* `FindMax` function to test and run what has been written, we just need a function that *acts* like it is: A "fake" `FindMax` that accepts the proper number and types of parameters and returns values of the proper form for the function call is all we need to allow initial testing. This fake function is called a stub. A **stub** is the beginning of a final function that can be used as a placeholder for the final unit until the unit is completed. A stub for `FindMax` is as follows:

```
void FindMax(int x, int y)
{
  cout << "In FindMax()\n";
  cout << "The value of x is " << x << endl;
  cout << "The value of x is " << y << endl;
}
```

This stub function can now be compiled and linked with the previously completed code to obtain an executable program. The code for the function can then be further developed with the "real" code when it is completed, replacing the stub portion.

The minimum requirement of a stub function is that it compile and link with its calling module. In practice, it is a good idea to have a stub display a message that it has been entered successfully and the value(s) of its received parameters, as in the stub for `FindMax()`.

As the function is refined, you let it do more and more, perhaps allowing it to return intermediate or incomplete results. This incremental, or stepwise, refinement is an important concept in efficient program development that provides you with the means to run a program that does not yet meet all of its final requirements.

Functions with Empty Parameter Lists

Although useful functions having an empty parameter list are extremely limited (one such function is provided in Exercise 11), they can occur. The function prototype for such a function requires either writing the keyword `void` or nothing at all between the parentheses following the function's name. For example, both prototypes

```
int display();
```

and

```
int display(void);
```

indicate that the `display()` function takes no parameters and returns an integer. A function with an empty parameter list is called by its name with nothing written within the required parentheses following the function's name. For example, the statement `display();` correctly calls the `display()` function whose prototype is given above.

Default Arguments[3]

A convenient feature of C++ is its flexibility of providing default arguments in a function call. The primary use of default arguments is to extend the parameter list of existing functions without requiring any change in the calling argument lists already in place within a program.

Default argument values are listed in the function prototype and are automatically transmitted to the called function when the corresponding arguments are omitted from the function call. For example, the function prototype

```
void example(int, int = 5, float = 6.78);
```

provides default values for the last two arguments. If any of these arguments are omitted when the function is actually called, the C++ compiler will supply these default values. Thus, all of the following function calls are valid:

```
example(7, 2, 9.3)    // no defaults used
example(7, 2)         // same as example(7, 2, 6.78)
example(7)            // same as example(7, 5, 6.78)
```

Four rules must be followed when using default parameters. The first is that default values should be assigned in the function prototype.[4] The second is that if any parameter is given a default value in the function prototype, all parameters following it must also be supplied with default values. The third rule is that if one argument is omitted in the actual function call, then all arguments to its right must also be omitted. These two rules make it clear to the C++ compiler which arguments are being omitted and permits the compiler to

---

[3]This topic may be omitted on first reading with no loss of subject continuity.

[4]Some compilers accept default assignments in the function definition.

supply correct default values for the missing arguments, starting with the rightmost argument and working in towards the left. The last rule specifies that the default value used in the function prototype may be an expression consisting of both constants and previously declared variables. If such an expression is used, it must pass the compiler's check for validly declared variables, even though the actual value of the expression is evaluated and assigned at run time.

Default arguments are extremely useful when extending an existing function to include more features that require additional arguments. Adding the new arguments to the right of the existing arguments and providing each new argument with a default value permits all existing function calls to remain as they are. Thus, the effect of the new changes are conveniently isolated from existing code in the program.

Function Templates[5]

In most high-level languages, including C++'s immediate predecessor, C, each function requires its own unique name. In theory this makes sense, but in practice it can lead to a profusion of function names, even for functions that perform essentially the same operations. For example, consider determining and displaying the absolute value of a number. If the number passed into the function can be either an integer, a floating-point, or a double precision value, three distinct functions must be written to correctly handle each case. Certainly, we could give each of these functions a unique name, such as abs(), fabs(), and dabs(), respectively, having the function prototypes:

```
Void abs(int);
void fabs(long);
void dabs(double);
```

Clearly, each of these three functions performs essentially the same operation, but on different parameter data types. A much cleaner and more elegant solution is to write a general function that handles all cases, but whose parameters, variables, and even return type can be set by the compiler based on the actual function call. This is possible in C++ using function templates.

A **function template** is a single, complete function that serves as a model for a family of functions. Which function from the family that is actually created depends on subsequent function calls. To make this more concrete, consider a function template that computes and displays the absolute value of a passed argument. An appropriate function template is:

```
template <class T>
void showabs(T number)
{
  if (number < 0)
    number = -number;
  cout << "The absolute value of the number "
       << " is " << number << endl;

  return
}
```

---

[5]This topic may be omitted on first reading with no loss of subject continuity.

For the moment, ignore the first line `template <class T>`, and look at the second line, which consists of the function header `void showabs(T number)`. Notice that this header line has the same syntax that we have been using for all of our function definitions, except for the T in place of where a data type is usually placed. For example, if the header line were `void showabs(int number)`, you should recognize this as a function named `showabs` that expects one integer argument to be passed to it, and that returns no value. Similarly, if the header line were `void showabs(float number)`, you should recognize it as a function that expects one floating point argument to be passed when the function is called.

The advantage in using the T within the function template header line is that it represents a general data type that is replaced by an actual data type, such as `int`, `float`, `double`, etc., when the compiler encounters an actual function call. For example, if a function call with an integer argument is encountered, the compiler will use the function template to construct the code for a function that expects an integer parameter. Similarly, if a call is made with a floating point argument, the compiler will construct a function that expects a floating point parameter. As a specific example of this, consider program 6.3.

Program 6.3

```
#include <iostream.h>

template <class T>
void showabs(T number)
{

  if (number < 0)
    number = -number;
  cout << "The absolute value of the number is "
       << number << endl;

  return;
}

int main()
{
  int num1 = -4;
  float num2 = -4.23;
  double num3 = -4.23456;

  showabs(num1);
  showabs(num2);
  showabs(num3);

  return 0;
}
```

First notice the three function calls made in the main() function shown in Program 6.3, which call the function showabs() with an integer, float, and double value, respectively. Now review the function template for showabs() and let us consider the first line template <class T>. This line, which is called a **template prefix**, is used to inform the compiler that the function immediately following is a template that uses a data type named T. Within the function template the T is used in the same manner as any other data type, such as int, float, double, etc. Then, when the compiler encounters an actual function call for showabs(), the data type of the argument passed in the call is substituted for T throughout the function. In effect, the compiler creates a specific function, using the template, that expects the argument type in the call. Since Program 6.3 makes three calls to showabs, each with a different argument data type, the compiler will create three separate showabs() functions. The compiler knows which function to use based on the arguments passed at the time of the call. The output displayed when Program 6.3 is executed is:

```
The absolute value of the number is 4
The absolute value of the number is 4.23
The absolute value of the number is 4.23456
```

The letter T used in the template prefix template <class T> is simply a placeholder for a data type that is defined when the function is actually invoked. As such, any letter or non-keyword identifier can be used instead. Thus, the showabs() function template could just as well have been defined as:

```
template <class DTYPE>
void showabs(DTYPE number)
{
  if (number < 0)
    number = -number;
  cout << "The absolute value of the number is "
       << number << endl;

  return;
}
```

In this regard, it is sometimes simpler and clearer to read the word *class* in the template prefix as the words *data type*. Thus, the template prefix template <class T> can be read as "we are defining a function template that has a data type named T." Then, within both the header line and body of the defined function the data type T (or any other letter or identifier defined in the prefix) is used in the same manner as any built-in data type, such as int, float, double, etc..

Now suppose, we would like to create a function template to include both a return type and an internally declared variable. For example, consider the following function template:

```
template <class T> // template prefix
T abs(T value)     //header line
{
  T absnum;  // variable declaration
```

```
      if (value < 0)
        absnum = -value;
      else
        absnum = value;

      return absnum;
    }
```

In this template definition, we have used the date type T to declare three items: the return type of the function, the data type of a single function parameter named value, and one variable declared within the function. Program 6.4 illustrates how this function template could be used within the context of a complete program.

Program 6.4

```
#include <iostream.h>

template <class T> // template prefix
T abs(T value)     // header line
{
  T absnum;  // variable declaration

  if (value < 0)
    absnum = -value;
  else
    absnum = value;

  return absnum;
}
int main()
{
  int num1 = -4;
  float num2 = -4.23;
  double num3 = -4.23456;

  cout << "The absolute value of " << num1
       << " is " << abs(num1) << endl;
  cout << "The absolute value of " << num2
       << " is " << abs(num2) << endl;
  cout << "The absolute value of " << num3
       << " is " << abs(num3) << endl;

      return 0;
}
```

In the first call to `abs()` made within `main()`, an integer value is passed as an argument. In this case, the compiler substitutes an int data type for the `T` data type in the function template and creates the following function:

```
int showabs(int value) // header line
{
  int absnum;  // variable declaration

  if (value < 0)
    absnum = -value;
  else
    absnum = value;

  return absnum;
}
```

Similarly, in the second and third function calls, the compiler creates two more functions, one in which the data type `T` is replaced by the keyword `float`, and one in which the data type `T` is replaced by the keyword `double`. The output produced by Program 6.4 is:

```
The absolute value of -4 is 4
The absolute value of -4.23 is 4.23
The absolute value of -4.23456 is 4.23456
```

The value of using the function template is that one function definition has been used to create three different functions, each of which uses the same logic and operations but operates on different data types.

Finally, although both Programs 6.3 and 6.4 define a function template that uses a single placeholder data type, function templates with more than one data type can be defined. For example, the template prefix

```
template <class DTYPE1, class DTYPE2, class DTYPE3>
```

can be used to create a function template that requires three different data types. As before, within the header and body of the function template the data types `DTYPE1`, `DTYPE2`, and `DTYPE3` would be used in the same manner as any built-in data type, such as an `int`, `float`, `double`, etc. Additionally, as noted previously, the names `DTYPE1`, `DTYPE2`, and `DTYPE3` can be any non-keyword identifier. Conventionally, the letter `T` followed by zero or more digits would be used, such as `T`, `T1`, `T2`, `T3`, etc.

Reusing Function Names (Overloading)[6]

C++ provides the capability of using the same function name for more than one function, which is referred to as **function overloading**. The only requirement in creating more than one function with the same name is that the compiler must be able to determine which function to use based on the data types of the parameters (not the data type of the return value, if any). For example, consider the three following functions, all named `cdabs()`.

---

[6]This topic may be omitted on first reading with no loss of subject continuity.

```
void cdabs(int x)  // compute and display the absolute value of an integer
{
  if ( x < 0 )
    x = -x
  cout << "The absolute value of the integer is " << x << endl;
}

void cdabs(float x)  // compute and display the absolute value of a float
{
  if ( x < 0 )
    x = -x;
  cout << "The absolute value of the float is " << x << endl;
}

void cdabs(double x)  // compute and display the absolute value of a double
{
  if ( x < 0 )
    x = -x;
  cout << "The absolute value of the double is " << x << endl;
}
```

Which of the three functions named cdabs() is actually called depends on the argument types supplied at the time of the call. Thus, the function call cdabs(10); would cause the compiler to use the function named cdabs() that expects an integer argument, and the function call cdabs(6.28f); would cause the compiler to use the function named cdabs() that expects a floating-point argument.[7]

Notice that overloading a function's name simply means using the same name for more than one function. Each function that uses the name must still be written and exists as a separate entity. The use of the same function name does not require that the code within the functions be similar, although good programming practice dictates that functions with the same name should perform essentially the same operations. All that is formally required in using the same function name is that the compiler can distinguish which function to select based on the data types of the arguments when the function is called. Clearly, however, if all that is different about the overloaded functions is the argument types, a better programming solution is to simply create a function template. The use of overloaded functions, however, is extremely useful with constructor functions, a topic that is presented in Section 8.3.

---

[7]This is accomplished by a process referred to as *name mangling*. Using this process the function name actually generated by the C++ compiler differs from the function name used in the source code. The compiler appends information to the source code function name depending on the type of data being passed, and the resulting name is said to be a mangled version of the source code name.

Exercises 6.1

1. For the following function headers, determine the number, type, and order (sequence) of the values that must be passed to the function:
    a. `void factorial(int n)`
    b. `void volts(int res, double induct, double cap)`
    c. `void power(int type, double induct, double cap)`
    d. `void flag(char type, float current, float time)`
    e. `void total(float amount, float rate)`
    f. `void roi(int a, int b, char c, char d, float e, float f)`
    g. `void get_val(int item, int iter, char decflag, char delim)`

2. a. Write a function named `check()` that has three parameters. The first parameter should accept an integer number, the second parameter a floating-point number, and the third parameter a double-precision number. The body of the function should just display the values of the data passed to the function when it is called. (NOTE: When tracing errors in functions, it is very helpful to have the function display the values it has been passed. Quite frequently, the error is not in what the body of the function does with the data, but in the data received and stored.)
    b. Include the function written in Exercise 2a in a working program. Make sure your function is called from `main()`. Test the function by passing various data to it.

3. a. Write a function named `find_abs()` that accepts a double-precision number passed to it, computes its absolute value, and displays the absolute value. The absolute value of a number is the number itself if the number is positive and the negative of the number if the number is negative.
    b. Include the function written in Exercise 3a in a working program. Make sure your function is called from `main()`. Test the function by passing various data to it.

4. a. Write a function called `mult()` that accepts two floating-point numbers as parameters, multiplies these two numbers, and displays the result.
    b. Include the function written in Exercise 4a in a working program. Make sure your function is called from `main()`. Test the function by passing various data to it.

5. a. Write a function named `sqr_it()` that computes the square of the value passed to it and displays the result. The function should be capable of squaring numbers with decimal points.
    b. Include the function written in Exercise 5a in a working program. Make sure your function is called from `main()`. Test the function by passing various data to it.

6. a. Write a function named `powfun()` that raises an integer number passed to it to a positive integer power and displays the result. The positive integer should be the second value passed to the function. Declare the variable used to store the result as a long-integer data type to ensure sufficient storage for the result.

b. Include the function written in Exercise 6a in a working program. Make sure your function is called from `main()`. Test the function by passing various data to it.

7. a. Write a C++ program that returns the fractional part of any user entered number. For example, if the number 256.879 is entered, the number .879 should be displayed. (*Hint*: Use an `int` cast.)

b. Enter, compile, and execute the program written for Exercise 7a.

8. a. Write a C++ program that accepts an integer argument and determines whether the passed integer is even or odd. (*Hint*: Use the `%` operator.)

b. Enter, compile, and execute the program written for Exercise 8a.

9. a. Write a function that produces a table of the numbers from 1 to 10, their squares, and their cubes. The function should produce the same display as that produced by Program 5.11.

b. Include the function written in Exercise 9a in a working program. Make sure your function is called from `main()`. Test the function by passing various data to it.

10. a. Modify the function written for Exercise 9 to accept the starting value of the table, the number of values to be displayed, and the increment between values. If the increment is not explicitly sent, the function should use a default value of 1. Name your function `sel_tab()`. A call to `sel_tab(6,5,2);` should produce a table of five lines, the first line starting with the number 6 and each succeeding number increasing by 2.

b. Include the function written in Exercise 10a in a working program. Make sure your function is called from `main()`. Test the function by passing various data to it.

11. A useful function that uses no parameters can be constructed to return a value for π that is accurate to the maximum number of decimal places allowed by your computer. This value is obtained by taking the arcsine of 1.0, which is $\pi/2$, and multiplying the result by 2. In C++, the required expression is 2.0 * asin(1.0), where the `asin()` function is provided in the standard C++ mathematics library (remember to include `math.h`). Using this expression, write a C++ function named `Pi()` that calculates and displays the value of π.

12. a. Write a function template named `display()` that displays the value of the single argument that is passed to it when the function is called.

b. Include the function template created in Exercise 12a within a complete C++ program that calls the function four times: once with a character argument, once with an integer argument, once with a floating-point argument, and once with a double-precision argument.

13. a. Write a function template named `whole()` that returns the integer value of any argument that is passed to it when the function is called.

b. Include the function template created in Exercise 13a within a complete C++ program that calls the function four times: once with a character argument, once with an integer argument, once with a floating-point argument, and once with a double-precision argument.

14. a. Write a function template named `maximum()` that returns the maximum value of three arguments that are passed to the function when it is called. Assume that all three arguments will be of the same data type.

b. Include the function template created for Exercise 14a within a complete C++ program that calls the function with three integers and then with three floating-point numbers.

15. a. Write a function template named `square()` that computes and returns the square of the single argument passed to the function when it is called.

b. Include the function template created for Exercise 15a within a complete C++ program.

6.2 RETURNING A SINGLE VALUE

Using the method of passing data into a function presented in the previous section, the called function only receives copies of the values contained in the arguments at the time of the call (review Figure 6.3 if this is unclear to you). When a value is passed to a called function in this manner, the passed argument is referred to as **passed by value** and is a distinct advantage of C++.[8] Since the called function does not have direct access to the variables used as arguments by the calling function, it cannot inadvertently alter the value stored in one of these variables.

The function receiving the passed by value arguments may process the values sent to it in any fashion desired and directly return at most one, and only one, "legitimate" value to the calling function (see Figure 6.7). In this section we see how such a value is returned to the calling function. As you might expect, given C++'s flexibility, there is a way of returning more than a single value, but that is the topic of the next section.

A function can receive many values

Only one value can
be directly returned

Figure 6.7 A function directly returns at most one value.

---

[8]This is also referred to as a **call by value**. The term, however, does not refer to the function call as a whole, but to how an individual argument is passed when the call to a function is made.

As with the calling of a function, directly returning a value requires that the interface between the called and calling functions be handled correctly. From its side of the return transaction, the called function must provide the following items:

- the data type of the returned value

- the actual value being returned

A function returning a value must specify, in its header line, the data type of the value that will be returned. Recall that the function header line is the first line of the function, which includes both the function's name and a list of parameter names. As an example, consider the `FindMax()` function written in the last section. It determined the maximum value of two numbers passed to the function. For convenience, the `FindMax()` code is listed again:

```
void FindMax(int x, int y)
{                         // start of function body
  int maxnum;             // variable declaration

  if (x >= y)             // find the maximum number
    maxnum = x;
  else
    maxnum = y;

  cout << "\nThe maximum of the two numbers is "
       << maxnum << endl;

}   // end of function body and end of function
```

As written, the function's header line is

```
void FindMax(int x,   int y)
```

where x and y are the names chosen for the function's parameters.

If `FindMax()` is now to return a value, the function's header line must be amended to include the data type of the value being returned. For example, if an integer value is to be returned, the proper function header line is

```
int FindMax(int x, int y)
```

Similarly, if the function is to return a floating-point value the correct function header line is

```
float FindMax(float x, float y)
```

and if the function is to return a double-precision value the header line would be[9]

```
double FindMax(double x, double y)
```

---

[9]The return data type is only related to the parameter data types in as much as the returned value is computed from parameter values. In this case, since the function is used to return the maximum value of its parameters, it would make little sense to return a data type that did not match the function's parameter types.

Let us now modify the function `FindMax()` to return the maximum value of the two numbers passed to it. To do this, we must first determine the data type of the value that is to be returned and include this data type in the function's header line.

Since the maximum value determined by `FindMax()` is stored in the integer variable maxnum, it is the value of this variable that the function should return. Returning an integer value from `FindMax()` requires that the function declaration be

```
int FindMax(int x, int y)
```

Observe that this is the same as the original function header line for `FindMax()` with the substitution of the keyword `int` for the keyword `void`.

Having declared the data type that `FindMax()` will return, all that remains is to include a statement within the function to cause the return of the correct value. To return a value, a function must use a **return** statement, which has the form:[10]

return expression;

When the return statement is encountered, the expression is evaluated first. The value of the expression is then automatically converted to the data type declared in the function header before being sent back to the calling function. After the value is returned, program control reverts to the calling function. Thus, to return the value stored in maxnum, all we need to do is add the statement `return maxnum;` before the closing brace of the `FindMax()` function. The complete function code is:

```
These should ──────►int FindMax(int x, int y)   // function header line
be the same          {                           // start of function body
data type              int maxnum;               // variable declaration

                       if (x >= y)
                         maxnum = x;
                       else
                         maxnum = y;

                       return maxnum;            // return statement
                     }
```

In this new code for the function `FindMax()`, note that the data type of the expression contained in the return statement correctly matches the data type in the function's header line. It is up to the programmer to ensure that this is so for every function returning a value. Failure to exactly match the return value with the function's declared data type may not result in an error when your program is compiled, but it may lead to undesired results because the return value is always converted to the data type declared in the function declaration. Usually this is a problem only when the fractional part of a returned floating-point or double-precision number is truncated because the function was declared to return an integer value.

---

[10]Many programmers place the expression within parentheses, yielding the statement `return (expression);`. Although either form can be used, for consistency only one should be adopted.

Having taken care of the sending side of the return transaction, we must now prepare the calling function to receive the value sent by the called function. On the calling (receiving) side, the calling function must

- be alerted to the type of value to expect

- properly use the returned value

Alerting the calling function as to the type of return value to expect is properly taken care of by the function prototype. For example, including the function prototype

```
int FindMax(int, int);
```

before the `main()` function is sufficient to alert `main()` that `FindMax()` is a function that will return an integer value.

To actually use a returned value we must either provide a variable to store the value or use the value directly in an expression. Storing the returned value in a variable is accomplished using a standard assignment statement. For example, the assignment statement

```
max = FindMax(firstnum, secnum);
```

can be used to store the value returned by `FindMax()` in the variable named `max`. This assignment statement does two things. First the right-hand side of the assignment statement calls `FindMax()`, then the result returned by `FindMax()` is stored in the variable `max`. Since the value returned by `FindMax()` is an integer, the variable `max` should also be declared as an integer variable within the calling function's variable declarations.

The value returned by a function need not be stored directly in a variable, but can be used wherever an expression is valid. For example, the expression `2 * FindMax(firstnum, secnum)` multiplies the value returned by `FindMax()` by two, and the statement

```
cout << FindMax(firstnum, secnum);
```

displays the returned value.

Program 6.5 illustrates the inclusion of both prototype and assignment statements for `main()` to correctly declare, call, and store a returned value from `FindMax()`. As before, and in keeping with our convention of placing the `main()` function first, we have placed the `FindMax()` function after `main()`.

Program 6.5

```cpp
#include <iostream.h>

int FindMax(int, int);   // the function prototype

int main()
{
  int firstnum, secnum, max;


  cout << "\nEnter a number: ";
  cin  >> firstnum;
  cout << "Great! Please enter a second number: ";
  cin  >> secnum;

  max = FindMax(firstnum, secnum); // the function is called here

  cout << "\nThe maximum of the two numbers is " << max << endl;

  return 0;
}

int FindMax(int x, int y)
{                       // start of function body
  int maxnum;           // variable declaration

  if (x >= y)           // find the maximum number
    maxnum = x;
  else
    maxnum = y;

  return maxnum;        // return statement
}
```

In reviewing Program 6.5 it is important to note the four items we have introduced in this section. The first item is the prototype for FindMax(). This statement, which ends with a semicolon as all declaration statements do, alerts main() and any subsequent functions that use FindMax() to the data type that FindMax() will be returning. The second item to notice in main() is the use of an assignment statement to store the returned value from the FindMax() call into the variable maxnum. We have also made sure to correctly declare maxnum as an integer within main()'s variable declarations so that it matches the data type of the returned value.

The last two items of note concern the coding of the `FindMax()` function. The first line of `FindMax()` declares that the function will return an integer value, and the expression in the return statement evaluates to a matching data type. Thus `FindMax()` is internally consistent in sending an integer value back to `main()`, and `main()` has been correctly alerted to receive and use the returned integer.

In writing your own functions you must always keep these four items in mind. For another example, see if you can identify these four items in Program 6.6.

Program 6.6

```
#include <iostream.h>

double tempvert(double);   // function prototype

int main()
{
  const CONVERTS = 4;   // number of conversions to be made
  int count;                     // start of declarations
  double fahren;

  for(count = 1; count <= CONVERTS; count++)
  {
    cout << "\nEnter a Fahrenheit temperature: ";
    cin  >> fahren;
    cout << "The Celsius equivalent is "
         << tempvert(fahren) << endl;
  }

  return 0;
}

// convert fahrenheit to celsius
double tempvert(double in_temp)
{
  return (5.0/9.0) * (in_temp - 32.0);
}
```

In reviewing Program 6.6 let us first analyze the `tempvert()` function. The complete definition of the function begins with the function's header line and ends with the closing brace after the return statement. The function is declared as a double; this means the expression in the function's return statement must evaluate to a double-precision number, which it does. Since a function header line is not a statement but the start of the code defining the function, the function header line does not end with a semicolon.

On the receiving side, `main()` has a prototype for the function `tempvert()` that agrees with `tempvert()`'s function definition. As with all declaration statements, multiple declarations of the same type may be made within the same statement. No additional variable is declared in `main()` to store the returned value from `tempvert()` because the returned value is immediately passed to `cout` for display.

One further point is worth mentioning here. One of the purposes of declarations, as we learned in Chapter 2, is to alert the computer to the amount of internal storage reserved for the data. The prototype for `tempvert()` performs this task and alerts the compiler to the type of storage needed for the returned value. Since we have chosen always to list `main()` as the first function in a file, we must include function prototypes for all functions called by `main()`and any subsequent functions.

In-Line Functions[11]

Calling a function places a certain amount of overhead on a computer. This consists of placing argument values in a reserved memory region that the function has access to (this memory region is referred to as the *stack*), passing control to the function, providing a reserved memory location for any returned value (again, the stack region of memory is used for this purpose), and finally returning to the proper point in the calling program. Paying this overhead is well justified when a function is called many times, because it can significantly reduce the size of a program. Rather than repeating the same code each time it is needed, the code is written once, as a function, and called whenever it is needed.

For small functions that are not called many times, however, paying the overhead for passing and returning values may not be warranted. It still would be convenient, though, to group repeating lines of code together under a common function name and have the compiler place this code directly into the program wherever the function is called. This capability is provided by `inline` functions.

Telling the C+ compiler that a function is `inline` causes a copy of the function code to be placed in the program at the point the function is called. For example, consider the function `tempvert()` defined in Program 6.6. Since this is a relatively short function it is an ideal candidate to be an `inline` function. To make this, or any other function, an `inline` one, simply requires placing the reserved word `inline` before the function name and defining the function before any calls are made to it. This is done for the `tempvert()` function in Program 6.7.

---

[11]This section is optional and may be omitted on first reading without loss of subject continuity.

Program 6.7

```
#include <iostream.h>

inline double tempvert(double in_temp)  // an in-line function
{
  return (5.0/9.0) * (in_temp - 32.0);
}

int main()
{
  const CONVERTS = 4;    // number of conversions to be made
  int count;                  // start of declarations
  double fahren;

  for(count = 1; count <= CONVERTS; count++)
  {
    cout << "\nEnter a Fahrenheit temperature: ";
    cin  >> fahren;
    cout << "The Celsius equivalent is "
         << tempvert(fahren) << endl;
  }

  return 0;
}
```

Observe in Program 6.7 that the `inline` function is placed ahead of any calls to it. This is a requirement of all `inline` functions and obviates the need for a function prototype before any subsequent calling function. Since the function is now an `inline` one, its code will be expanded directly into the program wherever it is called.

The advantage of using an `inline` function is an increase in execution speed. Since the `inline` function is directly expanded and included in every expression or statement calling it, there is no execution time loss due to the call and return overhead required by a non-`inline` function. The disadvantage is the increase in program size when an `inline` function is called repeatedly. Each time an `inline` function is referenced the complete function code is reproduced and stored as an integral part of the program. A non-`inline` function, however, is stored in memory only once. No matter how many times the function is called, the same code is used. Therefore, `inline` functions should only be used for small functions that are not extensively called in a program.

Exercises 6.2

1. Rewrite Program 6.5 so that the function `FindMax()` accepts two floating-point arguments and returns a floating-point value to `main()`. Make sure to modify `main()` in order to pass two floating-point values to `FindMax()` and accept and store the floating-point value returned by `FindMax()`.

2. For the following function headers, determine the number, type, and order (sequence) of values that should be passed to the function when it is called and the data type of the value returned by the function.
   a. `int factorial(int n)`
   b. `double volts(int res, double induct, double cap)`
   c. `double power(int type, double induct, double cap)`
   d. `char flag(char type, float current, float time)`
   e. `int total(float amount, float rate)`
   f. `float roi(int a, int b, char c, char d, float e, float f)`
   g. `void get_val(int item, int iter, char decflag, char delim)`

3. Write function headers for the following:
   a. a function named `check` that has three parameters. The first parameter should accept an integer number, the second parameter a floating-point number, and the third parameter a double-precision number. The function returns no value.
   b. a function named `find_abs()` that accepts a double-precision number passed to it and returns its absolute value.
   c. a function named `mult` that accepts two floating-point numbers as parameters, multiplies these two numbers, and returns the result.
   d. a function named `sqr_it()` that computes and returns the square of the integer value passed to it.
   e. a function named `powfun()` that raises an integer number passed to it to a positive integer (as an argument) power and returns the result.
   f. a function that produces a table of the numbers from 1 to 10, their squares, and their cubes. No arguments are to be passed to the function and the function returns no value.

4. a. Write a function named `RightTriangle()` that accepts the lengths of two sides of a right triangle as the arguments a, and b, respectively. The subroutine should determine and return the hypotenuse, c, of the triangle. (*Hint:* Use Pythagoras' theorem, $c^2 = a^2 + b^2$).
   b. Include the function written for Exercise 4a in a working program. The `main()` function unit should correctly call `RightTriangle()` and display the value returned by the function.

5. a. Write a C++ function named `find_abs()` that accepts a double-precision number passed to it, computes its absolute value, and returns the absolute value to the calling function. The absolute value of a number is the number itself if the number is positive and the negative of the number if the number is negative.

b. Include the function written in Exercise 5a in a working program. Make sure your function is called from `main()` and correctly returns a value to `main()`. Have `main()` use a `cout` statement to display the value returned. Test the function by passing various data to it.

6. a. The volume, v, of a cylinder is given by the formula

$$v = \pi r^2 l$$

where r is the cylinder's radius and l is its length. Using this formula write a C++ function named `cylvol()` that accepts the radius and length of a cylinder and returns its volume.

b. Include the function written in Exercise 6a in a working program. Make sure your function is called from `main()` and correctly returns a value to `main()`. Have `main()` use a `cout` statement to display the value returned. Test the function by passing various data to it.

7. a. The surface area, s, of a cylinder is given by the formula

$$s = 2\pi r l$$

where r is the cylinder's radius and l is its length. Using this formula write a C++ function named `surfarea()` that accepts the radius and length of a cylinder and returns its surface.

b. Include the function written in Exercise 7a in a working program. Make sure your function is called from `main()` and correctly returns a value to `main()`. Have `main()` use a `cout` statement to display the value returned. Test the function by passing various data to it.

8. A second-degree polynomial in x is given by the expression $ax^2 + bx + c$, where a, b, and c are known numbers and a is not equal to zero. Write a C++ function named *poly_two(a, b, c, x)* that computes and returns the value of a second-degree polynomial for any passed values of a, b, c, and x.

9. a. The maximum allowable deflection of a beam depends on its function. For a floor, the typical maximum allowable deflection, in inches, is $D_{max} = L / 240$, while for a roof beam $D_{max} = L / 180$, where L is the length of the beam in inches. Using these formulas, write and test a function named `maxdeflect()` that accepts the length of a beam, in feet, and the type of beam (floor or roof) as a character code, and returns the maximum allowable deflection.

b. Include the function written in Exercise 9a in a working program. Make sure your function is called from `main()` and correctly returns a value to `main()`. Have `main()` use a `cout` statement to display the value returned. Test the function by passing various data to it.

10. a. The load, P_{cr}, in units of kips, applied to a column that will cause the column to buckle is referred to as the critical buckling load. This load can be determined using the equation

$$P_{cr} = \pi^2 \, E \, A \, / \, (L \, / \, r)^2$$

where E is the modulus of elasticity of the material used in the column, A is the cross-sectional area, L is the length of the column, and r is its radius of gyration. Using this formula write a C++ function named `CLoad()` that accepts values of E, A, L, and r, and returns the critical load.

b. Include the function written in Exercise 10a in a working program. Make sure your function is called from `main()` and correctly returns a value to `main()`. Have `main()` use a `cout` statement to display the value returned. Test the function by passing various data to it.

11. a. An extremely useful programming algorithm for rounding a real number to n decimal places is

Step 1: Multiply the number by 10^n
Step 2: Add 0.5
Step 3: Delete the fractional part of the result
Step 4: Divide by 10^n

For example, using this algorithm to round the number 78.374625 to three decimal places yields:

Step 1: $78.374625 \times 10^3 = 78374.625$
Step 2: $78374.625 + 0.5 = 78375.125$
Step 3: Retaining the integer part = 78375
Step 4: 78375 divided by $10^3 = 78.375$

Using this algorithm, write a C++ function that accepts a user entered value and returns the result rounded to two decimal places.

b. Enter, compile, and execute the program written for Exercise 11a.

12. a. Write a C++ function named `whole()` that returns the integer part of any number passed to the function. (*Hint*: Assign the passed argument to an integer variable.)

b. Include the function written in Exercise 12a in a working program. Make sure your function is called from `main()` and correctly returns a value to `main()`. Have `main()` use a `cout` statement to display the value returned. Test the function by passing various data to it.

13. a. Write a C++ function named `fracpart()` that returns the fractional part of any number passed to the function. For example, if the number 256.879 is passed to `fracpart()`, the number .879 should be returned. Have the function `fracpart()` call the function `whole()` that you wrote in Exercise 12. The number returned can then be determined as the number passed to `fracpart()` less the returned value when the same argument is passed to `whole()`. The completed program should consist of `main()` followed by `fracpart()` followed by `whole()`.

b. Include the function written in Exercise 13a in a working program. Make sure your function is called from `main()` and correctly returns a value to `main()`. Have `main()` use a `cout` statement to display the value returned. Test the function by passing various data to it.

14. All years that are evenly divisible by 400 or are evenly divisible by four and not evenly divisible by 100 are leap years. For example, since 1600 is evenly divisible by 400, the year 1600 was a leap year. Similarly, since 1988 is evenly divisible by four but not by 100, the year 1988 was also a leap year. Using this information, write a C++ function that accepts the year as a user input and returns a one if the passed year is a leap year or a zero if it is not.

6.3 RETURNING MULTIPLE VALUES

In a typical function invocation the called function receives values from its calling function, stores and manipulates the passed values, and directly returns at most one single value. When data is passed in this manner it is referred to as a **pass by value**.

Calling a function and passing arguments by value is a distinct advantage of C++. It allows functions to be written as independent entities that can use any variable or parameter name without concern that other functions may also be using the same name. It also alleviates any concern that altering a parameter or variable in one function may inadvertently alter the value of a variable in another function. Under this approach, parameters can be considered as either initialized variables or variables that will be assigned values when the function is executed. At no time, however, does the called function have direct access to any variable defined in the calling function, even if the variable is used as an argument in the function call.

There are times, however, when it is necessary to alter this approach by giving a called function direct access to the variables of its calling function. This allows one function, which is the called function, to use and change the value of variables that have been defined in the calling function. To do this requires that the address of the variable be passed to the called function. Once the called function has the variable's address, it "knows where the variable lives," so to speak, and can access and change the value stored there directly.

Passing addresses is referred to as a function **pass by reference**,[12] since the called function can reference, or access, the variable whose address has been passed. C++ provides two types of address parameters, references and pointers. In this section we describe the method that uses reference parameters.

Passing and Using Reference Parameters

As always, in exchanging data between two functions we must be concerned with both the sending and receiving sides of the data exchange. From the sending side, however, calling a function and passing an address as an argument that will be accepted as a reference

---

[12]It is also referred to as a **call by reference**, where again, the term applies only to the arguments whose address has been passed.

parameter is exactly the same as calling a function and passing a value; the called function is summoned into action by giving its name and a list of arguments. For example, the statement `newval(firstnum, secnum);` both calls the function named `newval` and passes two arguments to it. Whether a value or an address is actually passed depends on the parameter types declared for `newval()`. Let us now write the `newval` function and prototype so that it receives the addresses of the variables `firstnum` and `secnum`, which we will assume to be floating-point variables, rather than their values.

One of the first requirements in writing `newval()` is to declare two reference parameters for accepting passed addresses. In C++ a reference parameter is declared using the syntax

data-type& reference-name

For example, the reference declaration

```
float& num1;
```

declares that `num1` is a reference parameter that will be used to store the address of a `float`. Similarly, `int& secnum` declares that `secnum` is a reference to an integer and `char& key` declares that `key` is a reference to a character.

Recall from Section 2.4 that the ampersand, &, symbol in C++ means "the address of." Additionally, when an & symbol is used within a declaration it refers to "the address of" the preceding data type. Using this information, declarations such as `float& num1` and `int& secnum` are sometimes more clearly understood if they are read backwards. Reading the declaration `float& num1` in this manner yields the information that "num1 is the address of a floating-point value."

Since we need to accept two addresses in the parameter list for `newval()`, the declarations `float& num1, float& num2` can be used. Including these declarations within the parameter list for `newval()`, and assuming that the function returns no value (`void`), the function header for `newval()` becomes:

```
void newval(float& num1, float& num2)
```

For this function header line, an appropriate function prototype is

```
void newval(float&, float&);
```

This prototype and header line are included in Program 6.8, which includes a completed `newval()` function body that both displays and directly alters the values stored in these reference variables from within the called function.

Program 6.8

```cpp
#include <iostream.h>

void newval(float&, float&);   // prototype with two references parameters

int main()
{
  float firstnum, secnum;

  cout << "Enter two numbers: ";
  cin  >> firstnum >> secnum;
  cout << "\nThe value in firstnum is: " << firstnum << endl;
  cout << "The value in secnum is: " << secnum << "\n\n";

  newval(firstnum, secnum);   // call the function

  cout << "The value in firstnum is now: " << firstnum << endl;
  cout << "The value in secnum is now: " << secnum << endl;

  return 0;
}

void newval(float& xnum, float& ynum)
{
   cout << "The value in xnum is: " << xnum << endl;
   cout << "The value in ynum is: " << ynum << "\n\n";
   xnum = 89.5;
   ynum = 99.5;

   return;
}
```

In calling the newval() function within Program 6.8 it is important to understand the connection between the arguments, firstnum and secnum, used in the function call and the parameters, xnum and ynum, used in the function header. *Both refer to the same data items.* The significance of this is that the values in the arguments (firstnum and secnum) can now be altered from within newval() by using the parameter names (xnum and ynum). Thus, the parameter xnum and ynum do not store copies of the values in firstnum and secnum, but directly access the locations in memory set aside for these two arguments. The equivalence of argument names in Program 6.8, which is the essence of a pass by reference, is illustrated in Figure 6.8. As illustrated in this figure, the argument names and their matching parameter names are simply different names referring to the same memory storage areas. In main() these memory locations are referenced by the names firstnum and secnum, respectively, while in `newval()` the same locations are referenced by the parameter names `xnum` and `ynum`, respectively.

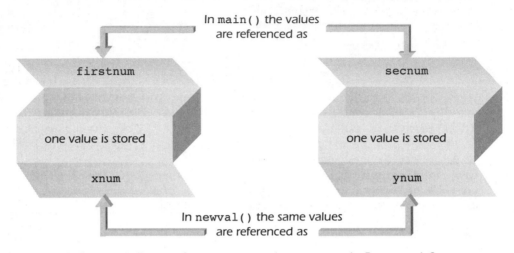

In `main()` the values are referenced as

firstnum

one value is stored

xnum

secnum

one value is stored

ynum

In `newval()` the same values are referenced as

Figure 6.8 The equivalence of arguments and parameters in Program 6.8.

The following sample run was obtained using Program 6.8:

```
Enter two numbers: 22.5 33.0

The value in firstnum is: 22.5
The value in secnum is:    33

The value in xnum is: 22.5
The value in ynum is: 33

The value in firstnum is now: 89.5
The value in secnum is now: 99.5
```

In reviewing this output notice that the values initially displayed for the parameters `xnum` and `ynum` are the same as those displayed for the arguments `firstnum` and `secnum`. Since `xnum` and `ynum` are reference parameters, however, `newval()` now has direct access to the arguments `firstnum` and `secnum`. Thus, any change to `xnum` within `newval()` directly alters the value of `firstnum` in `main()` and any change to `ynum` directly changes `secnum`'s value. As illustrated by the final displayed values, the assignment of values to `xnum` and `ynum` within `newval()` is reflected in `main()` as the altering of `firstnum`'s and `secnum`'s values.

The equivalence between actual calling arguments and function parameters illustrated in Program 6.8 provides the basis for returning multiple values from within a function. For example, assume that a function is required to accept three values, compute these values' sum and product, and return these computed results to the calling routine. By naming the function `calc()` and providing five parameters (three for the input data and two references for the returned values), the following function can be used.

```
void calc(float num1, float num2, float num3, float& total, float& product)
{
  total = num1 + num2 + num3;
  product = num1 * num2 * num3;
  return;
}
```

This function has five parameters, named num1, num2, num3, total, and product, of which only the last two are declared as references. Thus, the first three arguments are passed by value and the last two arguments are passed by reference. Within the function only the last two parameters are altered. The value of the fourth parameter, total, is calculated as the sum of the first three parameters and the last parameter, product, is computed as the product of the parameters num1, num2, and num3. Program 6.9 includes this function in a complete program.

Program 6.9

```
#include <iostream.h>

void calc(float, float, float, float&, float&);  // prototype

int main()
{
  float firstnum, secnum, thirdnum, sum, product;

  cout << "Enter three numbers: ";
  cin  >> firstnum >> secnum >> thirdnum;

  calc(firstnum, secnum, thirdnum, sum, product);  // function call

  cout << "\nThe sum of the numbers is: " << sum << endl;
  cout << "The product of the numbers is: " << product << endl;

  return 0;
}

void calc(float num1, float num2, float num3, float& total, float& product)
{
  total = num1 + num2 + num3;
  product = num1 * num2 * num3;
  return;
}
```

Within main(), the function calc() is called using the five arguments firstnum, secnum, thirdnum, sum, and product. As required, these arguments agree in number and data type with the parameters declared by calc(). Of the five arguments passed, only `firstnum`, `secnum`, and `thirdnum` have been assigned values when the call to `calc()` is made. The remaining two arguments have not been initialized and will be used to receive values back from `calc()`. Depending on the compiler used in compiling the program, these arguments will initially contain either zeros or "garbage" values. Figure 6.9 illustrates the relationship between actual and parameter names and the values they contain after the return from `calc()`.

Figure 6.9 Relationship between argument and parameter names.

Once `calc()` is called, it uses its first three parameters to calculate values for `total` and `product` and then returns control to `main()`. Because of the order of its actual calling arguments, `main()` knows the values calculated by `calc()` as `sum` and `product`, which are then displayed. Following is a sample run using Program 6.9.

```
Enter three numbers: 2.5 6.0 10.0

The sum of the entered numbers is: 18.5
The product of the entered numbers is: 150
```

As a final example illustrating the usefulness of passing references to a called function, we will construct a function named `swap()` that exchanges the values of two of `main()`'s floating-point variables. Such a function is useful when sorting a list of numbers.

Since the value of more than a single variable is affected, `swap()` cannot be written as a pass by value function that returns a single value. The desired exchange of `main()`'s variables by `swap()` can only be obtained by giving `swap()` access to `main()`'s variables. One way of doing this is using reference parameters.

We have already seen how to pass references to two variables in Program 6.8. We will now construct a function to exchange the values in the passed reference arguments. Exchanging values in two variables is accomplished using the three-step exchange algorithm:

1. Store the first parameter's value in a temporary location (see Figure 6.10a).

2. Store the second parameter's value in the first variable (see Figure 6.10b).

3. Store the temporary value in the second parameter (see Figure 6.10c).

Figure 6.10a Save the first value.

Figure 6.10b Replace the first value with the second value.

Figure 6.10c Change the second value.

Following is the function **swap** written according to these specifications:

```
void swap(float& num1, float& num2)
{
  float temp;

  temp = num1;      // save num1's value
  num1 = num2;      // store num2's value in num1
  num2 = temp;      // change num2's value

  return;
}
```

Notice that the use of references in **swap()**'s header line gives **swap()** access to the equivalent arguments in the calling function. Thus, any changes to the two reference parameters in `swap()` automatically changes the values in the calling function's arguments. Program 6.10 contains `swap()` in a complete program.

Program 6.10

```cpp
#include <iostream.h>

void swap(float&, float&);   // function receives 2 references

int main()
{
  float firstnum = 20.5, secnum = 6.25;

  cout << "The value stored in firstnum is: " << firstnum << endl;
  cout << "The value stored in secnum is: "<< secnum << "\n\n";

  swap(firstnum, secnum);   // call the function with references

  cout << "The value stored in firstnum is now: "
       << firstnum << endl;
  cout << "The value stored in secnum is now: "
       << secnum << endl;

  return 0;
}

void swap(float& num1, float& num2)
{
  float temp;

  temp = num1;      // save num1's value
  num1 = num2;      // store num2's value in num1
  num2 = temp;      // change num2's value

  return;
}
```

The following sample run was obtained using Program 6.10:

```
The value stored in firstnum is: 20.5
The value stored in secnum is: 6.25

The value stored in firstnum is now: 6.25
The value stored in secnum is now: 20.5
```

As illustrated by this output, the values stored in `main()`'s variables have been modified from within `swap()`, which was made possible by the use of reference parameters. If a pass by value had been used instead, the exchange within `swap()` would only affect `swap()`'s parameters and would accomplish nothing with respect to `main()`'s variables. Thus, a function such as `swap()` can only be written using references or some other means that provides access to `main()`'s variables (this other means is by pointers, the topic of Chapter 11).

In using reference arguments two cautions need to be mentioned. The first is that reference arguments must be variables (that is, they *cannot* be used to change constants). For example, calling `swap()` with two constants, such as in the call `swap(20.5, 6.5)` passes two constants to the function. Although `swap()` may execute, it will not change the values of these constants.[13]

The second caution to note is that a function call itself gives no indication that the called function will be using reference arguments. The default in C++ is to make passes by value rather than passes by reference, precisely to limit a called function's ability to alter variables in the calling function. This calling procedure should be adhered to whenever possible, which means that reference parameters should only be used in very restricted situations that actually require multiple return values, such as in the `swap()` function illustrated in Program 6.10. The `calc()` function, included in Program 6.9, while useful for illustrative purposes, could also be written as two separate functions, each returning a single value.

Exercises 6.3

1. Write parameter declarations for the following:
   a. a parameter named `amount` that will be a reference to a floating-point value.
   b. a parameter named `price` that will be a reference to a double-precision number.
   c. a parameter named `minutes` that will be a reference to an integer number.
   d. a parameter named `key` that will be a reference to a character.
   e. a parameter named `yield` that will be a reference to a double-precision number.

2. Three integer arguments are to be used in a call to a function named `time()`. Write a suitable function header for `time()`, assuming that `time()` accepts these variables as the reference parameters `sec`, `min`, and `hours`, and returns no value to its calling function.

3. Rewrite the `FindMax()` function in Program 6.5 so that the variable `max`, declared in `main()`, is used to store the maximum value of the two passed numbers. The value of `max` should be set directly from within `FindMax()`. (*Hint*: A reference to `max` will have to be accepted by `FindMax()`.)

4. Write a function named `change()` that has an integer parameter and six integer reference parameters named `hundreds`, `fifties`, `twenties`, `tens`, `fives` and `ones`, respectively. The function is to consider the passed integer value as a dollar amount and convert the value into the fewest number of equivalent bills. Using the

---

[13]Most compilers will catch this error.

references the function should directly alter the respective arguments in the calling function.

5. Write a function named `time()` that has an integer parameter named `seconds` and three integer reference parameters named `hours`, `min`, and `sec`. The function is to convert the passed number of seconds into an equivalent number of hours, minutes, and seconds. Using the references the function should directly alter the respective arguments in the calling function.

6. Write a function named `yr_calc()` that has a long integer parameter representing the total number of days from the date 1/1/1900 and reference parameters named `year`, `month`, and `day`. The function is to calculate the current year, month, and day for the given number of days passed to it. Using the references the function should directly alter the respective arguments in the calling function. For this problem assume that each year has 365 days and each month has 30 days.

7. The following program uses the same argument and parameter names in both the calling and called function. Determine if this causes any problem for the computer.

```
#include <iostream.h>

void time(int&, int&);   // function prototype

int main()
{
  int min, hour;

  cout << "Enter two numbers :";
  cin  >> min >> hour;
  time(min, hour);

  return 0;
}

void time(int& min, int& hour)   // accept two references
{
  int sec;

  sec = (hour * 60 + min) * 60;
  cout << "The total number of seconds is " << sec << endl;

  return;
}
```

6.4 ▷ APPLICATIONS

Preparing a well-designed computer program is very much like preparing a well-designed term paper, in that both should start with an outline. This outline can either be written down or, for very small programs, may simply be kept in mind as the program is being developed. As with a term-paper outline, however, which lists the paper's main topics, a computer program's initial outline must provide a listing of the primary tasks that the program must accomplish.

In written form, a computer program's initial outline is typically either a pseudocode description (see Section 1.3) or a first-level structure diagram (see Section 1.2). This initial outline begins the process of defining a more complicated problem into a set of smaller, more manageable tasks. Each of these tasks can be further subdivided or refined, into even smaller tasks, if required. Once the tasks are well defined, the actual work of coding can begin, starting with any task, in any order. If there are more tasks than can be handled by one programmer, they can be distributed among as many programmers as required. This is equivalent to having many people work on a large research project, with each person responsible for an individual topic. A general outline applicable to many engineering and scientific tasks is the following algorithm:

> ***Get the inputs to the problem***
> ***Calculate the desired result***
> ***Report the results of the calculation***

These three tasks are the primary responsibilities of every program, and we shall refer to this algorithm as the **Problem-Solver Algorithm.** A first-level structure diagram of this algorithm is shown in Figure 6.11.

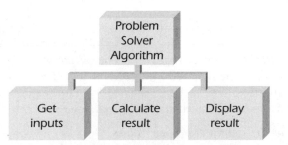

Figure 6.11 First-level structure diagram of the Problem-Solver Algorithm.

Each task in the Problem-Solver Algorithm can be worked on independently as a function—a sort of "mini" C++ program that typically is easier to complete than a whole program. Each of these function tasks can be refined and coded in any desired order, although completing the input section first usually makes testing and development easier. We now apply this development procedure to an actual programming problem.

Application 1: Rectangular to Polar Coordinate Conversion

Assume that we must write a C++ program to convert the rectangular (x,y) coordinates of a point into polar form. That is, given an x and y position on a Cartesian coordinate system, as illustrated in Figure 6.12, we must calculate the distance from the origin, r, and the angle from the x axis, θ, specified by the point. The values of r and θ are referred to as the point's *polar coordinates*.

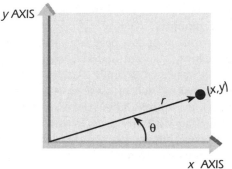

Figure 6.12 Correspondence between polar (distance and angle) and Cartesian (x,y) coordinates.

When the x and y coordinates of a point are known, the equivalent r and θ coordinates can be calculated using the formulas:

$$r = \sqrt{x^2 + y^2}$$

$$\theta = \tan^{-1}(y/x) \quad x \neq 0$$

We begin the development of our program with an outline of what the program is to accomplish. An initial pseudocode description of the desired program can be constructed using our Problem-Solver Algorithm as it pertains to the specifics of this application. For this application the required inputs are an x and y coordinate, the calculation is to convert the input values to their polar coordinate form, and the display is the calculated polar coordinates. Thus the initial pseudocode description is

> *Get the x and y coordinate values*
> *Calculate the polar (r and θ) coordinate values*
> *Display the polar coordinate values*

The equivalent first- or top-level structure diagram for this algorithm is illustrated in Figure 6.13.

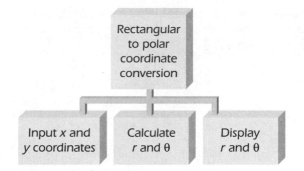

Figure 6.13 Top-level structure diagram.

As this is a relatively simple program and each task described by the algorithm needs no further refinement, coding of each task can begin. To illustrate that any task may be coded independently of any other task, we will arbitrarily start coding the function that performs the calculation of polar coordinates. As an added feature, we will have this function return the angle θ in degrees rather than the radian measure returned by the intrinsic `atan()` function. Since this function must receive two inputs, the *x* and *y* coordinates, and return two outputs, the *r* and θ coordinates, we provide the function with four parameters, two for its inputs and two for its outputs. Arbitrarily selecting the parameter names of `x`, `y`, `r`, and `theta`, and naming the function `polar()`, the following code performs the required calculation of polar coordinates.

```
void polar(float x, float y, float& r, float& theta)
{
  const float TODEGREES = 180.0/3.141593;

  r = sqrt(x * x + y * y);
  theta = atan(y/x) * TODEGREES;

  return;
}
```

The `polar()` function is rather straightforward. The function's header line declares that the function will directly return no value and each of its parameters is declared as a floating-point data type. The first two parameters will be used to accept an *x* and *y* value, while the last two parameters, which are reference parameters, will be used to pass the converted distance and angle values back to the calling function. Within the function's body a named constant `TODEGREES` is defined as the factor 180.0 / 3.142593. The next two assignment statements use the two parameters, `x` and `y`, to assign values to the `r` and `theta` parameters. The `TODEGREES` named constant is used to convert the returned radian value from the `atan()` function into degrees. As written, the `polar()` function may be compiled to check for any compile-time errors.

To understand how the return values are passed it is helpful to think of the reference parameters `r` and `theta` as containers (or variables) through which values may be passed in either direction. This situation is shown in Figure 6.14, which is helpful in understanding the fundamental characteristics of reference parameters: *they simply provide the ability for both a called and a calling function to access the same storage area using different names.*

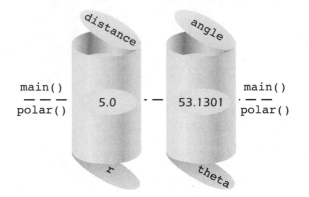

Figure 6.14 Parameter values when `polar()` is called.

As shown in Figure 6.14, the values assigned to r and `theta` within `polar()` can be accessed by the calling function using the argument names `distance` and `angle`, or any other programmer selected argument names.

Testing the Function

Once `polar()` is written it can be tested independently of any other function. This is done by writing a dedicated driver function that only calls `polar()`, as is done in Program 6.11.

Program 6.11

```
#include <iostream.h>
#include <math.h>

void polar(float, float, float&, float&); // function prototype

int main()
{
  float distance, angle;
  polar(3.0, 4.0, distance, angle);
  cout << "r = " << distance << endl;
  cout << "angle = " << angle << endl;

  return 0;
}
```

(Continued)

(Continued)

```
void polar(float x, float y, float& r, float& theta)
{
  const float TODEGREES = 180.0/3.141593;

  r = sqrt(x * x + y * y);
  theta = atan(y/x) * TODEGREES;

  return;
}
```

Notice that in `main()` we pass the constants 3.0 and 4.0 into `polar()`. The function accepts these inputs as the parameters `x` and `y`, and uses these parameters in calculating values for the parameters `r` and `theta`. Within `main()`, these last two parameters are known as `distance` and `angle`, whose values are displayed immediately after the call to `polar()` is made. The output produced when Program 6.11 is executed is

```
r = 5
angle = 53.1301
```

These are the same results that would be obtained from a hand calculation. As the function preforms only two calculations, and the result displayed by our test program agrees with those obtained from a hand calculation, the function has been completely tested by itself. It still remains to be group tested with the remaining two functions required for the complete program to ensure that correct argument values are exchanged between each function.

Completing the Program

The structure diagram for our complete program (Figure 6.13) requires that functions also be written for accepting two rectangular coordinates and displaying the calculated polar coordinates, respectively. The following function, `getrec()`, can be used to accept the input data.

```
void getrec(float&x, float &y)
{
  cout << "Rectangular to  Polar Coordinate"
       << " Conversion Program\n" << endl;
  cout << "Enter the x coordinate: ";
  cin  >> x;
  cout << "Enter the y coordinate: ";
  cin  >> y;

  return;
}
```

In this function the reference parameters `x` and `y` are used to return the values that are entered in response to the two `cin` prompts. As with the `polar()` function, this function may be tested by itself using a small dedicated driver program. The function with its driver program is illustrated in Program 6.12.

Program 6.12

```cpp
#include <iostream.h>

void getrec(float&, float&); // function prototype

int main()
{
  float xcoord, ycoord;

  getrec(xcoord, ycoord);
  cout << "The entered value for x is " << xcoord << endl;
  cout << "The entered value for y is " << ycoord << endl;

  return 0;
}


void getrec(float&x, float &y)
{
  cout << "Rectangular to Polar Coordinate"
       << " Conversion Program\n" << endl;
  cout << "Enter the x coordinate: ";
  cin  >> x;
  cout << "Enter the y coordinate: ";
  cin  >> y;

  return;
}
```

Notice that the dedicated driver program, which is also referred to as a "front-end" driver, has been used to both call `getrec()` and display the values returned by this function. The following output produced by Program 6.12 verifies the correct operation of the `getrec()` function:

```
Rectangular to Polar Coordinate Conversion Program

Enter the x coordinate: 3
Enter the y coordinate: 4
The entered value for x is 3
The entered value for y is 4
```

In a similar manner, the function for displaying polar coordinates is constructed. Program 6.13 contains both the function, which we have named `showit()`, and a front-end driver used for testing the function. Notice that the parameter names used in the header line for `showit()` need not be the same as those used in any other function. `showit()` is constructed to simply display the values in its two parameters, which in this case have been named `radius` and `angle`.

Program 6.13

```cpp
#include <iostream.h>

void showit(float, float); // function prototype

int main()
{
  showit(5.0, 53.1301);

  return 0;
}

void showit(float radius, float angle)
{
  cout << "\nThe polar coordinates are: " << endl;
  cout << "  Distance from origin: " << radius << endl;
  cout << "  Angle (in degrees) from x-axis: " << angle << endl;

  return;
}
```

The output of Program 6.13, which follows, verifies that `showit()` correctly displays the values passed to it.

```
The polar coordinates are:
   Distance from origin: 5
   Angle (in degrees) from x-axis: 53.1301
```

It now remains to create one `main()` program that calls each of the developed functions in the correct order. This is done in Program 6.14, which also includes the functions `getrec()`, `polar()`, and `showit()`.

Program 6.14

```
// This program converts rectangular coordinates to polar coordinates
// Functions used: getrec() - obtain the rectangular coordinates
//                : polar() - calculate the polar coordinates
//                : showit() - display the polar coordinates
//
#include <iostream.h>
#include <math.h>

void getrec(float&, float&);              // function prototype
void polar(float, float, float&, float&); // function prototype
void showit(float, float);                // function prototype

int main()
{
  float x, y, distance, angle;

  getrec(x, y);
  polar(x, y, distance, angle);
  showit(distance, angle);

  return 0;
}

void getrec(float&x, float &y)
{
  cout << "Rectangular to Polar Coordinate"
       << " Conversion Program\n" << endl;
  cout << "Enter the x coordinate: ";
  cin  >> x;
  cout << "Enter the y coordinate: ";
  cin  >> y;

  return;
}
```

(Continued)

(Continued)

```cpp
void polar(float x, float y, float& r, float& theta)
{
  const float TODEGREES = 180.0/3.141593;

  r = sqrt(x * x + y * y);
  theta = atan(y/x) * TODEGREES;

  return;
}

void showit(float radius, float angle)
{
  cout << "\nThe polar coordinates are: " << endl;
  cout << "  Distance from origin: " << radius << endl;
  cout << "  Angle (in degrees) from x-axis: " << angle << endl;

  return;
}
```

The following output was produced from one run using Program 6.14:

```
Rectangular to Polar Coordinate Conversion Program

Enter the x coordinate: 3
Enter the y coordinate: 4

The polar coordinates are:
  Distance from origin: 5
  Angle (in degrees) from x-axis: 53.1301
```

Before leaving Program 6.14, it should be noted that an alternative to writing driver programs for each subroutine as the subroutine was developed is to write a `main()` program first and add the subroutines later as they are developed. This is accomplished by using stubs for each function (see Section 6.1) and then replacing each stub, one at a time, with the completed function.

Application 2: Simulation

There are many scientific and engineering simulation problems in which probability must be considered or statistical sampling techniques must be used. For example, in simulating automobile traffic flow or telephone usage patterns, statistical models are required. Additionally, applications such as simple computer games and more involved engineering scenarios can only be described statistically. All of these statistical models require the generation of **random numbers**; that is, a series of numbers whose order cannot be predicted.

In practice, there are no truly random numbers. Dice never are perfect; cards are never shuffled completely randomly; the supposedly random motions of molecules are influenced by the environment; and digital computers can handle numbers only within a finite range and with limited precision. The best one can do is generate **pseudorandom** numbers, which are sufficiently random for the task at hand.

Some computer languages contain a library function that produces random numbers; others do not. The functions provided by C++ are named `rand()` which generates random numbers, and `srand()`, which sets initial random "seed" values. We present these two functions and then use them in an application that simulates the tossing of a coin to determine the number of resulting heads and tails.

Generating Pseudorandom Numbers

Two functions are provided by C++ compilers for creating random numbers: `rand()` and `srand()`. The `rand()` function produces a series of random numbers in the range $0 \leq$ `rand()` $\leq$ `RAND_MAX`, where the constant `RAND_MAX` is defined in the `stdlib.h` header file. The `srand()` function provides a starting "seed" value for `rand()`. If `srand()` or some other equivalent "seeding" technique is not used, `rand()` will always produce the same series of random numbers.

The general procedure for creating a series of n random numbers using C++'s library functions is illustrated by the following code:

```
srand(time(NULL));  // this generates the first "seed" value

for (int i = 1; i <= N; i++)  // this generates N random numbers
{
  rvalue = rand();
  cout << rvalue << endl;
}
```

Here, the argument to the `srand()` function is a call to the `time()` function with a `NULL` argument. With this argument the `time()` function reads the computer's internal clock time, in seconds. The `srand()` function then uses this time, converted to an unsigned `int`, to initialize the random number generator function `rand()`.[14] Program 6.15 uses this code to generate a series of 10 random numbers.

---

[14]Alternatively, many C++ compilers have a `randomize()` routine that is defined using the `srand()` function. If this routine is available, the call `randomize()` can be used in place of the call `srand(time(NULL))`. In either case, the initializing "seed" routine is only called once, after which the `rand()` function is used to generate a series of numbers.

Program 6.15

```cpp
#include <iostream.h>
#include <iomanip.h>
#include <stdlib.h>
#include <time.h>

// this program generates ten pseudo-random numbers
// using C++'s rand() function

int main()
{
  const int NUMBERS = 10;

  float randvalue;
  int i;

  srand(time(NULL));
  for (i = 1; i <= NUMBERS; i++)
  {
    randvalue = rand();
    cout << setw(20) << randvalue << endl;
  }

  return 0;
}
```

The following is the output produced by one run of Program 6.15:

```
               20203
               21400
               15265
               26935
                8369
               10907
               31299
               15400
                5074
               20663
```

Because of the srand() function call in Program 6.15 the series of ten random numbers will differ each time the program is executed. Without the randomizing "seeding" effect of this function the same series of random numbers would be always be produced. Note also the inclusion of the stdlib.h and time.h header files. The stdlib.h file contains the function prototypes for the srand() and rand() functions, while the time.h header file contains the function prototype for the time() function.

Scaling

One modification to the random number produced by the rand() function typically must be made in practice. In most applications either the random numbers are required to be floating-point values within the range 0.0 to 1.0 or to be integers within a specified range, such as 1 to 100. The method for adjusting the random numbers produced by a random number generator to reside within such ranges is called **scaling**.

Scaling random numbers to reside within the range 0.0 to 1.0 is accomplished easily by dividing the returned value of rand() by RAND_MAX. Thus, the expression float(rand())/RAND_MAX produces a floating-point random number between 0.0 and 1.0.

Scaling a random number as an integer value between 0 and n is accomplished by using either of the expressions rand() % (N+1) or int((rand()/RAND_MAX) * N). For example, the expression int(rand()/RAND_MAX * 100) produces a random integer between 0 and 100.[15]

To produce an integer random number between 1 and n the expression 1 + rand() % N can be used. For example, in simulating the roll of a die, the expression 1 + rand() % 6 produces a random integer between 1 and 6. The more general scaling expression a + rand() % (b + 1 - a) can be used to produce a random integer between the numbers a and b.

A common use of random numbers is to simulate events using a program, rather than going through the time and expense of constructing a real-life experiment. For example, statistical theory tells us that the probability of having a single tossed coin turn up heads is $\frac{1}{2}$. Similarly, there is a 50-percent probability of having a single tossed coin turn up tails.

Using these probabilities we would expect a single coin that is tossed 1000 times to turn up heads 500 times and tails 500 times. In practice, however, this is never exactly realized for a single experiment consisting of 1000 tosses. Instead of actually tossing a coin 1000 times we can use a random number generator to simulate these tosses.

Step 1   Analyze the Problem

For this problem two outputs are required: the percentage of heads and the percentage of tails that result when a simulated coin is tossed 1000 times. No input item will be required for the random number generator function.

---

[15]Many C++ compilers have a routine named random() that can be used to produce the same result. For example, if your compiler has the random() function, the call random(100) will produce a random integer between 0 and 100.

Step 2   Develop a Solution

The percentage of heads and tails are determined as

$$\text{percentage of heads} = \frac{\text{number of heads}}{1000} \times 100\%$$

$$\text{percentage of tails} \ = \frac{\text{number of tails}}{1000} \times 100\%$$

To determine the number of heads and tails, we will have to simulate 1000 random numbers in such a manner that we can define a result of "heads" or "tails" from each generated number. There are a number of ways to do this.

One way is to use the `rand()` function to generate integers between 0 and `RAND_MAX`. Knowing that any single toss has a 50% chance of being either a head or a tail, we could designate a "head" as an even random number and a "tail" as an odd random number. A third method would be to scale the return value from `rand()` to reside between 0.0 and 1.0 as described above. Then we could define a "head" as any number greater than 0.5 and any other result as a "tail." This is the algorithm we will adopt.

Having defined how we will create a single toss that has a 50% chance of turning up heads or tails, the generation of 1000 tosses is rather simple: we use a fixed-count loop that generates 1000 random numbers. For each generation we identify the result as either a head or tail and accumulate the results in a heads and tails counter. Thus, the complete simulation algorithm is given by the pseudocode

> *Initialize a heads count to zero*
> *Initialize a tails count to zero*
> *For 1000 times*
>   *generate a random number between 0 and 1*
>   *If the random number is greater than 0.5*
>   *consider this as a head and*
>   *add one to the heads count*
>   *Else*
>   *consider this as a tail and*
>   *add one to the tails count*
>   *Endif*
> *Endfor*
> *Calculate the percentage of heads as the number of heads divided by 1000 × 100%*
> *Calculate the percentage of tails as the number of tails divided by 1000 × 100%*
> *Print the percentage of heads and tails obtained*

Step 3 Code the Solution

Program 6.16 codes this algorithm in C++.

Program 6.16

```cpp
#include <iostream.h>
#include <iomanip.h>
#include <stdlib.h>
#include <time.h>

// a program to simulate the tossing of a coin NUM TOSSES times
int main()
{
  const int NUMTOSSES = 1000;

  int heads = 0;  // initialize heads count
  int tails = 0;  // initialize tails count
  int i;
  float flip, perheads, pertails;

    // simulate NUMTOSSES tosses of a coin
  srand(time(NULL));
  for (i = 1; i <= NUM TOSSES; i++)
  {
    flip = float(rand())/RAND_MAX;   // scale the number between 0 and 1
    if (flip > 0.5)
      heads = heads + 1;
    else
      tails = tails + 1;
  }
  perheads = (heads / float (NUM TOSSES)) * 100.0;  // calculate heads percentage
  pertails = (tails / float (NUM TOSSES)) * 100.0;  // calculate tails percentage
  cout << "\nHeads came up " << perheads << " percent of the time";
  cout << "\nTails came up " << pertails << " percent of the time" << endl;

  return 0;
}
```

Following are two sample runs using Program 6.16.

```
Heads came up 51.599998 percent of the time
Tails came up 48.400002 percent of the time
```

and

```
Heads came up 47.299999 percent of the time
Tails came up 52.700001 percent of the time
```

Writing and executing Program 6.16 is certainly easier than manually tossing a coin 1000 times. It should be noted that the validity of the results produced by the program depends on how random the numbers produced by `rand()` actually are.

Step 4   Test and Debug the Program

There are really two tests that Program 6.16 must pass. The more important test concerns the randomness of each generated number. This, of course, is really a test of the random number function. For our purposes, we have used a previously written function supplied by the compiler. So at this point we accept the "randomness" of the generator (see Exercise 13 for a method of verifying the function's randomness).

Once the question of the random number generator has been settled, the second test requires that we correctly generate 1000 numbers and accumulate a head and tail count. That this is correctly accomplished is adequately verified by a simple desk check of the `for` loop within Program 6.16. Also, we do know that the result of the simulation must be close to 50% heads and 50% tails. The results of the simulation verify this to be the case.

Exercises 6.4

1. **a.** The volume, v, and surface area, s, of a cylinder are given by the formulas $v = \pi r^2 l$ and $s = 2\pi r l$, where r is the cylinder's radius and l is its length. Using these formulas write and test a function named `cylinder()` that accepts the radius and length of a cylinder and returns its volume and surface area.

2. Write and test a C++ function that calculates the radius, r, and area, a, of a circle when its circumference, c, is given. The relevant formulas are $r = c/(2\pi)$ and $a = \pi r^2$. Test your function using a program having a dedicated driver function.

3. Fluid flowing in a pipe will either flow in a smooth pattern known as *laminar* flow or in a turbulent pattern known as *turbulent* flow. The velocities that clearly produce each type of flow within the pipe can be determined using the formulas:

   $v_{lam} = 2100\mu / \rho\, d$ and $v_{tur} = 4000\mu / \rho\, d$,

   where

   v_{lan} is the velocity of the fluid, in feet/sec, that produces a definite laminar flow

   v_{tur} is the velocity of the fluid, in feet/sec, that produces a definite turbulent flow

   μ is the viscosity of the fluid, in foot-pound sec /ft^2

   ρ is the density of the fluid, in slug/ft^3

   d is the inside diameter of the pipe, in feet

   Using these formulas, write and tests a C++ function named `flow()` that returns both the laminar flow velocity, v_{lan}, and the turbulent flow velocity, v_{tur}, using reference parameters. The function should calculate these velocities for water, which has a viscosity, μ, of 1.9×10^5 foot-pound sec /ft^2 and a density, ρ, of 1.94 slug/ft^3. The pipe diameter should be passed by value into the `flow()` function.

4. The viscosity and densities of three common fluids are listed below:

	Viscosity (foot-pound sec /ft^2)	Density (slug/ft^3)
Ethyl alcohol	2.29×10^5	1.527
Methyl alcohol	1.17×10^5	1.531
Propyl alcohol	4.01×10^5	1.556

Using this data, write and test a C++ function named `ViscDen()` that returns the viscosity and density of the selected fluid using reference parameters. The type of fluid should be input to the function as a character that is passed by value.

5. Write a C++ program that accepts the rectangular coordinates of two points (x_1, y_1) and (x_2, y_2), calculates the distance of each point from the origin, and the distance between the two points. The distance, d, between two points is given by the formula

$$d = \sqrt{(x_2 - x_1)^2 + (y_2 - y_1)^2}$$

6. Modify Program 6.16 so that it requests the number of tosses from the user. (*Hint*: Make sure to have the program correctly determine the percentages of heads and tails obtained.)

7. Many algorithms have been developed for generating pseudorandom numbers. Some of these algorithms utilize a counting scheme, such as counting bits beginning at some arbitrary location in a changing memory. Another scheme, which creates pseudorandom numbers by performing a calculation, is the power residue method.

The **power residue method** begins with an odd n-digit integer, which is referred to as the "seed" number. The seed is multiplied by the value $(10^{n/2} - 3)$. Using the lowest n digits of the result (the "residue") produces a new seed. Continuing this procedure produces a series of random numbers, with each new number used as the seed for the next number. If the original seed has four or more digits (n equal to or greater than 4) and is not divisible by either two or five, this procedure yields $5 \times 10^{(n-2)}$ random numbers before a sequence of numbers repeats itself. For example, starting with a 6 digit seed ($n = 6$), such as 654321, a series of $5 \times 10^4 = 50,000$ random numbers can be generated.

As an algorithm, the specific steps in generating pseudorandom numbers using a power-residue procedure consists of the following steps:

Step 1: Have a user enter a six digit integer seed that is not divisible by 2 or 5— this means the number should be an odd number not ending in 5.

Step 2: Multiply the seed number by 997, which is $10^3 - 3$.

Step 3: Extract the lower 6 digits of the result produced by step 2. Use this random number as the next seed.

Step 4: Repeat Steps 2 and 3 for as many random numbers as needed.

Thus, if the user entered seed number is 654321 (step 1), the first random number generated is calculated as follows:

Step 2: 654321 * 997 = 652358037
Step 3: Extract the lower 6 digits of the number obtained in step 2. This is accomplished using a standard programming "trick."

The trick involves:

Step 3a: Dividing the number by 10^6 = 1000000.
    For example, 652358037 / 1000000 = 652.358037
Step 3b: Taking the integer part of the result of step 3a.
    For example, the integer part of 652.358037 = 652
Step 3c: Multiplying the previous result by 10^6
    For example, 652 $\times$ 10^6 = 652000000
Step 3d: Subtracting this result from the original number.
    For example, 652358037 – 652000000 = 358037

The integer part of a floating-point number can either be taken by assigning the floating-point number to an integer variable, or by a C++ cast (see Section 3.3). In our procedure we will use the cast mechanism. Thus, the algorithm for producing a random number can be accomplished using the following code:

```
i = int(997.0 * x / 1.e6);     // take the integer part
x = 997.0 * x - i * 1.e6;
```

Using this information,

a. Create a function named `randnum()` that accepts a floating-point "seed" as a parameter and returns a floating-point random number between 0 and 1.e6.
b. Incorporate the `randnum()` function created in Exercise 7a into a working C++ program that produces ten random numbers between 0 and 1.e6.
c. Test the randomness of the `randnum()` function created in Exercise 7a using the method described in Exercise 13. Try some even seed values and some odd seed values that end in 5 to determine whether these affect the randomness of the numbers.

8. Write a C++ function that determines in which quadrant a line drawn from the origin resides. The determination of the quadrant is made using the angle that the line makes with the positive x axis as follows:

Angle from the positive x axis	Quadrant
Between 0 and 90 degrees	1
Between 90 and 180 degrees	2
Between 180 and 270 degrees	3
Between 270 and 360 degrees	4

NOTE: If the angle is exactly 0, 90, 180, or 270 degrees the corresponding line does not reside in any quadrant but lies on an axis. For this case your function should return a zero.

9. Write a program to simulate the roll of two dice. If the total of the two dice is 7 or 11 you win; otherwise, you lose. Embellish this program as much as you like, with betting, different odds, different combinations for win or lose, stopping play when you have no money left or reach the house limit, displaying the dice, etc. (*Hint:* Calculate the dots showing on each die by the expression `dots = (int)(6.0 * random number + 1)`, where the random number is between 0 and 1.)

10. A value that is sometimes useful is the greatest common divisor of two integers $n1$ and $n2$. A famous mathematician, Euclid, discovered an efficient method to do this over two thousand years ago. Right now, however, we'll settle for a stub. Write the integer function `stub gcd(n1, n2)`. Simply have it return a value that suggests it received its parameters correctly. (*Hint:* $n1 + n2$ is a good choice of return values. Why isn't $n1/n2$ a good choice?).

11. Euclid's method for finding the greatest common divisor (GCD) of two positive integers consists of the following steps:
    a. Divide the larger number by the smaller and retain the remainder.
    b. Divide the smaller number by the remainder, again retaining the remainder.
    c. Continue dividing the prior remainder by the current remainder until the remainder is zero, at which point the last nonzero remainder is the greatest common divisor.

    For example, assume the two positive integers are 84 and 49, we have:

    Step a: 84/49 yields a remainder of 35
    Step b: 49/35 yields a remainder of 14
    Step c: 35/14 yields a remainder of 7
    Step d: 14/7 yields a remainder of 0

    Thus, the last nonzero remainder, which is 7, is the greatest common divisor of 84 and 49.

    Using Euclid's algorithm, replace the stub function written for Exercise 10 with an actual function that determines and returns the GCD of its two integer parameters.

12. The following program uses the same variable names in both the calling and called function. Determine if this causes any problem for the compiler.

```
#include <iostream.h>

int time(int, int);  // function prototype

int main()
```

```
{
  int min, hour, sec;

  cout << "Enter two numbers: ";
  cin  >> min, hour;
  sec = time(min, hour);
  cout << "The total number of seconds is " << sec << endl;

  return 0;
}

int time(int min, int hour)
{
  int sec;

  sec = (hour * 60 + min) * 60;
  return sec;
}
```

13. Write a program that tests the effectiveness of the rand () library function. Start by initializing 10 counters, such as zerocount, onecount, twocount,..., ninecount to 0. Then generate a large numger of pseudorandom integers between 0 and 9. Each time a 0 occurs increment zerocount, when a 1 occurs increment onecount, etc. Finally, print out the number of 0s, 1s, 2s, ect. that occured and the percentage of the time they occured.

14. The determinant of the 2 by 2 matrix

$$\begin{vmatrix} a_{11} & a_{12} \\ a_{21} & a_{22} \end{vmatrix}$$

is $a_{11}a_{22} - a_{21}a_{12}$.

Similarly, the determinant of a 3 by 3 matrix

$$\begin{vmatrix} a_{11} & a_{12} & a_{13} \\ a_{21} & a_{22} & a_{23} \\ a_{31} & a_{32} & a_{33} \end{vmatrix} =$$

$$a_{11}\begin{vmatrix} a_{22} & a_{23} \\ a_{32} & a_{33} \end{vmatrix} - a_{21}\begin{vmatrix} a_{12} & a_{13} \\ a_{32} & a_{33} \end{vmatrix} + a_{31}\begin{vmatrix} a_{12} & a_{13} \\ a_{22} & a_{23} \end{vmatrix}$$

Using this information write and test two functions, named det2() and det3(). The det2() function should accept the four coefficients of a 2 by 2 matrix and return its determinant. The det3() function should accept the nine coefficients of a 3 by 3 matrix and return its determinant by calling det2() to calculate the required 2 by 2 determinants.

6.5 VARIABLE SCOPE

Now that we have begun to write programs containing more than one function, we can look more closely at the variables declared within each function and their relationship to variables in other functions.

By their very nature, C++ functions are constructed to be independent modules. As we have seen, values are passed to a function using the function's argument list and a value is returned from a function using a return statement. Seen in this light, a function can be thought of as a closed box, with slots at the top to receive values and a single slot at the bottom of the box to return a value (see Figure 6.15).

Values into the function

A single value directly
returned by the function

Figure 6.15 A function can be considered a closed box.

The metaphor of a closed box is useful because it emphasizes the fact that what goes on inside the function, including all variable declarations within the function's body, are hidden from the view of all other functions. Since the variables created inside a function are conventionally available only to the function itself, they are said to be local to the function or **local variables**. This term refers to the scope of an identifier, where **scope** is defined as the section of the program where the identifier, such as a variable, is valid or "known." This section of the program is also referred to as where the variable is visible. A variable can have either a local scope or a global scope. A variable with a **local scope** is simply one that has had storage locations set aside for it by a declaration statement made within a function body. Local variables are only meaningful when used in expressions or statements inside the function that declared them. This means that the same variable name can be declared and used in more than one function. For each function that declares the variable, a separate and distinct variable is created.

All the variables we have used until now have been local variables. This is a direct result of placing our declaration statements inside functions and using them as definition statements that cause the computer to reserve storage for the declared variable. As we shall see, declaration statements can be placed outside functions and also need not act as definitions that cause new storage areas to be reserved for the declared variable.

A variable with **global scope**, more commonly termed a **global variable**, is one whose storage has been created for it by a declaration statement located outside any function.

These variables can be used by all functions that are physically placed after the global variable declaration. This is shown in Program 6.17, where we have purposely used the same variable name inside both functions contained in the program.

Program 6.17

```cpp
#include <iostream.h>

int firstnum;     // create a global variable named firstnum

void valfun(void);    // function prototype (declaration)

int main()
{
  int secnum;             // create a local variable named secnum

  firstnum = 10; // store a value into the global variable
  secnum = 20;    // store a value into the local variable

  cout << "From main(): firstnum = " << firstnum << endl;
  cout << "From main(): secnum =  " << secnum << endl;

  valfun();       // call the function valfun

  cout << "\nFrom main() again: firstnum = " << firstnum << endl;
  cout << "From main() again: secnum = " << secnum << endl;

  return 0;
}

void valfun(void)    // no values are passed to this function
{
  int secnum;  // create a second local variable named secnum

  secnum = 30; // this only affects this local variable's value

  cout << "\nFrom valfun(): firstnum = " << firstnum << endl;
  cout << "From valfun(): secnum = " << secnum << endl;

  firstnum = 40;     // this changes firstnum for both functions

  return;
}
```

The variable firstnum in Program 6.17 is a global variable because its storage is created by a definition statement located outside a function. Since both functions, main()

and valfun(), follow the definition of firstnum, both of these functions can use this global variable with no further declaration needed.

Program 6.17 also contains two separate local variables, both named secnum. Storage for the secnum variable named in main() is created by the definition statement located in main(). A different storage area for the secnum variable in valfun() is created by the definition statement located in the valfun() function. Figure 6.16 illustrates the three distinct storage areas reserved by the three definition statements found in Program 6.17.

Figure 6.16 The three storage areas created by Program 6.17.

Each of the variables named secnum are local to the function in which their storage is created, and each of these variables can only be used from within the appropriate function. Thus, when secnum is used in main(), the storage area reserved by main() for its secnum variable is accessed, and when secnum is used in valfun(), the storage area reserved by valfun() for its secnum variable is accessed. The following output is produced when Program 6.17 is run:

```
From main(): firstnum = 10
From main(): secnum = 20

From valfun(): firstnum = 10
From valfun(): secnum = 30

From main() again: firstnum = 40
From main() again: secnum = 20
```

Let's analyze this output. Since `firstnum` is a global variable, both the `main()` and `valfun()` functions can use and change its value. Initially, both functions print the value of 10 that `main()` stored in `firstnum`. Before returning, `valfun()` changes the value of `firstnum` to 40, which is the value displayed when the variable `firstnum` is next displayed from within `main()`.

Because each function only "knows" its own local variables, `main()` can only send the value of its `secnum` to the `cout` object, and `valfun()` can only send the value of its `secnum` to the `cout` object. Thus, whenever `secnum` is obtained from `main()` the value of 20 is displayed, and whenever `secnum` is obtained from `valfun()` the value 30 is displayed.

C++ does not confuse the two `secnum` variables because only one function can execute at a given moment. While a function is executing, only those variables and parameters that are "in scope" for that function (global and local) can be accessed.

The scope of a variable in no way influences or restricts the data type of the variable. Just as a local variable can be a character, integer, float, double, or any of the other data types (long/short) we have introduced, so can global variables be of these data types, as illustrated in Figure 6.17. The scope of a variable is determined by the placement of the definition statement that reserves storage for it and optionally by a declaration statement that makes it visible, whereas the data type of the variable is determined by using the appropriate keyword (`char`, `int`, `float`, `double`, etc.) before the variable's name in a declaration statement.

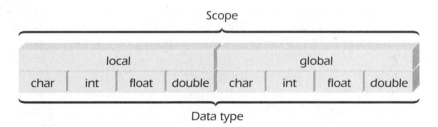

Figure 6.17 *Relating the scope and type of a variable.*

Scope Resolution Operator

When a local variable has the same name as a global variable, all references to the variable name made within the scope of the local variable refer to the local variable. This situation in illustrated in Program 6.18, where the variable name `number` is defined as both a global and local variable.

Program 6.18

```
#include <iostream.h>

float number = 42.8;        // a global variable named number

int main()
{
  float number = 26.4;      // a local variable named number

  cout << "The value of number is " << number << endl;

  return 0;
}
```

When Program 6.18 is executed, the following output is displayed.

```
The value of number is 26.4
```

As shown by this output, the local variable name takes precedence over the global variable. In such cases, we can still access the global variable by using C++'s scope resolution operator. This operator, which has the symbol ::, must be placed immediately before the variable name, as in ::number. When used in this manner, the :: tells the compiler to use the global variable. As an example, the scope resolution operator is used in Program 6.18a.

Program 6.18a

```
#include <iostream.h>

float number = 42.5;        // a global variable named number

int main()
{
  float number = 26.4;      // a local variable named number

  cout << "The value of number is " << ::number << endl;

  return 0;
}
```

The output produced by Program 6.18a is:

```
The value of number is 42.5
```

As indicated by this output, the scope resolution operator causes the global, rather than the local variable to be accessed.

Misuse of Globals

Global variables allow the programmer to "jump around" the normal safeguards provided by functions. Rather than passing variables to a function, it is possible to make all variables global ones. **Do not do this.** By indiscriminately making all variables global, you instantly destroy the safeguards C++ provides to make functions independent and insulated from each other, including the necessity of carefully designating the type of arguments needed by a function, the variables used in the function, and the value returned.

Using only global variables can be especially disastrous in larger programs that have many user-created functions. Since all variables in a function must be declared, creating functions that use global variables requires that you remember to write the appropriate global declarations at the top of each program using the function—they no longer come along with the function. More devastating than this, however, is the horror of trying to track down an error in a large program using global variables. Since a global variable can be accessed and changed by any function following the global declaration, it is a time-consuming and frustrating task to locate the origin of an erroneous value.

Global definitions, however, are sometimes useful in creating variables and constants that must be shared between many functions. Rather than passing the same variable to each function, it is easier to define the variable once as a global. Doing so also alerts anyone reading the program that many functions use the variable. Most large programs almost always make use of a few global variables or constants. Smaller programs containing a few functions, however, should almost never contain global variables.

The misuse of globals does not apply to function prototypes, which typically are global. It should be noted that all of the function prototypes we have used have been of global scope, which declares the prototype to all subsequent functions. Placing a function prototype within a function makes the prototype a local declaration available only to the function it is declared within.

Exercises 6.5

1. **a.** For the following section of code, determine the data type and scope of all declared variables. To do this use a separate sheet of paper and list the three column headings that follow (we have filled in the entries for the first variable):

Variable name	Data type	Scope
volts	int	global to main, roi, and step

```
#include <iostream.h>
int volts;
long int resistance;
double current;

int main()
{
   int power;
   double factor, time;
        .
        .
   return 0;
}

double roi(int mat1, int mat2)
{
   int count;
   double weight;
      .
      .
   return weight;
}

int step(float first, float last)
{
   int hours;
   float fracpart;
      .
      .
   return 10*hours;
}
```

b. Draw boxes around the appropriate section of the above code to enclose the scope of each variable.

c. Determine the data type of the parameters that the functions roi and step expect, and the data type of the value returned by these functions.

2. a. For the following section of code, determine the data type and scope of all declared variables. To do this, use a separate sheet of paper and list the three column headings that follow (we have filled in the entries for the first variable):

Variable name	Data type	Scope
key	char	global to main, func1, and func2

```
#include <iostream.h>
char key;
long int number;

int main()
{
  int a,b,c;
  double x,y;
    .
    .

  return 0;
}

double secnum;

int func1(int num1, int num2)
{
  int o,p;
  float q;
    .
    .

  return p;
}

double func2(float first, float last)
{
  int a,b,c,o,p;
  float r;
  double s,t,x;
    .
    .

  return s * t;
}
```

  b. Draw a box around the appropriate section of the above code to enclose the scope of the variables key, secnum, y, and r.

  c. Determine the data type of the arguments that functions func1 and func2 expect, and the data type of the value returned by these functions.

3. Besides speaking about the scope of a variable, we can also apply the term to a function's parameters. What do you think is the scope of all function parameters?

4. Consider the following program structure:

```cpp
#include <iostream.h>
int a, b;
float One(float);
void Two(void);
int main()
{
  int c, d;
  float e, f;
    .
    .
  return 0;
}

float One(float p2)
{
  char m, n;
    .
    .
}

void Two(void)
{
  int p, d;
  float q, r;
    .
    .
}
```

Define the scope of the parameter p2 and the variables a, b, c, d, m, n, p, d, q, and r.

5. Determine the values displayed by each cout statement in the following program:

```cpp
#include <iostream.h>

int firstnum = 10;  // declare and initialize a global variable
void display(void);  // function prototype
int main()
{
  int firstnum = 20;    // declare and initialize a local variable
  cout << "\nThe value of firstnum is " << firstnum << endl;
  display();

  return 0;
}
```

```
void display(void)
{
  cout << "The value of firstnum is now " << firstnum << endl;
  return;
}
```

6.6 VARIABLE STORAGE CLASS

The scope of a variable defines the location within a program where that variable can be used. Given a program, you could take a pencil and draw a box around the section of the program where each variable is valid. The space inside the box would represent the scope of a variable. From this viewpoint, the scope of a variable can be thought of as the space within the program where the variable is valid.

In addition to the space dimension represented by its scope, variables also have a time dimension. The time dimension refers to the length of time that storage locations are reserved for a variable. This time dimension is referred to as the variable's "lifetime." For example, all variable storage locations are released back to the computer when a program is finished running. However, while a program is still executing, interim variable storage areas are reserved and subsequently released back to the computer. Where and how long a variable's storage locations are kept before they are released can be determined by the **storage class** of the variable.

Besides having a data type and scope, every variable also has a storage class. The four available storage classes are called `auto`, `static`, `extern`, and `register`. If one of these class names is used, it must be placed before the variable's data type in a declaration statement. Examples of declaration statements that include a storage class designation are

```
auto int num;        // auto storage class and int data type
static int miles;    // static storage class and int data type
register int dist;   // register storage class and int data type
extern int volts;    // extern storage class and int data type
auto float coupon;   // auto storage class and float data type
static double yrs;   // static storage class and double data type
extern float yld;    // extern storage class and float data type
auto char in_key;    // auto storage class and char variable
```

To understand what the storage class of a variable means, we will first consider local variables (those variables created inside a function) and then global variables (those variables created outside a function).

Local Variable Storage Classes

Local variables can only be members of the `auto`, `static`, or `register` storage classes. If no class description is included in the declaration statement, the variable is automatically assigned to the `auto` class. Thus, `auto` is the default class used by C++. All the local variables we have used, since the storage class designation was omitted, have been auto variables.

The term auto is short for **automatic**. Storage for automatic local variables is automatically reserved or created each time a function declaring automatic variables is called. As long as the function has not returned control to its calling function, all automatic variables local to the function are "alive"—that is, storage for the variables is available. When the function returns control to its calling function, its local automatic variables "die"—that is, the storage for the variables is released back to the computer. This process repeats itself each time a function is called. For example, consider Program 6.19, where the function testauto() is called three times from main().

Program 6.19

```cpp
#include <iostream.h>

void testauto(void);      // function prototype

int main()
{
  int count;                // count is a local auto variable

  for(count = 1; count <= 3; count++)
    testauto();

  return 0;
}

void testauto(void)
{
  int num = 0;      // num is a local auto variable
                    // initialized to zero
  cout << "The value of the automatic variable num is "
      << num << endl;
  num++;

  return;
}
```

The output produced by Program 6.19 is:

```
The value of the automatic variable num is 0
The value of the automatic variable num is 0
The value of the automatic variable num is 0
```

Each time `testauto()` is called, the automatic variable num is created and initialized to zero. When the function returns control to `main()`, the variable num is destroyed along with any value stored in num. Thus the effect of incrementing num in `testauto()`, before the function's return statement, is lost when control is returned to `main()`.

For most applications, the use of automatic variables works just fine. There are cases, however, where we would like a function to remember values between function calls. This is the purpose of the `static` storage class. A local variable that is declared as `static` causes the program to keep the variable and its latest value even when the function that declared it is through executing. Examples of `static` variable declarations are

```
static int rate;
static float taxes;
static double amount;
static char in_key;
static long resistance;
```

A local `static` variable is not created and destroyed each time the function declaring the `static` variable is called. Once created, local `static` variables remain in existence for the life of the program. This means that the last value stored in the variable when the function is finished executing is available to the function the next time it is called.

Because local `static` variables retain their values, they are not initialized within a declaration statement in the same way as automatic variables. To understand why, consider the automatic declaration `int num = 0;`, which causes the automatic variable num to be created and set to zero each time the declaration is encountered. This is called a **run-time initialization** because initialization occurs each time the declaration statement is encountered. This type of initialization would be disastrous for a `static` variable, because resetting the variable's value to zero each time the function is called would destroy the very value we are trying to save.

The initialization of `static` variables (both local and global) is done only once, when the program is first compiled. At compilation time the variable is created and any initialization value is placed in it.[16] Thereafter, the value in the variable is kept without further initialization. To see how this works, consider Program 6.20.

---

[16]Some compilers initialize static local variables the first time the definition statement is executed rather than when the program is compiled.

Program 6.20

```
#include <iostream.h>

void teststat(void);      // function prototype

int main()
{
  int count;                // count is a local auto variable

  for(count = 1; count <= 3; count++)
    teststat();

  return 0;
}

void teststat(void)
{
  static int num = 0;       // num is a local static variable
  cout << "The value of the static variable num is now "
       << num << endl;
  num++;

  return;
}
```

The output produced by Program 6.20 is

```
The value of the static variable num is now 0
The value of the static variable num is now 1
The value of the static variable num is now 2
```

As illustrated by this output, the `static` variable num is set to zero only once. The function `teststat()` then increments this variable just before returning control to `main()`. The value that num has when leaving the function `teststat()` is retained and displayed when the function is next called.

Unlike automatic variables that can be initialized by either constants or expressions using both constants and previously initialized variables, `static` variables can only be initialized using constants or constant expressions, such as `3.2 + 8.0`. Also, unlike automatic variables, all `static` variables are set to zero when no explicit initialization is given. Thus, the specific initialization of num to zero in Program 6.19 is not required.

The remaining storage class available to local variables, the `register` class, is not used as extensively as either `auto` or `static` variables. Examples of `register` variable declarations are

```
register int time;
register double diffren;
register float coupon;
```

The `register` variables have the same time duration as `auto` variables; that is, a local `register` variable is created when the function declaring it is entered and is destroyed when the function completes execution. The only difference between `register` and `auto` variables is where the storage for the variable is located.

Storage for all variables (local and global), except `register` variables, is reserved in the computer's memory area. Most computers have a few additional high-speed storage areas located directly in the computer's processing unit that can also be used for variable storage. These special high-speed storage areas are called **registers**. Since registers are physically located in the computer's processing unit, they can be accessed faster than the normal memory storage areas located in the computer's memory unit. Also, computer instructions that reference registers typically require less space than instructions that reference memory locations because there are fewer registers that can be accessed than there are memory locations. When the compiler substitutes the location of a register for a variable during program compilation, less space in the instruction is needed than is required to address a memory having millions of locations.

Besides decreasing the size of a compiled C++ program, using `register` variables can also increase the execution speed of a C++ program, if the computer you are using supports this data type. Variables declared with the `register` storage class are automatically switched to the `auto` storage class if your computer does not support `register` variables or if the declared `register` variables exceed the computer's register capacity.

The only restriction in using the `register` storage class is that the address of a `register` variable, using the address operator `&`, cannot be taken. This is easily understood when you realize that registers do not have standard memory addresses.

Global Variable Storage Classes

Global variables are created by definition statements external to a function. By their nature, these externally defined variables do not come and go with the calling of any function. Once a global variable is created, it exists until the program in which it is declared is finished executing. Thus, global variables cannot be declared as either `auto` or `register` variables that are created and destroyed as the program is executing. Global variables may additionally be declared as members of the `static` or `extern` storage classes (but not both). Examples of declaration statements including these two class descriptions are

```
extern int sum;
extern double volts;
static double current;
```

The `static` and `extern` classes affect only the scope, not the time duration, of global variables. As with `static` local variables, all global variables are initialized to zero at compile time.

The purpose of the `extern` storage class is to extend the scope of a global variable beyond its normal boundaries. To understand this, we must first note that all of the programs we have written so far have always been contained together in one file. Thus, when you have saved or retrieved programs you have only needed to give the computer a single name for your program. This is not required by C++.

Larger programs typically consist of many functions that are stored in multiple files. An example of this is shown in Figure 6.18, where the three functions `main()`, `func1()`, and `func2()` are stored in one file and the two functions `func3()` and `func4()` are stored in a second file.

file1

```
int volts;
float current;
static double power;

        .
        .
        .

int main( )
{
    func1( );
    func2( );
    func3( );
    func4( );
}
int func1( )
{
        .
        .
        .

}
int func2( )
{
        .
        .
        .

}
```

file2

```
double factor;
int func3( )
{
        .
        .
        .

}
int func4( )
        .
        .
        .

}
```

Figure 6.18 A program may extend beyond one file.

For the files illustrated in Figure 6.18, the global variables `volts`, `current`, and `power` declared in file1 can only be used by the functions `main()`, `func1()`, and `func2()` in this file. The single global variable, `factor`, declared in file2 can only be used by the functions `func3()` and `func4()` in file2.

Although the variable `volts` has been created in file1, we may want to use it in file2. Placing the declaration statement `extern int volts;` in file2, as shown in Figure 6.19, allows us to do this. Putting this statement at the top of file2 extends the scope of the variable `volts` into file2 so that it may be used by both `func3()` and `func4()`. Thus, the `extern` designation simply declares a global variable that is defined in another file. So placing the statement `extern float current;` in `func4()` extends the scope of this global variable, created in file1, into `func4()`, and the scope of the global variable `factor`, created in file2, is extended into `func1()` and `func2()` by the declaration statement `extern double factor;` placed before `func1()`. Notice that `factor` is not available to `main()`.

file1

```
int volts;
float current;
static double power;
        .
        .
        .
int main( )
{
    func1( );
    func2( );
    func3( );
    func4( );
}
extern double factor;
int func1( )
{
        .
        .
        .
}
int func2( )
{
        .
        .
        .
}
```

file2

```
double factor;
extern int volts;
int func3( )
{
        .
        .
        .
}
int func4( )
{
        extern float current;
        .
        .
        .
}
```

Figure 6.19 *Extending the scope of global variables.*

A declaration statement that specifically contains the word `extern` is different from every other declaration statement in that it does not cause the creation of a new variable by reserving new storage for the variable. An `extern` declaration statement simply informs the computer that a global variable already exists and can now be used. The actual storage for the variable must be created somewhere else in the program using one, and only one, global declaration statement in which the word `extern` has not been used. Initialization of the global variable can, of course, be made with the original declaration of the global variable. Initialization within an `extern` declaration statement is not allowed and will cause a compilation error.

> ### Point of Information
>
> **Storage Classes**
>
> Variables of the type `auto` and `register` are always local variables.
>
> Only nonstatic global variables may be `externed`, which extends the variable's scope into another file or function.
>
> Making a global variable `static` makes the variable private to the file in which it is declared. Thus, `static` variables cannot be `externed`. Except for `static` variables, all variables are initialized each time they come into scope.

The existence of the `extern` storage class is the reason we have been so careful to distinguish between the creation and declaration of a variable. Declaration statements containing the word `extern` do not create new storage areas; they only extend the scope of existing global variables.

The last global class, `static` global variables, is used to prevent the extension of a global variable into a second file. Global `static` variables are declared in the same way as local `static` variables, except that the declaration statement is placed outside any function.

The scope of a global `static` variable cannot be extended beyond the file in which it is declared. This provides a degree of privacy for `static` global variables. Since they are only "known" and can only be used in the file in which they are declared, other files cannot access or change their values. Thus, `static` global variables cannot be subsequently extended to a second file using an `extern` declaration statement. Trying to do so will result in a compilation error.

Exercises 6.6

1. **a.** List the storage classes available to local variables.
   b. List the storage classes available to global variables.

2. Describe the difference between a local `auto` variable and a local `static` variable.

3. What is the difference between the following functions?

```
void init1(void)
{
  static int yrs = 1;
  cout << "The value of yrs is " << yrs << endl;
  yrs = yrs + 2;
}

void init2(void)
{
  static int yrs;
  yrs = 1;
  cout << "The value of yrs is " << yrs << endl;
  yrs = yrs + 2;
}
```

4. a. Describe the difference between a `static` global variable and an `extern` global variable.

b. If a variable is declared with an `extern` storage class, what other declaration statement must be present somewhere in the program?

5. The declaration statement `static double resistance;` can be used to create either a local or global `static` variable. What determines the scope of the variable `resistance`?

6. For the function and variable declarations illustrated in Figure 6.20, place an `extern` declaration to individually accomplish the following:

a. Extend the scope of the global variable `choice` into all of file2.
b. Extend the scope of the global variable `flag` into function `average()` only.
c. Extend the scope of the global variable `date` into `average()` and `variance()`.
d. Extend the scope of the global variable `date` into `roi()` only.
e. Extend the scope of the global variable `factor` into `roi()` only.
f. Extend the scope of the global variable `b_type` into all of file1.
g. Extend the scope of the global variable `resistance` into both `watts()` and `thrust()`.

file1
```
char choice;
int flag;
long date, time;
int main( )
{
     .
     .
     .
}
double factor;
double watts( )
{
     .
     .
     .
}
double thrust( )
{
     .
     .
     .
}
```

file2
```
char b_type;
double resistance;
double roi( )
{
     .
     .
     .
}
double average( )
{
     .
     .
     .
}
double variance
{
     .
     .
     .
}
```

Figure 6.20 Files for Exercise 6.

6.7 COMMON PROGRAMMING ERRORS

An extremely common programming error related to functions is passing incorrect data types. The values passed to a function must correspond to the data types of the parameters declared for the function. One way to verify that correct values have been received is to display all passed values within a function's body before any calculations are made. Once this verification has taken place, the display can be dispensed with.[17]

Another common error can occur when the same variable is declared locally within both the calling and called functions. Even though the variable name is the same, a change to one local variable *does not* alter the value in the other local variable.

Related to this error is the error that can occur when a local variable has the same name as a global variable. Within the function declaring it, the use of the variable's name only affects the local variable's contents unless the scope resolution operator, : :, is used.

Another common error is omitting the called function's prototype either before or within the calling function. The called function must be alerted to the type of value that will be returned, and this information is provided by the function prototype. The prototype can be omitted if the called function is physically placed in a program before its calling function. Although it is also permissible to omit the prototype and return type for functions returning an integer, it is poor documenting practice to do so. The actual value returned by a function can be verified by displaying it both before and after it is returned.

The last two common errors are terminating a function's header line with a semicolon and forgetting to include the data type of a function's parameters within the header line.

6.8 CHAPTER SUMMARY

1. A function is called by giving its name and passing any data to it in the parentheses following the name. If a variable is one of the arguments in a function call, the called function receives a copy of the variable's value.

2. The commonly used form of a user-written function is

   return-type function-name(parameter list)

   {

      declarations and other C++ statements;

      return expression;

   }

---

[17]In practice a good debugger program should be used.

The first line of the function is called the **function header**. The opening and closing braces of the function and all statements in between these braces constitute the function's **body**. The returned data type is, by default, an integer when no returned data type is specified. The parameter list is a comma separated list of parameter declarations.

3. A function's return type is the data type of the value returned by the function. If no type is declared the function is assumed to return an integer value. If the function does not return a value it should be declared as a void type.

4. Functions can directly return at most a single data type value to their calling functions. This value is the value of the expression in the return statement.

5. Using reference arguments a function can be passed the address of a variable. If a called function is passed an address it has the capability of directly accessing the respective calling function's variable. Using passed addresses permits a called function to effectively return multiple values.

6. Functions can be declared to all calling functions by means of a **function prototype**. The prototype provides a declaration for a function that specifies the data type returned by the function, its name, and the data types of the arguments expected by the function. As with all declarations, a function prototype is terminated with a semicolon and may be included within local variable declarations or as a global declaration. The most common form of a function prototype is:

data-type function-name(parameter data type list);

If the called function is placed physically above the calling function no further declaration is required because the function's definition serves as a global declaration to all following functions.

7. Every variable used in a program has a **scope**, which determines where in the program the variable can be used. The scope of a variable is either local or global and is determined by where the variable's definition statement is placed. A local variable is defined within a function and can only be used within its defining function or block. A global variable is defined outside a function and can be used in any function following the variable's definition. All global variables that are not specifically initialized by the user are initialized to zero by the compiler and can be shared between files using the keyword extern.

8. Every variable has a **class**. The class of a variable determines how long the value in the variable will be retained: auto variables are local variables that exist only while their defining function is executing; register variables are similar to auto variables but are stored in a computer's internal registers rather than in memory; static variables can be either global or local and retain their values for the duration of a program's execution. All static variables are set to zero when they are defined if they are not explicitly initialized by the user.

Chemical Engineering

Chemical engineering is the application of the knowledge or techniques of science, particularly chemistry, to industry. Chemical engineers are responsible for the design and operation of large-scale manufacturing plants for materials that undergo chemical changes in their production. These materials include all the new and improved products that have so profoundly affected society such as petrochemicals, rubbers and polymers, new metal alloys, industrial and fine chemicals, foods, paints, detergents, cements, pesticides, industrial gases, and medicines. Chemical engineers also play an important role in pollution abatement and the management of existing energy resources. Because the field of chemical engineering has grown to be so broad, it is difficult to classify the activities of chemical engineers. A rough subdivision is into large-scale production systems, or chemical processing, and smaller scale, or molecular, systems.

Chemical Processing

Chemical processing concerns all aspects of the design and operation of large chemical-processing plants. It includes the following areas.

1. Petrochemicals. The distillation and refinement of fuels such as gasoline, synthetic natural gas, coal liquefaction and gasification, and the production of an infinite variety of products made from petroleum, from cosmetics to pharmaceuticals.

2. Synthetic materials The process of polymerization, a joining of simpler molecules into large complex molecules, is responsible for many modern materials such as nylon, synthetic rubbers, polystyrene, and a great variety of plastics and synthetic fibers.

3. Food and biochemical engineering. The manufacture of packaged food, improved food additives, sterilization, and the utilization of industrial bacteria, fungi, and yeasts in processes like fermentation.

4. Unit operations. The analysis of the transport of heat or fluid, such as the pumping of chemicals through a pipeline or the transfer of heat between substances. This area also includes the effect of heat transfer on chemical reactions such as oxidation, chlorination, and so on.

5. Cryogenic engineering. The design of plants operating at temperatures near absolute zero.

6. Electrochemical engineering. The use of electricity to alter chemical reactions, such as electroplating, or the design of batteries or energy cells.

7. Pollution control. A rapidly growing field that seeks to monitor and reduce the harmful effects of chemical processing on the environment. Topics of concern are waste-water control, air pollution abatement, and the economics of pollution control.

(Continued)

Looking at Career Choices

Molecular Systems

This field involves the application of laboratory techniques to large-scale processes. It includes the following areas:

1. Biochemical engineering. Application of enzymes, bacteria, and so on to improve large-scale chemical processes.

2. Polymer synthesis. Molecular basis for polymer properties and the chemical synthesis of new polymers adapted for large-scale production.

3. Research and development in all areas of chemical processing.

Preparation for a career in chemical engineering requires a thorough background in physics, chemistry, and mathematics and a knowledge of thermodynamics and physical, analytic, and organic chemistry. Although extensively trained in chemistry, chemical engineers differ from chemists in that their main concern is the adaptation of laboratory techniques to large-scale manufacturing plants.

Part Two

Object-Oriented Programming

CHAPTERS

7 I/O File Streams and Data Files

8 Introduction to Classes

9 Class Functions and Conversions

CHAPTER **7**

I/O File Streams and Data Files

TOPICS

7.1 I/O FILE STREAM OBJECTS AND METHODS
FILES   EMBEDDED AND INTERACTIVE FILE NAMES
FILE STREAM OBJECTS AND MODES   CLOSING A FILE
FILE STREAM METHODS

7.2 READING AND WRITING FILES
STANDARD DEVICE FILES   OTHER DEVICES

7.3 RANDOM FILE ACCESS

7.4 FILE STREAMS AS FUNCTION ARGUMENTS

7.5 COMMON PROGRAMMING ERRORS

7.6 CHAPTER SUMMARY

7.7 CHAPTER APPENDIX: THE `iostream` CLASS LIBRARY
FILE STREAM TRANSFER MECHANISM
COMPONENTS OF THE `iostream` CLASS LIBRARY
IN-MEMORY FORMATTING
LOOKING AT CAREER CHOICES: MATERIALS SCIENCE AND
                                     METALLURGICAL ENGINEERING

The data for the programs we have seen so far has either been assigned internally within the programs or entered interactively during program execution. This type of data entry is fine for small amounts of data.

In this chapter we learn how to store data outside of a program using C++'s object-oriented capabilities. This external data storage permits a program to use the data without the user having to interactively recreate it each time the program is executed. This provides the basis for sharing data between programs so that the data output by one program can be input directly to another program. Additionally, it serves as an introduction to the stream objects used in delivering data to and from a program. As such, this provides an early presentation to the more general topic of object-oriented programming.

7.1 ▷ I/O FILE STREAM OBJECTS AND METHODS

To store and retrieve data on a file in C++ three items are required:

- A file
- A file stream object
- A mode

Files

A **file** is a collection of data that is stored together under a common name, usually on a disk, magnetic tape or CD-ROM. For example, the C++ programs that you store on disk are examples of files. The stored data in a program file is the program code that becomes input data to the C++ compiler.

A file is physically stored on an external medium such as a disk, using a unique file name referred to as the external file name. The **external file name** is the name of the file as it is known by the operating system. It is the external name that is displayed when you use an operating command such as `dir` or `ls` or display the contents of a directory.

Each computer operating system has its own specification as to the maximum number of characters permitted for an external file name. Table 7.1 lists these specifications for the more commonly used operating systems.

Table 7.1 Maximum Allowable File Name Characters

Operating System	Maximum length
DOS	8 characters plus an optional period and 3 character extension
VMX	8 characters plus an optional period and 3 character extension
Windows 3.1[1]	8 characters plus an optional period and 3 character extension
Windows 95	255 characters
UNIX Early Versions Current Versions	14 characters 255 characters

To ensure that the examples presented in this text are compatible with all of the operating systems listed in Table 7.1 we will adhere to the more restrictive DOS and VMX specifications. If you are using one of the other operating systems, however, you should take

---

[1]Since Windows 3.1 runs under DOS, it has the same restrictions as DOS. Technically, Windows 3.1 is not an operating system at all, but an application that runs under DOS. It more properly should be referred to as a dynamic linker and file managing application.

advantage of the increased length specification to create descriptive file names within the context of a manageable length (generally considered to be no more that 12 to 14 characters). Very long file names should be avoided. Although such names can be extremely descriptive they do take more time to type and are prone to typing errors.

Using the DOS convention then, the following are all valid computer data file names:

`bessel.dat`	`records`	`info.txt`
`exper1.dat`	`volts.dat`	`math.mem`

Computer file names should be chosen to indicate both the type of data in the file and the application for which it is used. Frequently, the first eight characters are used to describe the data itself and an extension (the three characters after the decimal point) are used to describe the application. For example, the Lotus 123 spreadsheet program automatically applies an extension of `wk3` to all spreadsheet files, Microsoft's Word and the WordPerfect word processing programs use the extensions `doc` and `wpx` (where x refers to the version number), respectively, and most C++ compilers require a program file to have the extension `cpp`. When creating your own file names you should adhere to this practice. For example, the name `exper1.dat` is appropriate in describing a file of data corresponding to experiment number 1.

File Stream Objects and Modes

A **file stream** is a one-way transmission path that is used to connect a file stored on a physical device, such as a disk or CD-ROM, to a program. Associated with every file stream is a **mode**, which determines the direction of data on the transmission path; that is, whether the path will be used for moving data from a file into a program or whether the path will be used for moving data from a program to a file. A file stream with a mode designated as **input** is referred to as an **input file stream** and is used to receive or read data from a file. A file stream with an **output** mode designation is referred to as an **output file stream** and is used to send or write data to a file.

Figure 7.1 illustrates the data flow from and to a file using input and output streams.

Figure 7.1 Input and output file streams.

For each file that your program uses, a distinct file stream object must be created. If you are going to both read and write to a file, both an input and output file stream object is required. Input file stream objects are declared to be of type `ifstream` while output file streams are declared to be of type `ofstream`. For example, the declaration

```
ifstream in_stream;
```

declares an input file stream object named `in_stream` that is of type `ifstream`. Similarly, the declaration

```
ofstream out_stream;
```

declares an output file stream object named `out_stream` that is of type `ofstream`. Within a C++ program a file stream is always accessed by its appropriate stream object name, one name for reading the file and one name for writing to the file. Object names, such as `in_stream` and `out_stream`, can be any programmer chosen names that conform to C++'s identifier rules.

File Stream Methods

Each file stream object has access to prewritten functions defined for its respective `ifstream` or `ofstream` class. These functions, include connecting a stream to an external file name (called *opening a file*), determining if a successful connection has been made, closing a connection (called *closing a file*), getting the next data item into the program from an input stream, putting a new data item from the program onto an output stream, and detecting when the end-of-a-file has been reached.

Opening a file connects each file stream object to a specific external file name. This is accomplished using a file stream's `open()` function, which is a "cookbook" procedure that accomplishes two purposes. First, opening a file establishes the physical connecting link between a program and a file. Since details of this link are handled by the computer's operating system and are transparent to the program, the programmer normally need not consider them.

From a coding perspective, the second purpose of opening a file is more relevant. Besides establishing the actual physical connection between a program and a data file, opening a file equates the file's external computer name to the stream object name used internally by the program. The function that performs this task is named `open()` and is provided by both the `ifstream` and `ofstream` classes.

In using the `open()` function to connect the file's external name to its internal object stream name, only one argument is required, which is the external file name. For example, the statement

```
in_file.open("test.dat");
```

connects the external file named `test.dat` to the internal program file stream object named `in_file`. This assumes, of course, that `in_file` has been declared as either an `ifstream` or `ofstream` object. Although this statement may look a little strange for a function call, there is a good reason for it. The name to the left of the required period identifies a specfic object, while the name to the right of the period identifies the function being called. This notation is used because, when dealing with objects, such as a file stream, more than one function with the same name typically exists. For example, there is more than one `open()` function.

Point of Information

Input and Output Streams

A *stream* is a one-way transmission path between a source and a destination. What gets sent down this transmission path is a stream of bytes. A good analogy to this "stream of bytes" is a stream of water that provides a one-way transmission path of water from a source to a destination.

Two stream objects that we have already used extensively are the input stream object named `cin` and the output stream object named `cout`. The `cin` object provides a transmission path from keyboard to program while the `cout` object provides a transmission path from program to terminal screen. These two objects are created from the stream classes named `istream` and `ostream`, respectively. When the `iostream.h` header file is included in a program using the `#include <iostream.h>` directive, the `cin` and `cout` stream objects are automatically declared as belonging to these streams and are opened by the C++ compiler for use by the compiled program.

File streams objects provide the same capabilities as the `cin` and `cout` objects, except they connect a program to a file rather than the keyboard or terminal screen. Also file stream objects must be explicitly declared. File stream objects that will be used for input must be declared as type `ifstream`, while file stream objects that will be used for output must be declared as type `ofstream`. These two classes, as well as the capability for automatically constructing the `cin` and `cout` objects, are made available to a program by inclusion of the `fstream.h` header file using the directive `#include <fstream.h>`.

Specifically, there is a function named `open()` that is used for opening input streams and a different function, also named `open()`, that is used for opening output streams. Although both functions clearly perform a similar "opening" task: one effectively opens a file for input while the other one is used to open a file for output. The compiler correctly determines which `open()` function to use by the name that appears to the left of the period. Functions such as `open()`, which are associated with objects, are referred to as both **member functions** and **methods** (the terms are used interchangeably), and using such functions requires that the function name be preceded by a period and an object name.

Once an input stream has been opened with the above statement, the program accesses the file using the internal object name `in_file`, while the computer saves the file under the external name `test.dat`. Notice that the external file name argument passed to `open()` is a string contained between double quotes.

When an existing file is connecting to an input file stream the file's data is made available for input, starting at the first data item in the file. Similarly, a file connected to an output file stream creates a new file and makes the file available for output. If a file exists with the same name as a file opened in output mode, the old file is erased and all its data is lost.

When opening a file, for input or output, good programming practice requires that you check that the connection has been established before attempting to use the file in any way. The check can be made using the `fail()` method. This method will return a true value, which is a 1, if the `open` was successful, or a false value, which is a 0, if the `open` failed. Typically the fail method is used in code similar to the following, which attempts to open a file named `test.dat`, checks that a valid connection was made, and reports an error message if the file was not successfully opened for input:[2]

```
ifstream in_file;  // any object name can be used here

in_file.open("test.dat");  // open the file

// check that the connection was successfully opened
if (in_file.fail())
{
  cout << "\nThe file was not successfully opened"
       << "\n Please check that the file currently exists."
       << endl;
  exit(1);
}
```

If the `fail()` method returns a true, which indicates that the open failed, a message is displayed by this code and the `exit()` function, which is a request to the operating system to end program execution immediately, is called. The `exit()` function requires inclusion of the `stdlib.h` header function in any program that uses this function, and `exit()`'s single integer argument is passed directly to the operating system for possible further operating system program action or user inspection. Throughout the remainder of the text we will include this type of error checking whenever a file is opened.

Program 7.1 illustrates the statements required to open a file in read mode, including an error checking routine to ensure that a successful open was obtained.

---

[2]To correctly use the `fail()` method on some compilers you must open input files using the `ios::nocreate` mode, for example, as `in_file.open("test.dat", ios::nocreate)`; this prevents a new file from being created if the named file does not exist and correctly sets the bit tested by `fail()` to indicate the file was not opened.

Checking for a Successful Connection

It is important to check that the open() method successfully established a connection between a file stream and an external file. This is because the open() call is really a request to the operating system that can fail for a variety of reasons. (Chief among these reasons is a request to open an existing file for reading that the operating system cannot locate.) If the operating system cannot satisfy the open request you need to know about it and gracefully terminate your program. Failure to do so almost always results some abnormal program behavior or a subsequent program crash. There are two styles of coding for checking the return value.

The most common method for checking that a fail did not occur is the one coded in Program 7.1. It is used to clearly distinguish the open() request from the check made via the fail() call and is repeated below for convenience:

```
in_file.open("test.dat");  // request to open the file

if (in_file.fail())   // check for a failed connection
{
  cout << "\nThe file was not successfully opened"
       << "\n Please check that the file currently exists."
       << endl;
  exit(1);
}
```

Alternatively, you may encounter programs that use fstream objects in place of both ifstream and ofstream objects. When using fstream's open() method two arguments are required; a file's external name and an explicit mode indication. If the open() function is not successful the fstream stream object is assigned the named constant NULL. Using this named constant, the open request and check typically appear as follows:

```
fstream in_file;

infile.open("external file name", ios::in);
if (in_file == NULL)
{
  cout << "\nThe file was not successfully opened"
       << "\n Please check that the file currently exists."
       << endl;
  exit(1);
}
```

Many times the conditional expression in_file==NULL is replaced by the equivalent expression !in_file. Although we will always use ifstream and ofstream objects, be prepared to encounter the styles that use fstream objects.

Program 7.1

```
#include <fstream.h>
#include <stdlib.h>    // needed for exit()

int main()
{
  ifstream in_file;

  in_file.open("test.dat");  // open the file with the
                             // external name test.dat
  if (in_file.fail())  // check for a successful open
  {
    cout << "\nThe file was not successfully opened"
         << "\n Please check that the file currently exists."
         << endl;
    exit(1);
  }

  cout << "\nThe file has been successfully opened for reading"
       << endl;

  return 0;
}
```

A sample run using Program 7.1 produced the output:

    The file has been successfully opened for reading.

Although Program 7.1 can be used to open an existing file in read mode, it clearly lacks statements to either read the file's data or close the file. These topics are discussed shortly. Before leaving Program 7.1, however, two items should be noted. First, the `iostream.h` header file did not have to be included in the program to use the `cout` object because its definition is incorporated within the `fstream.h` header file. Next, it is possible to combine the declaration of an `fstream` object and its associated `open` statement into one statement. For example, the two statements in Program 7.1

        ifstream in_file;
        in_file.open("test.dat");   // open the file

can be combined into the single statement

        ifstream in_file("test.dat");

In this text we will continue to declare all `ifstream` and `ofstream` objects at the top of the program and explicitly call the `open()` method in a separate statement. You may, however, choose to use the alternative single statement form.

Point of Information

Using `fstream` Objects

In using both `ifstream` and `ofstream` objects the mode, input or output, is implied by the object. Thus `ifstream` objects can only be used for input while `ofstream` objects can only be used for output.

Another means of creating file streams is to use `fstream` objects that can be used for input or output but require an explicit mode assignment. An `fstream` object is declared using the syntax

fstream object-name;

When using the `fstream` class' `open()` member function two arguments are required: a file's external name and a mode indicator. Permissible mode indicators are

Indicator	Description
`ios::in`	Open in input mode
`ios::out`	Open in output mode
`ios::app`	Open in append mode
`ios::ate`	Go to the end of the opened file
`ios::binary`	Open in binary mode (default is text)
`ios::trunc`	Delete file contents if it exists
`ios::nocreate`	If file does not exist, open fails
`ios::noreplace`	If file exists, open for output fails

As with `ofstream` objects, an `fstream` object in output mode creates a new file and makes the file available for writing. If a file exists with the same name as a file opened for output, the old file is erased. For example, assuming that file1 has been declared as an object of type `fstream` using the statement

    fstream file1;

then the statement

    file1.open("test.dat",ios::out);

attempts to open the file named `test.dat` for output. Once this file has been opened the program accesses the file using the internal object name `file1`, while the computer saves the file under the external name `test.dat`.

An `fstream` file object opened in append mode means that an existing file is available for data to be added to the end of the file. If the file opened for appending does not exist, a new file with the designated name is created and made available to receive output from the program. For example, again assuming that `file1` has been declared to be of type `fstream`, the statement

    file1.open("test.dat",ios::app);

attempts to open a file named `test.dat` and makes it available for data to be appended to the end of the file.

Finally, an `fstream` object opened in input mode means that an existing external file has been connected and its data is available as input. For example, assuming that `file1` has been declared to be of type `fstream`, the statement

    file1.open("test.dat",ios::in);

attempts to open a file named `test.dat` for input.

Embedded and Interactive File Names

Two practical problems with Program 7.1 are

1. The external file name is embedded within the program code.

2. There is no provision for a user to enter the desired file name while the program is executing.

As Program 7.1 is written, if the file name is to change a programmer must modify the external file name in the call to open() and recompile the program. Both of these problems can be alleviated by assigning the file name to string variable.

A *string variable* is a variable that can hold a string value, which is any sequence of zero or more characters enclosed within double quotes. For example, "Hello World", "test.dat", and "" are all strings. Notice that strings are always written with double quotes that delimit the beginning and end of a string but are not stored as part of the string. The declaration of a string variable is extremely simple. For example, while the declaration

```
char filename = 'a';
```

declares a character variable named filename and initializes this character variable to the single letter a, the declaration

```
char filename[21] = "test.dat";
```

declares a string variable capable of holding 21 characters in total and initializes the string variable with the string value test.dat.

In declaring and initializing a string variable three items must be considered. First, the maximum length of the string must be specified within brackets immediately after the variable's name. This is the function of the [21] in the above declaration. Secondly, *the number in brackets always represents one more than* the maximum number of characters that you can assign to the variable. This is because the compiler always adds a final end-of-string character to terminate the string. Thus the string value test.dat, which consists of 8 characters is actually stored as 9 characters. The extra character is an end-of-string marker supplied by the compiler. Finally, each initializing string value can be any sequence of characters from zero to one less than the maximum length specifier in brackets. Thus the maximum string value assignable to the string variable filename is a string value consisting of 20 characters.

Once a string variable is declared to store a filename it can be used in one of two ways. First, as shown in Program 7.1a, it can placed at the top of a program to clearly identify a file's external name, rather than embedded within an open() method call.

Point of Information

Character and String Variables

The primary difference between character and string variables is that a character variable can only store a single character value while a string variable can store a string value of zero or more characters. The stored value, however, always contains an additional end-of-string symbolic constant named NULL. For example, consider the declarations

```
char nameOne = 'x';
char nameTwo[2] = "x";
```

First notice that the initializing character value is enclosed within single quotes while the initializing string value is enclosed in double quotes. In the first case only one character, an x, is stored in the character variable nameOne. In the second case two characters are stored. These consist of the x character plus an end-of-string termination character supplied by the compiler. For all string variables this character is the named constant NULL, which has the value '\0'. Because of this terminating NULL, a string value such as "" is not stored as an empty string, but consists of the single NULL terminating character.

One other very important difference between character and string variables is that assignment to a string variable is always invalid except within a declaration statement. Assignment in nondeclarative statements is accomplished using the strcopy() function.

Program 7.1a

```
include <fstream.h>
include <stdlib.h>

int main()
{
  const int MAXLENGTH = 21;  // maximum file name length
  char file1[MAXLENGTH] = "test.dat";   // place the file name up front
  ifstream in_file;

  in_file.open(file1);  // open the file

  if (in_file.fail())  // check for successful open
  {
    cout << "\nThe file named " << file1 << " was not successfully opened"
         << "\n Please check that the file currently exists." << endl;
    exit(1);
  }

  cout << "\nThe file has been successfully opened for reading.\n";

  return 0;
}
```

In reviewing Program 7.1a notice that we have used a symbolic constant named MAXLENGTH to define the length of the string variable file1 and that we have declared and initialized this string variable at the top of the program for easy file identification. Next notice that when a string variable is used, as opposed to a string value, the variable name *is not* enclosed within double quotes in the open() method call. Finally, notice that in the fail() method code we can display the file's external name by inserting the string variable name in the cout standard output stream. For all of these reasons we will continue to identify the external names of files in this manner.

Another extremely useful role played by string variables is to permit the user to enter the file name as the program is executing. For example, the code

```
const int MAXLENGTH = 21;
char file1[MAXLENGTH];

cout << "Please enter the name of the file you wish to open: ";
cin  >> file1;
```

allows a user to enter a file's external name at runtime. The only restriction in this code is that the user must not enclose the entered string value in double quotes, which is a plus, and that the entered string value cannot contain any blanks. The reason for this is that the compiler will terminate the string when it encounters a blank.

Program 7.1b uses this code in the context of a complete program.

Program 7.1b

```
#include <fstream.h>
#include <stdlib.h>

int main()
{
  const int MAXLENGTH = 21;    // maximum file name length
  char file1[MAXLENGTH];
  ifstream in_file;

  cout << "Please enter the name of the file you wish to open: ";
  cin  >> file1;
```

(Continued)

(Continued)

```
    in_file.open(file1);   // open the file

    if (in_file.fail())   // check for successful open
    {
      cout << "\nThe file named " << file1 << " was not successfully opened"
           << "\n Please check that the file currently exists." << endl;
      exit(1);
    }

    cout << "\nThe file has been successfully opened for reading.\n";

    return 0;
}
```

Following is a sample output provided by Program 7.1b.

```
    Please enter the name of the file you wish to open: foobar

    The file named foobar was not successfully opened
      Please check that the file currently exists.
```

Closing a File

A file is closed using the `close()` method. This method breaks the connection between the file's external name and the file stream object, which can then be used for another file. For example, the statement

```
    in_file.close();
```

closes the `in_file` stream's connection to its current file. As indicated, the `close()` method takes no argument.

Since all computers have a limit on the maximum number of files that can be open at one time, closing files that are no longer needed makes good sense. Any open files existing at the end of normal program execution will be automatically closed by the operating system.

Exercises 7.1

1. **a.** Enter and execute Program 7.1 on your computer.
   b. Add a `close()` method to Program 7.1 and then execute the program.

2. **a.** Enter and execute Program 7.1a on your computer.
   b. Add a `close()` method to Program 7.1a and then execute the program.

3. **a.** Enter and execute Program 7.1b on your computer.
   b. Add a `close()` method to Program 7.1b and then execute the program.

4. Using the reference manuals provided with your computer's operating system, determine:
   a. the maximum number of characters that can be used to name a file for storage by the computer system.
   b. the maximum number of data files that can be open at the same time.

5. Would it be appropriate to call a saved C++ program a file? Why or why not?

6. **a.** Write a suitable declaration statement for each of the following `ifstream` objects: `in_data`, `prices`, `coupons`, and `file1`.
   b. Write a suitable declaration statement for each of the following `ofstream` objects: `out_date`, `rates`, `distance`, and `file2`.

7. Write individual declaration and open statements to link the following external data file names to their corresponding internal object names.

External Name	Object Name	Mode
coba.mem	memo	output
book.let	letter	output
coupons.bnd	coups	append
yield.bnd	pt_yield	append
test.dat	pri_file	input
rates.dat	rates	input

8. Write close statements for each of the files opened in Exercise 7.

7.2 ▷ READING AND WRITING FILES

Reading or writing to a file involves almost the identical operations for reading input from a terminal and writing data to a display screen. For writing to a file, the `cout` object is replaced by the `ofstream` object declared in the program. For example, if `out_file` is declared as an object of type `ofstream` the following output statements are valid.

```
out_file << 'a';
out_file << "Hello World!";
out_file << descrip << ' ' << price;
```

The file name in each of these statements, in place of cout, simply directs the output stream to a specific file instead of to the standard display device. Program 7.2 illustrates the use of a file write function to write a list of descriptions and prices to a file.

Program 7.2

```cpp
#include <fstream.h>
#include <stdlib.h>
#include <iomanip.h>

int main()
{
  const int MAXLENGTH = 21;  // maximum file name length
  char filename[MAXLENGTH] = "test.dat";  // put the filename up front
  ofstream out_file;

  out_file.open(filename);

  if (out_file.fail())
  {
    cout << "The file was not successfully opened" << endl;
    exit(1);
  }

    // set the output file stream formats
  out_file << setiosflags(ios::fixed)
           << setiosflags(ios::showpoint)
           << setprecision(2);

    // send data to the file
  out_file << "Batteries " << 39.95 << endl
           << "Bulbs "   << 3.22 << endl
           << "Fuses "   << 1.00;

  out_file.close();

  return 0;
}
```

Formatting Output File Stream Data

Output file streams can be formatted in the same manner as the `cout` standard output stream. For example, if an output stream named `file_out` has been declared, the statement

```
file_out << setiosflags(ios::fixed)
         << setiosflags(ios::showpoint)
         << setprecision(2);
```

formats all data inserted in the `file_out` stream in the same way that these parameterized manipulators work for the `cout` stream. The first manipulator parameter, `ios::fixed`, causes the stream to output all numbers in conventional fixed-point notation (not exponential). The next parameter, `ios::showpoint`, tells the stream to always provide a decimal point. Thus, a value such as 1.0 will appear as 1.0, and not 1. Finally, the `setprecision` manipulator tells the stream to always display 2 decimal values after the decimal point. Thus, the number 1.0 for example, will appear as 1.00.

Instead of using manipulators, you can also used the stream methods `setf()` and `precision()`. For example, the previous formatting can also be accomplished using the code:

```
file_out.setf(ios::fixed);
file_out.setf(ios::showpoint);
file.out.precision(2);
```

Which style you select is a matter of preference. In both cases the formats need only be specified once and remain in effect for every number subsequently inserted into the file stream.

When Program 7.2 is executed, a file named `test.dat` is created and saved by the computer. The file is a sequential file consisting of the following data:

```
Batteries 39.95
Bulbs 3.22
Fuses 1.00
```

The actual storage of characters in the file depends on the character codes used by the computer. Although only 35 characters appear to be stored in the file, corresponding to the descriptions, blanks, and prices written to the file, the file actually contains 38 characters. The extra characters consist of the newline escape sequence at the end of the first two lines and the special end-of-file marker placed as the last item in the file when the file is closed. Assuming characters are stored using the ASCII code, the `test.dat` file is physically stored as illustrated in Figure 7.2. For convenience, the character corresponding to each hexadecimal code is listed below the code. A code of 20 represents the blank character. Although the actual code used for the end-of-file marker depends on the system you are using, the hexadecimal code 26, corresponding to Control-Z, is common for the DOS operating system.

```
42 61 74 74 65 72 69 65 73 20 33 39 2e 32 35 0A 42 75 6c 62 73
 B  a  t  t  e  r  i  e  s     3  9  .  2  5 \n  B  u  l  b  s

20 33 2e 32 32 0A 46 75 73 65 73 20 31 2e 30 32 26
    3  .  2  2 \n  F  u  s  e  s     1  .  0  0  ^z
```

Figure 7.2 The `test.dat` file as stored by the computer.

Reading data from a file is almost identical to reading data from a standard keyboard, except that the `cin` object is replaced by the `fstream` object declared in the program. For example, if `in_file` is declared as an object of type `fstream` that is opened for input, the input statement

```
in_file >> descrip >> price;
```

will read the next two items in the file and store them in the variables `descrip` and `price`.

The file stream name in this statement, in place of `cin`, simply directs the input to come from the file stream rather than the standard input device stream, `cin`. Other methods that can be used for stream I/O are listed in Table 7.2. Each of these methods must, of course, be preceded by a stream object name.

Table 7.2 `fstream` **Methods**

Method Name	Description
`get(character-variable)`	Extract the next character from the input stream.
`getline(string var,int n,'\n')`	Extract characters from the input stream until either $n - 1$ characters are read or a newline is encountered (terminates the input with a '\0')
`peek(character-variable)`	Return the next character in the input stream without extracting it from the stream.
`put(character-expression)`	Put a character on the output stream.
`putback(character-expression)`	Push back a character onto the input stream. Does not alter the data in the file.
`eof(void)`	Returns a true if a read has been attempted past the EOF (end-of-file).
`ignore(int n)`	Skip over the next n characters; If n is omitted, the default is to skip over the next single character.

Reading data from a file requires that the programmer knows how the data appears in the file. This is necessary for correct "stripping" of the data from the file into appropriate variables for storage. All files are read sequentially, so that once an item is read the next item in the file becomes available for reading.

Point of Information

The `istream get()` **and** `putback()` **Methods**

All input streams have a `get()` method that permits character-by-character input from the stream. This method works in a similar manner to character extraction using the `>>` operator with two important differences: if a newline character, `'\n'`, or a blank character, `' '`, are encountered, these characters are read in the same manner as any other alphanumeric character. The syntax of this method call is

istream-name.get(character-variable);

For example, the following code can be used to read the next character from the standard input stream and store the character into the variable `ch`:

```
char ch;
cin.get(ch);
```

In a similar manner, if `in_file` is an `istream` object that has been opened to a file, the following code reads the next character in the stream and assigns it to the character keycode:

```
char keycode;
in_file.get(keycode);
```

In addition to the `get()` method, all input streams have a `putback()` method that can be used to put the last character read from an input stream back on the stream.. This method has the syntax

istream-name.putback(character-expression);

where character-expression can be any character variable of character value.

The `putback()` method provides an output capability to an input stream. It should be noted that the putback character need not be the last character read; rather, it can be any character. All putback characters, however, have no effect on the data file but only on the open input stream. Thus, the data file characters remain unchanged, although the characters subsequently read from the input stream can change. For this reason `putback()` is typically used to permit pre-scanning a character from an input stream using `get()` followed by an immediate return of the same character to the stream.

Program 7.3 illustrates reading the `test.dat` file that was created in Program 7.2. The program also illustrates how the EOF marker, which is the NULL character, can be detected by the `peek()` function. As long as the EOF has not been detected, the program will continue to read characters from the file.

Program 7.3

```cpp
#include <fstream.h>
#include <stdlib.h>
#include <iomanip.h>

int main()
{
  const int MAXLENGTH = 21;    // maximum file name length
  const int MAXCHARS = 31;     // maximum description length
  char filename[MAXLENGTH] = "test.dat";
  char descrip[MAXCHARS];
  int ch;
  float price;
  ifstream in_file;

  in_file.open(filename);

  if (in_file.fail())  // check for successful open
  {
    cout << "\nThe file was not successfully opened"
         << "\n Please check that the file currently exists."
         << endl;
    exit(1);
  }

    // set the format for the standard output stream
  cout << setiosflags(ios::fixed)
       << setiosflags(ios::showpoint)
       << setprecision(2);

  cout << endl;  // start on a new line

    // read and display the file's contents
  while ( (ch = in_file.peek()) != EOF ) // check next character
  {
    in_file >> descrip >> price;  // input the data
    cout << descrip << ' ' << price << endl;
  }

  in_file.close();

  return 0;
}
```

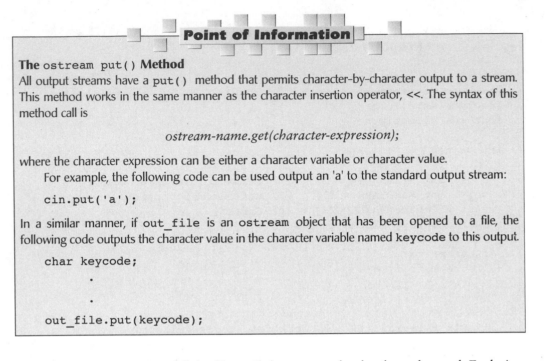

Point of Information

The ostream put() Method

All output streams have a put() method that permits character-by-character output to a stream. This method works in the same manner as the character insertion operator, <<. The syntax of this method call is

ostream-name.get(character-expression);

where the character expression can be either a character variable or character value.

For example, the following code can be used output an 'a' to the standard output stream:

```
cin.put('a');
```

In a similar manner, if out_file is an ostream object that has been opened to a file, the following code outputs the character value in the character variable named keycode to this output.

```
char keycode;
    .

    .

out_file.put(keycode);
```

Program 7.3 continues to read the file until the EOF marker has been detected. Each time the file is read, a string and a floating-point number are input to the program. The display produced by Program 7.3 is

```
Batteries 39.95
Bulbs 3.22
Fuses 1.00
```

In place of the in_file extraction, >>, used in Program 7.3, a getline() method call can be used. The getline() requires three arguments: a string variable where the characters read from the file will be stored, the maximum number of characters to be input in a single read, and a terminating character. For example, the function call

```
in_file.getline(line,80,'\n');
```

causes a maximum of 79 characters (one less than the specified number) to be read from the file named in_file and stored starting in the string variable named line. The function getline() continues reading characters until 79 characters have been read or a new-line character has been encountered. If a newline character is encountered it is included with the other entered characters before the string is terminated with the end-of-string NULL marker, \0. Program 7.4 illustrates the use of getline() in a working program.

Program 7.4

```cpp
#include <fstream.h>
#include <stdlib.h>
#include <iomanip.h>

int main()
{
  const int MAXLENGTH = 21;  // maximum file name length
  const int MAXCHARS = 80;   // maximum line length
  char file1[MAXLENGTH] = "test.dat";
  char line[MAXCHARS];
  int ch;
  ifstream in_file;

  in_file.open(file1);

  if (in_file.fail())   // check for successful open
  {
    cout << "\nThe file was not successfully opened"
         << "\n Please check that the file currently exists."
         << endl;
    exit(1);
  }

  cout << endl;   // start on a new line

    // now read the file
  while( (ch = in_file.peek()) != EOF )
  {
    in_file.getline(line,MAXCHARS,'\n');
    cout << line << endl;
  }

  in_file.close();

  return 0;
}
```

Program 7.4 is really a line-by-line text-copying program, reading a line of text from the file and then displaying it on the terminal. The output of Program 7.4 is

```
Batteries 39.95
Bulbs 3.22
Fuses 1.00
```

If it were necessary to obtain the description and price as individual variables, either Program 7.3 should be used or the string returned by `getline()` in Program 7.4 must be processed further to extract the individual data items.

Standard Device Files

The file stream objects we have used have all been logical file objects. A **logical file object** is a stream that connects a file of logically related data such as a data file to a program. In addition to logical file objects, C++ also supports physical file objects. A **physical file object** is a stream that connects to a hardware device, such as a keyboard, screen, or printer.

The actual physical device assigned to your program for data entry is formally called the **standard input file**. Usually this is the keyboard. When a `cin` object method call is encountered in a C++ program, a request goes to the operating system to this standard input file for the expected input. Similarly, when a `cout` object method call is encountered, the output is automatically displayed or "written to" a device that has been assigned as the standard output file. For most systems this is a terminal screen, although it can be a printer.

When a program is executed, the standard input stream `cin` is automatically connected to the standard input device. Similarly, the standard output stream `cout` is automatically connected to the standard output device. These two object streams are always available for programmer use.

Other Devices

The keyboard, display, and error-reporting devices are automatically connected to the internal stream objects named `cin`, `cout`, and `cerr`, respectively, by a C++ program using either the `iostream.h` or `fstream.h` header files. Additionally, other devices can be used for input or output if the name assigned by the system is known. For example, most IBM or IBM-compatible personal computers assign the name `prn` to the printer connected to the computer. For these computers a statement such as `out_file.open("prn")` connects the printer to the `ofstream` object named `out_file`. A subsequent statement, such as `out_file << "Hello World!";` would then cause the string `Hello World!` to be printed directly on the printer. Notice that as the name of an actual file, `prn` must be enclosed in double quotes in the `open()` function call.

Exercises 7.2

1. **a.** Write a C++ program that accepts lines of text from the keyboard and writes each line to a file named **text.dat** until an empty line is entered. An empty line is a line with no text—just a new line caused by pressing the ENTER (or RETURN) key.

   b. Modify Program 7.4 to read and display the data stored in the **text.dat** file created in Exercise 1a.

2. Determine the operating system command provided by your computer to display the contents of a saved file. Compare its operation with the program developed for Exercise 1b. (*Hint*: Typically the operating system command is called LIST, TYPE, or CAT.)

3. Write, compile, and run a C++ program that writes the four real numbers 92.65, 88.72, 77.46, and 82.93 to a text file named `result`. After writing the data to the file your program should read the data from the file, determine the average of the four numbers read, and display the average. Verify the output produced by your program by manually calculating the average of the four input numbers.

4. **a.** Write, compile, and execute a C++ program that creates a text file named `points` and writes the following numbers to the file:

6.3	8.2	18.25	24.32
4.0	4.0	10.0	−5.0
−2.0	5.0	4.0	5.0

   b. Using the data in the points file created in Exercise 4a write, compile, and run a C++ program that reads each record and interprets the first and second numbers in each record as the coordinates of one point and the third and fourth numbers as the coordinates of a second point. Have your program compute and display the slope and midpoint of the two points entered.

5. **a.** Write, compile, and run a C++ program that creates a text file named `volts` and writes the following 5 records to the file:

120.3	122.7	90.3	99.8
95.3	120.5	127.3	120.8
123.2	118.4	123.8	115.6
122.4	95.6	118.2	120.0
123.5	130.2	123.9	124.4

   b. Using the data in the `volts` file created in Exercise 5a write, compile, and run a C++ program that reads each record in the file, computes the average for each record, and displays the average.

6. **a.** Create a file containing the following car numbers, number of miles driven, and number of gallons of gas used by each car:

Car No.	Miles Driven	Gallons Used
54	250	19
62	525	38
71	123	6
85	1322	86
97	235	14

b. Write a C++ program that reads the data in the file created in Exercise 6a and displays the car number, miles driven, gallons used, and the miles per gallon for each car. The output should additionally contain the total miles driven, total gallons used, and average miles per gallon for all the cars. These totals should be displayed at the end of the output report.

7. a. A file named `polar.dat` contains the polar coordinates needed in a graphics program. Currently this file contains the following data:

Distance (inches)	Angle (degrees)
2.0	45.0
6.0	30.0
10.0	45.0
4.0	60.0
12.0	55.0
8.0	15.0

Write a C++ program to create this file on your computer system.

b. Using the `polar.dat` file created in Exercise 7a, write a C++ program that accepts distance and angle data from the user and adds the data to the end of the file.

c. Using the `polar.dat` file created in Exercise 7a, write a C++ program that reads this file and creates a second file named `xycord.dat`. The entries in the new file should contain the rectangular coordinates corresponding to the polar coordinates in the `polar.dat` file. Polar coordinates are converted to rectangular coordinates using the equations

$$x = r \cos\theta$$
$$y = r \sin\theta$$

where r is the distance coordinate and θ is the radian equivalent of the angle coordinate in the `polar.dat` file.

8. a. Store the following data in a file:
    5 96 87 78 93 21 4 92 82 85 87 6 72 69 85 75 81 73

b. Write a C++ program to calculate and display the average of each group of numbers in the file created in Exercise 8a. The data is arranged in the file so that each group of numbers is preceded by the number of data items in the group. Thus, the first number in the file, 5, indicates that the next five numbers should be grouped together. The number 4 indicates that the following four numbers are a group, and the 6 indicates that the last six numbers are a group. (*Hint*: Use a nested loop.)

Point of Information

A Way to Clearly Identify a File's Name and Location

During program development test files are usually placed in the same directory as the program. Therefore a method call such as `in_file.open("exper.dat")` causes no problems to the operating system. In production systems, however, it is not uncommon for data files to reside in one directory while program files reside in another. For this reason it is always a good idea to include the full path name of any file opened.

For example, if the `exper.dat` file resides in the directory `/test/files`, the `open()` call should include the full path name, viz: `in_file.open("/test/files/exper.dat")`. Then, no matter where the program is run from, the operating system will know where to locate the file.

Another important convention is to list all file names at the top of a program instead of embedding the names deep within the code. This can easily be accomplished by string variables to store each file name. For example, if the statements:

```
const int MAXLENGTH = 31;
char file1[MAXLENGTH] = "\test\files\exper.dat";
```

are placed at the top of a program file, the declaration statement clearly lists both the name of the desired file and its location. Then, if some other file is to be tested, all that is required is a simple one line change at the top of the program.

Using a string variable for the file's name is also useful for the `fail()` method check. For example, consider the following code:

```
ifstream infile;

in_file.open(file1);

if (in_file.fail())
{
  cout << "\n The file named " << file1 << " was not successfully opened"
       <<\n Please check that this file currently exists."
  exit(1);
}
```

In this code the name of the file that failed to open is directly displayed within the error message without the name being embedded as a string value.

7.3 RANDOM FILE ACCESS

File organization refers to the way data is stored in a file. All the files we have used have **sequential organization**. This means that the characters in the file are stored in a sequential manner, one after another. Additionally, we have read the files in a sequential manner. The way data is retrieved from the file is called **file access**. The fact that the characters in the file are stored sequentially, however, does not force sequential file access.

In **random access** any character in the file can be read directly, without first having to read all the characters stored ahead of it. To provide random access to files, each `ifstream` object establishes a file position marker. This marker is a long integer that represents an offset from the beginning of each file and keeps track of where the next character is to be read from or written to. The member functions that are used to access and change the file position marker are listed in Table 7.3.

Table 7.3 File Position Marker Functions

Name[3]	Description
`seekg(offset, mode)`	For input files, move to the offset position as indicated by the mode
`seekp(offset, mode)`	For output files, move to the offset position as indicated by the mode
`tellg(void)`	For input files, return the current value of the file position marker
`tellp(void)`	For output files, return the current value of the file position marker

The `seek()` functions allow the programmer to move to any position in the file. In order to understand this function, you must first clearly understand how data is referenced in the file using the file position marker.

Each character in a data file is located by its position in the file. The first character in the file is located at position 0, the next character at position 1, and so on. A character's position is also referred to as its offset from the start of the file. Thus, the first character has a 0 offset, the second character has an offset of 1, and so on for each character in the file.

The `seek()` functions require two arguments: the offset, as a long integer, into the file and where the offset is to be calculated from, as determined by the mode. The three possible alternatives for the mode are `ios::beg`, `ios::cur`, and `ios::end`, which denote the beginning, current position, and the end of the file, respectively. Thus, a mode of `ios::beg` means the offset is the true offset from the start of the file. A mode of `ios::cur` means that the offset is relative to the current position in the file, and an `ios::end` mode means the offset is relative to the end of the file. A positive offset means move forward in the file and a negative offset means move backward. Examples of

---

[3]The suffixes g and p denote get and put, respectively, where get refers to an input (get from) file and put refers to an output (put to) file.

seek() function calls are shown below. In these examples, assume that in_file has been opened as an input file and out_file as an output file:

```
in_file.seekg(4L,ios::beg);     // go to the fifth character in the input file
out_file.seekp(4L,ios::beg);    // go to the fifth character in the output file
in_file.seekg(4L,ios::cur);     // move ahead five characters in the input file
out_file.seekp(4L,ios::cur);    // move ahead five characters in the output file
in_file.seekg(-4L,ios::cur);    // move back five characters in the input file
out_file.seekp(-4L,ios::cur);   // move back five characters in the output file
in_file.seekg(0L,ios::beg);     // go to start of the input file
out_file.seekp(0L,ios::beg);    // go to start of the output file
in_file.seekg(0L,ios::end);     // go to end of the input file
out_file.seekp(0L,ios::end);    // go to end of the output file
in_file.seekg(-10L,ios::end);   // go to 10 characters before the input file's end
out_file.seekp(-10L,ios::end);  // go to 10 characters before the output file's end
```

Notice, in these examples, that the offset passed to seekg() and seekp() must be a long integer.

As opposed to the seek() functions that move the file position marker, the tell() functions simply return the offset value of the file position marker. For example, if ten characters have already been read from an input file named in_file, the function call

```
in_file.tellg();
```

returns the long integer 10. This means that the next character to be read is offset 10 byte positions from the start of the file and is the eleventh character in the file.

Program 7.5 illustrates the use of seekg() and tellg() to read a file in reverse order, from last character to first. As each character is read it is also displayed.

Assuming the file test.dat contains the following data,

```
The grade was 92.5
```

the output of Program 7.5 is:

```
5 : . : 2 : 9 :   : s : a : w :   : e : d : a : r : g :   : e : h : T :
```

Program 7.5 initially goes to the last character in the file. The offset of this character, which is the end-of-file character, is saved in the variable last. Since tellg() returns a long integer, last has been declared as long integer.

Starting from the end of the file, seekg() is used to position the next character to be read, referenced from the end of the file. As each character is read, the character is displayed and the offset adjusted in order to access the next character. It should be noted that the first offset used is −1, which represents the character immediately preceding the EOF marker.

Program 7.5

```cpp
#include <fstream.h>
#include <stdlib.h>

int main()
{
  const int MAXLENGTH = 31;
  char filename[MAXLENGTH] = "test.dat";
  char ch;
  long offset, last;

  ifstream in_file(filename);

  if (in_file.fail())    // check for successful open
  {
    cout << "\nThe file was not successfully opened"
         << "\n Please check that the file currently exists"
         << endl;
    exit(1);
  }

  in_file.seekg(0L,ios::end);    // move to the end of the file
  last = in_file.tellg();        // save the offset of the last character

  for(offset = 1L; offset <= last; offset++)
  {
    in_file.seekg(-offset, ios::end);
    ch = in_file.get();
    cout << ch << " : ";
  }

  in_file.close();

  return 0;
}
```

Exercises 7.3

1. **a.** Either using a text editor or copying the file `test.dat` on the program source disk provided with this book, create a file named `test.dat` on the directory that contains your program files.

b. Enter and execute Program 7.5 on your computer.

2. Rewrite Program 7.5 so that the origin for the `seekg()` function used in the `for` loop is the start of the file rather than the end.

3. The `seek()` functions return a 0 if the position specified has been reached, or a 1 if the position specified was beyond the file's boundaries. Modify Program 7.5 to display an error message if `seekg()` returns a 1.

4. Write a program that will read and display every second character in a file named `test.dat`.

5. Using the `seek()` and `tell()` functions, write a function named `f_chars()` that returns the total number of characters in a file.

6. Write a function named `r_bytes()` that reads and displays *n* characters starting from any position in a file. The function should accept three arguments: a file object name, the offset of the first character to be read, and the number of characters to be read (*NOTE*: the prototype for `r_bytes` should be `void r_bytes(fstream&, long, long)`).

7.4 FILE STREAMS AS FUNCTION ARGUMENTS

A file stream object can be a function argument. The only requirement is that the function's formal parameter be a reference to an the appropriate stream, either as `ifstream&` or `ofstream&`. For example, in Program 7.6 an `ofstream` object named `out_file` is opened in `main()` and this stream object is passed to the function `in_out()`. Notice that the function prototype and header line for `in_out()` both declare the formal parameter as a reference to an `ostream` object type. The `in_out()` function is then used to write five lines of user-entered text to the file.

Within `main()` the file `ostream` object is named `out_file`. This object is passed to the `in_out()` function and is accepted as the formal parameter named `file_out`, which is declared to be a reference to an `ostream` object type. The function `in_out()` then uses its reference parameter `file_out` as an output file stream name in an identical manner as `main()` would use the `out_file` stream object. Notice also that Program 7.6 uses the `getline()` method introduced in Section 7.2 (see Table 7.2). Although we have explicitly included the newline character as the third argument passed to `getline()`, this argument can be omitted. This is because the `'\n'` is a default value for the third formal parameter.

Program 7.6

```cpp
#include <fstream.h>
#include <stdlib.h>

void in_out(ofstream&);     // function prototype

int main()
{
  const int MAXCHARS = 21;
  char fname[MAXCHARS] = "list.dat";  // here is the file we are working with
  ofstream out_file;

  out_file.open(fname);
  if (out_file.fail())    // check for a successful open
  {
    cout << "\nThe output file " << fname << " was not successfully opened"
         << endl;
    exit(1);
   }

  in_out(out_file);  // call the function

  return 0;
}

void in_out(ofstream& file_out)
{
  const int LINELEN = 80;  // longest length of a line of text
  const int NUMLINES = 5;  // number of lines of text
  int count;
  char line[LINELEN];  // enough storage for one line of text

  cout << "Please enter five lines of text:" << endl;
  for (count = 0; count < NUMLINES; count++)
  {
    cin.getline(line,LINELEN,'\n');
    file_out << line << endl;
  }

  return;
}
```

In Program 7.7 we have expanded on Program 7.6 by adding a get_open() function to perform the open. Notice that get_open(), like in_out(), accepts a reference argument to an ofstream object. After the get_open() function completes execution, this reference is passed to in_out(), as it was in Program 7.6. Although you might be tempted to write get_open() to return a reference to an ofstream, this will not work because it ultimately results in an attempt to assign a returned reference to an existing one.

Program 7.7

```
#include <fstream.h>
#include <stdlib.h>

int get_open(ofstream&);   // pass a reference to an fstream
void in_out(ofstream&);    // pass a reference to an fstream

int main()
{

  ofstream out_file;    // file1 is an fstream object

  get_open(out_file);   // open the file
  in_out(out_file);     // write to it
}

int get_open(ofstream& file_out)
{
  const int MAXCHARS = 13;
  char name[MAXCHARS];

  cout << "\nEnter a file name: " << endl;
  cin.getline(name,MAXCHARS,'\n');

  file_out.open(name);       // open the file

  if (file_out.fail())       // check for successful open
  {
    cout << "Cannot open the file" << endl;
    exit(1);
  }
  else
    return 0;
}
```

(Continued)

(Continued)

```
void in_out(ofstream& file_out)
{
  const int NUMLINES = 5;   // number of lines
  const int LINELEN = 80;   // maximum line length
  int count;
  char line[LINELEN];    // enough storage for one line of text

  cout << "Please enter five lines of text:" << endl;
  for (count = 0; count < NUMLINES; ++count)
  {
    cin.getline(line,LINELEN,'\n');
    file_out << line << endl;
  }

  return;
}
```

Program 7.7 is simply a modified version of Program 7.6 that now allows the user to enter a file name from the standard input device and then opens the `ostream` connection to the external file. If the name of an existing data file is entered, the file will be destroyed when it is opened for output. A useful "trick" that you may encounter to prevent this type of mishap is to open the entered file using an input file stream. Then if the file exists, the `fail()` method will indicate a successful open (i.e., the open does not fail), which indicates that the file is available for input. This can be used to alert the user that a file with the entered name currently exists in the system and to request confirmation that the data in the file can be destroyed and the file reopened for output. Before the file is reopened for output the input file stream should be closed. The implementation of this algorithm is left as an exercise.

Exercises 7.4

1. A function named `p_file()` is to receive a file name as a reference to an `ifstream` object. What declarations are required to pass a file name to `p_file()`?

2. Write a function named `fcheck()` that checks whether a file exists. The function should accept an `ifstream` object as a formal reference parameter. If the file exists, the function should return a value of 1, otherwise the function should return a value of zero.

3. Rewrite the function `get_open()` used in Program 7.7 to incorporate the file-checking procedures described in this section. Specifically, if the entered file name exists, an appropriate message should be displayed. The user should then be presented with the option of entering a new file name or allowing the program to overwrite the existing file. Use the function written for Exercise 2 in your program.

4. Assume that a data file consisting of a group of individual lines has been created. Write a function named `print_line()` that will read and display any desired line of the file. For example, the function call `print_line(fstream& f_name,5);` should display the fifth line of the passed object stream.

7.5 ▷ COMMON PROGRAMMING ERRORS

Three programming errors are common when using files. The most common error is to use the file's external name in place of the internal file stream object name when accessing the file. The only stream method that uses the data file's external name is the `open()` function. As always, all stream methods presented in this chapter must be preceded by a stream object name and the dot operator.

A second error occurs when using the EOF marker to detect the end of a file. Any variable used to accept the EOF must be declared as an integer variable. For example, if `ch` is declared as a character variable the expression

```
while ( (ch = in.file.peek()) != EOF )
```

produces an infinite loop.[4] This occurs because a character variable can never take on an EOF code. The value of EOF is an integer value (usually –1) that has no character representation. This ensures that the EOF code can never be confused with any legitimate character encountered as normal data in the file. To terminate the loop created by the above expression, the variable `ch` must be declared as an integer variable.

The last error concerns the offset argument sent to the `seekg()` and `seekp()` functions. This offset must be a long integer constant or variable. Any other value passed to these functions can result in an unpredictable effect.

7.6 ▷ CHAPTER SUMMARY

1. A data file is any collection of data stored together in an external storage medium under a common name.

2. A data file is connected to a file stream using `fstream`'s `open()` method. This function connects a file's external name with an internal object name. After the file is opened, all subsequent accesses to the file require the internal object name.

3. A file can be opened in input or output mode. An opened output file stream either creates a new data file or erases the data in an existing opened file. An opened input file stream makes an existing file's data available for input. An error condition results if the file does not exist and can be detected using the `fail()` method.

---

[4]This will not occur on UNIX systems where characters are stored as signed integers.

4. All file streams must be declared as objects of either the `ifstream` or `ofstream` classes. This means that a declaration similar to either

```
ifstream in_file;
ofstream out_file;
```

must be included with the declarations in which the file is opened. The stream object names `in_file` and `out_file` can be replaced with any user-selected object name.

5. In addition to any files opened within a function, the standard stream objects `cin`, `cout`, and `cerr` are automatically declared and opened when a program is run. The object name of an input file stream used for data entry (usually from the keyboard) is `cin`, `cout` is the object name of an output file stream used for default data display (usually the terminal screen), and `cerr` is the object name of an output file stream used for displaying system error messages (usually the terminal screen).

6. Data files can be accessed randomly using the `seekg()`, `seekp()`, `tellg()`, and `tellp()` methods. The g versions of these functions are used to alter and query the file position marker for input file streams, while the p versions do the same for output file streams.

7. Table 7.4 lists the methods supplied by the `fstream` class for file manipulation.

Table 7.4 `fstream` **Methods**

Method Name	Description
`get(character-variable)`	Extract the next character from the input stream.
`getline(string var,int n,'\n')`	Extract characters from the input stream until either $n - 1$ characters are read or a newline is encountered (terminates the input with a '\0').
`peek(character-variable)`	Return the next character in the input stream without extracting it from the stream.
`put(character-expression)`	Put a character on the output stream.
`putback(character-expression)`	Push back a character onto the input stream. Does not alter the data in the file.
`eof(void)`	Returns a True if a read has been attempted past the EOF (end-of-file).
`ignore(int n)`	Skip over the next n characters; If n is omitted, the default is to skip over the next single character.

7.7 ◆ CHAPTER APPENDIX: THE `iostream` CLASS LIBRARY

The `iostream` class library provided as part of each C++ compiler is not part of the C++ language. By convention each C++ compiler provides an Input/Output library named `iostream` that contains a number of classes that adhere to a common ANSI specification.

As we have already seen, the classes contained within the `iostream` class library access files using entities called streams. For most systems the data bytes transferred on a stream represent either ASCII characters or binary numbers.

When the data transfer between a computer and an external data file modifies the data, so that the data stored in the file *is not* an exact representation of the data as it is stored internally within the computer, the file is referred to as a **formatted file**. Examples of this are files that store their data using ASCII codes. Such files are also referred to as **text files**, and the terms text and formatted are sometimes used interchangeably.

When the data transfer between a computer and an external data file is done without modification, so that the data stored in the file *is* an exact representation of the data as it is stored internally within the computer, the file is referred to as a **binary** *or* **unformatted file**.

The mechanism for reading a byte stream from a file or writing a byte stream to a file, with or without formatting, is always hidden when using a high-level language such as C++. Nevertheless, it is useful to understand this mechanism so that we can place the services provided by the `iostream` class library in their appropriate context.

File Stream Transfer Mechanism

The mechanism for transferring data between a program and a data file is illustrated in Figure 7.3.

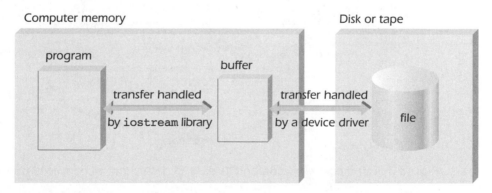

Figure 7.3 The data transfer mechanism.

As illustrated in Figure 7.3, transferring data between a program and a file involves an intermediate file buffer contained in the computer's memory. Each opened file is assigned its own file buffer, which is simply a storage area that is used by the data as it is transferred between the program and the file.

From its side, the program either writes a set of data bytes to the file buffer or reads a set of data bytes from the file buffer using a stream object.

On the other side of the buffer the transfer of data between the device storing the actual data file (usually a tape, disk, or CD-ROM drive) and the file buffer is handled by special operating system programs that are referred to as **device drivers**.[5] Typically a disk device driver will only transfer data between the disk and file buffer in fixed sizes, such as 1024 bytes at a time. Thus, the file buffer provides a convenient means of permitting a device driver to transfer data in blocks of one size while the program can access them using a different size (typically as individual characters or as a fixed number of characters per line).

Components of the `iostream` Class Library[6]

The iostream class library consists of two primary base classes, the `streambuf` class and the `ios` class. The `streambuf` class provides the file buffer illustrated in Figure 7.3 and a number of general routines for transferring data when little or no formatting is required. The `ios` class contains a pointer to the file buffers provided by the `streambuf` class and a number of general routines for transferring data with formatting. From these two base classes a number of other classes are derived and included in the `iostream` class library.

Figure 7.4 illustrates an inheritance diagram for the `ios` family of classes as it relates to the `ifstream`, `ofstream`, and `fstream` classes. The inheritance diagram for the `streambuf` family of classes is shown in Figure 7.5. As described in Chapter 9, the convention adopted for inheritance diagrams is that the arrows point from a derived class to a base class.

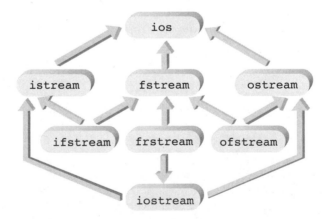

Figure 7.4 The base class `ios` and its derived classes (not all derived classes are shown).

---

[5]Device drivers are not stand-alone programs but are an integral part of the operating system. Essentially the device driver is a section of operating system code that accesses a hardware device, such as a disk unit, and handles the data transfer between the device and the computer's memory. As such it must correctly synchronize the speed of the data transferred between the computer and the device sending or receiving the data. This is because the computer's internal data transfer rate is generally much faster than any device connected to it.

[6]Although this appendix contains material directly relating to file streams, an understanding of it requires the material presented in Chapter 9. As such, this section should not be read until Chapter 9 has been completed.

Figure 7.5 The base class `streambuf` and its derived classes (not all derived classes are shown).

The correspondence between the classes illustrated in Figures 7.4 and 7.5, including the header files that define these classes, is listed in Table 7.5.

Table 7.5

ios Class	streambuf Class	Header File
istream ostream iostream	streambuf	iostream.h or fstream.h
ifstream ofstream fstream	filebuf	fstream.h

Thus, the `ifstream`, `ofstream`, and `fstream` classes that we have used for file access all use a buffer provided by the `filebuf` class that is defined in the `fstream.h` header file. Similarly, the `cin`, `cout`, and `cerr iostream` objects that we have been using throughout the text use a buffer provided by the `streambuf` class and defined in both the `iostream.h` and `fstream` header files.

In-Memory Formatting

In addition to the classes illustrated in Figure 7.4, a class named `strstream` is also derived from the `ios` class. This class uses the `strstreambuf` class illustrated in Figure 7.5, requires the `strstream.h` header file, and provides capabilities for writing and reading strings to and from in-memory defined streams.

As an output stream, such streams are typically used to "assemble" a string from smaller pieces until a complete line of characters is ready to be written, either to `cout` or to a file. Attaching a `strstream` object to a buffer for this purpose is done in a similar manner as attaching an `fstream` object to an output file. For example, the statement

```
strstream inmem(buf, 72, ios::out);
```

attaches a `strstream` object to an existing buffer of 72 bytes in output mode. Program 7.10 illustrates using this statement within the context of a complete program.

Program 7.8

```cpp
#include <strstream.h>
#include <iomanip.h>

int main()
{
  const int MAXCHARS = 81;   // one more than the maximum characters in a line
  char buf[MAXCHARS];
  int units = 10;
  float price = 36.85;

  strstream inmem(buf, MAXCHARS, ios::out);   // open an in-memory stream

    // write to the buffer through the stream
  inmem << "No. of units = "
        << setw(3) << units
        << "  Price per unit = $"
        << setw(8) << setprecision(2) << price << '\0';
  cout << '|' << buf << '|';

  return 0;
}
```

The output produced by Program 7.8 is:

```
|No. of units =  10  Price per unit = $   36.85|
```

As illustrated by this output, the character buffer has been correctly filled in by insertions to the `inmem` stream (note that the end-of-string NULL, \0, which is the last insertion to the stream, is required to correctly close off the string). Once the `buf` string variable has been filled, it would typically be written out to a file as a single string.

In a similar manner a `strstream` object can be opened in input mode. Typically such a stream would be used as a working storage area, or buffer, for storing a complete line of text from either a file or standard input. Once the buffer has been filled, the extraction operator would be used to "disassemble" the string into component parts and convert each data item into its designated data type. Doing this permits inputting data from a file on a line-by-line basis prior to assigning individual data items to their respective variables.

Materials Science and Metallurgical Engineering

To a large extent, advances in many areas of engineering in the twentieth century have been made possible by discoveries of new materials and a better understanding of the properties of existing materials. Knowledge of the physical and chemical principles determining the electrical properties of exotic materials called semiconductors have resulted in the fantastic progress in the field of solid-state devices, from transistors to integrated-circuit chips to large computers. Better understanding of the origins of metallic properties such as hardness, strength, ductility, corrosiveness, and others have led to improved design of automobiles, aircraft, spacecraft, and all types of machinery. The field is basically subdivided into metals and nonmetals, although there is often considerable overlap of interests and activities.

Materials Science

Materials science concerns the behavior and properties of materials, both metals and nonmetals, from both microscopic and macroscopic perspectives. It includes the following areas

1. Ceramics. Noncrystalline materials, such as glass, that are nonmetallic and that require high temperatures in their processing. Ceramics can be made brittle or flexible, hard or soft, or stronger than steel. They can be made to have a variety of chemical properties.

2. Polymers. Structural and physical properties of organic, inorganic, and natural polymers that are useful in engineering applications.

3. Materials fabrication, processing, and treatment. All aspects of the manufacture of ceramics, metals, and polymer synthesis, from the growth of crystals and fibers to metal forming.

4. Corrosion. Reaction mechanism and thermodynamics of corrosion of metals in the atmosphere or submerged under water or chemicals, whether standing or under stress.

5. Stress-strain, and fatigue-fracture of engineering materials. Physical properties governing the deformation and fracture of materials and their improvement and use in construction and design.

(Continued)

Metallurgical Engineering

Metallurgical engineering is the branch engineering responsible for the production of metals and metal alloys, from the discovery of ore deposits to the fabrication of the refined metal into useful products. Metallurgical engineers are important in every step in the production of metal from metal ore. Metallurgical engineering includes the following areas

1. Mining engineering. Usually a separate branch of engineering. However, the concerns of mining engineers and metallurgists frequently overlap in the processes of extraction of metals from metal ores and the refinement into usable products. Extraction metallurgy makes use of physical and chemical reactions to optimize metal production.

2. Metals fabrication. Metal forming into products such as cans, wires, and tubes; casting and joining of metals—for example, by welding.

3. Physical metallurgy. Analysis of stress-strain, fatigue-fracture characteristics of metals and metal alloys to prevent engineering component failures.

CHAPTER 8

Introduction to Classes

TOPIC

8.1 ABSTRACT DATA TYPES IN C++ (classes)
ABSTRACT DATA TYPES
CLASS CONSTRUCTION
TERMINOLOGY

8.2 CONSTRUCTORS
CALLING CONSTRUCTORS
OVERLOADED AND INLINE CONSTRUCTORS
DESTRUCTORS

8.3 APPLICATIONS
APPLICATION 1: CONSTRUCTING AN ELEVATOR OBJECT
APPLICATION 2: A SINGLE OBJECT GAS PUMP SIMULATION

8.4 COMMON PROGRAMMING ERRORS

8.5 CHAPTER SUMMARY

Besides being an improved version of C, the distinguishing characteristic of C++ is its support of object-oriented programming. Central to this object orientation is the concept of an abstract data type, which is a programmer-defined data type. In this chapter we explore the implications of permitting programmers to define their own data types and then present C++'s mechanism for constructing abstract data types. As we will see, the construction of a data type is based on both variables and functions; variables provide the means for creating new data configurations and functions provide the means for preforming operations on these structures. What C++ provides is a unique way of combining variables and functions together in a self-contained, cohesive unit from which objects can be created.

Point of Information

Procedural, Hybrid, and Pure Object-Oriented Languages

Most high-level programming languages can be categorized into one of three main categories: procedural, hybrid, or object-oriented. FORTRAN, which was the first commercially available high-level programming language, is procedural. This makes sense because FORTRAN was designed to perform mathematical calculations that used standard algebraic formulas. Formally, these formulas were described as algorithms and then the algorithms were coded using function and subroutine procedures. Other procedural languages that followed FORTRAN included BASIC, COBOL, and Pascal.

Currently there are only two pure object-oriented languages; Smalltalk and Eiffel. The first requirement of a pure object-oriented language is that it contain three specific features: classes, inheritance, and polymorphism (each of these features is described in this and the next chapter). In addition to providing these features, however, a "pure" object-oriented language must, as a minimum, always use classes. In a pure object-oriented language all data types are constructed as classes, all data values are objects, all operators can be overloaded, and every data operation can only be executed using a class member function. *It is impossible in a pure object-orientated language not to use object-oriented features* throughout a program. This is not the case in a hybrid language.

In a hybrid language, such as C++, *it is impossible not to use elements of a procedural program.* This is because the use of any built-in data type or operation effectively violates the pure object-oriented paradigm. Although a hybrid language must have the ability to define classes, the distinguishing feature of a hybrid language is that it is possible to write a complete program using only procedural code. Additionally, hybrid languages need not even provide inheritance and polymorphic features—but they must provide classes. Languages that use classes but do not provide inheritance and polymorphic features are referred to as *object-based* languages rather than *object-oriented*. All versions of Visual Basic prior to Version 4, are examples of object-based hybrid languages.

8.1 ▷ ABSTRACT DATA TYPES IN C++ (classes)

We live in a world full of objects—planes, trains, cars, telephones, books, computers, etc. Until quite recently, however, programming techniques have not reflected this at all. The primary programming paradigm[1] has been procedural, defining a program as an algorithm written in a machine readable language. The reasons for this emphasis on procedural programming are primarily historical.

When computers were developed in the 1940s they were used by mathematicians for military purposes—for computing bomb trajectories and decoding enemy orders and diplomatic transmissions. After World War II computers were still primarily used by mathematicians for mathematical computations. This reality was reflected in the name of the first commercially available high-level language introduced in 1957. The language's name was FORTRAN, which was an acronym for FORmula TRANslation.

---

[1]A *paradigm* is a standard way of thinking about or doing something.

Further reflecting this predominant use was the fact that in the 1960s almost all computer courses were taught in either engineering or mathematics departments. The term computer science was not yet in common use and computer science departments were just being formed.

This situation has changed dramatically, primarily for two reasons. One of the reasons for disenchantment with procedural-oriented programs has been the failure of traditional procedural languages to provide an adequate means of containing software costs. Software costs include all costs associated with initial program development and subsequent program maintenance. As illustrated in Figure 8.1, the major cost of most computer projects today, whether technical or commercial, is for software.

Figure 8.1 Software is the major cost of most computer projects.

Software costs contribute so heavily to total project costs because they are directly related to human productivity (they are labor intensive), while the equipment associated with hardware costs is related to manufacturing technologies. For example, microchips that cost over $500 ten years ago can now be purchased for less than $1.

It is far easier, however, to dramatically increase manufacturing productivity a thousandfold, with the consequent decrease in hardware costs, than it is for programmers to double either the quantity or quality of the code they produce. So as hardware costs have plummeted, software productivity and its associated costs have remained relatively constant. Thus, the ratio of software costs to total system costs (hardware plus software) has increased dramatically.

One way to significantly increase programmer productivity is to create code that can be reused without extensive revision, retesting, and revalidation. The inability of procedurally structured code to provide this type of reusability has led to the search for other software approaches.

The second reason for disenchantment with procedural-based programming has been the emergence of graphical screens and the subsequent interest in window applications. Providing a graphical user interface (GUI) where a user can easily move around in even a single window is a challenge using procedural code. Programming multiple and possibly overlapping windows on the same graphical screen simply increases the complexity enormously when procedural code is used.

Unlike a procedural approach, however, an object-oriented approach fits well to graphical windowed environments, where each window can be specified as a self-contained rectangular object that can be moved and resized in relation to other objects on the screen. Additionally, within each window other graphical objects, such as check boxes, option buttons, labels, and text boxes can easily be placed and moved.

To provide this object-creation capability, extensions to the procedural language C were developed. This extension became the new language named C++, which permits a programmer to both use and create new objects.

Central to the creation of objects is the concept of an abstract data type, which is simply a user-defined data type, as opposed to the built-in data types provided by all languages (such as integer and floating-point types). Permitting a programmer to define new data types, such as a rectangular type, out of which specific rectangular objects can be created and displayed on a screen, forms the basis of C++'s object orientation.

Abstract Data Types

To gain a clear understanding of what an abstract data type is, consider the following three built-in data types supplied in C++: integers, floats, and characters. In using these data types we typically declare one or more variables of the desired type, use them in their accepted ways, and avoid using them in ways that are not specified. Thus, for example, we would not use the modulus operator on two floating-point numbers. Since this operation makes no sense for floating-point numbers it is never defined, in any programming language, for such numbers. Thus, although we typically don't consider it, each data type consists of *both* a type of data, such as integer or float, *and* specific operational capabilities provided for each type.

In computer terminology, the combination of data and their associated operations is defined as a **data type**. That is, a data type defines *both* the types of data and the types of operations that can be performed on the data. Seen in this light the integer data type, the floating-point data type, and the character data type provided in C++ are all examples of *built-in* data types that are defined by a type of data and specific operational capabilities provided for initializing and manipulating the type. In a simplified form this relationship can be described as

data type = allowable data + operational capabilities

Thus, the operations that have been using in C++ are an inherent part of each data type we have been using. For each of these data types the designers of C++ had to carefully consider, and then implement, specific operations.

To understand the importance of the operational capabilities provided by a programming language, let's take a moment to list some of those supplied with C++'s built-in data types (`ints`, `floats`, and `chars`). The minimum set of the capabilities provided by C++'s built-in data types is listed in Table 8.1.[2]

---

[2]You might notice the absence of reading and writing operations. In both C and C++, except for very primitive operations, input and output is provided by standard library routines and class functions.

Table 8.1 C++ Built-In Data Type Capabilities

Capability	Example
Define one or more variables of the data type	`int a, b;`
Initialize a variable at definition	`int a = 5;`
Assign a value to a variable	`a = 10;`
Assign one variable's value to another variable	`a = b;`
Perform mathematical operations	`a + b`
Perform relational operations	`a > b`
Convert from one data type to another	`a = int (7.2);`

Now let's see how all of this relates to abstract data types (ADTs). By definition an **abstract data type** is simply a user-defined type that defines both a type of data and the operations that can be performed on them. Such user-defined data types are required when we wish to create objects that are more complex than simple integers and characters. If we are to create our own data types we must be aware of both the type of data we are creating and the capabilities that we will provide to initialize and manipulate the data.

As a specific example, assume that we are programming an application that uses dates extensively. Clearly, from a data standpoint a date must be capable of accessing and storing a month, day, and year designation. Although from an implementation standpoint there are a number of means of storing a date, from a user viewpoint the actual implementation is not relevant. For example, a date can be stored as three integers, one for the month, day, and year, respectively. Alternatively, a single long integer in the form *yyyymmdd* can also be used. Using the long integer implementation the date 5/16/02 would be stored as the integer 20020516. For sorting dates the long integer format is very attractive, because the numerical sequence of the dates corresponds to their calendar sequence.

The method of internally structuring the date, unfortunately, supplies only a partial answer to our programming effort. We must still supply a set of operations that can be used with dates. Clearly, such operations could include assigning values to a date, subtracting two dates to determine the number of days between them, comparing two dates to determine which is earlier and which is later, and displaying a date in a form such as 12/03/01.

Notice that the details of how each operation works is dependent on how we choose to store a date (formally referred to as its data structure) and is only of interest to us as we develop each operation. For example, the implementation of comparing two dates will differ if we store a date using a single long integer as opposed to using separate integers for the month, day, and year, respectively.

The combination of the storage structure used for dates with a set of available operations appropriate to dates would then define an abstract Date data type. Once this date type is developed, programmers that want to use it need never be concerned with *how* dates are stored or *how* the operations are performed. All that they need to know is *what* each operation does and how to invoke it, much as they use C++'s built-in operations.

For example, we don't really care how the addition of two integers is performed but only that it is done correctly.

In C++ an abstract data type is referred to as a **class**. Construction of a class is inherently easy and we already have all the necessary tools in variables and functions. What C++ provides is a mechanism for packaging these two items together in a self-contained unit. Let's see how this is done.

Class Construction

A `class` defines both data and functions. This is usually accomplished by constructing a `class` in two parts, consisting of a declaration section and an implementation section. As illustrated in Figure 8.2, the declaration section declares both the data types and functions of the class. The implementation section is then used to define the functions whose prototypes have been declared in the declaration section.[3]

```
// class declaration section
class class_name
{
    data members
    (instance and variables)
    function members
    (inline or prototypes)
};
// class implementation section
function definitions
```

Figure 8.2 Format of a `class` definition.

Both the variables and functions listed in the `class` declaration section are collectively referred to as **class members**. Individually, the variables are referred to as both **data members** and as **instance variables** (the terms are synonymous), while the functions are referred to as **member functions**. A member function name may not be the same as a data member name.

As a specific example of a `class`, consider the following definition of a `class` named `Date`.

---

[3]This separation into two parts is not mandatory as the implementation can be included within the declaration section if inline functions are used.

```
//--- class declaration section

class Date
{
  private:         // notice the colon after the word private
      int month;    // a data member
      int day;      // a data member
      int year;     // a data member
    public:         // again, notice the colon here
      Date(int = 7, int = 4, int = 2001); // a member function - the constructor
      void setdate(int, int, int);      // a member function
      void showdate(void);              // a member function
};

//--- class implementation section

Date::Date(int mm, int dd, int yyyy)
{
  month = mm;
  day = dd;
  year = yyyy;
}

void Date::setdate(int mm, int dd, int yyyy)
{
  month = mm; day = dd; year = yyyy;

  return;
}

void Date::showdate(void)
{
  cout << "The date is ";
  cout << setfill('0')
       << setw(2) << month << '/'
       << setw(2) << day << '/'
       << setw(2) << year % 100; // extract the last 2 year digits
  cout << endl;

  return;
}
```

Since this definition may initially look overwhelming, first simply notice that it does consist of two sections—a declaration section and an implementation section. Now consider each of these sections individually.

The class declaration section begins with the keyword class followed by a class name. Following the class name are the class's variable declarations and function prototypes, enclosed in a brace pair that is terminating with a semicolon. Thus, the general structure of the form that we have used is[4]

```
class Name
{
  private:
    a list of variable declarations
  public:
    a list of function prototypes
};
```

Notice that this format is followed by our `Date` class, which for convenience we have listed below with no internal comments.

```
//--- class declaration section

class Date
{
  private:
      int month;
      int day;
      int year;
  public:
      Date(int = 7, int = 4, int = 2001);
      void setdate(int, int, int);
      void showdate(void);
};   // this is a declaration - don't forget the semi-colon
```

The name of this `class` is `Date`. Although the initial capital letter is not required, it is conventionally used to designate a `class`. The body of the declaration section, which is enclosed within braces, consists of variable and function declarations. In this case the data members `month`, `day`, and `year` are declared as integers and three functions named `Date()`, `setdate()`, and `showdate()` are declared via prototypes. The keywords `private` and `public` are access specifiers that define access rights. The `private` keyword specifies that the `class` members following, in this case the data members `month`, `day`, and `year`, may only be accessed by using the `class` functions (or friend functions, as will be discussed in Section 9.2).[5] The purpose of the `private` designation is specifically meant to enforce data security by requiring all access to `private` data members through the provided member functions. This type of access, which restricts a user from seeing how the data is actually stored is referred to as **data hiding**. Once a class category such as `private` is designated it remains in force until a new category is listed.

---

[4]Other forms are possible. As this form is one of the most commonly used and easily understood, it will serve as our standard model throughout the text.

[5]Note that the default membership category in a `class` is `private`, which means that this keyword can be omitted. In this text we will explicitly use the `private` designation to reinforce the idea of access restrictions inherent in `class` membership.

Specifically, we have chosen to store a date using three integers: one for the month, day, and year, respectively. We will also always store the year as a four-digit number. Thus, for example, we will store the year 1998 as 1998 and not as 98. Making sure to store all years with their correct century designation will eliminate a multitude of problems that can crop up if only the last two digits, such as 98, are stored. For example, the number of years between 2002 and 1999 can be quickly calculated as 2002 − 1999 = 3 years, while this same answer is not so easily obtained if only the year values 02 and 99 are used. Additionally, we are sure of what the year 2000 refers to, while a two-digit value such as 00 could refer to either 1900 or 2000.[6]

Following the `private class` data members, the function prototypes listed in the `Date class` have been declared as `public`. This means that these `class` functions *can* be called by any objects and functions not in `class` (outside). In general, all `class` functions should be `public`; as such they furnish capabilities to manipulate the class variables from outside of the class. For our `Date class` we have initially provided three functions named `Date()`, `setdate()`, and `showdate()`. Notice that one of these member functions has the same name, `Date`, as the `class` name. This particular function is referred to as a **constructor** function, and it has a specially defined purpose: it can be used to initialize `class` data members with values. The default values that are used for this function are the numbers 7, 4, and 2001, which, as we will shortly see, are used as the default `month`, `day`, and `year` values, respectively. The only point to notice here is that the default year is correctly represented as a four-digit integer that retains the century designation. Also notice that the constructor function has no return type, which is a requirement for this special function. The two remaining functions declared in our declaration example are `setdate()` and `showdate()`, both of which have been declared as returning no value (`void`). In the implementation section of the class these three member functions will be written to permit initialization, assignment, and display capabilities, respectively.

The **implementation section** of a `class` is where the member functions declared in the declaration section are written.[7] Figure 8.3 illustrates the general form of functions included in the implementation section. This format is correct for all functions except the constructor, which, as we have stated, has no return type.

```
return-type  class-name::function-name(parameter list)
{
     function body
}
```

Figure 8.3 Format of a member function.

---

[6]These problems are all included under the designation "The year 2000 problem."

[7]It is also possible to define these functions within the declaration section by declaring and writing them as inline functions. Examples of inline member functions are presented in Section 8.2.

As shown in Figure 8.3 member functions defined in the implementation section have the same format as all user-written C++ functions with the addition of the `class` name and scope resolution operator, `::`, that identifies the function as a member of a particular `class`. Let us now reconsider the implementation section of our `Date class`, which is repeated below for convenience.

```
//--- class implementation section

Date::Date(int mm, int dd, int yyyy)
{
  month = mm;
  day = dd;
  year = yyyy;
}

void Date::setdate(int mm, int dd, int yyyy)
{
  month = mm;
  day = dd;
  year = yyyy;

  return;
}

void Date::showdate(void)
{
  cout << "The date is ";
  cout << setfill('0')
       << setw(2) << month << '/'
       << setw(2) << day << '/'
       << setw(2) << year % 100; // extract the last 2 year digits
  cout << endl;

  return;
}
```

Notice that the first function in this implementation section has the same name as the `class`, which makes it a constructor function. As such, it has no return type. The `Date::` included at the beginning of the function header line identifies this function as a member of the `Date class`. The rest of the header line,

```
        Date(int mm, int dd, int yyyy)
```

defines the function as having three integer parameters. The body of this function simply assigns the data members `month`, `day`, and `year` with the values of the parameters `mm`, `dd`, and `yyyy`, respectively.

The next function header line

```
void Date::setdate(int mm, int dd, int yyyy)
```

defines this as the `setdate()` function belonging to the `Date class` (`Date::`). This function returns no value (`void`) and expects three integer parameters, `mm`, `dd`, and `yyyy`. In a manner similar to the `Date()` function, the body of this function assigns the data members month, day, and year with the values of its parameters. In a moment we will see the difference between `Date()` and `setdate()`.

Finally, the last function header line in the implementation section defines a function named `showdate()`. This function has no parameters, returns no value, and is a member of the `Date class`. The body of this function, however, needs a little more explanation.

Although we have chosen to internally store all years as four-digit values that retain century information, users are accustomed to seeing dates where the year is represented as a two-digit value, such as 12/15/99. To display the last two digits of the year value, the expression `year % 100` can be used. For example, if the year is 1999, the expression `1999 % 100` yields the value 99, and if the year is 2001, the expression `2001 % 100` yields the value 1. Notice that if we had used an assignment such as `year = year % 100`; we would actually be altering the stored value of `year` to correspond to the last two digits of the year. Since we want to retain the year as a four-digit number, we must be careful to only manipulate the displayed value using the expression `year % 100` within the cout stream. The `setfill` and `setw` manipulators are used to ensure that the displayed values correspond to conventionally accepted dates. For example, the date March 9, 2002 should appear as either 3/9/02 or 03/09/02. The `setw` manipulator forces each value to be displayed in a field width of 2. Since this manipulator only remains in effect for the next insertion, we have included it before the display of each date value. As the `setfill` manipulator, however, remains in effect until the fill character is changed, we only have to include it once.[8] We have used the `setfill` manipulator here to change the fill character from its default of a blank space to the character 0. Doing this ensures that a date such as December 9, 2002 will appear as 12/09/02 and not 12/ 9/ 2.

To see how our `Date class` can be used within the context of a complete program, consider Program 8.1. To make the program easier to read it has been shaded in light and darker areas. The lighter area contains the `class` declaration and implementation sections that we have already considered. The darker area contains the header and `main()` function. For convenience we will retain this shading convention for all programs using classes.[9]

---

[8]This type of information is easily obtained using the on-line Help facility, as described in Section 2.8.

[9]This shading is not accidental. In practice the lighter shaded region containing the `class` definition would be placed in a separate file. A single `#include` statement would then be used to include this `class` declaration in the program. Thus, the final program would consist of the two darker shaded regions illustrated in Program 8.1 with the addition of one more `#include` statement in the first region.

Program 8.1

```cpp
#include <iostream.h>
#include <iomanip.h>

// class declaration

class Date
{
  private:
    int month;
    int day;
    int year;
  public:
    Date(int = 7, int = 4, int = 2001);   // constructor
    void setdate(int, int, int);          // member function to copy a date
    void showdate(void);                  // member function to display a date
};

// implementation section

Date::Date(int mm, int dd, int yyyy)
{
  month = mm;
  day = dd;
  year = yyyy;
}
void Date::setdate(int mm, int dd, int yyyy)
{
  month = mm;
  day = dd;
  year = yyyy;

  return;
}
void Date::showdate(void)
{
  cout << "The date is ";
  cout << setfill('0')
       << setw(2) << month << '/'
       << setw(2) << day << '/'
       << setw(2) << year % 100; // extract the last 2 year digits
  cout << endl;

  return;
}
```

(Continued)

(Continued)

```
int main()
{
  Date a, b, c(4,1,1998);  // declare 3 objects - initializes 1 of them

  b.setdate(12,25,2002);   // assign values to b's data members
  a.showdate();            // display object a's values
  b.showdate();            // display object b's values
  c.showdate();            // display object c's values

  return 0;
}
```

The declaration and implementation sections contained in the lighter shaded region of Program 8.1 should look familiar to you, as they contain the class declaration and implementation sections that we have already discussed. Notice, however, that this region only declares the class, it does not create any variables of this class type. This is true of all C++ types, including the built-in types such as integers and floats. Just as a variable of an integer type must be defined, variables of a user-declared class must also be defined. Variables defined to be of a user-declared class are referred to as **objects**.

Using this new terminology, the first statement in the Program 8.1 main() function, contained in the darker area, defines three objects, named a, b, and c, to be of class type Date. In C++ whenever a new object is defined, memory is allocated for the object and its data members are automatically initialized. This is done by an automatic call to the class constructor function. For example, consider the definition Date a, b, c(4,1,1998); contained in main(). When the object named a is defined the constructor function Date is automatically called. Since no parameters have been assigned to a, the default values of the constructor function are used, resulting in the initialization:

```
a.month = 7
a.day = 4
a.year = 2001
```

Notice the notation that we have used here. It consists of an object name and an attribute name separated by a period. This is the standard syntax for referring to an object's attribute, namely

object-name.attribute-name

where *object-name* is the name of a specific object and *attribute-name* is the name of a data member defined for the object's class.

Thus, the notation a.month = 7 refers to the fact that object a's month data member has been set to the value 7. Similarly, the notation a.day = 4 and a.year = 2001 refers to the fact that a's day and year data members have been set to the values 4 and 2001, respectively. In the same manner, when the object named b is defined the same default parameters are used, resulting in the initialization of b's data members as

```
b.month = 7
b.day = 4
b.year = 2001
```

The object named c, however, is defined with the arguments 4, 1, and 1998. These three arguments are passed into the constructor function when the object is defined, resulting in the initialization of c's data members as

```
c.month = 4
c.day = 1
c.year = 1998
```

The next statement in main(), b.setdate(12,25,2002), calls b's setdate function, which assigns the argument values 12, 25, 2002 to b's data members, resulting in the assignment

```
b.month = 12
b.day = 25
b.year = 2002
```

Notice the syntax for referring to an object's method. This syntax is

object-name.method-name(parameters)

where *object-name* is the name of a specific object and *method-name* is the name of one of the functions defined for the object's class. Since we have defined all class functions as public, a statement such as b.setdate(12,25,2002) is valid inside the main() function and is a call to the class' setdate() function. This statement tells the setdate() function to operate on the b object with the arguments 12, 25, and 2002. It is important to understand that because all class data members were specified as private, a statement such as b.month = 12 would be invalid from within main(). We are, therefore, forced to rely on member functions to access data member values.

The last three statements in main() call the showdate() function to operate on the a, b, and c objects. The first call results in the display of a's data values, the second call in the display of b's data values, and the third call in the display of c's data values. Thus, the output of Program 8.1 is

```
The date is 02/04/01
The date is 12/25/02
The date is 04/01/98
```

Notice that a statement such as cout << a; is invalid within main() because cout does not know how to handle an object of class Date. Thus, we have supplied our class with a function that can be used to access and display an object's internal values.

Point of Information

Interfaces, Implementations, and Information Hiding

The terms interface and implementation are used extensively in object-oriented programming literature. Each of these terms can be equated to specific parts of a `class'` declaration and implementation sections.

An *interface* consists of a `class'` `public` member function declarations and any supporting comments. As such, the interface should be all that is required to tell a programmer how to use the `class`.

The *implementation* consists of both the `class'` implementation section, which consists of both `private` and `public` member definitions *and* the `class'` `private` data members, which is contained in a `class'` declaration section.

The implementation is the essential means of providing information hiding. In its most general context *information hiding* refers to the principal that *how* a `class` is internally constructed is not relevant to any programmer who wishes to use the `class`. That is, the implementation can and should be hidden from all `class` users precisely to ensure that the `class` is not altered or compromised in any way. All that a programmer need know to correctly use `class` should be provided by the interface.

Terminology

As there is sometimes confusion about the terms classes, objects, and other terminology associated with object-oriented programming, we will take a moment to clarify and review the terminology.

A **class** is a programmer-defined data type out of which objects can be created. **Objects** are created from classes; they have the same relationship to classes as variables do to C++'s built-in data types. For example, in the declaration

    int a;

a is said to be a variable, while in the Program 8.1 declaration

    Date a;

a is said to be an object. If it initially helps you to think of an object as a variable, do so.

Objects are also referred to as **instances** of a `class` and the process of creating a new object is frequently referred to as an **instantiation** of the object. Each time a new object is instantiated (created), a new set of data members belonging to the object is created.[10] The particular values contained in these data members determines the object's **state**.

Seen in this way, a `class` can be thought of as a blueprint out of which particular instances (objects) can be created. Each instance (object) of a class will have its own set of particular values for the set of data members specified in the `class` declaration section.

---

[10]Note that only one set of class functions is created. These functions are shared between objects.

In addition to the data types allowed for an object, a `class` also defines **behavior**—that is, the operations that are permitted to be performed on an object's data members. Users of the object need to know *what* these functions can do and how to activate them through function calls, but unless runtime or space implications are relevant, they do not need to know *how* the operation is done. The actual implementation details of an object's operations are contained in the class implementation, which can be hidden from the user. Other names for the operations defined in a class implementation section are procedures, functions, services, and methods. We will use these terms interchangeably throughout the remainder of the text.

Exercises 8.1

1. Define the following terms:
   a. class
   b. object
   c. declaration section
   d. implementation section
   e. instance variable
   f. member function
   g. data member
   h. constructor
   i. class instance
   j. services
   k. methods
   l. interface
   m. state
   n. behavior

2. **a.** In place of specifying a rectangle's location by listing the position of two corner points, what other attributes could be used?
   b. What other attributes, besides length and width, might be used to describe a rectangle if the rectangle is to be drawn on a color monitor?
   c. Describe a set of attributes that could be used to define circles that are to be drawn on a black and white monitor?
   d. What additional attributes would you add to those selected in response to Exercise 2c if the circles were to be drawn on a color monitor?

3. **a.** The attributes of a `class` represent how objects of the `class` appear to the outside world. The behavior represents how an object of a `class` reacts to an external stimulus. Given this, what do you think is the mechanism by which one object "triggers" the designated behavior in another object?
   b. If behavior in C++ is constructed by defining an appropriate function, how do you think the behavior is activated in C++?

4. Write a `class` declaration section for each of the following specifications. In each case include a prototype for a constructor and a member function named `showdata()` that can be used to display member values.
   a. A `class` named `Time` that has integer data members named `secs`, `mins`, and `hours`.
   b. A `class` named `Complex` that has floating-point data members named `real` and `imaginary`.
   c. A `class` named `Circle` that has integer data members named `xcenter` and `ycenter` and a floating-point data member named `radius`.

d. A `class` named `System` that has character data members named `computer`, `printer`, and `screen`, each capable of holding 30 characters (including the end of string `NULL`), and floating-point data members named `comp_price`, `print_price`, and `scrn_price`.

5. a. Construct a `class` implementation section for the constructor and `showdate()` function members corresponding to the `class` declaration created for Exercise 4a.

b. Construct a `class` implementation section for the constructor and `showdate()` function members corresponding to the `class` declaration created for Exercise 4b.

c. Construct a `class` implementation section for the constructor and `showdate()` function members corresponding to the `class` declaration created for Exercise 4c.

d. Construct a `class` implementation section for the constructor and `showdate()` function members corresponding to the `class` declaration created for Exercise 4d.

6. a. Include the `class` declaration and implementation sections prepared for Exercises 4a and 5a in a complete working program.

b. Include the `class` declaration and implementation sections prepared for Exercises 4b and 5b in a complete working program.

c. Include the `class` declaration and implementation sections prepared for Exercises 4c and 5c in a complete working program.

d. Include the `class` declaration and implementation sections prepared for Exercises 4d and 5d in a complete working program.

7. Determine the errors in the following class declaration section:

```
class employee
  {
  public:
    int empnum;
    char code;
  private:
    class(int = 0);
    void showemp(int, char);
  };
```

8. a. Construct a `class` named `Rectangle` that has floating-point data members named `length` and `width`. The class should have a member function named `perimeter()` and `area()` to calculate the perimeter and area of a rectangle, a member function named `getdata()` to set a rectangles `length` and `width`, and a member function named `showdata()` that displays a rectangle's `length`, `width`, `perimeter`, and `area`.

b. Include the `Rectangle class` constructed in Exercise 8a within a working C++ program.

9. a. Modify the `Date class` defined in Program 8.1 to include a `nextDay()` function that increments a date by one day. Test your function to ensure that it correctly increments days into a new month and into a new year.

   b. Modify the `Date class` defined in Program 8.1 to include a `priorDay()` function that decrements a date by one day. Test your function to ensure that it correctly decrements days into a prior month and into a prior year.

10. Modify the `Date class` in Program 8.1 to contain a function that compares two `Date` objects and returns the larger of the two. The function should be written according to the following algorithm:

> *Comparison function*
> > *Accept two* `Date` *values as parameters*
> > *Determine the later date using the following procedure:*
> > > *Convert each date into an integer value having the form yyyymmdd*
> > > *This can be accomplished using the formula* year*100000 + month*100 + day
> > > *Compare the corresponding integers for each date*
> > > *The larger integer corresponds to the later date*
> > *Return the later date*

11. a. Add a member function to Program 8.1's class definition named `da_of_wk()` that determines the day of the week for any date object. An algorithm for determining the day of the week, known as Zeller's algorithm, is the following:

> *If the month is greater than 2*
> > *Set the variable mp = 0 and yp = year – 1*
> *Else*
> > *Set mp = int(0.4 * month + 2.3) and yp = year*
> *Endif*
> *Set the variable t = int(yp/4) – int(yp/100) + int(yp/400)*
> *Day-of-week = (365L*year + 31L*(month – 1) + day + t – mp) % 7*

Using this algorithm the `Day-of-week` will have a value of 0 if the date is a Sunday, 1 if a Monday, etc.

   b. Include the class definition constructed for Exercise 11a in a complete C++ program. The `main()` function should display the name of the day (Sun, Mon, Tue, etc.) for the `Date` object being tested.

8.2 CONSTRUCTORS

A **constructor** function is any function that has the same name as its `class`. Multiple constructors can be defined for each `class` as long as they are distinguishable by the number and types of their parameters.

The intended purpose of a constructor is to initialize a new object's data members. As such, depending on the number and types of supplied arguments, one constructor function is automatically called each time an object is created. If no constructor function is written, the compiler supplies a default constructor. In addition to its initialization role, a constructor function may also perform other tasks when it is called and can be written in a variety of ways. In this section we present the possible variations of constructor functions and introduce another function, the destructor, which is automatically called whenever an object goes out of existence.

Figure 8.4 illustrates the general format of a constructor. As shown in this figure, a constructor

- must have the same name as the class to which it belongs

- must have no return type (not even void)

```
class-name::class-name(parameter list)
{
   function body
}
```

Figure 8.4 Constructor Format

If you do not include a constructor in your class definition, the compiler supplies a do-nothing default one for you. For example, consider the following class declaration:

```
class Date
{
  private:
    int month, day, year;
  public:
    void setdate(int, int, int);
    void showdate(void)
};
```

Because no user-defined constructor has been declared here, the compiler creates a default constructor. For our `Date class` this default constructor is equivalent to the implementation `Date::Date(void){}`—that is, the compiler-supplied default constructor expects no parameters and has an empty body. Clearly this default constructor is not very useful, but it does exist if no other constructor is declared.

The term **default constructor** is used quite frequently in C++. It refers to any constructor that does not require any arguments when it is called. This can be because no arguments are declared, which is the case for the compiler-supplied default, or because all arguments have been given default values. For example the constructor `Date(int mm = 7, int dd = 4, int yyyy = 2001)` is a valid prototype for a default constructor also. Here, each argument has been given a default value, and an object can be declared as type `Date` without supplying any further arguments. Using such a constructor, the declaration `Date a;` initializes the `a` object with the default values 7, 4, and 2001.

To verify that a constructor function is automatically called whenever a new object is created, consider Program 8.2. Notice that in the implementation section the constructor function uses `cout` to display the message `Created a new object with data` values. Thus, whenever the constructor is called this message is displayed. Since the `main()` function creates three objects, the constructor is called three times and the message is displayed three times.

The following output is produced when Program 8.2 is executed:

```
Created a new data object with data values 7, 4, 2001
Created a new data object with data values 7, 4, 2001
Created a new data object with data values 4, 1, 2002
```

Although any legitimate C++ statement can be used within a constructor function, such as the `cout` statement used in Program 8.2, it is best to keep constructors simple and use them only for initializing purposes. One further point needs to be made with respect to the constructor function contained in Program 8.2. According to the rules of C++, object members are initialized in the order they are declared in the class declaration section and *not* in the order they may appear in the function's definition within the implementation section. Usually this will not be an issue, unless one member is initialized using another data member's value.

Program 8.2

```cpp
#include <iostream.h>

// class declaration section

class Date
{
  private:
    int month;
    int day;
    int year;
  public:
    Date(int = 7, int =4, int = 2001);    // constructor
};

// implementation section

Date::Date(int mm, int dd, int yyyy)
{
  month = mm;
  day = dd;
  year = yyyy;
  cout << "Created a new data object with data values "
       << month << ", " << day << ", " << year << endl;
}
```

(Continued)

(Continued)

```
int main()
{
  Date a;              // declare an object
  Date b;              // declare an object
  Date c(4,1,2002);    // declare an object

  return 0;
}
```

Calling Constructors

As we have seen, constructors are called whenever an object is created. The actual declaration, however, can be made in a variety of ways.

For example, the declaration

```
Date c(4,1,2002);
```

used in Program 8.2 could also have been written as

```
Date c = Date(4,1,2002);
```

This second form declares c as being of type Date and then makes a direct call to the constructor function with the arguments 4, 1, and 2002. This second form can be simplified when only one argument is passed to the constructor. For example, if only the month data member of the c object needed to be initialized with the value 8 and the day and year members can use the default values, the object can be created using the declaration

```
Date c = 8;
```

Since this resembles declarations in C, it and its more complete form using the equal sign is referred to as the *C style of initialization*. The form of declaration used in Program 8.2 is referred to as the *C++ style of initialization,* and is the form we will use predominantly throughout the remainder of the text.

Regardless of which initialization form you use, in no case should an object be declared with empty parentheses. For example, the declaration Date a(); is not the same as the declaration Date a;. The latter declaration uses the default constructor values while the former declaration results in no object being created.

Overloaded and inline Constructors

The primary difference between a constructor and other user-written functions is how the constructor is called: Constructors are called automatically each time an object is created, while other functions must be explicitly called by name.[11] As a function, however, a constructor must still follow all of the rules applicable to user-written functions

---

[11]This is true for all functions except destructors, which are described later in this section. A destructor function is automatically called each time an object is destroyed.

that were presented in Chapter 6. This means that constructors may have default arguments, as was illustrated in Program 8.1, may be overloaded, and may be written as inline functions.

Recall from Section 6.1 that function overloading permits the same function name to be used with different argument lists. Based on the supplied argument types the compiler determines which function to use when the call is encountered. Let's see how this can be applied to our `Date class`. For convenience the appropriate `class` declaration is repeated below:

```
// class declaration section
class Date
{
  private:
    int month;
    int day;
    int year;
  public:
    Date(int = 7, int = 4, int = 2001);     // constructor
};
```

Here, the constructor prototype specifies three integer parameters, which are used to initialize the month, day, and year data members.

An alternate method of specifying a date is to use a long integer in the form year · 10000 + month · 100 + day. For example, the date 12/24/1998 using this form is 19981224 and the date 2/5/2002 is 20020205.[12] A suitable prototype for a constructor that uses dates of this form is:

```
Date(long);   // an overloaded constructor
```

Here, the constructor is declared as receiving one long integer argument. The code for this new `Date` function must, of course, correctly convert its single argument into a month, day, and year, and would be included within the class implementation section. The actual code for such a constructor is:

```
Date::Date(long yyyymmdd)    // a second constructor
{
  year = int(yyyymmdd/10000.0);    // extract the year
  month = int( (yyyymmdd - year * 10000.0) / 100.00 ); // extract the month
  day = int(yyyymmdd - year * 10000.0 - month * 100.0); // extract the day
}
```

Do not be overly concerned with the actual conversion code used within the function's body. The important point here is the concept of overloading the `Date()` function to provide two constructors. Program 8.3 contains the complete class definition within the context of a working program.

---

[12]The reason for specifying dates in this manner is that only one number needs to be used per date and that sorting the numbers automatically puts the corresponding dates into chronological order.

Program 8.3

```
#include <iostream.h>
#include <iomanip.h>

// class declaration

class Date
{
  private:
    int month;
    int day;
    int year;
  public:
    Date(int = 7, int = 4, int = 2001);   // constructor
    Date(long);               // another constructor
    void showdate(void);      // member function to display a date
};

// implementation section

Date::Date(int mm, int dd, int yyyy)
{
  month = mm;
  day = dd;
  year = yyyy;
}

Date::Date(long yyyymmdd)
{
  year = int(yyyymmdd/10000.0);     // extract the year
  month = int( (yyyymmdd - year * 10000.0)/100.00 ); // extract the month
  day = int(yyyymmdd - year * 10000.0 - month * 100.0); // extract the day
}

void Date::showdate(void)
{
  cout << "The date is ";
  cout << setfill('0')
       << setw(2) << month << '/'
       << setw(2) << day << '/'
       << setw(2) << year % 100; // extract the last 2 year digits
  cout << endl;

  return;
}
```

(Continued)

(Continued)

```
int main()
{
  Date a, b(4,1,1998), c(20020515L); // declare three objects

  a.showdate();          // display object a's values
  b.showdate();          // display object b's values
  c.showdate();          // display object c's values

  return 0;
}
```

The output provided by Program 8.3 is:

```
The date is 07/04/01
The date is 04/01/98
The date is 05/15/02
```

Three objects are created in the Program 8.3 `main()` function. The first object, a, is initialized with the default constructor using its default arguments. Object b is also initialized with the default constructor but uses the arguments 4, 1, and 1998. Finally, object c, which is initialized with a long integer, uses the second constructor in the class implementation section. The compiler knows to use this second constructor because the argument specified, 20020515L, is clearly designated as a long integer. It is worthwhile pointing out that a compiler error would occur if both `Date` constructors had default values. In such a case a declaration such as `Date d;` would be ambiguous to the compiler, as it would not be able to determine which constructor to use. Thus, in each implementation section only one constructor can be written as the default.

Just as constructors may be overloaded, they may also be written as `inline` functions. Doing so simply means defining the function in the `class` declaration section. For example, making both of the constructors contained in Program 8.3 inline is accomplished by the declaration section:

```
// class declaration

class Date
{
  private:
    int month;
    int day;
    int year;
  public:
    Date(int mm = 7, int dd = 4, int yyyy = 2001)
    {
      month = mm;
      day = dd;
      year = yyyy;
    }
```

Constructors

A **constructor** is any function that has the same name as its class. The primary purpose of a constructor is to initialize an object's member variables when an object is created. As such, a constructor is automatically called when an object is declared.

A class can have multiple constructors provided that each constructor is distinguishable by having a different formal parameter list. A compiler error results when unique identification of a constructor is not possible. If no constructor is provided the compiler will supply a do-nothing default constructor.

Every constructor function must be declared *with no return type* (not even void). Since they are functions, constructors may also be explicitly called in nondeclarative statements. When used in this manner the function call requires parentheses following the constructor name, even if no parameters are used. However, when used in a declaration, parentheses *must not* be included for a zero parameter constructor. For example, the declaration Date a(); is incorrect. The correct declaration is Date a;. When parameters are used, however, they must be enclosed within parentheses in both declarative and nondeclarative statements. Default parameter values should be included within the constructor's prototype.

```
Date(long yyyymmdd)    // here is the overloaded constructor
{
   year = int(yyyymmdd/10000.0);      // extract the year
   month = int( (yyyymmdd - year * 10000.0)/100.00 );  // extract the month
   day = int(yyyymmdd - year * 10000.0 - month * 100.0); // extract the day
}
};
```

The keyword `inline` is not required in this declaration because member functions defined inside the `class` declaration are `inline` by default.

Generally, only functions that can be coded on a single line are good candidates for `inline` functions. This reinforces the convention that `inline` functions should be small. Thus, the first constructor is more conventionally written as

```
Date(int mm = 7, int dd = 4, int yyyy = 2001)
   { month = mm; day = dd; year = yyyy; }
```

The second constructor, which extends over three lines, should not be written as an `inline` function.

Destructors

The counterpart to constructor functions are destructor functions. Destructors are functions having the same `class` name as constructors, but preceded with a tilde(~). Thus, for our `Date class`, the destructor name is `~Date()`. Like constructors, a default do-nothing destructor is provided by the C++ compiler in the absence of an explicit destructor. Unlike constructors, however, there can only be one destructor function per `class`. This is because destructors take no parameters—they also return no values.

> ## Point of Information
>
> ### Accessor Functions
>
> An *accessor function* is any non-constructor member function that accesses a class' private data members. For example, the function `showdate()` in the `Date class` is an accessor function. Such functions are extremely important because they provide a means of displaying `private` data member's stored values.
>
> When you construct a `class` make sure to provide a complete set of accessor functions. Each accessor function does not have to return a data member's exact value, but it should return a useful representation of the value. For example, assume that a date such as 12/25/2002 is stored as a long-integer member variable in the form 20022512. Although an accessor function could display this value, a more useful representation would typically be either 12/25/02, or December 25, 2002.
>
> Besides being used for output, accessor functions can also provide a means of data input. For example, the `setdate()` function in the `Date class` is an example of an input accessor function. Constructor functions, whose primary purpose is to initialize an object's member variables, are not considered as accessor functions.

Destructors are automatically called whenever an object goes out of existence and are meant to "clean up" any undesirable effects that might be left by the object. Generally such effects only occur when an object contains a pointer member.

Exercises 8.2

1. Determine whether the following statements are true or false.
   a. A constructor function must have the same name as its `class`.
   b. A `class` can only have one constructor function.
   c. A `class` can only have one default constructor function.
   d. A default constructor can only be supplied by the compiler.
   e. A default constructor can have no parameters or all parameters must have default values.
   f. A constructor must be declared for each `class`.
   g. A constructor must be declared with a return type.
   h. A constructor is automatically called each time an object is created.
   i. A `class` can only have one destructor function.
   j. A destructor must have the same name as its `class`, preceded by a tilde(~).
   k. A destructor can have default arguments.
   l. A destructor must be declared for each class.
   m. A destructor must be declared with a return type.
   n. A destructor is automatically called each time an object goes out of existence.
   o. Destructors are not useful when the class contains a pointer data member.

2. For Program 8.3, what date would be initialized for object `c` if the declaration `Date c(15);` were used in place of the declaration `Date c(20020515L);`?

3. Modify Program 8.3 so that the only data member of the class is a long integer named yyyymmdd. Do this by substituting the declaration

```
long yyyymmdd;
```

for the existing declarations

```
int month;
int day;
int year;
```

Then, using the same constructor function prototypes currently declared in the class declaration section, rewrite them so that the Date(long) function becomes the default constructor and the Date(int, int, int) function converts a month, day, and year into the proper form for the class data member.

4. a. Construct a Time class containing integer data members seconds, minutes, and hours. Have the class contain two constructors: the first should be a default constructor having the prototype time(int, int, int), which uses default values of 0 for each data member. The second constructor should accept a long integer representing a total number of seconds and disassemble the long integer into hours, minutes, and seconds. The final function member should display the class data members.

b. Include the class written for Exercise 4a within the context of a complete program.

5. a. Construct a class named Student consisting of an integer student identification number, an array of five floating point grades, and an integer representing the total number of grades entered. The constructor for this class should initialize all Student data members to zero. Included in the class should be member functions to (1) enter a student ID number, (2) enter a single test grade and update the total number of grades entered, and (3) compute an average grade and display the student ID followed by the average grade.

b. Include the class constructed in Exercise 5a within the context of a complete program. Your program should declare two objects of type Student and accept and display data for the two objects to verify operation of the member functions.

6. a. In Exercise 4 you were asked to construct a Time class. For such a class include a tick() function that increments the time by one second. Test your function to ensure that it correctly increments into a new minute and a new hour.

b. Modify the Time class written for Exercise 6a to include a detick() function that decrements the time by one second. Test your function to ensure that it correctly decrements time into a prior hour and into a prior minute.

8.3 ▷ APPLICATIONS

Now that you have an understanding of how classes are constructed and the terminology used in describing them, let us apply this knowledge to two new applications. In the first application we construct a single elevator object. We assume that the elevator can travel between the 1st and 15th floors of a building and that the location of the elevator must be known at all times. In the second application we simulate the operation of a gas pump.

Application 1: Constructing an Elevator Object

In this application you are required to simulate the operation of an elevator. What is required is an output that describes the current floor that the elevator is either stationed at or is passing by and an internal elevator request button that is pushed as a request to move to another floor. The elevator can travel between the 1st and 15th floor of the building it is situated in.

Step 1   Analyze the Problem

For this application we have one object, which is an elevator. The only attribute of interest is the location of the elevator. The single requested service is the ability to request a change in the elevator's position (state). Additionally, we must be able to establish the initial floor position when a new elevator is put in service.

Step 2   Develop a Solution

For this application the location of the elevator, which corresponds to its current floor position, can be represented by an integer member variable ranging between 1 and 15. The value of this variable, which we will name `cur_floor`, for current floor, effectively represents the current state of the elevator. The services that we will provide for changing the state of the elevator will be an initialization function to set the initial floor position when a new elevator is put in service, and a request function to change the elevator's position (state) to a new floor. Putting an elevator in service is accomplished by declaring a single `class` instance (declaring an object of type `Elevator`), while requesting a new floor position is equivalent to pushing an elevator button.

Step 3   Code the Solution

From the design, a suitable class declaration is

```
// class declaration section
class Elevator
{
  private:
    int cur_floor;
  public:
    Elevator(int = 1);        // constructor
    void request(int);
};
```

Notice that we have declared one data member, `cur_floor`, and two `class` functions. The data member, `cur_floor` is used to store the current floor position of the elevator. As a `private` member it can only be accessed through member functions. The two declared public member functions, `Elevator()` and `request()`, will be used to define the external services provided by each `Elevator` object. The `Elevator()` function, which has the same name as its `class`, becomes a constructor function that is automatically called when an object of type `Elevator` is created. We will use this function to initialize the starting floor position of each elevator. The `request()` function is used to alter the position of the elevator. To accomplish these services a suitable class implementation section is

```
// class implementation section

Elevator::Elevator(int cfloor)    // constructor
{
  cur_floor = cfloor;
}

void Elevator::request(int newfloor)  // access function
{
  if (newfloor < 1 || newfloor > MAXFLOOR || newfloor == cur_floor)
    ;  // do nothing
  else if ( newfloor > cur_floor)  // move elevator up
  {
    cout << "\nStarting at floor " << cur_floor << endl;
    while (newfloor > cur_floor)
    {
      cur_floor++;     // add one to current floor
      cout << "   Going Up - now at floor " << cur_floor << endl;
    }
    cout << "Stopping at floor " << cur_floor << endl;
  }
  else  // move elevator down
  {
    cout << "\nStarting at floor " << cur_floor << endl;
    while (newfloor < cur_floor)
    {
      cur_floor--;    // subtract one from current floor
      cout << "   Going Down - now at floor " << cur_floor << endl;
    }
    cout << "Stopping at floor " << cur_floor << endl;
  }

  return;
}
```

The constructor function is straightforward. When an `Elevator` object is declared it is initialized to the floor specified; if no floor is explicitly given the default value of 1 will be used. For example, the declaration

```
Elevator a(7);
```

initializes the variable `a.cur_floor` to 7, while the declaration

```
Elevator a;
```

uses the default argument value and initializes the variable `a.cur_floor` to 1.

The `request()` function defined in the implementation section is more complicated and provides the class' primary service. Essentially this function consists of an `if-else` statement having three parts: if an incorrect service is requested no action is taken, if a floor above the current position is selected the elevator is moved up, and if a floor below the current position is selected the elevator is moved down. For movement up or down the function uses a `while` loop to increment the position one floor at a time, and reports the elevator's movement using a `cout` object stream. Program 8.4 includes this `class` in a working program.

Step 4   Test and Correct the Program

Testing the `Elevator class` entails testing each `class` operation. To do this we first include the `Elevator class` within the context of a working program, which is listed as Program 8.4.

Program 8.4

```cpp
#include <iostream.h>
const int MAXFLOOR = 15;

// class declaration

class Elevator
{
  private:
    int cur_floor;
  public:
    Elevator(int = 1);          // constructor
    void request(int);
};

// implementation section

Elevator::Elevator(int cfloor)
{
  cur_floor = cfloor;
}
```

(Continued)

(Continued)

```
void Elevator::request(int newfloor)
{
  if (newfloor < 1 || newfloor > MAXFLOOR || newfloor == cur_floor)
    ;   // do nothing
  else if ( newfloor > cur_floor)  // move elevator up
  {
    cout << "\nStarting at floor " << cur_floor << endl;
    while (newfloor > cur_floor)
    {
      cur_floor++;     // add one to current floor
      cout << "   Going Up - now at floor " << cur_floor << endl;
    }
    cout << "Stopping at floor " << cur_floor << endl;
  }
  else  // move elevator down
  {
    cout << "\nStarting at floor " << cur_floor << endl;
    while (newfloor < cur_floor)
    {
      cur_floor--;   // subtract one from current floor
      cout << "   Going Down - now at floor " << cur_floor << endl;
    }
    cout << "Stopping at floor " << cur_floor << endl;
  }

  return;
}


int main()
{
  Elevator a;    // declare 1 object of type Elevator

  a.request(6);
  a.request(3);

  return 0;
}
```

The lightly shaded portion of Program 8.4 contains the class construction that we have already described. To see how this class is used, concentrate on the darker shaded section of the program. At the top of the program we have included the iostream.h header file and declared a named constant MAXFLOOR, which corresponds to the highest floor that can be requested.

Within the main() function three statements are included. The first statement creates an object named a of type Elevator. Since no explicit floor has been given, this elevator will begin at floor 1, which is the default constructor argument.

A request is then made to move the elevator to floor 6, which is followed by a request to move to floor 3. The output produced by Program 8.4 is:

```
Starting at floor 1
   Going Up - now at floor 2
   Going Up - now at floor 3
   Going Up - now at floor 4
   Going Up - now at floor 5
   Going Up - now at floor 6
Stopping at floor 6

Starting at floor 6
   Going Down - now at floor 5
   Going Down - now at floor 4
   Going Down - now at floor 3
Stopping at floor 3
```

The basic requirements of object-oriented programming are evident in even as simple a program as Program 8.4. Before the `main()` function can be written a useful `class` must be constructed. This is typical of programs that use objects. For such programs the design process is front-loaded with the requirement that careful consideration of the class—its declaration and implementation—be given. Code contained in the implementation section effectively removes code that would otherwise be part of `main()`'s responsibility. Thus, any program that uses the object does not have to repeat the implementation details within its `main()` function. Rather, the `main()` function and any function called by `main()` is only concerned with sending messages to its objects to activate them appropriately. How the object responds to the messages and how the state of the object is retained is not `main()`'s concern—these details are hidden within the `class` construction.

One further point should be made concerning Program 8.4, which is the control provided by the `main()` function. Notice that this control is sequential, with two calls made to the same object operation using different argument values. This control is perfectly correct for testing purposes. However, by incorporating calls to `request()` within a `while` loop and using the random number function `rand()` to generate random floor requests, a continuous simulation of the elevator's operation is possible (see Exercise 3).

Application 2: A Single Object Gas Pump Simulation

We have been requested to write a program that simulates the operation of a gas pump. At any time during the simulation we should be able to determine, from the pump, the price-per-gallon of gas and the amount remaining in the supply tank from which the gas is being pumped. If a request for gas, in gallons, is less than the amount of gas in the tank, the request should be filled; otherwise only the available amount in the supply tank should be used. Once the gas is pumped, the total price of the gallons pumped should be displayed and the amount of gas, in gallons, that was pumped should be subtracted from the amount in the supply tank.

For the simulation assume that the pump is randomly idle between 1 to 15 minutes between customer arrivals and that a customer randomly requests between 3 and 20 gallons of gas. Although the tank capacity is 500 gallons, assume that the initial amount of gas in the tank is only 300 gallons. Initially, the program should simulate a one-half hour time frame.

Additionally, for each arrival and request for gas we want to know the idle time before the customer arrived, how many gallons of gas were pumped, and the total price of the transaction. The pump itself must keep track of the price per gallon of gas and the amount of gas remaining in the tank. Typically, the price per gallon is $1.00, but the price used for the simulation should be $1.25.

For this part of the simulation, we will construct a gas-pump `class` that can be used in the final simulation, which is completed in Section 9.5.

Step 1   Analyze the Problem

This problem involves two distinct object types. The first is a person who can arrive randomly between 1 and 15 minutes and can randomly request between 3 and 20 gallons of gas. The second object type is the gas pump. For this part of the problem our goal is to create a suitable gas pump class.

The model for constructing a gas pump class that meets the requirements of the simulation are easily described in pseudocode as

> *Put pump in service*
>   *Initialize the amount of gas in the tank*
>   *Initialize the price per gallon of gas*
>
> *Display values*
>   *Display the amount of gas in the tank*
>   *Display the price per gallon*
>
> *Pump an amount of gas*
>   *If the amount in the tank = amount to be pumped*
>   *Set pumped amount equal to the amount in the tank*
>   *Else*
>   *Set pumped amount equal to the amount to be pumped*
>   *Endif*
>   *Subtract the pumped amount from the amount in the tank*
>   *Calculate the total price as (price per gallon * pumped amount)*
>   *Display the pumped amount*
>   *Display the amount remaining in the tank*
>   *Display the total price*

Step 2   Develop a Solution

From the pseudocode description the implementation of a `Pump` class is rather straightforward. The attributes of interest for the pump are the amount of gallons in the tank and the price per gallon. The required operations include supplying initial values for the pump attributes, interrogating the pump for its attribute values, and satisfying a request for gas.

Since the two attributes, the amount-in-the-tank and the price-per-gallon, can have fractional values, it is appropriate to make them floating-point values. Additionally, three services need to be provided. The first consists of initializing a pump's attributes, which consists of setting values for the amount in the supply tank and the price per gallon. The second consists of satisfying a request for gas, while the third service simply provides a reading of the pump's current attribute values.

Step 3   Code the Solution

A suitable class declaration is

```
// class declaration
class Pump
{
  private:
    float amtInTank;
    float price;
  public:
    Pump(float = 500.00, float = 1.00);        // constructor
    void values(void);
    void request(float);
};
```

Notice that we have declared two data members and three member functions. As private members, the two data attributes can only be accessed through the class' declared member functions: Pump(), values(), and request(). It is these functions that provide the external services available to each Pump object.

The Pump() function, which has the same name as its class, is the constructor function that is automatically called when an object of type Pump is created. The values() function simply provides a readout of the current attribute values, while the request() function handles the logic for fulfilling a customer's request for gas. To accomplish these services a suitable class implementation section is

```
// class implementation

Pump::Pump(float start, float todaysPrice)
{
  amtInTank = start;
  price = todaysPrice;
}

void Pump::values(void)
{
  cout << setiosflags(ios::fixed) << setiosflags(ios::showpoint)
       << setprecision(2) << endl;
  cout << "The gas tank has " << amtInTank
       << " gallons of gas." << endl;
  cout << "The price per gallon of gas is $" << price << endl;
```

```
    return;
}

void Pump::request(float pumpAmt)
{
  float pumped;

  if (amtInTank >= pumpAmt)
     pumped = pumpAmt;
  else
     pumped = amtInTank;

  amtInTank -= pumped;
  cout << setiosflags(ios::fixed) << setiosflags(ios::showpoint)
       << setprecision(2) << endl;
  cout << pumpAmt << " gallons were requested " << endl;
  cout << pumped << " gallons were pumped" << endl;
  cout << amtInTank << " gallons remain in the tank" << endl;
  cout << "The total price is $" << (pumped * price) << endl;

  return;
}
```

The constructor function is straightforward. When a Pump object is declared it will be initialized to a given amount of gas in the supply tank and a given price per gallon. If no values are given, the defaults of 500 gallons and $1 per gallon will be used.

The values() function defined in the implementation section simply provides a readout of the current attribute values. It is the request() function that is the most complicated because it provides the primary Pump service. The code follows the requirements that the pump provides all of the gas required unless the amount remaining in the supply tank is less the requested amount. Finally, it subtracts the amount pumped from the amount in the tank and calculates the total dollar value of the transaction.

Step 4 Test and Correct the Program

Testing the Pump class entails testing each class operation. To do this we first include the Pump class within the context of a working program, which is listed as Program 8.5.

The lightly shaded portion of Program 8.5 contains the class construction that we have already described. To see how this class is used, concentrate on the darker shaded section of the program. At the top of the program we have included the required include files and two constants AMT_IN_TANK and TODAYS_PRICE, which corresponds to the data that is to be used in the simulation.

Within the main() function six statements are included. The first statement creates an object named a of type Pump. The supply tank for this pump contains AMT_IN_TANK gallons and the price per gallon is set to TODAYS_PRICE.

Program 8.5

```cpp
#include <iostream.h>
#include <iomanip.h>
const float AMT_IN_TANK = 300;  // initial gallons in the tank
const float TODAYS_PRICE = 1.25;  // price-per-gallon


// class declaration

class Pump
{
  private:
    float amtInTank;
    float price;
  public:
    Pump(float = 500.0, float = 1.00);       // constructor
    void values(void);
    void request(float);
};
// implementation section

Pump::Pump(float start, float todaysPrice)
{
  amtInTank = start;
  price = todaysPrice;
}

void Pump::values(void)
{
  cout << setiosflags(ios::fixed) << setiosflags(ios::showpoint)
       << setprecision(2) << endl;
  cout << "The gas tank has " << amtInTank << " gallons of gas." << endl;
  cout << "The price per gallon of gas is $" << price << endl;

  return;
}

void Pump::request(float pumpAmt)
{
  float pumped;

  if (amtInTank >= pumpAmt)
     pumped = pumpAmt;
  else
     pumped = amtInTank;
```

(Continued)

(Continued)

```
   amtInTank -= pumped;

   cout << setiosflags(ios::fixed) << setiosflags(ios::showpoint)
        << setprecision(2) << endl;
   cout << pumpAmt << " gallons were requested " << endl;
   cout << pumped << " gallons were pumped" << endl;
   cout << amtInTank << " gallons remain in the tank" << endl;
   cout << "The total price is $" << (pumped * price) << endl;

   return;
}
```

```
int main()
{
   Pump a(AMT_IN_TANK, TODAYS_PRICE);    // declare 1 object of type Pump

   a.values();
   cout << endl;
   a.request(30.0);
   cout << endl;
   a.request(280.0);

   return 0;
}
```

A request is then made to `values()` to display the pump's attribute values, which are correctly set at 300 gallons and $1.25 per gallon. The next `cout` statement simply provides a blank line.

The first request for gas is for 30 gallons, followed by a `cout` statement to again provide a blank line. Finally, the last statement is a request for 280 gallons, which should exceed the available gas in the supply tank. The output produced by Program 8.5 is

```
The gas tank has 300 gallons of gas.
The price per gallon of gas is $1.25

30.00 gallons were requested
30.00 gallons were pumped
270.00 gallons remain in the tank
The total price is $37.50

280.00 gallons were requested
270.00 gallons were pumped
0.00 gallons remain in the tank
The total price is $337.50
```

Point of Information

Encapsulation

The term **encapsulation** refers to the packaging of a number of items into a single unit. For example, a function is used to encapsulate the details of an algorithm. Similarly, a `class` encapsulates both variables and functions together in a single package.

Although the term encapsulation is sometimes used to refer to the process of information hiding, this usage is technically not accurate. The correct relationship between terms is that information hiding refers to the encapsulation and hiding of all implementation details.

Exercises 8.3

1. Enter Program 8.4 in your computer and execute it.

2. **a.** Modify the `main()` function in Program 8.4 to put a second elevator in service starting at the 5th floor. Have this second elevator move to the 1st floor and then move to the 12th floor.

   b. Verify that the constructor function is called by adding a message within the constructor that is displayed each time a new object is created. Run your program to ensure its operation.

3. Modify the `main()` function in Program 8.4 to use a `while` loop that calls the `Elevator`'s request function with a random number between 1 and 15. If the random number is the same as the elevator's current floor, generate another request. The `while` loop should terminate after 5 valid requests have been made and satisfied by movement of the elevator. (*Hint:* Review Section 6.4 for the use of random numbers.)

4. **a.** Modify the `main()` function in Program 8.5 to use a `while` loop that calls the `Pump`'s request function with a random number between 3 and 20. The `while` loop should terminate after 5 requests have been made.

   b. Modify the `main()` function written for Exercise 4a to provide a 30 minute simulation of the gas pump's operation. To do this you will have to modify the `while` loop to select a random number between 1 and 15 that represents the idle time between customer requests. Have the simulation stop once the idle time exceeds 30 minutes.

5. **a.** Construct a `class` definition of a Person `object` type. The `class` is to have no attributes, a single constructor function and two additional member functions named `arrive()` and `gallons()`.The constructor function should simply call `srand()` with the argument `time(NULL)` to initialize the `rand()` function. The `arrive()` function should provide a random number between 1 and 15 as a return value, while the `gallons()` function should provide a random number between 3 and 20.

   b. Test the `Person` class functions written for Exercise 5a in a complete working program.

c. Use the `Person` class function to simulate a random arrival of a `Person` and a random request for gallons of gas within the program written for Exercise 4b.

6. Modify Program 8.5 so that the `Pump class` definition resides in a file named `PUMP.H`. Then have Program 8.5 use an `#include` statement to `include` the `class` definition within the program. Make sure to use a full path name in the `include` statement. For example, if `PUMP.H` resides in the directory named `FOO` on the C drive, the include statement should be `#include <C:\FOO\PUMP.C>`.

7. Construct a `class` named `Light` that simulates a traffic light. The color attribute of the `class` should change from `Green` to `Yellow` to `Red` and then back to `Green` by the `class' change()` function. When a new `Light` object is created its initial color should be `Red`.

8. a. Construct a `class` definition that can be used to represent an employee of a company. Each employee is defined by an integer ID number, a floating-point pay rate, and the maximum number of hours the employee should work each week. The services provided by the class should be the ability to enter data for a new employee, the ability to change data for a new employee, and the ability to display the existing data for a new employee.

b. Include the class definition created for Exercise 8a in a working C+ program that asks the user to enter data for 3 employees and displays the entered data.

c. Modify the program written for Exercise 8b to include a menu that offers the user the following choices:

1. Add an employee
2. Modify employee data
3. Delete an employee
4. Exit this menu

In response to a choice the program should initiate appropriate action to implement the choice.

9. a. Construct a `class` definition that can be used to represent types of food. A type of food is classified as basic or prepared. Basic foods are further classified as either `Dairy`, `Meat`, `Fruit`, `Vegetable`, or `Grain`. The services provided by the class should be the ability to enter data for a new food, the ability to change data for a new food, and the ability to display the existing data for a new food.

b. Include the `class` definition created for Exercise 9a in a working C++ program that asks the user to enter data for four food items and displays the entered data.

c. Modify the program written for Exercise 9b to include a menu that offers the user the following choices:

1. Add a food item
2. Modify a food item
3. Delete a food item
4. Exit this menu

In response to a choice the program should initiate appropriate action to implement the choice.

8.4 ▷ COMMON PROGRAMMING ERRORS

The more common programming errors initially associated with the construction of classes are

1. Failing to terminate the `class` declaration section with a semicolon.

2. Including a return type with the constructor's prototype or failing to include a return type with the other functions' prototypes.

3. Using the same name for a data member as for a member function.

4. Defining more than one default constructor for a `class`.

5. Forgetting to include the `class` name and scope operator, `::`, in the header line of all member functions defined in the `class` implementation section.

All of these errors will result in a compiler error message.

8.5 ▷ CHAPTER SUMMARY

1. A **class** is a programmer-defined data type. **Objects** of a `class` may be defined and have the same relationship to their class as variables do to C++'s built-in data types.

2. A `class` definition consists of a declaration and implementation section. The most common form of a `class` definition is

```
// class declaration section
class name
{
  private:
   a list of variable declarations;
  public:
   a list of function prototypes;
};

// class implementation section
class function definitions
```

The variables and functions declared in the class declaration section are collectively referred to as **class members**. The variables are individually referred to as class data members and the functions as class member functions. The terms `private` and `public` are access specifiers. Once an access specifier is listed it remains in force until another access specifier is given. The `private` keyword specifies that the class members following it are `private` to the class and can only be accessed by member functions. The `public` keyword specifies that the class members following may be accessed from outside the class. Generally all data members should be specified as `private` and all member functions as `public`.

3. `Class` functions listed in the declaration section may either be written inline or their definitions included in the class implementation section. Except for constructor and destructor functions, all class functions defined in the class implementation section have the header line form

   return-type   class-name::function-name(parameter list);

   Except for the addition of the class name and scope operator, `::`, which are required to identify the function name with the class, this header line is identical to the header line used for any user-written function.

4. A **constructor function** is a special function that is automatically called each time an object is declared. It must have the same name as its class and cannot have any return type. Its purpose is to initialize each declared object.

5. If no constructor is declared for a class the compiler will supply a default constructor. This is a do-nothing function having the definition
   `class-name::class-name(void){}.`

6. The term **default constructor** refers to any constructor that does not require any arguments when it is called. This can be because no parameters are declared (as is the case for the compiler-supplied default constructor) or because all parameters have been given default values.

7. Each class may only have one default constructor. If any user-defined constructor is defined the compiler will not create its default constructor.

8. Objects are created using either a C++ or C style of declaration. The C++ style of declaration has the form:

   class-name list of object names(list of initializers);

   where the list of initializers is optional. An example of this style of declaration, including initializers, for a `class` named `Date` is

   `Date a, b, c(12,25,1999);`

   Here the objects `a` and `b` are declared to be of type `Date` and are initialized using the default constructor while the object `c` is initialized with the values 12, 25, and 1999.

   The equivalent C style of declaration, including the optional list of initializers, has the form

   class-name object-name = class-name(list of initializers);

   An example of this style of declaration for a `class` named `Date` is

   `Date c = Date(12,25,1999)`

Here the object c is created and initialized with the values 12, 25, and 1999.

9. Constructors may be overloaded in the same manner as any other user-written C++ function.

10. If a constructor is defined for a class, a user-defined default constructor also should be written, as the compiler will not supply it.

11. A destructor function is called each time an object goes out of scope. Destructors must have the same name as their class, but preceded with a tilde (~). There can only be one destructor per class.

12. A **destructor function** takes no arguments and returns no value. If a user-defined destructor is not included in a class the compiler will provide a do-nothing destructor.

CHAPTER 9

Class Functions and Conversions

TOPICS

9.1 ASSIGNMENT
COPY CONSTRUCTORS
BASE/MEMBER INITIALIZATION

9.2 ADDITIONAL CLASS FEATURES
CLASS SCOPE
STATIC CLASS MEMBERS
FRIEND FUNCTIONS

9.3 OPERATOR FUNCTIONS
OPERATOR FUNCTIONS AS FRIENDS

9.4 DATA TYPE CONVERSIONS
BUILT-IN TO BUILT-IN CONVERSION
BUILT-IN TO CLASS CONVERSION
CLASS TO BUILT-IN CONVERSION
CLASS TO CLASS CONVERSION

9.5 APPLICATION—A MULTI-OBJECT GAS PUMP SIMULATION

9.6 CLASS INHERITANCE
ACCESS SPECIFICATIONS
AN EXAMPLE

9.7 POLYMORPHISM

9.8 COMMON PROGRAMMING ERRORS

9.9 CHAPTER SUMMARY

The creation of a class requires that we provide the capability to declare, initialize, assign, manipulate, and display data members. In the previous chapter the declaration, initialization, and display of objects was presented. In this chapter we continue our construction of classes by providing the ability to create operator and conversion capabilities similar to those inherent in C++'s built-in types. With these additions our user-defined types will have all of the functionality of built-in types.

9.1 > ASSIGNMENT

In Chapter 3 we saw how C++'s assignment operator, =, performs assignment between variables. In this section we see how assignment works when it is applied to objects and how to define our own assignment operator to override the default provided for user-defined classes.

For a specific assignment example, consider the `main()` function of Program 9.1.

Notice that the implementation section of the `Date` class in Program 9.1 contains no assignment function. Nevertheless, we would expect the assignment statement `a = b;` in `main()` to assign b's data member values to their counterparts in a. This is, in fact, the case and is verified by the output produced when Program 9.1 is executed:

```
The date stored in a is originally 04/01/99
After assignment the date stored in a is 12/18/01
```

The type of assignment illustrated in Program 9.1 is referred to as **memberwise assignment**. In the absence of any specific instructions to the contrary, the C++ compiler builds this type of default assignment operator for each class. If the class *does not* contain any pointer data members this default assignment operator is adequate and can be used without further consideration. Before considering the problems that can occur with pointer data members, let's see how to construct our own explicit assignment operators.

Assignment operators, like all class members, are declared in the class declaration section and defined in the class implementation section. For the declaration of operators, however, the keyword `operator` must be included in the declaration. Using this keyword, a simple assignment `operator` declaration has the form:

void operator=(class-name&);

Here the keyword `void` indicates that the assignment returns no value, the `operator=` indicates that we are overloading the assignment operator with our own version, and the class name and ampersand within the parentheses indicates that the argument to the `operator` is a class reference. For example, to declare a simple assignment operator for our `Date` class, the declaration:

```
void operator=(Date& );
```

can be used.

The actual implementation of the assignment operator is defined in the implementation section. For our declaration, a suitable implementation is

```
void Date::operator=(Date& newdate)
{
  day = newdate.day;        // assign the day
  month = newdate.month;    // assign the month
  year = newdate.year;      // assign the year
}
```

Program 9.1

```cpp
#include <iostream.h>
#include <iomanip.h>

// class declaration
class Date
{
  private:
      int month;
      int day;
      int year;
    public:
      Date(int = 7, int = 4, int = 2001);     // constructor
      void showdate(void);        // member function to display a Date
};

// implementation section
Date::Date(int mm, int dd, int yyyy)
{
  month = mm;
  day = dd;
  year = yyyy;
}

void Date::showdate(void)
{
  cout << setfill('0')
       << setw(2) << month << '/'
       << setw(2) << day << '/'
       << setw(2) << year % 100;
  return;
}
```

```cpp
int main()
{
  Date a(4,1,1999), b(12,18,2001); // declare two objects

  cout << "The date stored in a is originally ";
  a.showdate();  // display the original date
  a = b;           // assign b's value to a
  cout << "After assignment the date stored in a is ";
  a.showdate();  // display a's values

  return 0;
}
```

The use of the reference argument in the definition of this operation is not accidental. In fact, one of the primary reasons for adding reference variables to C++ was to facilitate the construction of overloaded operators and make the notation more natural.[1] In this definition `newdate` is defined as a reference to a `Date` class. Within the body of the definition the `day` member of the object referenced by `newdate` is assigned to the `day` member of the current object, which is then repeated for the `month` and `year` members. Assignments such as `a.operator=(b);` can then be used to call the overloaded assignment operator and assign b's member values to a. For convenience, the expression `a.operator=(b)` can be replaced with `a = b;`. Program 9.2 contains our new assignment `operator` within the context of a complete program.

Except for the addition of the overloaded assignment operator declaration and definition, Program 9.2 is identical to Program 9.1 and produces the same output. Its usefulness to us is that it illustrates how we can explicitly construct our own assignment definitions. Before moving on, however, two simple modifications to our assignment operator need to be made.

Program 9.2

```cpp
#include <iostream.h>
#include <iomanip.h>

// class declaration
class Date
{
  private:
    int month;
    int day;
    int year;
  public:
    Date(int = 7, int = 4, int = 2001);     // constructor
    void operator=(Date&);    // define assignment of a date
    void showdate(void);      // member function to display a date
};

// implementation section
Date::Date(int mm, int dd, int yyyy)
{
  month = mm;
  day = dd;
  year = yyyy;
}
```

(Continued)

---

[1] Passing a reference is preferable to passing an object by value because it reduces the overhead required in making a copy of each object's data members.

(Continued)

```
void Date::operator=(Date& newdate)
{

  day = newdate.day;       // assign the day
  month = newdate.month;   // assign the month
  year = newdate.year;     // assign the year
  return;
}

void Date::showdate(void)
{
  cout << setfill('0')
       << setw(2) << month << '/'
       << setw(2) << day << '/'
       << setw(2) << year % 100;
  return;
}
```

```
int main()
{
  Date a(4,1,1999), b(12,18,2001); // declare two objects

  cout << "The date stored in a is originally ";
  a.showdate();  // display the original date
  a = b;         // assign b's value to a
  cout << "After assignment the date stored in a is ";
  a.showdate();  // display a's values

  return 0;
}
```

First, to preclude any inadvertent alteration to the object used on the right-hand side of the assignment, a constant reference argument should be used. For our Date class, this takes the form:

```
void Date::operator=(const Date& newdate);
```

The final modification concerns the operation's return value. As constructed, our simple assignment operator returns no value, which precludes us from using it in multiple assignments such as a = b = c. The reason for this is that overloaded operators retain the same precedence and associativity as their equivalent built-in versions. Thus, an expression such as a = b = c is evaluated in the order a = (b = c). As we have defined assignment, unfortunately, the expression b = c returns no value, making subsequent assignment to a an error. To provide for multiple assignments a more complete assignment operation would return a reference to its class type. As the implementation of such an assignment requires a special class pointer, the presentation of this more complete assignment operator is deferred until the material presented in Chapter 11 is introduced. Until then, our simple assignment operator will be more than adequate for our needs.

Copy Constructors

Although assignment looks similar to initialization, it is worthwhile noting that they are two entirely different operations. In C++ an initialization occurs every time a new object is created. In an assignment no new object is created—the value of an existing object is simply changed. Figure 9.1 illustrates this difference.

Figure 9.1 *Initialization and assignment.*

One type of initialization that closely resembles assignment occurs in C++ when one object is initialized using another object of the same class. For example, in the declaration

        Date b = a;

or its entirely equivalent form

        Date b(a);

the b object is initialized to a previously declared a object. The constructor that performs this type of initialization is called a **copy constructor**, and if you do not declare one the compiler will construct one for you. The compiler's **default copy constructor** performs in a similar manner to the default assignment `operator` by doing a memberwise copy between objects. Thus, for the declaration `Date b = a;` the default copy constructor sets b's month, day, and year values to their respective counterparts in a. As with default assignment operators, default copy constructors work just fine unless the class contains pointer data members. Before considering the complications that can occur with pointer data members and how to handle them, it will be helpful to see how to construct our own copy constructors.

Copy constructors, like all class functions, are declared in the class declaration section and defined in the class implementation section. The declaration of a copy constructor has the general form:

class-name(const class-name&);

As with all constructors, the function name must be the class name. As further illustrated by the declaration, the argument is a reference to the class, which is a characteristic of all copy constructors.[2] To ensure that the argument is not inadvertently altered, it is always specified as a constant. Applying this general form to our `Date` class, a copy constructor can be explicitly declared as

        Date(const Date&);

---

[2]A copy constructor is frequently defined as a constructor whose first argument is a reference to its class type, with any additional arguments being defaults.

The actual implementation of this constructor, if it were to perform the same member-wise initialization as the default copy constructor, would take the form:

```
Date:: Date(const Date& olddate)
{
  month = olddate.month;
  day = olddate.day;
  year = olddate.year;
}
```

As with the assignment operator, the use of a reference argument for the copy constructor is no accident: The reference argument again facilitates a simple notation within the body of the function. Program 9.3 contains this copy constructor within the context of a complete program.

Program 9.3

```
#include <iostream.h>
#include <iomanip.h>


// class declaration

class Date
{
  private:
    int month;
    int day;
    int year;
  public:
    Date(int = 7, int = 4, int = 2001);    // constructor
    Date(const Date&);        // copy constructor
    void showdate(void);      // member function to display a date
};

// implementation section

Date::Date(int mm, int dd, int yyyy)
{
  month = mm;
  day = dd;
  year = yyyy;
}
```

(Continued)

(Continued)

```
Date::Date(const Date& olddate)
{
  month = olddate.month;
  day = olddate.day;
  year = olddate.year;
}

void Date::showdate(void)
{
  cout << setfill('0')
       << setw(2) << month << '/'
       << setw(2) << day << '/'
       << setw(2) << year % 100;

  return;
}
```

```
int main()
{
  Date a(4,1,1999), b(12,18,2002); // use the constructor
  Date c(a);    // use the copy constructor
  Date d = b;   // use the copy constructor

  cout << "The date stored in a is ";
  a.showdate();
  cout << "The date stored in b is ";
  b.showdate();
  cout << "The date stored in c is ";
  c.showdate();
  cout << "The date stored in d is ";
  d.showdate();

  return 0;
}
```

The output produced by Program 9.3 is:

```
The date stored in a is 04/01/99
The date stored in b is 12/18/02
The date stored in c is 04/01/99
The date stored in d is 12/18/02
```

As illustrated by this output, c's and d's data members have been initialized by the copy constructor to a's and b's values, respectively. Although the copy constructor defined in Program 9.3 adds nothing to the functionality provided by the compiler's default copy constructor, it does provide us with the fundamentals of defining our own copy constructors.

Base/Member Initialization[3]

Except for the reference names `olddate` and `newdate`, a comparison of Program 9.3's copy constructor to Program 9.2's assignment operator shows them to be essentially the same function. The difference in these functions is that the copy constructor first creates an object's data members before the body of the constructor uses assignment to specify member values. Thus, the copy constructor does not perform a true initialization, but rather a creation followed by assignment.

A true initialization would have no reliance on assignment whatsoever and is possible in C++ using a **base/member initialization list**. Such a list can only be applied to constructor functions and may be written in two ways.

The first way to construct a base/member initialization list is within a class' declaration section using the form

class-name(argument list) : list of data members(initializing values) {}

For example, using this form a default constructor that performs true initialization is

```
// class declaration section

public:
  Date(int mo = 4, int da = 1, int yr = 2001) : month(mo), day(da), year(yr) {}
```

The second way is to declare a function prototype with defaults in the class' declaration section followed by the initialization list in the implementation section. For our `Date` constructor this takes the form:

```
// class declaration section

public:
  Date(int = 4, int = 1, int = 2001);  // prototype with defaults

// class implementation section

Date::Date(int mo, int da, int yr) : month(mo), day(da), year(yr) {}
```

Notice that in both forms the body of the constructor function is empty. This is not a requirement, and the body can include any subsequent operations that you would like the constructor to perform. The interesting feature of this type of constructor is that it clearly differentiates between the initialization tasks performed in the member initialization list contained between the colon and the braces, and any subsequent assignments that might be contained within the function's body. Although we will not be using this type of initialization subsequently, it is required whenever there is a `const class` instance variable.

---

[3]The material in this section is presented for completeness only and may be omitted without loss of subject continuity.

Exercises 9.1

1. Describe the difference between assignment and initialization.

2. **a.** Construct a class named `Time` that contains three integer data members named `hrs`, `mins`, and `secs`, which will be used to store `hours`, `minutes`, and `seconds`. The function members should include a constructor that provides default values of 0 for each data member, a display function that prints an object's data values, and an assignment operator that performs a memberwise assignment between two time objects.

   b. Include the `Time` class developed in Exercise 2a in a working C++ program that creates and displays two `Time` objects, the second of which is assigned the values of the first object.

3. **a.** Construct a class named `Complex` that contains two floating-point data members named `real` and `imag`, which will be used to store the real and imaginary parts of a complex number. The function members should include a constructor that provides default values of 0 for each member function, a display function that prints an object's data values, and an assignment operator that performs a memberwise assignment between two complex number objects.

   b. Include the class written for Exercise 3a in a working C++ program that creates and displays the values of two `Complex` objects, the second of which is assigned the values of the first object.

4. **a.** Construct a class named `Cartesian` that contains two floating-point data members named `x` and `y`, which will be used to store the `x` and `y` values of a point in rectangular coordinates. The function members should include a constructor that initializes the `x` and `y` values of an object to 0 and functions to input and display an object's `x` an `y` values. Additionally, there should be an assignment function that performs a memberwise assignment between two `Cartesian` objects.

   b. Include the class written for Exercise 4a in a working C++ program that creates and displays the values of two `Cartesian` objects, the second of which is assigned the values of the first object.

5. **a.** Construct a class named `Car` that contains the following four data members: a floating-point variable named `engine_size`, a character variable named `body_style`, and an integer variable named `color_code`. The function members should include a constructor that provides default values of 0 for each numeric data member and an `X` for each character variable; a display function that prints the engine size, body style, and color code; and an assignment operator that performs a memberwise assignment between two car objects for each instance variable.

   b. Include the class written for Exercise 5a in a working C++ program that creates and displays two `Car` objects, the second of which is assigned the values of the first object.

Point of Information

Values and Identities

Apart from any behavior that an object is supplied with, a characteristic feature of objects that they share with variables is that they always have a unique identity. It is an object's identity that permits distinguishing one object from another. This is not true of a value, such as the number 5, because all occurrences of 5 are indistinguishable from one another. As such, values are not considered as objects in object-oriented programming languages such as C++.

Another distinguishing feature between an object and a value is that a value can never be container whose value can change, while an object clearly can. A value is simply an entity that stands for itself.

Now consider a string such as "Chicago." As a string this is a value. However, since Chicago could also be a specific and identifiable object of type `city`, the context in which the name is used is important. Notice that if the string "Chicago" were assigned to an object's name attribute, it reverts to being a value.

9.2 ADDITIONAL CLASS FEATURES

This section presents additional features pertaining to classes. These include the scope of a class, creating static class members, and granting access privileges to nonmember functions. Each of these topics may be read independently of the others.

Class Scope

We have already encountered local and global scope in Section 6.5. As we saw, the scope of a variable defines the portion of a program where the variable can be accessed.

For local variables this scope is defined by any block contained within a brace pair, `{}`. This includes both the complete function body and any internal subblocks. Additionally, all parameters of a function are considered as local function variables.

Global variables are accessible from their point of declaration throughout the remaining portion of the file containing them, with three exceptions:

1. If a local variable has the same name as a global variable, the global variable can only be accessed within the scope of the local variable by using the scope resolution operator, `::`.

2. The scope of a global variable can be extended into another file by using the keyword `extern`.

3. The same global name can be reused in another file to define a separate and distinct variable by using the keyword `static`. `static` global variables are unknown outside of their immediate file.

In addition to local and global scopes, each class also defines an associated **class scope**. That is, the names of the data and function members are local to the scope of their class. Thus, if a global variable name is reused within a class, the global variable is hidden by the class data member in the same manner as a local function variable hides a global variable of the same name. Similarly, member function names are local to the class they are declared in and can only be used by objects declared for the class. Additionally, local function variables also hide the names of class data members having the same name. Figure 9.2 illustrates the scope of the variables and functions for the following declarations.

```
float rate;    // global
// class declaration
class Test
{
  private:
    float amount, price, total;  // class scope
  public:
    float extend(float, float);  // class scope
};
```

Figure 9.2 Example of scopes.

Static Class Members

As each **class** object is created it gets its own block of memory for its data members. In some cases, however, it is convenient for every instantiation of a class to share the *same* memory location for a specific variable. For example, consider a class consisting of employee records, where each employee is subject to the same state sales tax. Clearly we could make the sales tax a global variable, but this is not very safe. Such data could be modified anywhere in the program, could conflict with an identical variable name within a function, and certainly violates C++'s principle of data hiding.

This type of situation is handled in C++ by declaring a class variable to be `static`. **Static class data members** share the same storage space for all objects of the class; as such, they act as global variables for the class and provide a means of communication between objects.

C++ requires that static variables be declared as such within the class' declaration section. Since a static data member requires only a single storage area, regardless of the number of class instantiations, it is defined in a single place outside of the class definition. This is typically done in the global part of the program where the class implementation section is provided. For example, assuming the class declaration

```
//class declaration

class Employee
{
  private:
    static float tax_rate;
    int id_num;
  public:
    Employee(int);    //constructor
    void display();
};
```

the definition and initialization of the `static` variable `tax_rate` is accomplished using a statement such as

```
float Employee::tax_rate = 0.0025;
```

Here the scope resolution operator, `::`, is used to identify `tax_rate` as a member of the class `Employee` and the keyword `static` is not included. Program 9.4 uses this definition within the context of a complete program.

The output produced by Program 9.4 is

```
Employee number 11122 has a tax rate of 0.0025
Employee number 11133 has a tax rate of 0.0025
```

Although it might appear that the initialization of `tax_rate` is global, it is not. Once the definition is made, any other definition will result in an error. Thus, the actual definition of a `static` member remains the responsibility of the class creator. The storage sharing produced by the `static` data member and the objects created in Program 9.4 is illustrated in Figure 9.3.

Program 9.4

```cpp
#include <iostream.h>

// class declaration

class Employee
{
  private:
    static float tax_rate;
    int id_num;
  public:
    Employee(int = 0);    // constructor
    void display();   // access function
};

// static member definition
float Employee::tax_rate = 0.0025;

// implementation section

Employee::Employee(int num)
{
  id_num = num;
}

void Employee::display()
{
  cout << "Employee number " << id_num
       << " has a tax rate of " << tax_rate << endl;

  return;
}

int main()
{
  Employee emp1(11122), emp2(11133);

  emp1.display();
  emp2.display();

  return 0;
}
```

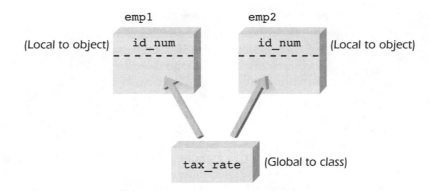

Figure 9.3 Sharing the `static` data member `tax_rate`.

In addition to `static` data members, `static` member functions can also be created. Such functions apply to a class as a whole rather than for individual class objects and can only access static data members and other static member functions of the class. An example of such a function is provided by Program 9.5.

Program 9.5

```
#include <iostream.h>

// class declaration

class Employee
{
  private:
    static float tax_rate;
    int id_num;
  public:
    Employee(int = 0);     // constructor
    void display();        // access function
    static void disp();    // static function
};
// static member definition
float Employee::tax_rate = 0.0025;
```

(Continued)

(Continued)

```
// implementation section

Employee::Employee(int num)
{
  id_num = num;
}

void Employee::display()
{
  cout << "Employee number " << id_num
       << " has a tax rate of " << tax_rate << endl;

  return;
}

void Employee::disp()
{
  cout << "The static tax rate is " << tax_rate << endl;

  return;
}
```

```
int main()
{
  Employee::disp();    // call the static functions
  Employee emp1(11122), emp2(11133);

  emp1.display();
  emp2.display();

  return 0;
}
```

The output produced by Program 9.5 is

```
The static tax rate is 0.0025
Employee number 11122 has a tax rate of 0.0025
Employee number 11133 has a tax rate of 0.0025
```

When reviewing Program 9.5 notice that the keyword static is used only when static data and function members are declared; it is not included in the definition of these members. Also notice that the static member function is called using the resolution operator with the function's class name. Finally, since static functions access only static variables that are not contained within a specific object, static functions may be called before any instantiations are declared.

Friend Functions

The only method we currently have for accessing and manipulating private class' data members is through the class' member functions. Conceptually, this arrangement can be viewed as illustrated in Figure 9.4a. There are times, however, when it is useful to provide such access to selected nonmember functions.

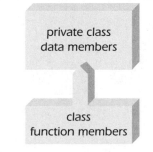

Figure 9.4a Direct access is provided to member functions.

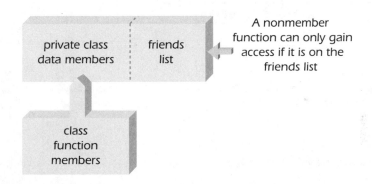

Figure 9.4b Access provided to nonmember functions.

The procedure for providing this external access is rather simple—the class maintains its own approved list of nonmember functions that are granted the same privileges as member functions. The nonmember functions on the list are called **friend functions**, and the list is referred to as a **friends list**.

Figure 9.4b conceptually illustrates the use of such a list for nonmember access. Any function attempting access to an object's private data members is first checked against the friends list: if the function is on the list, access is approved, otherwise access is denied.

From a coding standpoint the friends list is simply a series of function prototype declarations that are preceded with the keyword `friend` and included in the class' declaration section. For example, if the functions named `addreal()` and `addimag()` are to be allowed access to the private members of a class named `Complex`, the following prototypes would be included within `Complex`'s declaration section.

```
friend float addreal(Complex&, Complex&);
friend float addimag(Complex&, Complex&);
```

Here the friends list consists of two declarations. The prototypes indicate that each function returns a floating-point number and expects two references to objects of type Complex as arguments. Program 9.6 includes these two friend declarations in a complete program.

Program 9.6

```
#include <iostream.h>
#include <math.h>

// class declaration

class Complex
{
  // friends list
  friend float addreal(Complex&, Complex&);
  friend float addimag(Complex&, Complex&);
  private:
    float real;
    float imag;
  public:
    Complex(float = 0, float = 0);   // constructor
    void display();

};

// implementation section

Complex::Complex(float rl, float im)
{
  real = rl;
  imag = im;
}

void Complex::display()
{
  char sign = '+';

  if(imag < 0) sign = '-';
  cout << real << sign << fabs(imag) << 'i';

  return;
}
```

(Continued)

(Continued)

```
// friend implementations

float addreal(Complex &a, Complex &b)
{
  return(a.real + b.real);
}

float addimag(Complex &a, Complex &b)
{
  return(a.imag + b.imag);
}
```

```
int main()
{
  Complex a(3.2, 5.6), b(1.1, -8.4);
  float re, im;

  cout << "\nThe first complex number is ";
  a.display();
  cout << "\nThe second complex number is ";
  b.display();

  re = addreal(a,b);
  im = addimag(a,b);
  Complex c(re,im);  // create a new Complex object
  cout << "\n\nThe sum of these two complex numbers is ";
  c.display();

  return 0;
}
```

The output produced by Program 9.6 is

```
The first complex number is 3.2+5.6i
The second complex number is 1.1-8.4i

The sum of these two complex numbers is 4.3-2.8i
```

In reviewing Program 9.6 notice four items. The first is that since friends are not class members, they are unaffected by the access section in which they are declared—*they may be declared anywhere within the declaration section*. The convention we have followed is to include all friend declarations immediately following the class header. The second item to notice is that the keyword `friend` (like the keyword `static`) is used only within the class declaration and not in the actual function definition. Third, since a friend function is intended to have access to an object's private data members, at least one of the friend's arguments should be a reference to an object of the class that has made it a friend. Finally, as illustrated by Program 9.6, it is the class that grants friend status to a function and not the other way around. The function can never confer friend status on itself, because to do so would violate the concepts of data hiding and access provided by a class.

Exercises 9.2

1. **a.** Rewrite Program 9.5 to include an integer `static` data member named `numemps`. This variable should act as a counter that is initialized to zero and is incremented by the class constructor each time a new object is declared. Rewrite the `static` function `disp()` to display the value of this counter.
   b. Test the program written for Exercise 1a. Have the `main()` function call `disp()` after each `Employee` object is created.

2. **a.** Construct a class named `Circle` that contains two integer data members named `x_cent` and `y_cent`, and a floating-point data member named `radius`. Additionally, the `class` should contain `static` data member named `scale_factor`. Here the `x_cent` and `y_cent` values represent the center point of a circle, `radius` represents the circle's actual radius, and `scale_factor` represents a scale factor that will be used to scale the circle to fit on a variety of display devices.
   b. Include the class written for Exercise 2a in a working C++ program.

3. **a.** Could the following three statements in Program 9.6

   ```
   re = addreal(a,b);
   im = addimag(a,b);
   complex c(re,im);  // create a new complex object
   ```

   be replaced by the single statement

   ```
   complex(addread(a,b), addimag(a,b));
   ```

   b. Verify your answer to Exercise 3a by running Program 9.6 with the suggested replacement statement.

4. **a.** Rewrite the program written for Exercise 2a, but include a friend function that multiples an object's `radius` by a static `scale_factor` and then displays the actual radius value and the scaled value.
   b. Test the program written for Exercise 4a.

5. Rewrite Program 9.6 to have only one `friend` function named `addcomplex()`. This function should accept two complex objects and return a complex object. The real and imaginary parts of the returned object should be the sum of the real and imaginary parts, respectively, of the two objects passed to `addcomplex()`.

6. a. Construct a class named `Coord` that contains two floating-point data members named `xval` and `yval`, which will be used to store the x and y values of a point in rectangular coordinates. The function members should include appropriate constructor and display functions and a `friend` function named `conv_pol()`. The `conv_pol()` function should accept two floating-point numbers that represent a point in polar coordinates and convert them into rectangular coordinates. For conversion from polar to rectangular coordinates use the formulas

$x = r \cos \theta$
$y = r \sin \theta$

b. Include the class written for Exercise 6a in a working C++ program.

7. a. Construct two classes named `Rec_coord` and `Pol_coord`. The class named `Rec_coord` should contain two floating-point data members named `xval` and `yval`, which will be used to store the x and y values of a point in rectangular coordinates. The function members should include appropriate constructor and display functions and a `friend` function named `conv_pol()`.

The class named `Pol_coord` should contain two floating-point data members named `dist` and `theta`, which will be used to store the distance and angle values of a point represented in polar coordinates. The function members should include appropriate constructor and display functions and a `friend` function named `conv_pol()`. The `friend` function should accept an integer argument named `dir`; two floating point arguments named `val1` and `val2`; and two reference arguments named `recref` and `polref`, the first of which should be a reference to an object of type `rec_coord`, and the second to an object of type `pol_coord`. If the value of `dir` is 1, `val1` and `val2` are to be considered as x and y rectangular coordinates that are to be converted to polar coordinates; if the value of `dir` is any other value, `val1` and `val2` are to be considered as distance and angle values that are to be converted to rectangular coordinates. For conversion from rectangular to polar, coordinates are

$r = \sqrt{x^2 + y^2}$
$\theta = \tan (y/x)^{-1}$

For conversion from polar to rectangular coordinates, use the formulas:

$x = r \cos \theta$
$y = r \sin \theta$

b. Include the class written for Exercise 7a in a working C++ program.

9.3 ▷ OPERATOR FUNCTIONS

A simple assignment operator was constructed in Section 9.1. In this section we extend this capability and show how to broaden C++'s built-in operators to work with class objects. As we will discover, class operators are themselves either member or friend functions.

The only symbols permitted for user-defined purposes are the subset of C++'s built-in symbols listed in Table 9.1. Each of these symbols may be adopted for class use with no limitation as to its meaning.[4] This is done by making each operation a function that can be overloaded like any other function.

The operation of the symbols listed in Table 9.1 can be redefined as we see fit for our classes, subject to the following restrictions.

- Symbols not in Table 9.1 cannot be redefined. For example, the ., ::, and ?: symbols cannot be redefined.

- New operator symbols cannot be created. For example, since %% is not an operator in C++ it cannot be defined as a class operator.

- Neither the precedence nor the associativity of C++'s operators can be modified. Thus, you cannot give the addition operator a higher precedence than the multiplication operator.

- Operators cannot be redefined for C++'s built-in types.

- A C++ operator that is unary cannot be changed to a binary operator and a binary operator cannot be changed to a unary operator.

- The operator must either be a member of a class or be defined to take at least one class member as an operand.

The first step in providing a class with operators from Table 9.1 is to decide which operations make sense for the class and how they should be defined. As a specific example, we continue to build on the `Date` class introduced previously. For this class a small, meaningful set of class operations is defined.

Clearly the addition of two dates is not meaningful. The addition of a date with an integer, however, does make sense if the integer is taken as the number of days to be added to the date. Likewise, the subtraction of an integer from a date makes sense. Also, the subtraction of two dates is meaningful if we define the difference to mean the number of days between the two dates. Similarly, it makes sense to compare two dates and determine if the dates are equal or one date occurs before or after another date. Let's now see how these operations can be implemented using C++'s operator symbols.

---

[4]The only limitation is that the syntax of the operator cannot be changed. Thus, a binary operator must remain binary and a unary operator must remain unary. Within this syntax restriction an operator symbol can be used to produce any operation, whether or not the operation is consistent with the symbol's accepted usage. For example, we could redefine the addition symbol to provide multiplication. Clearly this violates the intent and spirit of making these symbols available to us. We shall be very careful to redefine each symbol in a manner consistent with its accepted usage.

Table 9.1 Operators Available for Class Use

Operator	Description
( ) [ ] -> new delete	Function call Array element Structure member pointer reference dynamically allocate memory dynamically deallocate memory
++ -- - ! ~ *	Increment Decrement Unary minus Logical negation One's complement Indirection
* / % + -	Multiplication Division Modulus (remainder) Addition Subtraction
<< >>	Left shift Right shift
< <= > >= == != && ||	Less than Less than or equal to Greater than Greater than or equal to Equal to Not equal to Logical AND Logical OR
& ^ |	Bitwise AND Bitwise exclusive OR Bitwise inclusive OR
= += -= *= /= %= &= ^= |= <<= >>=	Assignment Assignment Assignment Assignment Assignment
,	Comma

A user-defined operation is created as a function that redefines C++'s built-in operator symbols for class use. Functions that define operations on class objects and use C++'s built-in operator symbols are referred to as **operator functions**.

Operator functions are declared and implemented in the same manner as all member functions, with one exception: It is the function's name that connects the appropriate operator symbol to the operation defined by the function. An operator function's name is always of the form operator<symbol> where <symbol> is one of the operators listed in Table 9.1. For example, the function name operator+ is the name of the addition function, while the function name operator== is the name of the equal-to comparison function.

Once the appropriate function name is selected the process of writing the function simply amounts to having it accept the desired inputs and produce the correct returned value.[5] For example, in comparing two Date objects for equality we would select C++'s equality operator. Thus, the name of our function becomes operator==. We would want our comparison operation to accept two Date objects, internally compare them, and return an integer value indicating the result of the comparison: 1 for equality and 0 for inequality. As a member function a suitable prototype that could be included in the class declaration section is

```
int operator==(Date& );
```

This prototype indicates that the function is named operator==, that it returns an integer, and that it accepts a reference to a Date object.[6] Only one Date object is required here because the second Date object will be the object that calls the function. Let's now write the function definition to be included in the class implementation section. Assuming our class is named Date, a suitable definition is

```
int Date::operator==(Date& Date2)
{
  if( day == date2.day && month == date2.month && year == date2.year)
    return 1;
  else
    return 0;
}
```

Once this function has been defined, it may be called using the same syntax as for C++'s built-in types. For example, if a and b are objects of type Date, the expression if (a == b) is valid. Program 9.7 includes this if statement as well as the declaration and definition of this operator function within the context of a complete program.

The output produced by Program 9.7 is:

```
Dates a and b are not the same.
Dates a and c are the same.
```

The first new feature to be illustrated in Program 9.7 is the declaration and implementation of the function named operator==( ). Except for its name, this operator function is constructed in the same manner as any other member function: it is declared in the declaration section and defined in the implementation section. The second new feature is how the function is called. Operator functions may be called using their associated symbols rather than in the way other functions are called. Since operator functions are true functions, however, the traditional method of calling them can also be used—by specifying their name and including appropriate arguments. Thus, in addition to being called by the expression a == b in Program 9.7, the call a.operator==(b) could also have been used.

---

[5]As previously noted, this implies that the specified operator can be redefined to perform any operation. Good programming practice, however, dictates against such redefinitions.

[6]The prototype int operator==(Date) also works. Passing a reference, however, is preferable to passing an object because it reduces the function call's overhead. This is because passing an object means that a copy of the object must be made for the called function, while passing a reference gives the function direct access to the object whose address is passed.

Program 9.7

```cpp
#include <iostream.h>

// class declaration
class Date
{
  private:
    int month;
    int day;
    int year;
  public:
    Date(int = 7, int = 4, int = 2001);  // constructor
    int operator==(Date &);  // declare the operator== function
    void showdate(void);  // member function to display a date
};

// implementation section
Date::Date(int mm, int dd, int yyyy)
{
  month = mm;
  day = dd;
  year = yyyy;
}

int Date::operator==(Date &date2)
{
  if(day == date2.day && month == date2.month && year == date2.year)
    return 1;
  else
    return 0;
}

int main()
{
  Date a(4,1,1999), b(12,18,2001), c(4,1,1999); // declare 3 objects

  if (a == b)
    cout << "Dates a and b are the same." << endl;
  else
    cout << "Dates a and b are not the same." << endl;

  if (a == c)
    cout << "Dates a and c are the same." << endl;
  else
    cout << "Dates a and c are not the same." << endl;

  return 0;
}
```

Let's now create another operator for our `Date` class—an addition operator. As before, creating this operator requires that we specify three items:

1. The name of the operator function

2. The processing that the function is to perform

3. The data type, if any, that the function is to return

Clearly, for addition we will use the operator function named `operator+`. Having selected the function's name we must now determine what we want this function to do, as it specifically relates to `Date` objects. As we noted previously, the sum of two dates makes no sense. Adding an integer to a date is meaningful, however, when the integer represents the number of days either before or after the given date. Here the sum of an integer to a `Date` object is simply another `Date` object, which should be returned by the addition operation. Thus, a suitable prototype for our addition function is

```
Date operator+(int);
```

This prototype would be included in the class declaration section. It specifies that an integer is to be added to a class object and the operation returns a `Date` object. Thus, if `a` is a `Date` object, the function call `a.operator+(284)`, or its more commonly used alternative, `a + 284`, should cause the number 284 to be correctly added to `a`'s date value. We must now construct the function to accomplish this.

Constructing the function requires that we first select a specific date convention. For simplicity we will adopt the financial date convention that considers each month to consist of 30 days and each year to consist of 360 days. Using this convention, our function will first add the integer number of days to the `Date` object's day value and then adjust the resulting day value to lie within the range 1 to 30 and the month value to lie within the range 1 to 12. A function that accomplishes this is

```
Date Date::operator+(int days)
{
  Date temp;  // a temporary Date to store the result

  temp.day = day + days;  // add the days
  temp.month = month;
  temp.year = year;
  while (temp.day > 30)    // now adjust the months
  {
    temp.month++;
    temp.day -= 30;
  }
  while (temp.month > 12)  // adjust the years
  {
    temp.year++;
    temp.month -= 12;
  }
  return temp;      // the values in temp are returned
}
```

The important feature to notice here is the use of the `temp` object. The purpose of this object is to ensure that none of the function's arguments, which become the operator's operands, are altered. To understand this consider a statement such as `b = a + 284;` that uses this operator function, where a and b are `Date` objects. This statement should never modify a's value. Rather, the expression `a + 284` should yield a `Date` value that is then assigned to b. The result of the expression is, of course, the `temp Date` object returned by the `operator+()` function. Program 9.8 uses this function within the context of a complete program.

Program 9.8

```cpp
#include <iostream.h>
#include <iomanip.h>

// class declaration

class Date
{
  private:
    int month;
    int day;
    int year;
  public:
    Date(int = 0, int = 0, int = 0);     // constructor
    Date operator+(int);     // overload the + operator
    void showdate(void);       // member function to display a date
};
// implementation section
Date::Date(int mm, int dd, int yyyy)
{
  month = mm;
  day = dd;
  year = yyyy;
}

Date Date::operator+(int days)
{
  Date temp;  // a temporary date to store the result

  temp.day = day + days;  // add the days
  temp.month = month;
  temp.year = year;
  while (temp.day > 30)     // now adjust the months
```

(Continued)

(Continued)

```
  {
    temp.month++;
    temp.day -= 30;
  }
  while (temp.month > 12)  // adjust the years
  {
    temp.year++;
    temp.month -= 12;
  }
  return temp;      // the values in temp are returned
}
void Date::showdate(void)
{
  cout << setfill('0')
       << setw(2) << month << '/'
       << setw(2) << day << '/'
       << setw(2) << year % 100
  return;
}
```

```
int main()
{
  Date a(4,1,1999), b; // declare two objects

  cout << "The initial date is ";
  a.showdate();
  b = a + 284;   // add in 284 days = 9 months and 14 days
  cout << "The new date is ";
  b.showdate();

  return 0;
}
```

The output produced by Program 9.8 is

```
The initial date is 04/01/99
The new date is 01/15/00
```

Operator Functions as Friends

The operator functions in both Programs 9.7 and 9.8 have been constructed as class members. An interesting feature of operator functions is that, except for the operator functions =, ( ), [ ], and ->, they may also be written as friend functions. For example, if the `operator+()` function used in Program 9.8 were written as a friend, a suitable declaration section prototype is

```
friend Date operator+(Date& , int);
```

Notice that the friend version contains a reference to a `Date` object that is not contained in the member function version. In all cases the equivalent friend version of a member operator function *must* contain an additional class reference that is not required by the member function.[7] This equivalence is listed in Table 9.2 for both unary and binary operators.

Table 9.2 Operator Function Argument Requirements

	Member Function	Friend Function
Unary operator	1 implicit	1 explicit
Binary operator	1 implicit and 1 explicit	2 explicit

Program 9.8's `operator+()` function, written as a friend function is

```
Date Date::operator+(Date& op1, int days)
{
  Date temp;  // a temporary Date to store the result

  temp.day = op1.day + days;  // add the days
  temp.month = op1.month;
  temp.year = op1.year;
  while (temp.day > 30)    // now adjust the months
  {
    temp.month++;
    temp.day -= 30;
  }
  while (temp.month > 12)  // adjust the years
  {
    temp.year++;
    temp.month -= 12;
  }
  return temp;       // the values in temp are returned
}
```

The only difference between this version and the member version is the explicit use of a `Date` argument named op1 (the choice of this name is entirely arbitrary) in the friend version. This means that within the body of the friend function the first three assignment statements explicitly reference op1's data members as `op1.day`, `op1.month`, and `op1.year`, whereas the member function simply refers to its arguments as `day`, `month`, and `year`.

In making the determination to overload a binary operator as either a friend or member operator function, the following convention can be applied: *friend functions are more appropriate for binary functions that modify neither of their operands, such as ==, +, –, etc., while member functions are more appropriate for binary functions, such as =, +=, –=, etc., that are used to modify one of their operands.*

---

[7]This extra argument is necessary to identify the correct object. This argument is not needed when using a member function because the member function "knows" which object it is operating on. The mechanism of this "knowing" is supplied by an implied member function argument named `this`.

Exercises 9.3

1. **a.** Define a *greater than* relational operator function named `operator>()` that can be used with the `Date` class declared in Program 9.7.

   b. Define a *less than* operator function named `operator<()` that can be used with the `Date` class declared in Program 9.7.

   c. Include the operator functions written for Exercises 1a and 1b in a working C++ program.

2. **a.** Define a subtraction operator function named `operator-()` that can be used with the `Date` class defined in Program 9.7. The subtraction should accept a long-integer argument that represents the number of days to be subtracted from an object's date and return a `Date`. In doing the subtraction use the financial assumption that all months consist of 30 days and all years of 360 days. Additionally, an end-of-month adjustment should be made, if necessary, that converts any resulting day of 31 to a day of 30, except if the month is February. If the resulting month is February and the day is either 29, 30, or 31, it should be changed to 28.

   b. Define another subtraction operator function named `operator-()` that can be used with the `Date` class defined in Program 9.7. The subtraction should yield a long integer that represents the difference in days between two dates. In calculating the day difference use the financial-day count basis that assumes that all months have 30 days and all years have 360 days.

   c. Include the overloaded operators written for Exercises 2a and 2b in a working C++ program.

3. **a.** Determine if the following addition operator function provides the same result as the function used in Program 9.8.

```
Date Date::operator+(int days)    // return a Date object
{
  Date temp;

  temp.day = day + days;    // add the days in
  temp.month = month + int(day/30);  // determine total months
  temp.day = temp.day % 30;           // determine actual day
  temp.year = year + int(temp.month/12);  // determine total years
  temp.month = temp.month % 12;       // determine actual month

  return temp;
}
```

   b. Verify your answer to Exercise 3a by including the function in a working C++ program.

4. **a.** Rewrite the equality relational operator function in Program 9.7 as a friend function.

   b. Verify the operation of the friend operator function written for Exercise 4a by including it within a working C++ program.

5. **a.** Construct an addition operator for the `Complex` class declared in Program 9.6. This should be a member function that adds two complex numbers and returns a complex number.

   b. Add a member multiplication operator function to the class used in Exercise 5a that multiplies two complex numbers and returns a complex number.

   c. Verify the operation of the operator functions written for Exercises 5a and 5b by including them within a working C++ program.

6. **a.** Rewrite the addition operator function in Program 9.8 to account for the actual days in a month, neglecting leap years. (*NOTE*: This requires an array to store the days in each month.)

   b. Verify the operation of the operator function written for Exercise 6a by including it within a working C++ program.

9.4 ▷ DATA TYPE CONVERSIONS

The conversion from one built-in data type to another was previously described in Section 3.2. With the introduction of user-defined data types the possibilities for conversion between data types expands to the following cases:

- Conversion from built-in type to built-in type

- Conversion from built-in type to class type

- Conversion from class type to built-in type

- Conversion from class type to class type

The first conversion is handled either by C++'s built-in implicit conversion rules or its explicit cast operator. The second conversion type is made using a **type conversion constructor**. The third and fourth conversion types are made using a **conversion operator function**. In this section the specific means of performing each of these conversions is presented.

Built-in to Built-in Conversion

The conversion from one built-in data type to another has already been presented in Section 3.1 and 3.3. To review this case briefly, this type of conversion is either implicit or explicit.

An implicit conversion occurs in the context of one of C++'s operations. For example, when a floating-point value is assigned to an integer variable only the integer portion of the value is stored. The conversion is implied by the operation and is performed automatically by the compiler.

An explicit conversion occurs whenever a cast is used. In C++ two cast notations exist. Using the older C notation, a cast has the form *(data-type) expression* while the newer C++ notation has the function-like form *data-type(expression)*. For example, both of the expressions (int)24.32 and int(24.32) cause the floating-point value 24.32 to be truncated to the integer value 24.

Built-In to Class Conversion

User-defined casts for converting a built-in to a class data type are created using constructor functions. A constructor whose first argument is not a member of its class and whose remaining arguments, if any, have default values is a **type conversion constructor**. If the first argument of a type conversion constructor is a built-in data type, the constructor can be used to cast the built-in data type to a class object. Clearly, one restriction of such functions is that, as constructors, they must be member functions.

Although this type of cast occurs when the constructor is invoked to initialize an object, it is actually a more general cast than might be evident at first glance. This is because a constructor function can be explicitly invoked after all objects have been declared, whether or not it was invoked previously as part of an object's declaration. Before exploring this further, let's first construct a type conversion constructor. We will then see how to use it as a cast independent of its initialization purpose.

The cast we will construct will convert a long integer into a Date object. Our Date object will consist of dates in the form month/day/year and use our by now familiar Date class. The long integer will be used to represent dates in the form year * 10000 + month * 100 + day. For example, using this representation the date 12/31/2001 becomes the long integer 20001231. Dates represented in this fashion are very useful for two reasons: First, it permits a date to be to stored as a single integer, and second, such dates are in numerically increasing date order, making sorting extremely easy. For example, the date 01/03/2002, which occurs after 12/31/2001 becomes the integer 20020103, which is larger than 20011231. Since the integers representing dates can exceed the size of a normal integer, the integers are always declared as longs.

A suitable constructor function for converting from a long-integer date to a date stored as a month, day, and year is

```
// type conversion constructor from long to Date

Date::Date(long findate)
{
  year = int(findate/10000.0);
  month = int((findate - year * 10000.0)/100.0);
  day = int(findate - year * 10000.0 - month * 100.0);
}
```

Program 9.9 uses this type conversion constructor both as an initialization function at declaration time and as an explicit cast later on in the program.

Program 9.9

```
#include <iostream.h>
#Include <iomanip.h>

// class declaration

class Date
{
  private:
    int month, day, year;
  public:
    Date(int = 7, int = 4, int = 2001);  // constructor
    Date(long);              // type conversion constructor
    void showdate(void);
};

// implementation section

// constructor
Date::Date(int mm, int dd, int yyyy)
{
  month = mm;
  day = dd;
  year = yyyy;
}

// type conversion constructor from long to date
Date::Date(long findate)
{
  year = int(findate/10000.0);
  month = int((findate - year * 10000.0)/100.0);
  day = int(findate - year * 10000.0 - month * 100.0);
}

// member function to display a date
void Date::showdate(void)
{
  cout << setfill('0')
       << setw(2) << month << '/'
       << setw(2) << day << '/'
       << setw(2) << year % 100;

  return;
}
```

(Continued)

(Continued)

```
int main()
{
  Date a, b(20011225L), c(4,1,1999);  // declare 3 objects - initialize 2 of them

  cout << "Dates a, b, and c are ";
  a.showdate();
  cout << ", ";
  b.showdate();
  cout << ", and ";
  c.showdate();
  cout << ".\n";

  a = Date(20020103L);  // cast a long to a date

  cout << "Date a is now ";
  a.showdate();
  cout << ".\n";

  return 0;
}
```

The output produced by Program 9.9 is

```
Dates a, b, and c are 07/04/01, 12/25/01, and 04/01/99.
Date a is now 01/03/02.
```

The change in a's date value illustrated by this output is produced by the assignment expression a = Date(20020103L), which uses a type conversion constructor to perform the cast from long to Date.

Class to Built-in Conversion

Conversion from a user-defined data type to a built-in data type is accomplished using a conversion operator function. A **conversion operator function** is a member operator function having the name of a built-in data type or class. When the operator function has a built-in data type name it is used to convert from a class to a built-in data type. For example, a conversion operator function for casting a class object to a long integer would have the name operator long(). Here the name of the operator function indicates that a conversion to a long will take place. If this function were part of a Date class it would be used to cast a Date object into a long integer. This usage is illustrated by Program 9.10.

The output produced by Program 9.10 is:

```
a's date is 04/01/99
This date, as a long integer, is 19990401
```

Program 9.10

```cpp
#include <iostream.h>
#include <iomanip.h>

// class declaration

class Date
{
  private:
    int month, day, year;
  public:
    Date(int = 7, int = 4, int = 2001);    // constructor
    operator long();         // conversion operator function
    void showdate(void);
};

// implementation section

// constructor
Date::Date(int mm, int dd, int yyyy)
{
  month = mm;
  day = dd;
  year = yyyy;
}

// conversion operator function converting from Date to long
Date::operator long()    // must return a long
{
  long yyyymmdd;

  yyyymmdd = year * 10000.0 + month * 100.0 + day;

  return(yyyymmdd);
}

// member function to display a date
void Date::showdate(void)
{
   cout << setfill('0')
        << setw(2) << month << '/'
        << setw(2) << day << '/'
        << setw(2) << year % 100;
  return;
}
```

(Continued)

(Continued)

```
int main()
{
  Date a(4,1,1999);   // declare and initialize one object of type date
  long b;             // declare an object of type long

  b = a;              // a conversion takes place here

  cout << "a's date is ";
  a.showdate();
  cout << "\nThis date, as a long integer, is " << b << endl;

  return 0;
}
```

The change in a's date value to a long integer illustrated by this output is produced by the assignment expression b = a. This assignment, which also could have been written as b = long(a), calls the conversion operator function long() to perform the cast from Date to long. In general, since explicit conversion more clearly documents what is happening, its use is preferred to implicit conversion.

Notice that the conversion operator has no explicit argument and has no explicit return type. This is true of all conversion operators: The implicit argument will always be an object of the **class** being cast from, and the return type is implied by the name of the function. Additionally, as previously indicated, a conversion operator function *must* be a member function.

Class to Class Conversion

Converting from a class data type to a class data type is performed in the same manner as a cast from a class to built-in data type—it is done using a member **conversion operator function**. In this case, however, the operator function uses the class name being converted to rather than a built-in data name. For example, if two classes named Date and Intdate exist, the operator function named operator Intdate() could be placed in the Date class to convert from a Date object to an Intdate object. Similarly, the operator function named Date() could be placed in the Intdate class to convert from an Intdate to a Date.

Notice that as before, in converting from a class data type to a built-in data type, *the operator function's name determines the result of the conversion*; the class containing the operator function determines the data type being converted from.

Before providing a specific example of a class to class conversion, one additional point must be noted. Converting between classes clearly implies that we have two classes, one of which is always defined first and one of which is defined second. Having, within the second class, a conversion operator function with the name of the first class poses no problem because the compiler knows of the first class' existence. However, including a conversion operator function with the second class' name in the first class does pose a problem because the second class has not yet been defined. This is remedied by including a declaration for the second class prior to the first class' definition. This declaration, which is formally referred to as a **forward declaration**, is illustrated in Program 9.11, which also includes conversion operators between the two defined classes.

Program 9.11

```
#include <iostream.h>
#include <iomanip.h>

// forward declaration of class Intdate
class Intdate;

// class declaration for Date
class Date
{
  private:
    int month, day, year;
  public:
    Date(int = 7, int = 4, int = 2001);     // constructor
    operator Intdate();      // conversion operator Date to Intdate
    void showdate(void);
};
// class declaration for Intdate
class Intdate
{
  private:
    long yyyymmdd;
  public:
    Intdate(long = 0);     // constructor
    operator Date();  // conversion operator intdate to date
    void showint(void);
};

// implementation section for Date
Date::Date(int mm, int dd, int yyyy)  // constructor
{
  month = mm;
  day = dd;
  year = yyyy;
}
// conversion operator function converting from Date to Intdate class
Date::operator Intdate()    // must return an Intdate object
```

(Continued)

(Continued)

```
{
  long temp;

  temp = year * 10000.0 + month * 100.0 + day;
  return(Intdate(temp));
}
// member function to display a Date
void Date::showdate(void)
{
   cout << setfill('0')
        << setw(2) << month << '/'
        << setw(2) << day << '/'
        << setw(2) << year % 100;
   return;
}

// implementation section for Intdate
Intdate::Intdate(long ymd)  // constructor
{
  yyyymmdd = ymd;
}
// conversion operator function converting from Intdate to Date class
Intdate::operator Date()    // must return a Date object
{
  int mo, da, yr;

  yr = int(yyyymmdd/10000.0);
  mo = int((yyyymmdd - yr * 10000.0)/100.0);
  da = int(yyyymmdd - yr * 10000.0 - mo * 100.0);
  return(Date(mo,da,yr));
}
// member function to display an Intdate
void Intdate::showint(void)
{
  cout << yyyymmdd;
  return;
}
```

```
int main()
{
  Date a(4,1,1999), b;       // declare two Date objects
  Intdate c(20011215), d;    // declare two Intdate objects

  b = Date(c);        // cast c into a Date object
  d = Intdate(a);     // cast a into an Intdate object
```

(Continued)

```
    cout << " a's date is ";
    a.showdate();
    cout << "\n   as an Intdate object this date is ";
    d.showint();

    cout << "\n c's date is ";
    c.showint();
    cout << "\n   as a Date object this date is ";
    b.showdate();
    cout << endl;

    return 0;
}
```

The output produced by Program 9.11 is

```
a's date is 04/01/99
   as an Intdate object this date is 19990401
c's date is 20011215
   as a Date object this date is 12/15/01
```

As illustrated by Program 9.11, the cast from Date to Intdate is produced by the assignment b = Date(c) and the cast from Intdate to Date is produced by the assignment d = Intdate(a). Alternatively, the assignments b = c and d = a would produce the same results. Notice also the forward declaration of the Intdate class prior to the Date class' declaration. This is required so that the Date class can reference Intdate in its operator conversion function.

Exercises 9.4

1. **a.** Define the four data type conversions available in C++ and the method of accomplishing each conversion.
   b. Define the terms type conversion constructor and conversion operator function and describe how they are used in user-defined conversions.

2. Write a C++ program that declares a class named Time having integer data members named hours, minutes, and seconds. Include in the program a type conversion constructor that converts a long integer, representing the elapsed seconds from midnight, into an equivalent representation as hours:minutes:seconds. For example, the long integer 30336 should convert to the time 8:25:36. Use a military representation of time so that 2:30 pm is represented as 14:30:00. The relationship between time representations is

*elapsed seconds = hours * 3600 + minutes * 60 + seconds.*

3. A Julian date is a date represented as the number of days from a known base date. One algorithm for converting from a Gregorian date, in the form month/day/year, to a Julian date with a base date of 0/0/0 is given below. All of the calculations in this algorithm use integer arithmetic, which means that the fractional part of all divisions must be discarded. In this algorithm M = month, D = day, and Y = year.

> *If M is less than or equal to 2*
>   *Set the variable MP = 0 and YP = Y–1*
> *Else*
>   *Set MP = int(0.4 * M + 2.3) and YP = Y*
> *EndIf*
> *T = int(YP/4) – int(YP/100) + int(YP/400)*
> *Julian date = 365 * Y + 31 * (M – 1) + D + T – MP*

Using this algorithm modify Program 9.10 to cast from a Gregorian date object to its corresponding Julian representation as a long integer. Test your program using the Gregorian dates 1/31/85 and 3/16/86, which correspond to the Julian dates 31077 and 31486, respectively.

4. Modify the program written for Exercise 2 to include a member conversion operator function that converts an object of type `Time` into a long integer representing the number of seconds from twelve midnight.

5. Write a C++ program that has a `Date` class and a `Julian` class. The `Date` class should be the same `Date` class as that used in Program 9.11, while the `Julian` class should represent a date as a long integer. For this program include a member conversion operator function within the `Date` class that converts a `Date` object to a `Julian` object, using the algorithm presented in Exercise 3. Test your program by converting the dates 1/31/95 and 3/16/96, which correspond to the Julian dates 34729 and 35139, respectively.

6. Write a C++ program that has a `Time` class and an `Ltime` class. The `Time` class should have integer data members named `hours`, `minutes`, and `seconds`, while the `Ltime` class should have a long data member named `elsecs`, which represents the number of elapsed seconds since midnight. For the `Time` class include a member conversion operator function named `Ltime()` that converts a `Time` object to an `Ltime` object. For the `Ltime` class include a member conversion operator function named `Time()` that converts an `Ltime` object to a `Time` object.

9.5 APPLICATION–A MULTI-OBJECT GAS PUMP SIMULATION

In Application 2 of Section 8.4 we presented a requirement to construct a C++ program that simulated a gas pump's operation over the course of one-half hour. In Section 8.4 we constructed a gas pump class to model the operation of a gas pump. In this section we use this gas pump class within the context of a complete simulation. For convenience we repeat the complete program requirement here.

We have been requested to write a program that simulates the operation of a gas pump. At any time during the simulation we should be able to determine, from the pump, the price-per-gallon of gas and the amount remaining in the supply tank from which the gas is being pumped. If a request for gas, in gallons, is less than the amount of gas in the tank, the request should be filled; otherwise only the available amount in the supply tank should be used. Once the gas is pumped, the total price of the gallons pumped should be displayed and the amount of gas, in gallons, that was pumped should be subtracted from the amount in the supply tank.

For the simulation assume that the customers randomly arrive between 1 to 15 minutes and that a customer randomly requests between 3 and 20 gallons of gas. Although the tank capacity is 500 gallons, assume that the initial amount of gas in the tank is only 300 gallons. Initially, the program should simulate a one-half hour time frame.

Additionally, for each arrival and request for gas we want to know the idle time before the customer arrived, how many gallons of gas were pumped, and the total price of the transaction. The pump itself must keep track of the price per gallon of gas and the amount of gas remaining in the tank. Typically, the price per gallon is $1.00, but the price used for the simulation should be $1.25.

In Section 8.4 we constructed a `Pump` class that can be used for this simulation. In this problem we complete the simulation by providing a `Customer` class and the controlling code within a `main()` function to create an actual multi-object simulation program consisting of both `Customer` and `Pump` objects.

Step 1   Analyze the Problem

As specified, the problem entails two types of objects: a gas pump and a customer. Let's consider these object types separately.

The Pump. A `Pump` class was designed and implemented in Section 8.4 and is repeated below for convenience.

```
// class declaration

class Pump
{
  private:
    float amtInTank;
    float price;
  public:
    Pump(float = 500.00, float = 1.00);        // constructor
    void values(void);
    void request(float);
};


// implementation section

Pump::Pump(float start, float todaysPrice)
```

```
{
  amtInTank = start;
  price = todaysPrice;
}

void Pump::values(void)
{
  cout << setiosflags(ios::fixed) << setiosflags(ios::showpoint)
       << setprecision(2) << endl;
  cout << "The gas tank has " << amtInTank
       << " gallons of gas." << endl;
  cout << "The price per gallon of gas is $" << price << endl;

  return;
}

void Pump::request(float pumpAmt)
{
  float pumped;

  if (amtInTank >= pumpAmt)
     pumped = pumpAmt;
  else
     pumped = amtInTank;

  amtInTank -= pumped;
  cout << setiosflags(ios::fixed) << setiosflags(ios::showpoint)
       << setprecision(2) << endl;
  cout << pumpAmt << " gallons were requested " << endl;
  cout << pumped << " gallons were pumped" << endl;
  cout << amtInTank << " gallons remain in the tank" << endl;
  cout << "The total price is $" << (pumped * price) << endl;

  return;
}
```

You should review Application 2 in Section 8.4 if either the data or function members of this Pump class are not clear. For later convenience in writing the required simulation program assume that the code for the Pump class has been stored in a file named PUMP.H within a directory named CLASSES on the C drive. Once this is done, including the Pump class definition within a program simply requires the single line preprocessor directive #include <C:\CLASSES\PUMP.H>.[8]

---

[8]The reason for using a full path name in the #include statement is to ensure that the preprocessor accesses the PUMP.H class that we have placed in the named directory. We do not want the preprocessor to either search its default directory and possibly locate some other PUMP.H that we do not know about or be unable to locate the PUMP.H file at all.

The Customer. For this problem there are multiple instances of customers arriving randomly between 1 and 15 minutes and requesting gas in amounts that vary randomly between 3 and 20 gallons. From an object viewpoint, however, we are not interested in storing the arrival and number of gallons requested by each customer. We simply need a customer object to present us with an arrival time and a request for gas, in gallons.

Notice that our `Customer` object type will have no attributes and will simply consist of two operations. The first operation, called `arrival()`, will be used to provide a random arrival time between 1 and 15 minutes. The second operation, called `gallons()`, will be used to provide a random request of between 3 and 20 gallons of gas. This class is relatively simple and its design and implementation are coded as

```
#include <stdlib.h>
#include <time.h>

//class declaration and implementation
class Customer
{
  public:
    Customer(void) {srand(time(NULL));};
    int arrive(void) {return(1 + rand() % 16);};
    int gallons(void) {return(3 + rand() % 21);};
};
```

In reviewing this code notice that the class constructor is used to randomize the `rand()` function (review Section 6.4 if you are unfamiliar with either the `srand()` or `rand()` functions). The `arrive()` function simply returns a random integer between 1 and 15, while the `gallons()` function returns a random integer between 3 and 20 (we leave it as an exercise for you to rewrite the `gallons()` function to return a floating-point value). Since all of the functions are single line, we have included their definitions within the declaration section as inline functions.

Again, for later convenience in writing the complete simulation program, assume that the code for the `Customer` class is placed in a file named `CUSTOMER.H` within a directory named `CLASSES` on the C drive. Once this is done, including the `Customer` class definition within a program requires the single line preprocessor directive `#include <C:\CLASSES\CUSTOMER.H>`.

Program Logic. Having analyzed and defined the two classes that we will be using, we still need to analyze and define the logic to correctly control the interaction between these two objects for a valid simulation.

In this particular case the only interaction between a `Customer` object and the single `Pump` object is that a customer's arrival, followed by a request, determines when the pump is activated and how much gas it delivers. Thus, each interaction between a `Customer` and the `Pump` can be expressed by the pseudocode

Obtain a customer arrival time
Obtain a customer request for gas
Activate the pump with the request

Although this repetition of events takes place continuously over the course of a day, we are only interested in a one-half hour period. Therefore, we must place these three events in a loop that is executed until the required simulation time has elapsed.

Step 2   Develop a Solution

We have already developed and coded the two required classes, `Pump` and `Customer`, for the simulation. What remains to be developed is the control logic within the `main()` function for correctly activating class events. From the analysis we know that a loop controlled by the total arrival time for all customers is required. A suitable control structure for `main()` is described by the algorithm

Create a pump object with the required initial gallons of gas display the values in the initialized pump
Set the total time to 0
Obtain a customer arrival time // first arrival
Add the arrival time to the total time
While the total time does not exceed the simulation time
    Display the total time
    Obtain a customer request for gas
    Activate the pump with the request
    Obtain a customer arrival time // next arrival
    Add the arrival time to the total time
Endwhile
Display a message that the simulation is over

Step 3   Code the Solution

The C++ code corresponding to our design is illustrated in Program 9.12.

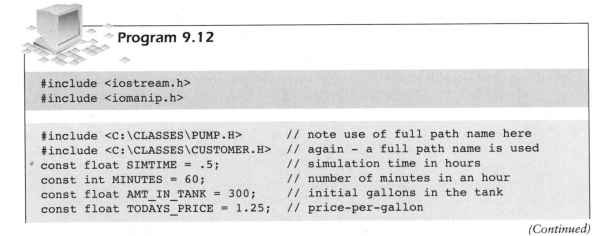

Program 9.12

```
#include <iostream.h>
#include <iomanip.h>


#include <C:\CLASSES\PUMP.H>         // note use of full path name here
#include <C:\CLASSES\CUSTOMER.H>     // again - a full path name is used
const float SIMTIME = .5;            // simulation time in hours
const int MINUTES = 60;              // number of minutes in an hour
const float AMT_IN_TANK = 300;       // initial gallons in the tank
const float TODAYS_PRICE = 1.25;     // price-per-gallon
```

(Continued)

(Continued)

```
int main()
{
  Pump a(AMT_IN_TANK, TODAYS_PRICE);    // declare 1 object of type Pump
  Customer b;                           // declare 1 object of type Customer
  int totalTime = 0;
  int idleTime;
  int amtRequest;
  int SimMinutes;  // simulation time in minutes

  SimMinutes = SIMTIME * MINUTES;
  cout << "\nStarting a new simulation - simulation time is "
       << SimMinutes << " minutes" << endl;
  a.values();

  // get the first arrival
  idleTime = b.arrive();
  totalTime += idleTime;

  while (totalTime <= SimMinutes)
  {
    cout << "\nThe idle time is " << idleTime << " minutes" << endl
         << "    and we are " << totalTime
         << " minutes into the simulation." << endl;
    amtRequest = b.gallons();
    a.request(float(amtRequest));

    // get the next arrival
    idleTime = b.arrive();
    totalTime += idleTime;
  }
  cout << "\nThe idle time is " << idleTime << " minutes." << endl
       << "As the total time now exceeds the simulation time, " << endl
       << "    this simulation run is over." << endl;

  return 0;
}
```

Step 4   Test and Correct the Program

Assuming that the `Pump` and `Customer` classes have been thoroughly tested and debugged, testing and debugging Program 9.12 is really restricted to testing and debugging the `main()` function. This specificity of testing is precisely one of the advantages of using an object-oriented approach.

Program and Class Libraries

The concept of a program library began with FORTRAN, which was the first commercial high-level language introduced in 1954. The FORTRAN library consisted of a group of completely tested and debugged mathematical routines that were provided with the compiler. Since that time every programming language has provided its own library of functions. In both C and C++, this library is referred to as the standard program library and includes more than 100 functions declared in fifteen different header files. Examples of standard library functions include `sqrt()`, `pow()`, `abs()`, `rand()`, `srand()`, and `time()`. The advantage of library functions is that they significantly enhance program development and design by providing code that is known to work correctly without the need for additional testing and debugging.

   With the introduction of object-oriented languages the concept of a program library has been extended to include `class` libraries. A *class library* is a library of tested and debugged `classes` that includes both interfaces and implementations. Generally, the interface portion is placed in a header file and the implementation in a separate implementation file.

   One of the key practical features of `class` libraries is that they help realize the goal of code reuse in a significant way. By providing tested and debugged code consisting of both data and function members, `class` libraries furnish large sections of prewritten and reusable code ready for incorporation within new applications. This shifts the focus of writing application programs from the creation of new code to understanding how to use predefined objects and stitch them together in a cohesive and useful way. A prime example of this is the visual object `classes` consisting of check boxes, list boxes, dialogs, command buttons, and option buttons provided in both Visual C++ and Visual Basic.

Typically, all prewritten and tested classes are included in a **class library,** just as library functions are included in a function library. By using previously written and tested `class` definitions in a program we can focus our attention on the remaining code that controls the flow of events between objects. In this case then, assuming that the `Pump` and `Customer classes` correctly meet their respective specifications, testing and debugging Program 9.12 centers on the `main()` function.

   By itself, the `main()` function in Program 9.12 is a straightforward `while` loop where the `Pump` idle time corresponds to the time between customer arrivals. The output of a sample run, shown below, verifies that the loop is operating correctly.

```
Starting a new simulation - simulation time is 30 minutes

The gas tank has 300 gallons of gas.
The price per gallon of gas is $1.25

The idle time is 12 minutes
    and we are 12 minutes into the simulation.

15.00 gallons were requested
15.00 gallons were pumped
```

```
          285.00 gallons remain in the tank
          The total price is $18.75

          The idle time is 15 minutes
              and we are 27 minutes into the simulation.

          7.00 gallons were requested
          7.00 gallons were pumped
          278.00 gallons remain in the tank
          The total price is $8.75

          The idle time is 10 minutes.
          As the total time now exceeds the simulation time,
              this simulation run is over.
```

Exercises 9.5

1. Enter Program 9.12 on your computer and execute it.

2. **a.** Remove the `inline` functions in the `Customer` class declaration and implementation section by constructing individual declaration and implementation sections. Discuss which form of the `Customer` class you prefer and why.

   b. Rewrite the `gallons()` function in the `Customer class` so that it returns a floating-point number between 3.0 and 20.0 gallons.

3. In place of the `main()` function used in Program 9.12, a student proposed the following:

```cpp
int main()
{
  Pump a(AMT_IN_TANK, TODAYS_PRICE);   // declare 1 object of type Pump
  Customer b;                          // declare 1 object of type Customer
  int totalTime = 0;
  int idleTime;
  int amtRequest;
  int SimMinutes;  // simulation time in minutes

  SimMinutes = SIMTIME * MINUTES;
  cout << "\nStarting a new simulation - simulation time is "
       << SimMinutes << " minutes" << endl;
  a.values();

  do
  {
    idleTime = b.arrive();
    totalTime += idleTime;
    if (totalTime > (SIMTIME * MINUTES))
    {
```

```
        cout << "\nThe idle time is " << idleTime << " minutes." << endl
                << "As the total time now exceeds the simulation time, " << endl
                << "   this simulation run is over." << endl;
        break;
      }
      else
      {
        cout << "\nThe idle time is " << idleTime << " minutes" << endl
            << "    and we are " << totalTime
            << " minutes into the simulation." << endl;
        amtRequest = b.gallons();
        a.request(float(amtRequest));
      }
  } while (1);   // always true

  return 0;
}
```

Determine if this `main()` function produces a valid simulation. If it does not, discuss why not. If it does, discuss which version you prefer and why.

4. Using the `Elevator` class defined in Section 8.4 and defining a new class named `Person`, construct a simulation whereby a person randomly arrives at any time from 1 to 10 minutes on any floor and calls the elevator. If the elevator is not on the floor that the person is, it must move to the floor that the person is on. Once inside the elevator the person can select any floor. Run the simulation for three randomly arriving people and have the simulation display the movement of the elevator.

9.6 CLASS INHERITANCE

The ability to create new classes from existing ones is the underlying motivation and power behind class- and object-oriented programming techniques. Doing so facilitates reusing existing code in new ways without the need for retesting and validation. It permits the designers of a class to make it available to others for additions and extensions, without relinquishing control over the existing class features.

Constructing one class from another is accomplished using a capability called inheritance. Related to this capability is an equally important feature named polymorphism. Polymorphism provides the ability to redefine how member functions of related classes operate based on the class object being referenced. In fact, for a programming language to be classified as an object-oriented language it must provide the features of classes, inheritance, and polymorphism. In this section we describe the inheritance and polymorphism features provided in C++.

Inheritance is the capability of deriving one class from another class. The initial class used as the basis for the derived class is referred to as either the **base**, **parent**, or **superclass**. The derived class is referred to as either the **derived**, **child**, or **subclass**.

Point of Information

Object-Based versus Object-Oriented Languages

An *object-based* language is one in which data and operations can be incorporated together in such a way that data values can be isolated and accessed through the specified `class` functions. The ability to bind the data members with operations in a single unit is referred to as *encapsulation*. In C++ encapsulation is provided by its class capability.

For a language to be classified as *object-oriented* it must also provide inheritance and polymorphism. *Inheritance* is the capability to derive one `class` from another. A derived class is a completely new data type that incorporates all of the data members and member functions of the original class with any new data and function members unique to itself. The class used as the basis for the derived type is referred to as the *base* or *parent* class and the derived data type is referred to as the *derived* or *child* class.

Polymorphism permits the same method name to invoke one operation in objects of a parent class and a different operation in objects of a derived class.

C++, which provides encapsulation, inheritance, and polymorphism, is a true object-oriented language. Because C, which is C++'s predecessor, does not provide these features, it is neither an object-based nor object-oriented language.

A derived class is a completely new class that incorporates all of the data and member functions of its base class. It can, and usually does, however, add its own additional new data and function members and can override any base class function.

As an example of inheritance, consider three geometric shapes consisting of a circle, a cylinder, and a sphere. All of these shapes share a common characteristic, a radius. Thus, for these shapes we can make the circle a base type for the other two shapes, as illustrated in Figure 9.5. By convention, arrows always point from the derived class to the base class. Reformulating these shapes as class types we would make the circle the base class and derive the cylinder and sphere classes from it.

The relationships illustrated in Figure 9.5 are examples of simple inheritance. In **simple inheritance** each derived type has only one immediate base type. The complement to simple inheritance is multiple inheritance. In **multiple inheritance** a derived type has two or more base types. Figure 9.6 illustrates an example of multiple inheritance. In this text we will only consider simple inheritance.

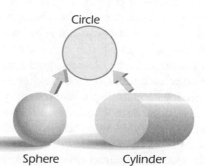

Figure 9.5 Relating object types.

Figure 9.6 *An example of multiple inheritance.*

The `class` derivations illustrated in both Figures 9.5 and 9.6 are formally referred to as **class hierarchies**, because they illustrate the hierarchy, or order, in which one class is derived from another. Let's now see how to derive one class from another.

A derived class has the same form as any other class in that it consists of both a declaration and an implementation. The only difference is in the first line of the declaration section. For a derived class this line is extended to include an access specification and a base class name and has the form:

class derived-class-name : class-access base-class-name

For example, if `Circle` is the name of an existing class, a new class named `Cylinder` can be derived as follows:

```
class Cylinder : public Circle
{
    // add any additional data and
    // function members in here
};  // end of Cylinder class declaration
```

Except for the class-access specifier after the colon and the base class name, there is nothing inherently new or complicated about the construction of the `Cylinder` class. Before providing a description of the `Circle` class and adding data and function members to the derived `Cylinder` class, we will need to reexamine access specifiers and how they relate to derived `class`es.

Access Specifications

Until now we have only used private and public access specifiers within a class. Giving all data members `private` status ensured that they could only be accessed by either class member functions or friends. This restricted access prevents access by any nonclass functions (except friends), *which also precludes access by any derived class functions*. This is a sensible restriction because if it did not exist anyone could "jump around" the `private` restriction by simply deriving a class.

To retain a restricted type of access across derived classes, C++ provides a third access specification—`protected`. A `protected` access behaves identically to `private` access in that it only permits member or friend function access, but it permits this restriction to be inherited by any derived class. The derived class then defines the type of inheritance it is willing to take on, subject to the base class' access restrictions. This is done by the class-access specifier, which is listed after the colon at the start of its declaration section. Table 9.3 lists the resulting derived class member access based on the base class member specifications and the derived class-access specifier.

Table 9.3 Inherited Access Restrictions

Base class Member	Derived class Access	Derived class Member
private ——————▶	: private ——————▶	inaccessible
protected ——————▶	: private ——————▶	private
public ——————▶	: private ——————▶	private
private ——————▶	: public ——————▶	inaccessible
protected ——————▶	: public ——————▶	protected
public ——————▶	: public ——————▶	public
private ——————▶	: protected ——————▶	inaccessible
protected ——————▶	: protected ——————▶	protected
public ——————▶	: protected ——————▶	protected

Using Table 9.3 it can be seen (shaded region), that if the base class member has a `protected` access and the derived class specifier is `public`, then the derived class member will be `protected` to its class. Similarly, if the base class has a `public` access and the derived class specifier is `public`, the derived class member will be `public`. As this is the most commonly used type of specification for base class data and function members respectively, it is the one we will use. This means that for all classes intended for use as a base class we will use a `protected` data member access in place of a `private` designation.

An Example

To illustrate the process of deriving one class from another we will derive a `Cylinder` class from a base `Circle` class. The definition of the `Circle` class is:

```
// class declaration

class Circle
{
  protected:
    double radius;
  public:
    Circle(double = 1.0);  // constructor
    double calcval();
};

// class implementation

// constructor
Circle::Circle(double r)  // constructor
{
  radius = r;
}
```

```
// calculate the area of a circle
double Circle::calcval(void)
{
   return(PI * radius * radius);
}
```

Except for the substitution of the access specifier `protected` in place of the usual `private` specifier for the data member, this is a standard class definition. The only variable not defined is `pi`, which is used in the `calcval()` function. We will define this as

```
const double PI = 2.0 * asin(1.0);
```

This is simply a "trick" that forces the computer to return the value of `PI` accurate to as many decimal places as allowed by your computer. This value is obtained by taking the arcsin of 1.0, which is $\pi/2$, and multiplying the result by 2.

Having defined our base class, we can now extend it to a derived class. The definition of the derived class is

```
// class declaration where
// Cylinder is derived from Circle

class Cylinder : public Circle
{
  protected:
    double length;  // add one additional data member and
  public:           // two additional function members
    Cylinder(double r = 1.0, double l = 1.0) : Circle(r), length(l) {}
    double calcval();
};

// class implementation

double Cylinder::calcval(void)   // this calculates a volume
{
  return (length * Circle::calcval()); // note the base function call
}
```

This definition encompasses several important concepts relating to derived classes. First, as a derived class, `Cylinder` contains all of the data and function members of its base class, `Circle`, plus any additional members that it may add. In this particular case the `Cylinder` class consists of a `radius` data member, inherited from the `Circle` class, plus an additional `length` member. Thus, each `Cylinder` object contains *two* data members, as is illustrated in Figure 9.7.

Figure 9.7 Relationship between `circle` and `cylinder` data members.

In addition to having two data members the `Cylinder` class also inherits `Circle`'s function members. This is illustrated in the `Cylinder` constructor, which uses a base member initialization list (see Section 9.1) that specifically calls the `Circle` constructor. It is also illustrated in `Cylinder`'s `calcval()` function, which makes a call to `Circle::calcval()`.

In both classes the same function name, `calcval()`, has been specifically used to illustrate the overriding of a base function by a derived function. When a `Cylinder` object calls `calcval()` it is a request to use the `Cylinder` version of the function, while a `Circle` object call to `calcval()` is a request to use the `Circle` version. In this case the `Cylinder` class can only access the class version of `calcval()` using the scope resolution operator, as is done in the call `Circle::calcval()`. Program 9.13 uses these two classes within the context of a complete program. The output produced by Program 9.13 is:

```
The area of circle_1 is 3.141593
The area of circle_2 is 12.566371
The volume of cylinder_1 is 113.097336

The area of circle_1 is now 28.274334
```

Program 9.13

```cpp
#include <iostream.h>
#include <math.h>

const double PI = 2.0 * asin(1.0);

// class declaration

class Circle
{
  protected:
    double radius;
  public:
    Circle(double = 1.0);  // constructor
    double calcval();
};
// implementation section for Circle

// constructor
Circle::Circle(double r)
{
  radius = r;
}
```

(Continued)

(Continued)

```
// calculate the area of a circle
double Circle::calcval(void)
{
  return(PI * radius * radius);
}

// class declaration for the derived class
// Cylinder which is derived from Circle
class Cylinder : public Circle
{
  protected:
    double length;   // add one additional data member and
  public:            // two additional function members
    Cylinder(double r = 1.0, double l = 1.0) : Circle(r), length(l) {}
    double calcval();
};

// implementation section for Cylinder

double Cylinder::calcval(void)    // this calculates a volume
{
  return (length * Circle::calcval()); // note the base function call
}
```

```
int main()
{
  Circle circle_1, circle_2(2);  // create two Circle objects
  Cylinder cylinder_1(3,4);      // create one Cylinder object

  cout << "The area of circle_1 is " << circle_1.calcval() << endl;
  cout << "The area of circle_2 is " << circle_2.calcval() << endl;
  cout << "The volume of cylinder_1 is " << cylinder_1.calcval() << endl;

  circle_1 = cylinder_1;  // assign a cylinder to a Circle

  cout << "\nThe area of circle_1 is now " << circle_1.calcval() << endl;

  return 0;
}
```

The first three output lines are all straightforward and are produced by the first three cout statements in the program. As the output shows, a call to calcval() using a Circle object activates the Circle version of this function, while a call to calcval() using a Cylinder object activates the Cylinder version.

The assignment statement circle_1 = cylinder_1; introduces another important relationship between a base and derived class: *A derived class object can be assigned to a base class object.* This should not be surprising because both base and derived classes share a common set of data member types. In this type of assignment it is only this set of data members, which consist of all the base class data members, that are assigned. Thus, as illustrated in Figure 9.8, our `Cylinder` to `Circle` assignment results in the following memberwise assignment:

```
circle_1.radius = cylinder_1.radius;
```

The length member of the `Cylinder` object is not used in the assignment because it has no equivalent variable in the `Circle` class. The reverse cast, from base to derived class, is not as simple and requires a constructor to correctly initialize the additional derived class members not in the base class.

Figure 9.8 Assignment from derived to base `class`.

Before leaving Program 9.13 one additional point should be made. Although the `Circle` constructor was explicitly called using a base/member initialization list for the `Cylinder` constructor, an implicit call could also have been made. In the absence of an explicit derived class constructor the compiler will automatically call the default base class constructor first, before the derived class constructor is called. This works because the derived class contains all of the base class data members. In a similar fashion the destructor functions are called in the reverse order—first derived class and then base class.

Exercises 9.6

1. Define the following terms:

   a. inheritance   **d.** simple inheritance

   b. base class   **e.** multiple inheritance

   c. derived class   **f.** class hierarchy

2. Describe the difference between a `private` and a `protected` class member.

3. What three features must a programming language provide for it to be classified as an object-oriented language?

4. **a.** Modify Program 9.13 to include a derived class named `Sphere` from the base `Circle` class. The only additional class members of `Sphere` should be a constructor and a `calcval()` function that returns the volume of the sphere. (NOTE: *volume* = 4/3 $\pi radius^3$)

   b. Include the class constructed for Exercise 4a in a working C++ program. Have your program call all of the member functions in the `Sphere` class.

5. a. Create a base class named `Point`, that consists of an x and y coordinate. From this class derive a class named `Circle` having an additional data member named `radius`. For this derived class the x and y data members represent the center coordinates of a circle. The function members of the first class should consist of a constructor, an area function named area that returns zero, and a distance function that returns the distance between two points, where

$$\text{distance} = \sqrt{(x_2 - x_1)^2 + (y_2 - y_1)^2}$$

Additionally, the derived class should have a constructor and an override function named `area` that returns the area of a circle.

b. Include the classes constructed for Exercise 5a in a working C++ program. Have your program call all of the member functions in each class. In addition call the base class `distance` function with two `Circle` objects and explain the result returned by the function.

6. a. Using the classes constructed for Exercise 5a, derive a class named `Cylinder` from the derived `Circle` class. The `Cylinder` class should have a constructor and a member function named `area` that determines the surface area of the cylinder. For this function use the algorithm *surface area = 2 π r (l + r)*, where *r* is the radius of the cylinder and *l* is the length.

b. Include the classes constructed for Exercise 6a in a working C++ program. Have your program call all of the member functions in the `Cylinder` class.

c. What do you think might be the result if the base class `distance()` function was called with two `Cylinder` objects?

7. a. Create a base class named `Rectangle`, that contains length and width data members. From this class derive a class named `Box` having an additional data member named `depth`. The function members of the base `Rectangle` class should consist of a constructor and an area function. The derived `Box` class should have a constructor, a volume function, and an override function named `area` that returns the surface area of the box.

b. Include the classes constructed for Exercise 7a in a working C++ program. Have your program call all of the member functions in each class and explain the result when the `distance()` function is called using two `Circle` objects.

9.7 > POLYMORPHISM

The overriding of a base member function using an overloaded derived member function, as was illustrated by the `calcval()` function in Program 9.13, is an example of polymorphism. **Polymorphism** permits the same function name to invoke one response in objects of a base class and another response in objects of a derived class. In some cases, however, this method of overriding does not work as one might desire. To understand why this is so, consider Program 9.14.

Program 9.14

```
#include <iostream.h>
#include <math.h>


// class declaration for the base class

class One
{
  protected:
    float a;
  public:
    One(float = 2.0);    // constructor
    float f1(float);    // a member function
    float f2(float);    // another member function
};

// class implementation for One

One::One(float val)    // constructor
{
  a = val;
}

float One::f1(float num)  // a member function
{
  return(num/2);
}
float One::f2(float num)  // another member function
{
  return( pow(f1(num),2) );  // square the result of f1()
}

// class declaration for the derived class

class Two : public One
{
  public:
    float f1(float);    // this overrides class One's f1()
};

// class implementation for Two

float Two::f1(float num)
{
  return(num/3);
}
```

(Continued)

(Continued)

```
int main()
{
  One object_1;  // object_1 is an object of the base class
  Two object_2;  // object_2 is an object of the derived class

    // call f2() using a base class object call
  cout << "The computed value using a base class object call is "
      << object_1.f2(12) << endl;

    // call f2() using a derived class object call
  cout << "The computed value using a derived class object call is "
      << object_2.f2(12) << endl;

  return 0;
}
```

The output produced by this program is

```
The computed value using a base class object call is 36
The computed value using a derived class object call is 36
```

As this output shows, the same result is obtained no matter which object type calls the f2() function. This result is produced because the derived class does not have an override to the base class f2() function. Thus, both calls to f2() result in the base class f2() function being called.

Once invoked, the base class f2() function will always call the base class version of f1() rather than the derived class override version. This behavior is due to a process referred to as **function binding**. In normal function calls static binding is used. In **static binding** the determination of which function is called is made at compile time. Thus, when the compiler first encounters the f1() function in the base class it makes the determination that whenever f2() is called, either from a base or derived class object, it will subsequently call the base class f1() function.

In place of static binding we would like a binding method that is capable of determining which function should be invoked at run time, based on the object type making the call. This type of binding is referred to as **dynamic binding**. To achieve dynamic binding C++ provides virtual functions.

A **virtual function** specification tells the compiler to create a pointer to a function, but not fill in the value of the pointer until the function is actually called. Then, at run time, *and based on the object making the call*, the appropriate function address is used. Creating a **virtual** function is extremely easy—all that is required is that the keyword virtual be placed before the function's return type in the declaration section. For example, consider Program 9.15, which is identical to Program 9.14 except for the virtual declaration of the f1() function.

Program 9.15

```cpp
#include <iostream.h>
#include <math.h>


// class declaration for the base class

class One
{
  protected:
    float a;

  public:
    One(float = 2.0);   // constructor
    virtual float f1(float);   // a member function
    float f2(float);   // another member function
};

// class implementation for One

One::One(float val)   // constructor
{
  a = val;
}

float One::f1(float num)  // a member function
{
  return(num/2);
}

float One::f2(float num)  // another member function
{
  return( pow(f1(num),2) );  // square the result of f1()
}

// class declaration for the derived class

class Two : public One
{
  public:
    virtual float f1(float);     // this overrides class One's f1()
};

// class implementation for Two
```

(Continued)

(Continued)

```
float Two::f1(float num)
{
  return(num/3);
}
```

```
int main()
{
  One object_1;  // object_1 is an object of the base class
  Two object_2;  // object_2 is an object of the derived class

    // call f2() using a base class object call
  cout << "The computed value using a base class object call is "
     << object_1.f2(12) << endl;

   // call f2() using a derived class object call
  cout << "The computed value using a derived class object call is "
     << object_2.f2(12) << endl;

  return 0;
}
```

The output produced by Program 9.15 is

```
The computed value using a base class object call is 36
The computed value using a derived class object call is 16
```

As illustrated by this output the `f2()` function now calls different versions of the over-loaded `f1()` function based on the object type making the call. This selection, based on the object making the call, is the classic definition of polymorphic function behavior and is caused by the dynamic binding imposed on `f1()` by virtue of its being a virtual function.

Once a function is declared as virtual *it remains virtual for the next derived class with or without a virtual declaration in the derived class.* Thus, the second virtual declaration in the derived class is not strictly needed, but should be included both for clarity and to ensure that any subsequently derived classes correctly inherit the function. To understand why, consider the inheritance diagram illustrated in Figure 9.9, where class C is derived from class B and class B is derived from class A.[9] In this situation, if function `f1()` is virtual in class A, but is not declared in class B, it will not be virtual in class C. The only other requirement is that once a function has been declared as virtual the return type and parameter list of all subsequent derived class override versions *must be* the same.

---

[9]By convention, as previously noted in Section 9.6, arrows always point from the derived class to the base class.

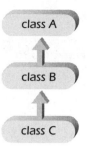

Figure 9.9 *An inheritance diagram.*

Exercises 9.7

1. Enter and execute both Program 9.14 and 9.15 on your computer so that you understand the relationship between function calls in each program.

2. Describe the two methods C++ provides for implementing polymorphism.

3. Describe the difference between static binding and dynamic binding.

4. Describe the difference between a virtual function and a nonvirtual function.

5. Describe what polymorphism is and provide an example of polymorphic behavior.

6. Discuss, with reasons, whether the multiplication operator provided for both the integer and float built-in types is an example of overloading or polymorphism.

9.8 COMMON PROGRAMMING ERRORS

1. Using a user defined assignment operator in a multiple assignment expression when the operator has not been defined to return an object.

2. Using the keyword `static` when defining either a static data or function member. Here, the `static` keyword should be used only within the class declaration section.

3. Using the keyword `friend` when defining a friend function. The `friend` keyword should be used only within the class declaration section.

4. Failing to instantiate static data members before creating class objects that must access these data members.

5. Attempting to redefine an operator's meaning as it applies to C++'s built-in data types.

6. Redefining an overloaded operator to perform a function not indicated by its conventional meaning. Although this will work, it is an example of extremely bad programming practice.

7. Attempting to make a conversion operator function a friend, rather than a member function.

8. Attempting to specify a return type for a member conversion operator function.

9. Attempting to override a virtual function without using the same type and number of arguments as the original function.

10. Using the keyword `virtual` in the class implementation section. Functions are only declared as `virtual` in the class declaration section.

9.9   CHAPTER SUMMARY

1. An assignment operator may be declared for a `class` with the function prototype

   void operator=(class-name&);

   Here, the argument is a reference to the class name. The return type of void precludes using this operator in multiple assignment expressions such as a = b = c.

2. A type of initialization that closely resembles assignment occurs in C++ when one object is initialized using another object of the same class. The constructor that performs this type of initialization is called a *copy constructor* and has the function prototype

   class-name(const class-name&);

   This is frequently represented using the notation *X(X&)*.

3. Each class has an associated class scope, which is defined by the brace pair, { }, containing the class declaration. Data and function members are local to the scope of their class and can only be used by objects declared for the class. If a global variable name is reused within a class, the global variable is hidden by the class variable. Within the scope of the class variable the global variable may be accessed using the scope resolution operator, ::.

4. For each class object a separate set of memory locations is reserved for all data members, except those declared as `static`. A static data member is a shared by all class objects and provides a means of communication between objects. Static data members must be declared as such within the class declaration section and are defined outside of the declaration section.

5. `static` function members apply to the class as a whole, rather than individual objects. As such, a `static` function member can access only `static` data members and other `static` function members. Any `static` function members must be declared as such within the class declaration section and are defined outside of the declaration section.

6. A nonmember function may access a class' `private` data members if it is granted friend status by the class. This is accomplished by declaring the function as a friend within the class' declaration section. Thus, it is always the class that determines which nonmember functions are friends; a function can never confer friend status on itself.

7. User-defined operators can be constructed for classes using member operator functions. An operator function has the form *operator<symbol>*, where <symbol> is one of the following:

```
() [] -> new delete ++ -- ! ~ * / % + -
<< >> < <= > >= ++ != && || & ^ | = +=
-= *= /= %= &= ^= |= <<= >>= ,
```

For example, the function prototype `Date operator+(int);` declares that the addition operator will be defined to accept an integer and return a `Date` object.

8. User-defined operators may be called in either of two ways—as a conventional function with arguments or as an operator expression. For example, for an operator having the header line

```
Date Date::operator+(int)
```

if `dte` is an object of type `Date`, the following two calls produce the same effect:

```
dte.operator+(284)
dte + 284
```

9. Operator functions may also be written as friend functions. The equivalent friend version of a member operator function will always contain an additional class reference that is not required by the member function.

10. There are four categories of data type conversions. They are conversions from

- Built-in types to built-in types
- Built-in types to user-defined (class) types
- User-defined (class) types to built-in types
- User-defined (class) types to user-defined (class) types

Built-in to built-in type conversions are done using C++'s implicit conversion rules or explicitly using casts. Built-in to user-defined type conversions are done using type conversion constructors. Conversions from user-defined types to either built-in or other user-defined types are done using conversion operator functions.

11. A **type conversion constructor** is a constructor whose first argument is not a member of its class and whose remaining arguments, if any, have default values.

12. A **conversion operator function** is a member operator function having the name of a built-in data type or class. It has no explicit arguments or return type; rather, the return type is the name of the function.

13. Inheritance is the capability of deriving one class from another class. The initial class used as the basis for the derived class is referred to as the base, parent, or superclass. The derived class is referred to as either the derived, child, or subclass.

14. Base member functions can be overridden by derived member functions with the same name. The override function is simply an overloaded version of the base member function defined in the derived class.

15. Polymorphism is the capability of having the same function name invoke different responses based on the object making the function call. It can be accomplished using either override functions or virtual functions.

16. In **static binding** the determination of which function actually is invoked is made at compile time. In **dynamic binding** the determination is made at run time.

17. A **virtual function** specification designates that dynamic binding should take place. The specification is made in the function's prototype by placing the keyword `virtual` before the function's return type. Once a function has been declared as `virtual` it remains so for all derived classes as long as there is a continuous trail of function declarations through the derived chain of classes.

Part Three
Data Structures

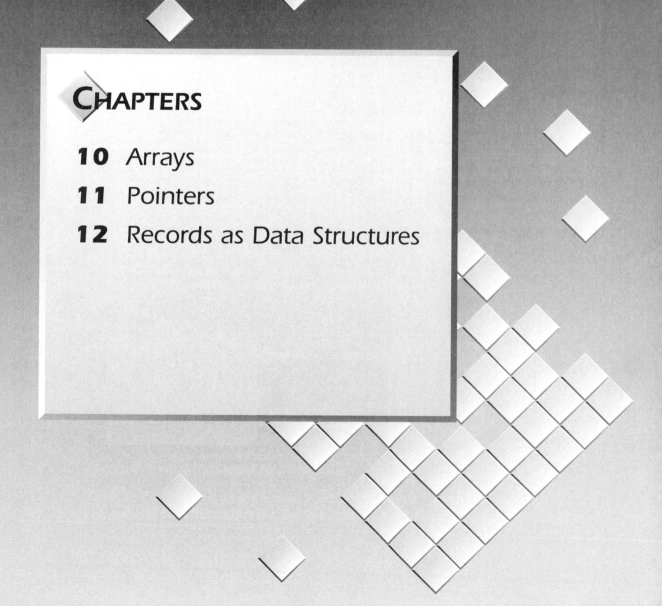

CHAPTERS

10 Arrays

11 Pointers

12 Records as Data Structures

CHAPTER 10

Arrays

TOPICS

10.1 ONE-DIMENSIONAL ARRAYS
INPUT AND OUTPUT OF ARRAY VALUES

10.2 ARRAY INITIALIZATION

10.3 DECLARING AND PROCESSING TWO-DIMENSIONAL ARRAYS
LARGER DIMENSIONAL ARRAYS

10.4 APPLICATIONS
APPLICATION 1: STATISTICAL ANALYSIS   APPLICATION 2: CURVE PLOTTING

10.5 ARRAYS AS ARGUMENTS

10.6 COMMON PROGRAMMING ERRORS

10.7 CHAPTER SUMMARY

10.8 CHAPTER APPENDIX: SEARCHING AND SORTING
SEARCH ALGORITHMS   SORT ALGORITHMS
BIG O NOTATION

The variables that we have used so far have all had a common characteristic: each variable could only be used to store a single value at a time. For example, although the variables key, count, and grade declared in the statements

```
char key;
int count;
float grade;
```

are of different data types, each variable can only store one value of the declared data type. These types of variables are called atomic variables. An **atomic variable**, which is also referred to as a **scalar variable**, is a variable whose value cannot be further subdivided or separated into a legitimate data type.

Frequently we may have a set of values, all of the same data type, that form a logical group. For example, Figure 10.1 illustrates three groups of items. The first group is a list of five floating-point temperatures, the second group is a list of four character codes, and the last group is a list of six integer voltages.

Temperatures	Codes	Voltages
95.75	Z	98
83.0	C	87
97.625	K	92
72.5	L	79
86.25		85
		72

Figure 10.1 Three lists of items.

A simple list containing individual items of the same data type is called a one-dimensional array. In this chapter we describe how one-dimensional arrays are declared, initialized, stored inside a computer, and used. Additionally, we explore the use of one-dimensional arrays with example programs and present the procedures for declaring and using multidimensional arrays.

10.1 ONE-DIMENSIONAL ARRAYS

A **one-dimensional array**, which is also referred to as either a **single-dimensional array** or a vector, is a list of related values with the same data type that is stored using a single group name.[1] In C++, as in other computer languages, the group name is referred to as the array name. For example, consider the list of temperatures illustrated in Figure 10.2.

Temperatures
95.75
83.0
97.625
72.5
86.25

Figure 10.2 A list of temperatures.

---

[1]Note that lists can be implemented in a variety of ways. An array is simply one implementation of a list in which all of the list elements are of the same type and each element is stored consecutively in a set of contiguous memory locations.

All the temperatures in the list are floating-point numbers and must be declared as such. However, the individual items in the list do not have to be declared separately. The items in the list can be declared as a single unit and stored under a common variable name called the array name. For convenience, we will choose temp as the name for the list shown in Figure 10.2. To specify that temp is to store five individual floating-point values requires the declaration statement `float temp[5]`. Notice that this declaration statement gives the array (or list) name, the data type of the items in the array, and the number of items in the array. It is a specific example of the general array declaration statement having the syntax:

data-type array-name[number-of-items]

Good programming practice requires defining the number-of-items in the array as a constant before declaring the array. Thus, the previous array declaration for temp would, in practice, be declared using two statements, such as:

```
const int NUMELS = 5; // define a constant for the number of items
float temp[NUMELS];    // declare the array
```

Further examples of array declarations using this two-line syntax are:

```
        const int NUMELS = 6;
        int volts[NUMELS];

        const int ARRAYSIZE = 4;
        char code[ARRAYSIZE];

        const int SIZE = 100;
        float amount[SIZE];
```

In these declaration statements, each array is allocated sufficient memory to hold the number of data items given in the declaration statement. Thus, the array named volts has storage reserved for six integers, the array named code has storage reserved for four characters, and the array named amount has storage reserved for 100 floating-point numbers. The constant identifiers, NUMELS, ARRAYSIZE, and SIZE are programmer selected names.

Figure 10.3 illustrates the storage reserved for the volts and code arrays.

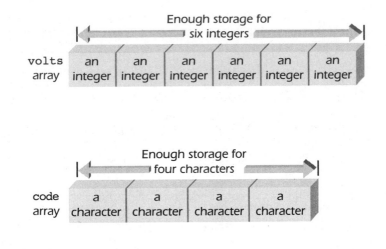

Figure 10.3 The `volts` and `code` arrays in memory.

Each item in an array is called an *element* or *component* of the array. The individual elements stored in the arrays illustrated in Figure 10.3 are stored sequentially, with the first array element stored in the first reserved location, the second element stored in the second reserved location, and so on until the last element is stored in the last reserved location. This contiguous storage allocation for the list is a key feature of arrays because it provides a simple mechanism for easily locating any single element in the list.

Since elements in the array are stored sequentially, any individual element can be accessed by giving the name of the array and the element's position. This position is called the element's **index** or **subscript** value (the two terms are synonymous). For a single-dimensional array, the first element has an index of 0, the second element has an index of 1, and so on. In C++, the array name and index of the desired element are combined by listing the index in braces after the array name. For example, given the declaration `float temp[5]`,

`temp[0]` refers to the first temperature stored in the `temp` array

`temp[1]` refers to the second temperature stored in the `temp` array

`temp[2]` refers to the third temperature stored in the `temp` array

`temp[3]` refers to the fourth temperature stored in the `temp` array

`temp[4]` refers to the fifth temperature stored in the `temp` array

Figure 10.4 illustrates the `temp` array in memory with the correct designation for each array element. Each individual element is referred to as an **indexed variable** or a **subscripted variable**, since both a variable name and an index or subscript value must be used to reference the element. Remember that the index or subscript value gives *the position* of the element in the array.

Figure 10.4 *Identifying individual array elements.*

The subscripted variable, `temp[0]`, is read as "temp sub zero." This is a shortened way of saying "the temp array subscripted by zero" and distinguishes the first element in an array from an atomic variable that could be declared as `temp0`. Similarly, `temp[1]` is read as "`temp` sub one", `temp[2]` as "`temp` sub two," and so on.

Although it may seem unusual to reference the first element with an index of zero, doing so increases the computer's speed when it accesses array elements. Internally, unseen by the programmer, the computer uses the index as an offset from the array's starting position. As illustrated in Figure 10.5, the index tells the computer how many elements to skip, starting from the beginning of the array, to get to the desired element.

Figure 10.5 *Accessing an individual array element—element 3.*

Subscripted variables can be used anywhere that scalar variables are valid. Examples using the elements of the temp array are:

```
temp[0] = 95.75;
temp[1] = temp[0] - 11.0;
temp[2] = 5.0 * temp[0];
temp[3] = 79.0;
temp[4] = (temp[1] + temp[2] - 3.1) / 2.2;
sum = temp[0] + temp[1] + temp[2] + temp[3] + temp[4];
```

The subscript contained within brackets need not be an integer constant; any expression that evaluates to an integer may be used as a subscript.[2] In each case, of course, the value of the expression must be within the valid subscript range defined when the array is declared. For example, assuming that i and j are int variables, the following subscripted variables are valid:

```
temp[i]
temp[2*i]
temp[j-i]
```

One extremely important advantage of using integer expressions as subscripts is that it allows sequencing through an array by using a loop. This makes statements like

```
sum = temp[0] + temp[1] + temp[2] + temp[3] + temp[4];
```

unnecessary. The subscript values in this statement can be replaced by a for loop counter to access each element in the array sequentially. For example, the code

```
sum = 0;                    // initialize the sum to zero
for (i = 0; i < 5; i++)
  sum = sum + temp[i];   // add in a temperature
```

sequentially retrieves each array element and adds the element to sum. Here the variable i is used both as the counter in the for loop and as a subscript. As i increases by one each time through the loop, the next element in the array is referenced. The procedure for adding the array elements within the for loop is similar to the accumulation procedure we have used many times before.

The advantage of using a for loop to sequence through an array becomes apparent when working with larger arrays. For example, if the temp array contained 100 values rather than just five, simply changing the number 5 to 100 in the for statement is sufficient to sequence through the 100 elements and add each temperature to the sum.

As another example of using a for loop to sequence through an array, assume that we want to locate the maximum value in an array of 1000 elements named volts. The procedure we will use to locate the maximum value is to assume initially that the first element in the array is the largest number. Then, as we sequence through the array, the maximum is compared to each element. When an element with a higher value is located, that element becomes the new maximum. The following code does the job.

```
const int NUMELS = 1000;

maximum = volts[0];          // set the maximum to element zero
for (i = 1; i < NUMELS; i++) // cycle through the rest of the array
  if (volts[i] > maximum)    // compare each element to the maximum
    maximum = volts[i];      // capture the new high value
```

In this code the for statement consists of one if statement. The search for a new maximum value starts with element 1 of the array and continues through the last element. Each element is compared to the current maximum, and when a higher value is encountered it becomes the new maximum.

---

[2]Note: Some compilers permit floating-point variables as subscripts; in these cases the floating-point value is truncated to an integer value.

Input and Output of Array Values

Individual array elements can be assigned values interactively using a `cin` stream object. Examples of individual data entry statements are:

```
cin >> temp[0];
cin >> temp[1] >> temp[2] >> temp[3];
cin >> temp[4] >> volts[6];
```

In the first statement a single value will be read and stored in the variable named `temp[0]`. The second statement will cause three values to be read and stored in the variables `temp[1]`, `temp[2]`, and `temp[3]`, respectively. Finally, the last `cin` statement can be used to read values into the variables `temp[4]` and `volts[6]`.

Alternatively, a `for` loop can be used to cycle through the array for interactive data input. For example, the code

```
const int NUMELS = 5;

for (i = 0; i < NUMELS; i++)
{
  cout << "Enter a temperature: ";
  cin  >> temp[i];
}
```

prompts the user for five temperatures. The first temperature entered is stored in `temp[0]`, the second temperature entered in `temp[1]`, and so on until five temperatures have been input.

One caution should be mentioned about storing data in an array. C++ does not check the value of the index being used (called a **bounds check**). If an array has been declared as consisting of 10 elements, for example, and you use an index of 12, which is outside the bounds of the array, C++ will not notify you of the error when the program is compiled. The program will attempt to access element 12 by skipping over the appropriate number of bytes from the start of the array. Usually this results in a program crash—but not always. If the referenced location itself contains a value of the correct data type, the new value will simply overwrite the value in the referenced memory locations. This leads to more errors, which are particularly troublesome to locate when the variable legitimately assigned to the storage location is used at a different point in the program.

During output, individual array elements can be displayed using the `cout` object or complete sections of the array can be displayed by including a `cout` statement within a for loop. Examples of this are

```
cout << volts[6];
```

and

```
cout << "The value of element " << i << " is " << temp[i];
```

Point of Information

Aggregate Data Types

In contrast to atomic types, such as integer and floating-point data, there are aggregate types. An aggregate type, which is also referred to as both a *structured type* and a *data structure,* is any type whose values can be decomposed and are related by some defined structure. Additionally, operations must be available for retrieving and updating individual values in the data structure.

Single-dimensional arrays are examples of a structured type. In a single-dimensional array, such as an array of integers, the array is composed of individual integer values, where integers are related by their position in the list. Indexed variables provide the means of accessing and modifying values in the array.

---

and

```
const int NUMELS = 20;

for (k = 5; k < NUMELS; k++)
  cout <<  k << "  " << amount[k] << endl;
```

The first statement displays the value of the subscripted variable `volts[6]`. The second statement displays the value of the subscript `i` and the value of `temp[i]`. Before this statement can be executed, `i` would have to have an assigned value. Finally, the last example includes a `cout` object within a `for` loop. Both the value of the index and the value of the elements from 5 to 20 are displayed.

Program 10.1 illustrates these input and output techniques using an array named `temp` that is defined to store five integer numbers. Included in the program are two `for` loops. The first `for` loop is used to cycle through each array element and allows the user to input individual array values. After five values have been entered, the second `for` loop is used to display the stored values.

Program 10.1

```cpp
#include <iostream.h>

int main()
{
  const int MAXTEMPS = 5;
  int i, temp[MAXTEMPS];

  for (i = 0; i < MAXTEMPS; i++)    // Enter the temperatures
  {
    cout << "Enter a temperature: ";
    cin  >> temp[i];
  }

  cout << endl;

  for (i = 0; i < MAXTEMPS; i++)    // Print the temperatures
    cout << "temperature " << i << " is " << temp[i] << endl;

  return 0;
}
```

A sample run of Program 10.1 follows:

```
Enter a temperature: 85
Enter a temperature: 90
Enter a temperature: 78
Enter a temperature: 75
Enter a temperature: 92

temperature 0 is 85
temperature 1 is 90
temperature 2 is 78
temperature 3 is 75
temperature 4 is 92
```

In reviewing the output produced by Program 10.1, pay particular attention to the difference between the index value displayed and the numerical value stored in the corresponding array element. The index value refers to the location of the element in the array, while the subscripted variable refers to the value stored in the designated location.

In addition to simply displaying the values stored in each array element, the elements can also be processed by appropriately referencing the desired element. For example, in Program 10.2, the value of each element is accumulated in a total, which is displayed upon completion of the individual display of each array element.

Program 10.2

```cpp
#include <iostream.h>

int main()
{
  const int MAXTEMPS = 5;
  int i, temp[MAXTEMPS], total = 0;

  for (i = 0; i < MAXTEMPS; i++)        // Enter the temperatures
  {
    cout << "Enter a temperature: ";
    cin  >> temp[i];
  }

  cout << "\nThe total of the temperatures";

  for (i = 0; i < MAXTEMPS; i++)        // Display and total the temperatures
  {
    cout << "   " << temp[i];
    total =  total + temp[i];
  }

  cout << " is " << total << endl;

  return 0;
}
```

A sample run of Program 10.2 follows:

```
Enter a temperature: 85
Enter a temperature: 90
Enter a temperature: 78
Enter a temperature: 75
Enter a temperature: 92

The total of the temperatures  85  90  78  75  92 is 420
```

Notice that in Program 10.2, unlike Program 10.1, only the values stored in each array element are displayed and not the index numbers. Although the second for loop was used to accumulate the total of each element, the accumulation could also have been accomplished in the first loop by placing the statement total = total + temp[i]; after the cin statement used to enter a value. Also notice that the cout statement used to display the total is made outside of the second for loop, so that the total is displayed only once, after all values have been added to the total. If this cout statement were placed inside of the for loop five totals would be displayed, with only the last displayed total containing the sum of all of the array values.

Exercises 10.1

1. Write array declarations for the following.
   a. a list of 100 floating-point voltages
   b. a list of 50 floating-point temperatures
   c. a list of 30 characters, each representing a code
   d. a list of 100 integer years
   e. a list of 32 floating-point velocities
   f. a list of 1000 floating-point distances
   g. a list of 6 integer code numbers

2. Write appropriate notation for the first, third, and seventh elements of the following arrays:
   a. `int grades[20]`
   b. `float volts[10]`
   c. `float amps[16]`
   d. `int dist[15]`
   e. `float velocity[25]`
   f. `float time[100]`

3. a. Write individual input statements using `cin` that can be used to enter values into the first, third, and seventh elements of each of the arrays declared in Exercises 2a through 2f.
   b. Write a `for` loop that can be used to enter values for the complete array declared in Exercise 2a.

4. a. Write individual output statements using `cout` that can be used to print the values from the first, third, and seventh elements of each of the arrays declared in Exercises 2a through 2f.
   b. Write a `for` loop that can be used to display values for the complete array declared in Exercise 2a.

5. List the elements that will be displayed by the following sections of code:
   a. ```
for (m = 1; m <= 5; m++)
   cout << a[m] << " ";
```
   b. ```
for (k = 1; k <= 5; k = k + 2)
   cout <<  a[k] << " ";
```
   c. ```
for (j = 3; j <= 10; j++)
    cout << b[j] << " ";
```
   d. ```
for (k = 3; k <= 12; k = k + 3)
    cout << b[k] << " ";
```
   e. ```
for (i = 2; i < 11; i = i + 2)
    cout << c[i] << " ";
```
```

6. **a.** Write a program to input the following values into an array named `volts`: 10.95, 16.32, 12.15, 8.22, 15.98, 26.22, 13.54, 6.45, 17.59. After the data has been entered, have your program output the values.

   b. Repeat Exercise 6a, but after the data has been entered, have your program display it in the following form:

10.95	16.32	12.15
8.22	15.98	26.22
13.54	6.45	17.59

7. Write a program to input eight integer numbers into an array named `temp`. As each number is input, add the numbers into a total. After all numbers are input, display the numbers and their average.

8. **a.** Write a program to input 10 integer numbers into an array named `fmax` and determine the maximum value entered. Your program should contain only one loop and the maximum should be determined as array element values are being input. (*Hint*: Set the maximum equal to the first array element, which should be input before the loop used to input the remaining array values.)

   b. Repeat Exercise 8a, keeping track of both the maximum element in the array and the index number for the maximum. After displaying the numbers, print these two messages

   ```
   The maximum value is:
   This is element number _____ in the list of numbers
   ```

   Have your program display the correct values in place of the underlines in the messages.

   c. Repeat Exercise 8b, but have your program locate the minimum of the data entered.

9. **a.** Write a program to input the following integer numbers into an array named `grades`: 89, 95, 72, 83, 99, 54, 86, 75, 92, 73, 79, 75, 82, 73. As each number is input, add the numbers to a total. After all numbers are input and the total is obtained, calculate the average of the numbers and use the average to determine the deviation of each value from the average. Store each deviation in an array named `deviation`. Each deviation is obtained as the element value less the average of all the data. Have your program display each deviation alongside its corresponding element from the `grades` array.

   b. Calculate the variance of the data used in Exercise 9a. The variance is obtained by squaring each individual deviation and dividing the sum of the squared deviations by the number of deviations.

10. Write a program that specifies three one-dimensional arrays named `current`, `resistance`, and `volts`. Each array should be capable of holding 10 elements. Using a `for` loop, input values for the `current` and `resistance` arrays. The entries in the `volts` array should be the product of the corresponding values in the `current` and `resistance` arrays (thus, `volts[i] = current[i] * resistance[I]`). After all of the data has been entered, display the following output:

    ```
    Current          Resistance          Volts
    ```

    Under each column heading display the appropriate value.

10.2 ARRAY INITIALIZATION

Array elements can be initialized within their declaration statements in the same manner as scalar variables, except that the initializing elements must be included in braces. Examples of such initializations are

```
int temp[5] = {98, 87, 92, 79, 85};
char codes[6] = {'s', 'a', 'm', 'p', 'l', 'e'};
double slopes[7] = {10.96, 6.43, 2.58, .86, 5.89, 7.56, 8.22};
```

Initializers are applied in the order they are written, with the first value used to initialize element 0, the second value used to initialize element 1, and so on, until all values have been used. Thus, in the declaration

```
    int temp[5] = {98, 87, 92, 79, 85};
```

`temp[0]` is initialized to 98, `temp[1]` is initialized to 87, `temp[2]` is initialized to 92, `temp[3]` is initialized to 79, and `temp[4]` is initialized to 85.

Because white space is ignored in C++, initializations may be continued across multiple lines. For example, the declaration

```
int gallons[20] = {19, 16, 14, 19, 20, 18,  // initializing values
                   12, 10, 22, 15, 18, 17,  // may extend across
                   16, 14, 23, 19, 15, 18,  // multiple lines
                   21, 5};
```

uses four lines to initialize all of the array elements.

If the number of initializers is less than the declared number of elements listed in square brackets, the initializers are applied starting with array element zero. Thus, in the declaration

```
    float length[7] = {7.8, 6.4, 4.9, 11.2};
```

only `length[0]`, `length[1]`, `length[2]`, and `length[3]` are initialized with the listed values. The other array elements will be initialized to zero.

Unfortunately, there is no method of either indicating repetition of an initialization value or initializing later array elements without first specifying values for earlier elements.

A unique feature of initializers is that the size of an array may be omitted when initializing values are included in the declaration statement. For example, the declaration

```
    int gallons[] = {16, 12, 10, 14, 11};
```

reserves enough storage room for five elements. Similarly, the following two declarations are equivalent:

```
    char codes[6] = {'s', 'a', 'm', 'p', 'l', 'e'};
    char codes[] = {'s', 'a', 'm', 'p', 'l', 'e'};
```

Both of these declarations set aside six character locations for an array named `codes`. An interesting and useful simplification can also be used when initializing character arrays. For example, the declaration

```
    char codes[] = "sample";   // no braces or commas
```

uses the string "sample" to initialize the codes array. Recall that a string is any sequence of characters enclosed in double quotes. This last declaration creates an array named codes having seven elements and fills the array with the seven characters illustrated in Figure 10.6. The first six characters, as expected, consist of the letters s, a, m, p, l, and e. The last character, which is the escape sequence \0, is called the **null character**. The null character is automatically appended to all strings by the C++ compiler. This character has an internal storage code that is numerically equal to zero (the storage code for the zero character has a numerical value of decimal 48, so the two cannot be confused by the computer), and is used as a marker, or sentinel, to mark the end of a string.

codes [0] codes [1] codes [2] codes [3] codes [4] codes [5] codes [6]

s	a	m	p	l	e	\0

Figure 10.6 A string is terminated with a special sentinel.

Once values have been assigned to array elements, either through initialization within the declaration statement or using interactive input, the array elements can be processed as described in the previous section. For example, Program 10.3 illustrates the initialization of array elements within the declaration of the array and then uses a for loop to locate the maximum value stored in the array.

Program 10.3

```cpp
#include <iostream.h>

int main()
{
  const int MAXELS = 5;

  int i, max, nums[MAXELS] = {2, 18, 1, 27, 16};

  max = nums[0];

  for (i = 1; i < MAXELS; i++)
    if (max < nums[i])
      max = nums[i];

  cout << "The maximum value is " << max << endl;

  return 0;
}
```

The output produced by Program 10.3 is

```
The maximum value is 27
```

Exercises 10.2

1. Write array declarations, including initializers, for the following
   a. a list of 10 integer voltages: 89, 75, 82, 93, 78, 95, 81, 88, 77, 82
   b. a list of five double-precision slopes: 10.62, 13.98, 18.45, 12.68, 14.76
   c. a list of 100 double-precision distances; the first six distances are 6.29, 6.95, 7.25, 7.35, 7.40, 7.42
   d. a list of 64 floating-point temperatures; the first 10 temperatures are 78.2, 69.6, 68.5, 83.9, 55.4, 67.0, 49.8, 58.3, 62.5, 71.6
   e. a list of 15 character codes; the first seven codes are f, j, m, q, t, w, z

2. Write an array declaration statement that stores the following values in an array named `volts`: 16.24, 18.98, 23.75, 16.29, 19.54, 14.22, 11.13, 15.39. Include these statements in a program that displays the values in the array.

3. Write a program that uses an array declaration statement to initialize the following numbers in an array named `slopes`: 17.24, 25.63, 5.94, 33.92, 3.71, 32.84, 35.93, 18.24, 6.92. Your program should locate and display both the maximum and minimum values in the array.

4. Write a program that stores the following prices in an array named `resistance`: 16, 27, 39, 56, and 81. Your program should also create two arrays named `current` and `power`, each capable of storing five double-precision numbers. Using a `for` loop and a `cin` statement, have your program accept five user-input numbers into the `current` array when the program is run. Your program should store the product of the corresponding values of the square of the `current` array and the `resistance` array in the `power` array (for example, `power[1] = resistance[1] * pow(current[1],2)` and display the following output (fill in the table appropriately):

Resistance	Current	Power
16	•	•
27	•	•
39	•	•
56	•	•
81	•	•

Total:		•

5. a. Write a declaration to store the string `"This is a test"` into an array named `strtest`. Include the declaration in a program to display the message using the following loop:

```
for (i = 0; i < NUMDISPLAY; i++)
  cout << strtest[i];
```

   where `NUMDISPLAY` is a named constant for the number 15.
   b. Modify the `for` statement in Exercise 5a to display only the array characters t, e, s, and t.

   c. Include the array declaration written in Exercise 5a in a program that uses the `cout` object to display characters in the array. For example, the statement `cout << strtest;` will cause the string stored in the `strtest` array to be displayed. Using this statement requires that the last character in the array is the end of string marker `\0`.

   d. Repeat Exercise 5a using a `while` loop. (*Hint*: Stop the loop when the `\0` escape sequence is detected. The expression `while (strtest[i] != '\0')` can be used.)

10.3 DECLARING AND PROCESSING TWO-DIMENSIONAL ARRAYS

A **two-dimensional array,** which is sometimes referred to as a table, consists of both rows and columns of elements. For example, the array of numbers

8	16	9	52
3	15	27	6
14	25	2	10

is called a two-dimensional array of integers. This array consists of three rows and four columns. To reserve storage for this array, both the number of rows and the number of columns must be included in the array's declaration. Calling the array `val`, the correct specification for this two-dimensional array is

```
int val[3][4];
```

Similarly, the declarations

```
float volts[10][5];
char code[6][26];
```

declare that the array `volts` consists of 10 rows and 5 columns of floating-point numbers and that the array `code` consists of 6 rows and 26 columns, with each element capable of holding one character.

Figure 10.7 Each array element is identified by its row and column position.

To locate each element in a two-dimensional array, an element is identified by its position in the array. As illustrated in Figure 10.7, the term `val[1][3]` uniquely identifies the element in row 1, column 3. As with single-dimensional array variables, double-dimensional array variables can be used anywhere that scalar variables are valid. Examples using elements of the `val` array are

```
watts = val[2][3];
val[0][0] = 62;
newnum = 4 * (val[1][0] - 5);
sumRow0 = val[0][0] + val[0][1] + val[0][2] + val[0][3];
```

The last statement causes the values of the four elements in row 0 to be added and the sum to be stored in the scalar variable `sumRow0`.

As with single-dimensional arrays, two-dimensional arrays can be initialized from within their declaration statements. This is done by listing the initial values within braces and separating them by commas. Additionally, braces can be used to separate individual rows. For example, the declaration

```
int val[3][4] = { {8,16,9,52},
                  {3,15,27,6},
                  {14,25,2,10} };
```

declares `val` to be an array of integers with three rows and four columns, with the initial values given in the declaration. The first set of internal braces contains the values for row 0 of the array, the second set of internal braces contains the values for row 1, and the third set of braces the values for row 2.

Although the commas in the initialization braces are always required, the inner braces can be omitted. Thus, the initialization for `val` may be written as

```
int val[3][4] = {8,16,9,52,
                 3,15,27,6,
                 14,25,2,10};
```

The separation of initial values into rows in the declaration statement is not necessary since the compiler assigns values beginning with the `[0][0]` element and proceeds row by row to fill in the remaining values. Thus, the initialization

```
int val[3][4] = {8,16,9,52,3,15,27,6,14,25,2,10};
```

is equally valid but does not clearly illustrate to another programmer where one row ends and another begins.

As illustrated in Figure 10.8, the initialization of a two-dimensional array is done in row order. First, the elements of the first row are initialized, then the elements of the second row are initialized, and so on, until the initializations are completed. This row ordering is also the same ordering used to store two-dimensional arrays. That is, array element `[0][0]` is stored first, followed by element `[0][1]`, followed by element `[0][2]` and so on. Following the first row's elements are the second row's elements, and so on for all the rows in the array.

Figure 10.8 Storage and initialization of the `val[ ]` array.

As with single-dimensional arrays, two-dimensional arrays may be displayed by individual element notation or by using loops (either `while` or `for`). This is illustrated by Program 10.4, which displays all of the elements of a 3 by 4 two-dimensional array using two different techniques. Notice in Program 10.4 that we have used named constants to define the array's rows and columns.

The display produced by Program 10.4 follows.

```
Display of val array by explicit element
    8   16    9   52
    3   15   27    6
   14   25    2   10
Display of val array using a nested for loop
    8   16    9   52
    3   15   27    6
   14   25    2   10
```

The first display of the `val` array produced by Program 10.4 is constructed by explicitly designating each array element. The second display of array element values, which is identical to the first, is produced using a nested `for` loop. Nested loops are especially useful when dealing with two-dimensional arrays because they allow the programmer to designate and cycle through each element easily. In Program 10.4, the variable `i` controls the outer loop and the variable `j` controls the inner loop. Each pass through the outer loop corresponds to a single row, with the inner loop supplying the appropriate column elements. After a complete row is printed a new line is started for the next row. The effect is a display of the array in a row-by-row fashion.

Program 10.4

```cpp
#include <iostream.h>
#include <iomanip.h>

int main()
{

  const int NUMROWS = 3;
  const int NUMCOLS = 4;

  int i, j;
  int val[NUMROWS][NUMCOLS] = {8,16,9,52,3,15,27,6,14,25,2,10};

  cout << "\nDisplay of val array by explicit element"
       << '\n' << setw(4) << val[0][0] << setw(4) << val[0][1]
       << setw(4) << val[0][2] << setw(4) << val[0][3]
       << '\n' << setw(4) << val[1][0] << setw(4) << val[1][1]
       << setw(4) << val[1][2] << setw(4) << val[1][3]
       << '\n' << setw(4) << val[2][0] << setw(4) << val[2][1]
       << setw(4) << val[2][2] << setw(4) << val[2][3];

  cout << "\n\nDisplay of val array using a nested for loop";

  for (i = 0; i < NUMROWS; i++)
  {
    cout << '\n';        // print a new line for each row
    for (j = 0; j < NUMCOLS; j++)
      cout << setw(4) <<  val[i][j];
  }

  cout << endl;

  return 0;
}
```

Once two-dimensional array elements have been assigned, array processing can begin. Typically, for loops are used to process two-dimensional arrays because, as was previously noted, they allow the programmer to designate and cycle through each array element easily. For example, the nested for loop illustrated in Program 10.5 is used to multiply each element in the val array by the scalar number 10 and display the resulting value.

Following is the output produced by Program 10.5.

```
Display of multiplied elements
 80   160    90   520
 30   150   270    60
140   250    20   100
```

Program 10.5

```cpp
#include <iostream.h>
#include <iomanip.h>

int main()
{
  const int NUMROWS = 3;
  const int NUMCOLS = 4;

  int i, j;
  int val[NUMROWS][NUMCOLS] = {8,16,9,52,
                               3,15,27,6,
                               14,25,2,10};

// multiply each element by 10 and display it
  cout << "\nDisplay of multiplied elements";
  for (i = 0; i < NUMROWS; i++)
  {
    cout << endl;    // start each row on a new line
    for (j = 0; j < NUMCOLS; j++)
    {
      val[i][j] = val[i][j] * 10;
      cout << setw(5) << val[i][j];
    }  // end of inner loop
  }    // end of outer loop
  cout << endl;

  return 0;
}
```

Larger Dimensional Arrays

Although arrays with more than two dimensions are not commonly used, C++ does allow any number of dimensions to be declared. This is done by listing the maximum size of all dimensions for the array. For example, the declaration `int response [4][10][[6];` declares a three-dimensional array. The first element in the array is designated as `response[0][0][0]` and the last element as `response[3][9][5]`.

Conceptually, as illustrated in Figure 10.9, a three-dimensional array can be viewed as a book of data tables. Using this visualization, the first index can be thought of as the location of the desired row in a table, the second index value as the desired column, and the third index value, which is often called the "rank," as the page number of the selected table.

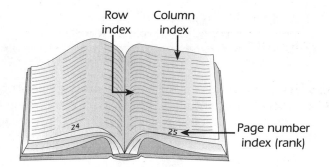

Figure 10.9 *Representation of a three-dimensional array.*

Similarly, arrays of any dimension can be declared. Conceptually, a four-dimensional array can be represented as a shelf of books, where the fourth dimension is used to declare a desired book on the shelf, and a five-dimensional array can be viewed as a book case filled with books where the fifth dimension refers to a selected shelf in the book case. Using the same analogy, a six-dimensional array can be considered as a single row of book cases where the sixth dimension references the desired bookcase in the row; a seven-dimensional array can be considered as multiple rows of book cases where the seventh dimension references the desired row, and so on. Alternatively, arrays of three, four, five, six, etc. dimensional arrays can be viewed as mathematical *n*-tuples of order three, four, five, six, etc., respectively.

Exercises 10.3

1. Write appropriate specification statements for
   a. an array of integers with 6 rows and 10 columns
   b. an array of integers with 2 rows and 5 columns
   c. an array of characters with 7 rows and 12 columns
   d. an array of characters with 15 rows and 7 columns
   e. an array of floating point numbers with 10 rows and 25 columns
   f. an array of floating point numbers with 16 rows and 8 columns

2. Determine the output produced by the following program:

```cpp
#include <iostream.h>

int main()
{
  int i, j, val[3][4] = {8,16,9,52,3,15,27,6,14,25,2,10};

  for (i = 0; i < 3; ++i)
    for (j = 0; j < 4; ++j)
      cout << "%2d  " << val[i][j];

  return 0;
}
```

3. a. Write a C++ program that adds the values of all elements in the `val` array used in Exercise 2 and displays the total.

    b. Modify the program written for Exercise 3a to display the total of each row separately.

4. Write a C++ program that adds equivalent elements of the two-dimensional arrays named `first` and `second`. Both arrays should have two rows and three columns. For example, element `[1][2]` of the resulting array should be the sum of `first[1][2]` and `second[1][2]`. The `first` and `second` arrays should be initialized as follows:

FIRST			SECOND		
16	18	23	24	52	77
54	91	11	16	19	59

5. a. Write a C++ program that finds and displays the maximum value in a two-dimensional array of integers. The array should be declared as a 4 by 5 array of integers and initialized with the data 16, 22, 99, 4, 18, –258, 4, 101, 5, 98, 105, 6, 15, 2, 45, 33, 88, 72, 16, 3

    b. Modify the program written in Exercise 5a so that it also displays the maximum value's row and column subscript numbers.

6. Write a C++ program to select the values in a four by five array of integers in increasing order and store the selected values in the single-dimensional array named sort. Use the data statement given in Exercise 5a to initialize the two-dimensional array.

7. a. An engineer has constructed a two dimensional array of real numbers having 3 rows and 5 columns. This array currently contains the test voltages of an amplifier. Write a C++ program that interactively inputs 15 array values and then determines the total number of voltages in the ranges less than 60, greater than or equal to 60 and less than 70, greater than or equal to 70 and less than 80, greater than or equal to 80 and less than 90, and greater or equal to 90.

    b. Entering 15 voltages each time the program written for Exercise 7a is run is cumbersome. What method, therefore, is appropriate for initializing the array during the testing phase?

    c. How might the program you wrote for Exercise 7a be modified to include the case of no voltage being present? That is, what voltage could be used to indicate an invalid voltage and how would your program have to be modified to exclude counting such a voltage?

10.4 Applications

Arrays are extremely useful in any application that requires multiple passes through the same set of data elements. Two such applications are presented in this section. The first application is a statistical data analysis requiring two passes through the data. The first pass is used to input the list and determine the average of the data, while the second pass uses the average to determine a standard deviation. The second application presents a simple but elegant method of plotting data on either a video screen or standard printer. Here a first pass is used to both initialize the array with the data points that are to be plotted and to determine maximum and minimum array values. These values are then used to calculate an appropriate scaling factor to ensure that the final plot fits within the area of the video screen or paper. Finally, a second pass through the array is made to produce the plot.

Application 1: Statistical Analysis

A program is to be developed that accepts a list of a maximum of 100 voltages as input, determines both the average and standard deviation of the input voltages, and then displays the results.

Step 1   Analyze the Problem

The statement of the problem indicates that two output values are required: an average and a standard deviation. In Step 2 we will verify that we know how these values are to be calculated. The input item defined in the problem statement is a maximum of 100 voltages. This means that any number of voltages, from zero to 100 could be input by the user when the program is executed. To accommodate for this, we will have to ask the user how many voltages he or she intends to input. Thus, the first input will be the number of voltages that will subsequently be entered.

Step 2   Develop a Solution

The I/O specifications determined in Step 1 define that the user will enter two types of input: the number of voltages followed by the actual data. Based on this input the program is to calculate and display the average and standard deviation of the data. These output items are determined as follows:

Calculate the average by adding the voltages and dividing by the number of voltages that were added
Determine the standard deviation by
  1. *Subtracting the average from each individual voltage: This results in a set of new numbers, each of which is called a **deviation***
  2. *Square each deviation found in the previous step*
  3. *Add the squared deviations and divide the sum by the number of deviations*
  4. *The square root of the number found in the previous step is the standard deviation*

Notice that the calculation of the standard deviation requires the average, which means that the standard deviation can be calculated only after the average has been computed. This is the advantage of specifying the algorithm, in detail, before any coding is done; it ensures that all necessary inputs and requirements are discovered early in the programming process.

To ensure that we understand the required processing we will do a hand calculation. For this calculation we will arbitrarily assume that the average and standard deviation of the following 10 voltages are to be determined: 98, 82, 67, 54, 78, 83, 95, 76, 68, and 63.

The average of this data is determined as

$$\text{Average} = (98 + 82 + 67 + 54 + 78 + 83 + 95 + 76 + 68 + 63)/10$$
$$= 76.4$$

The standard deviation is calculated by first determining the sum of the squared deviations. The standard deviation is then obtained by dividing the resulting sum by 10 and taking its square root.

$$
\begin{aligned}
\text{Sum of squared deviations} \; = \; & (98 - 76.4)^2 \\
+ \; & (82 - 76.4)^2 \\
+ \; & (67 - 76.4)^2 \\
+ \; & (54 - 76.4)^2 \\
+ \; & (78 - 76.4)^2 \\
+ \; & (83 - 76.4)^2 \\
+ \; & (95 - 76.4)^2 \\
+ \; & (76 - 76.4)^2 \\
+ \; & (68 - 76.4)^2 \\
+ \; & (63 - 76.4)^2 \\
= \; & 1730.4007
\end{aligned}
$$

$$\text{Standard Deviation} = \sqrt{1730.4007 / 10}$$

$$= \sqrt{173.04007}$$

$$= 13.154470$$

Having specified the algorithm required of each function, we are now in a position to code them.

Step 3   Code the Solution

Program 10.6 presents the C++ version of the selected algorithm. Notice that the program uses one `for` loop to enter and sum the individual voltages and a second `for` loop to determine the sum of the squared deviations. Because calculation of the squared deviations requires the average, the standard deviation can be calculated only after the average has been computed. Notice also that the termination value of the loop counter in both `for` loops is `numvolts`, which is the number of voltages input by the user. The use of this argument gives the program its generality and allows it to be used for lists of any number of voltages, up to `NUM_ELS`, which is defined as 100 by the `const` statement.

Program 10.6

```cpp
#include <iostream.h>
#include <iomanip.h>
#include <math.h>

int main()
{

  const int NUM_ELS = 100;

  int i, numvolts;
  double volt[NUM_ELS];
  double average, stddev;
  double sumvolts = 0.0, sumdevs = 0.0;

  cout << "Enter the number of voltages to be analyzed: ";
  cin  >> numvolts;

  // read the input voltages and total them
  for (i = 0; i < numvolts; i++)
  {
      cout << "Enter voltage " << i+1 << ": ";
      cin  >> volt[i];
    sumvolts = sumvolts + volt[i];
  }
  // calculate and display the average
  average = sumvolts / numvolts;
  cout << "\nThe average of the voltages is "
       << setw(11) << setiosflags(ios::showpoint)
       << setprecision(8) << average << endl;

  // calculate and display the standard deviation
  for (i = 0; i < numvolts; i++)
     sumdevs = sumdevs + pow((volt[i] - average),2);
  stddev = sqrt(sumdevs/numvolts);
  cout << "The standard deviation of the voltages is "
       << setw(11) << setiosflags(ios::showpoint)
       << setprecision(8) << stddev << endl;

  return 0;

}
```

Step 4   Test and Correct the Program

A test run using Program 10.6 produced the following display:

```
Enter the number of voltages to be analyzed: 10
Enter voltage 1: 98
Enter voltage 2: 82
Enter voltage 3: 67
Enter voltage 4: 54
Enter voltage 5: 78
Enter voltage 6: 83
Enter voltage 7: 95
Enter voltage 8: 76
Enter voltage 9: 68
Enter voltage 10: 63

The average of the voltages is   76.400000
The standard deviation of the voltages is 13.154467
```

Although this result agrees with our previous hand calculation, testing is really not complete without verifying the calculation at the boundary points. In this case such a test consists of checking the calculation with all of the same values, such as all 0s and all 100s. Another simple test would be to use five 0s and five 100s. We leave these tests as an exercise.

Application 2: Curve Plotting

Two basic constraints must be considered when graphing data on either a video screen or printer. The first constraint is that both devices automatically move in a forward direction, which means that our graphs should avoid the need to "back up" (although there are methods for reversing the cursor motion on a video screen, all of our programs will be constructed to work for both printers and screens). The second constraint is that both printer paper and video displays are restricted in the horizontal direction to displaying a maximum of either 80 or 132 characters. No such restriction exists in the vertical direction because the paper length is effectively unlimited and the video display scrolls forward. For this reason our plots will always be constructed "sideways" with the y axis horizontal and the x axis vertical. This means that the values must always be checked, and scaled if necessary, to fit across a page or screen across. With these two constraints in mind, consider the plot shown in Figure 10.10.

Figure 10.10 *A graph is plotted sideways.*

As illustrated in Figure 10.10, the graph is plotted sideways with the *y* axis displayed across the top of the graph and the *x* axis displayed down the side. Omitting, for the moment, the two header lines

the actual graph of the data points consists of 15 individual lines, as follows:

```
line 1: |                                          *
line 2: |                                  *
line 3: |                            *
line 4: |                      *
line 5: |                 *
line 6: |            *
line 7: |    *
line 8: | *
line 9: |    *
line 10:|      *
line 11:|            *
line 12:|                 *
line 13:|                      *
line 14:|                            *
line 15:|                                      *
```

Notice that individually, each line consists of only two printed symbols, a bar (|) and an asterisk (*). The bar is always displayed in column one and the asterisk is positioned to indicate an appropriate *y* value. With these points in mind, it is rather easy to construct these 15 lines. To do this we will first construct an exact image of the first line to be printed in an array of characters. After the array is constructed and printed it will be used to construct an image of the second line. After the second image is displayed, the same array is used to construct an image of the third line, and so on until all 15 lines have been displayed. To make sure that the elements in the array can be displayed on a page the array should be smaller than the maximum horizontal width of either the paper or video screen being used for the display.

As illustrated in Figure 10.11, the array, called **line**, is filled with blanks, except for the first element, which stores the bar symbol, and one other element, which stores an asterisk.

Line[0]

Figure 10.11 The **line** array.

Using the **line** array to store the image of each line before it is printed, our graphing approach is

Step 1. Store an asterisk in the desired array element

Step 2. Print the array

Step 3. Reset the element to a blank

Step 4. Repeat steps 1 through 3 until the required number of lines have been displayed

These four steps are easily implemented using a **for** loop having the form

```
for (x = 1; x <= 15; x++)
  {
    calculate a value for y
    line[y] = '*';      // set character to an asterisk
    cout << line << endl;
    line[y] = ' ';      // reset character to a blank
  }
```

The calculation of the y value, which is then used as a subscript for the line array, depends on the graph being plotted. For the graph illustrated in Figure 10.10, the equation $y = (x - 8)^2 + 3$ was used.[3] Incorporating this into the `for` loop yields the executable code

```
for (x = 1; x <= 15; ++x)
{
  y = pow((x-8),2.0) + 3;
  line[y] = '*';      // set character to an asterisk
  cout << line << endl;
  line[y] = ' ';      // reset character to a blank
}
```

Program 10.7 includes this code within a working program.

Program 10.7

```
#include <iostream.h>
#include <math.h>

int main()
{
  int x, y;
  char line[]="|                                                ";
  for (x = 1; x <= 15; x++)
  {
    y = pow((x-8),2.0) + 3;
    line[y] = '*';      // set character to an asterisk
    cout <<  line << endl;
    line[y] = ' ';      // reset character to a blank
  }

  return 0;
}
```

Notice in Program 10.7 that the `line` array is declared and initialized with a bar symbol and the remaining elements with blanks. The `for` loop then calculates a y value, uses this value as a subscript to locate where the asterisk should be placed in the line array, displays the array, and restores a blank in place of the asterisk. This process is repeated fifteen times, resulting in the plot illustrated in Figure 10.12.

---

[3]To use the y value as a subscript for the line array requires that this value be an integer between the numbers 0 and 72, inclusive. The curve $y = (x - 8)^2 + 3$ was selected precisely because it yielded y values within this range. Once the plotting algorithm is understood, an algorithm is presented for scaling all y values into the required range.

Figure 10.12 The display produced by Program 10.7.

In reviewing Program 10.7 first notice that an *y* axis has not been explicitly included on the output. This is a minor omission that is be corrected by Program 10.8.

Program 10.8

```
#include <iostream.h>
#include <math.h>

int main()
{
  int x,y;
  char label[]="                    y axis";
  char axis[]="+---------------------------------------------->";
  char line[]="|                                              ";
  cout << label << endl;
  cout << axis << endl;
  for (x = 1; x <= 15; x++)
  {
    y = pow((x-8),2.0) + 3;
    line[y] = '*';        // set character to an asterisk
    cout << line << endl;
    line[y] = ' ';        // reset character to a blank
  }

  return 0;
}
```

Notice that Program 10.8 is essentially the same as Program 10.7 with the addition of two array declarations for the y axis and **two** cout statements to display the label and y axis strings. These statements are placed before the **for** loop to display the header lines. Program 10.8 produces the completed plot shown in Figure 10.13.

Figure 10.13 *The ouput displayed by Program 10.8.*

A more serious problem with both Programs 10.7 and 10.8 is that negative y values and y values greater than the width of the line array cannot be accommodated as a subscript to the line array. To accommodate graphs with such values requires scaling of the y values to fit within the line array's subscript range. The scaling algorithm to do this, which ensures that out plotting program works for any y value, requires the use of an array, which is presented next.

Equation 1 provides a scaling formula that ensures that all plotted data will fit within the width of a paper or video screen. As such, it should be used before a plotting routine is employed.

$$Scaled\ y\ value = \frac{Original\ value - Minimum\ value}{Maximum\ value - Minimum\ value} \times (W{-}1) \qquad \text{(Eqn. 1)}$$

where the *Maximum* and *Minimum* values are the respective maximum and minimum values for the complete set of data values being plotted, and W is the desired width of the paper or video display.

The term

$$\frac{Original\ value - Minimum\ value}{Maximum\ value - Minimum\ value}$$

in Equation 1 forces each original y value to lie within the range zero to one, with the minimum data value corresponding to zero and the maximum data value to one. Multiplying this result by the term (W − 1) produces values between 0 and (W − 1), for a total width of W.

For example, the second column in Table 10.1 lists y values of the equation $y = -x^3$ for values of x between -5 and 5, in increments of 0.5. As shown in column two, the maximum and minimum y values are $+125$ and -125, respectively.

Table 10.1 Values of the Equation $y = -x^3$

x	y	Scaled y	Rounded
-5 0	-125.000	0.000	0
-4.5	-91.125	7.186	7
-4.0	-64.000	12.932	13
-3.5	-42.875	17.411	17
-3.0	-27.000	20.776	21
-2.5	-15.625	23.188	23
-2.0	-8.000	24.804	25
-1.5	-3.375	25.786	26
-1.0	-1.000	26.288	26
-0.5	-0.125	26.473	26
0.0	0.000	26.500	27
0.5	0.125	26.527	27
1.0	1.000	26.712	27
1.5	3.375	27.216	27
2.0	8.000	28.196	28
2.5	15.625	29.813	30
3.0	27.000	32.224	32
3.5	42.875	35.590	36
4.0	64.000	40.068	40
4.5	91.125	45.819	46
5.0	125.000	53.000	53

For purposes of illustration assume that the width of the display area for plotting each y value in column 2 is 55 characters. Also assume that a single character of this display area is to be used for an axis symbol, such as the bar (|). This leaves a total width, W, of 54 for the actual data display. Applying Equation 1 to the data of column two with $W = 54$, and using the correct minimum and maximum values of -125 and 125, respectively, yields the values listed in column three of the table. Notice that the minimum value of -125 is converted to the value 0.000 and the maximum value of 125 is converted to the value 53.000. The last column in the table is the rounded and integerized values of the scaled numbers listed in the third column. Notice that the values in column four

Program 10.9

```cpp
#include <iostream.h>
#include <math.h>

int main()
{
 const int MAXPOINTS = 100;
  int i, npts, nval[MAXPOINTS];
  float x, xinc, fval, ymin, ymax, width, sval[100];
  char label[]="                                y axis";
  char axis[]="+-------------------------------------------------->";
  char line[]="|                                                   ";
  ymax = 1.0e-5;
  ymin = 1.0e+5;
  x = -5.0;
  xinc = 0.5;
  npts = 21;
  width = 53;
  // load up the data to be plotted and find the max and min values
  for (i = 1; i <= npts; i++)
  {
    sval[i] = pow(x,3.0);
    if (sval[i] > ymax)
      ymax = sval[i];
    if (sval[i] < ymin)
      ymin = sval[i];
    x = x + xinc;
  }
  // scale all y values to be plotted
  for (i = 1; i <= npts; ++i)
  {
    fval = ( (sval[i] - ymin)/(ymax - ymin) ) * width;
    nval[i] = fval + 0.5;   // convert to an integer value
  }
  // produce the plot
  cout << "Minimum Y Value: " << ymin << endl;
  cout << "Maximum Y Value: " << ymax << endl;
  cout << label << endl;
  cout << axis << endl;
  for (i = 1; i <= npts; ++i)
  {
    line[nval[i] + 2] = '*';      // set character to an asterisk
    cout << line << endl;
    line[nval[i] + 2] = ' ';      // reset character to a blank
  }

  return 0;
}
```

range from 0 to 53, for a total range of 54 possible *y* values. These values can be used directly by the curve plotting routine presented in the previous application to create a graph similar to that shown in Figure 10.14.

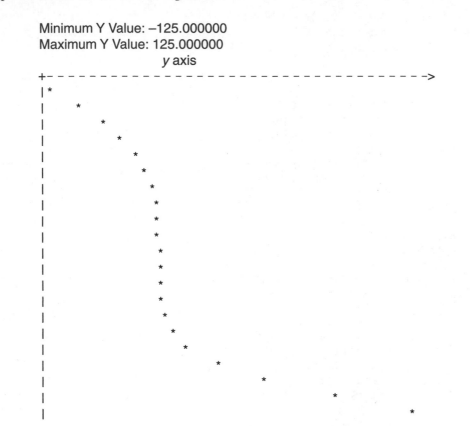

Figure 10.14 The output displayed by Program 10.9.

Program 10.9, which was used to create Figure 10.14, includes the data scaling algorithm and the curve plotting routine used in Program 10.8.

Exercises 10.4

1. Enter and run Program 10.6 on your computer.

2. Run Program 10.6 to determine the average and standard deviation of the following list of 15 voltages: 68, 72, 78, 69, 85, 98, 95, 75, 77, 82, 84, 91, 89, 65, 74.

3. Enter and run Program 10.8 on your computer system.

4. Modify Program 10.8 to plot the curve $y = x^3 - 4x^2 + 3x + 2$ for x equal to 0, 1, 2, 3, 4, 5, and 6.

5. Modify Program 10.8 to plot the curve $y = x^3 - 4x^2 + 3x + 2$ for x between -8 and $+8$, in increments of 0.5.

6. Modify Program 10.8 to plot the curve $y = 4x^3 - x^4$ for x between -10 and $+10$, in increments of 0.5.

7. When the switch illustrated in Figure 10.15 is closed at time $t = 0$, the voltage, V, across the capacitor is given by the equation $V = E[1 - e^{t/(RC)}]$, where E is the voltage of the battery, R is the circuit resistance, C is the value of the capacitance, and t is in seconds. Assuming that $E = 50$, $R = 4000$, and $C = 0.005$, modify Program 10.8 to plot the voltage across the capacitor from $t = 0$ to $t = 30$, in increments of 1 second.

Figure 10.15 A simple RC circuit.

8. Enter and run Program 10.9 on your computer system.

9. Figure 10.16 illustrates a *harmonic oscillator*, which consists of an object of mass m fastened to one end of a spring. The other end of the spring is attached to a wall, and the object is free to slide over a frictionless surface. Assuming the object is initially at rest (that is, the spring is neither stretched or compressed) and then pulled to position A at time $t = 0$, the position of the mass at any other time, t, is described by the equation

$$x = A \cos \left[(\sqrt{k/m})t \right]$$

where k is the spring constant in newtons/meter, m is the mass in units of kilograms, and A is the initial displacement in units of centimeters. Assuming A is 10 centimeters, k is 2000 newtons/meter, and m is 200 kilograms modify Program 10.9 to plot the displacement of the mass from $t = 0$ to $t = 60$ seconds, in increments of 1 second.

Figure 10.16 A harmonic oscillator.

10.5 ARRAYS AS ARGUMENTS

Individual array elements are passed to a called function in the same manner as individual scalar variables; they are simply included as subscripted variables when the function call is made. For example, the function call

```
find_min(volts[2], volts[6]);
```

passes the values of the elements `volts[2]` and `volts[6]` to the function `find_min()`.

Passing a complete array of values to a function is in many respects an easier operation than passing individual elements. The called function receives access to the actual array, rather than a copy of the values in the array. For example, if `volts` is an array, the function call `find_max(volts);` makes the complete `volts` array available to the `find_max()` function. This is different from passing a single variable to a function.

Recall that when a single scalar argument is passed to a function, the called function only receives a copy of the passed value, which is stored in one of the function's parameters. If arrays were passed in this manner, a copy of the complete array would have to be created. For large arrays, making duplicate copies of the array for each function call would be wasteful of computer storage and would frustrate the effort to return multiple-element changes made by the called program (recall that a function returns at most one direct value). To avoid these problems, the called function is given direct access to the original array.[4] Thus, any changes made by the called function are made directly to the array itself. For the following specific examples of function calls, assume that the arrays `nums`, `keys`, `volts`, and `current` are declared as:

```
int nums[5];                     // an array of five integers
char keys[256];                  // an array of 256 characters
double vots[500], current[500];  // two arrays of 500 doubles
```

For these arrays, the following function calls can be made:

```
find_max(nums);
find_ch(keys);
calc_tot(nums, volts, current);
```

In each case, the called function receives direct access to the named array.

On the receiving side, the called function must be alerted that an array is being made available. For example, suitable function header lines for the previous functions are

```
int find_max(int vals[5])
char find_ch(char in_keys[256])
void calc_tot(int arr1[5], double arr2[500], double arr3[500])
```

---

[4]This is accomplished because the starting address of the array is actually passed as an argument. The formal parameter receiving this address argument is a pointer. The intimate relationship between array names and pointers is presented in Chapter 11.

In each of these function header lines, the names in the parameter list are chosen by the programmer. However, the parameter names used by the functions still refer to the original array created outside the function. This is made clear in Program 10.10.

Program 10.10

```cpp
#include <iostream.h>

const int MAXELS = 5;
int find_max(int [MAXELS]);        // function prototype

int main()
{
  int nums[MAXELS] = {2, 18, 1, 27, 16};

  cout << "The maximum value is " << find_max(nums) << endl;

  return 0;
}

// find the maximum value
int find_max(int vals[MAXELS])
{
  int i, max = vals[0];
  for (i = 1; i < MAXELS; i++)
    if (max < vals[i]) max = vals[i];

  return max;
}
```

Notice that the function prototype for find_max() declares that find_max will return an integer and expects an array of five integers as an actual argument. It is also important to know that only one array is created in Program 10.10. In main() this array is known as nums, and in find_max() the array is known as vals. As illustrated in Figure 10.17, both names refer to the same array. Thus, in Figure 10.17 vals[3] is the same element as nums[3].

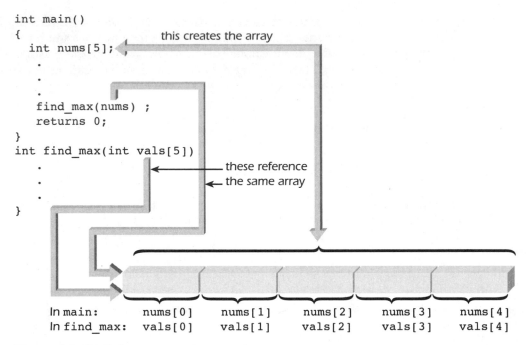

```
int main()
{
  int nums[5];                    this creates the array
     .
     .
     .
  find_max(nums) ;
  returns 0;
}
int find_max(int vals[5])
     .                            these reference
     .                            the same array
     .
}
```

In main:	nums[0]	nums[1]	nums[2]	nums[3]	nums[4]
In find_max:	vals[0]	vals[1]	vals[2]	vals[3]	vals[4]

Figure 10.17 Only one array is created.

The parameter declaration in the `find_max()` header line actually contains extra information that is not required by the function. All that `find_max()` must know is that the parameter `vals` references an array of integers. Since the array has been created in `main()` and no additional storage space is needed in `find_max()`, the declaration for `vals` can omit the size of the array. Thus, an alternative function header line is

```
int find_max(int vals[])
```

This form of the function header makes more sense when you realize that only one item is actually passed to `find_max` when the function is called, the starting address of the num array. This is illustrated in Figure 10.18.

```
  nums[0]   nums[1]   nums[2]   nums[3]   nums[4]
```

```
starting address
of nums array is &nums[0].
this is passed to
the function
```

```
find_max(nums);
```

Figure 10.18 The starting address of the array is passed.

Since only the starting address of `vals` is passed to `find_max`, the number of elements in the array need not be included in the declaration for `vals`.[5] In fact, it is generally advisable to omit the size of the array in the function header line. For example, consider the more general form of `find_max()`, which can be used to find the maximum value of an integer array of arbitrary size.

```
int find_max(int vals[], int num_els)    // find the maximum value
{
  int i, max = vals[0];

  for (i = 1; i < num_els; i++)
   if (max < vals[i])
     max = vals[i];

  return max;
}
```

The more general form of `find_max()` declares that the function returns an integer value. The function expects the starting address of an integer array and the number of elements in the array as arguments. Then, using the number of elements as the boundary for its search, the function's `for` loop causes each array element to be examined in sequential order to locate the maximum value. Program 10.11 illustrates the use of `find_max()` in a complete program.

The output displayed by both Programs 10.10 and 10.11 is

```
The maximum value is 27
```

Passing two-dimensional arrays into a function is a process identical to passing single-dimensional arrays. The called function receives access to the entire array. For example, assuming that `val` is a two-dimensional array, the function call `display(val);` makes the complete `val` array available to the function named `display()`. Thus, any changes made by `display()` will be made directly to the `val` array. As further examples, assume that the following two-dimensional arrays named `test`, `factors`, and `thrusts` are declared as:

```
int test[7][9];
float factors[26][10];
double thrusts[256][52];
```

then the following function calls are valid:

```
find_max(test);
obtain(factors);
average(thrusts);
```

---

[5]An important consequence of this is that `find_max()` has direct access to the passed array. This means that any change to an element of the `vals` array actually is a change to the `nums` array. This is significantly different than the situation with scalar variables, where the called function does not receive direct access to the passed variable.

Program 10.11

```
// this program displays a message
#include <iostream.h>

int find_max(int [], int);    // function prototype

int main()
{
  const int MAXELS = 5;
  int nums[MAXELS] = {2, 18, 1, 27, 16};

  cout << "The maximum value is "
       << find_max(nums, MAXELS) << endl;

  return 0;
}

// find the maximum value
int find_max(int vals[], int num_els)
{
  int i, max = vals[0];

  for (i = 1; i < num_els; i++)
    if (max < vals[i]) max = vals[i];

  return max;
}
```

On the receiving side, the called function must be alerted that a two-dimensional array is being made available. For example, assuming that each of the previous functions returns an integer, suitable function header lines for these functions are:

```
int find_max(int nums[7][9])
int obtain(float values[26][10])
int average(double vals[256][52])
```

In each of these function header lines, the parameter names chosen will be used internal to the function's body. However, these parameter names still refer to the original array created outside the function. Program 10.12 illustrates passing a two-dimensional array into a function that displays the array's values.

Program 10.12

```cpp
#include <iostream.h>
#include <iomanip.h>

const int ROWS = 3;
const int COLS = 4;
void display(int [ROWS][COLS]);     // function prototype

int main()
{
  int val[ROWS][COLS] = {8,16,9,52,
                         3,15,27,6,
                        14,25,2,10};

  display(val);

  return 0;
}

void display(int nums[ROWS][COLS])
{
  int row_num, col_num;
  for (row_num = 0; row_num < ROWS; row_num++)
  {
    for(col_num = 0; col_num < COLS; col_num++)
      cout << setw(4) <<nums[row_num][col_num];
    cout << endl;
  }

  return;
}
```

Only one array is created in Program 10.12. This array is known as val in main() and as nums in display(). Thus, val[0][2] refers to the same element as nums[0][2].

Notice the use of the nested for loop in Program 10.12 for cycling through each array element. In Program 10.12, the variable row_num controls the outer loop and the variable col_num controls the inner loop. For each pass through the outer loop, which corresponds to a single row, the inner loop makes one pass through the column elements. After a complete row is printed, a new line is started for the next row. The effect is a display of the array in a row-by-row fashion:

```
 8  16   9  52
 3  15  27   6
14  25   2  10
```

The parameter declaration for `nums` in `display()` contains extra information that is not required by the function. The declaration for `nums` can omit the row size of the array. Thus, an alternative function prototype is

```
display(int nums[][4]);
```

The reason the column size must be included while the row size is optional becomes obvious when you consider how the array elements are stored in memory. Starting with element `val[0][0]`, each succeeding element is stored consecutively, row by row, as `val[0][0]`, `val[0][1]`, `val[0][2]`, `val[0][3]`, `val[1][0]`, `val[1][1]`, etc., as illustrated in Figure 10.19.

Figure 10.19 Storage of the `val` array.

As with all array accesses, an individual element of the `val` array is obtained by adding an offset to the starting location of the array. For example, element `val[1][3]` of the `val` array illustrated in Figure 10.19 is located at an offset of 14 bytes from the start of the array. Internally, the compiler uses the row index, column index, and column size to determine this offset using the following calculation (again, assuming two bytes for an `int`):

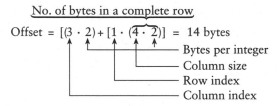

The column size is necessary in the offset calculation so that the compiler can determine the number of positions to skip over in order to get to the desired row.

Exercises 10.5

1. The following declaration was used to create the `volts` array:

```
int volts[500];
```

Write two different function header lines for a function named `sort_arr()` that accepts the `volts` array as a parameter named `in_array`.

2. The following declaration was used to create the `factors` array:

```
float factors[256];
```

Write two different function header lines for a function named `find_key()` that accepts the `factors` array as a parameter named `select`.

3. The following declaration was used to create the `power` array:

```
double power[256];
```

Write two different function header lines for a function named `prime()` that accepts the `power` array as an argument named `rates`.

4. a. Modify the `find_max()` function in Program 10.10 to locate the minimum value of the passed array.
   b. Include the function written in Exercise 4a in a complete program and run the program on a computer.

5. Write a program that has a declaration in `main()` to store the following numbers into an array named temps: 6.5, 7.2, 7.5, 8.3, 8.6, 9.4, 9.6, 9.8, 10.0. There should be a function call to `show()` that accepts the `temps` array as a parameter named `temps` and then displays the numbers in the array.

6. Write a program that declares three single-dimensional arrays named `volts`, `current`, and `resistance`. Each array should be declared in `main()` and should be capable of holding ten double-precision numbers. The numbers that should be stored in `current` are 10.62, 14.89, 13.21, 16.55, 18.62, 9.47, 6.58, 18.32, 12.15, 3.98. The numbers that should be stored in `resistance` are 4, 8.5, 6, 7.35, 9, 15.3, 3, 5.4, 2.9, 4.8. Your program should pass these three arrays to a function named `calc_volts()`, which should calculate the elements in the `volts` array as the product of the corresponding elements in the `current` and `resistance` arrays (for example, `volts[1] = current[1] * resistance[1]`). After `calc_volts()` has put values into the `volts` array, the values in the array should be displayed from within `main()`.

7. Write a program that includes two functions named `calc_avg()` and `variance()`. The `calc_avg()` function should calculate and return the average of the values stored in an array named `testvals`. The array should be declared in `main()` and include the values 89, 95, 72, 83, 99, 54, 86, 75, 92, 73, 79, 75, 82, 73. The `variance()` function should calculate and return the variance of the data. The variance is obtained by subtracting the average from each value in `testvals`, squaring the values obtained, adding them, and dividing by the number of elements in `testvals`. The values returned from `calc_avg()` and variance should be displayed using `cout` statements in `main()`.

10.6 COMMON PROGRAMMING ERRORS

Four common errors are associated with using arrays.

1. Forgetting to declare the array. This error results in a compiler error message equivalent to "invalid indirection" each time a subscripted variable is encountered within a program. The exact meaning of this error message will become clear when the correspondence between arrays and pointers is established in Chapter 11.

2. Using a subscript that references a nonexistent array element. For example, declaring the array to be of size 20 and using a subscript value of 25. This error is not detected by most C++ compilers. It will, however, result in a run-time error that results either in a program crash or a value that has no relation to the intended element being accessed from memory. In either case it is usually an extremely troublesome error to locate. The only solution to this problem is to make sure, either by specific programming statements or by careful coding, that each subscript references a valid array element.

3. Not using a large enough counter value in a `for` loop counter to cycle through all the array elements. This error usually occurs when an array is initially specified to be of size n and there is a `for` loop within the program of the form `for (i = 0; i < n; i++)`. The array size is then expanded but the programmer forgets to change the interior `for` loop parameters. Declaring an array's size using a named constant and consistently using the named constant throughout the function in place of the variable n eliminates this problem.

4. Forgetting to initialize the array. Although many compilers automatically set all elements of integer and real valued arrays to zero, and all elements of character arrays to blanks, it is up to the programmer to ensure that each array is correctly initialized before processing of array elements begins.

10.7 CHAPTER SUMMARY

1. A single-dimensional array is a data structure that can be used to store a list of values of the same data type. Such arrays must be declared by giving the data type of the values that are stored in the array and the array size. For example, the declaration:

```
int num[100];
```

creates an array of 100 integers. A preferable approach is to first use a named constant to set the array size, and then use this constant in the definition of the array. For example,

```
const int MAXSIZE = 100;
```

and

```
int num[MAXSIZE];
```

2. Array elements are stored in contiguous locations in memory and referenced using the array name and a subscript, for example, num[22]. Any nonnegative integer value expression can be used as a subscript and the subscript 0 always refers to the first element in an array.

3. A two-dimensional array is declared by listing both a row and a column size with the data type and name of the array. For example, the declaration

```
int mat[5][7];
```

creates a two-dimensional array consisting of five rows and seven columns of integer values.

4. Arrays may be initialized when they are declared. For two-dimensional arrays this is accomplished by listing the initial values, in a row-by row manner, within braces and separating them with commas. For example, the declaration

```
int vals[3][2] = { {1, 2},
                   {3, 4},
                   {5, 6} };
```

produces the following 3 row by 2 column array:

```
1   2
3   4
5   6
```

As C++ uses the convention that initialization proceeds in rowwise order, the inner braces can be omitted. Thus, an equivalent initialization is provided by the statement:

```
int vals[3][2] = { 1, 2, 3, 4,  5, 6};
```

5. Arrays are passed to a function by passing the name of the array as an argument. The value actually passed is the address of the first array storage location. Thus, the called function receives direct access to the original array and not a copy of the array elements. Within the called function a formal argument must be declared to receive the passed array name. The declaration of the formal argument can omit the row size of the array.

10.8 ◆ CHAPTER APPENDIX: SEARCHING AND SORTING

Most programmers encounter the need to both sort and search a list of data items at some time in their programming careers. For example, experimental results might have to be arranged in either increasing (ascending) or decreasing (descending) order for statistical analysis, lists of names may have to be sorted in alphabetical order, or a list of dates may have to be rearranged in ascending date order. Similarly, a list of names may have to be searched to find a particular name in the list, or a list of dates may have to be searched to locate a particular date. In this section we introduce the fundamentals of both sorting and searching lists. Note that it is not necessary to sort a list before searching it, although, as we shall see, much faster searches are possible if the list is in sorted order.

Search Algorithms

A common requirement of many programs is to search a list for a given element. For example, in a list of names and telephone numbers, we might search for a specific name so that the corresponding telephone number can be printed, or we might wish to search the list simply to determine if a name is there. The two most common methods of performing such searches are the linear and binary search algorithms.

Linear Search

In a **linear search**, which is also known as a **sequential search**, each item in the list is examined in the order in which it occurs in the list until the desired item is found or the end of the list is reached. This is analogous to looking at every name in the phone directory, beginning with Aardvark, Aaron, until you find the one you want or until you reach Zzxgy, Zora. Obviously, this is not the most efficient way to search a long alphabetized list. However, a linear search has these advantages:

1. The algorithm is simple.
2. The list need not be in any particular order.

In a linear search the search begins at the first item in the list and continues sequentially, item by item, through the list. The pseudocode for a function performing a linear search is

> *For all the items in the list*
>   *Compare the item with the desired item*
>   *If the item was found*
>   *Return the index value of the current item*
>   *Endif*
> *EndFor*
> *Return –1 because the item was not found*

Notice that the function's `return` value indicates whether the item was found or not. If the `return` value is –1, the item was not in the list; otherwise, the `return` value within the `for` loop provides the index of where the item is located within the list.

The function linearSearch() illustrates this procedure as a C++ function:

```
// this function returns the location of key in the list
// a -1 is returned if the value is not found
int linearSearch(int list[], int size, int key)
{
  int i;

  for (i = 0; i < size; i++)
  {
    if (list[i] == key)
      return i;
  }

  return -1;
}
```

In reviewing linearSearch() notice that the for loop is simply used to access each element in the list, from first element to last, until a match is found with the desired item. If the desired item is located the index value of the current item is returned, which causes the loop to terminate; otherwise, the search continues until the end of the list is encountered.

To test this function we have written a main() driver function to call it and display the results returned by linearSearch(). The complete test program is illustrated in Program 10.13.

Sample runs of Program 10.13 follow:

```
Enter the item you are searching for: 101
The item was found at index location 9
```

and

```
Enter the item you are searching for: 65
The item was not found in the list
```

As has already been pointed out, an advantage of linear searches is that the list does not have to be in sorted order to perform the search. Another advantage is that if the desired item is toward the front of the list, only a small number of comparisons will be done. The worst case, of course, occurs when the desired item is at the end of the list. On average, however, and assuming that the desired item is equally likely to be anywhere within the list, the number of required comparisons will be $n/2$, where n is the list's size. Thus, for a 10-element list, the average number of comparisons needed for a linear search is 5, and for a 10,000 element list, the average number of comparisons needed is 5000. As we show next, this number can be significantly reduced using a binary search algorithm.

Program 10.13

```cpp
#include <iostream.h>

const int NUMEL = 10;

int linearSearch(int [], int, int);

int main()
{
  int nums[NUMEL] = {5,10,22,32,45,67,73,98,99,101};
  int item, location;


  cout << "Enter the item you are searching for: ";
  cin  >> item;

  location = linearSearch(nums, NUMEL, item);

  if (location > -1)
    cout << "The item was found at index location " << location
         << endl;
  else
    cout << "The item was not found in the list\n";

  return 0;
}

// this function returns the location of key in the list
// a -1 is returned if the value is not found
int linearSearch(int list[], int size, int key)
{
  int i;

  for (i = 0; i < size; i++)
  {
    if (list[i] == key)
      return i;
  }

  return -1;
}
```

Binary Search

In a **binary search** the list must be in sorted order. Starting with an ordered list, the desired item is first compared to the element in the middle of the list (for lists with an even number of elements, either of the two middle elements can be used). Three possibilities present themselves once the comparison is made: the desired item may be equal to the middle element, it may be greater than the middle element, or it may be less than the middle element.

In the first case the search has been successful, and no further searches are required. In the second case, since the desired item is greater than the middle element, if it is found at all it must be in the second half of the list. This means that the first part of the list consisting of all elements from the first to the midpoint element can be discarded from any further search. In the third case, since the desired item is less than the middle element, if it is found at all it must be found in the first part of the list. For this case the second half of the list containing all elements from the midpoint element to the last element can be discarded from any further search.

The algorithm for implementing this search strategy is illustrated in Figure 10.20 and defined by the following pseudocode:

> *Set the lower index to 0*
> *Set the upper index to one less than the size of the list*
> *Begin with the first item in the list*
> *While the lower index is less than or equal to the upper index*
> > *Set the midpoint index to the integer average of the lower and upper index values*
> > *Compare the desired item to the midpoint element*
> > > *If the desired element equals the midpoint element*
> > > > *Return the index value of the current item*
> > > *Else If the desired element is greater than the midpoint element*
> > > > *Set the lower index value to the midpoint value plus 1*
> > > *Else if the desired element is less than the midpoint element*
> > > > *Set the upper index value to the midpoint value less 1*
> > > *Endif*
> > *EndWhile*
> *Return −1 because the item was not found*

As illustrated by both the pseudocode and the flowchart of Figure 10.20, a `while` loop is used to control the search. The initial list is defined by setting the left index value to 0 and the right index value to one less than the number of elements in the list. The midpoint element is then taken as the integerized average of the left and right values. Once the comparison to the midpoint element is made, the search is subsequently restricted by moving either the left index to one integer value above the midpoint, or by moving the right index one integer value below the midpoint. This process is continued until the desired element is found or the left and right index values become equal. The function `binarySearch()` presents the C++ version of this algorithm.

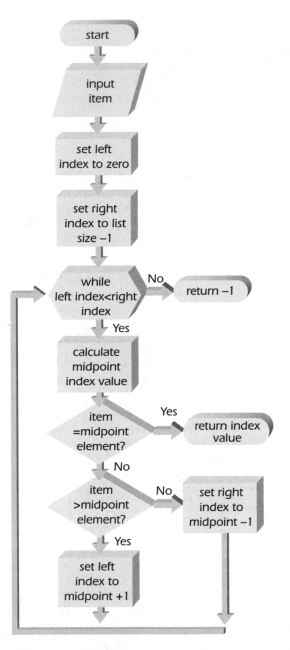

Figure 10.20 The binary search algorithm.

```
// this function returns the location of key in the list
// a -1 is returned if the value is not found
int binarySearch(int list[], int size, int key)
{
  int left, right, midpt;

  left = 0;
  right = size -1;

  while (left <= right)
  {
    midpt = (int) ((left + right) / 2);
    if (key == list[midpt])
    {
      return midpt;
    }
    else if (key > list[midpt])
      left = midpt + 1;
    else
      right = midpt - 1;
  }

  return -1;
}
```

For purposes of testing this function, Program 10-14 is used.

A sample run using Program 10.14 yielded the following:

```
Enter the item you are searching for: 101
The item was found at index location 9
```

The value of using a binary search algorithm is that the number of elements that must be searched is cut in half each time through the `while` loop. Thus, the first time through the loop n elements must be searched; the second time through the loop $n/2$ of the elements have been eliminated and only $n/2$ remain. The third time through the loop another half of the remaining elements has been eliminated, and so on.

In general, after p passes through the loop, the number of values remaining to be searched is $n/(2^p)$. In the worst case the search can continue until there is less than or equal to 1 element remaining to be searched. Mathematically, this can be expressed as $n/(2^p) \leq 1$. Alternatively, this may be rephrased as p is the smallest integer such that $2^p \geq n$. For example, for a 1000 element array, n is 1000 and the maximum number of passes, p, required for a binary search is 10. Table 10.2 compares the number of loop passes needed for a linear and binary search for various list sizes.

Program 10.14

```cpp
#include <iostream.h>

const int NUMEL = 10;
int binarySearch(int [], int, int);

int main()
{
  int nums[NUMEL] = {5,10,22,32,45,67,73,98,99,101};
  int item, location;
  cout << "Enter the item you are searching for: ";
  cin  >> item;
  location = binarySearch(nums, NUMEL, item);
  if (location > -1)
    cout << "The item was found at index location "
         << location << endl;
  else
    cout << "The item was not found in the array\n";

  return 0;
}

// this function returns the location of key in the list
// a -1 is returned if the value is not found
int binarySearch(int list[], int size, int key)
{
  int left, right, midpt;

  left = 0;
  right = size -1;

  while (left <= right)
  {
    midpt = (int) ((left + right) / 2);
    if (key == list[midpt])
    {
      return midpt;
    }
    else if (key > list[midpt])
      left = midpt + 1;
    else
      right = midpt - 1;
  }

  return -1;
}
```

Table 10.2 A Comparison of while Loop Passes for Linear and Binary Searches

Array Size	10	50	500	5000	50,000	500,000	5,000,000	50,000,000
Average Linear Search Passes	5	25	250	2500	25,000	250,000	2,500,000	25,000,000
Maximum Linear Search Passes	10	50	500	5000	50,000	500,000	5,000,000	50,000,000
Maximum Binary Search Passes	4	6	9	13	16	19	23	26

As illustrated, the maximum number of loop passes for a 50 item list is almost 10 times more for a linear search than for binary search, and even more spectacular for larger lists. As a rule of thumb, 50 elements are usually taken as the switch/over point: For lists smaller than 50 elements linear searches are acceptable; for larger lists a binary search algorithm should be used.

Big O Notation

On average, over a large number of linear searches with n items in a list, we would expect to examine half ($n/2$) of the items before locating the desired item. In a binary search the maximum number of passes, p, occurs when $n/(2)^p = 1$. This relationship can be algebraically manipulated to $2^p = n$, which yields $p = \log_2 n$, which approximately equals $3.33 \log_{10} n$.

For example, finding a particular name in an alphabetical directory with $n = 1000$ names would require an average of 500 ($=n/2$) comparisons using a linear search. With a binary search, only about 10 ($\approx 3.33 * \log_{10} 1000$) comparisons would be required.

A common way to express the number of comparisons required in any search algorithm using a list of n items is to give the order of magnitude of the number of comparisons required, on average, to locate a desired item. Thus, the linear search is said to be of order n and the binary search of order $\log_2 n$. Notationally, this is expressed as $O(n)$ and $O(\log_2 n)$, where the O is read as "the order of."

Sort Algorithms

For sorting data, two major categories of sorting techniques exist, called internal and external sorts, respectively. **Internal sorts** are used when the data list is not too large and the complete list can be stored within the computer's memory, usually in an array. **External sorts** are used for much larger data sets that are stored in large external disk or tape files and cannot be accommodated within the computer's memory as a complete unit. Here we present two internal sort algorithms that can be effectively used when sorting lists with less than approximately 50 elements. For larger lists more sophisticated sorting algorithms are typically employed.

Selection Sort

One of the simplest sorting techniques is the selection sort. In a **selection sort** the smallest value is initially selected from the complete list of data and exchanged with the first element in the list. After this first selection and exchange, the next smallest element in the revised list is selected and exchanged with the second element in the list. Since the smallest element is already in the first position in the list, this second pass need only consider the second through last elements. For a list consisting of n elements, this process is repeated $n - 1$ times, with each pass through the list requiring one less comparison than the previous pass.

For example, consider the list of numbers illustrated in Figure 10.21. The first pass through the initial list results in the number 32 being selected and exchanged with the first element in the list. The second pass, made on the reordered list, results in the number 155 being selected from the second through fifth elements. This value is then exchanged with the second element in the list. The third pass selects the number 307 from the third through fifth elements in the list and exchanges this value with the third element. Finally, the fourth and last pass through the list selects the remaining minimum value and exchanges it with the fourth list element. Although each pass in this example resulted in an exchange, no exchange would have been made in a pass if the smallest value were already in the correct location.

initial list	pass 1	pass 2	pass 3	pass 4
690	32	32	32	32
307	307	155	144	144
32	690	690	307	307
155	155	307	690	426
426	426	426	426	690

Figure 10.21 A sample selection sort.

In pseudocode, the selection sort is described as

> *Set interchange count to zero (not required, but done just to keep track of the interchanges)*
> *For each element in the list from first to next-to-last*
>   *Find the smallest element from the current element being referenced to the last element by;*
>   *Setting the minimum value equal to the current element*
>   *Saving (storing) the index of the current element*
>   *For each element in the list from the current element + 1 to the last element in the list*
>   *If element[inner loop index] < minimum value*
>   *Set the minimum value = element[inner loop index]*
>   *Save the index the new found minimum value*
>   *Endif*
>   *EndFor*
>   *Swap the current value with the new minimum value*
>   *Increment the interchange count*
> *EndFor*
> *Return the interchange count*

The function `selection_sort()` incorporates this procedure into a C++ function.

```
int selection_sort(int num[], int numel)
{
  int i, j, min, minidx, temp, moves = 0;

  for ( i = 0; i < (numel - 1); i++)
  {
    min = num[i];    // assume minimum is the first array element
    minidx = i;      // index of minimum element
    for(j = i + 1; j < numel; j++)
    {
      if (num[j] < min)    // if we've located a lower value
      {                    // capture it
      min = num[j];
      minidx = j;
      }
    }
    if (min < num[i])  // check if we have a new minimum
    {                        // and if we do, swap values
      temp = num[i];
      num[i] = min;
      num[minidx] = temp;
      moves++;
    }
  }

  return moves;
}
```

The `selection_sort()` function expects two arguments, the list to be sorted and the number of elements in the list. As specified by the pseudocode, a nested set of `for` loops performs the sort. The outer `for` loop causes one less pass through the list than the total number of data items in the list. For each pass, the variable `min` is initially assigned the value `num[i]`, where `i` is the outer `for` loop's counter variable. Since `i` begins at 0 and ends at one less than `numel`, each element in the list, except the last, is successively designated as the current element.

The inner loop cycles through the elements below the current element and is used to select the next smallest value. Thus, this loop begins at the index value `i + 1` and continues through the end of the list. When a new minimum is found, its value and position in the list are stored in the variables named `min` and `minidx`, respectively. Upon completion of the inner loop, an exchange is made only if a value less than that in the current position was found.

For purposes of testing `selection_sort()`, Program 10.15 was constructed. This program implements a selection sort for the same list of 10 numbers that was previously used to test our search algorithms. For later comparison to the other sorting algorithms that will be presented, the number of actual moves made by the program to get the data into sorted order is counted and displayed.

Program 10.15

```cpp
#include <iostream.h>

int selection_sort(int [], int);

int main()
{
  const int NUMEL = 10;
  int nums[NUMEL] = {22,5,67,98,45,32,101,99,73,10};
  int i, moves;

  moves = selection_sort(nums, NUMEL);

  cout << "The sorted list, in ascending order, is:\n";
  for (i = 0; i < NUMEL; i++)
    cout << "   " <<nums[i];

  cout << '\n' << moves << " moves were made to sort this list\n";

  return 0;
}

int selection_sort(int num[], int numel)
{
  int i, j, min, minidx, temp, moves = 0;

  for ( i = 0; i < (numel - 1); i++)
  {
    min = num[i];    // assume minimum is the first array element
    minidx = i;      // index of minimum element
    for(j = i + 1; j < numel; j++)
    {
      if (num[j] < min)    // if we've located a lower value
      {                    // capture it
      min = num[j];
      minidx = j;
      }
    }
    if (min < num[i])  // check if we have a new minimum
    {                    // and if we do, swap values
      temp = num[i];
      num[i] = min;
      num[minidx] = temp;
      moves++;
    }
  }

  return moves;
}
```

The output produced by Program 10.15 is as follows:

```
The sorted list, in ascending order, is:
  5  10  22  32  45  67  73  98  99  101
8 moves were made to sort this list
```

Clearly, the number of moves displayed depends on the initial order of the values in the list. An advantage of the selection sort is that the maximum number of moves that must be made is $n - 1$, where n is the number of items in the list. Further, each move is a final move that results in an element residing in its final location in the sorted list.

A disadvantage of the selection sort is that $n(n - 1)/2$ comparisons are always required, regardless of the initial arrangement of the data. This number of comparisons is obtained as follows: the last pass always requires one comparison, the next-to-last pass requires two comparisons, and so on, to the first pass, which requires $n - 1$ comparisons. Thus, the total number of comparisons is

$$1 + 2 + 3 + \cdots + n - 1 = n(n - 1)/2 = n^2/2 - n/2.$$

For large values of n the n^2 dominates, and the order of the selection sort is $O(n^2)$.

Exchange (Bubble) Sort

In an **exchange** or **bubble sort** adjacent elements of the list are exchanged with one another in such a manner that the list becomes sorted. One example of such a sequence of exchanges is provided by the bubble sort, where successive values in the list are compared, beginning with the first two elements. If the list is to be sorted in ascending (from smallest to largest) order, the smaller value of the two being compared is always placed before the larger value. For lists sorted in descending (from largest to smallest) order, the smaller of the two values being compared is always placed after the larger value.

For example, assuming that a list of values is to be sorted in ascending order, if the first element in the list is larger than the second, the two elements are interchanged. Then the second and third elements are compared. Again, if the second element is larger than the third, these two elements are interchanged. This process continues until the last two elements have been compared and exchanged, if necessary. If no exchanges were made during this initial pass through the data, the data is in the correct order and the process is finished; otherwise, a second pass is made through the data, starting from the first element and stopping at the next-to-last element. The reason for stopping at the next-to-last element on the second pass is that the first pass always results in the most positive value "sinking" to the bottom of the list.

As a specific example of this process, consider the list of numbers illustrated in Figure 10.22. The first comparison results in the interchange of the first two element values, 690 and 307. The next comparison, between elements two and three in the revised list, results in the interchange of values between the second and third elements, 690 and 32. This comparison and possible switching of adjacent values is continued until the last two elements have been compared and possibly switched. This process completes the first pass through the data and results in the largest number moving to the bottom of the list. As the largest value sinks to its resting place at the bottom of the list, the smaller elements slowly rise, or "bubble," to the top of the list. This bubbling effect of the smaller elements is what gave rise to the name "bubble" sort for this sorting algorithm.

690	307	307	307	307
307	690	32	32	32
32	32	690	155	155
155	155	155	690	426
426	426	426	426	690

Figure 10.22 The first pass of an exchange sort.

Because the first pass through the list ensures that the largest value always moves to the bottom of the list, the second pass stops at the next-to-last element. This process continues with each pass stopping at one higher element than the previous pass, until either $n - 1$ passes through the list have been completed or no exchanges are necessary in any single pass. In both cases the resulting list is in sorted order. The pseudocode describing this sort is

Set interchange count to zero (not required, but done just to keep track of the interchanges)
For the first element in the list to one less than the last element (i index)
  For the second element in the list to the last element (j index)
    If num[j] < num[j – 1]
    {
      Swap num[j] with num[j – 1]
      Increment interchange count
    }
  EndFor
EndFor
Return interchange count

This sort algorithm is coded in C++ as the function `bubble_sort()`, which included within Program 10.16 for testing purposes. This program tests `bubble_sort()` with the same list of 10 numbers used in Program 10.15 to test `selection_sort()`. For comparison to the earlier selection sort, the number of adjacent moves (exchanges) made by `bubble_sort()` is also counted and displayed.

Here is the output produced by Program 10.16.

```
The sorted list, in ascending order, is:
   5   10   22   32   45   67   73   98   99   101
18 moves were made to sort this list
```

As with the selection sort, the number of comparisons using a bubble sort is $O(n^2)$ and the number of required moves depends on the initial order of the values in the list. In the worst case, when the data is in reverse sorted order, the selection sort performs better than the bubble sort. Here both sorts require $n(n - 1)/2$ comparisons, but the selection sort needs only $n - 1$ moves while the bubble sort needs $n(n - 1)/2$ moves. The additional moves required by the bubble sort result from the intermediate exchanges between adjacent elements to "settle" each element into its final position. In this regard the selection sort is superior, because no intermediate moves are necessary. For random data, such as that used in Programs 10.15 and 10.16, the selection sort generally performs equal to or better than the bubble sort.

Program 10.16

```cpp
#include <iostream.h>

int bubble_sort(int [], int);

int main()
{
  const int NUMEL = 10;
  int nums[NUMEL] = {22,5,67,98,45,32,101,99,73,10};
  int i, moves;

  moves = bubble_sort(nums, NUMEL);

  cout << "The sorted list, in ascending order, is:\n";
  for (i = 0; i < NUMEL; ++i)
    cout << "   " <<nums[i];

  cout << '\n' << moves << " were made to sort this list\n";

  return 0;
}

int bubble_sort(int num[], int numel)
{
  int i, j, temp, moves = 0;

  for ( i = 0; i < (numel - 1); i++)
  {
    for(j = 1; j < numel; j++)
    {
      if (num[j] < num[j-1])
      {
      temp = num[j];
      num[j] = num[j-1];
      num[j-1] = temp;
      moves++;
      }
    }
  }

  return moves;
}
```

CHAPTER 11

Pointers

TOPICS

11.1 ADDRESSES AND POINTERS
STORING ADDRESSES
USING ADDRESSES
DECLARING POINTERS
REFERENCES AND POINTERS

11.2 ARRAY NAMES AS POINTERS
DYNAMIC ARRAY ALLOCATION

11.3 POINTER ARITHMETIC
POINTER INITIALIZATION

11.4 PASSING ADDRESSES
PASSING ARRAYS
ADVANCED POINTER NOTATION

11.5 COMMON PROGRAMMING ERRORS

11.6 CHAPTER SUMMARY

One of C++'s advantages is that it allows the programmer access to the addresses of variables used in a program. This permits programmers to directly enter into a computer's inner workings and access its basic storage structure. This gives the C++ programmer capabilities and programming power that is not available in other high-level languages. This is accomplished using a feature called pointers. Although other languages, such as Pascal and FORTRAN 90 also provide pointers, C++ extends this feature by providing pointer arithmetic; that is, pointer values can be added, subtracted, and compared.

Fundamentally, pointers are simply variables that are used to store memory addresses. This chapter presents the basics of declaring pointers, and then provides methods of applying pointer variables to access and use their stored addresses in meaningful ways.

11.1 ADDRESSES AND POINTERS

As we saw in Section 2.4, to display the address of a variable we can use C++'s address operator, &. To determine the address of num, we can use C++'s address operator, &, which means "the address of." When used in a nondeclarative statement, the address operator placed in front of a variable's name refers to the address of the variable.[1] For example, in a nondeclarative statement, &num means *the address of* num, &miles means *the address of* miles, and &foo means *the address of* foo. Program 11.1, which is copy of Program 2.9, uses the address operator to display the address of the variable num.

Program 11.1

```cpp
#include <iostream.h>

int main()
{
  int num;

  num = 22;
  cout << "num = " << num << endl;
  cout << "The address of num = " << &num << endl;

  return 0;
}
```

The output of Program 11.1 is

```
num = 22
The address of num = 0x8f5afff4
```

Figure 11.1 illustrates both the contents and address of the num variable provided by the output of Program 11.1.

---

[1]As we have seen in Chapter 6, when used in declaring reference arguments the ampersand refers to the data type *preceding* it. Thus, both the declarations float& num and float # are read as "num is the address of a float", or more commonly as "num is a reference to a float".

Figure 11.1 *A more complete picture of the variable* num.

As was mentioned in Section 2.4, address information will change depending on what computer is executing the program and how many other programs are currently loaded into memory.

Storing Addresses

Besides displaying the address of a variable, as was done in Program 11.1, we can also store addresses in suitably declared variables. For example, the statement

```
num_addr = &num;
```

stores the address corresponding to the variable num in the variable num_addr, as illustrated in Figure 11.2. Similarly, the statements

```
d = &m;
tab_point = &list;
chr_point = &ch;
```

store the addresses of the variables m, list, and ch in the variables d, tab_point, and chr_point, respectively, as illustrated in Figure 11.3.

Figure 11.2 *Storing num's address into* num_addr.

The variables num_addr, d, tab_point, and chr_point are formally called *pointer variables*, or *pointers* for short. **Pointers** are simply variables that are used to store the addresses of other variables.

Figure 11.3 Storing more addresses.

Using Addresses

To use a stored address, C++ provides us with an *indirection operator*, *. The * symbol, when followed by a pointer (with a space permitted both before and after the *), means *the variable whose address is stored in*. Thus, if num_addr is a pointer (remember that a pointer is a variable that stores an address), *num_addr means *the variable whose address is stored in* num_addr. Similarly, *tab_point means *the variable whose address is stored in* tab_point and *chr_point means *the variable whose address is stored in* chr_point. Figure 11.4 shows the relationship between the address contained in a pointer variable and the variable ultimately addressed.

Figure 11.4 Using a pointer variable.

Although *d literally means *the variable whose address is stored in* d, this is commonly shortened to the statement *the variable pointed to by d*. Similarly, referring to Figure 11.4, *y can be read as *the variable pointed to by y*. The value ultimately obtained, as shown in Figure 11.4, is qqqq.

When using a pointer variable, the value that is finally obtained is always found by first going to the pointer variable (or pointer, for short) for an address. The address contained in the pointer is then used to get the desired contents. Certainly, this is a rather indirect way of getting to the final value and, not unexpectedly, the term indirect addressing is used to describe this procedure.

Because use of a pointer requires the computer to do a double lookup (first the address is retrieved, then the address is used to retrieve the actual data), a worthwhile question is, why would you want to store an address in the first place? The answer to this question rests on the intimate relationship between pointers and arrays and the ability of pointers to create and delete new variable storage locations dynamically, as a program is running. Both of these topics are presented later in this chapter. For now, however, given that each variable has a memory address associated with it, the idea of actually storing an address should not seem overly strange.

Declaring Pointers

Like all variables, pointers must be declared before they can be used to store an address. When we declare a pointer variable, C++ requires that we also specify the type of variable that is pointed to. For example, if the address in the pointer num_addr is the address of an integer, the correct declaration for the pointer is

```
int *num_addr;
```

This declaration is read as *the variable pointed to by* num_addr (from the *num_addr in the declaration) *is an integer*.[2]

Notice that the declaration int *num_addr; specifies two things: first that the variable pointed to by num_addr is an integer, and second that num_addr must be a pointer (because it is used with the indirection operator *). Similarly, if the pointer tab_point points to (contains the address of) a floating-point number and chr_point points to a character variable, the required declarations for these pointers are

```
float *tab_point;
char *chr_point;
```

These two declarations can be read, respectively, as *the variable pointed to by* tab_point *is a* float and *the variable pointed to by* chr_point *is a* char. Because all addresses appear the same, this additional information is needed by the compiler to know how many storage locations to access when it uses the address stored in the pointer. Further examples of pointer declarations are

```
char *inkey;
int *num_pt;
float *dist_addr;
double *nm1Ptr
```

To understand pointer declarations, it is helpful to read them "backwards," starting with the indirection operator, the asterisk, *, and translating it either as *the variable whose address is stored in* or *the variable pointed to by*. Applying this to pointer declarations, the declaration char *inkey;, for example, can be read as either *the variable whose address is stored in* inkey *is a character* or *the variable pointed to by* inkey *is a character*. Both of these statements are frequently shortened to the simpler statement that inkey *points to a character*. Because all three interpretations of the declaration statement are correct, you can select and use whichever description makes more sense to you. We now put this together to construct a program using pointers. Consider Program 11.2.

---

[2]Pointer declarations may also be written in the form *data-type* * *pointer-name;* where a space is placed between the indirection operator symbol and the pointer variable name. This form, however, becomes error prone when multiple pointer variables are declared in the same declaration statement and the asterisk symbol is inadvertently omitted after the first pointer name is declared. For example, the declaration int* num1, num2; declares num1 as a pointer variable and num2 as an integer variable. In order to more easily accomodate multiple pointers in the same declaration and clearly mark a variable as a pointer, we will adhere to the convention that places an asterisk directly in front of each pointer variable name. This possible error rarely occurs with reference declarations because references are almost exclusively used as formal parameters and single declarations of parameters is mandatory.

Program 11.2

```cpp
#include <iostream.h>

int main()
{
  int *num_addr;      // declare a pointer to an int
  int miles, dist;    // declare two integer variables

  dist = 158;         // store the number 158 into dist
  miles = 22;         // store the number 22 into miles
  num_addr = &miles;  // store the 'address of miles' in num_addr

  cout << "The address stored in num_addr is " << num_addr << endl;
  cout << "The value pointed to by num_addr is " << *num_addr << "\n\n";

  num_addr = &dist;   // now store the address of dist in num_addr
  cout << "The address now stored in num_addr is " << num_addr << endl;
  cout << "The value now pointed to by num_addr is " << *num_addr << endl;

  return 0;
}
```

The output of Program 11.2 is:

```
The address stored in num_addr is 0x8f5ffff4
The value pointed to by num_addr is 22

The address now stored in num_addr is 0x8f5ffff2
The value now pointed to by num_addr is 158
```

The only use for Program 11.2 is to help us understand "what gets stored where." Let's review the program to see how the output was produced.

The declaration statement int *num_addr; declares num_addr to be a pointer variable used to store the address of an integer variable. The statement num_addr = &miles; stores the address of the variable miles into the pointer num_addr. The first activation of cout causes this address to be displayed. The second activation of cout in Program 11.2 uses the indirection operator to retrieve and print out *the value pointed to by* num_addr, which is, of course, the value stored in miles.

Because num_addr has been declared as a pointer to an integer variable, we can use this pointer to store the address of any integer variable. The statement num_addr = &dist illustrates this by storing the address of the variable dist in num_addr. The last two cout statements verify the change in num_addr's value and that the new stored address does point to the variable dist. As illustrated in Program 11.2, only addresses should be stored in pointers.

It certainly would have been much simpler if the pointer used in Program 11.2 could have been declared as `pointer num_addr;`. Such a declaration, however, conveys no information as to the storage used by the variable whose address is stored in `num_addr`. This information is essential when the pointer is used with the indirection operator, as it is in the second `cout` statement in Program 11.2. For example, if the address of an integer is stored in `num_addr`, then only two bytes of storage are typically retrieved when the address is used. If the address of a character is stored in `num_addr`, only 1 byte of storage would be retrieved, and a `float` typically requires the retrieval of four bytes of storage. The declaration of a pointer must, therefore, include the type of variable being pointed to. Figure 11.5 illustrates this concept.

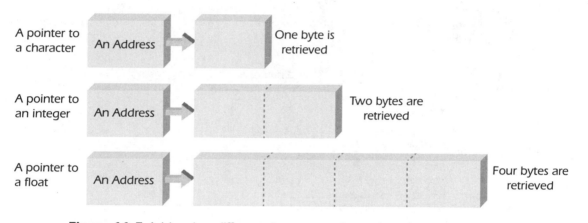

Figure 11.5 *Addressing different data types using pointers.*

References and Pointers

At this point you might be asking what the difference is between a pointer and a reference. Essentially, a reference is a named constant for an address; as such, the address named as a reference cannot be altered. Since a pointer is a variable, the address in the pointer can be changed. For most applications the use of references over pointers as arguments to functions is easier and clearly preferred. This is due to the simpler notation used in locating a reference parameter, which eliminates using the address operator, `&`, and the dereferencing operator, `*`, required for pointers. Technically, references are said to be *automatically dereferenced* or *implicitly dereferenced* (the two terms are used synonymously), while pointers must be explicitly dereferenced to locate the value being accessed.

For example, in passing a scalar variable's address as a function argument, references provide a simpler notational interface and are usually preferred. For other situations, such as dynamically allocating new sections of memory for additional variables as a program is running or using alternatives to array notation (both topics are presented in this chapter), pointers are required.

Reference Variables[3]

References are used almost exclusively as formal function parameters and return types. Nevertheless, reference variables are also available in C++. For completeness we now show how such variables can be declared and used.

Once a variable has been declared it may be given additional names. This is accomplished using a reference declaration, which has the form

data-type& new_name = existing_name;

For example, the reference declaration

```
float& sum = total;
```

equates the name `sum` to the name `total`—both now refer to the same variable, as illustrated in Figure 11.6.

Figure 11.6 `sum` is an alternative name for `total`.

Once another name has been established for a variable using a reference declaration, the new name, which is referred to as an alias, can be used in place of the original name. For example, consider Program 11.3.

The following output is produced by Program 11.3:

```
sum = 20.5
total = 18.6
```

Since the variable `sum` is simply another reference to the variable `total`, it is the value stored in `total` that is obtained by the first `cout` object in Program 11.3. Changing the value in `sum` then changes the value in `total`, which is displayed by the second `cout` object in Program 11.3.

---

[3]This section may be omitted with no loss of subject continuity.

Program 11.3

```
#include <iostream.h>

int main()
{
  float total = 20.5;    // declare and initialize total
  float& sum = total;    // declare another name for total

  cout << "sum = " << sum << endl;
  sum = 18.6;                  // this changes the value in total
  cout << "total = " << total << endl;

  return 0;
}
```

In constructing references, two considerations must be kept in mind. First, the reference should be of the same data type as the variable it refers to. For example, the sequence of declarations

```
        int num = 5;
        double& numref = num;
```

does not equate `numref` to `num`, since they are not the of the same data type. Rather, since the compiler cannot correctly associate the reference with a variable, it creates an unnamed variable of the reference type first, and then references this unnamed variable with the reference variable. Such unnamed variables are called **anonymous variables**. For example, consider Program 11.4, which illustrates the effect of creating an anonymous variable.

The output produced by Program 11.4 is:

```
The value of num is 10
The value of numref is 20.5
```

Notice that the value of num is not affected by the value stored in `numref`. This is because `numref` could not be created as a reference for num; rather, it is another name for an unnamed (anonymous) floating-point variable that can only be reached using the reference name `numref`.

Just as declaring a reference to an incorrect data type produces an anonymous variable, so does equating a reference to a constant. For example, the declaration

```
    int& val = 5;  // an anonymous variable is created
```

creates an anonymous variable with the number 5 stored in it. The only way to access this variable is by the reference name. Clearly, creating references to anonymous variables should be avoided. Once a reference name has been equated to either a legal variable or an anonymous one, the reference cannot be changed to refer to another variable.

Program 11.4

```
#include <iostream.h>

int main()
{
  int num = 10;
  float& numref = num;   // this does not equate numref to num
                         // instead, it equates numref to an
                         // anonymous floating point variable

  numref = 20.5;
  cout << "The value of num is " << num << endl;
  cout << "The value of numref is " << numref << endl;
  return 0;
}
```

As with all declaration statements, multiple references may be declared in a single statement as long as each reference name is preceded by the ampersand symbol. Thus, the declaration

```
float& sum = total, & average;
```

creates two reference variables named sum and average.[4]

Another way of looking at references is to consider them as pointers with restricted capabilities that implicitly hide a lot of dereferencing that is explicitly required with pointers.

For example, consider the statements

```
int b;       // b is an integer variable
int& a = b;  // a is a reference variable that stores b's address
a = 10;      // this changes b's value to 10
```

Here, a is declared as a reference variable that is effectively a named constant for the address of the b variable. Since the compiler knows from the declaration that a is a reference variable, it automatically assigns the address of b (rather than the contents of b) to a in the declaration statement. Finally, in the statement a = 10; the compiler uses the address stored in a to change the value stored in b to 10. The advantage of using the reference is that it automatically performs an indirect access of b's value without the need for explicitly using the indirection symbol, *. As we have noted previously, this type of access is referred to as an *automatic dereference*.

---

[4]Reference declarations may also be written in the form *data-type &new_name=existing name;* where a space is placed between the ampersand symbol and the data-type. This form is not much used, however, probably to distinguish reference variable address notation from that used in assigning addresses to pointer variables.

Implementing this same correspondence between a and b using pointers is done by the following sequence of instructions:

```
int b;        // b is an integer variable
int *a = &b;  // a is a pointer - store b's address in a
*a = 10;      // this changes b's value to 10 by explicit
              // dereference of the address in a
```

Here a is defined as a pointer that is initialized to store the address of b. Thus, *a, which can be read as either "the variable whose address is in a" or "the variable pointed to by a" is b, and the expression *a = 10 changes b's value to 10. Notice that in the pointer case that the stored address can be altered to point to another variable; in the reference case the reference variable cannot be altered to refer to any variable except the one it is initialized to. Also notice that to dereference a, we must explicitly use the indirection operator, *. As you might expect, the * is also referred to as the dereferencing operator.

Exercises 11.1

1. If average is a variable, what does &average mean?

2. For the variables and addresses illustrated in Figure 11.7, determine &temp, &dist, &date, and &miles.

Figure 11.7 Memory bytes for Exercise 2.

3. a. Write a C++ program that includes the following declaration statements. Have the program use the address operator and the cout object to display the addresses corresponding to each variable.

int num, count;
long date;
float slope;
double power;

    b. After running the program written for Exercise 3a, draw a diagram of how your computer has set aside storage for the variables in the program. On your diagram, fill in the addresses displayed by the program.

    c. Modify the program written in Exercise 3a to display the amount of storage your computer reserves for each data type (use the sizeof() operator). With this information and the address information provided in Exercise 3b, determine if your computer set aside storage for the variables in the order in which they were declared.

4. If a variable is declared as a pointer, what must be stored in the variable?

5. Using the indirection operator, write expressions for the following.

    a. The variable pointed to by x_addr
    b. The variable whose address is in y_addr
    c. The variable pointed to by pt_yld
    d. The variable pointed to by pt_miles
    e. The variable pointed to by mptr
    f. The variable whose address is in pdate
    g. The variable pointed to by dist_ptr
    h. The variable pointed to by tab_pt
    i. The variable whose address is in hours_pt

6. Write declaration statements for the following.

    a. The variable pointed to by y_addr is an integer.
    b. The variable pointed to by ch_addr is a character.
    c. The variable pointed to by pt_yr is a long integer.
    d. The variable pointed to by amt is a double-precision variable.
    e. The variable pointed to by z is an integer.
    f. The variable pointed to by qp is a floating-point variable.
    g. date_pt is a pointer to an integer.
    h. yld_addr is a pointer to a double-precision variable.
    i. amt_pt is a pointer to a floating-point variable.
    j. pt_chr is a pointer to a character.

7. a. What are the variables y_addr, ch_addr, pt_yr, amt, z, qp, date_ptr, yld_addr, amt_pt, and pt_chr used in Exercise 6 called?

    b. Why are the variable names amt, z, and qp used in Exercise 6 not good choices for pointer variable names?

8. Write English sentences that describe what is contained in the following declared variables.

   a. `char *key_addr;`
   b. `int *m;`
   c. `double *yld_addr;`
   d. `long *y_ptr;`
   e. `float *p_cou;`
   f. `int *pt_date;`

9. Which of the following are declarations for pointers.

   a. `long a;`
   b. `char b;`
   c. `char *c;`
   d. `int x;`
   e. `int *p;`
   f. `double w;`
   g. `float *k;`
   h. `float l;`
   i. `double *z;`

10. For the following declarations,

    ```
    int *x_pt, *y_addr;
    long *dt_addr, *pt_addr;
    double *pt_z;
    int a;
    long b;
    double c;
    ```

    determine which of the following statements is valid.

    a. `y_addr = &a;` **b.** `y_addr = &b;` **c.** `y_addr = &c;`
    d. `y_addr = a;` **e.** `y_addr = b;` **f.** `y_addr = c;`
    g. `dt_addr = &a;` **h.** `dt_addr = &b;` **i.** `dt_addr = &c;`
    j. `dt_addr = a;` **k.** `dt_addr = b;` **l.** `dt_addr = c;`
    m. `pt_z = &a;` **n.** `pt_addr = &b;` **o.** `pt_addr = &c;`
    p. `pt_addr = a;` **q.** `pt_addr = b;` **r.** `pt_addr = c;`
    s. `y_addr = x_pt;` **t.** `y_addr = dt_addr;` **u.** `y_addr = pt_addr;`

11. For the variables and addresses illustrated in Figure 11.8, fill in the appropriate data as determined by the following statements.

    a. `pt_num = &m;`
    b. `amt_addr = &amt;`
    c. `*z_addr = 25;`
    d. `k = *num_addr;`
    e. `pt_day = z_addr;`
    f. `*pt_yr = 1987;`
    g. `*amt_addr = *num_addr;`

Figure 11.8 Memory locations for Exercise 11.

12. Using the `sizeof()` operator, determine the number of bytes used by your computer to store the address of an integer, character, and double precision number. (*Hint:* `sizeof(*int)` can be used to determine the number of memory bytes used for a pointer to an integer.) Would you expect the size of each address to be the same? Why or why not?

11.2 ARRAY NAMES AS POINTERS

Although pointers are simply, by definition, variables used to store addresses, there is also a direct and intimate relationship between array names and pointers. In this section we describe this relationship in detail.

Figure 11.9 illustrates the storage of a single-dimensional array named `grade`, which contains five integers. Assume that each integer requires two bytes of storage.

Figure 11.9 The `grade` array in storage.

Using subscripts, the fourth element in the `grade` array is referred to as `grade[3]`. The use of a subscript, however, conceals the extensive use of addresses by the computer. Internally, the computer immediately uses the subscript to calculate the address of the desired element based on both the starting address of the array and the amount of storage used by each element. Calling the fourth element `grade[3]` forces the compiler, internally, to make the address computation

$$\&grade[3] = \&grade[0] + (3 * sizeof(int))$$

Remembering that the address operator, `&`, means "the address of," this last statement is read "the address of `grade[3]` equals the address of `grade[0]` plus 6." Figure 11.10 illustrates the address computation used to locate `grade[3]`.

Figure 11.10 Using a subscript to obtain an address.

Recall that a pointer is a variable used to store an address. If we create a pointer to store the address of the first element in the grade array, we can mimic the operation used by the computer to access the array elements. Before we do this, let us first consider Program 11.5.

When Program 11.5 is run, the following display is obtained:

```
Element 0 is 98
Element 1 is 87
Element 2 is 92
Element 3 is 79
Element 4 is 85
```

Program 11.5

```
#include <iostream.h>

int main()
{
  const int ARRAYSIZE = 5;

  int i, grade[ARRAYSIZE] = {98, 87, 92, 79, 85};

  for (i = 0; i < ARRAYSIZE; i++)
    cout << "\nElement " << i << " is " << grade[i];
  cout << endl;

  return 0;
}
```

Program 11.5 displays the values of the array grade using standard subscript notation. Now, let us store the address of array element 0 in a pointer. Then, using the indirection operator, *, we can use the address in the pointer to access each array element. For example, if we store the address of grade[0] into a pointer named g_ptr (using the assignment statement g_ptr = &grade[0];), then, as illustrated in Figure 11.11, the expression *g_ptr, which means "the variable pointed to by g_ptr," references grade[0].

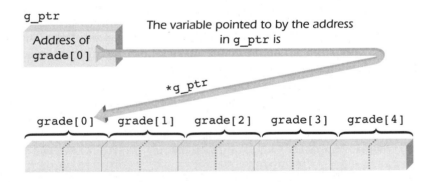

Figure 11.11 The variable pointed to by *g_ptr is grade[0].

One unique feature of pointers is that offsets may be included in expressions using pointers. For example, the 1 in the expression *(g_ptr + 1) is an *offset*. The complete expression references the integer that is one beyond the variable pointed to by g_ptr. Similarly, as illustrated in Figure 11.12, the expression *(g_ptr + 3) references the variable that is three integers beyond the variable pointed to by g_ptr. This is the variable grade[3].

Figure 11.12 An offset of 3 from the address in `g_ptr`.

Table 11.1 lists the complete correspondence between elements referenced by subscripts and by pointers and offsets. The relationships listed in Table 11.1 are illustrated in Figure 11.13.

Table 11.1 Array Elements May Be Referenced in Two Ways

Array Element	Subscript Notation	Pointer Notation
Element 0	`grade[0]`	`*g_ptr`
Element 1	`grade[1]`	`*(g_ptr + 1)`
Element 2	`grade[2]`	`*(g_ptr + 2)`
Element 3	`grade[3]`	`*(g_ptr + 3)`
Element 4	`grade[4]`	`*(g_ptr + 4)`

Figure 11.13 The relationship between array elements and pointers.

Using the correspondence between pointers and subscripts illustrated in Figure 11.13, the array elements previously accessed in Program 11.5 using subscripts can now be accessed using pointers. This is done in Program 11.6.

Program 11.6

```cpp
#include <iostream.h>

int main()
{

  const int ARRAYSIZE = 5;

  int *g_ptr;            // declare a pointer to an int
  int i, grade[ARRAYSIZE] = {98, 87, 92, 79, 85};

  g_ptr = &grade[0];     // store the starting array address
  for (i = 0; i < ARRAYSIZE; i++)
    cout << "\nElement " << i << " is " << *(g_ptr + i);
  cout << endl;

  return 0;
}
```

The following display is obtained when Program 11.6 is run:

```
Element 0 is 98
Element 1 is 87
Element 2 is 92
Element 3 is 79
Element 4 is 85
```

Notice that this is the same display produced by Program 11.5.

The method used in Program 11.6 to access individual array elements simulates how the compiler internally references all array elements. Any subscript used by a programmer is automatically converted to an equivalent pointer expression by the compiler. In our case, since the declaration of g_ptr included the information that integers are pointed to, any offset added to the address in g_ptr is automatically scaled by the size of an integer. Thus, *(g_ptr + 3), for example, refers to the address of grade[0] plus an offset of six bytes (3 * 2), where we have assumed that the sizeof(int) = 2. This is the address of grade[3] illustrated in Figure 11.13.

The parentheses in the expression *(g_ptr + 3) are necessary to correctly reference the desired array element. Omitting the parentheses results in the expression *g_ptr + 3. Due to the precedence of the operators, this expression adds 3 to "the variable pointed to by g_ptr." Since g_ptr points to grade[0], this expression adds the value of grade[0] and 3 together. Note also that the expression *(g_ptr + 3) does not change the address stored in g_ptr. Once the computer uses the offset to locate the correct variable from the starting address in g_ptr, the offset is discarded and the address in g_ptr remains unchanged.

Although the pointer g_ptr used in Program 11.5 was specifically created to store the starting address of the grade array, this was, in fact, unnecessary. When an array is created, the compiler automatically creates an internal pointer constant for it and stores the starting address of the array in this pointer. In almost all respects, a pointer constant is identical to a pointer variable created by a programmer; but, as we shall see, there are some differences.

For each array created, the name of the array becomes the name of the pointer constant created by the compiler for the array, and the starting address of the first location reserved for the array is stored in this pointer. Thus, declaring the grade array in Programs 11.5 and Program 11.6 actually reserved enough storage for five integers, created an internal pointer named grade, and stored the address of grade[0] in the pointer. This is illustrated in Figure 11.14.

Figure 11.14 Creating an array also creates a pointer.

The implication is that every reference to grade using a subscript can be replaced by an equivalent reference using grade as a pointer. Thus, wherever the expression grade[i] is used, the expression *(grade + i) can also be used. This is illustrated in Program 11.7, where grade is used as a pointer to reference all of its elements.

Executing Program 11.7 produces the same output previously produced by Program 11.5 and Program 11.6. However, using grade as a pointer made it unnecessary to declare and initialize the pointer g_ptr used in Program 11.6.

In most respects an array name and pointer can be used interchangeably. *A true pointer, however, is a variable and the address stored in it can be changed. An array name is a pointer constant and the address stored in the pointer cannot be changed by an assignment statement.* Thus, a statement such as grade = &grade[2]; is invalid. This should come as no surprise. Since the whole purpose of an array name is to correctly locate the beginning of the array, allowing a programmer to change the address stored in the array name would defeat this purpose and lead to havoc whenever array elements were referenced. Also, expressions taking the address of an array name are invalid because the pointer created by the compiler is internal to the computer, not stored in memory, as are pointer variables. Thus, trying to store the address of grade using the expression &grade results in a compiler error.

Program 11.7

```
#include <iostream.h>

int main()
{
  const int ARRAYSIZE = 5;

  int i, grade[ARRAYSIZE] = {98, 87, 92, 79, 85};

  for (i = 0; i < ARRAYSIZE; i++)
    cout << "\nElement " << i << " is " << *(grade + i);
  cout << endl;

  return 0;
}
```

An interesting sidelight to the observation that elements of an array can be referenced using pointers is that a pointer reference can always be replaced with a subscript reference. For example, if num_ptr is declared as a pointer variable, the expression *(num_ptr + i) can also be written as num_ptr[i]. This is true even though num_ptr is not created as an array. As before, when the compiler encounters the subscript notation, it replaces it internally with the pointer notation.

Dynamic Array Allocation[5]

As each variable is defined in a program, sufficient storage for it is assigned from a pool of computer memory locations made available to the compiler. Once specific memory locations have been reserved for a variable, these locations are fixed for the life of that variable, whether they are used or not. For example, if a function requests storage for an array of 500 integers, the storage for the array is allocated and fixed from the point of the array's definition. If the application requires less than 500 integers, the unused allocated storage is not released back to the system until the array goes out of existence. If, on the other hand, the application requires more than 500 integers, the size of the integer array must be increased and the function defining the array recompiled.

An alternative to this fixed or static allocation of memory storage locations is the dynamic allocation of memory. Under a **dynamic allocation** scheme, the amount of storage to be allocated is determined and adjusted as the program is run, rather than being fixed at compile time.

The dynamic allocation of memory is extremely useful when dealing with lists, because it allows the list to expand as new items are added and contract as items are deleted. For example, in constructing a list of grades, the exact number of grades ultimately needed may

---

[5]This topic may be omitted on first reading with no loss of subject continuity.

not be known. Rather than creating a fixed array to store the grades, it is extremely useful to have a mechanism whereby the array can be enlarged and shrunk as necessary. Two C++ operators, `new` and `delete`, that provide this capability are described in Table 11.2. (These operators require the `stdlib.h` header file.)

Table 11.2 The `new` and `delete` Operators

Operator Name	Description
new	Reserves the number of bytes requested by the declaration. Returns the address of the first reserved location or NULL if sufficient memory is not available.
delete	Releases a block of bytes previously reserved. The address of the first reserved location is passed as an argument to the function.

Explicit dynamic storage requests for scalar variables or arrays are made either as part of a declaration or assignment statement.[6] For example, the declaration statement `int *num = new int;` reserves an area sufficient to hold one integer and places the address of this storage area into the pointer `num`. This same dynamic allocation can be made by first declaring the pointer using the declaration statement `int *num;` and then subsequently assigning the pointer an address with the assignment statement `num = new int;`. In either case the allocated storage area comes from the computer's free storage area.[7]

In a similar manner and of more usefulness is the dynamic allocation of arrays. For example, the declaration

```
int *grades = new int[200];
```

reserves an area sufficient to store 200 integers and places the address of the first integer into the pointer `grades`. Although we have used the constant 200 in this example declaration, a variable dimension can be used. For example, consider the sequence of instructions

```
cout << "Enter the number of grades to be processed: ";
cin  >> numgrades;
int *grades = new int[numgrades];
```

In this sequence the actual size of the array that is created depends on the number input by the user. Since pointer and array names are related, each value in the newly created storage area can be accessed using standard array notation, such as `grades[i]`, rather than the equivalent pointer notation `*(grades + i)`. Program 11.8 illustrates this sequence of code in the context of a complete program.

---

[6]It should be noted that the compiler automatically provides this dynamic allocation and deallocation from the stack for all auto variables.

[7]The free storage area of a computer is formally referred to as the *heap*. The heap consists of unallocated memory that can be allocated to a program, as requested, while the program is running.

Program 11.8

```cpp
#include <iostream.h>
#include <stdlib.h>

int main()
{
  int numgrades, i;

  cout << "Enter the number of grades to be processed: ";
  cin  >> numgrades;

  int *grades = new int[numgrades];  // create the array

  for(i = 0; i < numgrades; i++)
  {
    cout << "  Enter a grade: ";
    cin  >> grades[i];
  }
  cout << "\nAn array was created for " << numgrades << "integers\n";
  cout << " The values stored in the array are:";
  for (i = 0; i < numgrades; i++)
    cout << "\n    " << grades[i];
  cout << endl;

  delete grades;    // return the storage to the heap

  return 0;
}
```

Notice in Program 11.8 that the `delete` operator has been used to restore the allocated block of storage back to the operating system while the programming is executing.[8] The only address required by `delete` is the starting address of the block of storage that was dynamically allocated. Thus, any address returned by `new` can subsequently be used by delete to restore the reserved memory back to the computer. The delete operator does not

---

[8]The allocated storage should automatically be returned to the heap, by the operating system, when the program has completed execution. Since this is not always the case, however, it is extremely important to formally restore dynamically allocated memory to the heap when the storage is no longer needed. The term **memory leak** is used to describe the condition that occurs when dynamically allocated memory is not formally returned using the delete operator and the operating system does not reclaim the allocated memory area.

alter the address passed to it, but simply removes the storage that the address references. Following is a sample run using Program 11.8:

```
Enter the number of grades to be processed: 4
   Enter a grade: 85
   Enter a grade: 96
   Enter a grade: 77
   Enter a grade: 92


An array was created for 4 integers
 The values stored in the array are:
    85
    96
    77
    92
```

Exercises 11.2

1. Replace each of the following references to a subscripted variable with a pointer reference.

   a. prices[5]   **b.** grades[2]   **c.** yield[10]
   d. dist[9]   **e.** mile[0]   **f.** temp[20]
   g. celsius[16]   **h.** num[50]   **i.** time[12]

2. Replace each of the following references using a pointer with a subscript reference.

   a. *(message + 6) **b.** *amount   **c.** *(yrs + 10)
   d. *(stocks + 2)   **e.** *(rates + 15) **f.** *(codes + 19)

3. **a.** List the three things that the declaration statement double slopes[5]; causes the compiler to do.
   b. If each double-precision number uses eight bytes of storage, how much storage is set aside for the slopes array?
   c. Draw a diagram similar to Figure 11.14 for the slopes array.
   d. Determine the byte offset relative to the start of the slopes array, corresponding to the offset in the expression *(slopes + 3).

4. Write a declaration to store the following values into an array named rates: 12.9, 18.6, 11.4, 13.7, 9.5, 15.2, 17.6. Include the declaration in a program that displays the values in the array using pointer notation.

11.3 POINTER ARITHMETIC

Pointer variables, like all variables, contain values. The value stored in a pointer is, of course, an address. Thus, by adding and subtracting numbers to pointers we can obtain different addresses. Additionally, the addresses in pointers can be compared using any of the relational operators (==, !=, < , >, etc.) that are valid for comparing other variables.

In performing arithmetic on pointers we must be careful to produce addresses that point to something meaningful. In comparing pointers we must also make comparisons that make sense. Consider the declarations:

```
int nums[100];
int *n_pt;
```

To set the address of nums[0] into n_pt, either of the following two assignment statements can be used:

```
n_pt = &nums[0];
n_pt = nums;
```

The two assignment statements produce the same result because nums is a pointer constant that itself contains the address of the first location in the array. This is, of course, the address of nums[0]. Figure 11.15 illustrates the allocation of memory resulting from the previous declaration and assignment statements, assuming that each integer requires two bytes of memory and that the location of the beginning of the nums array is at address 18934.

Figure 11.15 The nums array in memory.

Once n_pt contains a valid address, values can be added and subtracted from the address to produce new addresses. When adding or subtracting numbers to pointers, the computer automatically adjusts the number to ensure that the result still "points to" a value of the correct type. For example, the statement n_pt = n_pt + 4; forces the computer to scale the 4 by the correct number to ensure that the resulting address is the address of an integer. Assuming that each integer requires two bytes of storage, as illustrated in Figure 11.15, the computer multiplies the 4 by two and adds eight to the address in n_pt. The resulting address is 18942, which is the correct address of nums[4].

This automatic scaling by the computer ensures that the expression n_pt + i, where i is any positive integer, correctly points to the ith element beyond the one currently being pointed to by n_pt. Thus, if n_pt initially contains the address of nums[0], n_pt + 4 is the address of nums[4], n_pt + 50 is the address of nums[50], and n_pt + i is the address of nums[i]. Although we have used actual addresses in Figure 11.15 to illustrate the scaling process, the programmer need never know or care about the actual addresses used by the computer. The manipulation of addresses using pointers generally does not require knowledge of the actual address.

Addresses can also be incremented or decremented using both prefix and postfix increment and decrement operators. Adding one to a pointer causes the pointer to point to the next element of the type being pointed to. Decrementing a pointer causes the pointer to point to the previous element. For example, if the pointer variable p is a pointer to an integer, the expression p++ causes the address in the pointer to be incremented to point to the next integer. This is illustrated in Figure 11.16.

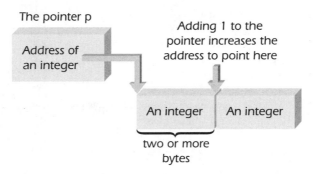

Figure 11.16 *Increments are scaled when used with pointers.*

In reviewing Figure 11.16, notice that the increment added to the pointer is correctly scaled to account for the fact that the pointer is used to point to integers. It is, of course, up to the programmer to ensure that the correct type of data is stored in the new address contained in the pointer.

The increment and decrement operators can be applied as both prefix and postfix pointer operators. All of the following combinations using pointers are valid:

```
*pt_num++    // use the pointer and then increment it
*++pt_num    // increment the pointer before using it
*pt_num--    // use the pointer and then decrement it
*--pt_num    // decrement the pointer before using it
```

Of the four possible forms, the most commonly used is the form *pt_num++. This is because such an expression allows each element in an array to be accessed as the address is "marched along" from the starting address of the array to the address of the last array element. The use of the increment operator is shown in Program 11.9. In this program each element in the nums array is retrieved by successively incrementing the address in n_pt.

The output produced by Program 11.9 is:

```
The total of the array elements is 115
```

The expression total = total + *n_pt++ used in Program 11.9 accumulates the values "pointed to" by the n_pt pointer variable. Within this expression, the term *n_pt++ first causes the computer to retrieve the integer pointed to by n_pt. This is done by the *n_pt part of the term. The postfix increment, ++, then adds one to the address in n_pt so that n_pt now contains the address of the next array element. The increment is, of course, scaled by the computer so that the actual address in n_pt is the correct address of the next element.

Program 11.9

```
#include <iostream.h>

int main()
{
  const int NUMS = 5;

  int nums[NUMS] = {16, 54, 7, 43, -5};
  int i, total = 0, *n_pt;

  n_pt = nums;     // store address of nums[0] in n_pt
  for (i = 0; i < NUMS; i++)
    total = total + *n_pt++;
  cout << "The total of the array elements is " << total << endl;

  return 0;
}
```

Pointers may also be compared. This is particularly useful when dealing with pointers that point to elements in the same array. For example, rather than using a counter in a `for` loop to access each element in an array correctly, the address in a pointer can be compared to the starting and ending address of the array itself. The expression

> `n_pt <= &nums[4]`

is true (nonzero) as long as the address in `n_pt` is less than or equal to the address of `nums[4]`. Since `nums` is a pointer constant that contains the address of `nums[0]`, the term `&nums[4]` can be replaced by the equivalent term `nums + 4`. Using either of these forms, Program 11.9 can be rewritten in Program 11.10 to continue adding array elements while the address in `n_pt` is less than or equal to the address of the last array element.

In Program 11.10 the compact form of the accumulating expression, `total += *n_pt++`, was used in place of the longer form, `total = total + *n_pt++`. Also, the expression `nums + 4` does not change the address in `nums`. Since `nums` is an array name and not a pointer variable, its value cannot be changed. The expression `nums + 4` first retrieves the address in `nums`, adds 4 to this address (appropriately scaled) and uses the result for comparison purposes. Expressions such as `*nums++`, which attempt to change the address, are invalid. Expressions such as `*nums` or `*(nums + i)`, which use the address without attempting to alter it, are valid.

Program 11.10

```
#include <iostream.h>

int main()
{
  const int NUMS = 5;

  int nums[NUMS] = {16, 54, 7, 43, -5};
  int total = 0, *n_pt;

  n_pt = nums;     // store address of nums[0] in n_pt
  while (n_pt < nums + NUMS)
    total += *n_pt++;
  cout << "The total of the array elements is " << total << endl;

  return 0;
}
```

Pointer Initialization

Like all variables, pointers can be initialized when they are declared. When initializing pointers, however, you must be careful to set an address in the pointer. For example, an initialization such as

```
int *pt_num = &miles;
```

is only valid if `miles` itself is declared as an integer variable before `pt_num` is. Here we are creating a pointer to an integer and setting the address in the pointer to the address of an integer variable. If the variable `miles` is declared after `pt_num` is declared, as follows,

```
int *pt_num = &miles;
int miles;
```

an error occurs. This is because the address of `miles` is used before `miles` has even been defined. Since the storage area reserved for `miles` has not been allocated when `pt_num` is declared, the address of `miles` does not yet exist.

Pointers to arrays can be initialized within their declaration statements. For example, if `volts` has been declared an array of floating-point numbers, either of the following two declarations can be used to initialize the pointer named `zing` to the address of the first element in `volts`:

```
float *zing = &volts[0];
float *zing = volts;
```

The last initialization is correct because `volts` is itself a pointer constant containing an address of the proper type. (The variable name `zing` was selected in this example to reinforce the idea that any variable name can be selected for a pointer.)

Exercises 11.3

1. Replace the `while` statement in Program 11.10 with a `for` statement.

2. **a.** Write a program that stores the following numbers in the array named `rates`: 6.25, 6.50, 6.8, 7.2, 7.35, 7.5, 7.65, 7.8, 8.2, 8.4, 8.6, 8.8, 9.0. Display the values in the array by changing the address in a pointer called `disp_pt`. Use a `for` statement in your program.
   b. Modify the program written in Exercise 2a to use a `while` statement.

3. Write a program that stores the following numbers in the array named `miles`: 15, 22, 16, 18, 27, 23, 20. Have your program copy the data stored in `miles` to another array named `dist` and then display the values in the `dist` array. Have your program use pointer rotation when copying and displaying array elements.

4. Write a program that declares three single-dimensional arrays named `miles`, `gallons,` and `mpg`. Each array should be capable of holding ten elements. In the miles array store the numbers 240.5, 300.0, 189.6, 310.6, 280.7, 216.9, 199.4, 160.3, 177.4, 192.3. In the gallons array store the numbers 10.3, 15.6, 8.7, 14, 16.3, 15.7, 14.9, 10.7, 8.3, 8.4. Each element of the `mpg` array should be calculated as the corresponding element of the `miles` array divided by the equivalent element of the `gallons` array: for example, `mpg[0]` = `miles[0]` / `gallons[0]`. Use pointers when calculating and displaying the elements of the `mpg` array.

5. Define an array of ten pointers to floating-point numbers. Then read ten numbers into the individual locations referenced by the pointers. Now add all of the numbers and store the result in a pointer-referenced location. Display the contents of all of the locations.

11.4 ▷ PASSING ADDRESSES

We have already seen one method of passing addresses to a function. This was accomplished using reference variables, as was described in Section 6.3. Although passing reference variables to a function provides the function with the address of the passed variables, it is an implied use of addresses because the function call does not reveal the fact that reference variables are being used. For example, the function call `swap(num1, num2);` does not reveal whether num1 or num2 is a reference variable. Only by looking at the declaration for these variables or by examining the function header line for `swap()` are the data types of num1 and num2 revealed.

In contrast to implicitly passing addresses using reference variables, addresses can be explicitly passed using pointer variables. Let us see how this is accomplished.

To explicitly pass an address to a function all that needs to be done is to place the address of operator, `&`, in front of the variable being passed. For example, the function call

```
swap(&firstnum, &secnum);
```

passes the addresses of the variables `firstnum` and `secnum` to `swap()`, as illustrated in Figure 11.17. Explicitly passing addresses using the address operator effectively is a *pass by reference* because the called function can reference, or access, variables in the calling function using the passed addresses. As we saw in Section 6.3 calls by reference are also accomplished using reference variables. Here we will use the passed addresses and pointers to directly access the variables `firstnum` and `secnum` from within `swap()` and exchange their values—a procedure that was previously accomplished in Program 6.8 using reference variables.

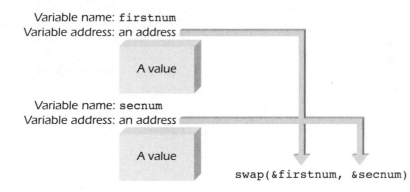

Figure 11.17 Explicitly passing addresses to `swap()`.

One of the first requirements in writing `swap()` is to construct a function header line that correctly receives and stores the passed values, which in this case are two addresses. As we saw in Section 11.1, addresses are stored in pointers, which means that the parameters of `swap()` must be declared as pointers.

Assuming that `firstnum` and `secnum` are double-precision variables, and that `swap()` returns no value, a suitable function header line for `swap` is

```
void swap(double *nm1_addr, double *nm2_addr)
```

The choice of the parameter names `nm1_addr` and `nm2_addr` is, as with all parameter names, up to the programmer. The declaration `double *nm1_addr`, however, declares that the parameter named `nm1_addr` will be used to store the address of a double-precision value. Similarly, the declaration `double *nm2_addr` declares that `nm2_addr` will also store the address of a double-precision value.

Before writing the body of `swap()` to exchange the values in `firstnum` and `secnum`, let's first check that the values accessed using the addresses in `nm1_addr` and `nm2_addr` are correct. This is done in Program 11.11.

The output displayed when Program 11.11 is run is

```
The number whose address is in nm1_addr is 20.5
The number whose address is in nm2_addr is 6.25
```

Program 11.11

```cpp
#include <iostream.h>

void swap(double *, double *);        // function prototype

int main()
{
  double firstnum = 20.5, secnum = 6.25;

  swap(&firstnum, &secnum);                 // call swap

  return 0;
}

// this function illustrates passing pointer arguments
void swap(double *nm1_addr, double *nm2_addr)
{

  cout << "The number whose address is in nm1_addr is "
      << *nm1_addr << endl;
  cout << "The number whose address is in nm2_addr is "
      << *nm2_addr << endl;

  return;
}
```

In reviewing Program 11.11, note two things. First, the function prototype for swap()

```cpp
void swap(double *, double *)
```

declares that swap() returns no value directly and that it's parameters are two pointers that "point to" double-precision values. As such, when the function is called it will require that two addresses be passed, and that each address is the address of a double-precision value.

The second item to notice is that within swap() the indirection operator is used to access the values stored in firstnum and secnum. The function swap() itself has no knowledge of these variable names, but it does have the address of firstnum stored in nm1_addr and the address of secnum stored in nm2_addr. The expression *nm1_addr used in the first cout statement means "the variable whose address is in nm1_addr." This is of course the variable firstnum. Similarly, the second cout statement obtains the value stored in secnum as "the variable whose address is in nm2_addr." Thus, we have successfully used pointers to allow swap() to access variables in main(). Figure 11.18 illustrates the concept of storing addresses in parameters.

Figure 11.18 *Storing addresses in parameters.*

Having verified that `swap()` can access `main()`'s local variables `firstnum` and `secnum`, we can now expand `swap()` to exchange the values in these variables. The values in `main()`'s variables `firstnum` and `secnum` can be interchanged from within `swap()` using the three-step interchange algorithm previously described in Section 6.3, which for convenience is relisted below:

1. Store `firstnum`'s value in a temporary location.

2. Store `secnum`'s value in `firstnum`.

3. Store the temporary value in `secnum`.

Using pointers from within `swap()`, this takes the form:

1. Store the value of the variable pointed to by `nm1_addr` in a temporary location. The statement `temp = *nm1_addr;` does this (see Figure 11.19).

2. Store the value of the variable whose address is in `nm2_addr` in the variable whose address is in `nm1_addr`. The statement `*nm1_addr = *nm2_addr;` does this (see Figure 11.20).

3. Move the value in the temporary location into the variable whose address is in `nm2_addr`. The statement `*nm2_addr = temp;` does this (see Figure 11.21).

Figure 11.19 *Indirectly storing* `firstnum`*'s value.*

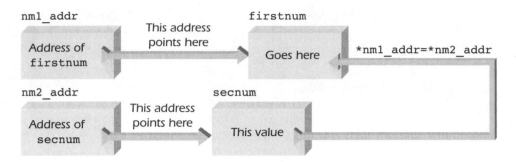

Figure 11.20 Indirectly changing `firstnum`'s value.

Figure 11.21 Indirectly changing `secnum`'s value.

Program 11.12 contains the final form of `swap()`, written according to our description. The following sample run was obtained using Program 11.12:

```
The value stored in firstnum is: 20.5
The value stored in secnum is: 6.25

The value stored in firstnum is now: 6.25
The value stored in secnum is now: 20.5
```

As illustrated in this output, the values stored in `main()`'s variables have been modified from within `swap()`, which was made possible by the use of pointers. The interested reader should compare this version of `swap()` with the version using references that was presented in Program 6.10. The advantage of using pointers in preference to references is that the function call itself explicitly designates that addresses are being used, which is a direct alert that the function will most likely alter variables of the calling function. The advantages of using references is that the notation is much simpler.

Generally, for functions such as `swap()`, the notational convenience wins out, and references are used. In passing arrays to functions, however, which is our next topic, the compiler automatically passes an address. This dictates that pointer variables will be used to store the address.

Program 11.12

```cpp
#include <iostream.h>

void swap(double *, double *);       // function prototype

int main()
{
  double firstnum = 20.5, secnum = 6.25;


  cout << "The value stored in firstnum is: " << firstnum << endl;
  cout << "The value stored in secnum is: " << secnum << "\n\n";

  swap(&firstnum, &secnum);           // call swap

  cout << "The value stored in firstnum is now: "
       << firstnum <<  endl;
  cout << "The value stored in secnum is now: "
       << secnum << endl;

  return 0;
}

// this function swaps the values in its two arguments
void swap(double *nm1_addr, double *nm2_addr)
{
  double temp;

  temp = *nm1_addr;             // save firstnum's value
  *nm1_addr = *nm2_addr;        // move secnum's value in firstnum
  *nm2_addr = temp;            // change secnum's value

  return;
}
```

Passing Arrays

When an array is passed to a function, its address is the only item actually passed. By this we mean the address of the first location used to store the array, as illustrated in Figure 11.22. Since the first location reserved for an array corresponds to element 0 of the array, the "address of the array" is also the address of element 0.

The address of the first location is passed as an argument

Figure 11.22 The address of an array is the address of the first location reserved for the array.

For a specific example in which an array is passed to a function, consider Program 11.13. In this program, the `nums` array is passed to the `find_max()` function using conventional array notation.

Program 11.13

```
#include <iostream.h>

int find_max(int [], int);     // function prototype

int main()
{
  const int NUMPTS = 5;

  int nums[NUMPTS] = {2, 18, 1, 27, 16};

  cout << "\nThe maximum value is "
       << find_max(nums,NUMPTS) << endl;
  return0;
}
// this function returns the maximum value in an array of ints
int find_max(int vals[], int num_els)
{
  int i, max = vals[0];

  for (i = 1; i < num_els; i++)
   if (max < vals[i])
     max = vals[i];

  return max;
}
```

The output displayed when Program 11.13 is executed is

```
The maximum value is 27
```

The parameter named `vals` in the header line declaration for `find_max()` actually receives the address of the array `nums`. As such, `vals` is really a pointer, since pointers are variables (or parameters) used to store addresses. Since the address passed into `find_max()` is the address of an integer, another suitable header line for `find_max()` is

```
int find_max(int *vals, int num_els) // here vals is declared as
                                     // a pointer to an integer
```

The declaration `int *vals` in the header line declares that `vals` is used to store an address of an integer. The address stored is, of course, the location of the beginning of an array. The following is a rewritten version of the `find_max()` function that uses the new pointer declaration for `vals`, but retains the use of subscripts to refer to individual array elements:

```
int find_max(int *vals, int num_els)    // find the maximum value
{
  int i, max = vals[0];

  for (i = 1; i < num_els; i++)
   if (max < vals[i])
     max = vals[i];

  return max;
}
```

Regardless of how `vals` is declared in the function header or how it is used within the function body, it is truly a pointer variable. Thus, the address in `vals` may be modified. This is not true for the name `nums`. Since `nums` is the name of the originally created array, it is a pointer constant. As described in Section 11.2, this means that the address in `nums` cannot be changed and that the address of `nums` itself cannot be taken. No such restrictions, however, apply to the pointer variable named `vals`. All the address arithmetic that we learned in the previous section can be legitimately applied to `vals`.

We shall write two additional versions of `find_max()`, both using pointers instead of subscripts. In the first version we simply substitute pointer notation for subscript notation. In the second version we use address arithmetic to change the address in the pointer.

As previously stated, access to an array element using the subscript notation `array_name[i]` can always be replaced by the pointer notation `*(array_name + i)`. In our first modification to `find_max()`, we make use of this correspondence by simply replacing all references to `vals[i]` with the equivalent expression `*(vals + i)`.

```
int find_max(int *vals, int num_els)    // find the maximum value
{
  int i, max = *vals;

  for (i = 1; i < num_els; i++)
   if (max < *(vals + i) )
     max = *(vals + i);

  return max;
}
```

Our next version of `find_max()` makes use of the fact that the address stored in `vals` can be changed. After each array element is retrieved using the address in `vals`, the address itself is incremented by one in the altering list of the `for` statement. The expression `max = *vals` previously used to set `max` to the value of `vals[0]` is replaced by the expression `max = *vals++`, which adjusts the address in `vals` to point to the second element in the array. The element assigned to `max` by this expression is the array element pointed to by `vals` before `vals` is incremented. The postfix increment, `++`, does not change the address in `vals` until after the address has been used to retrieve the array element.

```
int find_max(int *vals, int num_els)    // find the maximum value
{
  int i, max = *vals++;    // get the first element and increment
  for (i = 1; i < num_els; i++, vals++)
  {
    if (max < *vals)
      max = *vals;
  }
  return max;
}
```

Let us review this version of `find_max()`. Initially the maximum value is set to "the thing pointed to by `vals`." Since `vals` initially contains the address of the first element in the array passed to `find_max()`, the value of this first element is stored in `max`. The address in `vals` is then incremented by one. The one that is added to `vals` is automatically scaled by the number of bytes used to store integers. Thus, after the increment, the address stored in `vals` is the address of the next array element. This is illustrated in Figure 11.23. The value of this next element is compared to the maximum and the address is again incremented, this time from within the altering list of the `for` statement. This process continues until all the array elements have been examined.

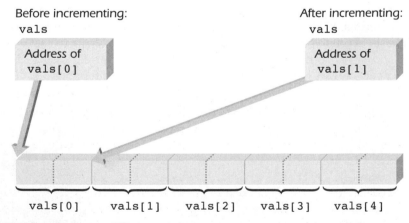

Figure 11.23 Pointing to different elements.

The version of find_max() that you should choose is a matter of personal style and taste. Generally, beginning programmers feel more at ease using subscripts rather than using pointers. Also, if the program uses an array as the natural storage structure for the application and data at hand, an array access using subscripts is more appropriate to clearly indicate the intent of the program. However, as we learn about data structures, the use of pointers becomes an increasingly useful and powerful tool in its own right. In these instances there is no simple or easy equivalence to the use of subscripts.

One further "neat trick" can be gleaned from our discussion. Since passing an array to a function really involves passing an address, we can just as well pass any valid address. For example, the function call find_max(&nums[2],3) passes the address of nums[2] to find_max(). Within find_max() the pointer vals stores the address and the function starts the search for a maximum at the element corresponding to this address. Thus, from find_max()'s perspective, it has received an address and proceeds appropriately.

Advanced Pointer Notation[9]

Access to multidimensional arrays can also be made using pointer notation, although the notation becomes more and more cryptic as the array dimensions increase. An extremely useful application of this notation occurs with two-dimensional character arrays. Here we consider pointer notation for two-dimensional numeric arrays. For example, consider the declaration

```
int nums[2][3] = { {16,18,20},
                   {25,26,27} };
```

This declaration creates an array of elements and a set of pointer constants named nums, nums[0], and nums[1]. The relationship between these pointer constants and the elements of the nums array are illustrated in Figure 11.24.

Figure 11.24 Storage of the nums array and associated pointer constants.

The availability of the pointer constants associated with a two-dimensional array allows us to access array elements in a variety of ways. One way is to consider the two-dimensional array as an array of rows, where each row is itself an array of three elements. Considered in this light, the address of the first element in the first row is provided by nums[0] and the address of the first element in the second row is provided by nums[1]. Thus, the variable pointed to by nums[0] is nums[0][0] and the variable pointed to

---

[9]This topic may be omitted with no loss of subject continuity.

by nums[1] is nums[1][0]. Once the nature of these constants is understood, each element in the array can be accessed by applying an appropriate offset to the appropriate pointer. Thus, the following notations are equivalent:

Pointer Notation	Subscript Notation	Value
*nums[0]	nums[0][0]	16
*(nums[0] + 1)	nums[0][1]	18
*(nums[0] + 2)	nums[0][2]	20
*nums[1]	nums[1][0]	25
*(nums[1] + 1)	nums[1][1]	26
*(nums[1] + 2)	nums[1][2]	27

We can now go even further and replace nums[0] and nums[1] with their respective pointer notations, using the address of nums itself. As illustrated in Figure 11.24, the variable pointed to by nums is nums[0]. That is, *nums is nums[0]. Similarly, *(nums + 1) is nums[1]. Using these relationships leads to the following equivalences:

Pointer Notation	Subscript Notation	Value
*(*nums)	nums[0][0]	16
*(*nums + 1)	nums[0][1]	18
*(*nums + 2)	nums[0][2]	20
((nums + 1))	nums[1][0]	25
((nums + 1) + 1)	nums[1][1]	26
((nums + 1) + 2)	nums[1][2]	27

The same notation applies when a two-dimensional array is passed to a function. For example, assume that the two-dimensional array nums is passed to the function calc() using the call calc(nums);. Here, as with all array passes, an address is passed. A suitable function header line for the function calc() is

```
calc(int pt[2][3])
```

As we have already seen, the parameter declaration for pt can also be

```
calc(int pt[][3])
```

Using pointer notation, another suitable declaration is

```
calc(int (*pt)[3])
```

In this last declaration the inner parentheses are required to create a single pointer to objects of three integers. Each object is, of course, equivalent to a single row of the `nums` array. By suitably offsetting the pointer, each element in the array can be accessed. Notice that without the parentheses the declaration becomes

```
int *pt[3]
```

which creates an array of three pointers, each one pointing to a single integer.

Once the correct declaration for `pt` is made (any of the three valid declarations can be used), the following notations within the function `calc()` are all equivalent:

Pointer Notation	Subscript Notation	Value
`*(*pt)`	`pt[0][0]`	16
`*(*pt+1)`	`pt[0][1]`	18
`*(*pt+2)`	`pt[0][2]`	20
`*(*(pt+1))`	`pt[1][0]`	25
`*(*(pt+1)+1)`	`pt[1][1]`	26
`*(*(pt+1)+2)`	`pt[1][2]`	27

The last two notations using pointers are encountered in more advanced C++ programs. The first of these occurs because functions can return any valid C++ scalar data type, including pointers to any of these data types. If a function returns a pointer, the data type being pointed to must be declared in the function's declaration. For example, the declaration

```
int *calc()
```

declares that `calc()` returns a pointer to an integer value. This means that an address of an integer variable is returned. Similarly, the declaration

```
float *taxes()
```

declares that `taxes()` returns a pointer to a floating-point value. This means that an address of a floating-point variable is returned.

In addition to declaring pointers to integers, floating-point numbers, and C++'s other data types, pointers can also be declared that point to (contain the address of) a function. Pointers to functions are possible because function names, like array names, are themselves pointer constants. For example, the declaration

```
int (*calc)()
```

declares `calc()` to be a pointer to a function that returns an integer. This means that `calc` will contain the address of a function, and the function whose address is in the variable `calc` returns an integer value. If, for example, the function `sum()` returns an integer, the assignment `calc = sum;` is valid.

Exercises 11.4

1. The following declaration was used to create the prices array:

   ```
   double prices[500];
   ```

   Write three different headers for a function named sort_arr() that accepts the prices array as a parameter named in_array and returns no value.

2. The following declaration was used to create the keys array:

   ```
   char keys[256];
   ```

   Write three different headers for a function named find_key() that accepts the keys array as a parameter named select and returns no value.

3. The following declaration was used to create the rates array:

   ```
   float rates[256];
   ```

   Write three different headers for a function named maximum() that accepts the rates array as a parameter named speed and returns a floating-point value.

4. Modify the find_max() function to locate the minimum value of the passed array. Write the function using only pointers.

5. In the last version of find_max() presented, vals was incremented inside the altering list of the for statement. Instead, suppose that we do the incrementing within the condition expression of the if statement as follows:

```
int find_max(int *vals, int num_els)     // incorrect version
{
  int i, max = *vals++;    // get the first element and increment

  for (i = 1; i < num_els; i++)
    if (max < *vals++)
      max = *vals;
  return (max);
}
```

   This version produces an incorrect result. Determine why.

6. **a.** Write a program that has a declaration in main to store the following numbers into an array named rates: 6.5, 7.2, 7.5, 8.3, 8.6, 9.4, 9.6, 9.8, 10.0. There should be a function call to show() that accepts rates in a parameter named rates and then displays the numbers using the pointer notation *(rates + i).

   b. Modify the show() function written in Exercise 6a to alter the address in rates. Always use the expression *rates rather than *(rates + i) to retrieve the correct element.

7. a. Determine the output of the following program:

```cpp
#include <iostream.h>

const int ROWS = 2;
const int COLS = 3;

void arr(int [][COLS]);

int main()
{
  int nums[ROWS][COLS] = { {33,16,29},
                           {54,67,99}};
  arr(nums);

  return 0;
}

void arr(int (*val)[COLS])
{
  cout << '\n' << *(*val);
  cout << '\n' << *(*val + 1);
  cout << '\n' << *(*(val + 1) + 2);
  cout << '\n' << *(*val) + 1;

  return;
}
```

b. Given the declaration for val in the arr() function, would the notation val[1][2] be valid within the function?

11.5 COMMON PROGRAMMING ERRORS

In using the material presented in this chapter, be aware of the following possible errors.

1. Attempting to store an address in a variable that has not been declared as a pointer.

2. Using a pointer to access nonexistent array elements. For example, if nums is an array of ten integers, the expression *(nums + 15) points to a location six integer locations beyond the last element of the array. Because C++ does not do any bounds checking on array accesses, this type of error is not caught by the compiler. This is the same error, disguised in pointer notation form, that occurs when using a subscript to access an out-of-bounds array element.

3. Incorrectly applying the address and indirection operators. For example, if `pt` is a pointer variable, the expressions

```
pt = &45
pt = &(miles + 10)
```

are both invalid because they attempt to take the address of a value. Notice that the expression `pt = &miles + 10`, however, is valid. Here, `10` is added to the address of `miles`. Again, it is the programmer's responsibility to ensure that the final address "points to" a valid data element.

4. Taking addresses of pointer constants. For example, given the declarations

```
int nums[25];
int *pt;
```

the assignment

```
pt = &nums;
```

is invalid. The constant `nums` is a pointer constant that is itself equivalent to an address. The correct assignment is `pt = nums`.

5. Taking addresses of a reference argument, reference variable or register variable. The reason for this is that reference arguments and variables are essentially the same as pointer constants, in that they are named address values. Similarly, the address of a register variables cannot be taken. Thus, for the declarations

```
register in total;
int *pt_tot;
```

the assignment

```
pt_tot = &total;   // INVALID
```

is invalid. The reason for this is that register variables are stored in a computer's internal registers, and these storage areas do not have standard memory addresses.

6. Initializing pointer variables incorrectly. For example, the initialization

```
int *pt = 5;
```

is invalid. Since `pt` is a pointer to an integer, it must be initialized with a valid address.

7. Becoming confused about whether a variable *contains* an address or *is* an address. Pointer variables and pointer arguments contain addresses. Although a pointer constant is synonymous with an address, it is useful to treat pointer constants as pointer variables with two restrictions:

- The address of a pointer constant cannot be taken.
- The address "contained in" the pointer constant cannot be altered.

Except for these two restrictions, pointer constants and pointer variables can be used almost interchangeably. Therefore, when an address is required, any of the following can be used:

- a pointer variable name

- a pointer argument name

- a pointer constant name

- a nonpointer variable name preceded by the address operator (e.g., `&variable`)

- a nonpointer argument name preceded by the address operator (e.g., `&argument`)

Some of the confusion surrounding pointers is caused by the cavalier use of the word *pointer*. For example, the phrase "a function requires a pointer argument" is more clearly understood when it is realized that the phrase really means "a function requires an address as an argument." Similarly, the phrase "a function returns a pointer" really means "a function returns an address."

If you are ever in doubt as to what is really contained in a variable or how it should be treated, use the `cout` object to display the contents of the variable, the "thing pointed to," or "the address of the variable." Seeing what is displayed frequently helps sort out what is really in the variable.

11.6 ▷ CHAPTER SUMMARY

1. Every variable has a data type, and address, and a value. In C++ the address of a variable can be obtained by using the address operator `&`.

2. A pointer is a variable that is used to store the address of another variable. Pointers, like all C++ variables, must be declared. The indirection operator, `*`, is used both to declare a pointer variable and to access the variable whose address is stored in a pointer.

3. An array name is a pointer constant. The value of the pointer constant is the address of the first element in the array. Thus, if `val` is the name of an array, `val` and `&val[0]` can be used interchangeably.

4. Any access to an array element using subscript notation can always be replaced using pointer notation. That is, the notation `a[i]` can always be replaced by the notation `*(a + i)`. This is true whether `a` was initially declared explicitly as an array or as a pointer.

5. Arrays can be dynamically created as a program is executing. For example, the sequence of statements

```
cout  << "Enter the array size: ";
cin   >> num;
int  *grades = new int[num];
```

creates an array named `grades` of size num. The area allocated for the array can be dynamically destroyed using the `delete` operator. For example, the statement `delete grades;` will return the allocated area for the `grades` array back to the computer.

6. Arrays are passed to functions as addresses. The called function always receives direct access to the originally declared array elements.

7. When a single-dimensional array is passed to a function, the parameter declaration for the function can be either an array declaration or a pointer declaration. Thus, the following parameter declarations are equivalent:

```
float a[];
float *a;
```

8. Pointers can be incremented, decremented, compared, and assigned. Numbers added to or subtracted from a pointer are automatically scaled. The scale factor used is the number of bytes required to store the data type originally pointed to.

CHAPTER 12

Records as Data Structures

TOPICS

12.1 SINGLE RECORDS

12.2 ARRAYS OF STRUCTURES

12.3 STRUCTURES AS FUNCTION ARGUMENTS
PASSING A POINTER
RETURNING STRUCTURES

12.4 LINKED LISTS

12.5 DYNAMIC DATA STRUCTURE ALLOCATION

12.6 UNIONS

12.7 COMMON PROGRAMMING ERRORS

12.8 CHAPTER SUMMARY

An array allows access to a list or table of data of the same data type using a single variable name. At times, however, we may want to store information of varying types—such as an integer part number, character part type, and floating-point supply voltage. A data structure that stores different types of data under a single variable name is called a record.

For example, assume that an integrated circuit (IC) manufacturer maintains a summary of information for each of the circuits it fabricates. The data items kept for each circuit are illustrated in Figure 12.1.

Part Number:

Integrated Circuit Family:

Function Type:

Supply Voltage:

Units in Stock:

Figure 12.1 An inventory record.

Each of the individual data items listed in Figure 12.1 is an entity by itself that is referred to as a **data field**. *Taken together, all the data fields form a single unit that is referred to as a* **record**. *In C++, a record is referred to as a* **structure**.

Although the integrated circuit manufacturer could keep track of hundreds of components, the form of each character's record is identical. In dealing with records it is important to distinguish between a record's form and its contents.

A record's form consists of the symbolic names, data types, and arrangement of individual data fields in the record. The record's contents refers to the actual data stored in the symbolic names. Figure 12.2 shows acceptable contents for the record form illustrated in Figure 12.1.

> Part Number: 23421
> Integrated Circuit Family: TTL
> Function Type: AND
> Supply Voltage: 6.0
> Units in Stock: 345

Figure 12.2 The form and contents of a record.

In this chapter, we describe the C++ statements required to create, fill, use, and pass records between functions.

12.1 SINGLE RECORDS

Using a record structure requires the same two steps needed for using any variable. First the record structure must be declared. Then specific values can be assigned to the individual record elements. Declaring a record requires listing the data types, data names, and arrangement of data items. For example, the definition

```
struct
{
 int month;
 int day;
 int year;
} birth;
```

gives the form of a record structure called `birth` and reserves storage for the individual data items listed in the structure. The `birth` structure consists of three data items or fields, which are called members of the structure.

Assigning actual data values to the data items of a structure is referred to as *populating the structure* and is a relatively straightforward procedure. Each member of a structure is accessed by giving both the structure name and individual data item name, separated by a period. Thus, `birth.month` refers to the first member of the `birth` structure, `birth.day` refers to the second member of the structure, and `birth.year` refers to the third member. Program 12.1 illustrates assigning values to the individual members of the birth structure.

Program 12.1

```cpp
// a program that defines and populates a record
#include <iostream.h>

int main()
{
  struct
  {
    int month;
    int day;
    int year;
  } birth;

  birth.month = 12;
  birth.day = 28;
  birth.year = 82;

  cout << "My birth date is "
       << birth.month << '/'
       << birth.day   << '/'
       << birth.year  << endl;

  return 0;
}
```

The output produced by Program 12.1 is

```
My birth date is 12/28/82
```

As in most C++ statements, the spacing of a structure definition is not rigid. For example, the birth structure could just as well have been defined

```cpp
struct {int month; int day; int year;} birth;
```

Also, as with all C++ definition statements, multiple variables can be defined in the same statement. For example, the definition statement

```cpp
struct
{
  int month;
  int day;
  int year;
} birth, current;
```

creates two structure variables having the same form. The members of the first structure are referenced by the individual names birth.month, birth.day, and birth.year, while the members of the second structure are referenced by the names `current.month`, `current.day`, and `current.year`. Notice that the form of this particular structure definition statement is identical to the form used in defining any program variable: the data type is followed by a list of variable names.

A useful and commonly used modification for defining structure types is listing the form of the structure with no following variable names. In this case, however, the list of structure members must be preceded by a user selected data type name. For example, in the declaration

```
struct Date
{
  int month;
  int day;
  int year;
};
```

the term `Date` is a structure type name: It defines a new data type that is a data structure of the declared form.[1] By convention the first letter of a user-selected data type name is uppercase, as in the name `Date`, which helps to identify it when it is used in subsequent definition statements. Here, the declaration for the `Date` structure creates a new data type without actually reserving any storage locations. As such it is not a definition statement. It simply declares a `Date` structure type and describes how individual data items are arranged within the structure. Actual storage for the members of the structure is reserved only when specific variable names are assigned. For example, the definition statement

```
Date birth, current;
```

reserves storage for two `Date` structure variables named `birth` and `current`, respectively. Each of these individual structures has the form previously declared for the `Date` structure.[2]

The declaration of a structure data types, like all declarations, may be global or local. Program 12.2 illustrates the global declaration of a `Date` data type. Internal to `main()`, the variable `birth` is defined as a local variable of `Date` type.

The output produced by Program 12.2 is identical to the output produced by Program 12.1.

The initialization of structures follows the same rules as for the initialization of arrays: global and local structures may be initialized by following the definition with a list of initializers. For example, the definition statement

```
Date birth = {12, 28, 72};
```

can be used to replace the first four statements internal to `main()` in Program 12.2. Notice that the initializers are separated by commas, not semicolons.

---

[1] For completeness it should be mentioned that a C++ structure can also be declared as a class with no member functions and all public data members. Similarly, a C++ class can be declared as a struct having all private data members and all public member functions. Thus, C++ provides two syntaxes for both structs and classes. The convention, however, is not to mix notations and always use structures for creating record types and classes for providing true information and implementation hiding.

[2] The type name in C++ for this declaration is `Date`. In C the type name would be `struct Date` and defining variables, such as `birth` and `current`, would be defined as `struct Date birth, current;`.

Program 12.2

```cpp
#include <iostream.h>

struct Date      // this is a global declaration
{
  int month;
  int day;
  int year;
};

int main()
{
  Date birth;

  birth.month = 12;
  birth.day = 28;
  birth.year = 82;

  cout << "My birth date is " << birth.month << '/'
       << birth.day   << '/'
       << birth.year  << endl;

  return 0;
}
```

The individual members of a structure are not restricted to integer data types, as illustrated by the Date structure. Any valid C++ data type can be used. For example, consider an employee record consisting of the following data items:

```
Name:
Identification Number:
Regular Pay Rate:
Overtime Pay Rate:
```

A suitable declaration for these data items is

```cpp
struct Pay_rec
{
  char name[20];
  int id_num;
  float reg_rate;
  float ot_rate;
};
```

Once the `Pay_rec` data type is declared, a specific structure variable using this type can be defined and initialized. For example, the definition

```
Pay_rec employee = {"H. Price",12387,15.89,25.50};
```

creates a structure named `employee` of the `Pay-rec` data type. The individual members of `employee` are initialized with the respective data listed between braces in the definition statement.

Notice that a single structure is simply a convenient method for combining and storing related items under a common name. Although a single structure is useful in explicitly identifying the relationship among its members, the individual members could be defined as separate variables. One of the real advantage to using structures is only realized when the same data type is used in a list many times over. Creating lists with the same data type is the topic of the next section.

Before leaving single structures, it is worth noting that the individual members of a structure can be any valid C++ data type, including both arrays and structures. An array of characters was used as a member of the employee structure defined previously. Accessing an element of a member array requires giving the structure's name, followed by a period, followed by the array designation. For example, `employee.name[4]` refers to the fifth character in the `employee.name` array.

Including a structure within a structure follows the same rules for including any data type in a structure. For example, assume that a structure is to consist of a name and a date of birth, where a `Date` structure has been declared as

```
struct Date
{
   int month;
   int date;
   int year;
};
```

A suitable definition of a structure that includes a `name` and a `Date` structure is

```
struct
{
   char name[20];
   Date birth;
} person;
```

Notice that in declaring the `Date` structure, the term `Date` is a data type name; thus it appears before the braces in the declaration statement. In defining the person structure variable, `person` is a variable name; thus it is the name of a specific structure. The same is true of the variable named `birth`. This is the name of a specific `Date` structure. Individual members in the `person` structure are accessed by preceding the desired member with the structure name followed by a period. For example, `person.birth.month` refers to the `month` variable in the `birth` structure contained in the `person` structure.

Exercises 12.1

1. Declare a structure data type named s_temp for each of the following records:
   a. a student record consisting of a student identification number, number of credits completed, and cumulative grade point average
   b. a student record consisting of a student's name, date of birth, number of credits completed, and cumulative grade point average
   c. an inventory record consisting of the items previously illustrated in Figure 12.1
   d. a stock record consisting of the stock's name, the price of the stock, and the date of purchase
   e. an inventory record consisting of an integer part number, part description, number of parts in inventory, and an integer reorder number

2. For the individual data types declared in Exercise 1, define a suitable structure variable name, and initialize each structure with the appropriate following data:
   a. Identification Number: 4672
      Number of Credits Completed: 68
      Grade Point Average: 3.01
   b. Name: Rhona Karp
      Date of Birth: 8/4/60
      Number of Credits Completed: 96
      Grade Point Average: 3.89
   c. Part Number: 54002
      IC Family: ECL
      Function Type: NAND
      Supply Voltage: −5
      Units in Stock: 123
   d. Stock: IBM
      Price Purchased: 134.5
      Date Purchased: 10/1/86
   e. Part Number: 16879
      Description: Battery
      Number in Stock: 10
      Reorder Number: 3

3. a. Write a C++ program that prompts a user to input the current month, day, and year. Store the data entered in a suitably defined record and display the date in an appropriate manner.
   b. Modify the program written in Exercise 3a to use a record that accepts the current time in hours, minutes, and seconds.

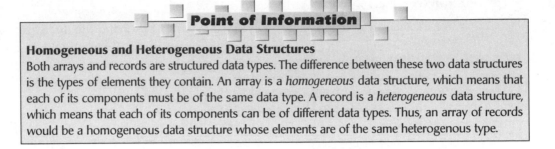

Homogeneous and Heterogeneous Data Structures

Both arrays and records are structured data types. The difference between these two data structures is the types of elements they contain. An array is a *homogeneous* data structure, which means that each of its components must be of the same data type. A record is a *heterogeneous* data structure, which means that each of its components can be of different data types. Thus, an array of records would be a homogeneous data structure whose elements are of the same heterogenous type.

4. Write a C++ program that uses a structure for storing the name of a stock, its estimated earnings per share, and its estimated price-to-earnings ratio. Have the program prompt the user to enter these items for five different stocks, each time using the same structure to store the entered data. When the data has been entered for a particular stock, have the program compute and display the anticipated stock price based on the entered earnings and price-per-earnings values. For example, if a user entered the data XYZ 1.56 12, the anticipated price for a share of XYZ stock is (1.56)*(12) = $18.72.

5. Write a C++ program that accepts a user-entered time in hours and minutes. Have the program calculate and display the time one minute later.

6. **a.** Write a C++ program that accepts a user-entered date. Have the program calculate and display the date of the next day. For purposes of this exercise, assume that all months consist of 30 days.

   b. Modify the program written in Exercise 6a to account for the actual number of days in each month.

12.2 ARRAYS OF STRUCTURES

The real power of structures is realized when the same structure is used for lists of data. For example, assume that the data shown in Figure 12.3 must be processed. Clearly, the employee numbers can be stored together in an array of integers, the names in an array of pointers, and the pay rates in an array of either floating-point or double-precision numbers. In organizing the data in this fashion, each column in Figure 12.3 is considered as a separate list, which is stored in its own array. The correspondence between items for each individual employee is maintained by storing an employee's data in the same array position in each array.

Employee Number	Employee Name	Employee Pay Rate
32479	Abrams, B.	6.72
33623	Bohm, P.	7.54
34145	Donaldson, S.	5.56
35987	Ernst, T.	5.43
36203	Gwodz, K.	8.72
36417	Hanson, H.	7.64
37634	Monroe, G.	5.29
38321	Price, S.	9.67
39435	Robbins, L.	8.50
39567	Williams, B.	7.20

Figure 12.3 A list of employee data.

The separation of the complete list into three individual arrays is unfortunate, since all of the items relating to a single employee constitute a natural organization of data into records, as illustrated in Figure 12.4. Using a structure, the integrity of the data organization as a record can be maintained and reflected by the program. Under this approach, the list illustrated in Figure 12.4 can be processed as a single array of ten structures.

	Employee Number	Employee Name	Employee Pay Rate
1st record ⟶	32479	Abrams, B.	6.72
2nd record ⟶	33623	Bohm, P.	7.54
3rd record ⟶	34145	Donaldson, S.	5.56
4th record ⟶	35987	Ernst, T.	5.43
5th record ⟶	36203	Gwodz, K.	8.72
6th record ⟶	36417	Hanson, H.	·7.64
7th record ⟶	37634	Monroe, G.	5.29
8th record ⟶	38321	Price, S.	9.67
9th record ⟶	39435	Robbins, L.	8.50
10th record ⟶	39567	Williams, B.	7.20

Figure 12.4 A list of records.

Declaring an array of structures is the same as declaring an array of any other variable type. For example, if the data type `Pay_rec` is declared as

```
struct Pay_rec {int idnum; char name[20]; float rate;};
```

then an array of ten such structures can be defined as

```
Pay_rec employee[10];
```

This definition statement constructs an array of ten elements, each of which is a structure of the data type `Pay_rec`. Notice that the creation of an array of ten structures has the same form as the creation of any other array. For example, creating an array of ten integers named employee requires the declaration

```
int employee[10];
```

In this declaration the data type is integer, while in the former declaration for `employee` the data type is `Pay_rec`.

Once an array of structures is declared, a particular data item is referenced by giving the position of the desired structure in the array followed by a period and the appropriate structure member. For example, the variable `employee[0].rate` references the `rate` member of the first `employee` structure in the `employee` array. Including structures as elements of an array permits a list of records to be processed using standard array programming techniques. Program 12.3 displays the first five employee records illustrated in Figure 12.4.

Program 12.3

```
#include <iostream.h>
#include <iomanip.h>

const int MAXNAME = 20;   // maximum characters in a name
const int NUMRECS = 5;    // maximum number of records

struct Pay_rec    // this is a global declaration
{
  long id;
  char name[MAXNAME];
  float rate;
};

int main()
{
  int i;
  Pay_rec employee[NUMRECS] = {
                               { 32479, "Abrams, B.", 6.72 },
                               { 33623, "Bohm, P.", 7.54},
                               { 34145, "Donaldson, S.",  5.56},
                               { 35987, "Ernst, T.", 5.43 },
                               { 36203, "Gwodz, K.", 8.72 }
                               };
```

(Continued)

(Continued)

```
    cout << endl;     // start on a new line
    cout << setiosflags(ios::left);  // left justify the output
    for ( i = 0; i < NUMRECS; i++)
      cout << setw(7)  << employee[i].id
           << setw(15) << employee[i].name
           << setw(6)  << employee[i].rate << endl;

    return 0;
}
```

The output displayed by Program 12.3 is:

```
32479   Abrams, B.      6.72
33623   Bohm, P.        7.54
34145   Donaldson, S.   5.56
35987   Ernst, T.       5.43
36203   Gwodz, K.       8.72
```

In reviewing Program 12.3, notice the initialization of the array of structures. Although the initializers for each structure have been enclosed in inner braces, these are not strictly necessary because all members have been initialized. As with all external and static variables, in the absence of explicit initializers, the numeric elements of both static and external arrays or structures are initialized to zero and their character elements are initialized to NULLs. The setiosflags(ios::left) manipulator included in the cout object stream forces each name to be displayed left justified in its designated field width.

Exercises 12.2

1. Define arrays of 100 structures for each of the data types described in Exercise 1 of the previous section.

2. **a.** Using the data type

```
struct Mon_days
{
  char name[10];
  int days;
};
```

define an array of 12 structures of type Mon_days. Name the array convert[ ], and initialize the array with the names of the 12 months in a year and the number of days in each month.

   b. Include the array created in Exercise 2a in a program that displays the names and number of days in each month.

3. Using the data type declared in Exercise 2a, write a C++ program that accepts a month from a user in numerical form and displays the name of the month and the number of days in the month. Thus, in response to an input of 3, the program would display `March has 31 days`.

4. **a.** Declare a single structure data type suitable for an employee record of the type illustrated below:

Number	Name	Rate	Hours
3462	Jones	4.62	40
6793	Robbins	5.83	38
6985	Smith	5.22	45
7834	Swain	6.89	40
8867	Timmins	6.43	35
9002	Williams	4.75	42

b. Using the data type declared in Exercise 4a, write a C++ program that interactively accepts the above data into an array of six structures. Once the data have been entered, the program should create a payroll report listing each employee's name, number, and gross pay. Include the total gross pay of all employees at the end of the report.

5. **a.** Declare a single structure data type suitable for a car record of the type illustrated:

Car Number	Miles Driven	Gallons Used
25	1450	62
36	3240	136
44	1792	76
52	2360	105
68	2114	67

b. Using the data type declared for Exercise 5a, write a C++ program that interactively accepts the above data into an array of five structures. Once the data have been entered, the program should create a report listing each car number and the miles per gallon achieved by the car. At the end of the report include the average miles per gallon achieved by the complete fleet of cars.

12.3 STRUCTURES AS FUNCTION ARGUMENTS

Individual structure members may be passed to a function in the same manner as any scalar variable. For example, given the structure definition

```
struct
{
  int id_num;
  double pay_rate;
  double hours;
} emp;
```

the statement

```
display(emp.id_num);
```

passes a copy of the structure member `emp.id_num` to a function named `display()`. Similarly, the statement

```
calc_pay(emp.pay_rate,emp.hours);
```

passes copies of the values stored in structure members `emp.pay_rate` and `emp.hours` to the function `calc_pay()`. Both functions, `display()` and `calc_pay()`, must declare the correct data types of their respective arguments.

Complete copies of all members of a structure can also be passed to a function by including the name of the structure as an argument to the called function. For example, the function call

```
calc_net(emp);
```

passes a copy of the complete `emp` structure to `calc_net()`. Internal to `calc_net()`, an appropriate declaration must be made to receive the structure. Program 12.4 declares a global data type for an employee record. This type is then used by both the `main()` and `calc_net()` functions to define specific structures with the names `emp` and `temp`, respectively.

The output produced by Program 12.4 is:

```
The net pay for employee 6782 is $361.66
```

In reviewing Program 12.4, observe that both `main()` and `calc_net()` use the same data type to define their individual structure variables. The structure variable defined in `main()` and the structure variable defined in `calc_net()` are two completely different structures. Any changes made to the local temp variable in `calc_net()` are not reflected in the `emp` variable of `main()`. In fact, since both structure variables are local to their respective functions, the same structure variable name could have been used in both functions with no ambiguity.

Program 12.4

```
#include <iostream.h>
#include <iomanip.h>

struct Employee          // declare a global type
{
  int id_num;
  double pay_rate;
  double hours;
};

double calc_net(Employee);    // function prototype

int main()
{
  Employee emp = {6782, 8.93, 40.5};
  double net_pay;

  net_pay = calc_net(emp);          // pass copies of the values in emp
    // set output formats
  cout << setw(10)
       << setiosflags(ios::fixed)
       << setiosflags(ios::showpoint)
       << setprecision(2);

  cout << "The net pay for employee " << emp.id_num
       << " is $" << net_pay << endl;;

  return 0;
}

double calc_net(Employee temp) // temp is of data type Employee
{
  return temp.pay_rate * temp.hours;
}
```

When `calc_net()` is called by `main()`, copies of emp's structure values are passed to the `temp` structure. `calc_net()` then uses two of the passed member values to calculate a number, which is returned to `main()`. Since `calc_net()` returns a noninteger number, the data type of the value returned must be included in all declarations for `calc_net()`.

An alternative to the pass-by-value function call illustrated in Program 12.4, in which the called function receives a copy of a structure, is a pass-by reference that passes a reference to a structure. Doing so permits the called function to directly access and alter values in the calling function's structure variable. For example, referring to Program 12.4, the prototype of `calc_net()` can be modified to

```
double calc_net(Employee &);
```

If this function prototype is used and the `calc_net()` function is rewritten to conform to it, the `main()` function in Program 12.4 may be used as is. Program 12.4a illustrates these changes within the context of a complete program.

Program 12.4a

```cpp
#include <iostream.h>
#include <iomanip.h>

struct Employee        // declare a global type
{
  int id_num;
  double pay_rate;

  double hours;
};

double calc_net(Employee &);   // function prototype

int main()
{
  Employee emp = {6782, 8.93, 40.5};
  double net_pay;

  net_pay = calc_net(emp);        // pass a reference

    // set output formats
  cout << setw(10)
       << setiosflags(ios::fixed)
       << setiosflags(ios::showpoint)
       << setprecision(2);

  cout << "The net pay for employee " << emp.id_num
       << " is $" <<  net_pay << endl;

  return 0;
}

double calc_net(Employee& temp)    // temp is a reference variable
{
  return temp.pay_rate * temp.hours;
}
```

Program 12.4a produces the same output as Program 12.4, except that the `calc_net()` function in Program 12.4a receives direct access to the `emp` structure rather than a copy of it. This means that the variable name `temp` within `calc_net` is an alternate name for the variable `emp` in `main()`, and any changes to `temp` are direct changes to `emp`. Although the same function call, `calc_net(emp)` is made in both programs, the call in Program 12.4a passes a reference while the call in Program 10.4 passes values.

Passing a Pointer

In place of passing a reference, a pointer can be used. Using a pointer requires, in addition to modifying the function's prototype and header line, that the call to `calc_net()` in Program 12.4 be modified to

    calc_net(&emp);

Here the function call clearly indicates that an address is being passed (which is not the case in Program 12.4a). The disadvantage, however, is in the dereferencing notation required internal to the function. However, as pointers are widely used in practice, it is worthwhile to become familiar with the notation used.

To correctly store the passed address, `calc_net()` must declare its parameter as a pointer. A suitable function definition for `calc_net()` is

    calc_net(Employee *pt)

Here, the declaration for `pt` declares this parameter as a pointer to a structure of type `Employee`. The pointer `pt` receives the starting address of a structure whenever `calc_net()` is called. Within `calc_net()`, this pointer is used to directly reference any member in the structure. For example, `(*pt).id_num` refers to the `id_num` member of the structure, `(*pt).pay_rate` refers to the `pay_rate` member of the structure, and `(*pt).hours` refers to the `hours` member of the structure. These relationships are illustrated in Figure 12.5.

Figure 12.5 A pointer can be used to access structure members.

The parentheses around the expression `*pt` in Figure 12.5 are necessary to initially access "the structure whose address is in `pt`." This is followed by an identifier to access the desired member within the structure. In the absence of the parentheses, the structure member operator `.` takes precedence over the indirection operator. Thus, the expression `*pt.hours` is another way of writing `*(pt.hours)`, which would refer to "the variable whose address is in the `pt.hours` variable." This last expression clearly makes no sense because there is no structure named `pt` and `hours` does not contain an address.

As illustrated in Figure 12.5, the starting address of the `emp` structure is also the address of the first member of the structure.

The use of pointers in this manner is so common that a special notation exists for it. The general expression `(*pointer).member` can always be replaced with the notation `pointer->member`, where the `->` operator is constructed using a minus sign followed by a right-facing arrow (greater than symbol). Either expression can be used to locate the desired member. For example, the following expressions are equivalent:

`(*pt).id_num`	can be replaced by `pt->id_num`
`(*pt).pay_rate`	can be replaced by `pt->pay_rate`
`(*pt).hours`	can be replaced by `pt->hours`

Program 12.5 illustrates passing a structure's address and using a pointer with the new notation to directly reference the structure.

The name of the pointer parameter declared in Program 12.5 is, of course, selected by the programmer. When `calc_net()` is called, `emp`'s starting address is passed to the function. Using this address as a starting point, individual members of the structure are accessed by including their names with the pointer.

Program 12.5

```cpp
#include <iostream.h>
#include <iomanip.h>

struct Employee   // declare a global type
{
  int id_num;
  double pay_rate;
  double hours;
};

double calc_net(Employee *);   //function prototype

int main()
{
  Employee emp = {6782, 8.93, 40.5};
  double net_pay;
  net_pay = calc_net(&emp);       // pass an address

    // set output formats
  cout << setw(10)
       << setiosflags(ios::fixed)
       << setiosflags(ios::showpoint)
       << setprecision(2);

  cout << "The net pay for employee " << emp.id_num
       << " is $" << net_pay << endl;

  return 0;
}

double calc_net(Employee *pt)   // pt is a pointer to a
{                               // structure of Employee type
  return(pt->pay_rate * pt->hours);
}
```

As with all C++ expressions that access a variable, the increment and decrement operators can also be applied to them. For example, the expression

        ++pt->hours

adds one to the hours member of the emp structure. Since the -> operator has a higher priority than the increment operator, the hours member is accessed first and then the increment is applied. Alternatively, the expression (++pt)->hours uses the prefix increment operator to increment the address in pt before the hours member is accessed.

Similarly, the expression (pt++)->hours uses the postfix increment operator to increment the address in pt after the hours member is accessed. In both of these cases, however, there must be sufficient defined structures to ensure that the incremented pointers actually point to legitimate structures.

As an example, Figure 12.6 illustrates an array of three structures of type employee. Assuming that the address of emp[1] is stored in the pointer variable pt, the expression ++pt changes the address in pt to the starting address of emp[2], while the expression --pt changes the address to point to emp[0].

Figure 12.6 *Changing pointer addresses.*

Returning Structures

In practice, most structure handling functions receive direct access to a structure by receiving a structure reference or address. Then any changes to the structure can be made directly from within the function. If you want to have a function return a separate structure, however, you must follow the same procedures for returning complete data structures as for returning scalar values. These procedures include declaring the function appropriately and alerting any calling function to the type of data structure being returned. For example, the function get_vals() in Program 12.6 returns a complete structure to main().

Program 12.6

```cpp
#include <iostream.h>
#include <iomanip.h>

struct  Employee        // declare a global type
{
  int id_num;
  double pay_rate;
  double hours;
};

struct Employee get_vals(void);    // function prototype

int main()
{
  Employee emp;

  emp = get_vals();
  cout << "\nThe employee id number is " << emp.id_num
       << "\nThe employee pay rate is $" << emp.pay_rate
       << "\nThe employee hours are " << emp.hours << endl;

  return 0;
}

struct Employee get_vals(void) // return an employee structure
{
  Employee next;

  next.id_num = 6789;
  next.pay_rate = 16.25;
  next.hours = 38.0;

  return next;
}
```

The following output is displayed when Program 12.6 is run:

```
The employee id number is 6789
The employee pay rate is $16.25
The employee hours are 38.0
```

Since the get_vals() function returns a structure, the function header for get_vals() must specify the type of structure being returned. Because get_vals() does not receive any arguments, the function header has no parameter declarations and consists of the line

```
Employee get_vals(void);
```

Within `get_vals()`, the variable `next` is defined as a structure of the type to be returned. After values have been assigned to the `next` structure, the structure values are returned by including the structure name within the parentheses of the return statement.

On the receiving side, `main()` must be alerted that the function `get_vals()` will be returning a structure. This is handled by including a function declaration for `get_vals()` in `main()`. Notice that these steps for returning a structure from a function are identical to the normal procedures for returning scalar data types previously described in Chapter 6.

Exercises 12.3

1. Write a C++ function named `days()` that determines the number of days from the turn of the century for any date passed as a structure. Use the `Date` structure

   ```
   struct Date
   {
     int month;
     int day;
     int year;
   };
   ```

   In writing the `days()` function, use the convention that all years have 360 days and each month consists of 30 days. The function should return the number of days for any `Date` structure passed to it. Make sure you declare the returned variable a long integer to reserve sufficient room for converting dates such as 12/19/02.

2. Write a C++ function named `dif_days()` that calculates and returns the difference between two dates. Each date is passed to the function as a structure using the following global type:

   ```
   struct Date
   {
     int month;
     int day;
     int year;
   };
   ```

   The `dif_days()` function should make two calls to the `days()` function written for Exercise 1.

3. **a.** Rewrite the `days()` function written for Exercise 1 to receive a reference to a `Date` structure, rather than a copy of the complete structure.
   b. Redo Exercise 3a using a pointer rather than a reference.

4. **a.** Write a C++ function named `larger()` that returns the later date of any two dates passed to it. For example, if the dates 10/9/99 and 11/3/99 are passed to `larger()`, the second date would be returned.

b. Include the `larger()` function that was written for Exercise 4a in a complete program. Store the `Date` structure returned by `larger()` in a separate `Date` structure and display the member values of the returned `Date`.

5. a. In two dimensions a vector is a pair of numbers that represent directed arrows in a plane, as shown by the vectors v_1 and v_2 in Figure 12.7.

Figure 12.7 Graph for Exercise 5.

Two-dimensional vectors can be written in the form (a,b), where a and b are called the x and y components of the vector, respectively. For example, for the vectors illustrated in Figure 12.17, $v_1 = (9, 4)$ and $v_2 = (3, 5)$. For vectors, the following operations apply:

If $v_1 = (a,b)$ and $v_2 = (c,d)$
$v_1 + v_2 = (a,b) + (c,d) = (a + c, b + d)$
$v_1 - v_2 = (a,b) - (c,d) = (a - c, b - d)$

Using this information write a C++ program that defines an array of two vector records, where each record consists of two floating-point components a and b. Your program should permit a user to enter two vectors, call two functions that return the sum and difference of the entered vectors, and display the results calculated by these functions.

b. In addition the operations defined in Exercise 5a, two additional vector operations are negation and absolute value. For a vector v_1 with components (a,b) these operations are defined as follows:

negation: $-v_1 = -(a,b) = (-a,-b)$
absolute value: $|v_1| = $ sqrt $(a * a + b * b)$

Using this information modify the program that you wrote for Exercise 5a to display the negation and absolute values of both vectors input by a user as well as the negation and absolute value of the sum of the two input vectors.

12.4 LINKED LISTS

A classic data-handling problem is making additions or deletions to existing records that are maintained in a specific order. This is best illustrated by considering the alphabetical telephone list shown in Figure 12.8. Starting with this initial set of names and telephone numbers, we desire to add new records to the list in the proper alphabetical sequence, and to delete existing records in such a way that the storage for deleted records is eliminated.

Acme, Sam
(555) 898-2392
Dolan, Edith
(555) 682-3104
Lanfrank, John
(555) 718-4581
Mening, Stephen
(555) 382-7070
Zemann, Harold
(555) 219-9912

Figure 12.8 A telephone list in alphabetical order.

Although the insertion or deletion of ordered records can be accomplished using an array of structures, these arrays are not efficient representations for adding or deleting records internal to the array. Arrays are fixed and prespecified in size. Deleting a record from an array creates an empty slot that requires either special marking or shifting up all elements below the deleted record to close the empty slot. Similarly, adding a record to the body of an array of structures requires that all elements below the addition be shifted down to make room for the new entry, or the new element could be added to the bottom of the existing array and the array then resorted to restore the proper order of the records. Thus, either adding or deleting records to such a list generally requires restructuring and rewriting the list—a cumbersome, time-consuming, and inefficient practice.

A linked list provides a convenient method for maintaining a constantly changing list, without the need to continually reorder and restructure the complete list. A linked list is simply a set of structures in which each structure contains at least one member whose value is the address of the next logically ordered structure in the list. Rather than requiring each record to be physically stored in the proper order, each new record is physically added wherever the computer has free space in its storage area. The records are "linked" together by including the address of the next record in the record immediately preceding it. From a programming standpoint, the current record being processed contains the address of the next record, no matter where the next record is actually stored.

The concept of a linked list is illustrated in Figure 12.9. Although the actual data for the `Lanfrank` structure illustrated in the figure may be physically stored anywhere in the computer, the additional member included at the end of the Dolan structure maintains the proper alphabetical order. This member provides the starting address of the location where the Lanfrank record is stored. As you might expect, this member is a pointer.

Figure 12.9 Using pointers to link structures.

To see the usefulness of the pointer in the Dolan record, let us add a telephone number for June Hagar into the alphabetical list shown in Figure 12.8. The data for June Hagar is stored in a data structure using the same type as that used for the existing records. To ensure that the telephone number for Hagar is correctly displayed after the Dolan telephone number, the address in the Dolan record must be altered to point to the Hagar record, and the address in the Hagar record must be set to point to the Lanfrank record. This is illustrated in Figure 12.10. Notice that the pointer in each structure simply points to the location of the next ordered structure, even if that structure is not physically located in the correct order.

Figure 12.10 Adjusting addresses to point to appropriate records.

Removal of a structure from the ordered list is the reverse process of adding a record. The actual record is logically removed from the list by simply changing the address in the structure preceding it to point to the structure immediately following the deleted record.

Each structure in a linked list has the same format; however, it is clear that the last record cannot have a valid pointer value that points to another record, because there is none. C++ provides a special pointer value called NULL that acts as a sentinel or flag to indicate when the last record has been processed. The NULL pointer value, like its end-of-string counterpart, has a numerical value of zero.

Besides an end-of-list sentinel value, a special pointer must also be provided for storing the address of the first structure in the list. Figure 12.11 illustrates the complete set of pointers and structures for a list consisting of three names.

Figure 12.11 *Use of the initial and final pointer values.*

The inclusion of a pointer in a structure should not seem surprising. As we discovered in Section 12.1, a structure can contain any C++ data type. For example, the structure declaration

```
struct Test
{
  int id_num;
  double *pt_pay
};
```

declares a structure type consisting of two members. The first member is an integer variable named `id_num`, and the second variable is a pointer named `pt_pay`, which is a pointer to a double-precision number. Program 12.7 illustrates that the pointer member of a structure is used like any other pointer variable.

The output produced by executing Program 12.7 is

```
Employee number 12345 was paid $456.20
```

Figure 12.12 illustrates the relationship between the members of the `emp` structure defined in Program 12.7 and the variable named `pay`. The value assigned to `emp.id_num` is the number 12345 and the value assigned to `pay` is 456.20. The address of the `pay` variable is assigned to the structure member `emp.pt_pay`. Since this member has been defined as a pointer to a double-precision number, placing the address of the double-precision variable `pay` in it is a correct use of this member. Finally, since the member operator `.` has a higher precedence than the indirection operator `*`, the expression used in the `cout` statement in Program 12.7 is correct. The expression `*emp.pt_pay` is equivalent to the expression `*(emp.pt_pay)`, which is translated as "the variable whose address is contained in the member `emp.pt_pay`."

Figure 12.12 *Storing an address in a structure member.*

Program 12.7

```
#include <iostream.h>
#include <iomanip.h>

struct Test
{
  int id_num;
  double *pt_pay;
};

int main()
{
  Test emp;
  double pay = 456.20;

  emp.id_num = 12345;
  emp.pt_pay = &pay;
    // set output formats
  cout << setw(6)
       << setiosflags(ios::fixed)
       << setiosflags(ios::showpoint)
       << setprecision(2);

  cout << "\nEmployee number " << emp.id_num << " was paid $"
       << *emp.pt_pay << endl;

  return 0;
}
```

Although the pointer defined in Program 12.7 has been used in a rather trivial fashion, the program does illustrate the concept of including a pointer in a structure. This concept can be easily extended to create a linked list of structures suitable for storing the names and telephone numbers listed in Figure 12.8. The following declaration creates a type for such a structure:

```
struct Tele_typ
{
  char name[30];
  char phone_no[15];
  Tele_typ *nextaddr;
};
```

The `Tele_typ` type consists of three members. The first member is an array of 30 characters, suitable for storing names with a maximum of 29 letters and an end-of-string

NULL marker. The next member is an array of 15 characters, suitable for storing telephone numbers with their respective area codes. The last member is a pointer suitable for storing the address of a structure of the `Tele_typ` type.

Program 12.8 illustrates the use of the `Tele_typ` type by specifically defining three structures having this form. The three structures are named `t1`, `t2`, and `t3`, respectively, and the name and telephone members of each of these structures are initialized when the structures are defined, using the data listed in Figure 12.8.

Program 12.8

```
#include <iostream.h>

const int MAXNAME = 30;   // maximum no. of characters in a name
const int MAXTEL = 16;    // maximum no. of characters in a telephone number

struct Tele_typ
{
  char name[MAXNAME];
  char phone_no[MAXTEL];
  Tele_typ *nextaddr;
};

int main()
{
  Tele_typ t1 = {"Acme, Sam","(555) 898-2392"};
  Tele_typ t2 = {"Dolan, Edith","(555) 682-3104"};
  Tele_typ t3 = {"Lanfrank, John","(555) 718-4581"};
  Tele_typ *first;      // create a pointer to a structure

  first = &t1;          // store t1's address in first
  t1.nextaddr = &t2;    // store t2's address in t1.nextaddr
  t2.nextaddr = &t3;    // store t3's address in t2.nextaddr
  t3.nextaddr = NULL;   // store a NULL address in t3.nextaddr

  cout << '\n' << first->name
       << '\n' << t1.nextaddr->name
       << '\n' << t2.nextaddr->name
       << endl;

  return 0;
}
```

The output produced by executing Program 12.8 is

```
Acme, Sam
Dolan, Edith
Lanfrank, John
```

Program 12.8 demonstrates the use of pointers to access successive structure members. As illustrated in Figure 12.13, each structure contains the address of the next structure in the list.

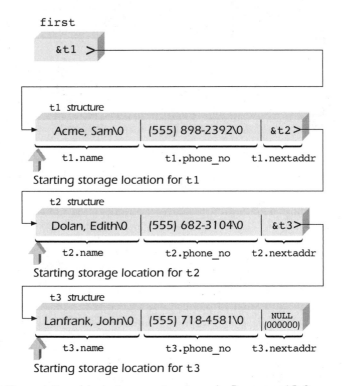

Figure 12.13 The relationship between structures in Program 12.8.

The initialization of the names and telephone numbers for each of the structures defined in Program 12.9 is straightforward. Although each structure consists of three members, only the first two members of each structure are initialized. As both of these members are arrays of characters, they can be initialized with strings. The remaining member of each structure is a pointer. To create a linked list, each structure pointer must be assigned the address of the next structure in the list.

The four assignment statements in Program 12.8 perform the correct assignments. The expression `first = &t1` stores the address of the first structure in the list in the pointer variable named `first`. The expression `t1.nextaddr = &t2` stores the starting address of the `t2` structure into the pointer member of the `t1` structure. Similarly, the expression `t2.nextaddr = &t3` stores the starting address of the `t3` structure into the pointer member of the `t2` structure. To end the list, the value of the NULL pointer, which is zero, is stored into the pointer member of the `t3` structure.

Once values have been assigned to each structure member and correct addresses have been stored in the appropriate pointers, the addresses in the pointers are used to access each structure's name member. For example, the expression `t1.nextaddr->name` refers to the `name` member of the structure whose address is in the `nextaddr` member of the `t1` structure. The precedence of the member operator `.` and the structure pointer operator `->` are equal and are evaluated from left to right. Thus, the expression `t1.nextaddr->name` is evaluated as `(t1.nextaddr)->name`. Since `t1.nextaddr` contains the address of the `t2` structure, the proper name is accessed.

The expression `t1.nextaddr->name` can, of course, be replaced by the equivalent expression `(*t1.nextaddr).name`, which uses the more conventional indirection operator. This expression also refers to "the name member of the variable whose address is in `t1.nextaddr`."

The addresses in a linked list of structures can be used to loop through the complete list. As each structure is accessed it can be either examined to select a specific value or used to print out a complete list. For example, the `display()` function in Program 12.9 illustrates the use of a `while` loop, which uses the address in each structure's pointer member to cycle through the list and successively display data stored in each structure.

The output produced by Program 12.9 is

```
Acme, Sam              (555) 898-2392
Dolan, Edith           (555) 682-3104
Lanfrank, John         (555) 718-4581
```

The important concept illustrated by Program 12.9 is the use of the address in one structure to access members of the next structure in the list. When the `display()` function is called, it is passed the value stored in the variable named `first`. Since `first` is a pointer variable, the actual value passed is an address (the address of the `t1` structure). The function `display()` accepts the passed value in the argument named `contents`. To store the passed address correctly, `contents` is declared as a pointer to a structure of the `tele_typ` type. Within `display()`, a `while` loop is used to cycle through the linked structures, starting with the structure whose address is in `contents`. The condition tested in the `while` statement compares the value in `contents`, which is an address, to the `NULL` value. For each valid address the name and phone number members of the addressed structure are displayed. The address in `contents` is then updated with the address in the pointer member of the current structure. The address in `contents` is then retested, and the process continues while the address in contents is not equal to the `NULL` value. The function `display()` "knows" nothing about the names of the structures declared in `main()` or even how many structures exist. It simply cycles through the linked list, structure by structure, until it encounters the end-of-list `NULL` address. Since the value of `NULL` is zero, the tested condition can be replaced by the equivalent expression `contents`.

A disadvantage of Program 12.9 is that exactly three structures are defined in `main()` by name and storage for them is reserved at compile time. Should a fourth structure be required, the additional structure would have to be declared and the program recompiled. In the next section we show how to have the computer dynamically allocate and release storage for structures at run time, as storage is required. Only when a new structure is to be added to the list, and while the program is running, is storage for the new structure created. Similarly, when a structure is no longer needed and can be deleted from the list, the storage for the deleted record is relinquished and returned to the computer.

Program 12.9

```cpp
#include <iostream.h>
#include <iomanip.h>

const int MAXNAME = 20;    // maximum no. of characters in a name
const int MAXTEL = 15;     // maximum no. of characters in a telephone number

struct Tele_typ
{
  char name[MAXNAME];
  char phone_no[MAXTEL];
  Tele_typ *nextaddr;
};

void display(Tele_typ *);        // function prototype

int main()
{
  Tele_typ t1 = {"Acme, Sam","(555) 898-2392"};
  Tele_typ t2 = {"Dolan, Edith","(555) 682-3104"};
  Tele_typ t3 = {"Lanfrank, John","(555) 718-4581"};
  Tele_typ *first;     // create a pointer to a structure

  first = &t1;        // store t1's address in first
  t1.nextaddr = &t2;  // store t2's address in t1.nextaddr
  t2.nextaddr = &t3;  // store t3's address in t2.nextaddr
  t3.nextaddr = NULL; // store the NULL address in t3.nextaddr

  display(first);     // send the address of the first structure

  return 0;
}

void display(Tele_typ *contents) // contents is a pointer to a structure
{                                // of type Tele_typ
  while (contents != NULL)   // display till end of linked list
  {
    cout << '\n' << setiosflags(ios::left)
         << setw(30) << contents->name
         << setw(20) << contents->phone_no ;
    contents = contents->nextaddr;    // get next address
  }
  cout << endl;

  return;
}
```

Exercises 12.4

1. Modify Program 12.9 to prompt the user for a name. Have the program search the existing list for the entered name. If the name is in the list, display the corresponding phone number; otherwise display this message:
   `The name is not in the current phone directory.`

2. Write a C++ program containing a linked list of ten integer numbers. Have the program display the numbers in the list.

3. Using the linked list of structures illustrated in Figure 12.13, write the sequence of steps necessary to delete the record for Edith Dolan from the list.

4. Generalize the description obtained in Exercise 3 to describe the sequence of steps necessary to remove the nth structure from a list of linked structures. The nth structure is preceded by the $(n - 1)$st structure and followed by the $(n + 1)$st structure. Make sure to store all pointer values correctly.

5. **a.** A doubly linked list is a list in which each structure contains a pointer to both the following and previous structures in the list. Define an appropriate type for a doubly linked list of names and telephone numbers.
   b. Using the type defined in Exercise 5a, modify Program 12.9 to list the names and phone numbers in reverse order.

12.5 ▷ DYNAMIC DATA STRUCTURE ALLOCATION

We have already encountered the concept of explicitly allocating and deallocating memory space using the new and delete operators (see Section 11.2). For convenience the description of these operators are repeated in Table 12.1.

Table 12.1

Operator Name	Description
new	Reserves the number of bytes required by the requested data type. Returns the address of the first reserved location or NULL if sufficient memory is not available.
delete	Releases a block of bytes previously reserved. The address of the first reserved location is passed as an argument to the function.

This dynamic allocation of memory is especially useful when dealing with a list of structures because it permits the list to expand as new records are added and contract as records are deleted.

In requesting additional storage space, the user must provide the new function with an indication of the amount of storage needed. This is done by requesting enough space for a particular type of data. For example, the expression `new(int)` or `new int` (the two forms may be used interchangeably) requests enough storage to store an integer number. A request for enough storage for a data structure is made in the same fashion. For example, using the declaration

```
struct Tel_typ
{
  char name[25];
  char phone_no[15];
};
```

both the expressions `new Tel_typ` and `new(Tel_typ)` reserve enough storage for one `Tel_typ` data structure.

In allocating storage dynamically, we have no advance indication as to where the computer system will physically reserve the requested number of bytes, and we have no explicit name to access the newly created storage locations. To provide access to these locations, `new` returns the address of the first location that has been reserved. This address must, of course, be assigned to a pointer. The return of a pointer by `new` is especially useful for creating a linked list of data structures. As each new structure is created, the pointer returned by `new` to the structure can be assigned to a member of the previous structure in the list.

Program 12.10 illustrates using `new` to create a structure dynamically in response to a user-input request.

Program 12.10

```
#include <iostream.h>
// a program illustrating dynamic structure allocation

#include <iostream.h>
#include <string.h>

const int MAXNAME = 30;  // maximum no. of characters in a name
const int MAXTEL = 15;   // maximum no. of characters in a telephone number

struct Tel_typ
{
  char name[MAXNAME];
  char phone_no[MAXTEL];
};

void populate(Tel_typ *);  // function prototype needed by main()
void disp_one(Tel_typ *);  // function prototype needed by main()
```

(Continued)

(Continued)

```cpp
int main()
{
  char key;
  Tel_typ *rec_point;    // rec_point is a pointer to a
                         // structure of type Tel_typ

  cout << "Do you wish to create a new record (respond with y or n): ";
  key = cin.get();
  if (key == 'y')
  {
    key = cin.get();        // get the Enter key in buffered input
    rec_point = new Tel_typ;
    populate(rec_point);
    disp_one(rec_point);

  }
  else
    cout << "\nNo record has been created.";

  return 0;
}

  // input a name and phone number
void populate(Tel_typ *record) // record is a pointer to a
  {                            // structure of type Tel_typ
    cout << "Enter a name: ";
    cin.getline(record->name,MAXNAME);
    cout << "Enter the phone number: ";
    cin.getline(record->phone_no,MAXTEL);

    return;
  }
  // display the contents of one record
void disp_one(Tel_typ *contents)  // contents is a pointer to a
{                                 // structure of type Tel_typ
    cout << "\nThe contents of the record just created is:"
         << "\nName: " << contents->name
         << "\nPhone Number: " << contents->phone_no << endl;

    return;
}
```

A sample session produced by Program 12.10 is

```
Do you wish to create a new record (respond with y or n): y
Enter a name: Monroe, James
Enter the phone number: (555) 617-1817
The contents of the record just created is:
Name: Monroe, James
Phone Number: (555) 617-1817
```

In reviewing Program 12.10, notice that only two variable declarations are made in main(). The variable key is declared as a character variable and the variable rec_point is declared as being a pointer to a structure of the Tel_typ type. Because the declaration for the type Tel_typ is global, Tel_typ can be used within main() to define rec_point as a pointer to a structure of the Tel_typ type.

If a user enters y in response to the first prompt in main(), a call to new is made for the required memory to store the designated structure. Once rec_point has been loaded with the proper address, this address can be used to access the newly created structure. The function populate() is used to prompt the user for data needed in filling the structure and to store the user-entered data in the correct members of the structure. The argument passed to populate() in main() is the pointer rec_point. Like all passed arguments, the value contained in rec_point is passed to the function. Since the value in rec_point is an address, populate() receives the address of the newly created structure and can directly access the structure members.

Within populate(), the value received by it is stored in the argument named record. Since the value to be stored in record is the address of a structure, record must be declared as a pointer to a structure. This declaration is provided by the statement Tel_typ *record;. The statements within populate() use the address in record to locate the respective members of the structure.

The disp_one() function in Program 12.10 is used to display the contents of the newly created and populated structure. The address passed to disp_one() is the same address that was passed to populate(). Because this passed value is the address of a structure, the argument name used to store the address is declared as a pointer to the correct structure type.

Once you understand the mechanism of calling new, you can use this function to construct a linked list of structures. As described in the previous section, the structures used in a linked list must contain at least one pointer member. The address in the pointer member is the starting address of the next structure in the list. Additionally, a pointer must be reserved for the address of the first structure, and the pointer member of the last structure in the list is given a NULL address to indicate that no more members are being pointed to. Program 12.11 illustrates the use of new to construct a linked list of names and phone numbers. The populate() function used in Program 12.11 is the same function used in Program 12.10, while the display() function is the same function used in Program 12.9.

Program 12.11

```cpp
#include <iostream.h>
#include <iomanip.h>

const int MAXNAME = 30;   // maximum no. of characters in a name
const int MAXTEL = 15;    // maximum no. of characters in a telephone number
const int MAXRECS = 3;    // maximum no. of records

struct Tel_typ
{
  char name[MAXNAME];
  char phone_no[MAXTEL];
  Tel_typ *nextaddr;
};

void populate(Tel_typ *);   // function prototype needed by main()
void display(Tel_typ *);    // function prototype needed by main()

int main()
{
  int i;
  Tel_typ *list, *current; // two pointers to structures of
                           // type Tel_typ

    // get a pointer to the first structure in the list
  list = new Tel_typ;
  current = list;

    // populate the current structure and create the remaining structures
  for(i = 0; i < MAXRECS - 1; i++)
  {
    populate(current);
    current->nextaddr = new Tel_typ;
    current = current->nextaddr;
  }

  populate(current);          // populate the last structure
  current->nextaddr = NULL;   // set the last address to a NULL address
  cout << "\nThe list consists of the following records:\n";
  display(list);   // display the structures

  return 0;
}
```

(Continued)

(Continued)

```
   // input a name and phone number
void populate(Tel_typ *record) // record is a pointer to a
{                               // structure of type Tel_typ

   cout << "Enter a name: ";
   cin.getline(record->name,MAXNAME);
   cout << "Enter the phone number: ";
   cin.getline(record->phone_no,MAXTEL);

   return;
}

void display(struct Tel_typ *contents) // contents is a pointer to a
{                                      // structure of type Tel_typ
   while (contents != NULL)      // display till end of linked list
   {
     cout << '\n' << setiosflags(ios::left)
         << setw(30) << contents->name
         << setw(20) << contents->phone_no;
     contents = contents->nextaddr;
   }
   cout << endl;

   return;
}
```

The first time new is called in Program 12.11 it is used to create the first structure in the linked list. As such, the address returned by new is stored in the pointer variable named list. The address in list is then assigned to the pointer named current. This pointer variable is always used by the program to point to the current structure. Because the current structure is the first structure created, the address in the pointer named list is assigned to the pointer named current.

Within main()'s for loop, the name and phone number members of the newly created structure are populated by calling populate() and passing the address of the current structure to the function. Upon return from populate(), the pointer member of the current structure is assigned an address. This address is the address of the next structure in the list, which is obtained from new. The call to new creates the next structure and returns its address into the pointer member of the current structure. This completes the population of the current member. The final statement in the for loop resets the address in the current pointer to the address of the next structure in the list.

After the last structure has been created, the final statements in `main()` populate this structure, assign a `NULL` address to the pointer member, and call `display()` to display all the structures in the list. A sample run of Program 12.11 is provided below:

```
Enter a name: Acme, Sam
Enter the phone number: (555) 898-2392
Enter a name: Dolan, Edith
Enter the phone number: (555) 682-3104
Enter a name: Lanfrank, John
Enter the phone number: (555) 718-4581

The list consists of the following records:

Acme, Sam                    (555) 898-2392
Dolan, Edith                 (555) 682-3104
Lanfrank, John               (555) 718-4581
```

Just as `new` dynamically creates storage while a program is executing, the `delete` function restores a block of storage back to the computer while the programming is executing. The only argument required by `delete` is the starting address of a block of storage that was dynamically allocated. Thus, any address returned by `new` can subsequently be passed to `delete` to restore the reserved memory back to the computer. The `delete` function does not alter the address passed to it, but simply removes the storage that the address references.

Exercises 12.5

1. As described in Table 12.1, the `new` operator returns either the address of the first new storage area allocated or `NULL` if insufficient storage is available. Modify Program 12.11 to check that a valid address has been returned before a call to `populate()` is made. Display an appropriate message if sufficient storage is not available.

2. Write a C++ function named `remove()` that removes an existing structure from the linked list of structures created by Program 12.11. The algorithm for removing a linked structure should follow the sequence developed for removing a structure developed in Exercise 4 in Section 12.4. The argument passed to `remove()` should be the address of the structure preceding the record to be removed. In the removal function, make sure that the value of the pointer in the removed structure replaces the value of the pointer member of the preceding structure before the structure is removed.

3. Write a function named `insert()` that inserts a structure into the linked list of structures created in Program 12.11. The algorithm for inserting a structure in a linked list should follow the sequence for inserting a record previously illustrated in Figure 12.10. The argument passed to `insert()` should be the address of the structure preceding the structure to be inserted. The inserted structure should follow this current structure. The `insert()` function should create a new structure dynamically, call the `populate` function used in Program 12.11, and adjust all pointer values appropriately.

4. We desire to insert a new structure into the linked list of structures created by Program 12.11. The function developed to do this in Exercise 3 assumed that the address of the preceding structure is known. Write a function called `find_rec()` that returns the address of the structure immediately preceding the point at which the new structure is to be inserted. (*Hint:* `find_rec()` must request the new name as input and compare the entered name to existing names to determine where to place the new name.)

5. Write a C++ function named `modify()` that can be used to modify the name and phone number members of a structure of the type created in Program 12.11. The argument passed to `modify()` should be the address of the structure to be modified. The `modify()` function should first display the existing name and phone number in the selected structure and then request new data for these members.

6. a. Write a C++ program that initially presents a menu of choices for the user. The menu should consist of the following choices:

Create an initial linked list of names and phone numbers
Insert a new structure into the linked list
Modify an existing structure in the linked list
Delete an existing structure from the list
Exit from the program

Upon the user's selection, the program should execute the appropriate functions to satisfy the request.

b. Why is the original creation of a linked list usually done by one program, and the options to add, modify, or delete a structure in the list provided by a different program?

12.6 UNIONS[3]

A union is a data type that reserves the same area in memory for two or more variables, each of which can be a different data type. A variable that is declared as a union data type can be used to hold a character variable, an integer variable, a double-precision variable, or any other valid C++ data type. Each of these types, but only one at a time, can actually be assigned to the union variable.

The definition of a union has the same form as a structure definition, with the keyword `union` used in place of the keyword `struct`. For example, the declaration

```
union
{
  char key;
  int num;
  double volts;
} val;
```

---

[3]This topic may be omitted on first reading with no loss of subject continuity.

creates a union variable named val. If val were a structure it would consist of three individual members. As a union, however, val contains a single member that can be either a character variable named key, an integer variable named num, or a double-precision variable named volts. In effect, a union reserves sufficient memory locations to accommodate its largest member's data type. This same set of locations is then referenced by different variable names depending on the data type of the value currently residing in the reserved locations. Each value stored overwrites the previous value, using as many bytes of the reserved memory area as necessary.

Individual union members are referenced using the same notation as structure members. For example, if the val union is currently being used to store a character, the correct variable name to access the stored character is val.key. Similarly, if the union is used to store an integer, the value is accessed by the name val.num, and a double-precision value is accessed by the name val.volts. In using union members, it is the programmer's responsibility to ensure that the correct member name is used for the data type currently residing in the union.

Typically a second variable is used to keep track of the current data type stored in the union. For example, the following code could be used to select the appropriate member of val for display. Here the value in the variable u_type determines the currently stored data type in the val union.

```
switch(u_type)
{
  case 'c': cout << val.key;
            break;
  case 'i': cout << val.num;
            break;
  case 'd': cout << val.volts;
            break;
  default : cout << "Invalid type in u_type : " << u_type;
}
```

As they are in structures, a data type can be associated with a union. For example, the declaration

```
union Date_time
{
   long int days;
   double time;

};
```

provides union data type without actually reserving any storage locations. This data type can then be used to define any number of variables. For example, the definition

```
Date_time first, second, *pt;
```

creates a union variable named first, a union variable named second, and a pointer that can be used to store the address of any union having the form of Date_time. Once a pointer to a union has been declared, the same notation used to access structure

members can be used to access union members. For example, if the assignment
`pt = &first;` is made, then `pt->date` references the `date` member of the union
named `first`.

Unions may themselves be members of structures or arrays. Structures, arrays, and
pointers may also be members of unions. In each case, the notation used to access a member
must be consistent with the nesting employed. For example, in the structure defined by

```
struct
{
  char u_type;
  union
  {
    char *text;
    float rate;
  } u_tax;
}  flag;
```

the variable `rate` is referenced as

```
flag.u_tax.rate
```

Similarly, the first character of the string whose address is stored in the pointer `text` is
referenced as

```
*flag.u_tax.text
```

Exercises 12.6

1. Assume that the following definition has been made

   ```
   union
   {
     float rate;
     double taxes;
     int num;
   } flag;
   ```

   For this union write appropriate `cout` stream activations to display the various
   members of the union.

2. Define a union variable named `car` that contains an integer named `year`, an
   array of 10 characters named `name`, and an array of 10 characters named `model`.

3. Define a union variable named `lang` that would allow a floating-point number
   to be referenced by both the variable names `volts` and `emf`.

4. Declare a union data type named `Amt` that contains an integer variable named
   `int_amt`, a double-precision variable named `dbl_amt`, and a pointer to a character named `pt_key`.

5. a. What do you think will be displayed by the following section of code?

```
union
{
  char ch;
  float btype;
} alt;
alt.ch = 'y';
cout << alt.btype;
```

b. Include the code presented in Exercise 5a in a program and run the program to verify your answer to Exercise 5a.

12.7 COMMON PROGRAMMING ERRORS

Three common errors are often made when using structures or unions. The first error occurs because structures and unions, as complete entities, cannot be used in relational expressions. For example, even if `Tel_typ` and `Phon_type` are two structures of the same type, the expression `Tel_typ == Phon_typ` is invalid. Individual members of a structure or union can, of course, be compared if they are of the same data type, using any of C++'s relational operators.

The second common error is really an extension of a pointer error as it relates to structures and unions. Whenever a pointer is used to "point to" either of these data types, or whenever a pointer is itself a member of a structure or a union, take care to use the address in the pointer to access the appropriate data type. Should you be confused about just what is being pointed to, remember, "If in doubt, print it out."

The final error relates specifically to unions. Since a union can store only one of its members at a time, you must be careful to keep track of the currently stored variable. Storing one data type in a union and accessing it by the wrong variable name can result in an error that is particularly troublesome to locate.

12.8 CHAPTER SUMMARY

1. A structure allows individual variables to be grouped under a common variable name. Each variable in a structure is accessed by its structure variable name, followed by a period, followed by its individual variable name. Another term for a data structure is a record. One form for declaring a structure is:

```
struct
{
  individual member declarations;
} structure_name;
```

2. A data type can be created from a structure using the declaration form

```
struct Data-type
{
  individual member declarations;
};
```

Individual structure variables may then be defined as this `Data-type`. By convention, the first letter of the `Data-type` name is always capitalized.

3. Structures are particularly useful as elements of arrays. Used in this manner, each structure becomes one record in a list of records.

4. Complete structures can be used as function arguments, in which case the called function receives a copy of each element in the structure. The address of a structure may also be passed, either as a reference or a pointer, which provides the called function with direct access to the structure.

5. Structure members can be any valid C++ data type, including other structures, unions, arrays, and pointers. When a pointer is included as a structure member a linked list can be created. Such a list uses the pointer in one structure to "point to" (contain the address of) the next logical structure in the list.

6. Unions are declared in the same manner as structures. The definition of a union creates a memory overlay area, with each union member using the same memory storage locations. Thus, only one member of a union may be active at a time.

Part Four
Additional Topics

CHAPTERS

13 Numerical Methods

14 Bit Operations

CHAPTER 13

Numerical Methods

TOPICS

13.1 INTRODUCTION TO ROOT FINDING

13.2 THE BISECTION METHOD

13.3 REFINEMENTS TO THE BISECTION METHOD
REGULA FALSI METHOD
MODIFIED REGULA FALSI METHOD
SUMMARY OF THE ALGORITHMS BASED ON BISECTION

13.4 THE SECANT METHOD

13.5 INTRODUCTION TO NUMERICAL INTEGRATION

13.6 THE TRAPEZOIDAL RULE
COMPUTATIONAL FORM OF THE TRAPEZOIDAL RULE EQUATION
EXAMPLE OF A TRAPEZOIDAL RULE CALCULATION

13.7 SIMPSON'S RULE
EXAMPLE OF SIMPSON'S RULE AS AN APPROXIMATION TO AN INTEGRAL

13.8 COMMON PROGRAMMING ERRORS

13.9 CHAPTER SUMMARY

One of the most common tasks in science and engineering is finding the roots of equations, that is, given a function f(x), finding values of x such that f(x) = 0.0. This type of problem also includes determining the points of intersection of two curves. If the curves are represented by functions f(x) and g(x), respectively, the intersection points correspond to the roots of the function F(x) = f(x) − g(x).

A second important task is numerical integration—where approximation methods are used to determine the integral's value when exact solutions do not exist. In this chapter we first present and apply several programming techniques for finding the roots of equations. This is followed by techniques commonly employed in numerical integration.

13.1 INTRODUCTION TO ROOT FINDING

Root-finding techniques are important for a number of reasons. They are useful, easy to understand and usually easy to carry out. Thus, with a minimum of instruction you are able to solve genuine problems in engineering. A vital element in numerical analysis is appreciating what can or cannot be solved and clearly understand the accuracy of the answers obtained. Since this appreciation and understanding come mostly from experience, you need to begin solving numerical problems immediately. Besides, you will find that root-solving problems are fun.

Some examples of the types of functions that are encountered in root solving problems are

$$ax^2 + bx + c = 0 \tag{13.1}$$

$$2x^4 - 7x^3 + 4x^2 + 7x - 6 = (x - 2)(x - 1)(x + 1)(2x - 3) = 0 \tag{13.2}$$

$$x^5 - 2x^3 - 5x^2 + 2 = 0 \tag{13.3}$$

$$\sin^5(x) + \sin^3(x) + 5\cos(x) - 7 = 0 \tag{13.4}$$

$$100e - x - \sin(2\pi x) = 0 \tag{13.5}$$

The general quadratic equation, Equation 13.1, can be solved easily and exactly by using the quadratic formula

$$r = \frac{-b \pm \sqrt{(b^2 - 4ac)}}{2a}$$

Equation 13.2 can be solved for x exactly by factoring the polynomial. The roots are then clearly 1, –1, 2, 3/2. However, most polynomials cannot be factored so easily, and other more general techniques are required. There are formulas for the exact solution of general cubic or quartric equations, but they are cumbersome and thus seldom used. No exact formula is possible for a polynomial like Equation 13.3, in which the highest power of x is greater than 4. For these polynomials numerical means must generally be used to determine the roots.

You will recall from high school algebra that a polynomial of degree n (i.e., the highest power of x^n) has precisely n roots, of which some may be complex numbers and others may be multiple roots. Thus Equation 13.3 has three real roots,

$$r_1 = -0.712780744625. . .$$

$$r_2 = 0.57909844162. . .$$

$$r_3 = 2.0508836199. . .$$

and two complex roots,

$$r_4 = 0.757225433526 + i(0.57803468208)$$

$$r_5 = 0.757225433526 - i(0.57803468208)$$

The equation

$$x^2 - 2x + 1 = 0$$

can be factored as

$$(x - 1)^2 = 0$$

and has two real roots, both of which happen to be the same. In this case the root is said to be a multiple root with multiplicity 2.

Equations 13.4 and 13.5 are called **transcendental equations** and represent an entirely different class of functions. Transcendental equations typically involve trigonometric, exponential, or logarithmic functions and cannot be reduced to any polynomial equation in x. The real roots of a polynomials are usually classified as being either rational numbers (that is, a simple fraction) or irrational for example, $\sqrt{2}$). The roots of transcendental equations are often transcendental numbers like π or e. Irrational numbers and transcendental numbers are represented by nonrepeating decimal fractions and cannot be expressed as simple fractions. These numbers are important to mathematics since they are responsible for the real number system being dense or continuous. Thus, the classification of equations as polynomials or transcendental and the roots of these equations as rational or irrational is vital to traditional mathematics; however, the distinction is of less consequence to the computer. In fact, not only is the number system available to the computer not continuous, it is a finite set.

At any rate, when finding the roots of equations, the distinction between polynomials and transcendental equations is unnecessary and the same numerical procedures are applied to both. The distinction between the two types of functions is, however, important in other regards. Many of the theorems you learned concerning roots of polynomials do not apply to transcendental equations. For instance both equations 13.4 and 13.5 have an infinite number of real roots.

All of the root-solving techniques discussed in this chapter are interactive; that is, you specify an interval that is known to contain a root or simply an initial guess for the root and the various routines will return a more limited interval or a better guess. Some of the schemes we will discuss will be guaranteed to find a root eventually but may take considerable computer time to arrive at the answer. Others may converge to a root much faster but are more susceptible to problems of divergence; that is, they come with no guarantees.

The common ingredient in all root-solving recipes is that potential computational difficulties of any nature are best avoided by mastering as much intelligence as possible in the initial choice of the method used and the accompanying initial guess. This part of the problem is often the most difficult and time consuming. The art involved in numerical analysis consists in balancing time spent optimizing the solution of the problem before computation against time spent correcting unforeseen errors during computation. If at all possible, the function should be roughly sketched before root solving is attempted, either by using graphing routines or by generating a table of function values that are then graphed by hand. These graphs are extremely useful to the programmer not only in estimating the first guess for the root, but also in anticipating potential difficulties. If a sketch is not feasible, some method of monitoring the function must be utilized to arrive at some understanding of what the function is doing before the actual computation is initiated. As an example of the general procedure we will follow, consider the transcendental function

$$f(x) = e^{-x} - \sin(\tfrac{1}{2}\pi x)$$

This equation, as we will shortly see, has an infinite number of positive roots. For the moment, we will concentrate on obtaining an initial guess for the first root, and then use this initial guess to find a more precise root value.

We begin by gathering as much information as possible before trying to construct a C++ program. This step almost always involves making a rough sketch of the function being considered. The second equation above can be written as

$$e^{-x} = \sin(\tfrac{1}{2}\pi x)$$

A root of this equation then corresponds to any value of x such that the left side and right side are equal. If the left and right sides are plotted independently, the roots of the original equation are then given by the points of intersection of the two curves (see Figure 13.1). From the sketch we see that the roots are

Roots $\approx$ 0.4, 1.9, 4.0, . . .

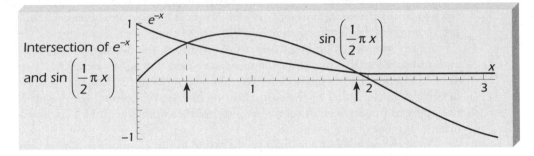

Figure 13.1 Graph of e^{-x} and $\sin(\tfrac{1}{2}\pi x)$ for locating the intersection points.

Since the sine oscillates, there will be an infinite number of positive roots. We will concentrate first on improving the estimate of the first root near 0.4. We begin by establishing a procedure, or algorithm, that is based on the most obvious method of attack when using a pocket calculator; that is, we begin at some value of x just before the root (say 0.3) and step along the x axis, carefully watching the magnitude and particularly the sign of the function.

Step	x	e^{-x}	$\sin(\tfrac{1}{2}\pi x)$	$f(x) = e^{-x} - \sin(\tfrac{1}{2}\pi x)$
0	0.3	0.741	0.454	0.297
1	0.4	0.670	0.588	0.082
2	0.5	0.606	0.707	−0.101

Notice that the function has changed sign between 0.4 and 0.5, indicating a root between these two x values. Thus, for the next approximation we will use the midpoint value, $x = 0.45$ for our next step:

Step	x	e^{-x}	$\sin(\frac{1}{2}\pi x)$	$f(x) = e^{-x} - \sin(\frac{1}{2}\pi x)$
3	0.45	0.638	0.649	−0.012

The function is again negative at 0.45, indicating that the root is between 0.4 and 0.45. The next approximation will, therefore, be the midpoint of this interval, 0.425. In this way we can proceed systematically to a computation of the root to any desired degree of accuracy.

Step	x	e^{-x}	$\sin(\frac{1}{2}\pi x)$	$f(x) = e^{-x} - \sin(\frac{1}{2}\pi x)$
4	0.425	0.654	0.619	0.0347
5	0.4375	0.6456	0.6344	0.01126
6	0.44365	0.6417	0.6418	−0.00014

The key element in the procedure is the monitoring of the sign of the function. When the sign changes, specific action is taken to refine the estimate of the root. This change in sign of the function, indicating the vicinity of a root has been located, forms the key element in the computer code for locating roots. In the next three sections consider a number of root finding methods that use this procedure as their basis.

Exercises 13.1

1. Use the iterative technique presented in this section to find a root of the equation

   $$f(x) = \sin x - x/3 = 0 \quad (x \text{ is in radians})$$

   To do this, first rewrite the equation as

   $$\sin x = x/3$$

   and plot the left and right sides independently on the same graph.

13.2 THE BISECTION METHOD

The root-solving procedure illustrated in the preceding section is suitable for hand calculations; however, a slight modification will make it more "systematic" and easier to adapt to computer coding.

Suppose we already know that there is a root between $x = a$ and $x = b$; that is, the function changes sign in this interval. For simplicity we will assume that there is only one root between $x = a$ and $x = b$ and that the function is continuous in this interval.

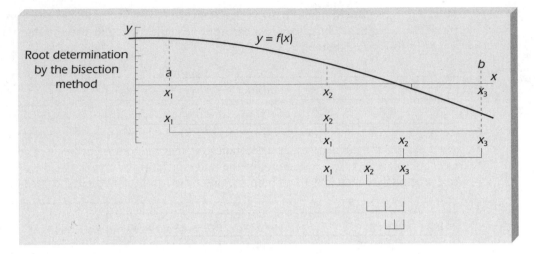

Root determination by the bisection method

Figure 13.2 A sketch of a function with one root between *a* and *b*.

The function might then resemble the sketch in Figure 13.2. If we next define $x_1 = a$ and $x_3 = b$ as the left and right ends of the interval, respectively, and $x_2 = \frac{1}{2}(x_1 + x_3)$ as the midpoint, in which half-interval does the function crosses the x-axis? In the figure, the crossing is on the right, so we replace the full interval by the right half-interval. Thus,

> x_2 now becomes x_1
>
> x_3 remains as it is
>
> x_2 is recalculated as the value $\frac{1}{2}(x_1 + x_3)$

and the question is again posed as "In which half-interval does the function cross the x axis?" After determining a second time whether the left half or the right half contains the root, the interval is once more replaced by either the left or right half-interval. This process is continued until we narrow in on the root to within some previously assigned accuracy. Each step halves the interval, and so after n iterations, the size of the interval contain the root will be $(b - a)/2^n$. If we are required to find a root to within a tolerance δ, that is, $|x - \text{root}| < \delta$, the number of iterations n required can be determined from

$$\frac{b - a}{2^n} < \delta$$

For example, the initial search interval in the example presented in the previous section was $(b - a) = 0.1$. If the root was required to an accuracy of $\delta = 10^{-5}$, then

$$\frac{0.1}{2^n} < 10^{-5}$$

or

$$2^n > 10^4$$

This can be solved for n as follows:

$$n > \frac{\log(10^4)}{\log(2)} > 13$$

Thus, the calculation reveals that the desired degree of accuracy is achieved after the 13th application of the interval halving procedure. The only element of the method that has been omitted is how the computer is to determine which half of the interval contains the axis crossing. To that end, consider the product of the function evaluated at the left, $f_1 = f(x_1)$, and the function evaluated at the midpoint, $f_2 = f(x_2)$.

If	Then
$f_1 f_2 > 0.0$	f_1 and f_2 are both positive or both negative. In either case, there is no crossing between x_1 and x_2, and no root lies within the interval.
$f_1 f_2 < 0.0$	$f(x)$ has changed sign between x_1 and x_2. In this case, there is a root within the interval bounded by x_1 and x_2.

A program to compute the roots of an equation using this procedure is illustrated by Program 13.1. In reviewing this program, the following features should be especially noted:

- In each iteration after the first, there is only one function evaluation. It would be highly inefficient to reevaluate $f(x_1)$, $f(x_2)$ and $f(x_3)$ for each iteration since two of them are already known. If the function were extremely complicated, redundant computations like this would be a serious problem. A great deal of computer time can be wasted by unnecessary function evaluations.

- The program contains several checks for potential problems along with diagnostic messages (e.g., excessive iteration, no roots in interval, etc.) even though the programmer may think these possibilities are remote. Generally, the more of these checks a program contains, the better. They take only a few minutes to a code and can save hours of debugging.

- The criterion for success is based on the size of the interval. Thus, even if the function were not close to zero at a point, x is changing very little, and continuing would not substantially improve the accuracy of the root.

Program 13.1

```cpp
#include <iostream.h>
#include <math.h>

void bisection(double, double, double, int); // function prototype
double f(double); // function prototype

int main()
{
  int imax;          // maximum number of iterations
  double a, b;       // left and right ends of the original interval
  double epsilon;    // convergence criterion

  // obtain the input data
  cout << "Enter the limits of the original search interval, a and b: ";
  cin  >> a >> b;
  cout << "Enter the convergence criteria: ";
  cin  >> epsilon;
  cout << "Enter the maximum number of iterations allowed: ";
  cin  >> imax;

  bisection(a, b, epsilon, imax);

  return 0;
}

// A bisection function that finds roots of a function
// The interval a < x < b is known to contain a root of f(x). The estimate
// of the root is successively improved by finding in which half of the interval
// the root lies and then replacing the original interval by that half-interval.
//
void bisection(double a, double b, double epsilon, int imax)
{
  int i;             // current iteration counter
  double x1, x2, x3; // left, right, and midpoint of current interval
  double f1, f2, f3; // function evaluated at these points
  double width;      // width of original interval = (b - a)
  double curwidth;   // width of current interval = (x3 - x1)

  // echo back the passed input data
  cout << "\nThe original search interval is from " << a << " to " << b << endl;
  cout << "The convergence criterion is: interval < " << epsilon << endl;
  cout << "The maximum number of iterations allowed is " << imax << endl;

  // calculate the root
```

(Continued)

(Continued)

```cpp
  x1 = a;
  x3 = b;
  f1 = f(x1);
  f3 = f(x3);
  width = (b - a);

  // verify there is a root in the interval
  if (f1 * f3 > 0.0)
    cout << "\nNo root in the original interval exists" << endl;
  else
  {
    for (i = 1; i <= imax; i++)
    {
      // find which half of the interval contains the root
      x2 = (x1 + x3) / 2.0;
      f2 = f(x2);
      if (f1 * f2 <= 0.0) // root is in left half interval
      {
        curwidth = (x2 - x1) / 2.0;
        f3 = f2;
        x3 = x2;
      }
      else // root is in right half interval
      {
        curwidth = (x3 - x2) / 2.0;
        f1 = f2;
        x1 = x2;
      }
      if (curwidth < epsilon)
      {
       cout << "\nA root at x = " << x2 << " was found "
            << "in " << i << " iterations" << endl;
       cout << "The value of the function is " << f2 << endl;
       return;
      }
    }
  }
  cout << "\nAfter " << imax << " iterations, no root was found "
       << "within the convergence criterion" << endl;

  return;
}

// function to evaluate f(x)
double f(double x)
{
      const double PI = acos(-1); // value of pi

      return (exp(-x) - sin(0.5 * PI * x));
}
```

A sample run using Program 13.1 produced the following:

```
Enter the limits of the original search interval, a and b: .4 .5
Enter the convergence criteria: .00001
Enter the maximum number of iterations allowed: 25

The original search interval is from 0.4 to 0.5
The convergence criterion is: interval < 1e-005
The maximum number of iterations allowed is 25


A root at x = 0.443567 was found in 13 iterations
The value of the function is 1.22595e-005
```

Although Program 13.1 is used to evaluate the roots of the equation $f(x) = e^x - \sin(\pi x/2)$, by changing the calculation in the return statement in the last function, $f(\ )$, listed in the program, this program can be used for any function.

One final comment: the bisection method used in Program 13.1 is an example of a so-called brute force method; that is, it possesses a minimum of finesse. Although it illustrates fundamental C++ techniques, much more powerful and clever numerical procedures are available. These techniques are presented next in the next section.

Exercises 13.2

1. Use the bisection procedure for finding the roots of an equation. First construct a table of the following form:

Step	x_1	x_2	x_3	$f(x_1)$	$f(x_2)$	$f(x_3)$	Crossing Left	Right
0	a	$\frac{1}{2}(a+b)$	b					
1								
.	.	.	.	.	.	.	.	.
.	.	.	.	.	.	.	.	.
.	.	.	.	.	.	.	.	.

Next, use the bisection procedure and a pocket calculator to obtain the roots of the following functions to an accuracy of five significant figures.

a. $f(x) = x^2 + 2x - 15$ (Use $a = 2.8$, $b = 3.1$. The exact answer $= 3.0$)

b. $g(x) = \frac{1}{2}\sin(x)(e^x - e^{-x})$ (This is the elliptic gear equation, with x in radians. Use $a = 1$, $b = 4$)

c. $E(x) = \sqrt{(R^2 - x^2)} - x\tan(x)$ (This is the equation for quantum energies of a particle in a box. Use $R = 10$, $a = 4.0$, $b = 4.7$)

d. Predict the number of steps needed to obtain the answer to the specified accuracy of five significant figures in parts a through c.

2. a. Modify Program 13.1 to solve for the indicated roots of each of the functions of Exercise 1.

   b. Modify Program 13.1 to produce a table similar to the one required in Exercise 1 for each of the functions listed in Exercise 1.

3. Write a C++ program to find the maximum of a function $f(x)$ over an interval $a \le x \le b$ by starting at $x = a$ with a step size Δx. Evaluate $f_1 = f(x)$ and $f_2 = f(x + \Delta x)$. If $f_1 < f_2$, replace x with $x + \Delta x$ and continue; otherwise, reduce the step size by half and repeat the comparison. The program should terminate successfully when $\Delta < 10^{-6}$.

13.3 REFINEMENTS TO THE BISECTION METHOD

The bisection method described in the previous section presents the basics upon which most root-finding methods are constructed. It is a so-called brute-force method that is rarely used in practice, since for almost any problem an alternative method that is faster, more accurate, and only slightly more complex is available. All of the refinements of the bisection method that might be devised are based on attempts to use as much information as is available about the behavior or the function at each iteration. In the ordinary bisection method, the only feature of the function that is monitored is its sign. Thus, if we were searching for roots of the function

$$f(x) = e^{-x} - \sin(\tfrac{1}{2}\pi x)$$

we would begin the search, as described in Section 13.1, by stepping along the x axis and watching for a change in sign of the function, as follows:

i	x_i	$f(x_i)$
0	0.0	2.0
1	0.1	1.33
2	0.2	0.75
3	0.3	0.29
4	0.4	−.05

The next step in the bisection procedure is to reduce the step size by half, that is, try, $x_5 = 0.35$. However, from the magnitude of the numbers above we would expect the root to be closer to 0.4 than to 0.3. Thus, by using information about the size of the functional value in addition to its sign, we may be able to speed up the convergence. In the present case we might interpolate the root to be approximately

$$\frac{0.29 - 0.0}{0.29 - (-0.05)} = \frac{f_3 - 0}{f_3 - f_4} = 0.853$$

of the distance from $x_3 = 0.3$ to $x_4 = 0.4$, or $x_5 = 0.3853$. Continuing in this manner and interpolating at each step, we would obtain the following results:

i	x_i	$f(x_i)$
3	0.30	0.29
4	0.40	−0.05
5	0.385	−0.0083
6	0.3823	−0.0013
7	0.3819	−0.00019
8	0.38185	−0.000028
9	0.38184	−0.000004

Comparing these results with the bisection method applied to a similar function in the previous section, we see that the convergence rate for the present method is significantly faster. The next task is to formalize this procedure into a method suitable for a general function.

Regula Falsi Method

The basic idea in the first refinement of the bisection algorithm is that the new method will be essentially the same as bisection except that in place of using the midpoint of the interval at each step of the calculation, an interpolated value for the root is used. The method is illustrated in Figure 13.3. In the figure a root is known to exist in the interval $(x_1 \leftrightarrow x_3)$, and in the drawing, f_1 is negative whereas f_3 is positive. The interpolated position of the root is x_2. Since the two triangles ABC and CDE are similar, the lengths of the sides are related by

$$\frac{DE}{AB} = \frac{CD}{BC}$$

or

$$\frac{0.0 - f_1}{f_3 - f_1} = \frac{x_2 - x_1}{x_3 - x_1}$$

which may be solved for the unknown position x_2 to yield

$$x_2 = x_1 - (x_3 - x_1)\frac{f_1}{f_3 - f_1}$$

This value of x_2 then replaces the midpoint used in the bisection algorithm, and the rest of the procedure remains exactly the same. Thus, the next step would be to determine whether the actual root is to the left or to the right of x_2. As before,

If $f_1 \times f_2 < 0$ then the root is on the left

If $f_2 \times f_3 < 0$ then the root is on the right

In the figure the root is to the left of x_2, so the interval used for the next iteration would be

$x_3 = x_2$

$f_3 = f_2$

$$x_2 = x_1 - (x_3 - x_1)\frac{f_1}{f_3 - f_1}$$

$f_2 = f(x_2)$

In other words, to employ this slightly faster algorithm, the only change that has to be made to the previous bisection code is to replace statements of the form

$x_2 = (x_1 + x_3) / 2.$

by a statement of the form

$$x_2 = x_1 - (x_3 - x_1)\frac{f_1}{f_3 - f_1}$$

This method is still guaranteed to obtain a root eventually and will almost always converge faster than the conventional bisection algorithm. We do, however, pay a small price. The values of f_1 and f_3 used in solving for x_2 may be very nearly equal, and we could be plagued by round-off errors in their difference. Also, in the bisection algorithm we could predict with some precision the number of iterations required to obtain the root to a desired accuracy (see Section 13.1). This prediction is no longer possible if we use the interpolated values, and the code must now include a check for excessive iterations.

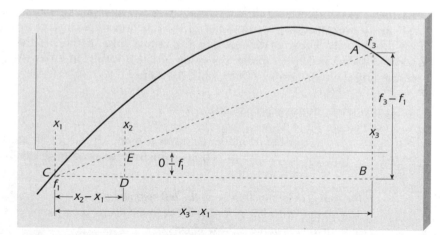

Figure 13.3 *Estimating the root by interpolation.*

This method illustrates that an almost trivial change in the algorithm, which is based on more intelligent monitoring of the function, can reap considerable rewards in more rapid convergence. The formal name of the method just described is the **regula falsi method** (the method of false position).

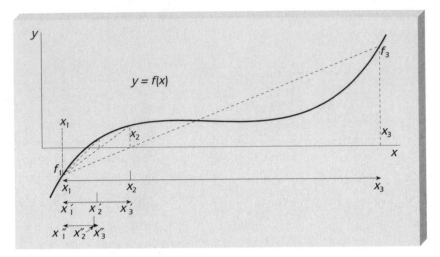

Figure 13.4 Graphical illustration of several iterations of the regula falsi algorithm.

Are there any additional improvements in the basic bisection algorithm that can be easily implemented? To answer this question we must examine in more detail the manner in which the regula falsi method arrives at a solution. This is best done graphically. The calculation begun in Figure 13.3 is continued in Figure 13.4. Notice that in this example, in which the function is concave downward near the root, the value of the left limit of the search interval near the root, x_1, never changes. The actual root always remains in the left segment in each iteration. The right segment of the interval, $x_3 - x_2$, shrinks quite rapidly; but the left segment, $x_2 - x_1$, does not. If the function were concave upward, the converse would be true. Thus, a drawback in the regula falsi method is that even though the method converges more rapidly to a value of x that results in a "small" $|f(x)|$, the interval containing the root does *not* diminish significantly.

Modified Regula Falsi Method

Perhaps the procedure can be made to converge more rapidly if the interval can somehow be made to collapse from both directions. One way to accomplish this is demonstrated in Figure 13.5. The idea is as follows:

> *If the root is determined to lie in the left segment $(x_2 - x_1)$*
>   *The interpolation line is drawn between the points $(x_1, \frac{1}{2}f_1)$ and (x_3, f_3)*
> *Else If the root is in the right segment*
>   *The interpolation line is drawn between the points (x_1, f_1) and $(x_3, \frac{1}{2}f_3)$*
> *Endif*

Using this algorithm, the slope of the line is *artificially* reduced. The effect of this reduction is that if the root is in the left of the original interval, it will eventually turn up in the right segment of a later interval and subsequently will alternate between left and right. The last modification to the bisection method in combination with the regula falsi method is known as the *modified regula falsi method*, a very powerful and popular procedure for finding rots of equations. The alternatives to the original bisection code presented in Program 13.1 are quite trivial and are incorporated within Program 13.2.

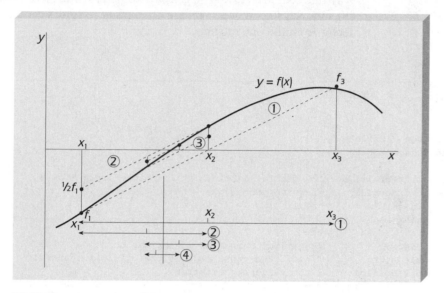

Figure 13.5 *Graphical illustration of the modified regula falsi method.*

The C++ code in Program 13.2 requires some explanation:

1. The function $f(x)$ is evaluated only once per cycle. If the function is complicated and therefore costly to compute, this measure of efficiency can be attractive, even decisive, in choosing the appropriate method of solution.

2. The code can terminate in only three ways.

    a. One success path: If the current fractional size of the search interval [i.e., (current interval)/(original interval)] is less than the user-supplied convergence criterion. If so, the original aim of the program, to narrowly bracket a root, has been achieved. There is no guarantee that this criterion will result in a value of $f(x)$ that is "small." The point is, however, that successive iterations have resulted in only small changes in the interval containing the root and so continuing the process is not necessary or productive.

    b. There are two failure paths: (1) If the number of iterations is greater than I_{max}, the maximum number of iterations set by the programmer, then the process is stopped. This test allows the programmer to specify the maximum cost that will be accepted for an attempted solution. Since in the regula falsi and modified regula falsi methods the number of iterations is not predictable, this form of safeguard is essential. It is also a prudent precaution against unforeseen errors in the construction of the problem that could cause the program to cycle forever and not obtain a solution. Statements of this type are required in any program in which there is a danger of infinite looping.

(2) If the function does not change sign ($f_1 \times f_3 > 0$), then the process is stopped. Since the original interval was known to contain a root, the only way this condition can arise is by error. Usually the error is in the code for the function $f(x)$; that is, you are attempting to find a root of a function different from the one intended.

Program 13.2

```cpp
#include <iostream.h>
#include <math.h>

void modregfalsi(double, double, double, int); // function prototype
double f(double); // function prototype

int main()
{
    int imax;          // maximum number of iterations
    double a, b;       // left and right ends of the original interval
    double epsilon;    // convergence criterion

    // obtain the input data
    cout << "Enter the limits of the original search interval, a and b: ";
    cin  >> a >> b;
    cout << "Enter the convergence criteria: ";
    cin  >> epsilon;
    cout << "Enter the maximum number of iterations allowed: ";
    cin  >> imax;

    modregfalsi(a, b, epsilon, imax);

    return 0;
}

// A modified regula falsi function that finds roots of a function
// The maximum number of iterations permitted is imax. The convergence
// criterion is the fractional size of the search interval (x3 - x1) / (b - a)
// is less than epsilon. A relaxation factor RELAX is used
void modregfalsi(double a, double b, double epsilon, int imax)
{
    const double RELAX = 0.9; // the relaxation factor

    int i;             // current iteration counter
    double x1, x2, x3; // left, right, and midpoint of current interval
    double f1, f2, f3; // function evaluated at these points
    double width;      // width of original interval = (b - a)
    double curwidth;   // width of current interval = (x3 - x1)
```

(Continued)

(Continued)

```
    // echo back the passed input data
    cout << "\nThe original search interval is from " << a << " to " << b
         << "\nThe convergence criterion is: interval < " << epsilon
         << "\nThe maximum number of iterations allowed is " << imax << endl;

    // calculate the root
    x1 = a;
    x3 = b;
    f1 = f(x1);
    f3 = f(x3);
    width = fabs(b - a);

    // iterations
    for (i = 1; i <= imax; i++)
    {
      curwidth = (x3 - x1) / width;
      x2 = x1 - width * curwidth * f1 / (f3 - f1);
      f2 = f(x2);
      if (fabs(curwidth) < epsilon) // root is found
      {
        cout << "\nA root at x = " << x2 << " was found "
             << "in " << i << " iterations" << endl;
        cout << "The value of the function is " << f2 << endl;
        return;
      }
      else // check for left and right crossing
      {
        if(f1 * f2 < 0.0) // check for crossing on the left
        {
          x3 = x2;
          f3 = f2;
          f1 = RELAX * f1;
        }
        else if (f2 * f3 < 0.0) // check for crossing on the right
        {
          x1 = x2;
          f1 = f2;
          f3 = RELAX * f3;
        }
        else // no crossing in the interval
        {
         cout << "The search for a root has failed due to no root in the interval\n"
              << "In step " << i << " of the iteration the function does not change sign"
            << endl;
        }
      }
    }
    cout << "\nAfter " << imax << " iterations, no root was found "
         << "within the convergence criterion\n"
         << "The search for a root has failed due to excessive iterations\n"
         << "after the maximum number of " << imax << " iterations" << endl;
```

(Continued)

(Continued)

```
    return;
}
// function to evaluate f(x)
double f(double x)
{
        const double PI = acos(-1); // value of pi

        return (exp(-x) - sin(0.5 * PI * x));
}
```

A sample run using Program 13.2 produced the following:

```
Enter the limits of the original search interval, a and b: .4 .5
Enter the convergence criteria: .00001
Enter the maximum number of iterations allowed: 25

The original search interval is from 0.4 to 0.5
The convergence criterion is: interval < 1e-005
The maximum number of iterations allowed is 25

A root at x = 0.443574 was found in 7 iterations
The value of the function is -2.25374e-009
```

In comparing the results from the sample run of Program 13.2 to those of Program 13.1, notice that a more exact root was located by the modified regula falsi function in five less iterations (7 as opposed to 13). The exactness of the root is indicated by the functional value at the root, which is closer to 0.0 in the output produced by Program 13.2. A more complete comparison of the rate of convergence for all three root finding methods presented so far, as these methods applied to the function

$$f(x) = 2e^{-2x} - \sin(\pi x)$$

is presented in Table 13.1.

A slope-reduction factor of one-half was used in constructing the drawing in Figure 13.5 and is an example of what is called a **relaxation factor**, a number used to alter the results of one iteration before inserting them into the next. Determining the optimum relaxation factor is almost always an extremely complex problem in any calculation and is well beyond the scope of this text. However, in this instance a little trial and error shows that a less drastic decrease in the slope will result in improved convergence. Using a reduction factor of 0.9 should be adequate for most problems; this factor was used to generate the values in Table 13.1.

Table 13.1 Comparison of Root-Finding Methods Using the Function $f(x) = 2e^{-2x} - \sin(\pi x)$

i	Bisection x_2	Regula Bisection x_2	Modified Regula Bisection x_2
1	0.35	0.385	0.385
2	0.375	0.3823	0.3820
3	0.3875	0.3819	0.38183
4	0.38125	0.38185	0.381843
5	0.38438	0.381844	0.38184267
6	0.38281	0.381843	0.38184276
7	0.38203	0.3818428	0.38184275
8	0.38164	0.38184275	0.38184275

Summary of the Algorithms Based on Bisection

The characteristic features of the three methods discussed in this and the previous section are listed below

Bisection	Success based on size of interval
	Slow convergence
	Predictable number of iterations
	Interval halved in each iteration
	Guaranteed to bracket a root
Regula falsi	Success based on size of function
	Faster convergence
	Unpredictable number of iterations
	Interval containing root is not small
	Monitors size of function as well as its sign
Modified regula falsi	Success based on size of interval
	Faster convergence
	Unpredictable number of iterations

Of the three methods, the modified regula falsi is probably the most efficient for common problems and is the recommended algorithm whenever the only information available is that the function changes sign between x_1 and x_3.

The requirement that the initial search interval be one in which the function changes sign (only once) can occasionally be troublesome. For example, the problem of finding the root of the function

$$f(x) = x^2 - 2x + 1 = (x - 1)^2$$

is not suited to any of the algorithms based on bisection since the function never changes sign. This difficulty occurs whenever the root of the function is a multiple root of even multiplicity. A method that overcomes this limitation is the secant method, which is the topic of the next section.

Exercises 13.3

1. Roughly reproduce the sketch in Figure 13.6 and then graphically apply the regula falsi method for three iterations.

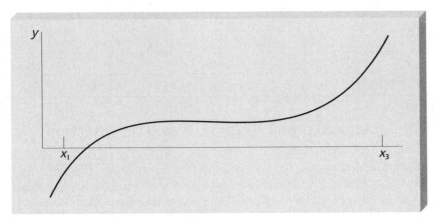

Figure 13.6 Function for Exercise 1.

2. Using a pocket calculator, apply the regula falsi procedure for three iterations to the following functions:
   a. $f(x) = xe^{-x^2} - \cos(x)$; $a = 0$, b = 2; exact root = 1.351491185. . .
   b. $g(x) = x^2 - 2x - 3$; $a = 0$, $b = 4$; exact root = 3.0
   c. $h(x) = e^x - (1 + x + x^2/2)$; $a = -1$, $b = 1$; exact root = 0.0
   d. $F(x) = x^3 - 2x - 5$; $a = 1$, $b = 3$; exact root = 2.0945514815. . .
   e. $G(x) = 10 \ln(x) - x$; $a = 1$, $b = 2$; exact root = 1.1183255916. . .

3. Roughly reproduce Figure 13.6 and then graphically apply the modified regula falsi method for three iterations.

4. **a.** Execute Program 13.2.
   b. Use Program 13.2 to find the root of one of the functions in Exercise 2 to an accuracy of 10^{-5}.
   c. Change the relaxation factor from 0.9 to 0.75 and rerun the program. Comment on the difference between the two calculations.

13.4 THE SECANT METHOD

The secant method is identical to the method of false position (regula falsi method) except that the sign of $f(x)$ need not be checked at each iteration. As in the regula falsi method, the values of x_0 and x_1 are required to start the procedure but then the following algorithm is employed to obtain an improvement for the next value of x:

Start with the interval defined by (x_0, x_1)
Compute the next value of x as

$$x_2 = \frac{f(x_0)}{f(x_0) - f(x_1)} (x_1 - x_0)$$

Replace the pair of values (x_0, x_1) by the pair (x_1, x_2)
Repeat steps 2 and 3 until the value of $f(x)$ is within an acceptable limit of zero

The secant method can be shown (see Exercise 2) to be equivalent to repeatedly replacing the function by straight lines drawn through the points $[x_0, f(x_0)]$ and $[x_1, f(x_1)]$—that is, secant lines. The C++ code for a function implementing the secant method is included within in Program 13.3.

A sample run using Program 13.2 produced the following:

```
Enter the limits of the original search interval, a and b: .4 .5
Enter the convergence criteria: .00001
Enter the maximum number of iterations allowed: 25

The original search interval is from 0.4 to 0.5
The convergence criterion is: interval < 1e-005
The maximum number of iterations allowed is 25

A root at x = 0.443567 was found in 4 iterations
The value of the function is -9.014174e-008
```

Although the secant method is probably the most popular method used to find the root of a function, it does posses divergence problems. As such, a check should be built into the C++ code for this method that detects when successive intervals start to become larger rather than smaller.

Program 13.3

```cpp
#include <iostream.h>
#include <math.h>

void secant(double, double, double, int); // function prototype
double f(double); // function prototype

int main()
{
  int imax;           // maximum number of iterations
  double a, b;        // left and right ends of the original interval
  double epsilon;     // convergence criterion

  // obtain the input data
  cout << "Enter the limits of the original search interval, a and b: ";
  cin  >> a >> b;
  cout << "Enter the convergence criteria: ";
  cin  >> epsilon;
  cout << "Enter the maximum number of iterations allowed: ";
  cin  >> imax;

  secant(a, b, epsilon, imax);

  return 0;
}

// This function implements the secant method for finding
// a root of a function
void secant(double a, double b, double epsilon, int imax)
{

  int i;              // current iteration counter
  double x0, x1;      // left and right x values of current interval
  double f0, f1;      // function evaluated at these points
  double dx0;         // delta x0
  double dx1;         // delta x1

  // echo back the passed input data
  cout << "\nThe original search interval is from " << a << " to " << b
       << "\nThe convergence criterion is: interval < " << epsilon
       << "\nThe maximum number of iterations allowed is " << imax << endl;
```

(Continued)

(Continued)

```cpp
  // determine the root
  x0 = a;
  f0 = f(x0);
  dx0 = fabs(b - a);

  // iterations
  for (i = 1; i <= imax; i++)
  {
    x1 = x0 + dx0;
    f1 = f(x1);
    if (fabs(f1) < epsilon) // root is found
    {
      cout << "\nA root at x = " << x1 + dx1 << " was found "
           << "in " << i << " iterations" << endl;
      cout << "The value of the function is " << f1 << endl;
      return;
    }
    else // do next iteration
    {
      dx1 = ( f1/(f0 - f1) ) * dx0;
      x0 = x1;
      dx0 = dx1;
      f0 = f1;
    }
  }
  cout << "\nAfter " << imax << " iterations, no root was found "
       << "within the convergence criterion\n"
       << "The search for a root has failed due to excessive iterations\n"
       << "after the maximum number of " << imax << " iterations" << endl;

  return;
}

// function to evaluate f(x)
double f(double x)
{
        const double PI = acos(-1); // value of pi

        return (exp(-x) - sin(0.5 * PI * x));
}
```

Exercises 13.4

1. **a.** Execute Program 13.3 on your computer.

   b. Use Program 13.3 to find the root of the function $f(x) = x^2 - 2x + 0.9$ starting with an initial guess of $x_0 = 0.6$ and $x_1 = 0.9$.

2. The function Secant of Program 13.3 was used to find a root of the function $f(x) = x^2 - 2x + 0.9$ starting with an initial guess of $x_0 = 0.6$, $x_1 = 1.0$ and the values of x_0 and $x_1 - x_0$ were printed for each iteration. The results are

Step	x_0	$x_1 - x_0$
0	0.600	0.300
1	0.900	−0.180
2	0.720	−0.057
3	0.663	0.022
4	0.685	−0.001

Carefully graph the function for $0.5 \leq x \leq 1.0$ and use the above numbers to graphically demonstrate how the secant method arrives at a root of the function.

3. Use Program 13.3 to find a root of the function $f(x) = x^2 - 2x - 3$.

13.5 ▷ INTRODUCTION TO NUMERICAL INTEGRATION

The integration of a function of a single variable can be thought of as either the opposite of differentiation—that is, the antiderivative—or as the area under a curve. Antiderivatives are ordinarily discussed in depth in a calculus course. Here we will concentrate instead on the less analytic, more visual approach of interpreting a definite integral as an area. That is, the integral of the function $f(x)$ from $x = a$ to $x = b$, designated as

$$I = \int_a^b f(x)\, dx$$

will be evaluated by devising schemes for measuring the area under the graph of the function over this interval (see Figure 13.7). This method of evaluating an integral lends itself so naturally to numerical computation that the most effective way to understand the process of integration is to learn the numerical approach first and later have these ideas reinforced by the more formal concepts of the antiderivative.

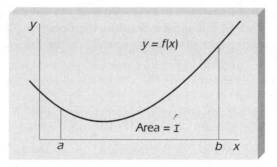

Figure 13.7 *An integral as an area under a curve.*

Another reason for studying numerical integration at this stage is that it is a so-called stable process; it almost always works. This is because numerical integration consists of expressing the area as the sum of areas of smaller segments, a procedure that is relatively safe from problems such as division by zero or round-off error caused by subtracting numbers of approximately the same magnitude.

Finally, it is unfortunately true that many, perhaps most, of the integrals that occur in actual engineering or science problems cannot be expressed in any closed form.

To formally integrate a function—that is, to obtain a closed expression for the answer—often takes considerable training and experience. Dozens of "tricks" must be learned and understood. On the other hand, the procedures of numerical integration are few in number, all quite easy to understand and remember. As in many earlier numerical procedures, we begin by replacing the function over a limited range by straight-line segments. The interval $x = a$ to $x = b$ is divided into subintervals or panels of size Δx, the function is replaced by line segments over each subinterval, and the area under the function is then approximated by the area under the line segments. This is the trapezoidal rule approximation for an integral and is described in the next section. The next order approximation is to replace the function by parabolic segments and is known as Simpson's rule, which is presented in Section 13.7.

13.6 THE TRAPEZOIDAL RULE

An approximation to the area under a complicated curve is obtained by assuming that the function can be replaced by simpler functions over a limited range. A straight line, the simplest approximation to a function, is the first to be considered and leads to what is called the **trapezoidal rule.**

The area under the curve $f(x)$ from $x = a$ to $x = b$ is approximated by the area beneath a straight line drawn between the points $x_a, f(a)$ and $x_b, f(b)$ (see Figure 13.8). The lighter area is then the approximation to the integral and is the area of a trapezoid, which is

$$I \simeq \text{(average value of } f \text{ over interval) (width of interval)}$$

or

$$I \simeq \tfrac{1}{2}\,[f(a) + f(b)]\,(b - a) = T_0 \qquad (13.6)$$

This is the trapezoidal rule for one panel, identified as T_0.

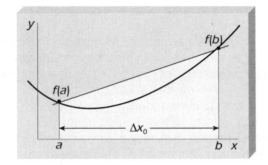

Figure 13.8 Approximating the area under a curve by a single trapezoid.

To improve the accuracy of the approximation to the area under a curve, the interval is next divided in half and the function approximated by straight-line segments over each half. The area in this case is approximated by the area of two trapezoids, as illustrated in Figure 13.9.

$$I \approx T_1 = \left[\tfrac{1}{2}\left(f(a) + f_1\right)\Delta x_L\right] + \left[\tfrac{1}{2}\left(f_1 + f(b)\right)\Delta x_L\right]$$

or

$$T_1 = \frac{\Delta x_L}{2}\left[f(a) + 2f_1 + f(b)\right] \qquad (13.7)$$

where

$$\Delta x_L = \frac{(b - a)}{2}$$

$$f_1 = f\left(x = a + \Delta x_L\right)$$

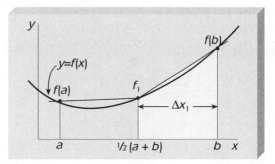

Figure 13.9 Two-panel approximation to the area.

Notice that when adding the areas of the trapezoids, the sides at $f(a)$ and $f(b)$ are sides of only the first and last trapezoid, whereas the side at f_1 is a side of two trapezoids and thus "counts twice," explaining the factor of 2 in Equation 13.7.

Furthermore, the two-panel approximation, T_1, can be related to the one-panel results, T_0, as

$$T_1 = \frac{T_0}{2} + \Delta x_1 f_1 \quad \textbf{(13.8)}$$

To increase the accuracy further, the interval is simply subdivided into a large number of panels. The result for n panels is clearly

$$I \approx T_n = \tfrac{1}{2}\Delta x_n \left[f(a) + 2 \sum_{i=1}^{n-1} f_i + f(b) \right] \quad \textbf{(13.9)}$$

where $\Delta x_n = (b - a)/n$ and f_i is the function evaluated at each of the interior points,

$$f_i = f(x = a + i\,\Delta x_n)$$

The reason for the extra factor of 2 in Equation 13.9 is the same as in the two-panel example. Equation 3.9 is known as the **Trapezoidal Rule**.

Computational Form of the Trapezoidal Rule Equation

Equation 13.9 was derived assuming that the widths of all the panels are the same and equal to Δx_n. However, equal panel widths are not required in the derivation, and the equation can easily be generalized to a partition of the interval into unequal panels of width Δx_i, $i = 1, \ldots, n - 1$. However, for reasons to explained a bit later, we will not only restrict the panel widths to be equal but the number of panels to be a power of 2—that is,

$$n = 2^k$$

The number of panels is n, the order of the calculation will be called k, and the corresponding trapezoidal rule approximation will be labeled as T_k. Thus, T_0 is the result for $n = 2^0 = 1$ panel. The situation for $k = 2$ or $2^2 = 4$ panels is illustrated in Figure 13.10.

In the figure the width of a panel is $\Delta x_2 = (b - a)/2^2$, and the value of the $k = 2$ trapezoidal rule approximation is

$$T_2 = (\Delta x_2/2)[f(a) + 2f(a + \Delta x_2) + 2f(a + \Delta x_2) + 2f(a + 3\Delta x_2) + f(b)] \quad (13.10)$$

However, since $2\Delta x_2 = \Delta x_1$, we see that

$$f(a + 2\Delta x_2) = f(a + x_1)$$

Figure 13.10 Four-panel trapezoidal approximation, T^2.

and $f(a + \Delta x_1)$ was already determined in the previous calculation of T_1, (Equation 13.8). The point is that by successively doubling the number of panels in each stage, the only new information we require to proceed to the next order trapezoidal rule approximation is the evaluation of the function at the midpoints of the current intervals.

To exploit this fact further, Equations 13.7 and 13.8 can be used to rewrite Equation 13.10 in the form

$$T_2 = (\Delta x_1/4)[f(a) + 2f(a + \Delta x_1) + f(b)] + \Delta x_2[f(a + \Delta x_2) + f(a + 3\Delta x_2)]$$

$$= T_1/2 + \Delta x_2[f(a + \Delta x_2) + f(a + 3\Delta x_2)]$$

This equation can easily be generalized to yield

$$T_k = \tfrac{1}{2} T_{k-1} + \Delta x_k \sum_{\substack{i=1 \\ \text{odd only}}}^{n-1} f(a + i\,\Delta x_k) \quad (13.11)$$

where

$$\Delta x_k = \frac{b - a}{2^k}$$

The procedure for using Equation 13.11 to approximate an integral by the trapezoidal rule is then:

1. Compute T_0 by using Equation 13.6.

2. Repeatedly apply Equation 13.11 for k = 1,2, ... until sufficient accuracy is obtained.

Example of a Trapezoidal Rule Calculation

To illustrate the ideas of this section, we use the integral

$$I = \int_1^2 (1/x)\, dx$$

The function $f(x) = 1/x$ can of course be integrated analytically to give $\ln(x)$, and since $\ln(1) = 0$, the value of the integral is $\ln(2) = 0.69314718$. The trapezoidal rule approximation to the integral with $a = 1$ and $b = 2$ begins with Equation 13.6 to obtain T_0.

$$T_0 = \frac{1}{2}\left(\frac{1}{1} + \frac{1}{2}\right)(2 - 1) = 0.75$$

Repeated use of Equation 13.11 then yields

$k = 1$ $\qquad \Delta x_1 = \tfrac{1}{2}$

$$T_1 = T_0/2 + \tfrac{1}{2}\left[f\left(1 + \tfrac{1}{2}\right)\right] = 0.75/2 + \tfrac{1}{2}\ (1/1.5)$$

$$= 0.708333$$

$k = 2$ $\qquad \Delta x_2 = \tfrac{1}{4}$

$$T_2 = T_1/2 + \tfrac{1}{4}\ (1/1.25 + 1/1.75)$$

$$= 0.6970238$$

$k = 3$ $\qquad \Delta x_3 = \tfrac{1}{8}$

$$T_3 = T_2/2 + \tfrac{1}{8}\ (1/1.25 + 1/1.375 + 1/1.625 + 1/1.875)$$

$$= 0.69412185$$

Continuing the calculation through $k = 5$ yields

k	T_k
0	0.75
1	0.70833
2	0.69702
3	0.69412
4	0.69339
5	0.693208
.	.
.	.
.	.
Exact	0.693147. . .

The convergence of the computed values of the trapezoidal rule is not particularly fast, but the method is quite simple.

Exercises 13.6

1. Evaluate the integrals below by using the trapezoidal rule.
   a. Evaluate T_0 for one panel by using Equation 13.6.
   b. Compute T_1 using the value of T_0 and Equation 13.11.
   c. Continue the calculation through T_4.

   Collect your results in the form of a table. (Be careful: errors in one step will carry over into the next.)

		Exact Result
a.	$\int_0^8 x^2 dx$	$170\frac{2}{3}$
b.	$\int_0^8 x^4 dx$	6553.6
c.	$\int_0^1 xe^{-x} dx$	$1 - 2/e = 0.2642411175\ldots$
d.	$\int_0^{\pi/2} x\,\sin(x)dx$	1.0
e.	$\int_0^1 (1+x^2)^{3/2} dx$	$1.567951963\ldots$
f.	$\int_0^1 e^{-x^2} dx$	$0.74682404\ldots$

13.7 SIMPSON'S RULE

The trapezoidal rule is based on approximating the function by straight line segments. To improve the accuracy and the convergence rate of the method, an obvious direction to take would be to approximate the function by parabolic segments in place of straight lines. This idea results in an approximation for the integral known as **Simpson's rule**, the simplest example of which is illustrated in Figure 13.11. To uniquely specify a parabola requires three points, and so the lowest-order Simpson's rule has two panels.

To proceed, we need to know the area under a parabola drawn through three points. Note that the corresponding step in the derivation of the trapezoidal rule was trivial: the area under a line through two points is simply $\Delta x[f(a) + f(b)])/2$.

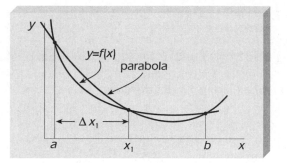

Figure 13.11 Area under a parabola drawn through three points.

If the curve $f(x)$ drawn in Figure 13.11 is approximated by a parabola drawn through the three points $f(a)$, $f(b)$, and the value of $f(x)$ at the midpoint of the interval f_{mid}, it can be shown using calculus that shaded area under the parabola, denoted as S_1, is

$$S_1 = \tfrac{1}{3} \Delta x_1 \left[f(a) + 4f(a + \Delta x_1) + f(b) \right]$$

where

$$\Delta x_1 = \frac{b-a}{2^2}$$

This is the first order Simpson's rule approximation where $k = 1$ and $n = 2^1$ panels. The next level of approximation is to halve the interval width and partition the interval into four panels, as shown in Figure 13.12. The area under the function $f(x)$ is then approximated as the area under the two parabolas shown in the figure. Again, using calculus, it can be shown that the area under the two parabolas is

$$S_2 = \tfrac{1}{3} \Delta x_2 \left\{ \left[f(a) + 4f(x_1) + f(x_2) \right] + \left[f(x_2) + 4f(x_3) + f(b) \right] \right\}$$

$$= \tfrac{1}{3} \Delta x_2 \left\{ f(a) + 4\left[f(x_1) + f(x_3) \right] + 2f(x_2) + f(b) \right\} \qquad (13.12)$$

where

$$\Delta x_2 = \frac{b-a}{2^2}$$

and

$$f_i = f\left(x = a + i\Delta x_2 \right)$$

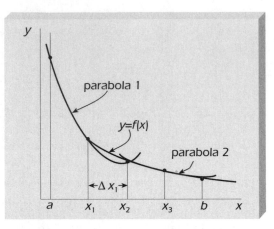

Figure 13.12 Second-order Simpson's rule approximation is the area under two parabolas.

This procedure can be extended to 8, 16, 32, and so on panels. The result is a rather simple generalization of Equation 13.12and for $n = 2^k$ panels is

$$S_k = \tfrac{1}{3}\Delta x_k \left[f(a) + 4\sum_{\substack{i=1 \\ \text{odd only}}}^{n-1} f(a + i\,\Delta x_k) + 2\sum_{\substack{i=2 \\ \text{even only}}}^{n-2} f(a + i\,\Delta x_k) + f(b) \right] \quad \textbf{(13.13)}$$

Equation 13.13, which is known as **Simpson's rule**, is an extremely popular method of evaluating integrals of functions that are smooth, and rightly so. As we shall see later in the chapter, Simpson's rule converges nicely in most instances and it is relatively easy to use. Also, Equation 13.13 can easily be adapted to handle an odd number of unevenly spaced points and is the most common method for estimating the integral of experimentally obtained data.

Example of Simpson's Rule as an Approximation to an Integral

Again consider the integral

$$I = \int_1^2 (1/x)\,dx$$

Using Equation 13.13 first for $k = 1$ yields

$$k = 1$$
$$n = 2^1 = 2$$
$$\Delta x_1 = \frac{b-a}{2^2} = \frac{1}{2}$$

$$S_1 = \tfrac{1}{3}(\tfrac{1}{2})[1 + 4(1/1.5) + \tfrac{1}{2}] = 0.6944444$$

Repeating for $k = 2$

   $k = 2$

   $n = 2^2 = 4$

   $\Delta x_2 = \frac{1}{4}$

   $S_2 = \frac{1}{3}(\frac{1}{4})[1 + 4(1/1.25 + 1/1.75) + 2(1/1.5) + \frac{1}{2}] = 0.69325397$

Continuing the calculation, we obtain the values listed in Table 13.2. For comparison, results are also included for the same integral obtained in the previous section using the Trapezoidal rule. Clearly, Simpson's rule converges much faster that the Trapezoidal rule, at least for this example.

Table 13.2 Trapezoidal and Simpson's Rule Results for the Integral $\int_1^2 (1/x)\, dx$

Order k	Number of Panels n	T_k	S_k
0	1	0.75	–
1	2	0.7083	0.6944
2	4	0.69702	0.69325
3	8	0.69412	0.69315
4	16	0.69339	0.6931466
5	32	0.693208	0.6931473
6	64	0.693162	0.6931472

Exercises 13.7

1. Using Equation 13.13, calculate the two-panel and the four-panel Simpson's rule results, S_1 and S_2 for the following integrals.

                              Exact Result

   a. $\int_0^8 x^2 dx$ $170\frac{2}{3}$

   b. $\int_0^8 x^4 dx$ 6553.6

   c. $\int_0^1 xe^{-x} dx$ $1 - 2/e = 0.2642411175\ldots$

   d. $\int_0^{\pi/2} x \sin(x)\, dx$ 1.0

e.
$$\int_0^1 \left(1+x^2\right)^{3/2} dx \qquad 1.567951962\ldots$$

f.
$$\int_0^1 e^{-x^2} dx \qquad 0.74682404\ldots$$

2. Using Equation 13.13, calculate S_1 through S_4 for the integrals listed in Exercise 1.

13.8 COMMON PROGRAMMING ERRORS

In using the modified bisection root-finding method, two problems can occur.

The first problem is round-off error, which can occur whenever the values of $f(x_1)$ and $f(x_3)$ used in the computation are very nearly equal. The second problem occurs because a prediction of the exact number of iterations required to achieve a desired accuracy is not available. To successfully counter these two problems, the code used in these two methods must detect their occurrence to prevent excessive and possibly infinite iterations.

With respect to numerical integration excessive computation times can also be a problem. This typically occurs whenever the number of iterations exceeds fifty. Frequently, it is possible to significantly reduce run-time by carefully inspecting each program loop to ensure that only those calculations that must be iteratively computed are included within the loop, and moving all other calculations to be computed either before or after the loop is completed.

13.9 CHAPTER SUMMARY

All of the root-solving methods described in this chapter are of an iterative nature and can be categorized within two classes of root-finding algorithms, depending on whether you are starting with an interval containing a root or with an initial estimate of the root. The bisection-based procedures begin with an interval that is known to contain a root and are guaranteed to converge to within a prescribed tolerance bracketing the root. Of the bisection methods, the modified regula falsi is the fastest converging and is recommended.

In algorithms based on the bisection method, the initial interval is refined by repeatedly evaluating the function at points within the interval and then, by monitoring the sign of the function, and determining in which subinterval the root lies. If the left and right ends of the current interval are x_1 and x_3, respectively, the standard bisection method uses the function evaluated at the midpoint, $x_2 = \frac{1}{2}(x_1 + x_3)$. The sign of the function at x_2 is compared with that at either end of the interval to determine which half of the interval contains the root. The full interval is then replaced by this half and the process repeated. After n iterations, the root will be contained in an interval of size $(x_3 - x_1)/2n$.

In the regula falsi method, the conditions are the same as for the bisection method. But instead of using the midpoint of the interval, a straight line connecting the points at the ends of the interval is used to interpolate the position of the root. The intersection of this line with the x axis determines the value of x_2 to be used in the next step. This value of x_2 is given by the equation

$$x_2 = x_1 - (x_3 - x_1)\frac{f(x_1)}{f(x_3) - f(x_1)}$$

in place of the equation for the midpoint. Convergence is faster than with the bisection method. However, it is likely that the interval will converge to the root from one side only.

The modified regula falsi method is the same as the regula falsi method except for the following change: in each iteration, when the full interval is replaced by the subinterval containing the root, a relaxation factor is used to first modify the value of the function at the fixed end of the subinterval. A relaxation factor of approximately 0.9 is suggested. This additional feature will cause the interval to converge from both ends, and convergence is then based on interval size. This method is the preferred procedure for finding a root of a function that is not too expensive to evaluate and that is known to have a root in a specified interval.

The secant method replaces the function by a secant line through two points and then finds the point of intersection of the line with the x axis. The algorithm requires two input numbers, x_0 and Δx_0, corresponding to initial guesses for the root and for an interval containing the root. This pair of values is then replaced by the pair $(x_1, \Delta x_1)$ where

$$x_1 = x_0 + \Delta x_0$$

and

$$\Delta x_1 = \frac{f(x_1)}{f(x_0) - f(x_1)} \Delta x_0$$

and the process is continued until the new interval Δx is sufficiently small.

Root-solving methods are amenable to C++ coding. However, the success of a program to find the root of a function usually depends on the quality of the information supplied by the user; that is, how accurate is the initial guess or search interval and how well does the method chosen match the circumstances of the problem. Execution-time problems are most frequently traceable to errors in coding the function or to inadequate user-supplied diagnostics for potential problems.

The integral of $f(x)$ from $x = a$ to $x = b$, written as

$$I = \int_a^b f(x)\,dx$$

is evaluated numerically by computing the area under the curve $f(x)$ over the specified range of x. The procedures for estimating this area consist of partitioning the interval $a \le x \le b$ into n panels of width $\Delta x_i (i = 1, n)$, and approximating the function $f(x)$ over each panel by a simpler function.

The trapezoidal rule results from replacing the function $f(x)$ by straight-line segments over the panels Δx_i. The approximate value for the integral is then given by the following formula, which is known as the trapezoidal rule:

$$\int_a^b f(x)\, dx \approx \tfrac{1}{2}\,\Delta x_n\left(f(a) + 2\sum_{i-1}^{n-1} f_i + f(b) \right)$$

If the panels are of equal size *and* the number of panels is $n = 2^k$, where k is a positive integer, the trapezoidal rule approximation is then labeled as T_k and satisfies the equation

$$T_k = \tfrac{1}{2}\,T_{k-1} + \Delta x_k \sum_{\substack{i=1 \\ \text{odd only}}}^{n-1} f\!\left(a + i\Delta x_k\right)$$

where

$$\Delta x_k = \frac{b-a}{2^k}$$

In the next level of approximation the function $f(x)$ is replace by $n/2$ parabolic segments over pairs of equal-size panels, $\Delta x = (b-a)/n$ and results in the formula for the area known as Simpson's rule:

$$\int_a^b f(x)\, dx \approx \tfrac{1}{3}\Delta x_k\left[f(a) + 4\sum_{\substack{i=1 \\ \text{odd only}}}^{n-1} f\!\left(a + i\Delta x_k\right) + 2\sum_{\substack{i=2 \\ \text{even only}}}^{n-2} f\!\left(a + i\Delta x_k\right) + f(b) \right]$$

CHAPTER **14**

Bit Operations

TOPICS

14.1 THE AND OPERATOR

14.2 THE INCLUSIVE OR OPERATOR

14.3 THE EXCLUSIVE OR OPERATOR

14.4 THE COMPLEMENT OPERATOR

14.5 DIFFERENT-SIZE DATA ITEMS

14.6 THE SHIFT OPERATORS

14.7 CHAPTER SUMMARY

C++ operates with data entities that are stored as one or more bytes, such as character, integer, and double-precision constants and variables. In addition, C++ provides for the manipulation of individual bits of character and integer values and variables. The operators that are used to perform bit manipulations are called bit operators, and are listed in Table 14.1.

All the operators listed in Table 14.1, except ~, are binary operators, requiring two operands. Each operand is treated as a binary number consisting of a series of individual 1s and 0s. The respective bits in each operand are then compared on a bit-by-bit basis and the result is determined based on the selected operation.

Table 14.1 Bit Operators

Operator	Description
&	Bitwise AND
|	Bitwise Inclusive OR
^	Bitwise Exclusive OR
~	Bitwise one's complement
<<	Left shift
>>	Right shift

14.1 THE AND OPERATOR

The AND operator causes a bit-by-bit AND comparison between its two operands. *The result of each bit-by-bit comparison is a 1 only when both bits being compared are 1s, otherwise the result of the AND operation is a 0.* For example, assume that the following two eight-bit numbers are to be ANDed:

```
1 0 1 1 0 0 1 1
1 1 0 1 0 1 0 1
— — — — — — — —
```

To perform an AND operation, each bit in one operand is compared to the bit occupying the same position in the other operand. Figure 14.1 illustrates the correspondence between bits for these two operands. As shown in the figure, when both bits being compared are 1s, the result is a 1, otherwise the result is a 0. The result of each comparison is, of course, independent of any other bit comparison.

```
    1 0 1 1 0 0 1 1
  & 1 1 0 1 0 1 0 1
    — — — — — — — —
    1 0 0 1 0 0 0 1
```

Figure 14.1 A sample AND operation.

Program 14.1 illustrates the use of an AND operation. In this program, the variable op1 is initialized to the octal value 325, which is the octal equivalent of the binary number 1 1 0 1 0 1 0 1, and the variable op2 is initialized to the octal value 263, which is the octal representation of the binary number 1 0 1 1 0 0 1 1. These are the same two binary numbers illustrated in Figure 14.1.

Program 14.1

```
#include <iostream.h>

int main()
{
  int op1 = 0325, op2 = 0263;

  int op3 = op1 & op2;
  cout << oct << op1 << " ANDed with "<< op2 << " is " << op3 << endl;

  return 0;
}
```

Program 14.1 produces the following output:

```
325 ANDed with 263 is 221
```

The result of ANDing the octal numbers 325 and 263 is the octal number 221. The binary equivalent of 221 is the binary number 1 0 0 1 0 0 0 1, which is the result of the AND operation illustrated in Figure 14.1.

AND operations are extremely useful in masking, or eliminating, selected bits from an operand. This is a direct result of the fact that ANDing any bit (1 or 0) with a 0 forces the resulting bit to be a 0, while ANDing any bit (1 or 0) with a 1 leaves the original bit unchanged. For example, assume that the variable op1 has the arbitrary bit pattern x x x x x x x x, where each x can be either 1 or 0, independent of any other x in the number. The result of ANDing this binary number with the binary number 0 0 0 0 1 1 1 1 is:

```
    op1 =   x x x x x x x x
    op2 =   0 0 0 0 1 1 1 1
            — — — — — — — -
 Result =   0 0 0 0 x x x x
```

As can be seen from this example, the zeros in op2 effectively mask, or eliminate, the respective bits in op1, while the ones in op2 filter, or pass, the respective bits in op1 through with no change in their values. In this example, the variable op2 is called a **mask**. By choosing the mask appropriately, any individual bit in an operand can be selected, or filtered, out of an operand for inspection. For example, ANDing the variable op1 with the mask 0 0 0 0 0 1 0 0 forces all the bits of the result to be zero, except for the third bit. The third bit of the result will be a copy of the third bit of op1. Thus, if the result of the AND is zero, the third bit of op1 must have been zero, and if the result of the AND is a nonzero number, the third bit must have been a 1.

Program 14.2 uses this masking property to convert lowercase letters into their uppercase form, assuming the letters are stored using the ASCII code. The algorithm for converting letters is based on the fact that the binary codes for lowercase and uppercase letters in ASCII are the same except for bit five, which is a 1 for lowercase letters and

0 for uppercase letters.[1] For example the binary code for the letter a is 01100001 (hex 61), while the binary code for the letter A is 01000001 (hex 41). Similarly, the binary code for the letter z is 01111010 (hex 7A), while the binary code for the letter Z is 01011010 (hex 5A). (See Appendix B for the hexadecimal values of the upper and lowercase letters.) Thus, given a lowercase letter, it can be converted into its uppercase form by forcing the fifth bit to zero. This is accomplished in Program 14.2 by masking the letter's code with the binary value 11011111, which has the hexadecimal value DF.

Program 14.2

```cpp
#include <iostream.h>

const int TO_UP = 0xDF;
void upper(char *);   // function prototype

int main()
{
  char word[81];        // enough storage for a complete line

  cout << "Enter a string of both upper and lowercase letters:\n";
  cin.getline(word,80,'\n');
  cout << "\nThe string of letters just entered is:\n"
       << word << endl;
  upper(word);
  cout << "\nThis string, in uppercase letters is:\n"
       << word << endl;
}
void upper(char *word)
{
  while (*word != '\0')
    *word++ &= TO_UP;
}
```

A sample run using Program 14.2 follows:

```
Enter a string of both upper and lowercase letters:
abcdefgHIJKLMNOPqrstuvwxyz

The string of letters just entered is:
abcdefgHIJKLMNOPqrstuvwxyz

This string, in uppercase letters is:
ABCDEFGHIJKLMNOPQRSTUVWXYZ
```

---

[1]This assumes the conventional numbering scheme starting with bit 0 as the rightmost bit. Using this convention the rightmost bit (or bit 0) is referred to as the least significant bit (LSB) and the leftmost bit is referred to as the most significant bit (MSB). Here the MSB is bit 7.

Notice that the lowercase letters are converted to uppercase form, while uppercase letters are unaltered. This is because bit five of all uppercase letters is zero to begin with, so that forcing this bit to zero using the mask has no effect. Only when bit five is a one, as it is for lowercase letters, is the input character altered.

14.2 THE INCLUSIVE OR OPERATOR

The inclusive OR operator, |, performs a bit-by-bit comparison of its two operands in a similar fashion to the bit-by-bit AND. The result of the OR comparison, however, is determined by the following rule:

The result of the comparison is 1 if either bit being compared is a 1, otherwise the result is a 0.

Figure 14.2 illustrates an OR operation. As shown in the figure, when either of the two bits being compared is a 1, the result is a 1, otherwise the result is a 0. As with all bit operations, the result of each comparison is, of course, independent of any other comparison.

```
    1 0 1 1 0 0 1 1
|   1 1 0 1 0 1 0 1
  — — — — — — — —
    1 1 1 1 0 1 1 1
```

Figure 14.2 A sample OR operation.

Program 14.3 illustrates an OR operation, using the octal values of the operands illustrated in Figure 14.2.

Program 14.3

```
#include <iostream.h>

int main()
{
  int op1 = 0325, op2 = 0263;

  int op3 = op1 | op2;
  cout << oct << op1 << " ORed with " << op2 << " is " << op3 << endl;
}
```

Program 14.3 produces the following output:

```
325 ORed with 263 is 367
```

The result of ORing the octal numbers 325 and 263 is the octal number 367. The binary equivalent of 367 is 1 1 1 1 0 1 1 1, which is the result of the OR operation illustrated in Figure 14.2.

Inclusive OR operations are extremely useful in forcing selected bits to take on a 1 value or for passing through other bit values unchanged. This is a direct result of the fact that ORing any bit (1 or 0) with a 1 forces the resulting bit to be a 1, while ORing any bit (1 or 0) with a 0 leaves the original bit unchanged. For example, assume that the variable op1 has the arbitrary bit pattern x x x x x x x x, where each x can be either 1 or 0, independent of any other x in the number. The result of ORing this binary number with the binary number 1 1 1 1 0 0 0 0 is

```
  op1 =    x x x x x x x x
  op2 =    1 1 1 1 0 0 0 0
           - - - - - - - -
Result =   1 1 1 1 x x x x
```

As can be seen from this example, the ones in op2 force the resulting bits to 1, while the zeros in op2 filter, or pass, the respective bits in op1 through with no change in their values. Thus, using an OR operation a similar masking operation can be produced as with an AND operation, except the masking bits are set to ones rather than to zeros. Another way of looking at this is to say that ORing with a zero has the same effect as ANDing with a one.

Program 14.4 uses this masking property to convert uppercase letters in a word into their respective lowercase form, assuming the letters are stored using the ASCII code. The algorithm for converting letters is similar to that used in Program 14.2, and converts uppercase letters into their lowercase form by forcing the fifth bit in each letter to a one. This is accomplished in Program 14.4 by masking the letter's code with the binary value 00100000, which has the hexadecimal value 20.

A sample run using Program 14.4 follows:

```
Enter a string of both upper and lowercase letters:
abcdefgHIJKLMNOPqrstuvwxyz

The string of letters just entered is:
abcdefgHIJKLMNOPqrstuvwxyz

This string, in lowercase letters is:
abcdefghijklmnopqrstuvwxyz
```

Notice that the uppercase letters are converted to lowercase form, while uppercase letters are unaltered. This is because bit five of all lowercase letters is one to begin with, so that forcing this bit to one using the mask has no effect. Only when bit five is a zero, as it is for uppercase letters, is the input character altered.

Program 14.4

```
#include <iostream.h>

const int TO_LOW = 0x20;
void lower (char *);   // function prototype

int main()
{
  char word[81];          // enough storage for a complete line

  cout << "Enter a string of both upper and lowercase letters:\n";
  cin.getline(word,81,'\n');
  cout << "\nThe string of letters just entered is:\n"
       << word << endl;
  lower(word);
  cout << "\nThis string, in lowercase letters is:\n"
       << word << endl;
}
void lower(char *word)
{
  while (*word != '\0')
    *word++ |= TO_LOW;
}
```

14.3 THE EXCLUSIVE OR OPERATOR

The exclusive OR operator, ^, performs a bit-by-bit comparison of its two operands. The result of the comparison is determined by the following rule:

The result of the comparison is 1 if one and only one of the bits being compared is a 1, otherwise the result is 0.

Figure 14.3 illustrates an exclusive OR operation. As shown in the figure, when both bits being compared are the same value (both 1 or both 0), the result is a zero. Only when both bits have different values (one bit a 1 and the other a 0) is the result a 1. Again, each pair or bit comparison is independent of any other bit comparison.

```
  1 0 1 1 0 0 1 1
^ 1 1 0 1 0 1 0 1
- - - - - - - -
  0 1 1 0 0 1 1 0
```

Figure 14.3 A sample exclusive OR operation.

An exclusive OR operation can be used to create the opposite value, or complement, of any individual bit in a variable. This is a direct result of the fact that exclusive ORing any bit (1 or 0) with a 1 forces the resulting bit to be of the opposite value of its original state, while exclusive ORing any bit (1 or 0) with a 0 leaves the original bit unchanged. For example, assume that the variable op1 has the arbitrary bit pattern x x x x x x x x, where each x can be either 1 or 0, independent of any other x in the number. Using the notation that $\bar{x}$ is the complement (opposite) value of x, the result of exclusive ORing this binary number with the binary number 0 1 0 1 0 1 0 1 is:

```
op1 =   x x x x x x x x
op2 =   0 1 0 1 0 1 0 1
        - - - - - - - -

        _   _   _   _
Result = x x x x x x x x
```

As can be seen from this example, the ones in op2 force the resulting bits to be the complement of their original bit values, while the zeros in op2 filter, or pass, the respective bits in op1 through with no change in their values.

Many encryption methods use the exclusive OR operation to code data. For example, the string Hello there world! initially used in Program 2.1 can be encrypted by exclusive ORing each character in the string with a mask value of 52. The choice of the mask value, which is referred to as the encryption key, is arbitrary, and any key value can be used.

Program 14.5 uses an encryption key of 52 to code a user-entered message.

Following is a sample run using Program 14.5.

```
Enter a sentence:
Good morning

The sentence just entered is:
Good morning

The encrypted version of this sentence is:
s[[P¶Y[FZ]ZS
```

Decoding an encrypted message requires exclusive ORing the coded message using the original encryption key, which is left as a homework exercise.

Program 14.5

```cpp
#include <iostream.h>

void encrypt(char *); // function prototype

int main()
{
  char message[81];      // enough storage for a complete line

  cout << "\nEnter a sentence:\n";
  cin.getline(message,81,'\n');
  cout << "\nThe sentence just entered is:\n"
       << message << endl;
  encrypt(message);
  cout << "\nThe encrypted version of this sentence is:\n"
       << message << endl;
}

void encrypt(char *message)
{
  while (*message != '\0')
    *message++ ^= 52;
}
```

14.4 THE COMPLEMENT OPERATOR

The complement operator, ~, is a unary operator that changes each 1 bit in its operand to 0 and each 0 bit to 1. For example, if the variable op1 contains the binary number 11001010, ~op1 replaces this binary number with the number 00110101. The complement operator is used to force any bit in an operand to zero, independent of the actual number of bits used to store the number. For example, the statement

        op1 = op1 & ~07;   // 07 is an octal number

or its shorter form,

        op1 &= ~07;   // 07 is an octal number

both set the last three bits of op1 to zero, regardless of how op1 is stored within the computer. Either of these two statements can, of course, be replaced by ANDing the last three bits of op1 with zeros, if the number of bits used to store op1 is known. In a computer that uses 16 bits to store integers, the appropriate AND operation is

```
op1 = op1 & 0177770;    // in octal
```

or

```
op1 = op1 & 0xFFF8;     // in hexadecimal
```

For a computer that uses 32 bits to store integers, the above AND sets the leftmost or higher order 16 bits to zero also, which is an unintended result. The correct statement for 32 bits is:

```
op1 = op1 & 027777777770;    // in octal
```

or

```
op1 = op1 & 0xFFFFFFF8;      // in hexadecimal
```

Using the complement operator in this situation frees the programmer from having to determine the storage size of the operand and, more importantly, makes the program portable between machines using different integer storage sizes.

14.5 DIFFERENT-SIZE DATA ITEMS

When the bit operators &, |, and ^ are used with operands of different sizes, the shorter operand is always increased in bit size to match the size of the larger operand. Figure 14.4 illustrates the extension of a 16-bit unsigned integer into a 32-bit number.

Figure 14.4 Extending 16-bit unsigned data to 32 bits.

As the figure shows, the additional bits are added to the left of the original number and filled with zeros. This is the equivalent of adding leading zeros to the number, which has no effect on the number's value.

When extending signed numbers, the original leftmost bit is reproduced in the additional bits that are added to the number. As illustrated in Figure 14.5, if the original leftmost bit is 0, corresponding to a positive number, 0 is placed in each of the additional bit positions. If the leftmost bit is 1, which corresponds to a negative number, 1 is placed in the additional bit positions. In either case, the resulting binary number has the same sign and magnitude of the original number.

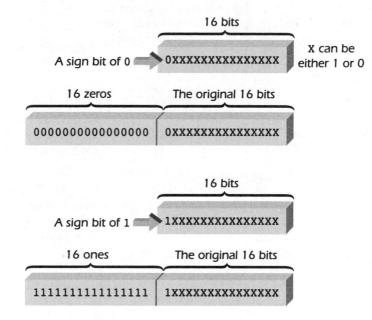

Figure 14.5 Extending 16-bit signed data to 32 bits.

14.6 THE SHIFT OPERATORS

The left shift operator, <<, causes the bits in an operand to be shifted to the left by a given amount. For example, the statement

```
op1 = op1 << 4;
```

causes the bits in op1 to be shifted four bits to the left, filling any vacated bits with a zero. Figure 14.6 illustrates the effect of shifting the binary number 1111100010101011 to the left by four bit positions.

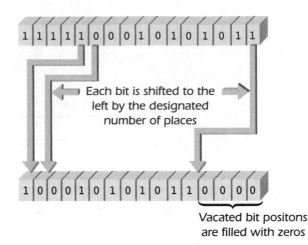

Each bit is shifted to the left by the designated number of places

Vacated bit positons are filled with zeros

Figure 14.6 *An example of a left shift.*

For unsigned integers, each left shift corresponds to multiplication by two. This is also true for signed numbers using two's complement representation, as long as the leftmost bit does not switch values. Since a change in the leftmost bit of a two's complement number represents a change in both the sign and magnitude represented by the bit, such a shift does not represent a simple multiplication by two.

The right shift operator, >>, causes the bits in an operand to be shifted to the right by a given amount. For example, the statement

```
op2 = op1 >> 3;
```

causes the bits in op1 to be shifted to the right by three bit positions. Figure 14.7a illustrates the right shift of the unsigned binary number 1111100010101011 by three bit positions. As illustrated, the three rightmost bits are shifted "off the end" and are lost.

For unsigned numbers, the leftmost bit is not used as a sign bit. For this type of number, the vacated leftmost bits are always filled with zeros. This is the case that is illustrated in Figure 14.7a.

For signed numbers, what is filled in the vacated bits depends on the computer. Most computers reproduce the original sign bit of the number. Figure 14.7b illustrates the right shift of a negative binary number by four bit positions, where the sign bit is reproduced in the vacated bits. Figure 14.7c illustrates the equivalent right shift of a positive signed binary number.

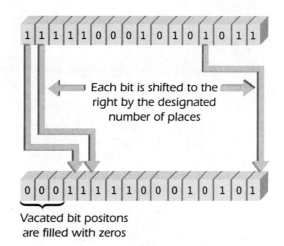

Figure 14.7a An unsigned arithmetic right shift.

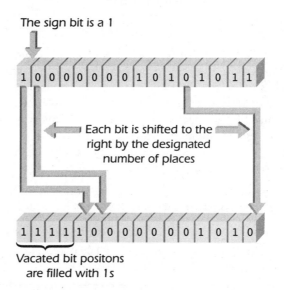

Figure 14.7b The right shift of a negative binary number.

The sign bit is a 0

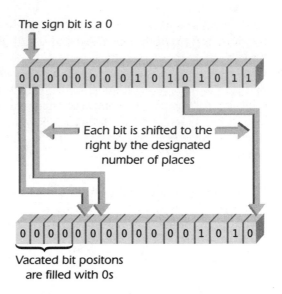

Each bit is shifted to the right by the designated number of places

Vacated bit positons
are filled with 0s

Figure 14.7c The right shift of a positive binary number.

The type of fill illustrated in Figures 14.7b and c, where the sign bit is reproduced in vacated bit positions, is called an **arithmetic right shift**. In an arithmetic right shift, each single shift to the right corresponds to a division by two.

Instead of reproducing the sign bit in right-shifted signed numbers, some computers automatically fill the vacated bits with zeros. This type of shift is called a **logical shift**. For positive signed numbers, where the leftmost bit is zero, both arithmetic and logical right shifts produce the same result. The results of these two shifts are only different when negative numbers are involved.

Exercises for Chapter 14

1. Determine the results of the following operations:

   a.   11001010   **b.**   11001010   **c.**   11001010
          & 10100101 | 10100101   ^ 10100101
        _____   _____   _____

2. Write the octal representations of the binary numbers given in Exercise 1.

3. Determine the octal results of the following operations, assuming unsigned numbers:
   a. the octal number 0157 shifted left by one bit position
   b. the octal number 0701 shifted left by two bit positions
   c. the octal number 0673 shifted right by two bit positions
   d. the octal number 067 shifted right by three bit positions

4. Repeat Exercise 3 assuming that the numbers are treated as signed values.

5. **a.** Assume that the arbitrary bit pattern xxxxxxxx, where each x can represent either 1 or 0, is stored in the integer variable named **flag**. Determine the

octal value of a mask that can be ANDed with the bit pattern to reproduce the third and fourth bits of `flag` and set all other bits to zero. The rightmost bit in `flag` is considered bit 0.

b. Determine the octal value of a mask that can be inclusively ORed with the bit pattern in `flag` to reproduce the third and fourth bits of `flag` and set all other bits to one. Again, consider the rightmost bit in `flag` to be bit 0.

c. Determine the octal value of a mask that can be used to complement the values of the third and fourth bits of `flag` and leave all other bits unchanged. Determine the bit operation that should be used with the mask value to produce the desired result.

6. a. Write the two's complement form of the decimal number –1, using eight bits. (*Hint*: Refer to Section 1.6 for a review of two's complement numbers.)

b. Repeat Exercise 6a using 16 bits to represent the decimal number –1 and compare your answer to your previous answer. Could the 16-bit version have been obtained by sign-extending the 8-bit version?

7. As was noted in the text, Program 14.2 has no effect on uppercase letters. Using the ASCII codes listed in Appendix B, determine what other characters would be unaffected by Program 14.2.

8. Modify Program 14.2 so that a complete sentence can be read in and converted to lowercase values. (*Hint*: When a space is masked by Program 14.2, the resulting character is \0, which terminates the output.)

9. Modify Program 14.4 to allow a complete sentence to be input and converted to uppercase letters. Make sure that your program does not alter any other characters or symbols entered.

10. Modify Program 14.5 to permit the encryption key to be a user-entered input value.

11. Modify Program 14.5 to have its output written to a file named `coded.dat`.

12. Write a C++ program that reads the encrypted file produced by the program written for Exercise 10, decodes the file, and prints the decoded values on your system's standard output device.

13. Write a C++ program that displays the first eight bits of each character value input into a variable named `ch`. (*Hint*: Assuming each character is stored using eight bits, start by using the hexadecimal mask 80, which corresponds to the binary number 10000000. If the result of the masking operation is a zero, display a zero; else display a one. Then shift the mask one place to the right to examine the next bit, and so on until all bits in the variable `ch` have been processed.)

14. Write a C++ program that reverses the bits in an integer variable named `okay` and stores the reversed bits in the variable named `rev_okay`. For example, if the bit pattern 11100101, corresponding to the octal number 0345, is assigned to `okay`, the bit pattern 10100111, corresponding to the octal number 0247, should be produced and stored in `rev_okay`.

14.7 CHAPTER SUMMARY

1. Individual bits of character and integer variables and constants can be manipulated using C++'s bit operators. These are the AND, inclusive OR, exclusive OR, one's complement, left shift, and right shift operators.

2. The AND and inclusive OR operators are useful in creating masks. These masks can be used to pass or eliminate individual bits from the selected operand. The exclusive OR operator is useful in complementing an operand's bits.

3. When the AND and OR operators are used with operands of different sizes, the shorter operand is always increased in bit size to match the size of the larger operand.

4. The shift operators produce different results depending on whether the operand is a signed or an unsigned value.

APPENDIX A
Operator Precedence Table

Table A.1 presents the symbols, precedence, descriptions, and associativity of C++'s operators. Operators toward the top of the table have a higher precedence than those toward the bottom. Operators within each box have the same precedence and associativity.

Table A.1 Summary of C++ Operators

Operator	Description	Associativity
( ) [ ] –> .	Function call Array element Structure member pointer reference Structure member reference	Left to right
++ -- — ! ~ (type) sizeof & *	Increment Decrement Unary minus Logical negation One's complement Type conversion (cast) Storage size Address of Indirection	Right to left
* / %	Multiplication Division Modulus (remainder)	Left to right
+ –	Addition Subtraction	Left to right
<< >>	Left shift Right shift	Left to right
< <= > >=	Less than Less than or equal to Greater than Greater than or equal to	Left to right

(Continued)

Table A.1 Summary of C++ Operators (Continued)

Operator	Description	Associativity
== !=	Equal to Not equal to	Left to right
&	Bitwise AND	Left to right
^	Bitwise exclusive OR	Left to right
|	Bitwise inclusive OR	Left to right
&&	Logical AND	Left to right
||	Logical OR	Left to right
?:	Conditional expression	Right to left
= += -= *= /= %= &= ^= |= <<= >>=	Assignment Assignment Assignment Assignment Assignment	Right to left
,	Comma	Left to right

APPENDIX B
ASCII Character Codes

Key(s)	Dec	Oct	Hex	Key	Dec	Oct	Hex	Key	Dec	Oct	Hex
Ctrl 1	0	0	0	Esc	27	33	1B	6	54	66	36
Ctrl A	1	1	1	Ctrl <	28	34	1C	7	55	67	37
Ctrl B	2	2	2	Ctrl /	29	35	1D	8	56	70	38
Ctrl C	3	3	3	Ctrl =	30	36	1E	9	57	71	39
Ctrl D	4	4	4	Ctrl –	31	37	1F	:	58	72	3A
Ctrl E	5	5	5	Space	32	40	20	;	59	73	3B
Ctrl F	6	6	6	!	33	41	21	<	60	74	3C
Ctrl G	7	7	7	"	34	42	22	=	61	75	3D
Ctrl H	8	10	8	#	35	43	23	>	62	76	3E
Ctrl I	9	11	9	$	36	44	24	?	63	77	3F
\n	10	12	A	%	37	45	25	@	64	100	40
Ctrl K	11	13	B	&	38	46	26	A	65	101	41
Ctrl L	12	14	C	'	39	47	27	B	66	102	42
RETURN	13	15	D	(	40	50	28	C	67	103	43
Ctrl N	14	16	E	)	41	51	29	D	68	104	44
Ctrl O	15	17	F	*	42	52	2A	E	69	105	45
Ctrl P	16	20	10	+	43	53	2B	F	70	106	46
Ctrl Q	17	21	11	,	44	54	2C	G	71	107	47
Ctrl R	18	22	12	–	45	55	2D	H	72	110	48
Ctrl S	19	23	13	.	46	56	2E	I	73	111	49
Ctrl T	20	24	14	/	47	57	2F	J	74	112	4A
Ctrl U	21	25	15	0	48	60	30	K	75	113	4B
Ctrl V	22	26	16	1	49	61	31	L	76	114	4C
Ctrl W	23	27	17	2	50	62	32	M	77	115	4D
Ctrl X	24	30	18	3	51	63	33	N	78	116	4E
Ctrl Y	25	31	19	4	52	64	34	O	79	117	4F
Ctrl Z	26	32	1A	5	53	65	35	P	80	120	50

(Continued)

725

(Continued)

Key(s)	Dec	Oct	Hex	Key	Dec	Oct	Hex	Key	Dec	Oct	Hex
Q	81	121	51	a	97	141	61	q	113	161	71
R	82	122	52	b	98	142	62	r	114	162	72
S	83	123	53	c	99	143	63	s	115	163	73
T		84	124	54	d	100	144	64	t	116	164	74
U		85	125	55	e	101	145	65	u	117	165	75
V		86	126	56	f	102	146	66	v	118	166	76
W		87	127	57	g	103	147	67	w	119	167	77
X		88	130	58	h	104	150	68	x	120	170	78
Y		89	131	59	i	105	151	69	y	121	171	79
Z		90	132	5A	j	106	152	6A	z	122	172	7A
[		91	133	5B	k	107	153	6B	{	123	173	7B
\		92	134	5C	l	108	154	6C	|	124	174	7C
]		93	135	5D	m	109	155	6D	}	125	175	7D
^		94	136	5E	n	110	156	6E	~	126	176	7E
–		95	137	5F	o	111	157	6F	del	127	177	7F
'		96	140	60	p	112	160	70				

APPENDIX C

Program Entry, Compilation, and Execution

In this appendix, we examine the steps required to enter, compile, and execute compiled versions of C++ programs. These steps are:

1. logging into (and eventually out of) the computer
2. creating and editing the program
3. compiling and linking the program
4. loading and executing the program.

Logging into and out of the Computer

As illustrated in Figure C.1, a computer can be thought of as a self-contained world that is entered by a special set of steps called a *login procedure*. For some computers such as IBM personal computers (PCs), and other desk-top computers, the login procedure is as simple as turning on the computer's power switch. Larger multiuser systems, such as DEC VAX computers, typically require a login procedure consisting of turning a terminal on and supplying an account number and password.

Once you have successfully logged in to your computer system you are automatically under the control of a computer program called the operating system (unless the computer is programmed to switch you into a specific application program). The *operating system* is the program that effectively runs the computer. It is used to gain access to the services provided by the computer, which include the programs needed for entering, compiling, and executing a C++ program.

Communicating with the operating system is accomplished either by using a specific set of commands that are recognized by the operating system or by selecting graphical icons presented in a window. Although each computer system type (IBM, Apple, DEC, etc.) has one or more available operating systems, all operating systems provide commands that permit logging on to the system, exiting from the system, creating programs and a means of quickly listing, deleting, copying, and renaming programs.

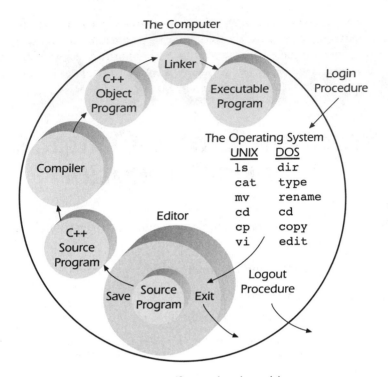

Figure C.1 Viewing a computer as a self-contained world.

The specific operating system commands and any additional steps used for exiting from a computer, such as turning the power off, are collectively referred to as the *logout procedure*. Make sure you know the logout procedure for your computer at the time you login to ensure that you can effectively "escape" when you are ready to leave the system. The operating system command for listing a program typically has a name such as List, Type, cat or PRINT; the command for deleting a program typically has a name such as DELETE, DEL, ERASE, UNSAVE, REMOVE, or rm; the command for copying a program typically has a name such as COPY, COP, or cp; and the operating system command for renaming a program typically has a name such as RENAME, REN, RN, or mv. Use Table C.1 to list the specific operating system command names used by your system to perform these tasks.

Table C.1 Operating System Commands (Fill in for your system)

Task	Command	Example
Log-in procedure		
Log-out procedure		
List a program		
Copy a program		
Delete a program		
Rename a program		

The commands to list, copy, delete, or rename a program are all concerned with manipulating existing programs. Let us now turn our attention to creating, compiling, an executing a new C++ program. The procedures for doing these tasks are illustrated in Figure C.2. As shown in this figure, the procedure for creating an executable C++ program consists of three distinct operations: editing, compiling, and linking.

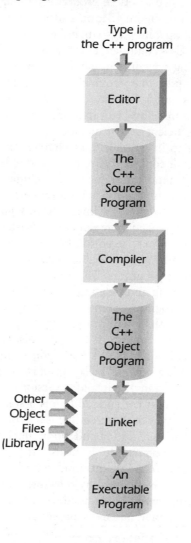

Figure C.2 Creating an executable C++ program.

Editing

Both the creation of a new C++ program and the modification of an existing C++ program require the use of an editor program. The function of such a program is to allow a user to type statements at a keyboard and to save the typed statements together under a common name, called a **source program file name.**

As illustrated in Figure C.1, an editor program is contained within the environment controlled by the operating system, either as a separate program or as part of the services provided with a C++ compiler. This means that the editor program can only be accessed using an operating system command, which either starts up the editor program directly or by a C++ compiler that provides its own editor.

Some editors handle one line at a time; to add, change, or delete text, you refer to a specific line by number and edit that line. Line editors are sometimes inconvenient to use, but they make efficient use of memory and CPU time. Fullscreen editors permit you to move the cursor to insert, delete, or change text at any point on the screen. Many C++ compilers for small computers are packaged with an editor; on larger machines you will have to use the general editor for that machine.

Once the editor program has been requested, the operating system relinquishes control to this program. Again, as illustrated in Figure C.1, this means that you temporarily leave the world controlled by the operating system and its commands and enter the world controlled by the editor. The editor, like the operating system, has its own set of services and commands, and you will need to become familiar with these commands to create and modify your source programs. The services provided by the editor include entering C++ statements, modifying and deleting existing C++ statements in a program, listing a program, naming a program, saving a program, and exiting from the editor back into the operating system with or without saving the program.

In using an editor you must carefully distinguish between entering a C++ statement and entering an editor command. Some editors make this distinction by using special keys to alert the editor that what is being typed is a command to the editor rather than the line of a program (for example, in older versions of BASIC the line number automatically informs the editor that the entered line is a statement and the absence of a line number informs the editor that the entered line is an editor command). Other editors contain two modes: a text mode for entering and modifying program statements and a command mode for entering editor commands. For this latter type of editor there is always a means of switching from text to command mode and back from command to text mode. In both cases the commands recognized by the editor depend on the editor being used. After filling in the operating system command needed to enter the editor, use Table C.2 to list the specific editor command names or procedures provided by your editor.

```
Operating system command
to enter the editor:_____
```

Table C.2 Editor Commands (Fill in for your system)

Task	Command(s)	Example
Save the program and exit from the editor		
Save the program without exiting from the editor		
Exit from the editor without saving the program		
Switch to text mode (if applicable)		
Switch to command mode (if applicable)		
List the complete program from within the editor		
Delete the complete program from within the editor		
Delete a set of lines from within the editor		
Delete a single line from within the editor		
Name a program from within the editor		
Search for text from within the editor		
Search and replace text from within the editor		

Compiling and Linking

The translation of a C++ source program into a form that can be executed by the computer is accomplished using a program called a **compiler**. The compiler, like the editor, is accessed using an operating system command. Each operating system uses a different command for calling the compiler into action and giving the compiler the name of the source file that is to be translated. Determine and then list the command used by your computer for performing this operation:

Command to compile a program:_____

The output produced by the compiler is called an object program. An **object program** is simply a translated version of the source program that can be executed by the computer system with one more processing step. Let us see why this is so.

Most C++ programs contain statements that use preprogrammed routines for input and output and for finding such quantities as square roots, absolute values, and other commonly encountered mathematical calculations. Additionally, a large C++ program may be stored in two separate program files. In such a case, each file can be compiled separately. However, both files must ultimately be combined to form a single program before the program can be executed. In both of these cases it is the task of the linker to combine all of the preprogrammed routines and individual object files into a single program ready for execution. This final program is called an **executable program**. Determine and then list the command used by your compiler for performing this operation:

Command to compile and link a program:_____

A Word of Caution

You will want to print the source code files to the screen or printer using operating system commands, such as `TYPE`, `PRINT`, or something similar—so that you can see and work with these files. This can be done because the source program is actually text consisting of a sequence of character codes. Do NOT, however try to print the object or executable files in the same manner, because these files consist of binary numbers, not text. If you attempt to print these files, at best, you will see unrecognizable characters on the screen or printer as the binary code comprising these files is displayed as text. Even worse, you may lock up the keyboard or print a ream of paper with one character on each page when some of the binary codes perform terminal control functions

Executing

Finally, once the C++ source program has been compiled and linked, it must be executed. To execute (or run) the program you simply type the name of the executable file in response to the operating system prompt. Determine and then list the command for performing this operation:

```
Command to execute a
compiled and linked program:_____
```

APPENDIX D

Floating-Point Number Storage

The two's complement binary code used to store integer values was presented in Section 1.6. In this appendix we present the binary storage format typically used in C++ to store single-precision and double-precision numbers, which are stored as floats and doubles, respectively. Collectively, both single- and double-precision values are commonly referred to as floating-point values.

Like their decimal number counterparts that use a decimal point to separate the integer and fractional parts of a number, floating-point numbers are represented in a conventional binary format with a binary point. For example, consider the binary number 1011.11. The digits to the left of the binary point (1011) represent the integer part of the number and the digits to the right of the binary point (11) represent the fractional part.

To store a floating-point binary number a code similar to decimal scientific notation is used. To obtain this code the conventional binary number format is separated into a mantissa and an exponent. The following examples illustrate floating-point numbers expressed in this scientific notation.

Conventional Binary Notation	Binary Scientific Notation
1010.0	1.01 exp 011
−10001.0	−1.0001 exp 100
0.001101	1.101 exp −011
−0.000101	−1.01 exp −100

In binary scientific notation, the term exp stands for exponent. The binary number in front of the exp term is the mantissa and the binary number following the exp term is the exponent value. Except for the number zero, the mantissa always has a single leading 1 followed immediately by a binary point. The exponent represents a power of 2 and indicates the number of places the binary point should be moved in the mantissa to obtain the conventional binary notation. If the exponent is positive, the binary point is moved to the right. If the exponent is negative, the binary point is moved to the left. For example, the exponent 011 in the number

```
1.01 exp 011
```

means move the binary point three places to the right, so that the number becomes 1010. The –011 exponent in the number

```
1.101 exp -011
```

means move the binary point three places to the left, so that the number becomes

```
.001101
```

In storing floating-point numbers, the sign, mantissa, and exponent are stored individually within separate fields. The number of bits used for each field determines the precision of the number. Single-precision (32 bit), double-precision (64 bit), and extended-precision (80 bit) floating-point data formats are defined by the Institute of Electrical and Electronics Engineers (IEEE) Standard 754-1985 to have the characteristics given in Table D.1. The format for a single-precision floating-point number is illustrated in Figure D.1.

Table D.1 IEEE Standard 754-1985 Floating-Point Specification

Data Format	Sign Bits	Mantissa Bits	Exponent Bits
Single-precision	1	23	8
Double-precision	1	52	11
Extended-precision	1	64	15

The sign bit shown in Figure D.1 refers to the sign of the mantissa. A sign bit of 1 represents a negative number and a zero sign bit represents a positive value. Since all mantissas, except for the number zero, have a leading 1 followed by their binary points, these two items are never stored explicitly. The binary point implicitly resides immediately to the left of mantissa bit 22, and a leading 1 is always assumed. The binary number zero is specified by setting all mantissa and exponent bits to 0. For this case only, the implied leading mantissa bit is also zero.

Figure D.1 Single-precision floating-point number storage format.

The exponent field contains an exponent that is biased by 127. For example, an exponent of 5 would be stored using the binary equivalent of the number 132 (127 + 5). Using eight exponent bits, this is coded as 100000100. The addition of 127 to each exponent allows negative exponents to be coded within the exponent field without the need for an explicit sign bit. For example, the exponent −011, which corresponds to −3, would be stored using the binary equivalent of +124 (127 − 3).

| 1 | 10000100 | 11011110000000000000000 |

Figure D.2 *The encoding and storage of the decimal number 59.75.*

Figure D.2 illustrates the encoding and storage of the decimal number 59.75 as a 64-bit single-precision binary number. The sign, exponent, and mantissa are determined as follows. The conventional binary equivalent of

    -59.75

is

    -111011.11

Expressed in binary scientific notation this becomes

    -1.1101111 exp 101

The minus sign is signified by setting the sign bit to 1. The mantissa's leading 1 and binary point are omitted and the 23-bit mantissa field is encoded as

    11011110000000000000000

The exponent field encoding is obtained by adding the exponent value of 101 to 1111111, which is the binary equivalent of the 127_{10} bias value:

$$
\begin{array}{rcl}
1\ 1\ 1\ 1\ 1\ 1\ 1 & = & 127_{10} \\
+\ 1\ 0\ 1 & = & 5_{10} \\
\hline
1\ 0\ 0\ 0\ 0\ 1\ 0\ 0 & = & 132_{10}
\end{array}
$$

APPENDIX E
Command Line Arguments

Arguments can be passed to any function in a program, including the `main()` function. In this section we describe the procedures for passing arguments to `main()` when a program is initially invoked and having `main()` correctly receive and store the arguments passed to it. Both the sending and receiving sides of the transaction must be considered. Fortunately, the interface for transmitting arguments to a `main()` function has been standardized in C++, so both sending and receiving arguments can be done almost mechanically.

All the programs that have been run so far have been invoked by typing the name of the executable version of the program after the operating system prompt is displayed. The command line for these programs consists of a single word, which is the name of the program. For computers that use the UNIX operating system, the prompt is usually the `$` symbol and the executable name of the program is `a.out`. For these systems, the simple command line

```
$a.out
```

begins program execution of the last compiled source program currently residing in `a.out`.

If you are using a C++ compiler on an IBM PC, the equivalent operating system prompt in DOS is either `A>` or `C>`, and the name of the executable program is typically the same name as the source program with an `.exe` extension rather than a `.cpp` extension. Assuming that you are using an IBM PC with the `C>` operating system prompt, the complete command line for running an executable program named `showad.exe` is `C> showad`. As illustrated in Figure E.1, this command line causes the `showad` program to begin execution with its `main()` function, but no arguments are passed to `main()`.

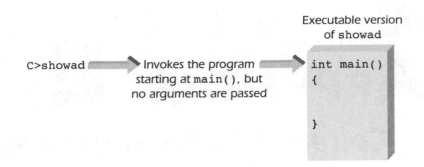

Figure E.1 Invoking the **showad** program.

Now assume that we want to pass the three separate string arguments **three blind mice** directly into **showad**'s main function. Sending arguments into a **main()** function is extremely easy. It is accomplished by including the arguments on the command line used to begin program execution. Because the arguments are typed on the command line, they are, naturally, called command line arguments. To pass the arguments **three blind mice** directly into the **main()** function of the **showad** program, we only need to add the desired words after the program name on the command line:

```
C> showad three blind mice
```

Upon encountering the command line **showad three blind mice**, the operating system stores it as a sequence of four strings. Figure E.2 illustrates the storage of this command line, assuming that each character uses one byte of storage. As shown in the figure, each string terminates with the standard C++ null character \0.

Figure E.2 The command line stored in memory.

Sending command line arguments to **main()** is always this simple. The arguments are typed on the command line and the operating system nicely stores them as a sequence of separate strings. We must now handle the receiving side of the transaction and let **main()** know that arguments are being passed to it.

Arguments passed to **main()**, like all function arguments, must be declared as part of the function's definition. To standardize argument passing to a **main()** function, only two items are allowed: a number and an array. The number is an integer variable, which conventionally is named **argc** (short for argument counter), and the array is a one-dimensional list, which is conventionally named **argv** (short for argument values). Figure E.3 illustrates these two arguments. The integer passed to **main()** is the total number of items on the command line. In our example, the value of **argc** passed to **main()** is 4, which includes the name of the program plus the three command line arguments. The one-dimensional list passed to **main()** is a list of pointers containing the starting storage address of each string typed on the command line, as illustrated in Figure E.4.

Figure E.3 An integer and an array are passed to `main()`.

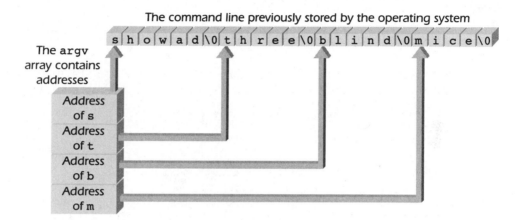

Figure E.4 Addresses are stored in the `argv` array.

We can now write the complete function definition for `main()` to receive arguments by declaring their names and data types. For `main`'s two arguments the names conventionally used are `argv` and `argc`, respectively.[1] Because `argc` will store an integer value, its declaration will be `int argc`. Because `argv` is the name of an array whose elements are addresses that point to where the actual command line arguments are stored, its proper declaration is `char *argv[]`. This is nothing more than the declaration of an array of pointers. It is read "`argv` is an array whose elements are pointers to characters." Putting all this together, the full function header for a `main()` function that will receive command line arguments is:

```
int main(int argc, char *argv[])
```

No matter how many arguments are typed on the command line, `main()` only needs the two standard pieces of information provided by `argc` and `argv`: the number of items on the command line and the list of starting addresses indicating where each argument is actually stored.

Program E.1 verifies our description by printing the data actually passed to `main()`. The variable `argv[i]` used in Program E.1 contains an address. The purpose of inserting the expression `(void *)argv[i]` into the first `cout` stream is to force the address value contained in `argv[i]` to be displayed. If this cast is not used, the address in `argv[i]` is automatically dereferenced by the insertion operator, `<<`, because this operator has been

---

[1]These names are not required, and any valid C++ identifier can be used in their place.

overloaded to perform dereferences on all pointer variables. Thus, in the absence of the cast, the string value pointed to by the address in `argv[i]` would be printed. Similarly, the string notation `*argv[i]` in the second `cout` stream refers to "the character pointed to" by the address in `argv[i]`.

Program E.1

```cpp
#include <iostream.h>
int main(int argc, char *argv[])
{
  int i;

  cout << "\nThe number of items on the command line is "
       << argc << '\n' << endl;
  for(i = 0; i < argc; i++)
  {
    cout << "The address stored in argv[" << i <<"] is "
         << (void *)argv[i] << endl;
    cout << "The character pointed to is " << *argv[i] << endl;
  }

  return 0;
}
```

Assuming that the executable version of Program E.1 is named `showad.exe`, a sample output for the command line `showad three blind mice` is:[2]

```
The number of items on the command line is 4

The address stored in argv[0] is 0x2412ffda
The character pointed to is s
The address stored in argv[1] is 0x2412ffeb
The character pointed to is t
The address stored in argv[2] is 0x2412fff1
The character pointed to is b
The address stored in argv[3] is 0x2412fff7
The character pointed to is m
```

The addresses displayed by Program E.1 clearly depend on the machine used to run the program. Figure E.5 illustrates the storage of the command line as displayed by the sample output. As anticipated, the addresses in the `argv` array "point" to the starting characters of each string typed on the command line.

---

[2]Some compilers store the full path name of the program in `argv[0]`.

Figure E.5 *The command line stored in memory.*

Once command line arguments are passed to a C++ program, they can be used like any other C++ strings. Program E.2 causes its command line arguments to be displayed from within `main()`.

Program E.2

```
// A program that displays its command line arguments
#include <iostream.h>
int main(int argc, char *argv[])
{
  int i;

  cout << "\nThe following arguments were passed to main(): ";
  for (i = 1; i < argc; i++)
    cout << argv[i] << " ";
  cout << endl;

  return 0;
}
```

Assuming that the name of the executable version of Program E.2 is `a.out`, the output of this program for the command line `a.out three blind mice` is:

```
The following arguments were passed to main(): three blind mice.
```

Notice that when the addresses in `argv[]` are inserted into the `cout` stream in Program E.2, the strings pointed to by these addresses are displayed. As was mentioned previously, this occurs because `cout` automatically dereferences these addresses and performs the required indirection to locate the actual string that is displayed.

One final comment about command line arguments is in order. Any argument typed on a command line is considered to be a string. If you want numerical data passed to `main()`, it is up to you to convert the passed string into its numerical counterpart. This is seldom an issue, however, since most command line arguments are used as flags to pass appropriate processing control signals to an invoked program.

APPENDIX F.
Namespaces

A new feature introduced as part of the ANSI/ISO draft C++ standard is the concept of namespaces, which essentially is a rather simple principle. A *namespace* is a space (or a section) of code that is given an explicit name; the named code must be enclosed in braces and can only include definitions or other **namespaces**. For example, the following section of code consists of two namespaces, named **screen** and **printer**, respectively, where each namespace consists of a single definition statement.

```
namespace screen    // the keyword namespace is required
{
   int lines = 5;
}  // end of screen namespace

namespace printer  // the keyword namespace is required
{
   int lines = 10;
}  // end of printer namespace
```

Notice that the namespace concept simply provides a means of explicitly naming a blocked section of definition statements. As such, namespaces are really a scoping mechanism that are used to clearly identify variables within different blocks of code. The only restriction on a namespace, however, is that it can consist only of definition statements and additional internally nested namespaces. The naming of the blocked code provides a means of identifying different variables that may have the same name but reside in different namespaces. This identification is accomplished by prefixing every variable name with its namespace name and the scope resolution operator, **::**. To illustrate how this is accomplished, consider Program F.1.

Program F.1

```
#include <iostream>

namespace screen
{
  int lines = 5;
}  // end of screen namespace

namespace printer
{
  int lines = 10;
}  // end of printer namespace

int main()
{
  std::cout << "\nThe screen lines are: "
            << screen::lines << std::endl;
  std::cout <<"\nThe printer lines are: "
            << printer::lines << std::endl;

  return 0;
}
```

In reviewing Program F.1 notice first that we have used the new style C++ header without the .h suffix. Each of these new C++ headers are members of a namespace named std, which is short for standard. Thus, whenever an identifier defined in this header is used, such as cout and endl, they must also be preceded by their namespace name and the scope resolution operator, as in std::cout and std::endl. This is also the case for the variables named lines defined in the namespaces screen and printer. To clearly identify which line variable is being accessed, it must be preceded by its namespace name and the scope resolution operator. The output produced when Program F.1 is executed is

```
The screen lines are: 5
The printer lines are: 10
```

The need to constantly append std:: to each standard library identifier can be quite annoying, although it may someday become the conventional programming style, the reason for which we will explain shortly. To avoid constantly including the std:: prefix, however, you can either use the old style .h header files, as we have done throughout the text, or include the following statement after the #include <iostream> preprocessor command:

```
using namespace std;
```

This statement declares the namespace `std` as a default, and any variables in this namespace can now be used without the `std::` prefix. Note that we could also use the statement `using namespace screen;` at any point after the `screen` namespace has been defined. Then, whenever the variable `lines` is encountered, it will refer to the `screens::lines` variable. However, if the statement `using namespace printer;` was also used, a conflict would arise when the variable `lines` is used. The compiler will flag this with a "`using ambiguous symbol`" error message.

Clearly, the `using` statement effectively defeats the explicit scope naming provided by namespaces. Since the primary motivation for namespaces was to avoid the possibility of scoping conflicts, especially as more and more third party libraries become available, the convention for writing C++ programs may eventually be to always include the namespace name when a standard library component is used. Finally, all namespaces must appear at file scope or immediately within another namespace. Since C++ now considers file scope as effectively another namespace, the terms **file scope** and **global namespace scope** are synonymous.

APPENDIX G
The Standard Template Library

A driving force behind object-oriented programming was the desire to create easily reusable source code. For example, recreating source code each time an array or queue is needed wastes both time and programming effort, which is added to by the additional time required for fully testing and verifying code that may have only been minimally modified. Suppose, for example, that a single program needs to use three arrays: an array of characters, an array of integers, and an array of double-precision numbers. Rather than coding three different arrays, it makes more sense to implement each array from a single, fully tested generic array class that comes complete with methods and algorithms for processing the array, such as sorting, inserting, finding maximum and minimum values, locating values, randomly shuffling values, copying arrays, comparing arrays, and dynamically expanding and contracting the array, as needed. This generic type of data structure, which is referred to as a container, forms the basis of the Standard Template Library (STL). In addition to providing seven types of generic data structures, one of which is the `array container` class (which is formally referred to as the `vector container` class), the STL provides methods and algorithms for appropriately operating on each of its generic data structures.

This generic programming approach for the STL was initially provided by Hewlett-Packard Corporation in 1994, and has subsequently been incorporated as part of the ANSI/ISO recommendations for inclusion into C++'s Standard Library.[1] In addition to the STL, the Standard Library provides two other majors sections, which are as follows.

- Input/Output headers: These provide support for conversions between text and encoded data, and input and output to external files. More specifically these headers consist of `<fstream>`, `<iomanip>`, `<ios>`, `<iosfwd>`, `<iostream>`, `<istream>`, `<ostream>`, `<stream>`, `<streambuf>`, and `<strstream>`.

- Other Standard C++ headers: These include language support for common type definitions, such as `<limits>`; diagnostic components for reporting exceptional conditions, such as `<stdexcept>`; string components for string classes, which is provided by `<string>`; and the 18 additional Standard C Library headers.

---

[1] The initial Hewlett-Packard STL developers were Alexander Stepanov and Meng Lee, with major contributions made by David Musser.

The **Standard Template Library,** which is the third major section of the standard library, is divided into the following three categories:

- **Containers,** which are the template classes from which individual data structures can be constructed. By definition a **container** is an STL template class that manages a sequence of elements. There are currently seven container classes that are used to construct vector, list, deque, stack, queue, set, and map data structures, respectively.

- **Algorithms,** which are template functions (see Section 6.1) that provide useful search, sort, location, and other numeric functions that can be applied to the various data structures created from the container classes.

- **Iterators,** which can be considered as generalized pointers for keeping track of the beginning, ending, and other positions within a data structure. Specifically, iterators are used to keep track of the first and last positions in a data structure and for establishing the boundaries of sequences of elements to which an algorithm is applied.

Table G.1 lists the 13 headers provided by the Standard Template Library. As seen, seven of the headers are container types, which are used to create data structures, three of the headers are concerned with providing algorithmic capabilities, and three of the headers are concerned with providing iterator capabilities.

Table G.1 Standard Template Headers

Name	Type	Description
`<algorithm>`	algorithm	defines numerous function templates that implement algorithms
`<functional>`	algorithm	defines templates required by `<algorithm>` and `<numeric>`
`<numeric>`	algorithm	defines several function templates that implement numeric functions
`<deque>`	container	defines a template class that implements a deque container
`<list>`	container	defines a template class for implementing a list container
`<map>`	container	defines template classes for implementing associative containers
`<queue>`	container	defines a template class for implementing a queue container
`<set>`	container	defines template classes for implementing associative containers having unique elements
`<stack>`	container	defines a template class for implementing a stack container
`<vector>`	container	defines a template class for implementing a vector container
`<iterators>`	iterator	defines templates for defining and manipulating iterators
`<memory>`	iterator	defines templates for allocating and freeing container class memory storage
`<utility>`	iterator	defines several general utility templates

In its most general usage, one or more container classes are first used to the desired construct data structures. Once these desired data structures have been created, both class methods and algorithms, both of which are always constructed as functions, can be applied to them. Iterators, which act like generalized pointers, are used as arguments by all of the algorithms to determine and keep track of which elements in the data structure are to be operated upon.

To make this more tangible and provide a meaningful introduction to using the STL we will use the vector container class to create two vectors: one for holding integers and one for holding characters. A vector is similar to a C++ array, except that it can automatically expand and contract as needed. We will then use two vector methods and two algorithms to operate on the instantiated vectors. Specifically, one method is used to change an existing element value and another to insert an element within each vector. The first algorithm is then used to sort the elements in each vector, while the second algorithm is used to randomly reshuffle each vector's elements. After each method and algorithm is applied a `cout` object is employed to display the results. To see how this is accomplished, consider Program G.1.

In reviewing Program G.1 first notice the inclusion of the three header files `<iostream>`, `<vector>`, and `<algorithm>` with the `using namespace std;` statement.[2] Here we need the `<iostream>` header to create and use the `cout` stream, the `<vector>` to create one or move vector objects, and the `<algorithm>` header for the two algorithms we will be using named `sort()` and `random_shuffle()`, respectively.

Program G.1

```cpp
#include <iostream>
#include <vector>
#include <algorithm>
using namespace std;

int main()
{
  const int NUMELS = 5;
  int a[NUMELS] = {1,2,3,4,5};
  char b[NUMELS] = {'a','b','c','d','e'};
  int i;

    // instantiate an integer and character vector
    // using a constructor to set the size of each vector
    // and initialize each vector with values
  vector<int> x(a, a + NUMELS);
  vector<char> y(b, b + NUMELS);
```

(Continued)

---

[2]Review Appendix F for the purpose of the `using namespace std;` statement.

(Continued)

```
  cout << "\nThe vector x initially contains the elements: "  << endl;
  for (i = 0; i < NUMELS; i++)
    cout << x[i] << "   ";
  cout << "\nThe vector y initially contains the elements: " << endl;
  for (i = 0; i < NUMELS; i++)
    cout << y[i] << "   ";

    // instantiate two ostream objects
  ostream_iterator<int> outint(cout, "   ");
  ostream_iterator<char> outchar(cout, "   ");

    // modify elements in the existing list
  x.at(3) = 6;     //set element at position 3 to a 6
  y.at(3) = 'f'; // set element at position 3 to an 'e'
    // add elements to the end of the list
  x.insert(x.begin() + 2,7);   // insert a 7 at position 2
  y.insert(y.begin() + 2,'g'); // insert an f at position 2

  cout << "\n\nThe vector x now contains the elements: "  << endl;
  copy(x.begin(), x.end(), outint);
  cout << "\nThe vector y now contains the elements: " << endl;
  copy(y.begin(), y.end(), outchar);

    //sort both vectors
  sort(x.begin(), x.end());
  sort(y.begin(), y.end());

  cout << "\n\nAfter sorting, vector x's elements are: "  << endl;
  copy(x.begin(), x.end(), outint);
  cout << "\nAfter sorting, vector y's elements are:" << endl;
  copy(y.begin(), y.end(), outchar);

    // random shuffle the existing elements
  random_shuffle(x.begin(), x.end());
  random_shuffle(y.begin(), y.end());
  cout << "\n\nAfter random shuffling, vector x's elements are:"  << endl;
  copy(x.begin(), x.end(), outint);
  cout << "\nAfter random shuffling, vector y's elements are:" << endl;
  copy(y.begin(), y.end(), outchar);

  cout << endl;
  return 0;
}
```

The two statements in Program G.1 that are used to create and initialize each vector are

```
        vector<int> x(a, a + NUMELS);
        vector<char> y(b, b + NUMELS);
```

Here, the vector x is declared as a vector of type int and is initialized with elements from array a starting with the first element of the array, located at address a, which is the element a[0], and ending with the element at one location less than a + NUMELS, which contains the element a[NUMELS - 1]. Thus, the vector x now has a size sufficient for five integers and has been initialized with the values 1, 2, 3, 4, and 5. Similarly, vector y now has an exact size for five characters and has been initialized with the values a, b, c, d, and e. The next set of statements in Program G.1 display the initial values in each vector, using standard subscripted vector notation that is identical to the notation used for accessing array elements. Displaying the vector values in this manner, however, requires knowing how many elements each vector contains. As we insert and remove elements we would like the vector class itself to keep track of where the first and last elements are, and this capability is, in fact, automatically provided by two iterators methods furnished for each vector, named begin() and end(). Before using these two functions we will construct two iterator dependent output objects for making the output display of elements rather simple with the statements:

```
ostream_iterator<int> outint(cout, "  ");
ostream_iterator<char> outchar(cout, "  ");
```

As we will see momentarily, the outint and outchar objects (the two names are programmer selected) can be used to display all vector values contained between two iterators with two spaces provided between each value, before the value is placed on the cout stream.

The next major set of statements

```
// modify elements in the existing list
x.at(3) = 6;    //set element at position 3 to a 6
y.at(3) = 'f'; // set element at position 3 to an 'e'
  // add elements to the end of the list
x.insert(x.begin() + 2,7);  // insert a 7 at position 2
y.insert(y.begin() + 2,'g'); // insert an f at position 2
```

are used to both modify existing vector values and insert a new value into each vector. Specifically, the at() method requires an integer value for its argument, while the insert() method requires an iterator and the value to be inserted as arguments. Specifically, the at() argument of 3 indicates that the 4th element in each vector will be changed (remember that vectors, like arrays, begin at index position 0). This means that the value 4, which is in the 4th position in the integer array, will be changed to a 6, and the value 'd' in the character array will be changed to an 'f'. The insert() method is then used to insert values of 7 and 'g' in the third position for both vectors. Notice that, like pointers, iterator arithmetic is allowed. Since the begin() method returns the iterator value corresponding to the start of the vector, adding 2 to it points to the third position in the array. It is at this position the new value is inserted with all subsequent values moved up by one position in the vector, the vector automatically expanding to accept the inserted value. At this point in the program, the vector x now contains the elements

1 2 7 3 6 5

and the vector y now contains the elements

    a b g c f e

For vector x, this arrangement was obtained by replacing the original value of 4 with a
6 and then inserting a 7 in the third position, which moved all subsequent elements up
by one position and increased the total vector size to accommodate 6 integers. A similar
process resulted in the arrangement shown for vector y's elements. To have the program
display these elements the statements

```
cout << "\n\nThe vector x now contains the elements: "  << endl;
copy(x.begin(), x.end(), outint);
cout << "\nThe vector y now contains the elements: " << endl;
copy(y.begin(), y.end(), outchar);
```

were used. The copy() algorithm uses two iterators, which are the values returned by
the begin() and end() methods to delimit the beginning and ending positions to copy.
In this case a copy of each complete vector is made to the outint and outchar objects,
respectively. As these objects are standard output objects, the values placed on them are
displayed on the screen, suitably interspaced with two spaces between each element.

Finally, the last section of code used in Program G.1 uses the sort() and
random_shuffle() algorithms to first sort the elements in each vector and then
randomly shuffle them. Notice that both of these algorithms use iterator values to determine the sequence of elements to be operated upon. After each algorithm is applied, the
copy() algorithm is once again used to force an output display. Following is the
complete output produced by Program G.1:

```
The vector x initially contains the elements:
1  2  3  4  5
The vector y initially contains the elements:
a  b  c  d  e

The vector x now contains the elements:
1  2  7  3  6  5
The vector y now contains the elements:
a  b  g  c  f  e

After sorting, vector x's elements are:
1  2  3  5  6 7
After sorting, vector y's elements are:
a  b  c  e  f  g

After random shuffling, vector x's elements are:
6  5  1  3  7  2
After random shuffling, vector y's elements are:
e  a  f  c  g  b
```

APPENDIX H

Solutions to Selected Odd-Numbered Exercises

Exercises 1.1

1. a. A **computer program** is a structured combination of data and instructions that is used to operate a computer.

b. **Programming** is the process of using a programming language to produce a computer program.

c. A **programming language** is the set of instructions, data, and rules that can be used to construct a program.

d. A **high-level language** is a programming language that uses instructions that resemble a written language, such as English, and can be translated to run on a variety of computer types.

e. A **low-level language** is a programming language that uses instructions that are directly tied to one type of computer. They consist of machine level and assembly languages.

f. A **machine language** contains the binary codes that can be executed by a computer. Such languages are frequently referred to as executables.

g. An **assembly language** permits symbolic names to be used for mathematical operations and memory addresses. Assembly languages are low-level.

h. A **procedure-oriented languages** has instructions that are used to create procedures, where a procedure is a logically consistent set of instructions that produce a specific result.

i. An **object-oriented language** permits the construction of objects, that can be manipulated and displayed. Such languages are gaining increased usage in graphical-oriented programs.

j. A **source program** consists of the program statements comprising a C++ or other programming language program.

k. A **compiler** is a program that is used to translate a high-level source program as a complete unit before any one statement is actually executed.

l. An **interpreter** is a program that translates individual source program statements, one at a time, into executable statements. Each statement is executed immediately after translation.

3. a. Low-level languages use instructions that are directly tied to one computer and generally execute at the fastest level possible. **High-level languages** are portable, but must be compiled into a low-level language before it can be executed.

  b. A **procedure-oriented language** uses instructions to create procedures, which are self-contained units that manipulate input values to produce resulting outputs. An **object-oriented language** permits the construction of objects, such as rectangles, that can be manipulated and displayed. Typically object-oriented languages are used for producing programs that have a graphical component.

4. All of these are translator programs used to translate source code into machine code. An **assembler** translates assembly language programs, while both compilers and interpreters translate high-level source programs. A **compiler** translate a high-level source program as a complete unit before any one statement is actually executed, while an **interpreter** translates individual source program statements one at a time into executable statements. Each statement is executed immediately after translation.

5. a. Add the data in memory location 1 to the data in memory location 2.
  Multiply the data in memory location 3 by the data in memory location 2.
  Subtract the data in memory location 4 from the data in memory location 3.
  Divide the data in memory location 3 by the data in memory location 5.

  b. $3 + 5 = 8$
  $6 \cdot 3 = 18$
  $14 - 6 = 8$
  $6 / 4 = 1.5$

Exercises 1.2

1. a. Clearly define the problem—To ensure that the problem is clearly understood, including what inputs will be given and what outputs are required.
  Develop a solution—Define an appropriate set of steps, called an algorithm, to solve the problem.
  Code the solution—Write the program by translating the solution into a source program.
  Test and correct the program—Test the completed computer program to ensure that it does provide a solution to the problem.

  b. Documentation—Provide adequate user documentation for people who will use the program and programmer documentation for people who will have to maintain the program.
  Maintenance—Keep the solution up to date by making modifications required whether due to changes in requirements or because errors are found during program execution.

3. If Phase I is 40% of the total effort, then coding represents 20% of 40% = $(0.2) \times (0.4) = 0.08 = 8\%$ of the total effort.

5. A fixed fee is a good choice if you have experience in exactly what is wanted, are selling an existing program to a new client, or both you and the client are in total agreement as to what will be produced; otherwise, it is generally a bad choice for both parties. On the positive side is that you do know how much you will receive for your work and the client knows how much they will have to pay. The disadvantage is that unless you both are very clear as to what will be produced, you may end up doing double and triple the amount of work contracted for very little if any additional funding. This occurs because after the client sees the program, new features immediately present themselves. You, as a programmer, may claim these are additional features, while the client may claim them as normal features that you should have incorporated as part of a useful program. No matter how the issue is resolved, generally, one or both sides may feel they have been deceived.

Exercises 1.3

1. a. One possible solution:
Make sure the car is parked, the engine is off, and the key is out of the ignition switch
Go to the trunk
Put the correct key into the trunk
Open the trunk
Remove the spare tire and the jack
Put the jack under the car . . . and so on
  b. Go to a phone
Remove the handset from the phone
Wait for the dial tone
Take out the correct change for the call
Put the correct change into the phone
Dial the number
  c. Arrive at the store
Walk through the door
Go to the bread aisle
Select the desired bread
Go to the cashier
Pay for the bread and leave
  d. Prepare the turkey
Preheat the oven
Open the oven door
Put the turkey in the oven
Close the oven door
Wait the appropriate time for the turkey to cook

3. Step 1: Pour the contents of the first cup into the third cup
Step 2: Rinse out the first cup
Step 3: Pour the contents of the second cup into the first cup

Step 4: Rinse out the second cup
Step 5: Pour the contents of the third cup into the second cup

5. Step 1: Compare the first number with the second number and use the smallest of these numbers for the next step
Step 2: Compare the smallest number found in step 1 with the third number. The smallest of these two numbers is the smallest of all three numbers.

7. **a.** Step 1: Compare the first name in the list with the name BARTER. If the names match, stop the search; else go to step 2.
Step 2: Compare the next name in the list with the name BARTER. If the names match, stop the search; else repeat this step.

Exercises 2.1

1. power	Valid. A mnemonic.
density	Valid. A mnemonic.
m1234	Valid. Not a mnemonic.
newamp	Valid. A mnemonic.
12345	Invalid. Violates Rule 1; starts with a number.
abcd	Valid. Not a mnemonic.
total	Valid. A mnemonic.
tangent	Valid. A mnemonic.
absval	Valid. A mnemonic.
computed	Valid. Not a mnemonic because it doesn't indicate what was computed.
b34a	Valid. Not a mnemonic.
34ab	Invalid. Violates Rule 1; starts with a number.
volts$	Invalid. Violates Rule 2; contains a special character.
a2-b3	Invalid. Violates Rule 2; contains a special character.
while	Invalid. Violates Rule 3; is a keyword.
minVal	Valid. A mnemonic.
sine	Valid. A mnemonic.
$sine.	Invalid. Violates Rule 1; does not start with a letter or underscore.
cosine	Valid. A mnemonic
speed	Valid. A mnemonic.
netdistance	Valid. A mnemonic
sum	Valid. A mnemonic.
return	Invalid. Violates Rule 3; is a keyword
stack	Valid. Could be a mnemonic

3. These functions might be used to determine the speed, distance, and acceleration achieved by some object, such as a car.

5. a. void main() or void main(void)
b. char main() or char main(void)
c. float main() or float main(void)
d. double main() or double main(void)

7. a.
```cpp
#include <iostream.h>
int main()
{
    cout << "The cosecant of an angle" << endl;
    cout << "        is equal to one over " << endl;
    cout << "            the sine of the angle" << endl;

    return 0;
}
```

This can also be constructed as:

```cpp
#include <iostream.h>
int main()
{
    cout << "The cosecant of an angle\n"
         << "        is equal to one over\n"
         << "            the sine of the angle" << endl;

    return 0;
}
```

9. The two operations are a line feed to bring the cursor down one line and a carriage return to bring the cursor to the first column of the current line.

NOTE for Exercises 11 through 15: Many solutions are possible for these exercises. The following are possible answers.

11. Determine the placement of the light fixtures
   If you are capable of doing so
      Purchase the necessary materials including the fixtures
      and wire the lights in accordance with local ordinances
   Else hire a licensed electrician

13. Determine the courses needed for graduate engineering school
   Take the right courses
   Maintain an appropriate grade average
   Prepare for the GMATs
   Contact engineering schools for admission interview requirements
   Determine what area of engineering you are interested in studying
   Get letters of recommendation

15. Select and reserve a camp site
   Prepare list of items to take along
   Purchase needed supplies
   Reserve a camper at the rental agency (optional)
   Arrange for someone to feed plants and watch house
   Make arrangements for care of pets (optional)
   Check and service automobile

Exercises 2.2

1. a. Yes.
   b. It is not in standard form. To make programs more readable and easier to debug, the standard form presented in Section 2.2 of the text should be used.

3. a. Two backslashes in a row causes one backslash to be displayed.
   b. `cout << "The escape sequence \\ will produce a backslash." << endl;`

Exercises 2.3

1. a. float or double
   b. integer
   c. float or double
   d. integer
   e. float or double
   f. characters

3. $1.26e^2$ $6.5623e^2$ $3.42695e^3$ $4.8932e^3$ $3.21e^{-1}$ $1.23e^{-2}$ $6.789e^{-3}$

5. Since all of the operands given are integers, the result of each expression is an integer value.
   a. $3 + 4 \cdot 6 = 3 + 24 = 27$
   b. $3 \cdot 4 / 6 + 6 = 12 / 6 + 6 = 2 + 6 = 8$
   c. $2 \cdot 3 / 12 \cdot 8 / 4 = 6 / 12 \cdot 8 / 4 = 0 \cdot 8 / 4 = 0 / 4 = 0$
   d. $10 \cdot (1 + 7 \cdot 3) = 10 \cdot (1 + 21) = 10 \cdot 22 = 220$
   e. $20 - 2 / 6 + 3 = 20 - 0 + 3 = 23$
   f. $20 - 2 / (6 + 3) = 20 - 2 / 9 = 20 - 0 = 20$
   g. $(20 - 2) / 6 + 3 = 18 / 6 + 3 = 3 + 3 = 6$
   h. $(20 - 2) / (6 + 3) = 18 / 9 = 3$
   i. $50 \% 20 = 10$
   j. $(10 + 3) \% 4 = 13 \% 4 = 1$

7. a. $10.0 + 15 / 2 + 4.3 = 10.0 + 7 + 4.3 = 21.3$
   b. $10.0 + 15.0 / 2 + 4.3 = 10.0 + 7.5 + 4.3 = 21.8$
   c. $3.0 \cdot 4 / 6 + 6 = 12.0 / 6 + 6 = 2.0 + 6.0 = 8.0$
   d. $3 \cdot 4.0 / 6 + 6 = 12.0 / 6 + 6 = 2.0 + 6 = 8.0$
   e. $20.0 - 2 / 6 + 3 = 20.0 - 0 + 3 = 23.0$
   f. $10 + 17 \cdot 3 + 4 = 10 + 51 + 4 = 65$
   g. $10 + 17 / 3.0 + 4 = 10 + 5.6666667 + 4 = 19.6666667$
   h. $3.0 \cdot 4 \% 6 + 6 = 12.0 \% 6 + 6 =$ invalid expression
   i. $10 + 17 \% 3 + 4 = 10 + 2 + 4 = 16$

11. answer1 is the integer 2
    answer2 is the integer 5

13.
```
#include<iostream.h>
int main()
{
    cout << "3.0 * 5.0 = " << 3.0*5.0 << endl;
    cout << "7.1 * 8.3 - 2.2 = " << 7.1 * 8.3 - 2.2 << endl;
    cout << "3.2 / (6.1 * 5) = " << 3.2 / (6.1*5) << endl;

    return 0;
}
```

15. **a.**   P   U   L   L   E   Y
         01010000 01010101 01001100 01001100 01000101 01011001
    b.   P   U   L   L   E   Y
         1101011 11100100 11010011 11010011 11000101 11101000

17. **a.** 'm' − 5 = 'h'
    b. 'm' + 5 = 'r'
    c. 'G' + 6 = 'M'
    d. 'G' − 6 = 'A'
    e. 'b' − 'a' = 1
    f. 'g' − 'a' + 1 = 6 + 1 = 7
    g. 'G' − 'A' + 1 = 6 + 1 = 7

19. **a.** $512 \cdot 1024 = 524{,}288$ bytes
    b. $2 \cdot 1{,}048{,}576 = 2{,}097{,}152$ bytes
    c. $8 \cdot 1{,}048{,}576 = 8{,}388{,}608$ bytes
    d. $16 \cdot 1{,}048{,}576 = 16{,}777{,}216$ bytes
    e. $4 \cdot 1{,}048{,}576 = 4{,}194{,}304$ words $\cdot$ 2 bytes/word $= 8{,}388{,}608$ bytes
    f. $4 \cdot 1{,}048{,}576 = 4{,}194{,}304$ words $\cdot$ 4 bytes/word $= 16{,}777{,}216$ bytes
    g. $1.44 \cdot 1{,}048{,}576 = 1{,}509{,}949$ bytes

Exercises 2.4

1. The following are not valid:
12345	does not begin with either a letter or underscore
$total	does not begin with either a letter or underscore
new al	cannot contain a space
9ab6	does not begin with either a letter or underscore
sum.of	contains a special character

3. **a.** int count;
   b. float volt;
   c. double power;
   d. char keychar;

5. **a.** int firstnum, secnum;
   b. float speed, acceleration, distance;
   c. double thurst;

7. a.

```
#include <iostream.h>  // includes the iostream.h header file
int main() // function header line
{  // start of function body
  int num1, num2, total; //declare the integer variables num1, num2, and total

  num1 = 25;    // assign the integer 25 to num1
  num2 = 30;    // assign the integer 30 to num2
  total = num1 + num2;  // assign the sum of num1 and num2 to total
  cout << "The total of " << num1 << " and " // displays:
      << num2 << " is " << total << endl;   // The total of 25 and 30 is 55.


   Return 0;  // returns control to the operating system
} // end of function body
```

        b. The total of 25 and 30 is 55.

9. a. Address:

159	160	161	162	163	164	165	166
				W	O	W	!

    rate   ch1   ch2   ch3   ch4

Address:

167	168	169	170	171	172	173	174

    taxes

Address:

175	176	177	178	179	180	181	182
		0	0				

    num   count

    The empty addresses above are usually filled with zeros or garbage values, meaning their contents are whatever happened to be placed there by the computer or by the previously run program.

    b. ch1 = 01110111
        ch2 = 01101111
        ch3 = 01110111
        ch4 = 00100001

11. miles begins at address 159
     count begins at address 163
     num   begins at address 165
     dist   begins at address 167
     temp begins at address 175

Exercises 2.5

    3. The amount of storage reserved for each data type does not depend on the value actually stored into the reserved memory locations.

Exercises 2.6

1. **a.** One output: the total resistance value
   b. Three inputs: the number of 56, 33, and 15 ohm resistors
   c. resistance = m · 56 + n · 33 + p · 15
   d. resistance = 17 · 56 + 24 · 33 + 12 · 15 = 952 + 792 + 180 = 1924 ohms

3. **a.** One output: the amount of Ergies
   b. Two inputs: Fergies, Lergies
   c. Ergies = Fergies · sqrt(Lergies)
   d. Ergies = 14.65 · sqrt(2 · 3.1416 · 2.7818$^{1.672}$) = 14.65 · sqrt(34.761) = 86.3743

5. **a.** One output: distance
   b. Three inputs: s, d, and t
   c. distance = $s - 0.5 \cdot d \cdot t \cdot t$

7. **a.** Three outputs: two individual voltages and the sum of the voltages
   b. Four inputs: the values of V and f for each circuit
   c. The first output is determined using the first formula and the second output is determined using the second formula. The third output is obtained by adding the first two outputs.

Exercises 2.7

1. **a.**

```
#include <iostream.h>
int main()
{
  double speed, f0, f1;

  f0 = 2e-10;
  f1 = 2.00000035e-10;

  speed = 6.685e8 * (f1 - f0) / (f1 + f0);
  cout << "The speed is " << speed << " miles/hour" << endl;

  return 0;
}
```

3. a.

```cpp
#include<iostream.h>
int main()
{
  unsigned long numin, lines;

  numin = 1000;
  lines = numin * (numin - 1) / 2;
  cout << "The number of lines needed is " << lines << ".\n";;

  return 0;
}
```

5. a.

```cpp
#include <iostream.h>
int main()
{
  float fahr, cel;

  fahr = 98.6;
  cel = (5.0 / 9.0) * (fahr - 32.0);
  cout << "For a fahrenheit temperature of " << fahr << "degrees,"
       << "the equivalent\n"
       << "celsius temperature is " << cel << " degrees" << endl;

  return 0;
}
```

7. a.

```cpp
#include <iostream.h>
int main()
{
  float speed = 58.0, dist = 183.67, time;

  time = dist / speed;
  cout << "The elapsed time for the trip is " << time << " hours.\n";

  return 0;
}
```

9. a.
```cpp
#include <iostream.h>
#include <math.h>
int main()
{
   int Tinit = 150, A = 60, t = 20;
   float e = 2.71828, k = 0.0367, Tfin;

   Tfin = (Tinit - A) * pow(e, -k * t) + A;
   cout << "The final temperature is " << Tfin << endl;

   return 0;
}
```

Exercises 3.1

1. `circum = 2.0 * 3.1416 * radius;`

3. `celsius = 5.0 / 9.0 * (fahrenheit - 32.0);`

5. `eltime = totdis / avspeed;`

7. `linexp = linzero * (1.0 + alfpha * (tempfin - tempinit));`

9. `m = x * w * (l - x) / l;`

11. a.
```cpp
#include <iostream.h>
int main()
{
                                              ← missing declaration for all variables
   width = 15 ←                               missing semicolon
   area = length * width; ←                   no value assigned to length
   cout << "The area is " << area ←           missing ;
                                              ← missing return statement
}
```

The corrected program is

```cpp
#include <iostream.h>
int main()
{
   int length, width, area;
   width = 15;
   length = 20;     // must be assigned some value
   area = length * width;
   cout << "The area is " << area;

   return 0;
}
```

b.
```
#include <iostream.h>
int main()
{
   int length, width, area;

   area = length * width;  ←—— this should come after the assign-
   length = 20;                  ment of values to length and width
   width = 15;
   cout << "The area is  \n" << area;
        ←——————————————————————— missing return statement

}
```

The corrected program is

```
#include <iostream.h>
int main()
{
   int length, width, area;

   length = 20;
   width = 15;
   area = length * width;
   cout << "The area is  \n" << area;

   return 0;
}
```

c.
```
#include <iostream.h>
int main()
{
   int length = 20, width = 15, area;

   length * width = area;  ←——— incorrect assignment statement
   cout << "The area is  " << area;
        ←——————————————————————— missing return statement
}
```

The corrected program is

```
#include <iostream.h>
int main()
{
   int length = 20, width = 15, area;

   area = length * width;
   cout << "The area is  \n" << area;

   return 0;
}
```

13.

Radius	Height	Volume
1.62	6.23	51.3652
2.86	7.52	193.241669
4.26	8.95	510.261932
8.52	10.86	2476.623291
12.29	15.35	7283.884277

Exercises 3.2

1. `answer1` is the integer 2
`answer2` is the integer 5

5. a. The double quote after the 2nd insertion symbol should come before the symbol and the parentheses at the end of the statement should be a semicolon.
   b. The `setw(4)` manipulator should not be enclosed in double quotes.
   c. The `setprecision(5)` manipulator should not be enclosed in double quotes.
   d. The statement should be `cout << "Hello World!";`
   e. The `setw(6)` manipulator should appear before the insertion of the number 47.
   f. The `setprecision(2)` manipulator should appear before the insertion of the number 526.768.

7. a. The number is 26.27
   The number is 682.30
   The number is 1.97

   b.   26.27
          682.30
            1.97
         ───────
          711.54

   c.   26.27
          682.30
            1.97
         ───────
          711.54

   d.   36.16
            10.00
         ───────

9.
```
#include <iostream.h>
#include <iomanip.h>
int main()
{
    float r1, r2, r3, resistance;

            r1 = 1000;
            r2 = 1000;
            r3 = 1000;
            resistance = 1 / (1/r1 + 1/r2 + 1/r3);
            cout << setw(7) << setiosflags(ios::fixed)
                 << setiosflags(ios::showpoint)
                 << setprecision(2)
                 << resistance << endl;

    return 0;
}
```

11.
```
#include <iostream.h>
#include <iomanip.h>
int main()
{
  int x1 = 3, y1 = 7;
      int x2 = 8, y2 = 12;
      float xmid, ymid;

      xmid = (x1 + x2) / 2.0;
      ymid = (y1 + y2) / 2.0;
      // set the display format
      cout << setw(5) << setiosflags(ios::fixed)
               << setiosflags(ios::showpoint)
                   << setprecision(2);
      cout << "The x midpoint is " << xmid
               << "\nThe y midpoint is " << ymid << endl;

    return 0;
}
```

Exercises 3.3

1. **a.** sqrt(6.37)
   b. sqrt(x−y)
   c. sin(30.0 · 3.1416 / 180.0)
   d. sin(60.0 · 3.1416 / 180.0)
   e. fabs(pow(a,2.0) − pow(b,2.0)) or fabs(a·a + b·b)
   f. exp(3.0)

3. a. b = sin(x) − cos(x);
   b. b = pow(sin(x),2.0) − pow(cos(x),2.0);
             or
      b = sin(x) · sin(x) − cos(x) · cos(x);
   c. area = (c · b · sin(a)) / 2.0;
   d. c = sqrt(pow(a,2.0) + pow(b,2.0));
             or
      c = sqrt(a·a + b·b));
   e. p = sqrt(fabs(m−n));
   f. sum = (a·(pow(r,n) − 1.0)) / (r − 1.0);

5.
```
#include <stdio.h>
#include <math.h>
int main()
{
    float dist, x1, y1, x2, y2;

    x1 = 7.0;
    y1 = 12.0;
    x2 = 3.0;
    y2 = 9.0;
    dist = sqrt(pow((x1-x2),2.0) + pow((y1-y2),2.0));
    cout << "The distance is " << dist << endl;

    return 0;
}
```

7.

```
#include <iostream.h>
#include <math.h>
#include <iomanip.h>
int main()
{
  float height, velocity, theta;

  velocity = 5.0 * 1609.0 / 3600.0 ;   // convert mph to meters/sec
  theta = 60.0 * 3.1416 / 180.0;   // convert degrees to radians
  height = 0.5 * pow(velocity,2.0) * pow(sin(theta),2.0) / 32.2 ;
  // set output format
      cout << setiosflags(ios::fixed)
           << setiosflags(ios::showpoint)
           << setprecision(2);
      cout << "The maximum height reached is " << height << " meters" << endl;

      return 0;
}
```

```
9. #include <iostream.h>
   #include <math.h>
   #include <iomanip.h>
   int main()
   {
     float x, y, r, theta;

     r = 10.0;
     theta = 30.0 * 3.1416 / 180.0;   // convert to radians
     x = r * cos(theta);
     y = r * sin(theta);
     // set output format
     cout << setiosflags(ios::fixed)
          << setiosflags(ios::showpoint)
          << setprecision(2);
     cout << "The x coordinate is " << x << endl;
     cout << "The y coordinate is " << y << endl;

         return 0;
   }
```

Exercises 3.4

```
1. a. cin >> firstnum;
   b. cin >> grade;
   c. cin >> secnum;
   d. cin >> keyval;
   e. cin >> month >> years >> average;
   f. cin >> num1 >> num2 >> grade1 >> grade2
   g. cin >> interest >> principal >> capital >> price >> yield;
   h. cin >> ch >> letter1 >> letter2 >> num1 >> num2 >> num3;
   i. cin >> temp1 >> temp2 >> temp3 >> volts1 >> volts2;
```

```
3. a. #include <iostream.h>
      int main()
      {
        float radius, circum;

        cout << "Enter the radius of a circle: ";
        cin  >> radius;
        circum = 2.0 * 3.1416 * radius;
        cout << "The circumference is " <<  circum << endl;

        return 0;
      }
```

5.
```cpp
#include <iostream.h>
int main()
{
    float num, total, average;

    total = 0;
    cout << "Enter a number: ";
    cin  >> num;
    total = total + num;
    cout << "Enter a second number: ";
    cin  >> num;
    total = total + num;
    cout << "Enter a third number: ";
    cin  >> num;
    total = total + num;
    cout << "Enter a fourth number: ";
    cin  >> num;
    total = total + num;
    cout << "The average is " << total / 4.0 << endl;

    return 0;
}
```

Exercises 3.5

1.
```cpp
#include <iostream.h>  // this line may be placed second instead of first
#include <math.h>      // this line may be placed first instead of second
int main()
{
  const float GRAV = 32.2;
  int height;
  double time;

  height = 800;
  time = sqrt(2 * height / GRAV);
  cout << "It will take " << time << " seconds to fall "
       << height << " feet." << endl;

  return 0;
}
```

```
3. #include <iostream.h>
   int main()
   {
       const float PRIME_RATE = .08;
       float amount, interest;
       cout << "Enter the amount: ";
       cin  >> amount;
       interest = PRIME_RATE * amount;
       cout << "The interest earned is $" << interest
            << " dollars" << endl;

       return 0;
   }
```

Exercises 3.6

3. The problem with the program is that the request for data comes between the heading and data lines produced by the program. For example, a typical output is

```
    e to the x           Approximation        Difference
  ------------          --------------        --------------
  Enter a value of x: 2
     7.389056               1.000000           6.389056
     7.389056               3.000000           4.389056
     7.389056               5.000000           2.389056
     7.389056               6.333333           1.055723
```

5.
```
#include <iostream.h>
int main()
{
  float x, mu, sigma, deviate;

  cout << "Enter a value of x: ";
  cin  >>  x;
  cout << "Enter the mean: ";
  cin  >>  mu;
  cout << "Enter the standard deviation: ";
  cin  >>  sigma;
  deviate = (x - mu) / sigma;
  cout << "The standard normal deviate is " << deviate << endl;

  return 0;
}
```

The computed standard normal deviate for the data is 1.325

Exercises 4.1

1. a. The relational expression is true. Therefore, its value is 1.
   b. The relational expression is true. Therefore, its value is 1.
   c. The final relational expression is true. Therefore, its value is 1.
   d. The final relational expression is true. Therefore, its value is 1.
   e. The final relational expression is true. Therefore, its value is 1.
   f. The arithmetic expression has a value of 10.
   g. The arithmetic expression has a value of 4.
   h. The arithmetic expression has a value of 0.
   i. The arithmetic expression has a value of 10.

3. a. `distance == 30`
   b. `temperature > 98.6`
   c. `speed == 55`
   d. `month == 12`
   e. `let_in == 'K'`
   f. `length > 2 && length < 3`
   g. `day == 15 && month == 1`
   h. `speed == 35 && acceleration > 4`
   i. `speed > 50 && time >= 5`
   j. `code < 500 && transmit > 2`

Exercises 4.2

1. a.
```
if (angle == 90)
   cout << "The angle is a right angle" << endl;
else
   cout << "The angle is not a right angle" << endl;
```
   b.
```
if (temperature > 100)
   cout << "above the boiling point of water" << endl;
else
   cout << "below the boiling point of water" << endl
```
   c.
```
if (number > 0)
   possum = possum + number;
else
   negsum = negsum + number;
```
   d.
```
if (slope < 0.5)
   flag = 0;
else
   flag = 1;
```
   e.
```
if (fabs(volts1 - volts2) < 0.001)
   approx = 0.0;
else
   approx = (volts1 - volts2) / 2.0;
```

f. `if (frequency > 60)`
        `cout << "Frequency is too high." << endl;`
g. `if (fabs(temp1 - temp2) > 2.3)`
        `error = (temp1 - temp2) * factor;`
h. `if ( x > y && x < 20)`
      `cin  >> p;`
i. `if (distance > 20 && distance < 35)`
        `cin  >> time;`

3.
```
#include <iostream.h>
int main()
{
  float num1, num2;

  cout << "Enter a number: ";
  cin  >> num1;
  cout << "Enter another number: ";
  cin  >> num2;
  if (num1 > num2)
      cout << "The first number is greater." << endl;
  else
      cout << "The first number is smaller." << endl;

  return 0;
}
```
If the two numbers entered are equal, the else statement will be executed, which would not be a true statement.

5.
```
#include <iostream.h>
int main()
{
  float voltage;

  cout << "Enter a voltage: ";
  cin  >> voltage;
  if (voltage > 600)
    cout << "PASSED VOLTAGE TEST" << endl;
  else
    cout << "FAILED VOLTAGE TEST" << endl;

  return 0;
}
```

```
7. #include <iostream.h>
   int main()
   {
    char code;

     cout << "Enter the takeoff code: ";
     cin  >> code;
     if (code == 'g')
      cout << "PROCEED WITH TAKEOFF" << endl;
     else
       cout << "ABORT TAKEOFF" << endl;

     return 0;
   }
```

Exercises 4.3

```
1. #include <iostream.h>

   int main()
   {
     char code;

     cout << "Enter a specification code: ";
     cin  >> code;

     if (code == 'S' || code == 's')
         cout << "The item is space exploration grade.";
     else if (code == 'M'|| code == 'm')
       cout << "The item is military grade.";
     else if (code == 'C'|| code == 'c')
       cout << "The item is commercial grade.";
     else if (code == 'T'|| code == 't)
       cout << "The item it toy grade.";
     else
       cout << "An invalid code was entered.";
     cout << endl;

     return 0;
   }
```

3.
```cpp
#include <iostream.h>
int main()
{
  float angle;

  cout << "Enter the angle: ";
  cin  >> angle;
  if (angle < 90.0)
    cout << "The angle is acute." << endl;
  else if (angle == 90.0)
    cout << "The angle is a right angle." << endl;
  else if (angle > 90.0)
    cout << "The angle is obtuse." << endl;

  return 0;
}
```

5.
```cpp
#include <iostream.h>
int main()
{
  float grade;
  char letter;

  cout << "Enter the student's numerical grade: ";
  cin  >> grade;
  if (grade >= 90.0) letter = 'A';
  else if (grade >= 80.0) letter = 'B';
  else if (grade >= 70.0) letter = 'C';
  else if (grade >= 60.0) letter = 'D';
  else letter = 'F';
  cout << "The student receives a grade of " << letter << endl;

  return 0;
}
```

Notice that an `if-else` chain is used. If simple `if` statements were used, a grade entered as 75.5, for example, would be assigned a 'C' because it was greater than 60.0. But, the grade would then be reassigned to 'D' because it is also greater than 60.0.

```
7. #include <iostream.h>
   int main()
   {
     float fahr, cels, in_temp;
     char letter;

     cout << "Enter a temperature followed by";
     cout << " one space and the temperature's type" << endl;
     cout << " (an f designates a fahrenheit temperature";
     cout << "  and a c designates a celsius temperature): ";
     cin  >> in_temp >> letter;
     if (letter == 'f' || letter == 'F')
     {
       cels = (5.0/9.0)*(in_temp - 32.0);
       cout << in_temp << " degrees Fahrenheit = "
            << cels << " degrees Celsius" << endl;
     }
     else if (letter == 'c' || letter == 'C')
     {
       fahr = (9.0/5.0)*in_temp + 32.0;
       cout << in_temp << " degrees Celsius = "
            << fahr << " degrees Fahrenheit" << endl;
     }
     else
       cout << "The data entered is invalid." << endl;

     return 0;
   }
```

9. **a.** This program will run. It will not, however, produce the correct result.

   b. and c. This program evaluates a correct output for an input of less than 70 lbs. If 70 or more were entered, the first else-if statement would be executed and all others would be ignored. Had if statements been used in place of the else-if statements, this program would work correctly, but inefficiently, since each if statement would be executed, rather than the single if-else statement being terminated when the correct condition had been located.

Exercises 4.4

1.

```cpp
switch (let_grad)
{
  case 'A':
    cout <<  "The numerical grade is between 90 and 100" << endl;
    break;
  case 'B':
    cout <<  "The numerical grade is between 80 and 89.9" << endl;
    break;
  case 'C':
    cout <<  "The numerical grade is between 70 and 79.9" << endl;
    break;
  case 'D':
    cout <<  "How are you going to explain this one" << endl;
    break;
  default:
    cout <<  "Of course I had nothing to do with the grade." << endl;
    cout <<  "It must have been the professors fault." << endl;
}
```

3.
```cpp
#include <iostream.h>
int main()
{

    int mfgcode;

    cout << "Enter the manufacture's code: ";
    cin >> mfgcode;
    switch (mfgcode)
    {
      case 1:
        cout << "3M Corporation" << endl;
        break;
      case 2:
        cout << "Maxell Corporation" << endl;
        break;
      case 3:
        cout << "Sony Corporation" << endl;
        break;
      case 4:
        cout << "Verbatim Corporation" << endl;
        break;
      default:
        cout << "Incorrect Code" << endl;
        break;
    }

    return 0;
}
```

5. The expression in the `switch` statement must evaluate to an integer quantity and be tested for equality. The `if-else` chain in Program 4.6 uses floating-point values and inequalities, violating both requirements of the `switch` statement's requirements.

Exercises 4.5

1. a.

```cpp
#include <iostream.h>
int main()
{
  int opselect;
  double fnum, snum;

  cout << "Please type in two numbers: ";
  cin  >> fnum >> snum;
  cout << "Enter a select code: " << endl;
  cout << "   a 1 for addition" << endl;
  cout << "   a 2 for multiplication" << endl;
  cout << "   or a 3 for division: ";
  cin  >> opselect;
  switch (opselect)
  {
    case 1:
      cout << "The sum of the numbers entered is " << fnum + snum << endl;
      break;
    case 2:
      cout << "The product of the numbers entered is " << fnum * snum << endl;
      break;
    case 3:
      cout << "The first number divided by the second is " << fnum / snum << endl;
      break;
  }        // end of switch

  return 0;
}
```

b. Typically a message such as "`Floating point error: Divide by 0`" will be displayed.

c.

```cpp
#include <iostream.h>
int main()
{
  int opselect;
  double fnum, snum;

  cout << "Please type in two numbers: ";
  cin  >> fnum >> snum;
  cout << "Enter a select code: " << endl;
  cout <<  "   a 1 for addition" << endl;
  cout <<  "   a 2 for multiplication" << endl;
  cout <<  "   or a 3 for division: ";
  cin  >> opselect;
  switch (opselect)
  {
    case 1:
      cout << "The sum of the numbers entered is " << fnum + snum << endl;
      break;
    case 2:
      cout << "The product of the numbers entered is " << fnum * snum << endl;
      break;
    case 3:
        if (snum == 0)
          cout <<  "Division by zero is not permitted!" << endl;
        else
          cout << "The first number divided by the second is "
               << fnum / snum << endl;
      break;
  }        // end of switch

  return 0;
}
```

3. a.
```cpp
#include <iostream.h>
int main()
{
  float angle;

  cout << "Enter an angle: ";
  cin  >> angle;

  if (angle < 0 || angle > 360)
    cout << "An incorrect angle was entered." << endl;
  else if (angle > 0 && angle < 90)
    cout << "The angle is in quadrant I." << endl;
  else if (angle > 90 && angle < 180)
    cout << "The angle is in quadrant II." << endl;
  else if (angle > 180 && angle < 270)
    cout << "The angle is in quadrant III." << endl;
  else if (angle > 270 && angle < 360)
    cout << "The angle is in quadrant IV." << endl;

  return 0;
}
```

b.
```cpp
#include <iostream.h>
int main()
{
  float angle;

  cout << "Enter an angle: ";
  cin  >> angle;

  if (angle < 0 || angle > 360)
    cout << "An incorrect angle was entered." << endl;
  else if (angle > 0 && angle < 90)
    cout << "The angle is in quadrant I." << endl;
  else if (angle > 90 && angle < 180)
    cout << "The angle is in quadrant II." << endl;
  else if (angle > 180 && angle < 270)
    cout << "The angle is in quadrant III." << endl;
  else if (angle > 270 && angle < 360)
    cout << "The angle is in quadrant IV." << endl;
  else if (angle == 0)
      cout << "The angle is on the positive X axis." << endl;
  else if (angle == 90)
      cout << "The angle is on the positive Y axis." << endl;
  else if (angle == 180)
      cout << "The angle is on the negative X axis." << endl;
  else if (angle == 270)
      cout << "The angle is on the negative Y axis." << endl;

  return 0;
}
```

5. a.
```cpp
#include <iostream.h>
#include <iomanip.h>
int main()
{
  int year, weight, wclass;
  float fee;

  cout << "Enter a model year: ";
  cin  >> year;
  cout << "Enter a weight in pounds: ";
  cin  >> weight;

  if (year <= 1970)
  {
    if (weight < 2700)
    {
      wclass = 1;
      fee = 16.50;
    }
```

```
      else if (weight >= 2700 && weight <= 3800)
      {
        wclass = 2;
        fee = 25.50;
      }
      else if (weight > 3800)
      {
        wclass = 3;
        fee = 46.50;
      }
    }
    else if (year >= 1971 && year <= 1979)
    {
      if (weight < 2700)
      {
        wclass = 4;
        fee = 27.00;
      }
      else if (weight >= 2700 && weight <= 3800)
      {
        wclass = 5;
        fee = 30.50;
      }
      else if (weight > 3800)
      {
        wclass = 6;
        fee = 52.50;
      }
    }
    else if (year >= 1980)
    {
      if (weight < 3500)
      {
        wclass = 7;
        fee = 19.50;
      }
      else if (weight >= 3500)
      {
        wclass = 8;
        fee = 52.50;
      }
    }

    cout << setiosflags(ios::fixed)
         << setiosflags(ios::showpoint)
         << setprecision(2);
    cout << "The weight class is " << wclass
         << " and the registration fee is $" << fee << endl;

    return 0;
}
```

7.
```cpp
#include <iostream.h>
int main()
{
  int card1, card2, card3, total;

  cout << "Enter three cards." << endl
       << "(Enter an ace as 1 and picture cards as 10): ";
  cin  >> card1 >> card2 >> card3;

  total = card1 + card2 + card3;
  if (total < 21 && (card1 == 1 || card2 == 1 || card3 == 1))
    if (total - 1 + 11 <= 21)
      total = total - 1 + 11;
  cout << "The total is " << total << endl;

  return 0;
}
```

NOTE: The only useful possibility of counting the ace as an 11 rather than as a 1 occurs when the total is less than 21 and one of the cards is an ace.

Exercises 5.2

1.
```cpp
#include <iostream.h>
int main()
{
  int count = 2;

  while (count <= 10)
  {
    cout << count << " ";
    count = count + 2;
  }

  return 0;
}
```

3. a. 21 items are displayed, which are the integers from 1 to 21
   c. 21 items are displayed, which are the integers from 0 to 20

```
5. #include <iostream.h>
   #include <iomanip.h>
   int main()
   {
     int feet;
     float meters;

     cout << "FEET      METERS" << endl;
     cout << "----      ------" << endl;
     feet = 3;

     while (feet <= 30)
     {
       meters = feet / 3.28;
       cout << setiosflags(ios::fixed)
            << setiosflags(ios:: showpoint);
       cout << setw(3) << feet
            << setw(11) << setprecision(2)
            << meters << endl;
       feet = feet + 3;
     }

     return 0;
   }
```

7.
```
#include <iostream.h>
#include <iomanip.h>
int main()
{
  float time, miles;
  cout << "TIME       MILES" << endl;
  cout << "----       -----" << endl;
  time = .5;

  while (time <= 4)
  {
    miles = 55 * time;
    cout << setiosflags(ios::fixed)
         << setiosflags(ios::showpoint);
    cout << setw(4) << setprecision(1) << time
         << setw(10) << setprecision(2) << miles << endl;
    time = time + .5;
  }

  return 0;
}
```

Exercises 5.3

1. The only modification that needs to be made is to change the named constant MAXNUMS to be equal to 8 instead of 4.

3. a.
```
#include <iostream.h>
#include <iomanip.h>
int main()
{
  float cels, fahr, incr;
  int num, count = 0;

  cout << "Enter the starting temperature ";
  cout << "in degrees Celsius: ";
  cin  >> cels;
  cout << "Enter the number of conversions to be made: ";
  cin  >> num;
  cout << "Now enter the increment between conversions ";
  cout << "in degrees Celsius: ";
  cin  >> incr;
  cout << "\nCelsius      Fahrenheit" << endl;
  cout << "---------------------" << endl;
  while (count <= num)
```

```
      {
        fahr = (9.0/5.0)*cels + 32.0;
        cout << setiosflags(ios::fixed)
             << setiosflags(ios::showpoint)
             << setprecision(2);
        cout << setw(6) << cels
             << setw(14)<< fahr << endl;
        cels = cels + incr;
        ++count;
      }

      return 0;
    }
```

5. The only modification that needs to be made is to change the named constant MAXNUMS to be equal to 10 instead of 4.

7. This program still calculates the correct values, but the average is now calculated four times. Since only the final average is desired, it is better to calculate the average once outside of the while loop.

9.
```
#include <iostream.h>
#include <iomanip.h>
#include <math.h>
const int MAXTERM = 10;
int main()
{
  int a = 1, n = 1;
  float  r = 0.5, nthTerm, total = 0;

  cout << "Term No.   Term Value\n";
  cout << "--------   ----------\n";
  while (n <= MAXTERM)
  {
      nthTerm = a * pow(r, n - 1);
    total = total + nthTerm;
    cout << setw(5) << n
         << setw(16) << nthTerm << endl;
    ++n;
  }
  cout << "\nThe total of the series is " << total <<endl;

  return 0;
}
```

Exercises 5.4

1. a. `for ( i = 1; i <= 20; ++i)`
   b. `for (icount = 1; icount <= 20;   icount = icount + 2)`
   c. `for (j = 1; j <= 100; j = j + 5)`
   d. `for (icount = 20; icount >= 1; --icount)`
   e. `for (icount = 20; icount >= 1; icount = icount - 2)`
   f. `for (count = 1.0; count <= 16.2; count = count + 0.2)`
   g. `for (xcnt = 20.0; xcnt >= 10.0; xcnt = xcnt - 0.5)`

3. a. 10
   b. 1024
   c. 75
   d. –5
   e. 40320
   f. 0.03125

5.
```
#include <iostream.h>
#include <iomanip.h>
const int MAXNUM = 20;
int main()
{
  int num;

  cout << "NUMBER    SQUARE     CUBE\n"
       << "------     ------      ----" << endl;
  for (num = 0; num <= MAXNUM; num += 2)
    cout << setw(3) << num << "          "
         << setw(3) << num * num << "        "
         << setw(4) << num * num * num << endl;

  return 0;
}
```

7.
```
#include <iostream.h>
#include <iomanip.h>
int main()
{
  int count;
  float fahr, celsius;

  cout << "Fahrenheit     Celsius\n";
       << "----------     -------" << endl;
  cout << setiosflags(ios::fixed)
       << setiosflags(ios::showpoint);
  for (fahr = 20.0, count = 1; count <= 20; ++count)
```

```
            {
              celsius = (5.0 / 9.0) * (fahr - 32.0);
              cout << setw(6) << setprecision(1) << fahr
                      << setw(16) << setprecision(2) << celsius << endl;

              fahr += 4;
            }

            return 0;
        }
```

9.

```cpp
#include <iostream.h>
#include <iomanip.h>
int main()
{
  int temp;
  int starttemp = 0;
  int endtemp = 40;
  int incr = 5;
  double length = 7365;
  double coefOfExpansion = 11.7e-6;
  double deltaLength;

  cout << "Initial Length: " << length << " meters\n" << endl;
  cout << "  Length\n"
       << " Increase          Temperature\n"
       << "(in meters)        (Celsius)\n"
       << "-----------        -----------" << endl;

  cout << setiosflags(ios::fixed)
       << setiosflags(ios::showpoint);

  for(temp = starttemp; temp <= endtemp; temp = temp + incr)
  {
    deltaLength = coefOfExpansion * length * (temp - starttemp);
    cout << setw(8) << setprecision(4) << deltaLength
         << setw(14) << temp << endl;
  }

  return 0;
}
```

11.

```
#include <iostream.h>
#include <iomanip.h>
#include <math.h>
int main()
{
  float prob, ex;
  int lamda = 3;  // average no. of arrivals per minute
  long factorial = 1;  // denominator of the probability expression
  int customer;

  cout << " No. of\n";
  cout << "Arriving\n";
  cout << "Customers     Probability\n";
       << "---------     -----------" << endl;

  ex = exp(-lamda);    // only need to do this calculation once
  for (customer = 1; customer <= 10; ++customer)
  {
     factorial = factorial * customer;
     prob = (pow(lamda,customer) * ex / factorial);
     cout << setw(5) << customer
              << setw(17) << setprecision(6) << prob << endl;
  }

  return 0;
}
```

Exercises 5.5

```
1. #include <iostream.h>
   const int MAXCOUNT = 6;
   int main()
   {
     int count;
     float fahren, celsius;

     for(count = 1; count <= MAXCOUNT; ++count)
     {
       cout << "Enter a fahrenheit temperature: ";
       cin  >>  fahren;
       celsius = (5.0/9.0)*(fahren - 32.0);
       cout << " The corresponding celsius temperature is "
                << celsius << " degrees" <<endl;
     }

     return 0;
   }
```

3.

```cpp
#include <iostream.h>
int main()
 {
   int count, reps;
   float gallons, liters;

   cout << "Please type in the total number of data values ";
   cout << "to be converted: ";
   cin  >>  reps;
   for(count = 1; count <= reps; ++count)
   {
     cout << "Enter the number of gallons: ";
     cin  >>  gallons;
     liters = 3.785 * gallons;
     cout << "  The corresponding number of liters is " << liters << endl;
   }

   return 0;
 }
```

5.
```cpp
#include <iostream.h>
int main()
{
  int i, reps, poscnt, negcnt;
  float usenum, postot, negtot, posavg, negavg;
  postot = 0;
  negtot = 0;
  poscnt = 0;
  negcnt = 0;

  cout << "Please type in the total number of data values ";
  cout << "to be added: ";
  cin  >>  reps;
  for(i = 1; i <= reps; ++i)
  {
    cout << "Enter a number (positive or negative) : ";
    cin  >>  usenum;
    if (usenum > 0)
    {
      ++poscnt;
      postot = postot + usenum;
    }
      else if (usenum < 0)
    {
        ++negcnt;
        negtot = negtot + usenum;
    }
```

```
      }
      posavg = postot / poscnt;
      negavg = negtot / negcnt;
      cout << "The positive average is " << posavg << endl;
      cout << "The negative average is " << negavg << endl;

      return 0;
    }
```

7.
```
#include <iostream.h>
int main()
{
  int count = 0, i = 0, num;

  cout << "The first 20 whole numbers divisible by 3 are:" << endl;
  while (count < 20)
  {
    ++i;
      if(i%3 == 0)   // can be replaced by if(!(i%3))
      {
        ++count;
        cout << i << "   ";
      }
  }

  return 0;
}
```

9. a.
```
     #include <iostream.h>
     #include <iomanip.h>
     #include <math.h>
     int main()
     {
       double x, y;

       cout << "x value       y value\n"
            << "-------       -------" << endl;
       cout << setiosflags(ios::fixed)
                    << setiosflags(ios::showpoint)
                       << setprecision(4);
       for (x = 5.0; x <= 10.0; x = x + 0.2)
       {
         y = 3 * pow(x,5) - 2 * pow(x,3) + x;
         cout << setw(8) << x
              << setw(14) << y << endl;
       }

       return 0;
     }
```

Exercises 5.6

1.

```
#include <iostream.h>
const int EXPERS = 4;
const int RESULTS = 6;
int main()
{
  int i, j;
  float total, avg, data;

  for (i = 1; i <= EXPERS; ++i)
  {
    cout << "Enter " << RESULTS << " results for experiment #" << i << ": ";
      for (j = 1, total = 0.0; j <= RESULTS; ++j)
      {
        cin >>  data;
        total += data;
      }
      avg = total/RESULTS;
      cout << "   The average for experiment #" << i << " is " << avg << endl;
  }

  return 0;
}
```

NOTE: When entering data for each experiment, the six individual results may be entered on one line with a space between each entry, on six individual lines, or any combination of these.

3. a.

```
#include <iostream.h>
int main()
{
  const int GENERATORS = 5;
  const int RESULTS = 3;
  int generator, result;
  float voltage, gentot, genavg;

  for(generator = 1; generator <= GENERATORS; ++generator)
  {
    for(result = 1, gentot = 0; result<= RESULTS; ++result)
    {
      cout << "Enter the voltage for generator " << generator << ": ";
      cin  >> voltage;
      gentot = gentot + voltage;
    }
    genavg = gentot / RESULTS;
    cout << "   The average for generator " << generator
         << " is " << genavg << endl;
  }

  return 0;
}
```

```
5. #include <iostream.h>
   #include <iomanip.h>
   #include <math.h>

   int main()
   {
     const float SMALLDIF = 0.00001;
     float x, y, z;

     cout << setiosflags(ios::fixed)
          << setiosflags(ios::showpoint)
          << setprecision(2);
     cout << "    x          z          y    \n"
          << "-------    -------    -------" << endl;
     for (x = 1.0; x <= 5.0; x += 1)
       for (z = 2.0; z <= 6.0; z += 1)
         if (fabs(x - z) > SMALLDIF)
         {
             y = x * z / (x - z);
             cout << setw(6) << x
                      << setw(6) << z
                      << setw(6) << y << endl;
         }
         else
            cout << setw(6) << x
                 << setw(6) << z
                 << " Function Undefined" << endl;

     return 0;
   }
```

Exercises 5.7

```
1. a. #include <iostream.h>
      int main()
      {
       const int LOWGRADE = 0;
       const int HIGHGRADE = 100;
       int grade;

         do
         {
           cout << "Enter a grade: ";
             cin >> grade;
         } while (grade < LOWGRADE || grade > HIGHGRADE);
             cout << "\nThe grade entered is " << grade << endl;

         return 0;
      }
```

b.
```cpp
#include <iostream.h>
int main()
{
  const int LOWGRADE = 0;
  const int HIGHGRADE = 100;
  int grade;

  do
  {
    cout << "Enter a grade: ";
    cin >>  grade;
    if (grade < LOWGRADE || grade > HIGHGRADE)
     cout << "Invalid grade - please retype it.\n";
  } while (grade < LOWGRADE || grade > HIGHGRADE);
    cout << "\nThe grade entered is " << grade << endl;

  return 0;
}
```

c.
```cpp
#include <iostream.h>
int main()
{
  const int LOWGRADE = 0;
  const int HIGHGRADE = 100;
  const int SENTINEL = 999;
  int grade;

  do
  {
    cout << "Enter a grade: ";
    cin >>  grade;
      if (grade == SENTINEL)
         return 0;
    else if (grade < LOWGRADE || grade > HIGHGRADE)
        cout << "Invalid grade - please retype it.\n";
  } while (grade < LOWGRADE || grade > HIGHGRADE);
    cout << "\nThe grade entered is " << grade << endl;

  return 0;
}
```

d.
```cpp
#include <iostream.h>
int main()
{
  const int LOWGRADE = 0;
  const int HIGHGRADE = 100;
  int grade, badGrade = 0;

  do
  {
    cout << "Enter a grade: ";
    cin >> grade;
    if (grade < LOWGRADE || grade > HIGHGRADE)
    {
      ++badGrade;
      if (badGrade == 5)
        return 0;
      else
        cout << "Invalid grade - please retype it.\n";
    }
  } while (grade < LOWGRADE || grade > HIGHGRADE);
  cout << "\nThe grade entered is " << grade << endl;

  return 0;
}
```

3. a.
```cpp
#include <iostream.h>
int main()
{
  int num, digit;

  cout << "Enter an integer: ";
  cin >> num;
  cout << "The number reversed is: ";
  do
  {
    digit = num % 10;
    num /= 10;
    cout << digit;
  } while (num > 0);

  return 0;
}
```

5.

```cpp
#include <iostream.h>
#include <math.h>
const float OKDIF = 0.00001;
int main()
{
  float num, root, approx;

  cout << "Enter a number for which you want the square root: ";
  cin >> num;
  cout << "Enter your best guess for this number's square root: ";
  cin >> approx;
  do
  {
    root = approx;    // save the approx
    approx = (num/root + root)/2.0;     // calculate a new approx
    cout << "new approx = " << approx << endl;
  }
  while ( fabs(approx - root) > OKDIF);
  cout << "The square root is " << approx << endl;

  return 0;
}
```

Exercises 6.1

1. **a.** factorial() expects to receive one integer value.
   b. price() expects to receive one integer and two double-precision values, in that order.
   c. An int and two double-precision values, in that order, must be passed to yield().
   d. A character and two floating-point values, in that order, must be passed to interest().
   e. Two floating-point values, in that order, must be passed to total().
   f. Two integers, two characters, and two floating-point values, in that order, are expected by roi().
   g. Two integers and two character values, in that order, are expected by get_val().

3. **a.** The findAbs() function is included in the program written for Exercise 3b.

b.

```cpp
#include <iostream.h>
void findAbs(double);  // function prototype
int main()
{
  double dnum;

  cout << "Enter a number: ";
  cin >> dnum;
  FindAbs(dnum);

  return 0;
}


void findAbs(double num)
{
  double val;

  if (num < 0)
    val = -num;
  else
    val = num;
  cout << "The absolute value of " << num << " is " << val << endl;

  return;
}
```

5. a. The `sqr_it()` function is included in the program written for Exercise 5b.
   b.

```cpp
#include <iostream.h>
void sqr_it(double);  // function prototype
int main()
{
  double first;

  cout << "\nEnter a number: ";
  cin  >> first;
  sqr_it(first);

  return 0;
}

void sqr_it(double num)
{
  cout << "The square of " << num << " is " << (num*num) << endl;

  return;
}
```

7. a. The function for producing the required table is included in the larger program written for Exercise 9.

b.
```cpp
#include <iostream.h>
double fracpart(double); // function prototype

int main()
{
  double number;

      cout << "Enter a number: ";
      cin  >> number;
      cout << "The fractional part of this number is "
           << fracpart(number) << endl;

      return 0;

}
double fracpart(double num)
{
  return num - long(num);
}
```

9. a. The function for producing the required table is included in the larger program written for Exercise 9b.

b.
```cpp
#include <iostream.h>
#include <iomanip.h>
void table(void);     // function prototype

  int main()
  {
    table();                 // call the function

    return 0;
  }

  void table(void)
  {
    int num;

  cout << endl; //display a blank line
  cout << "NUMBER    SQUARE    CUBE\n"
       << "------     ------     ----" << endl;

  for (num = 1; num <= 10; ++num)
    cout << setw(3) << num << "            "
         << setw(3) << num * num << "        "
         << setw(4) << num * num * num << endl;

  return;
  }
```

11. The function is included within the context of a complete program.

```cpp
#include <iostream.h>
#include <iomanip.h>
#include <math.h>
double PI(); // function prototype

int main()
{

  cout << setiosflags(ios::fixed | ios::showpoint)
       << setprecision(15);
  cout << "The value of pi is " << PI() << endl;

  return 0;

}

double PI()
{
`  return 2.0 * asin(1.0);
}
```

13. a. The required function template is included within the complete program created for Exercise 13b.

   b.
```cpp
#include <iostream.h>

template <class T>
int whole(T value)
{
   return int(value);
}

int main()
{
  char code = 'a';
  int num1 = 5;
  float num2 = -6.23;
  double num3 = 7.23456;

  cout << "The integer value of " << code << " is "
       << whole(code) << endl;
  cout << "The integer value of " << num1 << " is "
       << whole(num1) << endl;
  cout << "The integer value of " << num2 << " is "
       << whole(num2) << endl;
  cout << "The integer value of " << num3 << " is "
       << whole(num3) << endl;

  return 0;
}
```

15. a. The required function template is included within the complete program created for Exercise 15b.

b.
```cpp
#include <iostream.h>

template <class T>
T square(T value)
{
    return (value * value);
}

int main()
{

  int num1 = 5;
  float num2 = -6.23;
  double num3 = 7.23456;

  cout << "The square of " << num1 << " is "
       << square(num1) << endl;
  cout << "The square of " << num2 << " is "
       << square(num2) << endl;
  cout << "The square of " << num3 << " is "
       << square(num3) << endl;

  return 0;
}
```

Exercises 6.2

1.
```cpp
#include <iostream.h>
int main()
{
  float firstnum, secnum, max;
  float FindMax(float, float);   // the function prototype

  cout << "\nEnter a number: ";
  cin  >> firstnum;
  cout << "Great! Please enter a second number: ";
  cin  >> secnum;

  max = FindMax(firstnum, secnum); // the function is called here

  cout << "\nThe maximum of the two numbers is " << max << endl;
  return 0;
}
```

```
float find_max(float x, float y)
{                        // start of function body
  float maxnum;          // variable declaration

  if (x >= y)            // find the maximum number
    maxnum = x;
  else
    maxnum = y;

  return maxnum;         // return statement
}
```

3. **a.** void check(int num1, float num2, double num3)
   b. double find_abs(double x);
   c. float mult(float first, float second)
   d. int sqr_it(int number)
   e. int powfun(int num, int exponent)
   f. void table(void)

5. **a.** The find_abs() function is included in the program written for Exercise 5b.
   b.
```
#include <iostream.h>
int main()
{
  double number, absnum;
  double find_abs(double);   // function prototype

  cout << "Enter a number: ";
  cin  >> number;
  absnum = find_abs(number);
  cout << "The absolute value of this number is " << absnum;

  return 0;
}

double find_abs(double num)
{
  double val;

  if (num < 0)
    val = -num;
  else
    val = num;
  return val;
}
```

7. a. The surface() function is included in the program written for Exercise 7b.

b.
```cpp
#include <iostream.h>
double surface(double, double); // function prototype

int main()
{
  double radius, length;

  cout << "Enter a radius: ";
  cin  >> radius;
  cout << "Enter the length of the cylinder: ";
  cin  >>  length;
  cout << "The surface area of the cylinder is "
        << surface(radius, length) << endl;

  return 0;
}

double surface(double radius, double length)
{
  const double PI = 3.14157;

  return (2 * PI * radius * length);
}
```

9. a. The maxdeflect() function is included in the program written for Exercise 9b.

b.
```cpp
#include <iostream.h>
double maxdeflect(double length, char code);  //function prototype

int main()
{

  double length, deflect;
  char code;

  cout << "Enter the floor length (in inches): ";
  cin  >> length;
  cout << "Enter the type of floor\n"
              <<  "(f for floor or r for roof): ";
  cin  >> code;
  deflect = maxdeflect(length, code);
  if (deflect == -1)
    cout << "An incorrect code was entered" <<endl;
  else
    cout << "The maximum deflection is "
          <<  deflect << endl;

  return 0;
}
```

```
double maxdeflect(double length, char code)
{
      double deflect;

  if (code == 'r' || code == 'R')
    deflect = length / 240.0;
  else if (code == 'f' || code == 'F')
    deflect = length / 180.0;
  else
    deflect = -1;

  return deflect;
}
```

Exercises 6.3

1. **a.** `float &amount;`
   b. `double &price`
   c. `int &minutes;`
   d. `char &key;`
   e. `double &yield;`

3.
```
#include <iostream.h>
int main()
{
  int firstnum, secnum, max;
  void find_max(int, int, int &);  // function prototype

  cout << "Enter a number: ";
  cin >> firstnum;
  cout << "\nGreat! Please enter a second number: ";
  cin >> secnum;

  find_max(firstnum, secnum, max); // call the function

  cout << "\nThe maximum of the two numbers is " << max << endl;

  return 0;
}

void find_max(int x, int y, int &maxval)
{
  if (x >= y)
    maxval = x;
  else
    maxval = y;
  return;
}
```

5.
```cpp
void time(int tot_sec, int &hrs, int &mins, int &secs)
{
    hrs = tot_sec/3600; // 3600 seconds = 1 hour
                        // Integer division yields the whole
                        // number of times 3600 goes into
                        // tot_sec
    tot_sec -= hrs * 3600;
    mins = tot_sec/60;
    tot_sec -= mins * 60;
    secs = tot_sec;
    return;
}
```

7. In the `main()` function, the variables min and hour refer to integer quantities; in `time()` the variables min and hours are references to integers. Thus, there are four distinct variables in all, two of which are known in `main()` and two of which are known in `time()`. The variables in `time()` are, or course, references to the variables in `main()` having the same name. The compiler keeps track of each variable with no confusion.

Exercises 6.4

1.
```cpp
#include <iostream.h>
#include <math.h>
void cylinder(double, double, double&, double&); // prototype

int main()
{
    double radius, length;
    double surfarea, volume;

    cout << "Enter a radius: ";
    cin  >> radius;
    cout << "Enter the length of the cylinder: ";
    cin  >>  length;

    cylinder(radius, length, surfarea, volume);

    cout << "The surface area of the cylinder is "
         << surfarea << endl;

    cout << "The volume of the cylinder is "
         << volume << endl;

    return 0;
}
```

```
void cylinder(double r, double l, double& surf, double& vol)
{
   const double PI = 3.14157;

   surf = 2 * PI * r * l;
   vol = PI * pow(r,2) * l;

   return;
}
```

5.
```
#include <iostream.h>
#include <math.h>

// function prototype
void distance(float, float, float, float, float&, float&, float&);

int main()
{
  float dist1, dist2, dist3;

  distance(3.0, 4.0, 5.0, 6.0, dist1, dist2, dist3);

  cout << "Distance from origin of point 1 is " << dist1 << endl;
  cout << "Distance from origin of point 2 is " << dist2 << endl;
  cout << "Distance between the two points is " << dist3 << endl;

  return 0;
}

void distance(float x1, float y1, float x2, float y2, float& d1, float& d2, float& d3)
{
  d1 = sqrt(pow(x1,2) + pow(y1,2));
  d2 = sqrt(pow(x2,2) + pow(y2,2));
  d3 = sqrt(pow(x1-x2,2) + pow(y1-y2,2));

  return;
}
```

7.
```
float randnum(float seed)
{
   int i;

   i = int(997.0 * seed / 1.e6);
  return (997.0 * seed - i * 1.e6)
}
```

11.

```cpp
#include <iostream.h>
int gcd(int, int);  // function prototype
int main()
{
  int num1, num2, result;

  cout << "Enter two integer values: ";
  cin  >> num1 >> num2;
  result = gcd(num1, num2);
  cout << "The greatest common divisor of these numbers is " << result << endl;

  return 0;
}

int gcd(int n1, int n2)
{
  int smaller, larger, remainder;

  if(n1 < n2) // make sure the first number is not the smallest
  {
    smaller = n1;
    larger = n2;
  }
  else
  {
    smaller = n2;
    larger = n1;
  }
  while ((remainder = larger % smaller) != 0)
  {
    larger = smaller;
    smaller = remainder;
  }
  return smaller;  // the last smaller value is the gcd
}
```

Exercises 6.5

1. a.

Variable name	Data type	Scope
volts	integer	global to `main()`, `roi()`, and `step()`
resistance	long integer	global to `main()`, `roi()`, and `step()`
current	double precision	global to `main()`, `roi()`, and `step()`
power	integer	local to `main()` only
factor	double precision	local to `main()` only
time	double precision	local to `main()` only
count	integer	local to `roi()` only
weight	double precision	local to `roi()` only
hours	integer	local to `step()` only
fracpart	float	local to `step()` only

Note that although arguments of each function assume a value that is dependent on the calling function, these arguments can change values within their respective functions. This makes them behave as is they were local variables within the called function.

3. All function parameters have local scope with respect to their defined function.

5. The following is displayed:

```
20
10
```

Even though the global and local variables have the same name, `main()` cannot access the global variable firstnum because the declaration in `main()` has precedence over the global declaration. The global variable firstnum can, however, be accessed in `main()` by using the global scope resolution operator.

Exercises 6.6

1. a. Local variables may be automatic, static, or register. It is important to realize that not all variables declared inside of functions are necessarily local. An example of this is an external variable.

b. Global variables may be static or external.

3. The first function declares `yrs` to be a static variable and assigns a value of one to it only once when the function is compiled. Each time the function is called thereafter, the value in `yrs` is increased by two. The second function also declares `yrs` to be static, but assigns it the value one every time it is called, and the value of `yrs` after the function is finished will always be 3. By resetting the value of `yrs` to 1 each time it is called, the second function defeats the purpose of declaring the variable to be static.

5. The *scope of a variable* tells where the variable is recognized in the program and can be used within an expression. If, for example, the variable `resistance` is declared inside a function, it is local and its scope is inside that function only. If the variable is declared outside of any function, it is global and its scope is anywhere below the declaration but within that file, unless another file of the same program extends the scope of the variable by declaring the variable to be external.

Exercises 7.1

5. Yes. Anything stored on disk is referred to as a file. The two major divisions of files are data files and executable (program) files. Although source code files are sometimes called program files, strictly speaking they are data files used by a compiler program. A compiled C++ program is an example of an executable file.

7. **a.** ofstream memo;
      memo.open("coba.mem");
   b. ofstream letter;
      letter.open("book.let");
   c. ofstream coups;
      coups.open("coupons.bnd");
   d. ifstream pt_yield;
      pt_yield.open("yield.bnd");
   e. ifstream pri_file;
      pri_file.open("prices.dat");
   f. ifstream rates;
      rates.open("rates.dat", ios::in);

Exercises 7.2

1. a.

```
#include <fstream.h>7
#include <stdlib.h>
const int MAXCHARS = 80;
int main()
{
   int i;
   ofstream out;
   char strng[MAXCHARS];

   out.open("text.dat");
   if (out.fail())
   {
     cout << "The file was not successfully opened" << endl;
     exit(1);
   }
   cout << "Enter three lines of text to be stored in the file.\n";
     for (i = 1; i <= 3; i++)
     {
       cin.getline(strng, MAXCHARS, '\n');   // get input from cin stream
       out << strng << endl;
     }
     out.close();
     cout << "End of data input.\n"
          << "The file has been written." << endl;

     return 0;
}
```

b.
```
#include <fstream.h>
#include <stdlib.h>
const int MAXCHARS = 80;
int main()
{
  int ch;
  char line[MAXCHARS];
  ifstream in_file;

  in_file.open("text.dat");
  if (!in_file)   // check for successful open
  {
    cout << "\nThe file was not successfully opened"
         << "\n Please check that the file currently exists."
         << endl;
    exit(1);
  }
      // now read the file
  while( (ch = in_file.peek()) != EOF )
  {
    in_file.getline(line, MAXCHARS,'\n');
    cout << line << endl;
  }

  return 0;
}
```

3.
```
#include <fstream.h>
#include <stdlib.h>

int main()
{
  const int MAXCHARS = 7;
  const int DATAITEMS = 4;
  char filename[MAXCHARS] = "result";

  int i;
  float number, total, average;
  ifstream in_file;

  out_file.open(filename);
  if (out_file.fail())
  {
    cout << "The file was not successfully opened" << endl;
    exit(1);
  }

  out_file << 92.65 << ' ' << 88.72 << ' '
           << 77.46 << ' ' << 82.93 << endl;
  out_file.close();
  cout << "The data has been written to the file named "
             << filename << endl;

  in_file.open(filename);
  if (!in_file)    // check for successful open
```

```
  {
    cout << "\nThe file" <<filename << " was not successfully opened"
             << "\n Please check that the file currently exists."
             << endl;
    exit(1);
  }
      // now read each data item and add it to the total
      total = 0;
      cout << "The data read from the file is: ";
      for (i = 1; i <= DATAITEMS; i++)
  {
    in_file >> number;
    cout << number << "   ";
    total += number;
  }

  average = total / DATAITEMS;
  cout << "/nThe average is " << average << endl;
  return 0;
}
```

NOTE: In writing the four numbers to the file, it is necessary to separate the numbers by at least one space. If no spaces are placed between the numbers (or they are not written on separate lines) the data in the file will be 92.6588.7277.4682.93. If this data is then read in as four numbers, the numbers read from the file will be 92.6588, .7277, .4682, and .93. Alternatively, the output could also have been written using the statement

```
out_file << "92.65 88.72 77.46 82.93" << endl;
```

5. a.
```
   #include <fstream.h>
   #include <stdlib.h>

   int main()
   {
     const int MAXCHARS = 6;
     char filename[MAXCHARS] = "volts";
     ofstream out_file;

     out_file.open(filename);
     if (out_file.fail())
     {
       cout << "The file was not successfully opened" << endl;
       exit(1);
     }

     out_file << "120.3 122.7 90.3 99.8\n"
              << "95.3 120.5 127.3 120.8\n"
              << "123.2 118.4 123.8 115.6\n"
              << "122.4 95.6 118.2 120.0\n"
              << "123.5 130.2 123.9 124.4" << endl;
     out_file.close();
     cout << "The data has been written to the file named "
          << filename << endl;

     return 0;
   }
```

b.

```
#include <fstream.h>
#include <stdlib.h>

int main()
{
  const int MAXCHARS = 6;
  const int DATAITEMS = 4;
  const int RECORDS = 5;
  char filename[MAXCHARS] = "volts";

  int i, j;
  float voltage, total, average;
  ifstream in_file;

  in_file.open(filename);
  if (!in_file)    // check for successful open
  {
    cout << "\nThe file" <<filename << " was not successfully opened"
         << "\n Please check that the file currently exists."
         << endl;
    exit(1);
  }
    // now read each record and obtain the average
  for(i = 1; i <= RECORDS; i++)
  {
    total = 0;
    cout << "\nThe data for record " << i << " is: ";
    for (j = 1; j <= DATAITEMS; j++)
    {
      in_file >> voltage;
      cout << voltage << "   ";
      total += voltage;
    }

    average = total / DATAITEMS;
    cout << "\n   The average is " << average << endl;
  }

  return 0;
}
```

7. a. The data may be entered in a variety of ways. One possibility is to enter the data, line-by-line, and write each line to a file. A second method is to use a text editor to write the data to a file. A third possibility is to enter the data as individual items and write the file as individual items. The program below uses the first approach, where the data is included within the program itself, rather than being entered by the user to the program using cin statements before being printed to the file. Note that the header information is not included as part of the file.

```
#include <fstream.h>
#include <stdlib.h>
int main()
{
  const int MAXCHARS = 10;
  char filename[MAXCHARS] = "polar.dat";

  ofstream out_file;

  out_file.open(filename);
  if (out_file.fail())
  {
    cout << "The file was not successfully opened" << endl;
    exit(1);
  }

  out_file << " 2.0    45.0\n"
           << " 6.0    30.0\n"
           << "10.0    45.0\n"
           << " 4.0    60.0\n"
           << "12.0    55.0\n"
           << " 8.0    15.0"
           << endl;
  out_file.close();
  cout << "The data has been written to the file named "
       << filename << endl;

  return 0;
}
      b.
#include <fstream.h>
#include <stdlib.h>
#include <math.h>
int main()
{
  const int MAXCHARS = 10;
  const int RECORDS = 6;
  const float CONVERT = 3.14157 / 180.;   // radian conversion
  char filename[MAXCHARS] = "polar.dat";

  int i, j;
  float distance, angle;
    float x, y;
  ifstream in_file;

  in_file.open(filename);
  if (!in_file)    // check for successful open
  {
    cout << "\nThe file" <<filename << " was not successfully opened"
         << "\n Please check that the file currently exists."
         << endl;
    exit(1);
```

```
    }
    // now read each record and convert to cartesian coordinates
    for(i = 1; i <= RECORDS; i++)
    {
      in_file >> distance >> angle;
      cout << "distance = " << distance
           << "  angle = " << angle << endl;
      x = distance * cos(CONVERT * angle);
      y = distance * sin(CONVERT * angle);
      cout << "x = " << x << "   y = " << y << endl;
    }

    return 0;
}
```

Exercises 7.3

5. The f_chars() function is included in the program listed below:

```
#include <fstream.h>
#include <stdlib.h>
const int MAXLENGTH = 15;
void f_chars(ifstream&);  // function prototype needed by main()
int main()
{
  ifstream in;
  char f_name[MAXLENGTH];

  cout << "\nEnter a file name: ";
  cin  >> f_name;
  in.open(f_name);
  if (in.fail())    // check for successful open
  {
    cout << "\nThe file was not successfully opened"
         << "\n Please check that the file currently exits."
         << endl;
    exit(1);
  }
  f_chars(in);
  in.close();

  return 0;
}
void f_chars(ifstream& fname)
{
  fname.seekg(0L,ios::end);  // move to the end of the file
  cout << "\nThere are " << fname.tellg()
       << " characters in the file.\n";
  return;
}
```

Exercises 7.4

1. The filename referred to in the Exercise is a reference to an object of type `ifstream`. The function prototype for `p_file()` is `p_file(ifstream&);`.

3. The `get_open()` function is included below with a driver function used to test it.

```
#include <fstream.h>
#include <stdlib.h>
const int MAXCHARS = 15;
int get_open(ofstream&);    // function prototype
int main()     // driver function to test fcheck()
{
  ofstream out_file;

  get_open(out_file);

   return 0;
}

 int get_open(ofstream& file_out)
 {
   char key, name[MAXCHARS];
   ifstream file_in;

   cout << "\nEnter a file name: " << endl;
   cin.getline(name, MAXCHARS, '\n');

   file_in.open(name);
   if (file_in.fail())
    // the file doesn't exist - create it for writing
       file_out.open(name);
   else
   {
     file_in.close;
     cout << "\nThe file currently exists. Do you want to"
          << "\n overwrite it or exit."
          << "\nEnter an o, or e: ";
     cin  >> key;
     if(key == 'o')
        file_out.open(name);   // now open it for output
     if (file_out.fail())
     {
       cout << "The output file was not successfully opened" << endl;
       exit(1);
     }
   }
   return 1;
}
```

Exercises 8.1

1. **a.** A class is a programmer defined data type. The class specifies both the types of data and the types of operations that may be performed on the data.
   b. An object is a specific instance of a class.
   c. The declaration section declares both the data types and function prototypes of a class.
   d. The implementation section defines the class' functions.
   e. An instance variables is another name for a class data member.
   f. A member function is a function declared in the class declaration section.
   g. A data member is a variable declared in the class declaration section.
   h. A member function that has the same name as the class and is used to initialize an object's data members.
   i. Class instance is synonymous with an object.
   j. Services are synonyms for the functions defined in a class implementation section.
   k. Methods are synonyms for the functions defined in a class implementation section.
   l. The set of attributes and behavior defining a class is referred to as the class' *interface*.
   m. The state of an object defines how the object appears at the moment. It is specified by the values assigned to the object's data member variables.
   n. The behavior of an object defines how the object can be activated and the response that will be produced. It is specified by the object's member and friend functions.

3. Behavior is triggered in an object by calling one of its member functions. The call provides the stimulus that activates the function. The response to the call is whatever the function has been programmed to do.

5. **a.**
```
// implementation section
Time::Time(int hh = 0, int mm = 0, int ss = 0)
{
  hours = hh;
  mins = mm;
  secs = ss;
}
void Time::settime(int hh, int mm, int ss)
{
  hours = hh;
  mins = mm;
  secs = ss;
}
void Time::showdata(void)
{
  cout << "The time is "
       << setw(2) << setfill('0') << hours << ':'
       << setw(2) << setfill('0') << mins << ':'
       << setw(2) << setfill('0') << secs << endl;
}
```

b.
```cpp
// implementation section
Complex::Complex(float re = 0, float im = 0)
{
  real = re;
  imaginary = im;
}
void Complex::setvals(float re, float im)
{
  real = re;
  imaginary = im;
}
void Complex::showdata(void)
{
  float c;
  char sign = '+';

  c = imaginary;
  if (c < 0)
  {
    sign = '-';
    c = -c;
  }
  cout << "The complex number is "
       << setiosflags(ios::fixed)
       << real << ' ' << sign << ' ' << c << "i\n";

}
```

c.
```cpp
// implementation section
Circle::Circle(int xx = 1, int yy = 1, float rr = 1.0)
{
  xcenter = xx;
  ycenter = yy;
  radius = rr;
}
void Circle::setvals(int xx, int yy, float rr)
{
  xcenter = xx;
  ycenter = yy;
  radius = rr;
}
void Circle::showdata(void)
{
  cout << "The center of the circle is at "
       << '(' << setfill('0') << xcenter << ','
       << setfill('0') << ycenter << ')'
       << " and the radius is " << radius << endl;
}
```

7. The class name should begin with a capital letter (i.e., `Employee`). The data members should be declared as private and the function members should be declared as public. Additionally, the declaration for the constructor prototype should be `class(int, char *)`.

Exercises 8.2

1. a. true   **d.** false   **g.** false   **j.** true   **m.** false
   b. false   **e.** true   **h.** true   **k.** false   **n.** true
   c. true   **f.** false   **i.** true   **l.** false   **o.** false

3.

```cpp
#include <iostream.h>

// class declaration
class Date
{
  private:
     long yyyymmdd;
  public:
     Date(int, int, int);     // constructor
     Date(long = 200/0704L);              // default constructor
     void showdate(void);     // member function to display a Date
};

// implementation section
Date::Date(int mm, int dd, int yyyy)
{
  yyyymmdd = yyyy * 10000L + mm * 100L + dd;
}
Date::Date(long ymd)
{
  yyyymmdd = ymd;
}
void Date::showdate(void)
{
  int year, month, day;

  year = (int)(yyyymmdd/10000.0);     // extract the year
  month = (int)( (yyyymmdd - year * 10000.0)/100.00 ); // extract the month
  day = (int)(yyyymmdd - year * 10000.0 - month * 100.0); // extract the day
  cout << "The Date is " << month << "/" << day << "/" << year << endl;
}

int main()
{
   Date a, b(4,1,1998), c(20020515L); // declare three objects

   a.showdate();        // display object a's values
   b.showdate();        // display object b's values
   c.showdate();        // display object c's values

   return 0;
}
```

Exercises 8.3

3.

```cpp
#include <iostream.h>
#include <stdlib.h>
#include <time.h>
const int MAXFLOOR = 15;
const int NOMOVE = 0;  // code for no elevator movement
const int MOVEDUP = 1; // code for elevator moved up
const int MOVEDDOWN = 2; // code for elevator moved down
const int MAXREQS = 5;

// class declaration

class Elevator
{
  private:
    int cur_floor;
  public:
    Elevator(int = 1);    // constructor
    int request(int);
};

// implementation section

Elevator::Elevator(int cfloor)
{
  cur_floor = cfloor;
}

int Elevator::request(int newfloor)
{
  int code;
  if (newfloor < 1 || newfloor > MAXFLOOR || newfloor == cur_floor)
    code = NOMOVE;
  else if ( newfloor > cur_floor)  // move elevator up
  {
      cout << "\nStarting at floor " << cur_floor << endl;
    while (newfloor > cur_floor)
    {
      cur_floor++;    // add one to current floor
      cout << "  Going Up - now at floor " << cur_floor << endl;
    }
    cout << "Stopping at floor " << cur_floor << endl;
    code = MOVEDUP;
  }
  else  // move elevator down
  {
    cout << "\nStarting at floor " << cur_floor << endl;
    while (newfloor < cur_floor)
    {
      cur_floor--;   // subtract one from current floor
      cout << "  Going Down - now at floor " << cur_floor << endl;
```

```
        }
        cout << "Stopping at floor " << cur_floor << endl;
        code = MOVEDDOWN;
    }

    return code;
}

int main()
{
    Elevator a;    // declare an object of type Elevator
    int newfloor, moved, requests = 0;

    srand(time(NULL));
    while (requests < MAXREQS)
    {
        newfloor = (1 + rand() % 16);
        moved = a.request(newfloor);
        if (moved)
            requests++;
    }

    return 0;
}
```

5.
```
// class declaration
class Person
{
    public:
        Person(void);    //constructor
        int arrive(void);
        int gallons(void);
};

// implementation section

Person::Person()
{
    srand(time(NULL));
}

int Person::arrive()
{
    return (1 + rand() % 16);
}

int Person::gallons()
{
    return (3 + rand() % 21);
}
```

Exercises 9.1

1. Assignment stores a value into an existing variable or object; that is, it occurs after the variable or object has been created by a definition statement. Initialization occurs at the time a new variable or object is created and is part of the creation process.

3. a. The required class is contained within the program solution to Exercise 3b.

b.

```cpp
#include <iostream.h>
#include <iomanip.h>
// class declaration
class Complex
{
  private:
    float real;
    float imaginary;
  public:
    Complex(float = 0, float = 0);      // constructor
    void operator=(Complex& ); // overloaded assignment operator function
    void showdata(void);        // display member function
};

// implementation section
Complex::Complex(float re, float im)
{
  real = re;
  imaginary = im;
}
void Complex::operator=(Complex& oldnum)
{
  real = oldnum.real;
  imaginary = oldnum.imaginary;
  return;
}
void Complex::showdata(void)
{
  float c;
  char sign = '+';

  c = imaginary;
  if (c < 0)
  {
    sign = '-';
    c = -c;
  }
  cout << "The complex number is "
       << real << ' ' << sign << ' ' << c << "i\n";
  return;
}
```

```
int main()
{
  Complex a(4.2, 3.6), b;   // declare 2 objects

  a.showdata();        // display object a's values
  b.showdata();        // display object b's values
  b = a;               // assign a to b
  b.showdata();        // display object b's values

  return 0;
}
```

5. a. The required class is contained within the program solution to Exercise 5b.
  b.

```
#include <iostream.h>
#include <iomanip.h>
#include <string.h>
// class declaration
class Car
{
  private:
    float engine_size;
    char body_style;
    int color_code;
  public:
    Car(float = 0.0, char = 'X', int = 0);  // default constructor
    void operator=(Car& );       // overloaded assignment operator
    void showdata(void);         // member function to display a time
};

// implementation section

Car::Car(float eng, char styl, int cd)
{
  engine_size = eng;
  body_style = styl;
  color_code = cd;
}
void Car::operator=(Car& oldcar)
{
  engine_size = oldcar.engine_size;
  body_style = oldcar.body_style;
  color_code = oldcar.color_code;
  return;
}
```

```
void Car::showdata(void)
{
  cout << "\nThe values for this object are \n"
       << "  Engine size: " << engine_size << endl
       << "  Body style:  " << body_style << endl
       << "  Color code:  " << color_code << endl;
  return;
}

int main()
{
  Car a(250.0, 'S', 52), b;  // declare 2 objects

  a.showdata();    // display object a's values
  b.showdata();    // display object b's values
  b = a;           // assign a to b
  b.showdata();    // display object b's values

  return 0;
}
```

Exercises 9.2

1. a.
```
#include <iostream.h>
// class declaration
class Employee
{
  private:
    static float tax_rate;
    static int numemps;
    int id_num;
  public:
    Employee(int = 0);    // constructor
    void display();   // access function
};

// static member definition
float Employee::tax_rate = 0.0025;
int Employee::numemps = 0;
// class implementation
Employee::Employee(int num)
{
  id_num = num;
  numemps++;
}
```

```cpp
void Employee::display()
{
  cout << "Employee number " << id_num
       << " has a tax rate of " << tax_rate << endl;
  cout << "There are currently " << numemps
       << " Employee objects" << endl;
  return;
}

int main()
{
  Employee emp1(11122);

  emp1.display();

  Employee emp2(11133);   // create a second object
  emp2.display();

  return 0;
}
```

3. Yes, the three statements could be replaced by the single statement.

5.
```cpp
#include <iostream.h>
#include <math.h>

// class declaration
class Complex
{
  // friends list
  friend Complex addcomplex(Complex&, Complex&);
  private:
    float real;
    float imag;
  public:
    Complex(float = 0, float = 0);   // constructor
    void display();

};

// class implementation
Complex::Complex(float rl, float im)
{
  real = rl;
  imag = im;
}
```

```cpp
            void Complex::display()
            {
              char sign = '+';

              if(imag < 0) sign = '-';
              cout << real << sign << fabs(imag) << 'i';
              return;
            }

            // friend implementation
            Complex addcomplex(Complex& a, Complex& b)
            {
              Complex temp;

              temp.real = a.real + b.real;
              temp.imag = a.imag + b.imag;

              return temp;
            }

            int main()
            {
              Complex a(3.2, 5.6), b(1.1, -8.4), c;

              cout << "\nThe first complex number is ";
              a.display();
              cout << "\nThe second complex number is ";
              b.display();

              c = addcomplex(a,b);

              cout << "\n\nThe sum of these two complex numbers is ";
              c.display();

              return 0;
            }
```

7. a. The Rec_coord and Pol_coord classes are presented within the program solution to Exercise 7b.

   b.

```cpp
#include <iostream.h>
#include <iomanip.h>
#include <math.h>
const float DegToRad = 3.1416/180.0; // conversion from degrees to radians
const float RadToDeg = 1.0/DegToRad; // conversion from radians to degrees
const int RecToPolar = 1;
const int PolarToRec = 2;
```

```
// forward declaration of class Pol_coord
class Pol_coord;

//Rec_coord class declaration
class Rec_coord
{
  // friends list
  friend void conv_pol(int, Rec_coord&, Pol_coord&);
  private:
    float xval;
    float yval;
  public:
    Rec_coord(float = 0.0, float = 0.0); // constructor
    void input(float, float);  // input data member values
    void showdata(); // display data member values
};

// Pol_coord class declaration
class Pol_coord
{
  // friends list
  friend void conv_pol(int, Rec_coord&, Pol_coord&);
  private:
    float dist;
    float theta;
  public:
    Pol_coord(float = 0.0, float = 0.0); // constructor
    void input(float, float);  // input data member values
    void showdata(); // display data member values
};

// implementation section
Rec_coord::Rec_coord(float x, float y)
{
  xval = x;
  yval = y;
}

void Rec_coord::input(float newxval, float newyval)
{
  xval = newxval;
  yval = newyval;
  return;
}

void Rec_coord::showdata()
{
  cout << "(" << xval << ", " << yval << ")" << endl;
  return;
}
```

```
Pol_coord::Pol_coord(float r, float angle)
{
  dist = r;
  theta = angle;
}

void Pol_coord::input(float newdist, float newtheta)
{
  dist = newdist;
  theta = newtheta;
  return;
}

void Pol_coord::showdata()
{
  cout << "r = " << dist << ", angle = " << theta << endl;
  return;
}

// friend implementation
void conv_pol(int dir, Rec_coord& a, Pol_coord& b)
{
  if (dir == RecToPolar)
  {
    b.dist = sqrt(pow(a.xval,2) + pow(a.yval,2));
      b.theta = atan(a.yval/a.xval) * RadToDeg;
  }
  else if (dir == PolarToRec)
  {
    a.xval = b.dist * cos(b.theta * DegToRad);
    a.yval = b.dist * sin(b.theta * DegToRad);
  }
  return;
}

int main()
{
  Rec_coord a;   // declare one object for each class
  Pol_coord b;
  float newx, newy, newr, newtheta;

  cout << "Rectangular point a is initially located at ";
  a.showdata();      // display object a's values
  cout << "Polar point b is initially located at ";
  b.showdata();
  cout << "Enter a new distance and angle for point b: ";
  cin  >> newr >> newtheta;
  b.input(newr, newtheta);
  cout << "Polar point b is now located at ";
  b.showdata();
  conv_pol(PolarToRec, a, b);
  cout << "After conversion point a is now located at ";
  a.showdata();
  cout << "Enter a new x and y value for point a: ";
  cin  >> newx >> newy;
```

```
    a.input(newx, newy);
    cout << "Rectangular point a is now located at ";
    a.showdata();
    conv_pol(RecToPolar, a, b);
    cout << "After conversion, point b is now located at ";
    b.showdata();

    return 0;
}
```

Exercises 9.3

1. a. The required function is included within the following working program:

```
#include <iostream.h>
// class declaration
class Date
{
  private:
    int month;
    int day;
    int year;
  public:
    Date(int = 7, int = 4, int = 2001);      // constructor
    int operator>(Date& );   // declare the operator > function
    void showdate(void);   // member function to display a Date
};

// implementation section
Date::Date(int mm, int dd, int yyyy)
{
  month = mm;
  day = dd;
  year = yyyy;
}
int Date::operator>(Date& date2)
{
  long dt1, dt2;

  dt1 = year*10000L + month*100 + day;
  dt2 = date2.year*10000L + date2.month*100 + date2.day;
  if (dt1 > dt2)
    return 1;
  else
    return 0;
}

int main()
{
    Date a(4,1,1999), b(12,18,2001), c(4,1,1999); // declare 3 objects
```

```
    if (a > b)
      cout << "Date a greater than b \n";
    else
      cout << "Date a less than or equal to b \n";

    if (a > c)
      cout << "Date a greater than c \n";
    else
      cout << "Date a less than or equal to c \n";

  return 0;
}
```

3. a. This operator function provides the same result as the `operator()` function used in Program 9.8.

5. a. The required function is incorporated within the complete program written for Exercise 5b.

   b.

```
#include <iostream.h>
#include <math.h>
// class declaration
class complex
{
  private:
    float real;
    float imag;
  public:
    complex(float, float);  // constructor
    complex operator+(complex &); // declare the operator+ function
    void display();
};
// class implementation
complex::complex(float rl = 0, float im = 0)
{
  real = rl;
  imag = im;
}
void complex::display()
{
  char sign = '+';

  if(imag < 0) sign = '-';
  cout << real << sign << fabs(imag) << 'i';
}
complex complex::operator+(complex &newnum)
{
  complex temp;

  temp.real = real + newnum.real;
  temp.imag = imag + newnum.imag;

  return temp;    // return a complex number
}
```

```
int main()
{
  complex a(3.2, 5.6), b(1.1, -8.4), c;
  float re, im;

  cout << "\nThe first complex number is ";
  a.display();
  cout << "\nThe second complex number is ";
  b.display();
  c = a + b;   // can be written as a = a.operator+(b);
  cout << "\n\nThe sum of these two numbers is ";
  c.display();

  return 0;
}
```

Exercises 9.4

1. a. Conversion from a built-in type to a built-in type is accomplished by C++'s implicit conversion rules or by explicit casting. Conversion from a built-in type to a user-defined type is accomplished by a type conversion constructor. Conversion from a user-defined type to a built-in type is accomplished by a conversion operator function. Conversion from a user-defined type to a built-in type is accomplished by a conversion operator function.

b. A type conversion constructor is a constructor whose first parameter is not a member of its class and whose remaining parameters, if any, have default values. A conversion operator function is a class member operator function having the name of a built-in data type or class.

3.

```
#include <iostream.h>

// class declaration for Date
class Date
{
  private:
    int month, day, year;
  public:
    Date(int = 7, int = 4, int = 2001);    // constructor
    operator long();          // conversion operator function
    void showdate(void);
};
// constructor
Date::Date(int mm, int dd, int yyyy)
{
  month = mm;
  day = dd;
  year = yyyy;
}
```

```
// conversion operator function converting from Date to long
Date::operator long()    // must return a long
{
  int mp, yp, t;
  long julian;

  if (month <= 2)
  {
    mp = 0;
    yp = year - 1;
  }
  else
  {
    mp = int(0.4 * month + 2.3);
    yp = year;
  }
  t = int(yp/4) - int(yp/100) + int(yp/400);
  julian = 365L * year + 31L * (month - 1) + day + t - mp;
  return (julian);
}
// member function to display a Date
void Date::showdate(void)
{
  cout << setfill('0')
       << setw(2) << month << '/'
       << setw(2) << day << '/'
       << setw(2) << year % 100;
  return;
}
int main()
{
  Date a(1,31,1985);  // declare and initialize one object of type Date
  long b;             // declare an object of type long

  b = a;              // a conversion takes place here

  cout << "a's value, in the form month/day/year is ";
  a.showdate();
  cout << "\nThis value, as a Julian integer, is " << b << endl;

  return 0;
}
```

5.

```
#include <iostream.h>

// forward declaration of class Julian
class Julian;
// class declaration for Date
class Date
{
  private:
    int month, day, year;
```

```
    public:
      Date(int = 7, int = 4, int = 94);      // constructor
      operator Julian();       // conversion operator to Julian
      void showdate(void);
};

// class declaration for Julian
class Julian
{
  private:
    long yyyymmdd;
  public:
    Julian(long = 0);     // constructor
    void showjulian(void);
};
// class implementation for Date
Date::Date(int mm, int dd, int yyyy)   // constructor
{
  month = mm;
  day = dd;
  year = yyyy;
}
// conversion operator function converting from Date to Julian class
Date::operator Julian()    // must return an Julian object
{
  int mp, yp, t;
  long temp;

  if (month <= 2)
  {
    mp = 0;
    yp = year - 1;
  }
  else
  {
    mp = int(0.4 * month + 2.3);
    yp = year;
  }
  t = int(yp/4) - int(yp/100) + int(yp/400);
  temp = 365L * year + 31L * (month - 1) + day + t - mp;
  return temp;
}
// member function to display a Date
void Date::showdate(void)
{
  cout << setfill('0')
       << setw(2) << month << '/'
       << setw(2) << day << '/'
       << setw(2) << year % 100;
  return;
}
// class implementation for Julian
Julian::Julian(long ymd)   // constructor
{
  yyyymmdd = ymd;
}
```

```
// member function to display an Julian
void Julian::showjulian(void)
{
  cout << yyyymmdd;
  return;
}

int main()
{
  Date a(1,31,1995), b(3,16,1996);  // declare two Date objects
  Julian c, d;                      // declare two Julian objects

  c = Julian(a);    // cast a into an Julian object
  d = Julian(b);    // cast b into an Julian object
  cout << " a's date is ";
  a.showdate();
  cout << "\n   as a Julian object this date is ";
  c.showjulian();

  cout << "\n b's date is ";
  b.showdate();
  cout << "\n   as a Julian object this date is ";
  d.showjulian();
  cout << endl;

  return 0;
}
```

> NOTE: There is no conversion operator from Julian to Date. In general the Julian objects are extremely useful for determining actual day count differences between two dates and for sorting dates. In practice, the Julian date would be incorporated as a data member of the Date class. Also note that the forward reference to the Julian class could be omitted in this program if the Julian class were declared prior to the Date class.

Exercises 9.5

3. The main() function produces a valid simulation. The use of a do-while loop that is always true and which is exited using an internal if-else statement can be used in place of the while loop. Although students may sometimes encounter this type of loop in simulations, because of the always true condition while(1), it is considered inferior to a while loop that uses its tested condition in determining when loop execution is to end. Loops should exit via their tested condition rather than through a nonstandard internal decision point.

Exercises 9.6

1. a. Inheritance is the capability of deriving one class from another class.
   b. A base class is the class that is used as the basis for deriving subsequent classes.

c. A derived class is the class that inherits the characteristics of a base class.

d. Simple inheritance is a type of inheritance where the parent of each derived class is a single base class.

e. Multiple inheritance is a type of inheritance where a derived class has two or more parent base classes.

f. Class hierarchies are the order in which classes are derived.

3. The three features that must be provided for a programming language to be classified as object-oriented are classes, inheritance, and polymorphism. Object-based languages are languages that support objects but do not provide inheritance features.

5. a. The required classes are contained within the program solution to Exercise 5b.

   b.

```
#include <iostream.h>
#include <math.h>

const double PI = 2.0 * asin(1.0);

// class declaration

class Point
{
  protected:
    float x;
      float y;
  public:
    Point(float = 0.0, float = 0.0);   //constructor
    float distance(Point&);
};

// implementation section
Point::Point(float xval, float yval)
{
  x = xval;
  y = yval;
}

float Point::distance(Point& b)
{
  return (sqrt(pow((x-b.x),2) + pow((y-b.y),2)));
}

// class declaration for the derived Circle class
class Circle : public Point
{
  protected:
    double radius; // add an additional data member
  public:
    Circle(float = 0.0, float = 0.0, float = 1.0);   // constructor
    float distance(Circle&);
    float area();
};
```

```
// implementation section for Circle
Circle::Circle(float centerx, float centery, float r)  // constructor
{
  x = centerx;
  y = centery;
  radius = r;
}

float Circle::distance(Circle& b)
{
  return (Point::distance(b)); // note the base function call
}

float Circle::area()   // this calculates an area
{
  return (PI * pow(radius,2));
}

int main()
{
  Point a, b(4,4);
  Circle circ1, circ2(3,3,2);

  cout << "The distance between points is " << a.distance(b) << endl;
  cout << "The area of circ1 is " << circ1.area() << endl;
  cout << "The area of circ2 is " << circ2.area() << endl;
  cout << "The distance between circle centers is " << circ1.distance(circ2) << endl;

  return 0;
}
```

NOTE: An inline base member initialization for the Circle class' constructor using the Point class' constructor could also have been constructed.

Exercises 9.7

3. In static binding the determination of which function will be called is made at compile time, while in dynamic binding the determination of which function will be called is made at run time.

5. Polymorphism is the ability of a function or operator to have multiple forms. The particular form that will be invoked can be determined at run time depending on the object being used.

Exercises 10.1

1. a. `float voltages[100];`
   b. `float temp[50];`
   c. `int code[30];`
   d. `int years[100];`
   e. `float velocity[32];`
   f. `float dist[1000];`
   g. `int code_num[6];`

3. a. `cin >> grades[0] >> grades[2] >> grades[6];`
  b. `cin >> volts[0] >> volts[2] >> volts[6];`
  c. `cin >> amps[0] >> amps[2] >> amps[6];`
  d. `cin >> dist[0] >> dist[2] >> dist[6];`
  e. `cin >> velocity[0] >> velocity[2] >> velocity[6];`
  f. `cin >> time[0] >> time[2] >> time[6];`

5. a. `a[1]   a[2]   a[3]   a[4]   a[5]`
  b. `a[1]   a[3]   a[5]`
  c. `b[3]   b[4]   b[5]   b[6]   b[7]   b[8]   b[9]   b[10]`
  d. `b[3]   b[6]   b[9]   b[12]`
  e. `c[2]   c[4]   c[6]   c[8]   c[10]`

7.
```cpp
#include <iostream.h>
const int NUMELS = 8;
int main()
{
  int temp[NUMELS], sum, i;
  float average;

  sum = 0;    // initialize here or in the declaration
  for( i = 0; i < NUMELS; i++)
  {
    cout << "Enter a value for element number " << i << " : ";
    cin  >> temp[i];
    sum = sum + temp[i];
  }
  cout << "\nThe values stored in the array are:\n";
  for (i = 0; i < NUMELS; i++)
    cout << temp[i] << "   ";
  average = sum / NUMELS;

  cout << "\nThe average of these values is "
       << average << endl;

  return 0;
}
```

9. a.
```cpp
#include <iostream.h>
#include <iomanip.h>

int main()
{

  const int NUMELS = 14;
  int grades[NUMELS], total, i;
  float avg, deviation[NUMELS];

  total = 0;
  for(i = 0; i < NUMELS; i++)
```

```
    {
      cout << "Enter grade # " << (i + 1) << " : ";
      cin  >> grades[i];
      total += grades[i];
    }
    avg = total/NUMELS;
    cout << "\n The average of the grades is " << avg << '\n'
      << "Element        Element         Deviation\n"
      << "Number         Value          from Avg.\n"
      << "-------        -------         ----------\n";
    for(i = 0; i < NUMELS; i++)
    {
      deviation[i] = grades[i] - avg;
      cout << setiosflags(ios::showpoint) << setprecision(2);
      cout << setw(4) << i << "      "
           << setw(10) << grades[i] << "      "
           << setw(12) << deviation[i] << endl;
    }

    return 0;
}
```

Exercises 10.2

1. a. `int volts[10] = {89, 75, 82, 93, 78, 95, 81, 88, 77, 82};`
b. `double slopes[5] = {10.62, 13.98, 18.45, 12.68, 14.76};`
c. `double distances[100] = {6.29, 6.95, 7.25, 7.35, 7.40, 7.42};`
d. `float temp[64] = {78.2, 69.6, 68.5, 83.9, 55.4, 67.0, 49.8, 58.3, 62.5, 71.6};`
e. `char code[15] = {'f', 'j', 'm', 'q', 't', 'w', 'z'};`

3.
```
#include <iostream.h>
int main()
{
  const int NUMELS = 9;
  float slopes[NUMELS] = {17.24, 25.63,  5.94,
                          33.92,  3.71, 32.84,
                          35.93, 18.24,  6.92};

  int i;
  float max = 0.0, min = 999.9;

  for(i = 0; i < NUMELS; i++)
  {
    if (slopes[i] < min) min = slopes[i];
    if (slopes[i] > max) max = slopes[i];
  }
  cout << "\nThe minimum array value is " <<  min;
  cout << "\nThe maximum array value is " << max << endl;

  return 0;
}
```

5. a.
```
#include <iostream.h>
int main()
{
  char strtest[] = "This is a test";

  cout << endl;  // start on a new line
  cout << strtest << endl;

  return 0;
}
```

NOTE: The data can be initialized in any one of the following three ways:

```
char strtest1[15] =
  {'T','h','i','s',' ','i','s',' ','a',' ','t','e','s','t','\0'};
```

```
char strtest1[] =
  {'T','h','i','s',' ','i','s',' ','a',' ','t','e','s','t','\0'};
```

```
char strtest1[] = "This is a test";
```

This last declaration creates an array of characters and automatically add the null character, '\0', to the end of the string.

Exercises 10.3

1. a. `int array[6][10];`   **d.** `char letter[15][7];`
b. `int codes[2][5];`   **e.** `double vals[10][25];`
c. `char keys[7][12];`   **f.** `double test[16][8];`

3.
```
#include <iostream.h>
int main()
{
  const int ROWS = 3;
  const int COLS = 4;
  int i, j, total = 0;
  int val[ROWS][COLS] = {8,16,9,52,3,15,27,6,14,25,2,10};

  for (i = 0; i < ROWS; i++)
    for (j = 0; j < COLS; j++)
      total = total + val[i][j];
  cout << "\nThe total of the values is " << total << endl;

  return 0;
}
```

5. a.
```
#include <iostream.h>
int main()
{
  const int ROWS = 4;
  const int COLS = 5;
  int i, j;
```

```
        int max = -999;
        int val[ROWS][COLS] = {16, 22, 99, 4, 18,
                               -258, 4, 101, 5, 98,
                               105, 6, 15, 2, 45,
                               33, 88, 72, 16, 3};

        for (i = 0; i < ROWS; i++)
          for (j = 0; j < COLS; j++)
            if (val[i][j] > max)  max = val[i][j];
        cout << "\nThe maximum array value is " << max << endl;

        return 0;
      }
```

Exercises 10.5

1. ```
   void sort_arr(double in_array[500])
   void sort_arr(double in_array[])
   ```

3. ```
   float prime(float rates[256])
   float prime(float rates[])
   ```

5. ```
   #include <iostream.h>
   #include <iomanip.h>
   const int NUMS = 9;
   void show(float []);   // function prototype
   int main()
   {
       float rates[NUMS] = {6.5, 7.2, 7.5, 8.3, 8.6,
                            9.4, 9.6, 9.8, 10.0};

       show(rates);

       return 0;
   }

   void show(float rates[])
   {
     int i;

     cout << "\nThe elements stored in the array are:\n";
     cout << setiosflags(ios::showpoint) << setprecision(2);
     for(i = 0; i < NUMS; i++)
       cout << rates[i] << "   " << endl;
   }
```
```

7.
```cpp
#include <iostream.h>
const int NUMVALS = 14;
double calc_avg(int [], int);    // function prototype
double variance(int [], double, int); // function prototype
int main()
{
  int testvals[NUMVALS] = {89, 95, 72, 83, 99, 54, 86, 75,
                           92, 73, 79, 75, 82, 73};
  double avg,var;

  avg = calc_avg(testvals, NUMVALS);
  var = variance(testvals, avg, NUMVALS);
  cout << "\nThe average for the test values = " << avg << endl;
  cout << " and the variance = " << var << endl;
}

double calc_avg(int nums[], int num_els)
{
  int i;
  double total= 0.0;
  for( i = 0; i < num_els; i++)
    total += nums[i];

  return (total/num_els);
}

double variance(int vals[], double average, int num_els)
{
  int count;
  double total = 0;

  for(count = 0; count < num_els; count++)
    total += (vals[count] - average)*(vals[count] - average);

  return (total/num_els);
}
```

NOTE: Even though the global named constant NUMVALS could have been used directly, the number of elements is passed as an argument into both the average and variance functions. This permits the definitions of these functions to be used in any file and does not make them dependent on the precondition that a global constant named NUMVALS be defined.

Exercises 11.1

1. &average means "the address of the variable named average"

3. a.

```
#include <iostream.h>
int main()
{

    int num, count;
    long date;
    float slope;
    double power;

    cout << "The address of the variable num is " << &num << endl;
    cout << "The address of the variable count is " << &count << endl;
    cout << "The address of the variable date is " << &date << endl;
    cout << "The address of the variable yield is " << &slope << endl;
    cout << "The address of the variable price is " << &power << endl;

    return 0;
}
```

5. a. *x_addr
  b. *y_addr
  c. *pt_yld
  d. *pt_miles
  e. *mptr
  f. *pdate
  g. *dist_ptr
  h. *tab_pt
  i. *hours_pt

7. a. Each of these variables are pointers. This means that addresses will be stored in each of these variables.
  b. They are not very descriptive names and do not give an indication that they are pointers.

9. All pointer variable declarations must have an asterisk. Therefore, c, e, g, and i are pointer declarations.

11.

Variable: pt_num
Address: 500
| 8096 |

Variable: amt_addr
Address: 564
| 16256 |

Variable: z_addr
Address: 8024
| 20492 |

Variable: num_addr
Address: 10132
| 18938 |

Variable: pt_day
Address: 14862
| 20492 |

Variable: pt_yr
Address: 15010
| 694 |

Variable: years
Address: 694
| 1987 |

Variable: m
Address: 8096
| |

Variable: amt
Address: 16256
| 154 |

Variable: firstnum
Address: 18938
| 154 |

Variable: slope
Address: 20492
| 25 |

Variable: k
Address: 24608
| 154 |

Exercises 11.2

1. a. `*(prices + 5)`   **d.** `*(dist + 9)`   **g.** `*(celsius + 16)`
  b. `*(grades + 2)`   **e.** `*mile`   **h.** `*(num + 50)`
  c. `*(yield +10)`   **f.** `*(temp + 20)`   **i.** `*(time + 12)`

3. a. The declaration `double slopes [5];` causes storage space for five double precision numbers, creates a pointer constant named `slopes`, and equates the pointer constant to the address of the first element (`&slopes[0]`).

   b. Each element in slopes contains eight bytes and there are five elements for a total of 40 bytes.

   c.   slopes

   | &slopes[0] |

   slopes[0] or   slopes[1] or
   *slopes   *(slopes + 1)

   slopes[3] or   slopes[4] or
   *(slopes + 3)   *(slopes + 4)

   slopes[5] or
   *(slopes + 5)

   d. The byte offset for this element, from the beginning of the array, is 3 * 8 = 24 bytes.

Exercises 11.3

3.
```cpp
#include <iostream.h>
#include <iomanip.h>
int main()
{
  const int NUMELS = 7;
  int miles[NUMELS] = {15, 22, 16, 18, 27, 23, 20};
  int dist[NUMELS];
  int i;
    // copy the elements
  for (i = 0; i < NUMELS; i++)
    *(dist + i) = *(miles + i);
    // display the elements
  cout << "The elements in the dist array are:\n";
  for (i = 0; i < NUMELS; i++)
    cout << *(dist + i) << endl;

  return 0;
}
```

NOTE: Clearly, the display of the copied elements could have been included within the first for loop, immediately after the copy using the code:

```cpp
cout << "The elements in the dist array are:\n";
for (i = 0; i < NUMELS; i++)
{
  *(dist + i) = *(miles + i);  // copy elements
  cout << *(dist + i) << endl; // display elements
}
```

5.
```cpp
#include <iostream.h>
#include <iomanip.h>
int main()
{

  const int NUMELS = 10;
  float miles[NUMELS] = {240.5, 300.0, 189.6, 310.6, 280.7,
                         216.9, 199.4, 160.3, 177.4, 192.3 };
  float gallons[NUMELS] = {10.3, 15.6, 8.7, 14.0, 16.3,
                           15.7, 14.9, 10.7, 8.3, 8.4 };
  float mpg[NUMELS];
  int i;

    // set output format
  cout << setiosflags(ios::fixed)
       << setiosflags(ios::showpoint)
       << setprecision(2);

  cout << "The elements in the mpg array are:\n";
  for (i = 0; i < 10; i++)
```

```
  {
    *(mpg+i) = *(miles +i) / *(gallons + i);
    cout << *(mpg + i) << endl;
  }

  return 0;
}
```

Exercises 11.4

1. `void sort_arr(double in_array[500])`
`void sort_arr(double in_array[])` ·
`void sort_arr(double *in_array)`

3. `float maximum(double speed[256])`
`float maximum(double speed[])`
`float maximum(double *speed)`

5. The problem to this method of finding the maximum value lies in the statement

```
if(max < *vals++)
  max = *vals;
```

This statement compares the correct value to `max`, but then increments the address in the pointer before any assignment is made. Thus, the element assigned to `max` by the expression `max = *vals` is one element beyond the element pointed to within the parentheses.

7. a. The following output is obtained:

```
33
16
99
34
```

This is why:

```
*(*val) = *(val[0]) = val[0][0] = 33;
*(*val + 1) = *(val[1]) = val[1][0] = 16;
*(*(val + 1) + 2) = *(*(val[1]) + 2) = *(val[1][2]) = 99;
*(*val) + 1 = *(val[0]) + 1 = val[0][0] + 1 = 33 + 1 = 34.
```

In other words, for any two dimensional array, `arr[x][y]`, what we really have is two levels of pointers. What is meant by `*(arr + x)` is that there are `x` number of pointers, each successively pointing to `arr[1][0]`, `arr[2][0]`, `arr[3][0]`, . . . , `arr[x][0]`. So an expression such as `*(*(arr + x) + y)` translates to `arr[x][y]`.

b. The notation is valid. Currently this position is occupied by the number 99.

Exercises 12.1

1. a.
```
struct S_temp
  {
    int id_num;
    int credits;
    float avg;
  };
```
   b.
```
struct S_temp
  {
    char name[40];
    int month;
    int day;
    int year;
    int credits;
    float avg;
  };
```
   c.
```
struct S_temp
  {
    char name[40];
    char street[80];
    char city[40];
    char state[2];
    int zip;              // or char zip[5];
  };
```
   d.
```
struct S_temp
  {
    char name[40];
    float price;
    char date[8];    // Assumes a date in the form XX/XX/XX
  };
```
   e.
```
struct S_temp
  {
    int part_no;
    char desc[100];
    int quant;
    int reorder;
  };
```

3 a.
```
#include <iostream.h>
int main()
{
  struct Date
  {
    int month;
    int day;
    int year;
  };      // define a structure variable named date
```

```
        Date current;   // define a structure variable named current
        cout << "\nEnter the current month: ";
        cin  >> current.month;
        cout << "Enter the current day: ";
        cin  >> current.day;
        cout << "Enter the current year: ";
        cin  >> current.year;
        cout << "\nThe date entered is : "
             << current.month << '/' << current.day
             << '/' << current.year << endl;

      return 0;
    }
b. #include <iostream.h>
   #include <iomanip.h>
   int main()
   {
     struct Clock
     {
       int hours;
       int minutes;
       int seconds;
     };

     Clock time;     // define a structure variable named time

     cout << "\nEnter the current hour: ";
     cin  >> time.hours;
     cout << "Enter the current minute: ";
     cin  >> time.minutes;
     cout << "Enter the current second: ";
     cin  >> time.seconds;
     cout << "\nThe time entered is: "
          << setw(2) << setfill('0') << time.hours << ':'
          << setw(2) << time.minutes << ':'
          << setw(2) << time.seconds << endl;

     return 0;
   }
```

NOTE: the use of the setw and setfill manipulators. The fill character of 0 forces the field of 2 to be filled with leading zeros.

5.
```cpp
#include <iostream.h>
#include <iomanip.h>
int main()
{
  struct Clock
  {
    int hours;
    int minutes;
  };

    Clock time;

  cout << "Enter the current hour: ";
  cin  >> time.hours;
  cout << "Enter the current minute: ";
  cin  >> time.minutes;
  if(time.minutes != 59)
    time.minutes += 1;
  else
  {
    time.minutes = 0;
    if(time.hours != 12)
    time.hours += 1;
    else
    time.hours = 1;
  }
  cout << "\nThe time in one minute will be "
       << setiosflags(ios::showpoint) << setfill('0')
       << setw(2) << time.hours << ':'
       << setw(2) << time.minutes << endl;

  return 0;
}
```

NOTE: the use of the setw and setfill manipulators. The fill character of 0 forces the field of 2 to be filled with leading zeros.

Exercises 12.2

1. **a.** S_temp student[100];
   b. S_temp student[100];
   c. S_temp address[100];
   d. S_temp stock[100];
   e. S_temp inventory[100];

3.

```
#include <iostream.h>
const int MAXCHARS = 10;
const int MONTHS = 12;
struct Mon_days
{
  char name[MAXCHARS];
  int days;
};
#include <iostream.h>
int main()
{
  Mon_days convert[MONTHS] = {"January", 31, "February", 28, "March", 31,
                    "April", 30, "May", 31, "June", 30,
                    "July", 31, "August", 31, "September", 30,
                    "October", 31, "November", 30, "December", 31};
  int i;
  cout << "\nEnter the number of a month: ";
  cin  >> i;
  cout << convert[i-1].name << " has "
       << convert[i-1].days << " days\n";

 return 0;
}
```

NOTE: The structure declaration for Mon_days can either be global or local to main().

Exercises 12.3

1.
```
#include <iostream.h>
struct Date
{
  int month;
  int day;
  int year;
};
long days(Date);  // function prototype

int main()
{
  Date present;
  long num;

  cout << "Enter the month: ";
  cin  >> present.month;
  cout << "Enter the day: ";
  cin  >> present.day;
```

```
    cout << "Enter the year: ";
    cin  >> present.year;
    num = days(present);
    cout << "The number of days since the turn"
         << " of the century is " << num << endl;

    return 0;
}

long days(Date temp)
{
    return (temp.day + 30*(temp.month - 1) + 360*temp.year);
}
```

NOTE: The reference version of the function long **days( )** is written for Exercise 3a and the pointer version for Exercise 3b.

3. a.
```
    #include <iostream.h>
    struct Date
    {
      int month;
      int day;
      int year;
    };

    long days(Date& );   // function prototype

    int main()
    {
      Date present;
      long num;

      cout << "Enter the month: ";
      cin  >> present.month;
      cout << "Enter the day: ";
      cin  >> present.day;
      cout << "Enter the year: ";
      cin  >> present.year;
      num = days(present);
      cout << "The number of days since the turn"
           << " of the century is " << num << endl;
      return 0;
    }

    long days(Date& temp)
    {
      return (temp.day + 30*(temp.month - 1) + 360*temp.year);
    }
```

b.

```cpp
#include <iostream.h>
struct Date
{
  int month;
  int day;
  int year;
};

long days(Date *);    // function prototype

int main()
{
  Date present;
  long num;

  cout << "Enter the month: ";
  cin  >> present.month;
  cout << "Enter the day: ";
  cin  >> present.day;
  cout << "Enter the year: ";
  cin  >> present.year;
  num = days(&present);
  cout << "The number of days since the turn"
       << " of the century is " << num << endl;

  return 0;
}

long days(Date *temp)
{
  return (temp->day + 30*(temp->month - 1) + 360*temp->year);
}
```

NOTE: The **days()** function can also be written as:

```cpp
long days(Date *temp)
{
  return ((*temp).day + 30*((*temp).month - 1) + 360*(*temp).year);
}
```

5. a.

```cpp
#include <iostream.h>
const int MAXVECTS = 2;
struct VectorType
{
  int xcomp;
  int ycomp;
};
```

```cpp
void input(struct VectorType [], int); // function prototypes needed by main()
struct VectorType sum(struct VectorType, struct VectorType);
struct VectorType diff(struct VectorType, struct VectorType);

int main()
{
  struct VectorType vector[MAXVECTS], sumvect, difvect;

  input(vector, MAXVECTS);
  sumvect = sum(vector[0], vector[1]);
  difvect = diff(vector[0], vector[1]);
  cout << "\n(" << vector[0].xcomp << "," << vector[0].ycomp << ")"
       << " + (" << vector[1].xcomp << "," << vector[1].ycomp << ")"
       << " = (" << sumvect.xcomp << "," << sumvect.ycomp << ")\n";
  cout << "\n(" << vector[0].xcomp << "," << vector[0].ycomp << ")"
       << " - (" << vector[1].xcomp << "," << vector[1].ycomp << ")"
       << " = (" << difvect.xcomp << "," << difvect.ycomp << ")\n";

  return 0;
}

void input(struct VectorType vector[], int numvects)
{
  int i;

  for (i = 0; i < numvects; ++i)
  {
    cout << "Enter the x component for vector " << i + 1 << ": ";
    cin  >>  vector[i].xcomp;
    cout << "Enter the y component for vector " << i + 1 << ": ";
    cin  >>  vector[i].ycomp;
  }
  return;
}

struct VectorType sum(struct VectorType vector1, struct VectorType vector2)
{
  int i;
  struct VectorType temp;

  temp.xcomp = vector1.xcomp + vector2.xcomp;
  temp.ycomp = vector1.ycomp + vector2.ycomp;

  return temp;
}

struct VectorType diff(struct VectorType vector1, struct VectorType vector2)
{
  struct VectorType temp;
```

```
    temp.xcomp = vector1.xcomp - vector2.xcomp;
    temp.ycomp = vector1.ycomp - vector2.ycomp;
    return temp;
}
```

Notice that the input routine can be used for any number of vectors, while the sum and difference routines only work on the two specific vectors passed as arguments.

Exercises 12.4

1.
```
#include <iostream.h>
#include <string.h>
const int MAXNAME = 30;
const int MAXTEL = 15;

struct Tele_typ
{
  char name[MAXNAME];
  char phone_no[MAXTEL];
  Tele_typ *nextaddr;
};

void search(Tele_typ *, char *); // function prototype

int main()
{
  Tele_typ t1 = {"Acme, Sam", "(555) 898-2392"};
  Tele_typ t2 = {"Dolan, Edith", "(555) 682-3104"};
  Tele_typ t3 = {"Lanfrank, John", "(555) 718-4518"};
  Tele_typ *first;
  char strng[MAXNAME];

  first = &t1;
  t1.nextaddr = &t2;
  t2.nextaddr = &t3;
  t3.nextaddr = NULL;
  cout << "Enter a name: ";
  cin.getline(strng, MAXNAME);
  search(first, strng);
  cout << endl;

  return 0;
}

void search(Tele_typ *contents, char *strng)
{
  cout << strng;
  while(contents != NULL)
    {
```

```
            if(strcmp(contents->name,strng) == 0)
            {
              cout << "\nFound. The number is "
                    << contents->phone_no << endl;
              return;
            }
            else
            {
              contents = contents->nextaddr;
            }
        }
        cout << "\nThe name is not in the current phone directory.\n";
        return;
    }
```

3. To delete the second record, the pointer in the first record must be changed to point to the third record.

5. a.
```
    const int NAMECHARS = 30;
    const int PHONECHARS = 15;
    struct Phone_bk
    {
      char name[NAMECHARS];
      char phone_no[PHONECHARS];
      phone_bk *previous;
      phone_bk *next;
    };
```

Exercises 12.5

1. The check() function is included below in a complete program used to verify that check() works correctly.

```
#include <iostream.h>
#include <iomanip.h>
#include <stdlib.h>    // need this for the exit() function

const int NAMECHARS = 30;
const int PHONECHARS = 15;

struct Tel_typ
{
  char name[NAMECHARS];
  char phone_no[PHONECHARS];
  Tel_typ *nextaddr;
};

void populate(Tel_typ *);   // function prototype
void display(Tel_typ *);    // function prototype
int check(Tel_typ *);       // function prototype

int main()
{
```

```
   int i;

   Tel_typ *list, *current;

   list =  new (Tel_typ);
   check(list);
   current = list;
   for(i = 0; i < 2; i++)
   {
     populate(current);
     current->nextaddr = new (Tel_typ);

     if (check(current->nextaddr) == 0)
     {
       cout << "No available memory remains. Program terminating";
       exit(0); // terminate program and return to operating system
     }
     current = current->nextaddr;
   }
   populate(current);
   current->nextaddr = NULL;
   cout << "\nThe list consists of the following records:\n";
   display(list);

   return 0;
}

int check( Tel_typ *addr)
{

   if(addr == NULL)
     return 0;
   else
     return 1;
   }

void populate( Tel_typ *record)
{
   cout << "\nEnter a name: ";
   cin.getline(record->name, NAMECHARS);
   cout << "Enter the phone number: ";
   cin.getline(record->phone_no, PHONECHARS);
   return;
}

void display( Tel_typ *contents)
{
   while(contents != NULL)
   {
     cout << endl << setiosflags(ios::left)
          << setw(30) << contents->name
          << setw(20) << contents->phone_no;
     contents = contents->nextaddr;
   }
     return;
}
```

3. The `insert()` function in the complete program below is used to verify that `insert()` works correctly. As written, the function will insert a structure after the structure whose address is passed to it. Since the address of the first structure is passed to it, the new structure is inserted between the first and second structures.

```cpp
#include <iostream.h>
#include <iomanip.h>

const int NAMECHARS = 30;
const int PHONECHARS = 15;

struct Tel_typ
{
  char name[NAMECHARS];
  char phone_no[PHONECHARS];
  Tel_typ *nextaddr;
};

void insert(Tel_typ *);      // function prototype
void populate(Tel_typ *);    // function prototype
void display(Tel_typ *);     // function prototype

int main()
{
  Tel_typ *list, *current;

  list = new (Tel_typ);
  populate(list); // populate the first structure
  list->nextaddr = new (Tel_typ);
  current = list->nextaddr;
  populate(current); // populate the second structure
  current->nextaddr = NULL;
  cout << "\nThe list initially consists of the following records:";
  display(list);
  insert(list);    // insert between first and second structures
  cout << "\nThe new list now consists of the following records:";
  display(list);
  cout << endl;

  return 0;
}

void insert(Tel_typ *addr)
{
  Tel_typ *temp;
  void populate(Tel_typ *);  // function prototype

  temp = addr->nextaddr;      // save pointer to next structure
    // now change address to point to inserted structure
  addr->nextaddr = new (Tel_typ);
```

```
   populate(addr->nextaddr);   // populate the new structure
     // set address member of new structure to saved addr
   addr->nextaddr->nextaddr = temp;
   return;
}

void populate(Tel_typ *record)
{
  cout << "\nEnter a name: ";
  cin.getline(record->name, NAMECHARS);
  cout << "Enter the phone number: ";
  cin.getline(record->phone_no, PHONECHARS);
  return;
}

void display( Tel_typ *contents)
{
  while(contents != NULL)
  {
    cout << endl << setiosflags(ios::left)
         << setw(30) << contents->name
         << setw(20) << contents->phone_no;
    contents = contents->nextaddr;
  }
  return;
}
```

Notice if the populate function call is removed from the insert function, then `insert()` becomes a general insertion program that simply creates a structure and correctly adjusts the address members of each structure. Also, notice the notation used in `insert()`. The expression

```
    addr->nextaddr->nextaddr
```

is equivalent to

```
    (addr->nextaddr)->nextaddr
```

This notation was not used in `main()` because the pointer variable current is first used to store the address in `list->nextaddr` using the statement

```
    current = list->nextaddr;
```

The statement

```
    current->nextaddr = NULL;
```

in `int main()` however, could have been written as

```
    list->nextaddr->nextaddr = NULL;
```

An interesting exercise is to rewrite `main()` such that the pointer variable named current is removed entirely from the function.

5. The `modify()` function in the complete program below is used to verify that `modify()` works correctly. The driver function creates a single structure, populates it, and then calls `modify()`. `modify()` itself calls the function `repop()`. An interesting extension is to write `repop()` such that an ENTER key response retains the original structure member value.

```cpp
#include <iostream.h>
#include <iomanip.h>

const int NAMECHARS = 30;
const int PHONECHARS = 15;

struct Tel_typ
{
  char name[NAMECHARS];
  char phone_no[PHONECHARS];
  Tel_typ *nextaddr;
};

void populate(Tel_typ *);  // function prototype needed by main()
void modify(Tel_typ *);    // function prototype needed by main()
void display(Tel_typ *);   // function prototype needed by modify()
void repop(Tel_typ *);     // function prototype needed by modify()

int main()
{

  Tel_typ *list;

  list = new (Tel_typ);
  populate(list); // populate the first structure
  list->nextaddr = NULL;
  modify(list);   // modify the structure members

  return 0;
}

void modify(Tel_typ *addr)
{
  cout << "\nThe current structure members are:";
  display(addr);
  repop(addr);
  cout << "\nThe structure members are now:";
  display(addr);
  return;
}

void populate(Tel_typ *record)
{
  cout << "\nEnter a name: ";
  cin.getline(record->name, NAMECHARS);
  cout << "Enter the phone number: ";
  cin.getline(record->phone_no, PHONECHARS);
  return;
}
```

```
void repop(Tel_typ *record)
{
  cout << "\n\nEnter a new name: ";
  cin.getline(record->name, NAMECHARS);
  cout << "Enter a new phone number: ";
  cin.getline(record->phone_no, PHONECHARS);
  return;
}

void display(Tel_typ *contents)
{
  while(contents != NULL)
  {
    cout << endl << setiosflags(ios::left)
         << setw(30) << contents->name
         << setw(20) << contents->phone_no;
    contents = contents->nextaddr;
  }
  return;
}
```

Exercises 12.6

1. cout stream activations, with the correct control sequences, are contained within the following program.

```
union
{
  float rate;
  double taxes;
  int num;
} flag;

#include <iostream.h>
int main()
{
  flag.rate = 22.5;
  cout << "\nThe rate is " << flag.rate;
  flag.taxes = 44.7;
  cout << "\ntaxes are " << flag.taxes;
  flag.num = 6;
  cout << "\nnum is " << flag.num;

  return 0;
}
```

5. Since a value has not been assigned to alt.btype, the display produced is unpredictable (the code for a 'y' resides in the storage locations overlapped by the variables alt.ch and alt.btype). Thus, either a garbage value will be displayed or the program could even crash.

Exercises 13.1

1. The root is x = 2.2788626602. . . . .

Exercises 13.2

1. a.

i	x_1	x_2	x_3	f_1	f_2	f_3	cross
1	2.80000	2.95000	3.10000	−1.5600000	−0.3974991	0.8099995	R
2	2.95000	3.02500	3.10000	−0.3974991	0.2006254	0.8099995	L
3	2.95000	2.98750	3.02500	−0.3974991	−0.0998421	0.2006254	R
	. . .	. . .	. . .	. . .	. . .	. . .	. . .
	. . .	. . .	. . .	. . .	. . .	. . .	. . .
16	3.00000	3.00000	3.00001	−0.0000162	0.0000191	0.0000563	L
17	3.00000	3.00000	3.00000	−0.0000162	0.0000029	0.0000563	L
18	3.00000	3.00000	3.00000	−0.0000162	−0.0000076	0.0000029	R

b.

i	x_1	x_2	x_3	f_1	f_2	f_3	cross
1	1.00000	2.50000	4.00000	1.9888980	4.6208790	−42.991799	R
2	2.50000	3.25000	4.00000	4.6208790	−0.3930970	−42.991799	L
3	2.50000	2.87500	3.25000	4.6208790	3.3274150	−0.3930970	R
	. . .	. . .	. . .	. . .	. . .	. . .	. . .
	. . .	. . .	. . .	. . .	. . .	. . .	. . .
19	3.22158	3.22159	3.22160	0.0000550	−0.0000221	−0.0000993	L
20	3.22158	3.22159	3.22159	0.0000550	−0.0000163	−0.0000221	R
21	3.22159	3.22159	3.22160	0.0000163	−0.0000029	−0.0000221	L

c.

i	x_1	x_2	x_3	f_1	f_2	f_3	cross
1	4.00000	4.35000	4.70000	4.5338670	−2.4692450	−370.52332	R
2	4.00000	4.17500	4.35000	4.5338670	2.0803920	−2.4692450	R
3	4.17500	4.26250	3.35000	2.0803920	0.2194996	−2.4692450	R
	. . .	. . .	. . .	. . .	. . .	. . .	. . .
	. . .	. . .	. . .	. . .	. . .	. . .	. . .
17	4.27109	4.27109	4.27110	0.0001755	0.0000267	−0.0001097	R
18	4.27109	4.27110	4.27110	0.0000267	−0.0000477	−0.0001097	L
19	4.27109	4.27110	4.27110	0.0000267	−0.0000114	−0.0000477	L

d. $n_a > 16$, $n_b > 19$, $n_c > 16$

Exercises 13.3

1.
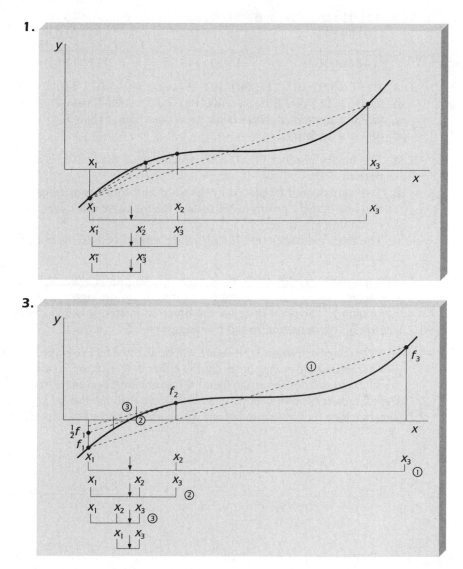

Exercises 13.4

3. The roots are x = 3 and x = −1.

Exercises 14

1. a. 11001010
  &10100101
  ‾‾‾‾‾‾‾‾
  10000000

b. 11001010
  |10100101
  ‾‾‾‾‾‾‾‾
  11101111

c. 11001010
  ^10100101
  ‾‾‾‾‾‾‾‾
  01101111

3. a. 0157 = 001 101 111; 001 101 111 << 1 = 011 011 110 = 0336
 b. 0701 = 111 000 001; 111 000 001 << 2 = 100 000 100 = 0404
 c. 0873 = undefined, there is no octal digit higher than 7.
 d. 087 = undefined.

5. a. The binary number 00001100, which equals octal 014, is the required mask pattern.
 b. Two zeros could be placed in the third and fourth positions to reproduce the flag bits in these positions. However, the inclusive OR operation cannot set the remaining bits to zero.
 c. The binary number 00001100, which equals octal 014, is the required mask pattern.

7. Any character whose sixth bit is zero will be unaffected, which corresponds to characters whose 2nd octal digit (counting from the right) is either 0, 1, 2, or 3. For example, the octal code for the brace character,], is 135. Since its 2nd octal digit is 3, it will be unaffected by Program 12.2.

Any character whose sixth bit is one will be affected by Program 12.2. This includes all characters whose 2nd octal digit is either a 4, 5, 6, or 7, which includes all of the characters from the space (octal 40) to the question mark (octal 77) and all of the characters from the apostrophe (octal 140) through the del key (octal 177). The latter include the lowercase letters, which are converted to uppercase.

INDEX

◆ A

abs() function, 133
abstract data type (ADT), 416, 419
access specifications, 506
accessor function, 440
accumulating, 108
addition operator (+), 55
address operator (&), 586
addresses,
    arrays as, 597
    decrementing, 607
    displaying, 72
    dynamic allocation of, 602
    incrementing, 607
    of variables, 584
    passing, 65
    storing, 585
    using, 586
aggregate data types, 530
algorithms, 17
anonymous variables, 591
American Standard Code for
  Information Interchange (ASCII), 52
AND operator (&&), 708
a.out, 737
application software, 4
argc, 739
argument(s), 38, 292
    command line, 737
    of functions, 292
argv[], 739
arithmetic and logic unit (ALU), 25
arithmetic with pointers, 605
arithmetic operations, 54
arithmetic operators, 55
    associativity, 59
    conversion rules for, 57
    integer division, 57
    negation, 58
    precedence, 59
    summary of, 59, 181, 723
arithmetic shift, 720
array(s), 523
    as addresses, 597
    as arguments, 558
    components of, 527
    dynamic allocation, 602
    elements of, 527
    index value, 526
    initialization of, 535
    larger dimensional, 542
    one-dimensional, 524
    passing, 558
    single-dimensional, 524
    of structures, 634
    two-dimensional, 538
array initialization, 535

array values, input and output of, 529
ASCII (American Code for Information
  Interchange), 52
assemblers, 3
assembly language, 2
assignment, 102, 458
assignment operations, 102
assignment operators, 105
assignment statements, 65
    accumulating statements, 108
    counting statements, 110
assignment variations, 107
associativity, 59
atomic data, 66
atomic variable, 523
auto(matic), 360
auto storage class, 359
auto variables, 360

◆ B

backslash character (/), 54
base class, 504
base member initialization list, 465
basic analysis, 81
behavior, 430
big O notation, 575
binary file, 571
binary search, 571,
binary subtraction, 55
bisection method, 675, 681
bit, 27
bit operators, 707
    AND operator, 708
    complement operator (NOT), 715
    different-size data items, 716
    exclusive OR operator, 713
    inclusive OR operator, 711
    shift operators, 717
block scope, 189
body of a function, 38, 294
boolean data, 53, 194
boot, 4
bootstrap loader, 4
bounds check, 529
break statement, 249
bubble sort, 579
built-in conversions, 487
bug, 14
bytes, 27

◆ C

C stye of initialization, 435
C++ style of initialization, 435
call by value, 310
called function, 291
calling constructors, 435
calling function, 291

case, 208
case sensitive, 36
cast(s), 135
central processing unit (CPU), 25
char, 69
character, 52
    escape, 54
    null, 536
character codes, 27
character constant, 52
character data type, 69
character value, 52
character variables, 69
child class, 504
cin, 140
class, 34-35, 420, 429
    assignment, 458
    access specifier, 422, 506
    construction, 420
    constructor, 423, 432
    conversion, 487
    declaration, 422
    destructor, 439
    implementation, 423
    inheritance, 504
    library, 502
    members, 420
    methods, 428
    scope, 467
class hierarchies, 506
class inheritance, 504
class library, 502
closing a file, 387
command line arguments, 739
comments, 46
compiled language, 4
compiler, 4
compile-time errors, 171
complement operator, 715
compound statement, 187
computer program, 2
conditions expressions, 178
const, 152
constructor, 423, 432, 439
    calling, 435
    conversion, 487
    copy, 462
    default, 433, 462
    inline, 435
    overloaded, 435
continue statement, 249
control unit, 25
conversion constructor, 487
conversion operator function, 487,
  490, 492
counting statement, 110
cout, 39

◆ D

data file, 375
    closing, 378
    opening, 378
data hiding, 422
data members, 420
data types, 65, 418
    conversions of, 79, 487
    user defined data types, 418
debugging, 84, 225
declarations, 65
    as definition statement, 70
    forward, 493
    of pointers, 587
    placement of, 66, 350
decrement operator (--), 112
default argument, 301
default constructor, 433, 462
defensive programming, 213
defining a function, 294
dereference, 589, 592
definition statement, 70
delete operator, 603
derived class, 504
design, 82
desk checking, 171
destructor, 439
development, 82
device drivers, 410
discriminant, 216
division operator (/), 55, 57
do statement, 279
do loops, 279
double, 66
double-precision numbers, 51
double quotes, to enclose strings, 40, 384
driver function, 37
dynamic allocation,
    of arrays, 602
    of structures, 647
dynamic binding, 514
dynamic memory allocation, 602, 647

◆ E

EBCDIC (Extended Binary Coded, Decimal Interchange Code), 52
echo printing, 17
equality operator (==), 179
errors,
    compile-time, 171
    logic, 172
    run-time, 171
    syntax, 171
    typos, 172
escape sequence, 54
exchange sort, 579
exit-controlled loop, 229
external sort, 575
extraction operator (>>), 141
exclusive OR operator (^), 713
executable program, 2
exponential function, 161
exponential notation, 51

expression, 57, 103
    relational, 178
    simple, 55
    value of, 105
Extended Binary Coded Decimal, Interchange Code (EBCDIC), 52
extern, 359
extern storage classes, 359
external file name, 376
external variable, 359

◆ F

file, 376
file access, 399
file names, passing and returning, 403, 405
file organization, 399
file stream, 377
file stream methods, 378
file stream transfer mechanism, 409
file streams as function arguments, 403
fixed count loop, 230
flag, 122
float, 66
floating point expression, 57
floating point numbers, 50
flowchart, 20
flow of control, 177
for loop, 253
formal parameters, 294
formatted file, 409
formatted output, 117
for statement, 253
FORTRAN (FORmula TRANslation), 502
forward declaration, 493
friend function, 473
fstream, 383
fstream methods, 391
functions, 34, 290
function binding, 514
    body, 294
    header, 37, 294
    names, 35
    overloading, 306
    prototype, 292, 296
    stubs, 299
    templates, 302
    with empty parameter lists, 301

◆ G

getline(), 391
global scope, 350
global variable, 350
    misuse of, 355
global variable storage class, 363
greater-than operator (>), 179
greater-than-or-equal-to operator (>=), 179

◆ H

header files, 39
    iomanip.h, 119
    iostream.h, 39
hexadecimal numbers, 124
high level languages, 3

◆ I

identifiers, 35
if-else statement, 184
    compound statements, 187
    one-way selection, 190
ifstream, 378, 410
implementation, 429
implementation section, 423
#include statement, 30
inclusive OR operator (|), 711
increment operator (++), 111
index, 526
indexed variable, 526
indirect addressing, 586
indirection operator (*), 586
infinite loop, 234
information hiding, 429
inheritance, 504
initialization, 69
inline function, 316
inner loop, 274
input, 377
input data validation, 213
input file stream, 377
input item, 83
input value, 83
input/output of array values, 529
input and output unit, 25
insertion operator (<<), 39
instances, 429
instance variable, 420
instantiation, 429
int, 65
integer division, 57
integer expression, 57
integer numbers, 49
integer qualifiers, 77
integer values, 49
integration, 464
interactive file names, 384
interactive while loops, 240
interface, 429
internal sort, 575
interpreted language, 3
interpreter, 3
invocation, 14
iomanip.h, 119
iostream, 375
iostream class library, 409
isolation testing, 300
iteration, 14

◆ K

keyword, 35

◆ L

languages
    high-level, 3
    low-level, 3
    middle-level, 3
    object-oriented, 4
    procedure oriented, 4
larger-dimensional arrays, 542
left justification, 122, 638
left shift operator (<<), 717

less-than operator (<), 179
library functions, 131
linear equations, 215
linear search, 568
linked lists, 649
linker, 731
local scope, 350
local variables, 350
local variable storage classes, 359
logic errors, 172
logical file object, 396
logical operators, 180
    AND (&&), 180
    NOT (!), 181
    OR (||), 180
logical shift, 720
login procedure, 727
long integer, 78
long qualifier, 78
looking at career choices, 30, 100, 175,
    226, 370, 371, 413, 414
loops, 229
    inner, 274
    nested, 274
    outer, 274
lvalue, 107
low-level languages, 3

◆ M
machine language, 2
magic numbers, 152
main() function, 37
manipulator, 67
    setiosflags, 118
    setprecision, 118
    setw, 118
mask, 709
mathematical library functions, 131
member function, 420
memberwise assignment, 458
memory allocation, 70
memory unit, 25
member functions, 379
memory, dynamic allocation of, 602, 647
memory leak, 604
methods, 379
microprocessor, 26
middle-level languages, 3
mixed mode expressions, 57
mnemonics, 36
mode, 377
modular programs, 34
modularity using functions, 379
modules, 34
modulus operator (%), 55
multiple declarations, 68
multiple inheritance, 505
multiplication operator (*), 55
multitasking, 5
multi-user, 5

◆ N
named constants, 153
namespaces, 743
negation, 58

negation operator (-), 58
nested if statements, 197
nested loops, 274
new operator, 603
newline escape sequence, 54
NOT operator (!), 181
null character, 536
null pointer, 650
null statement, 251
number codes, 27
numerical accuracy, 182
numerical results using cout, 117

◆ O
object(s), 427, 429
object-based, 505
object libraries, 6
object-oriented languages, 4, 505
object program, 729
octal numbers, 124
offsets, 598
ofstream, 378, 410
one-dimensional arrays, 524
one-way selection, 190
opcode, 2
opening a file, 378
operating system, 5, 727
operator functions, 478
    as friends, 484
operators,
    addition, 55
    address, 72
    arithmetic, 55
    assignment, 102
    associativity, 59
    bit, 707
    complement, 715
    decrement (--), 112
    delete, 603
    division, 55, 57
    equality (==), 179
    increment (++), 111
    indirection, 586
    left shift, 717
    logical, 180
    modulus, 55
    multiplication, 55
    negation, 58
    postfix decrement (--), 112
    postfix increment(++), 111
    precedence of, 59
    prefix decrement, 112
    prefix increment, 111
    relational, 178
    remainder, 55
    right shift, 717
    shift, 717
    sizeof(), 80
    subtraction, 55
    unary, 58
OR operator (||), 180
outer loop, 274
output, 377
output file stream, 377
output, formatted, 117

output insertion operator (>>), 140
overloaded functions, 306, 436
overloaded operators, 484

◆ P
parameter, 294
parent class, 504
pass by reference, 321, 611
pass by value, 310, 321
passing addresses, 610, 642
passing arrays, 615
passing file names, 403
passing structures, 639
percent sign (%), 55
physical file object, 396
point of information, 40, 52, 53, 66, 107,
    122, 123, 190, 194, 259, 261, 296,
    297, 300, 366, 379, 381, 383, 385,
    390, 392, 394, 399, 416, 429, 439,
    440, 452, 467, 502, 505, 530, 634
pointers, 585
    advanced notation, 619
    as array names, 596
    as structure members, 651
    declaring, 587
    decrementing, 607
    incrementing, 607
    passing, 642
    vs. references, 589
pointer arithmetic, 605
pointer declarations, 587
pointer initialization, 609
pointer variables, 587
polymorphism, 505, 512
precondition, 297
postfix decrement operator (--), 112
postfix increment operator (++), 111
posttest loop, 229
pound sign (#), 39
power residue method, 346
precedence, 59
precision, 52
precondition, 297
prefix decrement operator (--), 112
prefix increment operator (++), 111
preprocessor commands, 39
pretest loop, 229
private access rights, 422, 506
problem-solver algorithm, 331
procedure-oriented language, 4
procedures, 4
program requirements, 10
program tracing, 174
program verification and testing, 171
programming, 2
    object-oriented, 4
    procedural, 4
programming languages, 2, 5
programming style, 45
programming tracing, 174
prompt, 142
protected access rights, 506
protected derivation, 506
public access rights, 422, 506

public derivation, 506
pseudocode, 20
pseudorandom numbers, 340

◆ Q

quadratic equation, 215
qualifiers
    const, 152
    integer, 77

◆ R

radar speed traps, 87
random file access, 399, 400
random numbers, 339
reading files, 388
real numbers, 50
record, 628
regula falsi method, 682
references, 321
    variables, 590
    vs. pointers, 589
registers, 363
register storage class, 359, 363
relational expressions, 178
    logical operators, 180
    simple, 178
    value of, 179
relational operators, 178
remainder operator (%), 55
repetition statement, 228
repetition structures, 227
resolution operator, 353
return statement, 38, 312
returning file names, 405
returning structures, 645
returning multiple values, 310, 321
right justification, 122
right shift operator (>>), 717
root finding, 672
run-time errors, 171
run-time initialization, 361
rvalue, 107

◆ S

scalar variables, 523
scaling, 342
scientific method, 10
scope, 350
    block, 189
    class, 467
    global, 350
    local, 350
    variable, 190
scope resolution operator, 353
search algorithms, 568
    binary, 571
    linear, 568
seekg(), 400
seekp(), 400
secant method, 691
selection, 14
selection criteria, 178
selection sort, 575
sentinels, 248
sequence, 14

sequential organization, 399
sequential search, 568
setprecision(), 118
setw(), 118
shift operators, 717
short integer, 79
signed numbers, 78
simple arithmetic expression, 55
simple inheritance, 505
simple relational expression, 178
single-dimensional arrays, 524
single precision numbers, 50
single quotes, 52, 385
single records, 628
single structures, 628
simpson's rule, 700
sizeof() operator, 80
software, 2
software development procedure, 10
software engineering, 10
sort(s), 575
    bubble, 579
    exchange, 579
    external, 575
    internal, 575
    selection, 575
sort algorithms, 575
source code, 3
source program, 3
sqrt(), 131
standard device files, 396
standard input file, 396
standard library functions, 131
standard template library (STL), 747
state, 429
statements
    assignment, 65, 102
    break, 49
    compound, 187
    continue, 249
    declaration, 65
    definition, 70
    do, 279
    for, 253
    if-else, 184
    nested if, 197
    #include, 39
    null, 251
    return, 312
    switch, 207
    while, 231
static binding, 514
static storage class, 359
static variables, 361
storage class, 359, 366
string variable, 384, 385
structures, 628
    arrays of, 634
    content of, 628
    declaration of, 628
    initialization of, 632
    passing, 639
    returning, 645
    single, 628
structure pointer operator (->), 643

subclass, 504
subscript, 526
subscripted variable, 526
subtraction operator (-), 55
superclass, 504
switch statement, 207
symbolic constants, 153
syntax, 40
syntax error, 171
system software, 4
systems approach, 10

◆ T

telephone switching networks, 89
tellg(), 400
tellp(), 400
template prefix, 304
testing, 84, 225
text files, 409
token, 49
top-level structure diagram, 12
transcendental equations, 673
trapezoidal rule, 695
truncated, 100
two's complement numbers, 27
two-dimensional arrays, 538
type conversion constructor, 487

◆ U

unary operators, 58
union, 664
unsigned integer, 78
user-defined data types, 418
utilities, 4

◆ V

validity checks, 281
value box, 27
variable condition loop, 231
variables, 63, 64
    address of, 584
    anonymous, 591
    external, 359
    global, 350
    indexed, 526
    local, 350
    scalar, 523
    naming, 64
    scope, 190, 350
    storage class, 359
    subscripted, 526
virtual functions, 514
virtual memory, 5
void, 292, 301

◆ W

weighted sign, 28
while loop, 231
while statement, 231
white space, 45
words, 28
writing files, 388

Quick Reference

Standard I/O — Requires `iostream.h` header file

`cin`	Standard input stream
`cin.get()`	Input a single character
`cin.getline(str, ln, chr)`	Input a string of length ln or terminate if chr is detected
`cout`	Standard output stream

I/O Manipulators — Requires `iomanip.h` header file

`setfill(ch)`	Set the fill character to ch
`setw(n)`	Set the field width to n
`setprecision(n)`	Set the floating-point precision to n places
`setiosflags(flags)`	Set the format flags
`dec`	Set output for decimal display
`hex`	Set output for hexadecimal display
`oct`	Set output for octal display
`endl`	Insert newline and flush stream
`flush`	Flush an ostream

Format Flags for setiosflags()

`ios::showpoint`	Always show the decimal point (default of 6 significant digits)
`ios::showpos`	Display a leading + sign when the number is positive
`ios::fixed`	Always use fixed-point (conventional decimal point display) notation
`ios::scientific`	Use exponential display on output
`ios::showbase`	Show base indicator on output
`ios::dec`	Display in decimal format
`ios::oct`	Display in octal format
`ios::hex`	Display in hexadecimal format
`ios::left`	Left-justify output
`ios::right`	Right-justify output
`ios::stdio`	Flush `stdout` and `stderr` after insertion
`ios::skipws`	Skip whitespace on input

NOTE: *These flags may be combined by* OR *operators. For example,*
`setiosflags(ios::showpoint | ios::left)` *sets the showpoint and left flags together.*

Permissible File Modes

`ios::in`	Open in input mode
`ios::out`	Open in output mode
`ios::app`	Open in append mode
`ios::ate`	Go to end of file when opened
`ios::binary`	Open in binary mode (default is text)
`ios::trunc`	Delete file contents if it exists
`ios::nocreate`	If file does not exist, an open will fail
`ios::noreplace`	If file exists, an open for output will fail

Conversion Routines — Requires `stdlib.h` header file

`atof(string)`	Convert ASCII string to floating point
`atoi(string)`	Convert ASCII string to an integer
`itoa(num,string)`	Convert integer to ASCII string

Character Routines — Requires `ctype.h` header file

`isalpha(character)`	Is the character an alphanumeric
`isascii(character)`	Is the character an ASCII character
`islower(character)`	Is the character lowercase
`isupper(character)`	Is the character uppercase
`isdigit(character)`	Is the character a digit
`isspace(character)`	Is the character a whitespace
`isprint(character)`	Is this a printable character
`ispunct(character)`	Is this a punctuation character
`iscntrl(character)`	Is this a control character
`toupper(character)`	Convert character to uppercase
`tolower(character)`	Convert character to lowercase

String Routines — Requires `string.h` header file

`strcat(string1, string2)`	Concatenate two strings
`strcpy(tostring, fromstring)`	Copy `fromstring` to `tostring`
`strlen(string)`	Determine the length of a string
`strchr(string, character)`	Find a character in a string
`strcmp(string1, string2)`	Compare two strings

File I/O — Requires the `fstream.h` header file

`file.open(char*, mode)`	Open an `fstream` with given mode
`file.close()`	Close an `fstream`
`file.get()`	Extract the next character from the file
`file.getline(str, ln, ch)`	Extract a string from the file
`file.peek()`	Return the next file character without changing file position
`file.putback(ch)`	Push back a character to the file
`file.eof()`	Return a 1 if end-of-file has been reached

C++ Reference

Keywords

auto	default	goto	public	this
break	do	if	register	template
case	double	inline	return	typedef
catch	double	int	short	union
char	enum	long	signed	unsigned
class	extern	new	sizeof	virtual
const	float	overload	static	void
continue	for	private	struct	volatile
delete	friend	protected	switch	while

Operators

Type	Symbols	Associativity
Global resolution	::	right to left
Local resolution	::	left to right
Primary	-> . [] ()	left to right
Unary	sizeof ++ -- ~ ! + -* &()new delete	right to left
Arithmetic	* / %	left to right
Arithmetic	+ -	left to right
Shift	<< >>	left to right
Relational	< <= > >=	left to right
Relational	== !=	left to right
Bitwise	&	left to right
Bitwise	^	left to right
Bitwise	|	left to right
Logical	&&	left to right
Logical	||	left to right
Conditional	?:	right to left
Assignment	= += -= /= %= etc.	right to left
Comma	,	left to right

Scalar Data Types

char	*Examples:* char key;
int	int num = 10;
float	float sum, average, factor = 2.5;
double	double first, second, third;

NOTE: *Additionally, long, short, and unsigned qualifiers may be used with these data types.*

Arrays

An *array* is a list of elements, all of which are the same data type. The fist element in an array is referred to as the zeroth element.

```
Examples: int prices[5];
          char name[20];
          float rates [4][15];
```

Structures

A *structure* (or record) is a data type whose elements need not be of the same data type.

```
Examples: struct tel_record   // tel_record is an optional tag name
          {
              char name[20];
              int id;
              double rate;
          } phone;             // phone is an optional variable name
```

Comments

Line comments begin with a `//` and are terminated by the end of the line.

```
    Examples: // this is a sample line comment
```

Block comments can span multiple lines and are enclosed with an `/*` and `*/`.

```
    Examples: /*this is a sample block comment*/
```

Statements

A *null* statement consists of a semicolon only.

```
;        // the null statement
```

A *simple* statement is either a null statement, declaration, expression, or function statement.

```
Examples:  double a;               // declaration statement
           taxes = rate * income;  // expression statement
           void display(4.875);    // function statement
```

A *compound* statement consists of one or more statements enclosed within braces.

```
Example:  {                        // start of compound statement
              taxes = rate * income;
              count ++;
          }                        // end of compound statement
```

Flow control statements are structured statements consisting of a keyword (if, while, for, do, switch) followed by an expression within parentheses and a simple or compound statement.

```
if(expression)      if(expression)        switch(expression)      for (init; expression;alter)
    statement;          statement1;       {                           statement
                    else if(expression)       case value_1;
if(expression)          statement_2;              statement_1;    while (expression)
    statement1;             *                     break;              statement;
else                        *                 case value_2;
    statement2;         else                      statement_2;    do
                            statement_n;          break;              statement;
                                                  *                while (expression);
                                                  *
                                              default:
                                                  statement_n;
                                          }
```

Classes

A *class* is a user-defined data type that has both data and function members. An *object* is a variable created from a class.

```
Example:  // declaration section
          class Date
          {
            private:
              int month;
              int day;
              int year;
            public:
              Date(int=7, int=4, int=2001);    // a constructor prototype
              void showdate(void);   // another member function prototype
          ); // this is a declaration—don't forget the semicolon

          // implementation section
          Date::Date(int mm, int dd, int yy // a constructor
          {
            month = mm;
            day = dd;
            year = yy;
          }
          void showdate(void)
          {
            cout<<"the date is"<<month<<'/'<<day<<'/'<<year<<endl;
          }

          Date startdate, endate; // create two Date objects
```

NOTE: *Default arguments may be placed within the declarations section prototype. The function definition may also be included within the declaration section. Structures may also be extended to include member functions and define a class.*